enCYCLEpedia
Southern California

The Best Easy Scenic Bike Rides

3rd Edition

Richard Fox

enCYCLEpress

Copyright © 2021 by Richard Fox

Photography copyright © 2021 by Richard Fox and Steve Fisher except where otherwise credited.
Field Recon by Richard Fox and Steve Fisher

All rights reserved. No part of this publication may be reproduced or transmitted in any form or by any means, electronic or mechanical, including photocopy, recording, or any information storage and retrieval system, without permission in writing from the publisher.

Published by enCYCLEpress
U.S.A.
E-mail: info@enCYCLEpedia.net
www.enCYCLEpedia.net

Dedicated to Lisa Fisher. You are still with us on every ride. Photo: Ride DP1.

Library of Congress Control Number: 2014931110
ISBN: 978-1-63848-538-4
Printed in The United States of America

Disclaimer: Use the information contained within the pages of this book ONLY if you are willing to do so at your own risk. The information in this book is of a descriptive nature only, and is not intended to be relied upon as the sole source of information for any endeavors, including, but not limited to navigation to places. Neither the author, contributors, nor the publisher shall be liable for any personal, financial, or emotional damages, whether direct, incidental, or consequential, that persons using the information contained in this book incur. The author and publisher have used their best efforts in preparing this book, but make no representations or warranties with regard to the completeness or accuracy of the information provided. Although most known hazards associated with the activities described in this book have been identified, additional hazards may exist as well. This book was compiled in one particular period of time, and things will change after date of publication, or may have already changed. Some commercial establishments may close, others may open, and prices will differ. Call the respective establishments to verify any vital information before traveling. Transportation companies, their policies, and routes may change. Biking or hiking trails may become unsafe without warning, and some may be re-routed by their managing agency. Websites or telephone numbers may change or be discontinued. The author is committed to presenting the most correct information available. If you find something in the book that is in error or has changed, or if you would like to suggest additional rides for the next edition, please send a note to info@enCYCLEpedia.net. The book's website, enCYCLEpedia.net contains updates, additional rides, and features.

Front Cover: Ride SJ1 starts at Doheny State Beach (DP1). CV Link in Palm Springs (PS4). Lake Perris (LP1).

Contents

Rides are on pavement or concrete except mountain bike (MTB) paths on unpaved surfaces.

Acknowledgments 9

BEGINNINGS 10
   California Dreamin'—An Introduction 11
      Start Me Up!—Being Prepared 12
   Teach Me Tonight—How to Use This Book 13
      Help Me, Rhonda—The Maps, The Trails and What Everything Means . . . 13
   Fun Fun Fun—Exploring Southern California by Bike 17
      Cheeseburger in Paradise—Biking 'n Brunching. 17
      Surfin' Safari—Visit Some of SoCal's Best Beaches 19
      Come Fly With Me—Bird 'n Ride Adventures 20
      If I Could Turn Back Time—Pedaling Through SoCal's History 20
         Mission Bells—Cycle to SoCal's Missions 21
   I Get Around (SoCal) 22
      Drive My Car—Using Your Own Vehicle 22
      Big 'Ol Jet Airliner—SoCal's Airports. 22
      Take the "A" Train—Using Amtrak, Local Rail, and Bike-Carrying Buses . . 22
      Magic Bus—Other SoCal Bus Systems 24
   How Sweet It Is—The E-Bike Edge 25

FOOD FOR THE SOUL—The Best Easy Scenic Bike Rides 26
   1. San Luis Obispo County 27
      Cambria 28
         Cambria Bike 'n Brunch CA1 30
         North to San Simeon CA2 32
      Morro Bay and Montana de Oro State Park 32
         Morro Bay Bike 'n Brunch MB1 34
         Montana de Oro MTB—Ocean Bluffs and Creekside Cruise MB2 37
      San Luis Obispo 40
      Avila Beach 41
         Avila Bike Brunch 'n Beach AV1 42
      Pismo Beach 45
         Pismo Beach Ride on the Sand PB1 47
         Butterflies and Beyond—Flat Southbound Route PB2 47
         North Pismo Scenic Road Ride PB3 48
      Carrizo Plain National Monument—California's Serengeti 49
         Carrizo Plain Road & MTB Routes CP1, 2 and 3 50
   2. Santa Barbara County 52
      Santa Maria. 53
         Santa Maria River Trail SAM1 53
         Los Flores Ranch MTB SAM2 54

CONTENTS

Santa Barbara Wine Country 54
   Riding Sideways with Danish, Wine & Windmills SO1. 55
Lompoc. 59
   Lompoc to Surf Beach Road Ride LOM1. 59
Santa Barbara—Goleta 60
   Santa Barbara Waterfront and Beyond SB1. 60
   UC Santa Barbara and its Fabulous Coastal Trails SB2. 65

3. Ventura County 70
Ventura. 71
   Ventura Oceanfront and Harbor Tour VE1 72
   Ventura River Rail Trail VE2 75
   The Ojai Valley Trail VE3. 76
   Rincon Road Cruise and Seaside Path VE4 79

4. Los Angeles County 80
Los Angeles and the Beach Cities 82
   LA's Santa Monica and South Bay Beach Trails LA1 and LA2 82
San Pedro 89
   San Pedro and LA Harbor Tour LA3 89
Long Beach. 92
   The Long Beach World Class Waterfront LO1. 93
   Belmont Shore and Naples Island LO2. 96
Seal Beach. 99
   Seal Beach Ramble SE1 100
The San Gabriel River Trail (SGRT). 101
   Seal Beach to El Dorado Park SGR1. 103
   Whittier Narrows Recreation Area SGR2 104
   San Gabriel River—Santa Fe Dam Recreation Area SGR3 107
   West Fork San Gabriel River SGR4 111
San Fernando Valley. 111
   Griffith Park and LA River Loop LA4. 112
   Sepulveda Dam Recreation Area Loops LA5. 116
East County - Puddingstone Reservoir Loop - Road or MTB LA10 118
Pasadena and San Marino. 120
   Arroyo Seco Bike Trail & Heritage Square PA1 122
   Arroyo Seco Road Ride and the Rose Bowl PA2. 123
   San Marino and The Huntington PA3. 125
Catalina Island CAT1 125
   Avalon—A Mediterranean Island Village 126

5. Orange County 127
Huntington Beach 128
   Surf City Beach Trail HB1 128
   Huntington Beach Central Park HB2. 132
Newport Beach. 133
   Balboa Island and the Newport Ocean Beaches NB1 135
   Back Bay Wildlife Refuge Loop NB2 139
Crystal Cove State Park. 142
   Coastal Bluffs Trail NB3. 143
   El Moro Canyon Mountain Bike NB4. 145
Laguna Beach 146
   Top O' Laguna LB1. 147

Laguna Village to Crescent Bay LB2	148
Dana Point	149
Dana Point Cruise DP1	151
San Juan Capistrano	153
Cycling with the Swallows SJ1	154
San Clemente	157
San Clemente Beach Bike 'n Hike SC1	158
Bike Route Through San Clemente SC2	159
Surfin' USA! San Onofre State Beach and Camp Pendleton to Oceanside SC3	160
Santa Ana River Trail	163
Costa Mesa and Fountain Valley	164
Santa Ana River Trail—Costa Mesa Area SAR1	165
Mile Square Park in Fountain Valley FV1	168
Anaheim and Santa Ana	169
Santa Ana River Trail—Anaheim Area SAR2	170
Santa Ana River Trail—Anaheim to Yorba Linda SAR3	172
Yorba Linda	176
Yorba Linda Recreation Trail YL1	176
Irvine	177
San Diego Creek Trail IR1	179
Shady Canyon & Turtle Rock Loop IR2	182
OC Great Park and Jeffrey Open Space Loop IR3	184
Tustin	185
The Mountains to the Sea Trail TU1	185
Peters Canyon Regional Park MTB TU2	189
Orange	190
Old Towne Orange and the Santiago Creek Trail OR1	191
Santiago Oaks MTB and Irvine Regional Park OR2	195
Fullerton	198
Rail Trails, Hills 'n Brunch F1 and F2	199
Rail Trail MTB Loop with Downtown Option F1	201
The Fullerton MTB Loop with Downtown Option F2	202
Chino Hills State Park	204
Telegraph Canyon MTB Trail CH1	204
The Saddleback Valley	205
Aliso Creek National Recreation Trail SV1	206
Laguna Niguel Regional Park and Salt Creek Corridor to the Beach SV2	210
Aliso and Wood Canyons Wilderness Park	212
Weekend Aliso Canyon Road Ride SV3	213
Mountain Bike Ride in Wood Canyon SV4	214
Whiting Ranch Wilderness Park MTB SV5, SV6	215
Trabuco Canyon Area	216
O'Neil Park Ramble SV7	217
Arroyo Trabuco MTB Trail SV8	217
Trabuco Creek Bikeway SV9	218
Combination MTB and Class I Loop SV10	219
Caspers Wilderness Park MTB SV11	220

CONTENTS

6. San Diego County 221
  Oceanside 222
    Oceanside Tour: Your Mission—Boats, Beaches, and Birds OC1 224
  The North San Diego County Coast SDC1 229
  San Marcos 231
    South San Marcos Tour SMR1 231
    Inland Rail Trail SMR2 234
  Lake Hodges Area 235
    The East Lake Hodges Wetlands MTB LH1 238
    Dam Sweet MTB LH2 239
  San Diego 241
    Mission Bay & Ocean Front Walk SD1 241
    La Jolla Loop SD2 250
    Ocean Beach SD3 254
    San Diego Downtown & Harbor Tour SD4 257
    Point Loma Peninsula & Cabrillo National Monument SD5 261
    Balboa Park and Hillcrest SD6 262
    Coronado & The Bayshore Bikeway SD7 266
    Los Peñasquitos Canyon Preserve MTB SD8 273
    Lake Miramar Loop SD9 275
    Marian Bear Memorial Park SD10 and Rose Canyon SD11 Riparian MTB Adventures 277
    Mission Trails Regional Park—Mountain and Road Bike Combo SD12 278
    Lake Murray SD13 280
  Laguna Mountains 281
    Laguna Mountain MTB 'n Hike LM1 281

7. Kern County and the San Joaquin Valley 285
  Bakersfield 285
    The Kern River Parkway and Bakersfield BA1 286

8. The Inland Empire (IE) of Riverside and San Bernardino Counties 291
  Riverside 292
    Riverside and the Santa Ana River Trail R1 293
    Historic Victoria Avenue and the Citrus District R2 297
  Temecula and the Southern Wine Country 301
    Temecula Bike Routes T1 and T2 302
  Claremont 303
    Claremont Village and the Colleges CL1 304
    Thompson Creek Trail—City Loop or Trail Only CL2 305
  Lake Perris Loop Camp 'n Ride 306
  The Pacific Electric Trail (PET) - Inland Empire's Route 66 for Bikes 307
    Claremont to Montclair 310
    Upland 311
    Rancho Cucamonga 311
    Fontana and Rialto 313
  Big Bear Lake 314
    Alpine Pedal Path BB1 316
    Snow Summit to Bear Mountain Downhill MTB BB2 317
    Big Bear Bike 'n Brunch BB3 319

CONTENTS

9. The Deserts 319
   Palm Springs and the Coachella Valley 320
      The Bike-Friendly Cities of the Desert 321
      Sidewalks Under the Palms. 323
      Getting to and Around the Desert 324
   Palm Springs and Cathedral City 326
      Palm Springs Vintage Star Tour—Where YOU Are the Star! PS1. 327
      South Palm Springs PS2. 334
      Palm Springs' Tahquitz Creek Loop PS3 336
      Airport — Whitewater CV Link Loop PS4 338
      The Coachella Valley Bikeway/Whitewater Trail/CV Link CC1. 339
   Rancho Mirage and Palm Desert. 340
      Rancho Mirage and Palm Desert Sidepath Loop RM1 340
      The River Grand Sidepath/CV Link Loop RM2 345
      Desert Willow Loop PD1 349
      Mission Hills Loops of North Rancho Mirage RM3. 350
   La Quinta Indian Wells and Indio 350
      Indian Wells Connection IW1 and CV Link East Valley 351
      La Quinta Cove and Old Town LQ1 352
      The La Quinta Boulevards and Lake Cahuilla Regional Park LQ2 354
      Old Town La Quinta through Indian Wells to El Paseo LQ3. 356
   Beyond The Coachella Valley 357
   Joshua Tree National Park. 357
      Queen Valley—A Fabulous MTB 'n Hike JT1. 358
   Anza-Borrego Desert State Park and Borrego Springs 363
      Anza-Borrego and Borrego Springs Bike, Brunch 'n Hike AB1. 365
      Blair Valley MTB 'n Hike AB2. 365
      The Hawi-Vallecito Valley Cultural Preserve MTB AB3. 366
      Fish Creek Wash MTB 'n Hike AB4. 367

Encore—Additional Rides Ventura County: Pt Mugu State Park VE5 368
      Los Angeles County: Orange Line Busway LA6, Chandler Bikeway LA7,
      Malibu Creek SP LA8, Santa Clarita LA9, Whittier Rail Trail LA11

Index 369

Quick Reference: Ride Numbers 375

Ratings Our criteria for a Best Easy Scenic Bike Ride included: SoCal Scenery, quality of the ride including sufficient length but not too difficult, safety from traffic and crime, repeatability, seeing the SoCal sights, and general lack of "Knocks & Hazards."

    ⭐5 Don't miss! The Best of SoCal!   ⭐4 Awesome ride, highly recommended!
    ⭐3 Recommended. Maybe less length, exciting scenery or ride quality.
    ⭐2 Many may enjoy, perhaps involves more riding with traffic, is hilly,
       or has less stellar scenery. May be a mediocre ride to see a cool place.
  ⭐0 ⭐1 Options to get you from Point A to B, but has too many knocks.

Photos next page, clockwise from left:
Sea Otter in Morro Bay, ride MB1; Spring on Los Angeles beach path LA1;
Cabrillo National Monument at Point Loma SD5; Path up Mt. Rubidoux in Riverside R1 Opt 3;
Picnic spot at Lake Perris, LP1; The 2017 superbloom near Borrego Springs, AB1; shorebirds.

Acknowledgments

Dozens of entities were contacted while conducting the research for this book. Thanks to all that took the effort to provide information during the compilation of both editions, including many city managers, engineers and planners across the Southland.

Thanks to friends that helped evaluate the desirability and difficulty of rides or provided info: Rod Alan, Karin & Bryan Anderson, Stuart & Robin Bass, John Blando & Brian DeVries, John Conley & Bill MacMillan (Ride BB2), Ann Doherty, Lisa Fisher & Margot Bucholtz, Lew Fox & Elaine Galland, Hub Freeman, Gary Green, Jeff Green, Victor & Muriel Jones, Gary Leuders, Mary Ann Mills & Teddy, Frank Peters, Jim & Pam Petrie, Janice Radder, Janet & Kirk Stallman, Christine Tinsley, LeGrand Velez and Vic Yepello.

BEGINNINGS

Animated scarecrows by the Slabtown Rollers, Cambria (CA1)

California Dreamin'—An Introduction

Ahh, Southern California, land of sunshine, palm trees, the beckoning Pacific and year-round fun, a region so documented in television and motion pictures that when you visit even for the first time it seems familiar, kind of like New York or London. Tourists flock to the fabled beaches, expansive deserts, and attractions such as Disneyland, Hollywood, Hearst Castle and the San Diego Zoo, while the 22 million+ residents have year-round cycling opportunities at their disposal on fabulous networks of paved and dirt trails under the California sun.

Southern California, or SoCal as it is called, extends from the northern boundaries of San Luis Obispo, Kern, and San Bernardino Counties that line up at 35° 47′ 28″ north latitude, to the Mexican international border, and from the Pacific Ocean to the borders of Nevada and Arizona. Mountain ranges that form the backdrop to the coastal region, rising as high as 11,500 feet northeast of San Bernardino, produce multiple ecological zones, while a rainshadow effect creates vast deserts to their east.

The rides presented in this book let anyone who can operate a bicycle experience SoCal's wonderland of diverse regimes. Rather than focusing on individual bike trails, the rides showcase interesting SoCal places, with routes that may combine several bike trails or lightly traveled roads. Explore the region's history with rides to preserved historical sites and neighborhoods, such as the Spanish missions and town centers next to historic train depots, making many of the rides accessible via the regional rail systems. Cycle on epic trails along famous surfing beaches to vantage points to watch for whales and other sea mammals, and to some of the best bird-watching spots in North America. Explore the wine country of Santa Barbara in the north and Temecula in the south, and the preserved turn of the last century citrus culture in the Inland Empire region. Try a pedal through quintessential SoCal beach and resort towns like Santa Barbara and Ojai, or around busy and scenic harbors such as San Diego, Long Beach,

LA, and Newport Beach. Get a workout on one of the bicycle highways that parallel the region's channelized rivers. From fall through spring explore the desert rides near Palm Springs, which can be just sublime with perfect sunny weather and interesting desert landscapes, while a summer cycle in the pine-scented San Bernardino or Laguna Mountains can be a welcome relief from the desert heat. RV'ers and campers will appreciate the mention of campgrounds located near the rides, so that you can just pitch your tent or park your rig and hop on a trail without having to use your vehicle.

Best of all, these scenic rides are easy, fun, and relatively safe. The average cyclist should be able to navigate most of these rides with minimal difficulty. Those in better condition or with e-bikes can take advantage of the options that are added on to many of the rides to get even more of a workout. Since they make the perfect Bike 'n Brunch rides for social groups or individuals, restaurants are pointed out along the routes so that you can plan for your well-earned meal or coffee break.

This book presents the results of our exploration of easy scenic bike trails and routes around Southern California, and summarizes the rides that we feel are the best of the best. Our main criterion for determining a great ride was scenery, which could be either natural or man-made. We avoided rides that were too technical (for mountain biking) or strenuous, tried to steer clear of areas known to have high crime rates, and focused on rides that came in contact with a minimum of automobile traffic. We did make exceptions and stretched the criteria, where a fabulous ride included a hill or two along the way, or a bit of cycling in traffic, but for the most part it involved slow-moving traffic, such as in a quaint downtown or a park. We are exclusively easy scenic cyclists ourselves, so, as they say, if we can do it, you can do it! However, since every family is vastly different in their cycling experience and abilities, it is up to you to determine whether a particular ride is suitable for you and your kids, beyond the flat paved trails through municipal parks.

Falling behind on your exercise routine? Try one of these rides and let it inspire you to jump on your bike and experience the beautiful outdoor environment while enjoying the corresponding health benefits. If cycling is a new activity for you though, make sure to clear it with your doctor first.

Start Me Up!—Being Prepared

If you are new to cycling or need a refresher, check out some of the excellent articles at REI.com about bike selection, ride preparedness, equipment, and technique. For rules of the road when cycling with traffic, and requirements for bike safety equipment in California, do a web search for publication FFDL-37. State helmet law requires *that all persons under eighteen years of age are required to wear a properly fitting bicycle helmet in the state*, and we strongly recommend that everyone wear a helmet, even on trail or sidewalk rides. If you are concerned about messing up your hair, try wearing a "doo rag" like the motorcyclists. A bike headlight, rear red light or reflectors, and pedal reflectors are required for night riding. Bring energy snacks, water, clothing to anticipate changes in the weather (and dining options), spare inner tubes (and/or repair kit), tire levers, tire pump, bike repair tools, first aid kit, cell phone, road maps, transit schedule (just in case), your annual park passes, copies of the relevant pages in this book, perhaps the map downloaded from our website to your phone, and an upbeat, fun-loving attitude!

Teach Me Tonight—How to Use This Book

To find a ride, look at the county map at the beginning of each chapter, select the areas you wish to explore, then find the locale in that chapter using the ride number, table on page 375, or Table of Contents and Index. Orange County is included in the Los Angeles County map, and Ventura County is included in the Santa Barbara County map. The organization of the chapters is generally north to south, from San Luis Obispo County to San Diego County, moving down the coast. These are followed by the landlocked counties, which include Kern County, the western portions of San Bernardino and Riverside Counties, referred to as the Inland Empire, and the eastern portions of those counties plus eastern San Diego County, referred to as The Deserts.

In a couple of cases, border towns and/or rides fit in better with the adjacent county due to interconnecting rides. That is why Claremont is included with the Inland Empire, Seal Beach and all of the San Gabriel River Trail are grouped with Los Angeles County, and the San Onofre Ride through San Diego County's Camp Pendleton is lumped in with Orange County.

Help Me, Rhonda—The Maps, The Trails and What Everything Means

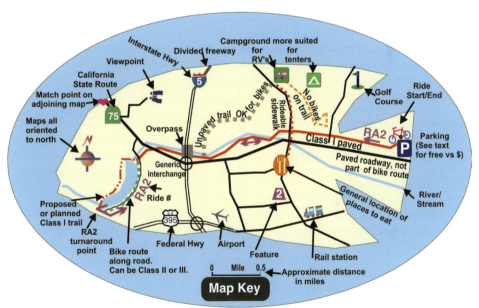

Detailed color maps accompany most of the rides. Each typically includes a bike symbol identifying the trailhead, the ride number, and arrows depicting the route. There may also be multiple rides on a single map, as well as options to extend the rides. Data for each ride includes the following:

Distance and Time: Ride distance is in miles. For approximate distance in kilometers multiply by 1.6. Assume distance given is the total ride mileage, unless indicated that it is one way only. Mileage for optional add-ons is listed separately. The time is a very rough estimate, as everyone cycles at a different speed. Expect that mountain bike trails will take longer than equivalent paved trails.

Route & Bike: All aspects of the bike route are summarized. The trail surface dictates the type of bike recommended. The majority of the rides are on paved surfaces, but a nice selection of novice or advanced novice-level mountain bike rides are also included, and those with a hybrid or mountain bike will enjoy the most options. Bikes with wider tires are also more forgiving on rough pavement, and on transitions between roads and trails or sidewalks, reducing the likelihood of a fall.

Difficulty is relative, depending on a cyclist's ability. Our rides are mainly "Easy," with routes fairly flat and distances mostly under 15 miles. "Moderate" rides can be longer or have a few hills. A few "Strenuous" options are included for those that feel like an extra workout. Topography is described, sometimes including elevations (feet above mean sea level) where hills are involved. Our ideal easy ride is mostly flat with perhaps a few small hills or gradual grades. E-bikes are a game changer, and rides where the extra umph comes in handy are labeled "E-bike edge." Class 1 & 2 e-bikes are allowed on most paved paths.

In general, mountain bike trails are more difficult than their paved counterparts. Where a mountain bike or hybrid is recommended for an unpaved surface it is spelled out, or abbreviated "MTB." Novice MTB trails are typically fairly flat fire roads or smooth paths with few obstacles, whereas advanced novice trails may include some hills, rocky terrain, stream crossings, or other elements that require a bit of skill. Some rides also mention optional trails that are for intermediate or advanced MTB riders. If you encounter conditions beyond your ability level, such as very rocky terrain or steep hills, you can walk your bike. E-bikes are not allowed on dirt MTB trails in some of the parks, as mentioned in each.

The paved trails are divided into categories that loosely correspond to the California Department of Transportation (Caltrans) "Class I, II, III & IV" designations:

Class I: Any paved path that is completely separated from traffic, indicated by a solid red line on our maps. Sometimes a sidewalk path is designated as a Class I path if it is a good enough quality route that it mimics a Class I path, such as many of the sidewalk paths in the Palm Springs area. Use extra caution if it is not an official Class I path, since there may not be as many warning signs regarding intersections or obstacles.

Sidewalk: Rideable sidewalks, indicated by a dotted red line on our maps, provide a safer option from a busy street. The legality of sidewalk riding is specified within most ride descriptions as well. If a jurisdiction has no specific rules on sidewalk riding, legality defers to California state law, which basically asserts that bike riding is allowed on sidewalks, but cyclists must be courteous to pedestrians who have the right of way. Sidewalk riding is frequently not allowed and not recommended in areas with a lot of pedestrian traffic, such as business districts and some beach areas. Pay close attention to the sidewalk safety tips referenced in The Deserts chapter (p 324), since it can be even more dangerous than street riding if you are careless. You may want to use a sidewalk as a detour from a bike trail to reach a restaurant, or other instances. A sidepath is a sidewalk that is more like a bike trail.

Class II: A paved city street with a Caltrans-approved bike lane, indicated by a dotted green line over a thin solid black line on our maps. We have tried to include sections of road with lower speed limits whenever possible. Along a high-speed road with a narrow bike lane, we tend to opt for a sidewalk if available.

Class III: A street that is enjoyable to cycle on, but does not have a bike lane. It could be a residential street, a park road, a downtown area with a low speed limit, or a popular bike route with no better off-road alternatives. Unlike the official Class III designation, our Class III is not necessarily a designated bike route. Any on-road route is indicated on the maps by a dotted green line over a thin solid black line, whether it is Class II or III. The distinction is typically made in the text. A sharrow is an arrow with a bike insignia painted onto the street, a cheap and easy way for cities to create phony bike lanes. They indicate that bikes and cars must share the lane, and they allow bikes to ride at a safe distance from parked cars (to avoid doors opening), which is welcome in downtown districts.

Class IV Cyclepath: A one or two way bike lane separated from traffic by a physical barrier. In this book they are marked as Class I paths on the maps except where noted otherwise.

Seasons and best time to ride: In most cases the rides can be cycled during all seasons, except for the mountain areas, which may have snow and freezing cold weather in the winter, and the deserts, which can be brutally hot in the summer. However, if you find yourself in the desert in summer, on many days you can plan to complete the ride early in the morning, before the heat is predicted to become uncomfortable, or at times dangerous. If you have sensitive lungs, try to avoid hot and smoggy conditions, most common in the Inland Empire and Bakersfield in summer and fall.

If you are planning a trip to Southern California, don't get off the plane in the winter wearing shorts and sandals, and end up on the local news saying, "I had no idea it could be this cold here!" While Southern California boasts one of the most desirable climates in the world, there is a lot of variability to be aware of. Climate charts are included with each chapter that depict what to expect in each region, on average. They show that precipitation decreases as you head south down the coast, increases in the foothills and the mountains, and decreases drastically east of the mountains. Pay attention to predictions of wind direction and intensity to avoid a brutal return ride. Cycling toward the ocean in the afternoon can be especially challenging at times if combating on-shore breezes. The rainy season is generally November through March, peaking in February, although in summer, thunderstorms can appear suddenly in the mountains and monsoons in the deserts causing flash floods. Mountain bike trails are typically closed during and several days after a significant rain event.

The best time to cycle in a business district to avoid vehicle traffic is early Sunday morning, and the best choice for cycling along the beach paths to avoid crowds is in the morning.

Facilities: Restrooms found along the route are mentioned, but keep in mind they can be locked, or in the case of portable toilets (porta-potties)—removed. Availability of water is sometimes mentioned, but do not depend on that in case the source is not working. Make sure to bring your own ample supply.

Knocks & Hazards: No ride is perfect, and this section explains why. Use your common sense, since there may be other hazards not listed, and conditions can change. Regional SoCal hazards such as earthquake and wildfire are not mentioned. The term "lurkers" used here refers to the likelihood that unsavory characters will "lurk" around the trail, whether they are harmless homeless persons, or others that may pose a more serious threat such as thugs or gang bangers. "Clueless peds" refers to a tendency for pedestrians to use the trail without regard for other users such as cyclists. That's where a loud bell comes in handy. Remember that peds and equestrians always have the right of way over cyclists on sidewalks and trails, and you should know never to spook a horse, of course, of course. Certain trails have speed limits, some more sensible than others, which can limit the extent of your workout.

Also noted are rides with many street crossings and segments that are in close proximity to automobile traffic. When you leave your bike for any reason, always secure it with the strongest lock practicable, and don't leave valuables in your car at trailheads or in touristy areas, since they are notorious for break-ins.

In the natural realm, venomous rattlesnakes can be found along many of the park trails except perhaps in the dead of winter. Mountain lions range throughout SoCal, and can be a concern in parks at the urban-wilderness interface. Attacks on humans are rare, but not unheard of, so keep children close at hand. Black bears (but not brown or grizzly bears) range in the higher elevation locales like Big Bear Lake, but also less frequently in the other SoCal mountain and foothill areas.

Bike 'n Brunch: The term Bike 'n Brunch can refer to any meal, not necessarily brunch. An optimal dining choice will have a delightful outdoor patio with a view of the scenery that you are already experiencing, good food and service, reasonable prices, and within close proximity to the bike route. The maps show general locations of restaurants, and usually indicate multiple restaurants at that location. In most cases only restaurants near the trails are noted.

Walking on Water Cafe
Ocean Beach Pier SD3

Camp 'n Ride: Many of the bike rides are in close proximity to campgrounds, and we love the Zen of being able to cycle directly from where we are staying. We mention campgrounds that are a short rideable distance from the trailhead, and only if they are worthwhile places to stay. Others that may require transporting your bikes may also be mentioned. Beach campgrounds are typically full most weekends and all through the summer months, so locals rush to reserve them the second the reservation window becomes available. Most are state park campgrounds that utilize reservecalifornia.com. A good source to get the lowdown on campgrounds is the the website campgroundeviews.com.

Hotels: Hotel accommodations are only noted when they are landmarks near the trail or perhaps contain an interesting restaurant. Hotel reservation websites usually have a mapping option so that you can see where they are located in relation to your ride. If you plot hotels or campgrounds on Googlemaps, you can select the "bicycling" layer to determine if there is a bike route between the accommodation and your intended ride.

Rent 'n Ride: Rentals tend to be readily available at the most popular urban trails and parks, but are less likely to be found elsewhere. Rentals identified near the trailhead and in the general vicinity are mentioned. Call to verify availability of the type of bike you need before traveling to a ride site. Bike shops that do not necessarily offer rentals are also listed. Many cities have been adopting Bike Share programs, where self-serve kiosks are placed at strategic locales so that cyclists can borrow a bike at one location and leave it at another. However, these services have come and gone frequently over the years and you should do a web search for one when making plans, and ensure it's still in business even if it shows up on Google. Finally, e-bikes have surged in popularity in recent years, and many rental options are available, with many listed in this book.

Further Info: Websites or phone numbers for obtaining additional information relevant to the ride, such as online maps, contact info to see if a park is open, commercial websites listing restaurants, hotels, and attractions, etc.

Access: The route to the start of the ride, by car or by rail if applicable. Bus routes are typically not mentioned since it is best to look up the current routes with the appropriate agency before traveling. GPS coordinates are included only for a few of the more rural areas.

Tunes and Eats: Every fabulous bike ride has a unique flavor, and what better way to compliment the ride than with paired music and food, just as a fine wine might be paired with a gourmet meal. Everyone has their own tastes in the culinary and musical realms, but we have suggested songs that we feel evoke the feeling of the rides, and a sample item from a popular nearby restaurant that we either have tried or read about. When there are no restaurants nearby, we suggest a picnic. Of course menus and even restaurants change, but this gives you an idea of what can be available.

Songs were chosen based on either the relevance of the title and/or lyrics to the ride, the local origin of the artist or group, movies filmed there, or as a soundtrack to the ride in general. Artists from the Southern California music scene through the years are well represented, especially the Beach Boys and other '60s surfer groups like Jan & Dean, Sunset Scene groups like The Byrds and Buffalo Springfield, contemporary artists such as Red Hot Chili Peppers, Katy Perry and No Doubt, Latin artists like Los Lobos and Quetzal, and more. Try to guess each song's relevance.

Remember that while bicycling it is illegal (CA Vehicle Code 27400) to wear a headset covering or earplugs or earphones inserted in both ears. Always keep the volume low so that it is background music, and you are aware of your surroundings for the safety of yourself and others. Better yet, just hum it in your head while you're cycling, as you listen to the ambient sounds of crashing waves, chirping birds, laughing children, or fellow cyclists chanting "on your left!"

Ratings: The rides are rated on a scale of ⭐0 to ⭐5 based on how each fits our critera for a "best" ride: Scenery; quality of path and ride; how enjoyable/repeatable; long enough to make it worthwhile; away from car traffic; low crime area; not too hilly; desirability of SoCal locale to visit. Ride options are also rated to help you decide whether to extend your outing. Lower rated rides may be included because they tour an interesting area, but are with traffic. They are sometimes presented in lesser detail due to space limits. Use an app (ie Google Maps) to help navigate those. Rides are graded on a curve; a ⭐2 is also worthwhile, but perhaps not for everyone.

Fun Fun Fun—Exploring Southern California by Bike

Follow us to the most interesting and beautiful places in Southern California that you can tour via an easy bike ride. You should be able to combine a bike ride with other wonderful activities at most locations, and for those in your party who do not ride at all, they can typically find something interesting to do while they eagerly await your tales of cycling bliss.

Cheeseburger in Paradise—Biking 'n Brunching

Southern California Cuisine is known for its fresh ingredients from locally farmed produce or animal products. Even if it's just a fruit garnish on a plate of free-range eggs,

Fisherman's Restaurant, San Clemente Pier (SC1)

the California touch is a welcome one. From the basic to elaborate, the use of international fusion cuisine makes many California restaurants unique. Cafés along our bike routes will most assuredly tempt you with these healthy creations. On the other extreme many prefer In-N-Out Burger with its long lines for its basic burger and fries menu. Surfing and burgers have gone together since the days of Gidget at the beach, and hamburger stands of all types still pack 'em in. Along your rides you may also encounter other tasty burgers at SoCal's famous Tommy's, chains such as Five Guys and Habit Burger, along with the surviving independents.

SoCal has been the melting pot of the U.S. for many decades, and the influx of people mostly from Latin America and Asia have infused their cuisines into every strip mall and Main Street in the region. Besides the ubiquitous Chinese restaurants there are Japanese/sushi places everywhere, Thai, Vietnamese, and others. The large Persian population supports restaurants that serve delicious roasted meat kabobs and wonderful rices mixed with berries or vegetables. With SoCal's estimated 40 percent Hispanic population, expect to find Mexican cuisine everywhere. Rubio's and Wahoo's Fish Tacos (counter service) chains, near many of our rides, are favorites for dependable inexpensive Mexican meals with fresh ingredients. El Torito, found along some of our oceanfront rides (LA2, DP1), serve Sunday buffet brunches. Many prefer independent mom and pop taquerias for tacos and burritos. Of course there's plenty of pizza along our bike routes, and Z Pizza is a chain that bakes unique gourmet pies. You'll find California Pizza Kitchens that also serves great salads al fresco and delicious thick crust pizza at BJ's Brewhouse. Old timey Ruby's diner franchises tend to be located at the end of many of the piers, a favorite with the kiddies.

There's nothing like a "fish lunch" near a pier amidst a day of beach cycling, and many rides have great seafood restaurant options that serve a fresh catch, including Fisherman's on San Clemente Pier (SC1) and Beach House Fish on the Ventura Pier (VE1). Did you know that the tri tip was invented in Santa Maria, California's barbeque capital? You can find several places to sample the authentic preparation in that north Santa Barbara County city. Vegetarians can choose from an increasing number of choices across SoCal including the Native Foods chain (PS2). For a coffee fix Starbucks are found everywhere along with other independent locals' favorites.

Finally, no place has better chicken restaurant chains than SoCal. Versailles (Cuban), near ride LA5, serves up half garlic chicken and roast pork entrées that are out of this world. Charo Chicken cooks sinfully delicious lemon butter chicken (SE1). El Pollo Loco is found near many of our rides, offering fabulous grilled citrus marinated chicken without the rich sauce of the others. Zankou Chicken around LA is famous for its middle-eastern style chicken, including Swarma.

Some of the best Bike 'n Brunch Rides are the Los Angeles beach trails (LA1, 2); San Diego's Mission Bay (SD1), Harbor Tour (SD4), and Coronado/Silver Strand

(SD7); The Desert Region's Palm Springs Star Tour (PS1), and Rancho Mirage/Palm Desert Loops (RM1, 2); and the Long Beach rides (LO1, 2). That's just an hors d'oeuvre. There are plenty more where that came from. Bon appetit!

Surfin' Safari—Visit Some of SoCal's Best Beaches

Wide tired e-bike on Lower Trestles Beach.

Learn to surf! This class is along Ocean Front Walk in Pacific Beach (SD1)

Dude! Put on your baggies or bikini and crank up the Beach Boys in your Woody then drive down PCH (Pacific Coast Highway) to some of the gnarliest surfing beaches in the Lower 48. Then get stoked for some radical easy scenic cycling along the beaches, watching those longboarders hang 10. Many surfers even have bikes equipped with surfboard racks to carry their surfboards from their ride to the beach. You can try your luck at surfing via one of the many surfing schools along the coast, or try bodyboarding, which is much easier to get into; all you need is an appropriate Styrofoam board and flippers, and during the summer months most crowded beach areas are segregated by a yellow flag with a black ball so that hard board surfers do not mingle with other ocean goers. And of course there's always skimboarding. The same beaches are great to just relax on and perhaps have your Bike 'n Brunch picnic. Watch for bottlenose dolphins skimming the waves, and if you are lucky, the spout of a winter migrating grey whale will appear farther out. Squadrons of pelicans cruise by as sanderlings scurry along the waters' edge.

Following are some of the beachiest rides. Those with an "*" indicate a better chance for mellower waves suitable for novices. Letters and numbers in parentheses indicated the ride number in this book. (Note: As in all oceans, there are sharks here.)

San Luis Obispo County: *Cambria (CA2)*: San Simeon State Beach; *Morro Bay (MB1)*: Surf Beach near Morro Rock and beaches to the north; *Pismo Beach (PB1)*: The Pier.

Santa Barbara County: *UCSB (SB2)*: Campus Point*, Coal Oil Point* (and yes, there is plenty of tar in these waters); *Santa Barbara (SB1)*: Leadbetter Point*.

Ventura County: *Rincon (VE4):* Rincon *(Also near south end SB1 Option 2).*

Los Angeles County: *Los Angeles Beaches (LA1)*: Sunset Point off Sunset Boulevard & PCH* (north of trail), Bay Street—Santa Monica* (south of pier, popular for lessons), Venice Beach; *(LA2)*: El Porto*, Manhattan Beach*, Hermosa Beach.

Orange County: *Seal Beach (SE1, listed under LA County)*: Seal Beach Pier; *Huntington Beach (HB1)*: Bolsa Chica State Beach, Huntington Pier; *Newport Beach (NB1)*: The Wedge (watch daredevils on high surf days); *Laguna Niguel (SV2)*: Salt Creek Beach; *Dana Point (DP1)*: Doheny Beach*; *San Clemente (SC1)*: The Pier*, T Street Beach;

San Clemente/San Onofre (SC3): Trestles is one of the premier breaks in the land, Old Man's* to its south at San Onofre Surf Beach is longboarders' heaven.

San Diego County: *Oceanside (OC1):* Oceanside Pier area; *San Diego North Coast Tour: (SDC1)*: Terra Mar (Hole in the Wall)—Carlsbad *, Cardiff Reef—Encinitas*, Swamis—Encinitas, Boneyard (north of Swamis)—Encinitas, Fletcher's Cove—Solana Beach*, Del Mar (15th Street)*, Blacks Beach (clothing optional, below Torrey Pines State Reserve), La Jolla Shores*; *La Jolla Loop (SD2)*: Windansea Beach; *Mission Bay/Pacific Beach (SD1)*: Tourmo (north end of Pacific Beach) *, Mission Beach*.

Come Fly With Me—Bird 'n Ride Adventures

The wide range of habitat in SoCal produces one of the most diverse bird watching locales in North America. You can watch sea and shore birds along the coast, another group in the large chaparral areas where most of the human settlement is located, others up in the mountains, and still others in the deserts. The Pacific Flyway is the West Coast's bird migratory route from South America to Canada during spring and fall, and wetlands or lakes along the way are typically a popular stopover point, while the Salton Sea is the southern terminus for many birds, with over 400 species recorded. Although we do not have a ride at the Salton Sea, many of these same birds can be seen during the winter in the Coachella Valley, including Lake Cahuilla in La Quinta, and around the lakes of the golf courses that are near most of our rides. Some notable birding rides along the Pacific Flyway are Morro Bay (MB1), Lake Balboa in Sepulveda Basin (LA5), Legg Lake at Whittier Narrows (SGR2), Bolsa Chica Ecological Reserve (HB1), Huntington Beach Central Park (HB2), Upper Newport Bay (NB2), Lake Hodges (LH1 and 2), Lake Perris (LP1), and the wildlife refuges of Mission Bay (SD1) and the Silver Strand (SD7).

If I Could Turn Back Time—Pedaling Through SoCal's History

The human history of Southern California began over ten thousand years ago when various groups of native peoples inhabited the land. Unlike the cave dwellings in other Southwest states, there is not much evidence remaining of the natives' time here except for some rock paintings and shell middens. Everything changed once the Europeans arrived, first in the 1500s as explorers, and later in the 1700s as settlers and governors. California was claimed by Spain, then Mexico in 1821 after its independence, and eventually became a U.S. state in 1850.

Our tours take you to ancient rock paintings at Carrizo Plain National Monument (CP1), and to historic buildings that still stand from the time of Spanish rule in the way of a series of preserved missions, described below. Other more recent historical districts from the late 1800s to mid 1900s are featured in rides in Orange County (Fullerton F1, Orange OR1, San Juan Capistrano SJ1), San Diego County (Mission Bay/Old Town SD1), Riverside County (Riverside R1 and 2), and San Bernardino County (Upland PET), all of which are accessible via local rail. The Pacific Electric Trail (PET) commemorates both the historic automobile Route 66, and the Pacific Electric rail line that was the most extensive electric rail line in the world in the early twentieth century.

Mission Bells—Cycle to SoCal's Missions

The Spanish missions were religious and military outposts established by the Spanish Catholics of the Franciscan Order during 1769 through 1823, of which fabled

Father Junípero Serra was one of the original missionaries. Their goal was to spread the Christian faith to the indigenous people and to colonize the Pacific Coast region, giving Spain a foothold in the new frontier. They would introduce ranching, livestock, and various crops to the mission communities that were situated at regular intervals along the coastal region. As with most endeavors of this kind, the results were not always positive, especially when it came to the natives succumbing to European diseases. However, the missions remain as some of the oldest and most visited historic structures in the region, and many have recently been restored.

Of the twenty-one missions in California, eleven are located in SoCal. Five of these can be visited as part of our rides, and another five are located a short drive from our ride locations. From north to south, the missions are as follows:

Mission San Miguel Arcángel, 775 Mission St, San Miguel, is along US 101 north of Paso Robles in San Luis Obispo County, not near our rides, but on your way north to the Bay Area.

Mission San Luis Obispo de Tolosa, 751 Palm St, downtown San Luis Obispo. Not on a featured ride, but easily accessible by a Class II jaunt around town and from the train depot.

Mission La Purísima Concepción, 2295 Purisima Rd, just northeast of Lompoc. Not on our bike routes, but reachable via a scenic road ride.

Mission Santa Inés, 1760 Mission Dr. in Solvang is where we recommend parking for the Wine Country Tour (SO1) and is worth visiting on its own.

Mission Santa Barbara, 2201 Laguna St, is located north of downtown, requiring a hilly bike ride to access it, or a short drive from the beach ride (SB1).

Mission San Luis Rey de Francia, Oceanside

Mission San Buenaventura, 211 E Main St. in Ventura is accessible from a Class I trail (VE1) via an easy Class II detour to downtown.

Mission San Fernando Rey de España, 15151 San Fernando Mission Blvd, Mission Hills, San Fernando Valley of Los Angeles. Drive to it from the vicinity of rides LA4 through 7.

Mission San Gabriel Arcángel, 428 S Mission Dr, San Gabriel. Short drive from the Pasadena or San Marino rides, PA1 through PA3.

Mission San Juan Capistrano, 26801 Ortega Hwy (at Camino Capistrano) is an easy ride or even a stroll from the train depot, and is part of our tour of the area (SJ1-3).

Mission San Luis Rey de Francia, 4050 Mission Ave in eastern Oceanside is accessible via a short detour from the San Luis Rey River Trail, and part of our tour (OC1-1).

Mission San Diego de Alcalá, 10818 San Diego Mission Rd, is a short drive from any of our San Diego rides, just east on I-8 from Old Town.

I Get Around (SoCal)

The optimal way to tour the region is with your own vehicle, carrying mountain or hybrid bikes on a sturdy bike rack, and stopping at the featured ride locations. It is an activity tailor made for RV'ers, and RV rentals are available from outfits such as cruiseamerica.com and elmonterv.com. Or, take advantage of SoCal's widespread bike-friendly rail service that makes your excursion greener and more fun, too.

Drive My Car—Using Your Own Vehicle

Highways and byways crisscross SoCal, including U.S. Interstates such as I-5, which are always access-controlled freeways. U.S. Highways like US 101, or California State Routes (such as SR1) can be either controlled access freeways or traditional undivided highways with traffic signals. To travel to SoCal from Sacramento or the San Francisco Bay Area in a hurry, take the direct I-5 or SR 99. From the Bay Area, the scenic US 101 freeway avoids the sometimes-snowy Tejon Pass along I-5, and SR1 along the dramatic Big Sur Coast is the ultimate scenic drive, except if you are an acrophobe. From I-80 at Reno or Lake Tahoe take scenic US 395 south in summer along the spectacular eastern side of the Sierra Nevada range, or I-80 west to the more lowland routes in winter. From Utah and Las Vegas take I-15 southwest. From the east, take I-8 west from Yuma, Arizona to San Diego, I-10 west from Phoenix to Palm Springs and Los Angeles, or I-40 west from the Flagstaff/Grand Canyon Area, meeting I-15 in Barstow.

Big 'Ol Jet Airliner—SoCal's Airports

SoCal's main airport is Los Angeles International, or LAX, located along the coast. Other airports that have regularly scheduled commercial flights to the vicinity of our rides include Lindbergh Field (San Diego), John Wayne (Santa Ana/Orange County), LA/Ontario, Bob Hope (Burbank/San Fernando Valley), Long Beach, Palm Springs, Meadows Field (Bakersfield), McClellan-Palomar (Carlsbad /North San Diego County), Oxnard, Santa Barbara, Santa Maria, and San Luis Obispo.

Take the "A" Train—Using Amtrak, Local Rail, and Bike-Carrying Buses

Metrolink's bicycle cars can hold 18 bikes

Get into the spirit of reducing greenhouse gases by leaving the old gas-guzzler behind and taking the train to your cycling destination. Several rail lines cross portions of So-Cal, giving you plenty of options to combine a fun train ride with your fabulous bike ride. After rolling your trusty steed off the train and onto the platform of your destination of choice, head out on your easy and scenic bike ride through the countryside. Ride back to the same station or do a one-way ride to another station and take the train back from there. Perhaps stay overnight at a local B&B or campground.

Granted, it does take some savoir-faire to be able to use the rail system, as some trains are more bike-friendly than others, and weekend schedules tend to be reduced significantly on the routes that are used primarily for commuting. Note that on most lines only standard single-rider bikes are allowed, as opposed to recumbent, tandem, trailers, etc. Make sure to buy your tickets in advance from the machines at the platform.

Amtrak: The national passenger line runs along the coastal area of our entire region, from San Luis Obispo to San Diego, accessing many of the best rides via the Pacific Surfliner line, the most bike-friendly of the Amtrak trains. Those trains typically have three roll-on bike spots per car, with some exceptions. A complimentary bike reservation is required to accompany your Amtrak ticket on the Surfliner, even if you are a Metrolink pass holder. The Coast Starlight runs the same route but from LA's Union Station north past San Luis Obispo all the way to Vancouver, BC. That train stops at fewer stations, and bikes typically need to be partially taken apart and put in an Amtrak box to ride on it. Other Amtrak lines head to points east, but Metrolink is a better bet for those routes locally. Info: www.amtrak.com; 1.800.USA.RAIL.

Metrolink: This regional line links LA's Union Station with routes through Los Angeles, Orange, portions of Ventura, Riverside, and San Bernardino Counties and connects to San Diego's Coaster and Sprinter rail systems at Oceanside. Metrolink mostly operates on the same tracks as Amtrak, but offers more local stops. The bike-friendly line allows three bikes on its cars (enter the door with a bike insignia next to it), and on select trains special bike cars are designed to hold 18 bikes on the lower level, as indicated by a yellow "Bike Car" sign or a car completely wrapped in a bike design. If you end up on the wrong car do not go between cars with your bike. Rather, notify the conductor and at the next stop get off the train and switch cars that way. See metrolinktrains.com for routes, rates and info on taking your bike on board, or call 800.371.5465 (LINK) for personalized travel planning.

View from Metrolink along San Clemente.

Metro Rail: These trains servicing Los Angeles County run above and below ground. Bikes are allowed on all of its cars. Look for either the symbol for bikes/strollers/

luggage or stand in the designated open area, and always remain with your bike. Never block the entrance to the conductor's area in the front car. Some lines, especially the Blue Line, go through some sketchy areas, but the system is regarded by most as safe, especially during the day. Most Metro buses are equipped to carry two bikes on a front-load rack. For information and trip planning on rail and bus see socaltransport.org.

Coaster and Sprinter: San Diego County's Coaster commuter train runs near the coast between downtown San Diego's Santa Fe Depot and the coastal towns up to Oceanside, taking about an hour for the entire route. Enjoy some segments with ocean views south of Carlsbad and south of Encinitas. Southbound the route leaves the ocean at Del Mar and heads into the Sorento Valley toward downtown San Diego. It overlaps with Amtrak's Surfliner route, which also stops at San Diego's Santa Fe and Old Town Depots and the Solana Beach and Oceanside stations, although select Surfliner trains stop at all 8 Coaster stations. In Oceanside the Coaster connects with LA's Metrolink system and North San Diego County's Sprinter line. Sprinter trains run along the Hwy 78 corridor between Oceanside and Escondido. Each Coaster and Sprinter car has a bike storage area. Enter the door with the bike emblem and use the Velcro straps provided. Breeze bus connections can get you closer to some of the rides, with buses that are equipped to carry two bikes on a front rack. Web: gonctd.com. Phone: 760.966.6500.

San Diego Trolley: The red light rail cars accommodate one or two bikes per car, but in tighter quarters than the Coaster, not recommended at rush hour. The blue, orange and green lines connect downtown with eastern and southern suburbs. MTS buses connect and carry two bikes on a front rack. For a route planner check sdmts.com.

Magic Bus—Other SoCal Bus Systems

San Luis Obispo County: Bus routes service all rides. Seasonal trollies to Avila Beach and Cambria carry 2–6 bikes. See slorta.org for routes and schedules. Phone: 805.541.2228.

Santa Barbara County: Check trafficsolutions.info/transit.htm for a summary of transit systems. Phone: 805.963.SAVE. Lompoc's Colt Transit bus runs between Lompoc and Solvang wine country.

Ventura County: The Coastal Express bus runs between Oxnard and UC Santa Barbara. Other routes run through Ventura County. See goventura.org. Phone: 800.438.1112.

Orange County: Orange County Transportation Authority (OCTA) operates buses with two-bike racks. See octa.net for routes and schedules. Other OC systems like Irvine Shuttle and Laguna Beach Transit also have bike racks. Phone: 714.636.RIDE.

Riverside & San Bernardino Counties: Riverside County Transit services most rides, including stops at Metrolink stations. Buses have bike racks. Route 210/220 is between Riverside's Metrolink station and Palm Desert. Route 208 is Riverside—Temecula. See riversidetransit.com for routes and details. In Coachella Valley (Palm Springs), local bus service is Sunbus, with bike racks. See sunline.org. Phone: 1.800.347.8628. San Bernardino County's Omnitrans buses have bike racks. See omnitrans.org for schedules, routes and fares. Mountain Area Regional Transit Authority operates bus service between the San Bernardino Metrolink station and Big Bear with easy access to our rides there. Each bus carries two bikes but spaces cannot be reserved. See marta.cc. Phone: 909.878.5200.

Kern County: Amtrak trains from Bakersfield go north only, through the San Joaquin Valley and to the Bay Area. Amtrak buses continue south over the mountain passes to the LA Basin, but call first to see if it is possible to take a bike along. For local travel, Bakersfield's Golden Empire Transit District's website is getbus.org.

How Sweet It Is — The E-Bike Edge

Hordes of casual cyclists have been snapping up e-bikes in recent years, redefining what an "easy" bike ride is. We revisited many of enCYCLEpedia's rides with Class I pedal-assist e-bikes to evaluate the differences and to see if rides could be added.

I-5 overpass, Oceanside, along San Luis Rey River Trail (OC1). E-bike edge for headwinds.

North San Diego coast vista along SDC1. E-bike edge for distance, headwinds, and hills.

The conclusions were obvious. Our e-bikes made hills fun rather than a chore, it was much easier to fight headwinds, and enabled us to go on longer rides, within the confines of the battery's capacity, which is important to gauge since many of these heavy steeds are difficult to pedal with no power assist. Most casual e-cyclists still enjoy safer low or no traffic scenic routes, so the rides remain mostly the same. Although we've added a few new fabulous rides in this edition, the only one added specifically for e-bikes is the ultra hilly car-free Mt. Hollywood ride option in Griffith Park (LA4).

E-bikes come in 3 basic varieties. Class I and II have a max assist speed of 20 mph and are allowed on most paved SoCal bike paths. Class II adds a throttle, helpful for easy starts and power without the need to pedal. Class III has a throttle with a max of 27 mph. They are banned from most paved SoCal bike paths, but enforcement is likely to be sporadic. Many public parks ban all e-bikes from their unpaved trails.

E-bike edges: Pismo Beach (PB3) for hills and Newport Beach (NB2) for short steep hills & headwinds.

FOOD FOR THE SOUL—
THE BEST EASY SCENIC BIKE RIDES

SC1

NB1

OC1

1. San Luis Obispo County

San Luis Obispo (SLO) County lies midway between Los Angeles and San Francisco, about 200 miles to either, and is accessible north-to-south by U.S. Highway 101 and scenic Highway 1. State highways from Kern County in the Central Valley to the east include routes 41, 46, 58, and 166. Of these, Hwy 46 between Lost Hills and Paso Robles is best for high profile vehicles; it is straighter with fewer grades and partially a 4-lane freeway. Monterey County is to the north and Santa Barbara County to the south. SLO County's total population of only around 275,000 over 3,304 square miles of land is an indication of its rural nature. Most of the population lives in the small coastal cities or along the US 101 corridor in the interior valley. Wine production is the number one industry in the county, and ranks third in California behind giants Napa and Sonoma Counties. Tourism in this beautiful region is also very important. The Amtrak line runs through SLO County, with stops in Grover Beach/Pismo Beach and SLO Town, the northern-most stop of the Pacific Surfliner.

The world-renowned Big Sur coastline descends southward out of Monterey County, and although the cliffs mellow by the time SLO County begins, the quintessential California coastline continues to enchant. The SLO coastline is also more accessible by both car and bike, with charming towns and popular attractions beckoning. While Hwy 1 through the Big Sur area is a very challenging cycle with steep hills, drop-offs, and winding roads with steady traffic and few bike lanes or shoulders, the Coast Highway through SLO typically has wide bike lanes with grades that are easier to navigate. Our routes for the most part do not include road rides such as these, but in the future watch for more Class I paths to be built parallel to Hwy 1in SLO to the Monterey County line, currently in the planning stages. For updates see the sites californiacoastaltrail.info and slocog.org/programs/active-transportation/regional-trails/.

The major attraction in SLO County is Hearst Castle, located near San Simeon, atop "La Cuesta Encantada" (The Enchanted Hill). The former William Randolph Hearst estate contains 165 rooms and 127 acres of gardens, terraces, pools, and walkways. It can be visited via a series of guided tours that cost about $25 each, reservable on reservecalifornia.com. Five miles farther north is a large elephant seal rookery, most active in the winter months, with a well-developed system of observation paths. The popular upscale destination of Cambria is about 5 miles south of Hearst Castle, containing the historic Main Street inland and dramatic coastal sections, which are explored in ride CA1. Scenic Hwy 1 connects Cambria to the points of interest farther north via on-road ride CA2. The fishing port and tourist town of Morro Bay is about 18 miles south of Cambria, which is a delightful place to visit, especially by bike on a mild sunny day in the off-season. Ride MB1 takes the cyclist on a tour of the town and out to its sentinel, Morro Rock. Morro Rock is actually a long extinct volcanic plug, part of the Nine Sisters of similar formations located between there and San Luis Obispo to the southeast. Nearby Montana de Oro State Park is a coastal jewel with a rarely allowed mountain bike ride along the seaside bluffs, and a flat creekside ride for contrast (MB2).

The county seat is also named San Luis Obispo, aka "SLO Town," a city of under 50,000 situated 9 miles inland from Morro Bay, and home of acclaimed California Polytechnic Institute. Although extended Class I trails are planned, it is not a destination for our brand of cycling at present, but worth a visit for its charming downtown core. Someday a Class I trail may run from there along San Luis Obispo Creek to Avila Beach, where the Bob Jones creekside trail currently exists, making for a great combination of trail ride and beach adventure.

Avila Beach is a quaint coastal community with a delightful Class I trail along a stream (ride AV1). A Class II route leads to Pismo Beach, a popular beach town, also with a charming downtown core next to a wide beach with sand so compact that it makes for a great bike ride—our only designated beach ride in the book (PB1). Pismo Beach falls short on Class I trails, but some are planned for the future. In the meantime, Class II road rides are offered to the south (PB2) and north (PB3) of downtown, with some spectacular ocean vistas en route.

The main wine-producing areas are in the interior valleys, which experience colder nights to stimulate grape production. You can explore wineries along the US 101 corridor around the towns of Atascadero, Templeton, and Paso Robles, which contains 2 miles of Salinas River Walk, planned to extend to 30 miles someday. Exploring wine country by bike here is mainly the on-road hilly variety. SLO County missions are Mission San Miguel Arcángel in San Miguel and Mission San Luis Obispo de Tolosa in downtown San Luis Obispo.

SLO County extends inland over the coastal mountain ranges that are mostly in the territory of Los Padres National Forest. The highest point in the county is 5,106-foot Caliente Mountain, at Carrizo Plain National Monument. This vast and isolated place can make for a great cycling adventure especially if wildflowers are peaking. (CP1, 2, and 3).

Climate Data for San Luis Obispo (Source: NOAA 1981 to 2010 normals)												
Month	Jan	Feb	Mar	Apr	May	Jun	Jul	Aug	Sep	Oct	Nov	Dec	Totals
Average High °F	61.1	62.0	63.6	66.4	69.3	73.0	76.0	76.9	76.8	73.7	67.3	61.1	69.0
Average Low °F	43.6	44.8	45.8	47.0	49.2	52.1	54.5	54.8	54.3	51.5	47.1	43.1	49.0
Precipitation, inches	4.95	5.12	3.97	1.39	0.47	0.10	0.02	0.04	0.26	0.93	2.16	3.71	23.12

Cambria

Cambria is an upscale jewel of a coastal community near the north end of San Luis Obispo County, with the nickname "Pines by the Sea." Check out their Halloween season Scarecrow Festival, when the whole town is decked out in the most elaborate takes on scarecrows, many with themes relating to the businesses that sponsored them. Cambria is always a treat to visit, and the hordes of visitors that flock here are a testament to the community's efforts of making the town attractive.

SAN LUIS OBISPO COUNTY

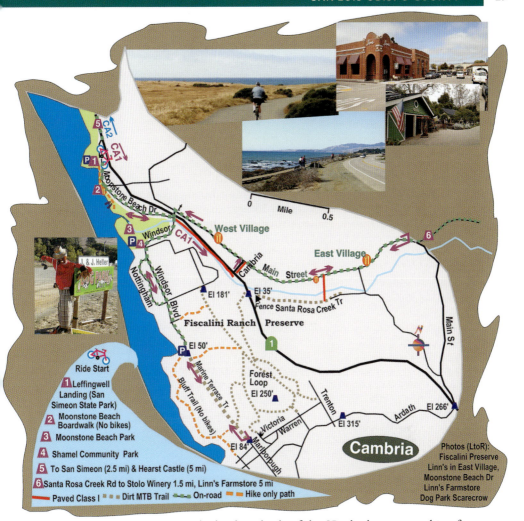

The downtown center is on the landward side of the SR1 highway, stretching for a full mile, with several cross streets, all worth exploring with its restored historic buildings. There are two main clusters of shops and restaurants, called East Village and West Village. Cambria's beautiful popular coastline featuring a mile of public access beaches is an easy bike ride from the downtown area, enabling a wonderful Bike 'n Brunch day.

The Fiscalini Ranch Preserve is accessible a half mile to the south of Moonstone Beach and contains a stunning coastal property with both hiking and mountain bike trails. Although most of the land was clearcut for grazing in the 1800s, one of the three remaining stands of

Moonstone Boardwalk

Monterey pine trees in the world remains up on the ridge. The ridge that separates downtown from the coast rises 200–300 feet in the area of the preserve, so traversing it requires some effort and mountain bike skills. However, the route between downtown and Moonstone Beach is relatively flat. Just north of town coastal Highway 1 has wide bike lanes most of the way to San Simeon with some scenic moments.

Cambria Bike 'n Brunch   CA1 ⭐

Since so many options and different types of riding are involved in your Cambria adventure, your best bet is to examine the map and make your own route depending on your bike type and the abilities in your group. Our suggested route is an easy one that is mostly flat and includes riding on 25 mph roads through town, some Class I path, and a gravel fire road. Those in good condition and with mountain bike skills will have more options. Much of the riding is on roadways with traffic, so it is not the greatest family ride.

Tunes: Whispering Pines by Dar Williams and Alison Krause; Feels So Good by Chuck Mangione; Mandoline Concerto in C Major RV425 by Vivaldi; San Simeon by Al Jardine

Eats: Olallieberry pie at Linn's *(also, their low-sugar olallieberry jam is excellent).*

Distance: 11.4 miles + options. Time: 1.25 hours.

Route & Bike: Easy. Class II and III paved roads; some Class I; flat dirt fire road and optional hilly dirt trails. Gradual grade up to Linn's farm store (e-bike edge). Any bike, hybrid or fatter tire for more options.

Seasons: Year round. Best on sunny uncrowded off-season weekday.

Facilities: Restrooms and water at Leffingwell Landing, Moonstone Beach, Shamel County Park, West Village (E of Chamber of Commerce, N of Main), East Village (W of Burton Dr, S of Main).

Knocks & Hazards: Road riding on low speed limit roads. Fog. Possible rattlesnakes in Preserve.

Rent 'n Ride: Check Morro Bay or San Luis Obispo.

Camp 'n Ride: San Simeon State Park, 1 mile north on Hwy 1: Tents/RV's (no hookups). Ride to Cambria on Hwy 1 in wide bike lane, or north to San Simeon and beyond along the coast (see ride CA2).

Bike 'n Brunch: Most restaurants are in East and West Villages along Main Street. In East Village, Linn's is a long-time standard, famous for home cooking and olallieberry pie, while local cyclists' favorite is Creekside Garden Café. For an ocean view, pricey Moonstone Beach Bar & Grill on Moonstone Beach Drive has a great patio. Sebastian's Café near WR Hearst State Beach north of town was once a great cycling destination via ride CA2. Check for current offerings there.

Bike Club: Slabtown Rollers: countrycoastclassic.org. Hosts Country Coast Classic.

Further Info: Fiscalini Ranch: ffrpcambria.org. Cambria: cambriachamber.org North SLO County coast: Elephant seal rookery: elephantseal.org; Tours of Piedras Blancas Lighthouse: piedrasblancas.org. Hearst Castle: hearstcastle.org

Access: Cambria is about 2.5 miles south along Hwy 1 from central San Simeon, and just 1 mile south of the San Simeon State Park's campground. Heading north on Hwy 1, Cambria is about 18 miles north of Morro Bay. Once reaching Cambria, turn west onto Windsor Avenue, and then immediately bear right onto Moonstone Beach Drive. Continue along the scenic drive about a mile and turn left into Leffingwell Landing (San Simeon State Park) where there is free parking and restrooms. If you are coming from the north you can save some distance by turning right onto Moonstone Beach Drive, then turn right into the parking lot.

The Ride: Unfortunately the beautiful wooden coastal boardwalk you see heading south is for pedestrians only, but a stroll along it is a very worthwhile post-ride activity. Pedal south along Moonstone Beach Drive, ogling the vistas and stopping at viewpoints, but being careful of parked and moving vehicles. Accommodations, a restaurant, and residences line the landward side of the road, but the seaward side is all open coastal parkland.

Once the road turns inland and reaches Windsor Avenue, turn to the right (mile 1.4). Cycle past Moonstone Beach Park toward Shamel County Park along the beach (1.7). Follow Windsor Boulevard to the left. You have the option of dropping down to Nottingham Dr for a few blocks and a scenic ocean viewpoint. At the end of Windsor is a trailhead for Fiscalini Ranch Preserve. The Bluff Trail to the right is hike-only (an option to lock and hike), however the Marine Terrace Trail is a fire road open to cycling that most bikes should be able to handle. There are great ocean views from this trail as well, just not close up bluff views. The trail ends at Marlborough Lane (3.2). Turn around here unless you are a mountain biker seeking some adventure (Option 1).

> **Option 1: Fiscalini Preserve MTB** 🌟 *2–4 miles, moderate, advanced novice skill.*
> Check the map for the trails that allow mountain bikes. Updated maps can also be found on line or posted on informational boards in the preserve. Ride the singletrack trail up the ridge over 200 feet in elevation gain, and around the forest loop through the rare Monterey pine trees. You can drop down to the other side of the ridge and reach Hwy 1, then make your way into town via Hwy 1 to Cambria Road. The grade in the preserve is more gradual on the ocean side compared to the inland side.

If you don't do Option 1, follow the route back along Windsor Blvd until almost reaching Hwy 1 (4.9). On the right is a paved Class I trail. Take it, parallel to Hwy 1. It ends at a signal to cross Hwy 1 at Cambria Rd (5.4) that leads to Main Street (5.5), with sharrows. The West Village area is a couple of blocks to the left and East Village is to the right. For a shorter trip, turn left at this point, and return to your start. Otherwise, turn right on Main Street. Reach the beginning of the East Village (6.3). Check this area out, and to continue for some more mileage ride along Main to Santa Rosa Creek Road (6.8). Main Street beyond here is a bike route, but it's very hilly with narrow shoulders. For a less trafficked and less hilly route, turn up Santa Rosa Creek Road, perhaps riding just past Coast Union High School (7.5). You can also visit Stolo Family Winery and Tasting Room, 1 mile farther up the road from the high school. Linn's Fruit Stand that sells pie and refreshments is another 3.5 miles up the scenic winding road from the winery. Beyond that point the road steepens.

Head back to Main Street and turn right (8.2). Ride back through East Village where there are some good dining options. After passing the Bluebird Inn on the left, there is paved path (8.9). This leads to a bike bridge across Santa Rosa Creek and a dirt trail. If you have a mountain bike, you can ride back and forth on the trail, however, a fence makes it difficult to continue toward Hwy 1, which you then must cross without a signal. Our route continues onward to Cambria Road, where you turned from before (9.4). You can return the same way or continue to West Village (9.7). The West Village is the main part of town, with diagonal parking that is such a menace to cyclists, so be extra careful here, or just walk your bike on the sidewalks to scout for shopping and dining. Turn left at Windsor Boulevard (10.0). Cross Hwy 1 with the signal, then bear right on Moonstone Beach Drive to return to your ride start (11.4).

North to San Simeon   CA2 ⭐

Details: About 12 to 23 miles round trip. Moderate. Class II, any bike, e-bike edge. Recommended for experienced cyclists only, especially past San Simeon.

The ride north of Cambria to San Simeon along Hwy 1, popular with road cyclists who don't mind riding next to fast-moving vehicles, begins at the north end of Moonstone Beach Dr. The most scenic section and widest shoulder is just north of Cambria. Closer to San Simeon the shoulder narrows and the ocean becomes more distant. Reach San Simeon State Park and its campground in 0.8 mile, and the hotel district of San Simeon in 2.2 miles, where you should divert onto the frontage road. The entrance to Hearst Castle is at 5.6 miles.

W.R. Hearst Memorial State Beach here is worth a visit. Check to see what has replaced the popular Sebastian's Café on the beach, and the wine tasting room. Stroll out on the pier and take in views back toward the castle on the hill. The bike lane narrows a bit, and the road pulls away from the seaside and up a small hill, but then returns to the ocean as you cycle next to the coast up to Piedras Blancas where the fascinating elephant seal rookery is located (10.1). Just beyond is the Piedras Blancas lighthouse (11.3) as the bike lane begins to disappear. The return ride can be even more scenic as you are cycling on the ocean side of the road.

Morro Bay and Montana de Oro State Park

The town of Morro Bay is a great place to visit, especially on a mild sunny day in the off-season, and even better if you can see it on two wheels. The tourist-oriented town features a main street of shops and restaurants situated next to a picture-perfect bay over which the distinctive Morro Rock, the "Gibraltar of the West Coast," stands sentinel. Fishing boats that dock at Morro Bay bring in a fresh catch served in a variety of seafood restaurants, while a huge PG&E power plant towers over the town competing for attention with The Rock.

Fishing boats and Morro Rock at Morro Bay

The bay is protected by the sand dunes of the north end of Montana de Oro State Park, a coastal jewel whose entrance is a 10-minute drive to the south. A fabulous easy mountain bike ride there takes you along a California coastal wonderland, and inland up a scenic riparian

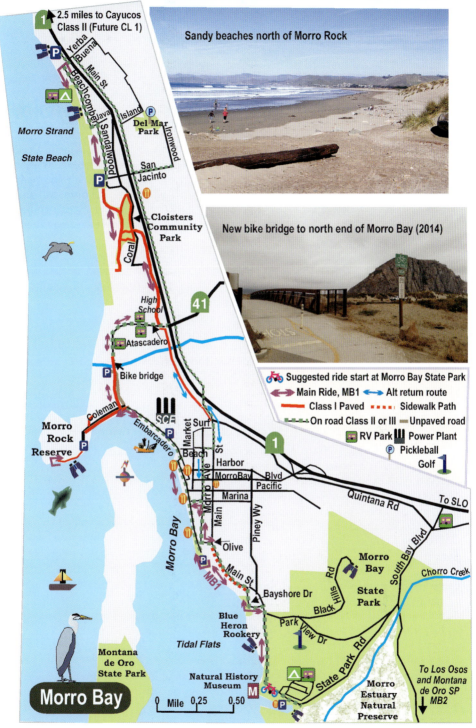

corridor. The Morro Bay area offers lots of sea mammal and bird watching opportunities, such as around Morro Estuary, one of the most prolific birding spots on the West Coast. Hiking, fishing, kayaking, and golfing are also popular in this area.

Morro Bay Bike 'n Brunch MB1

Embarcadero Harborwalk is short but sweet

Morro Bay is a wonderful town to cycle around on a variety of pathway types. An easy Bike 'n Brunch ride along the waterfront extends from beautiful Morro Bay State Park, through the main tourist strip, to Morro Rock. It continues across a new bike bridge to the oceanfront neighborhood at the north end of town. You can return the same way or tackle the hilly downtown district to add some variety.

Tunes: A Boat Like Gideon Brown by Great Big Sea; White Bird (long version) by It's A Beautiful Day; I Am A Rock by Simon and Garfunkel
Eats: Fresh fish lunch at one of the bayside restaurants or a beach picnic

Distance: 15 miles Time: 2 hours. Options to shorten ride. Extend: Road bikers can take Class II South Bay Blvd south to Los Osos (food) (4.4 mi), then either take Class III Pecho Valley Rd to MB2 (5 mi), or Class II Los Osos Valley Rd east to SLO (8 mi).
Route & Bike: Easy to moderate. Mix of Class I, II, and III. Paved for any bike. Mostly flat, some small hills. MTB'ers can try hilly trails in the State Park, see cccmb.org.
Seasons: All. Best on sunny uncrowded off-season weekday with no fog.
Facilities: Restrooms and water in Morro Bay State Park, Bayside Park, Cloisters Park, the Azure Avenue trailhead, and Morro Strand State Beach. Public restrooms in the Embarcadero tourist district.
Knocks & Hazards: Some clueless peds. Comingling with downtown tourist traffic—that portion may not be suitable for family rides. Be especially careful of car doors opening on Embarcadero. Street crossings. Potential for lurkers on secluded north end of Class I trails parallel to Hwy 1. Area tends to be foggy often. Possible flooding along creeks during winter storms.
Rent 'n Ride: Farmer's Kites, Surreys & More, 1108 Front St, 805.772.0113; Estero Adventures, 501 Embarcadero, 805.550.3165; The Bike Shop, 842 Main St, 805.772.2697.
Camp 'n Ride: Our ride starts at Morro Bay State Park (some partial hookups, dump station), 805.772.2560. Morro Strand State Beach (full hookups) is at north end of town, 805.772.2722. North of bike bridge: Morro Strand RV Park, 221 Atascadero Rd, 800.799.6030 and Morro Dunes RV Park, 1700 Embarcadero, 805.772.2722. Bay Pines Travel Park, 1501 Quintana Rd, 805.772.3223. El Choro Regional Park is 5 miles east on SR 1 toward San Luis Obispo. Reserve: 805.781.5930.
Bike 'n Brunch: Popular view restaurants on Embarcadero include The Galley at 899 for seafood and Blue Skye Coastal Café at 699 for breakfast and lunch. Tognazzini's Dockside at 1245 is popular for lunch, dinner, plus café on the dock and fresh fish market. On adjacent Front St, Frankie & Lola's at 1154 is good for breakfast/lunch. La Parisienne at 1140 is good for coffee, breakfast sandwiches. Popular coffee houses are Top Dog at 857 Main St and Rock Espresso Bar at 275 Morro Bay Blvd.
City Ordinance, bikes on sidewalks: Riding prohibited on sidewalks in business districts.

Event: July 4th Bike Parade
Further Info: Morro Bay State Park: www.parks.ca.gov/?page_id=594;
City: www.morro-bay.ca.us/; General: morrobay.org; morrobay.com.

Access: From SLO, take Hwy 1 north to the Los Osos–Baywood Park off ramp. Turn left, go about 1 mile and turn right, following a sign for Morro Bay State Park. Take park road for about 1.4 miles to park entrance. Turn right into park for camping, or left for free parking in marina area. Also find free parking all along route as described.

The Ride: Start from the campground entrance, or across the street at the marina lot, riding north along the 25 mph State Park Road that becomes Main Street. Mountain bikers can ride parallel to portions of the road on a lovely bayside trail with great views across Morro Bay to Morro Rock. On your right is the scenic and reasonably priced municipal golf course, while on the left is the Museum of Natural History.

Ride up a small hill to a fascinating blue heron rookery preserve in the eucalyptus trees. The loud noises you may hear are probably the males presenting gifts of nest materials to the females, accompanied by shrieks. They nest in late winter to spring on platforms atop the trees, laying 3–5 eggs, but just feeding the 1 or 2 most aggressive chicks.

In 0.6 mile make a left onto Bayshore Drive, which curves to the right. Turn left onto a sidewalk bike trail along the west side of Main Street (mile 0.8). Turn left again down Class II Olive Street (1.2), which ends down a hill at a nice Morro Bay viewpoint at Morro Avenue. Continue to the right down Morro Avenue, then make a left onto Marina Street (1.5). Ride down the short hill to Embarcadero, the main bayside tourist street in town. Be careful as you ride among the slow-moving traffic on this street. Cycle to the left, where the road ends at Bayside Park (2.0), which is mostly a boat launch facility, but it also has restrooms and some bayfront picnic tables.

Turn around and head north on Embarcadero, carefully riding through the main bayside downtown strip, with plenty of restaurants and shops to distract you. After the road jogs right, then left (2.6), you have the option of cycling through parking lots of several waterfront restaurants. Pass the gigantic outmoded PG&E power plant, and watch for a lovely short but sweet paved Class I trail on the bay side (3.0), the highlight of the ride. The Embarcadero Harborwalk runs along the bay to Morro Rock. The separated bike/ped trail crosses the road just before the rock (3.4) and ends soon after at Atascadero Beach, where you can pause and watch the surfers or stroll along the beach. You can also lock your bike at Morro Rock parking area and hike along the base of the rock. Morro Rock itself is a peregrine falcon sanctuary.

Coastal trail network of north Morro Bay

Return back down the path. Before it bends to the right (3.9), turn left on a path that crosses Coleman Drive to connect with a paved Class I path parallel to a dirt access road. It leads through the dunes to another parking area and a bike bridge (4.1). Cross the bridge and ride along the road with beach sands to the left and Morro Dunes RV Park to the right. The road curves to the right and passes a water treatment plant (4.4) and two entrances to Morro Strand RV Park. At the Motel 6 (4.7), cross Atascadero to a Class I path to the right of the Morro Bay High School entrance road. The trail follows the eastern perimeter of the school and then skirts a residential area, ending at Coral Avenue (5.3). Cross over Coral and enter Cloisters Community Park. Follow any of the paved trails toward the tall vegetated dunes and reach a path running parallel to them. Start by turning left on this path (5.5). The trail turns into a very pleasant beach boardwalk that ends after it curves to the right and daylights at a sandy beach with views of Morro Rock (5.8). Turn around and continue north along the dune path, skirting Cloisters Park, keeping to the left at junctions to remain next to the dunes, until the trail ends in a beautiful park with restrooms in a quiet residential neighborhood at the end of Azure Avenue (6.5).

From the park cycle north down sharrowed Sandalwood Avenue through the neighborhood. When it ends on Java Street, jog left then right on Beachcomber Drive (7.0). This spectacular stretch of road above the Morro Strand State Beach campground affords a panoramic view of the coastline and Morro Rock. You can enter the state park from the north end of Beachcomber (7.4). Cycle uphill on Yerba Buena Street, turning left on Toro Road just before SR1, and ride to a parking lot at the end of the street (7.7), where fat tired bikers can ride a short distance out to a beautiful precipice overlooking the beach. SLO County has proposed a Class I trail along the ocean side of Hwy 1 running 2.5 miles to Cayucos, a cute beach town with restaurants, but for now there is just a shoulder along the busy highway.

For the most scenic return, retrace your route. Assuming you skip the short jaunts to the beach at Cloisters Park and to Morro Rock, that will give you a ride of about 15 mostly easy miles. Otherwise you can try this alternate route as shown on the map: Once you reach the Motel 6 at Atascadero, ride to the left a short distance, then to the right after Morro Shores Inn on a Class I cypress-lined path that runs parallel to Hwy 1, past Lila Keiser Park. It empties onto a little-used access road to the power plant and then hilly Class II Main Street through downtown. From there you can skip the touristy waterfront area by turning right on Beach Street, left on Class II Morro Ave, and following that back, meeting up with our route farther to the south when it crosses Marina Street. This cuts off 2 miles from the ride but adds some car traffic and hills (e-bike edge).

Upon returning to Morro Bay State Park, turn right across from the campground entrance into the parking lot where the cozy Bayside Cafe is located.

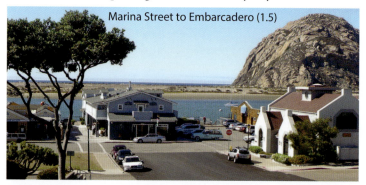

Marina Street to Embarcadero (1.5)

You can hike (no bikes) on short trails that begin at the south end of the parking lot, adjacent to marshlands with vistas of Morro Bay and Morro Rock. The Morro Bay Boardwalk that starts along the trail to the south is a great way to walk through the Morro Estuary Natural Preserve, one of the best bird watching spots on the West Coast.

Option 1: For a great bang for the buck option if time or ability is limiting, just do the portion of this ride between Morro Rock, Cloisters Park, and Morro Strand State Beach at the north end of town. This 7.5-8 mile round trip ride offers the most bike trails along with beautiful coastal scenery.

Montana de Oro MTB—Ocean Bluffs and Creekside Cruise   MB2

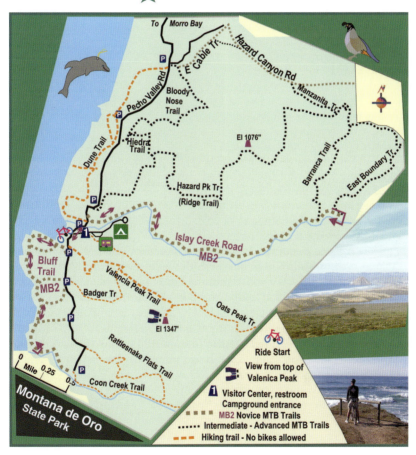

Montana de Oro State Park contains a rare jewel: its 2-mile long coastal bluff dirt trail actually allows bikes. The coastline here is classic California, with rocky bluffs above the pounding surf, sea otters frolicking in the kelp below, and pelicans patrolling the coastline. Landward are small but beautiful mountains that in springtime put on a dazzling wildflower display of orange California poppies, yellow mustard plant (non-native, but beautiful), and lavender, that peak in April and May, earning its namesake that means Mountain of Gold. Although the distance is short, you are guaranteed to spend ample time exploring the changing scenic vistas along the route.

To add some mileage, ride a 3.3-mile pleasant inland valley trail so that you can have more than a 10-mile scenic workout for the day. More adventurous mountain bikers can connect to some steep challenging trails. You can also hike to the summit of 1,347-foot Valencia Peak, a great trail with amazing views over the park and out to sea.

Tunes: Sting's Ocean Waltz and Mad About You (from *The Living Sea*) and Fields of Gold.
Eats: Picnic on an oceanfront bluff.

Distance: 10.5 miles (3.4 miles bluffs, 6.6 miles inland, 0.5 mile connector). Time: 1–2.5 hours.
Route & Bike: Easy except a short steep hill between the ocean and inland trailheads on paved park road, and some moderate hills on inland trail. Optional MTB trails are for advanced riders. Mostly flat packed dirt and gravel, single and double track. Hybrid or mountain bike. E-bike edge for hills. Main trails are non-technical.
Season: Year round. Best on sunny spring day with wildflowers peaking.
Facilities: Restrooms (no water) near the Visitor's Center. Water at main campground.
Knocks & Hazards: Bluff Trail may be crowded with hikers. Rattlesnakes and mountain lions, more so on inland trail. Connection between two trailheads is via 0.3-mile steep hilly pedal on paved park road. Diablo Canyon nuclear power plant, built on an earthquake fault, is just over the hill south along the coast. If you hear a steady siren for 3 to 5 minutes, return to your vehicle and tune to 920 or 1400 AM or 98.1 FM for instructions.

Bluff Trail, Montana de Oro State Park

Rent 'n Ride: See MB1.
Camp 'n Ride: Park campground is near the Visitor's Center—tents, RV's (to 27 feet), no hookups. Use dump station at Morro Bay State Park (See MB1). No ocean view from sites. Short ride from camp to both sections of this ride. Primitive and equestrian campsites elsewhere in the park.
Bike 'n Brunch: Picnic. Closest restaurants and supermarket in Los Osos.
Further Info: State Park: www.parks.ca.gov/?page_id=592; Central Coast Concerned Mountain Bikers posts current MTB maps: cccmb.org

Access: Montana de Oro State Park is a 10-minute drive south of Morro Bay past Los Osos. From Morro Bay State Park campground, take State Park Road northeast to South Bay Boulevard and turn right. From Highway 101 in San Luis Obispo, take Highway 1 toward Morro Bay, making a left onto South Bay Boulevard. Continue into Los Osos, making a right onto Los Osos Valley Road that leads into the park. The rides begin toward the end of the park road at the small Visitor's Center. The Islay Creek Road trail begins on the gated fire road on the left, just before the park road dips down to the beach, prior to the Visitor's Center. The Bluff Trail begins on the

Islay Creek Trail.

right, after the Visitor's Center and across the road from the Valencia Peak hike trailhead. No park entry fee.

The Ride: The Bluff Trail takes you through low brush along the beautiful bluffs above the rocky shoreline for almost 2 miles. Basically, stay on the wide, dirt and gravel trail, and choose to keep closer to the ocean at main trail junctions. At some places a narrower trail gets even closer to the edge of the bluffs, which we don't recommend to cycle on because of erosion and the proximity to the edge of the cliffs. The trail begins with a dip down to cross a small wooden bridge over a creek drainage. It then rises to bring you to Islay Point that overlooks Spooner's Cove Beach. Vistas northward are toward Morro Bay and Morro Rock. The trail descends gradually as it heads west, then levels out as it heads more southerly, with very gradual up and down grades. In about 0.5 mile notice a wide spur trail that leads to the right down to Corallina Cove, which is a nice spot to inspect some tide pools. You can lock your bike and walk down to it. The trail then heads inland and uphill for about 0.1 mile to go around the cove. Turn right onto a wooden bridge to cross over a ravine.

The trail then returns downhill to views of the open ocean. Below the bluffs are interesting rock formations and a plethora of sea life, from sea otters to elephant seals, and even perhaps the spouts of grey whales during the winter months. Watch sea and shore birds as well, including cormorants, western gulls, and the black oystercatcher with its crimson beak. Pigeon guillemots nest in inaccessible holes of the cliffs in summer. Look for their black breeding plumage, white wing-bars, and crimson legs. Raptors such as vultures and red-tail hawks patrol the coastal scrubland.

When the surf is up, the shoreline gets hammered with powerful breakers, and some surfers dare to tackle them. Around mile 1, a sole prized picnic table overlooks scenic Quarry Cove. The coastline becomes even more dramatic upon reaching the overlook to Grotto Rock, a stand-alone outcrop in a rocky cove with caverns at water level where the ocean surges through. The trail comes to an end at a roped off area at mile 1.7. A connector trail to the left enables you to ride up the small hill to the paved park road (Pecho Valley Road), but we recommend turning around and enjoying the spectacular scenery on the return. Consider riding up and down the connector trails to the park road to gain more mileage as shown on the map.

Our ride continues on Islay Creek Road, a wide multi-use dirt path that rises as it parallels Islay Creek. There is no parking at the trailhead. From the Visitor's Center, ride Pecho Valley Road 0.25 mile north down the hill, then up the short steep hill to the gated fire road on the right. On this trail you will pass conifer forest, riparian, chaparral, and coastal scrub habitats along the way. There is great birding along here, as the valley is home to 25 to 40 bird species. On one outing, a California quail led us down the trail, away from its nest. After the first mile it gets much hillier (e-bike edge).

The doubletrack path ends in 3.3 miles at a gate at the park boundary. Novices should turn around here, although experienced mountain bikers can attempt a more challenging return via the Barranca Trail (at mile 2.4) or the East Boundary Trail (at mile 3.3), both of which connect to the Hazard Peak/Ridge Trail that climbs over a 1,000 foot mountain and ends at the paved park road just north of the Islay Creek Road trailhead. This area is mountain lion habitat, so ride with a partner and keep children close by. Some bikers have also reported close encounters with rattlesnakes on the upper trails, but on the creek trail they should be easier to spot. Another trail considered novice level, accessible 1.5 miles farther to the north along Pecho Valley Road, is the Hazard Canyon Road Trail.

San Luis Obispo

San Luis Obispo ("SLO Town" or "SLO") is located along the US 101 freeway about 7 miles north of Pismo Beach. SR1, the Pacific Coast Highway, branches off from SLO at the Santa Rosa Street interchange and leads to Morro Bay and up along the fabulous Big Sur coast to Monterey. San Luis Obispo, Spanish for "St. Louis, the bishop," lies in a coastal valley to the west of the Santa Lucia Mountains, 11 miles from the ocean near Morro Bay and Avila Beach.

SLO Railroad Safety Trail bike bridge near Amtrak station.

Founded in 1772 by Spanish Father Junípero Serra, it is one of the oldest cities in California, and now has a population of about 45,000. Historic buildings include the restored Mission San Luis Obispo de Tolosa, downtown at 751 Palm Street, and the adjacent circa 1905 former Carnegie Library at 695 Monterey Street. SLO is also the San Luis Obispo County seat and home of highly rated California Polytechnic State University (Cal Poly) and its 20,000 staff and students, giving SLO the feel of a college town, which helps to have made it bike friendly, with many Class II lanes.

Morro Street is a bicycling boulevard with traffic calming that leads from a sidewalk connection at the northwest corner of Upham and Santa Barbara near the Amtrak station south to the downtown core, where many cycle, mingling with traffic. On the first Thursday of each month cyclists congregate after the Farmers' Market for Bike Happening (Bike Nite), where they ride en masse, many in costumes, around the city. The large market is held downtown on Higuera Street, between Osos and Nipomo Streets, every Thursday from 6 to 9 p.m. The historic downtown core is located southeast of US 101 between Nipomo Street and Grand Avenue, where beautiful tree-lined streets are full of interesting places to eat and shop.

SLO 's main Class I trail is the SLO Railroad Safety Trail, a rail trail. A new (2021) section connects Spanos Stadium on the Cal Poly campus with downtown, running south next to California Blvd and ending across US 101 near Pepper and Mill Streets. Bike routes are planned to connect to the existing trail section farther south, which starts near the Amtrak station at the south end of Santa Rosa Street near Upham. From Morro St cross at the light to Osos St and access the trail via an elaborate ramped bike bridge over the tracks. The trail runs about 1.3 miles south to Orcutt Road. Plans call for extending the trail about 2 miles farther south.

When/if the last 4.5-mile stretch of the Bob Jones Trail is completed from Avila Beach along San Luis Creek to southwest SLO, it will provide a true City to the Sea Class I ride (see Avila Beach). The SLO terminus will be at the Octagon Barn Center along Higuera Street about 0.4-mile south of Los Osos Valley Road. Higuera Street is currently the main Class II bike route heading south, parallel to US 101. The route crosses under the freeway at the See Canyon interchange and continues south on Ontario Road to the Bob Jones Trail that leads into Avila Beach. Future Class I trails may connect most of the way from the city's rail trail to the Bob Jones Trail, downtown, and other points of interest. More bicycle boulevards are planned as well.

Check the city's website, slocity.org, and the county site, rideshare.org/bike-maps. for maps and updates. Stop in at the Council of Governments building at 1114 Marsh Street for a printed copy of the county's bike map. Their website also has maps of a historic bike tour that passes the mission, Railroad Square, a 0.5-mile bike trail through Meadow Park, and a few other more obscure spots. A winery tour ride is also described on the site. SLO lies amid the Central Coast wine country that extends about 30 miles north to Paso Robles and 70 miles south to Santa Ynez in Santa Barbara County. From the SLO Amtrak station, one can set out south on the rail trail and link to road rides down Class II Orcutt Road that passes several wineries just south of town.

San Luis Obispo Bike Club offers many levels of rides, including those of the slow variety: slobc.org. Rentals: Wally's Bicycle Works, 306 Higuera St, 805.544.4116; Art's Cyclery, 181 Suburban Rd, 540.7969; Cambria Bicycle Outfitter, 1422 Monterey St, 543.1148; Foothill Cyclery, 767 E Foothill Blvd, 541.4101.
Bike 'n Brunch: Lots of interesting restaurants in the downtown core just east of the mission including a Splash Cafe, and in the Historic Railroad District, near the Amtrak station.

Avila Beach

The cute beach community of Avila Beach (photo) is located just northwest of Pismo Beach, about 16 miles south of Morro Bay and 5 miles southwest of San Luis Obispo via US 101. It faces south, and curves around San Luis Bay, which is known to have somewhat warmer water at this location. The Bob Jones Trail is the only Class I trail in the area. It is less than 3 miles long, but extensions are in the works.

Hiking trails lead from the end of Cave Landing Road to clothing-optional Pirates Cove Beach and up Ontario Ridge with fabulous views. A doubletrack gravel path with awesome views leads across a ridge and down a steep hill connecting to PB3.

SAN LUIS OBISPO COUNTY

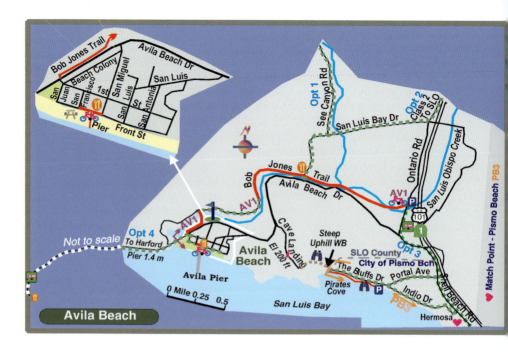

Avila Bike Brunch 'n Beach   AV1

The Bob Jones City to the Sea Bike Trail extends about 2.4 miles through a rural area resplendent in coastal riparian habitat, ending in town for a short but sweet Bike 'n Brunch or Bike 'n Beach experience. Along the way it passes a scenic golf course, orchards, and views of the surrounding hills that are reminiscent of the Tuscany region of Italy. It is a wonderful place to spend a day. The paved trail follows the right of way of the Pacific Coast Railroad, adjacent to San Luis Obispo Creek. Although the trail does not offer ocean views, the ride is very pleasant and is popular with families. It will eventually be a true City to the Sea ride when the extension to San Luis Obispo is completed someday. Options describe some scenic road riding available near town.

Tunes: Beachcombing by Mark Knopfler & Emmylou Harris; Mr. Jones by Counting Crows; El Jaguar by Strunz & Farah
Eats: Grilled fish sandwich with clam chowder on the Custom House patio.

Distance: 5.5 miles round trip + options. Time: 1 hour
Route & Bike: Easy, for any bike. Paved, mostly Class I with some easy Class III through a resort and downtown. Mostly flat with one hill around the golf course at west end of trail. E-bike edge for Options 1, 2, and 3b.
Seasons: Year round. Best on sunny uncrowded off-season weekday.
Facilities: Restroom at Ontario Rd trailhead. Restrooms with water at Avila Pier and Avila State Beach Park, and mid-trail at Woodstone Deli.
Knocks & Hazards: Slow moving bikes and clueless peds. Some on-street riding and road crossings. Possible rattlesnakes. Mountain lions have been spotted along the trail—keep children close by and best to ride with a friend.
Rent 'n Ride: BoltAbout eBike Rentals, 472 Front St, 805.234.2349; Pedego E-bikes, 445 1st St, 627.1414; Wally's at Avila Hot Springs Resort (See Camp 'n Ride).

Camp 'n Ride: San Luis Harbor RV Park, 1.2 miles west along Avila Beach Dr, 805.903.3395; Avila/Pismo KOA, 7075 Ontario Road, near the trailhead, 595.7111; Avila Hot Springs Resort (tent and cabins, no RV), southeast corner Avila Beach Dr. and Ontario Rd, 805.595.2359 (bike rentals). Numerous campgrounds around Pismo Beach.

Bike 'n Brunch: In town, try the Custom House or Ocean Grill restaurants on Front Street for a meal with great ocean views. There are several other restaurants in the small downtown grid as well. About 1.2 miles west on Avila Beach Drive is the Harford Pier with several restaurants to choose from including popular Fat Cats Cafe. Woodstone Deli is a popular place for a casual al fresco lunch, located midway along the Bob Jones trail, just west of the San Luis Bay Drive underpass. Picnic tables on the beach in Avila Beach also afford a great option. Several wineries have tasting rooms in town.

Further Info: visitavilabeach.com; avilabeachpier.com

Access: The eastern trailhead is located near US 101. Exit on Avila Beach Drive, westbound. In 0.25 mile, turn right on Ontario Road. The trailhead is 0.3 mile on the left, with parking across the street. We prefer to park in Avila Beach for safety regarding break-ins and for ending the ride at a place to eat, so instead of turning on Ontario Road continue west down Avila Beach Drive and turn left at the first light at 1st Street to go into town. There is free 3-hour parking on beachfront Front Street, and more unrestricted parking elsewhere in town, plus a large pay lot ($6/day). Our ride begins on the delightful pedestrian promenade at the pier.

The Ride: At the Avila Pier, fat-tired riders can ride out on the uneven wooden planks of the pier, and enjoy a view back toward town. Ride to the west along Front Street that bends right, next to the beach park. Bear left on 1st Street and cross Avila Beach Drive at the new interesting cyclist's light (mile 0.2). The Class I trail begins to the right and runs between the road and Avila Beach Golf Course. It turns away from the road and reaches a bike/ped/golf cart bridge (0.4) over the tidal portion of San Luis Obispo Creek, which is very scenic and a good place to watch for sea and shore birds.

The trail bends to the left and climbs a hill, reaching Blue Heron Drive (0.5). Turn right and continue to climb the moderate, though not steep, hill as you look down over the golf course with vacant hills to your left. Glide down the hill, next to the golf course, reaching a pleasant stretch next to the creek (0.9). At mile 1.2, continue straight onto a Class I path as the road veers left into the resort community. The next stretch is between the creek and resort facilities and dwellings.

At mile 1.6, a side path leads left to Woodstone Deli. This would be the access point for a cruise up See Canyon Road (see Option 1). The Bob Jones Trail continues with a dip under San Luis Bay Drive. Along the next scenic stretch are vistas to the north of orchards and Tuscan-style mansions on the hillsides, with the riparian ecosystem of the creek on the right. The trail continues along the creek, then rounds a bend and ends all too soon along Ontario Road (2.65). The east trailhead parking lot is across the street. Options 2 and 3 leave from this point. Otherwise, return the same way. When you come to the traffic light at 1st Street, cross diagonally with the bike signal. Or, at that point, see Option 4 to ride to Harford Pier. Upon returning to Avila Beach you can pedal around the small grid of streets for a while. Your total ride without trying any of the options will be about 5.5 miles.

Option 1: See Canyon Road *About 8 miles total. Moderate, any bike. E-bike edge.*
Many road cyclists enjoy biking on this rural road through vineyards and orchards. Once

Bob Jones Trail bridge over delta of San Luis Obispo Creek

you exit to the Woodstone Deli, make your way to San Luis Bay Drive and turn left. In about 0.5 mile turn left onto See Canyon Road (mile 0, 55-foot elevation). There are no bike lanes and you will probably want to turn back when the pitch of the road starts to increase significantly after about 4 miles. The quaint Kelsey See Canyon Vineyards is about 0.6 mile up the road (elevation 105 feet). At Black Walnut Road (mile 4), the elevation is 430 feet. This is a good turnaround point before the steep climb that follows.

Option 2: To SLO Town *About 7 miles each way. Moderate, any bike. E-bike edge.*
From the east trailhead you can cycle to SLO Town on a Class II bikeway until the Class I Bob Jones City to the Sea Trail is extended someday. Plans are underfoot to extend the trail about 5 miles, past San Luis Obispo's Octagon Barn Center to Los Osos Valley Road, running adjacent to the heavily wooded San Luis Obispo Creek drainage, parallel to US 101. See slocountyparks.org/planning-projects/ for details. Meanwhile, you'll need to ride next to fast-moving traffic along the existing fairly hilly route. Ontario Road eventually crosses under US 101 (mile 2.9) and becomes Class II Higuera Road that leads into downtown SLO around mile 7.0. See the section on SLO for further information.

Option 3: Combine with the Pismo Beach Rides *3a: 1 mile connector each way, easy.*
From the east trailhead, cycle down Class II Ontario Rd 0.3 mile to Avila Beach Drive. Carefully cross and turn left, up the hill. Just before the interchange with US 101 turn right onto Class II Shell Beach Rd (0.5). When you reach El Portal Rd (0.9), that is an intersection with the Pismo Beach area Class II tour (PB3). The Pismo Beach pier and entrance to the beach ride (PB1) is about 4.5 miles farther. *Opt 3b: See map for route up steep Cave Landing Rd, across ridge on an old road (wide tires) and down steep hill to PB3.*

Option 4: Ride to Harford Pier *About 4 miles round trip. Easy, any bike.*
From the west end of the Bob Jones Trail, ride west along the shoulder of Avila Beach Road, which begins a scenic stretch along the bay. First ride over a bridge, then past the oil company pier (no access), past Diablo Canyon Road (1.2), RV camping at the harbor, to the Harford Pier (1.5). Parking is allowed on the shoulders of Avila Beach Drive, so an off-peak day makes for a much better ride since you can ride off of the roadway. When there are a lot of parked cars be very careful of doors opening. Also, when the Diablo Canyon power plant shift is over in the late afternoon, there is fairly heavy eastbound traffic from Diablo Canyon Road eastward. The rewards of this option are great vistas of the bay and the restaurants on the Harford Pier. Cars and bikes (fat tires preferred) are allowed on the pier (1.7). There is plenty of parking here, which makes it another potential staging area. If the county completes the Bob Jones Trail out to this point as has been proposed, it will become a fabulous option and will become a part of the main Avila Beach ride.

Pismo Beach

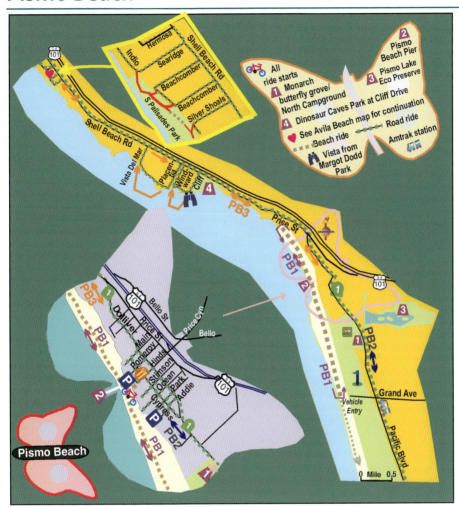

Are you ready for your Southern California beach ride? This classic central coast beach town boasts a beautiful shoreline and wide beaches with compact sand that make great riding at lower tides. You may have heard of the Pismo Clam, which were once harvested here by the bucket load. Although over-harvesting decimated them, they can still be picked in small numbers with a permit.

The Monarch butterfly may be seen wintering here en masse October through February to escape colder climes from Canada to the Sierra Nevada. The main place to see them is the Monarch Butterfly Grove, located 1 mile south of Pomeroy Avenue along SR 1. Free parking is available inside the North Beach Campground of Pismo State Beach, just north of the grove, and you can easily cycle there as well. When you look at the Monterey pine and eucalyptus trees, the yellow and orange leaves are actually butterflies. Sadly, numbers are down 90% since 1992 due to disappearing milkweed.

Pismo's downtown core is a few blocks square and contains plenty of options for a meal. The pier at the end of Pomeroy Avenue is the centerpiece, but bikes are not allowed on it. Since motor vehicles are not allowed on the beach within the Pismo

Beach city limits, its 2-mile stretch of beach is the most pleasant to cycle on. However, you can go as far as you like along the beach, even past where the vehicles are allowed. Road rides are also described here, including an easy jaunt around town and south to the Butterfly Grove, and a more difficult 12-mile coastal cruise north along Class II SR 1, which has some inclines, moderate traffic, and some great ocean vistas along the way. From the north end of town one can connect to the Class I Bob Jones Trail to Avila Beach.

Tunes: Elusive Butterfly by Bob Lind; Vacation by The Go-Go's; Surf Wax America by Weezer
Eats: Clam Chowder at the Splash Café.

Seasons: All. Best on sunny uncrowded off-season fogless weekday.
Facilities: Restrooms and water near the pier.
Knocks & Hazards: Beach can be very crowded at peak times, making an uninterrupted ride challenging. Ride PB1 can only be done when there is enough wet compacted sand during lower tides. If you go south along the beach past Pismo Beach city limits, motor vehicles are also allowed on the beach. Rides PB2 and 3 include road riding with street crossings. Area is commonly foggy.
Rent 'n Ride: Pismo Beach Bike Rentals, 160 Hinds Ave, 805.441.5792;
Pedal Up Bikes & Boards, 519 Cypress St, 805.295.6235.
Bike Shop: Trinity Cyclery, 1343 West Grand Avenue, Grover Beach, 805.473.8324.

Camp 'n Ride: Pismo Beach: Pismo Coast Village, 165 S Dolliver, 888.782.3224; Pismo State Beach, North Beach Campground, 400 S Dolliver, 805.773.7170; Holiday RV Park, 100 S Dolliver St, 805.773.1121. Oceano: Pismo State Beach—Oceano, Hwy 1 (35.106402, -120.627045), 805.489.1869; Oceano Dunes State Vehicular Recreation Area, 928 Pacific Blvd, 805.473.7220; Pacific Dunes RV Resort, 1205 Silver Spur Pl, 805.489.7787; Pismo Sands RV Park, 2220 Cienaga St, 805.481.3225; Oceano County Campground, 540 Air Park Dr, 805.781.4900. Grover Beach: Le Sage Riviera RV Park, 319 N Hwy 1, Grover Beach, 805.489.5506.
Bike 'n Brunch: Restaurants in downtown Pismo Beach and several spots along the SR 1 road ride to the north. A favorite is Splash Café downtown for their clam chowder. Also downtown is Mo's Smokehouse BBQ. Ventana Grill just north of downtown has great views and seafood.
Further Info (see also San Luis Obispo and Avila Beach): Tide tables and other local info: classiccalifornia.com/tides.htm; Pismo Beach info including a list of restaurants: pismochamber.com; Monarch Butterflies and current count at the grove: monarchbutterfly.org; Pismo State Beach: www.parks.ca.gov/?page_id=595.

Access: From US 101 southbound exit on Hinds Ave, or northbound exit on Price St/Business 101. Park in downtown Pismo Beach, either on the street following the posted time limits, or in lots. Two public parking lots are at the beach end of Pomeray Ave at the pier (pay lot; beach access at the end on Hinds Ave), and at the beach end of Park Street four blocks southeast (free; direct beach access).

Pismo Beach Ride on the Sand   PB1 ⭐3

Distance: 4 miles + options. Time: 1 hour
Route & Bike: Hard, flat sand beach. Use bike with fat tires, beach cruiser, or trike. Easy, with options that go to moderate.

The Ride: From either access point either wheel or carry (preferred) your bike through the soft sand until you reach the compacted wetter sand closer to the water. This is not a ride to be done at high tide when there is no hard sand exposed. Ride first to the northwest under the pier until you reach the dramatic white bluffs that block your way, then ride in the other direction, continuing onward until the point at which vehicles are allowed to enter the beach (Grand Avenue). Pier Avenue is the other vehicle entry point farther south in Oceano.

Turning around at Grand Avenue will give you a 4-mile beach ride. Or, you can continue for many more miles along the scenic coastline, even past where vehicles are allowed,

Cyclist & equestrian on the firm sands of Pismo Beach

depending on conditions. On a busy beach day this may become fairly obnoxious with all the vehicles, but it is still doable. It is also a popular beach for horseback riding, so be courteous of them. You can always make your way to Class II SR 1 for your return route if riding in the sand and perhaps an unfavorable breeze makes beach cycling too arduous. Then, return to Pismo Beach for lunch.

Butterflies and Beyond—Flat Southbound Route   PB2 ⭐2

Distance: Variable.
Route & Bike: Easy. Class II roads for any bike, fairly flat.

The Ride: For road riding, many people just stick to downtown Pismo Beach, its boardwalk, and a jaunt southbound on SR 1 to visit the Monarch butterfly grove in Pismo State Beach. If you have rented a heavy beach cruiser bike this is the recommended route because of the relatively flat topography. From the pier area take Cypress Street to the right (southeast). Cross the quaint one-lane wooden bridge on its sidewalk (mile 0.3) and reach SR 1. Bikes are banned from sidewalks along here so ride in the bike lane. Pass Pismo Coast Mobile Village and the entrance to Pismo State Beach and the North Campground (0.8). As SR 1 begins to bend, the Butterfly Grove is on the right. You can continue southbound on Class II SR 1 for several miles, but the route is not along the ocean and is not especially scenic.

North Pismo Scenic Road Ride   PB3

Distance: 11.6 miles + options. Time: 1–1.5 hours.
Route & Bike: Easy with options to moderate. Paved Class II and III roadways, park paths. Any bike with gears and good brakes. Flat to rolling hills. Grades between Hwy 1 and the residential streets that lead down to the coast: E-bike edge.

The Ride: Although the northern route is more difficult because of its topography consisting of rolling hills, that topography also enables some great ocean vistas. From the pier area in downtown Pismo Beach head out to the northwest along Dolliver Street to Price Street, or SR 1 (0.6). SR 1 is a frontage road through Pismo Beach that is adjacent to the US 101 freeway. Pass by oceanfront resorts, with some nice views occasionally out to sea.

Path between Pismo Beach and Cave Landing

At 1.1 miles, past the Best Western Shore Cliff Lodge, the road becomes more scenic as it is next to the bluffs. Pass the Best Western Shelter Cove Lodge (1.5), and then reach the beautiful oceanfront Dinosaur Caves Park (1.7). Either take a shortcut on paths through the park or continue to Cliff Avenue and turn left (1.9). Ride down the gradual hill, with a residential area on your right and awesome vistas of the ocean to your left. The road follows the beautiful bluffs around to the right and becomes Ocean Boulevard as it reaches Margot Dodd Park (2.2), a great place to stop and take in the ocean vistas. The awesome stretch soon ends as your route turns inland and becomes Windward Ave (2.4). Ride up the hill through the residential neighborhood, returning to Hwy 1 that is now Shell Beach Rd (2.6). Turn left on the Class II road and in two blocks at Placentia Ave is Zorro's Cantina with its fun patio (2.7).

Repeat the same routine by turning left down Placentia Ave, and glide down the hill to Ocean Boulevard (3.0). Turn right, and after passing a few residences, the fabulous ocean view reappears at Eldwayan Ocean Park (3.1). Your beachfront cycling treat ends at mile 3.4, as you turn inland up Vista Del Mar Avenue. Ride up the hill to Shell Beach Road (3.6). You can either turn to the right here to return to your start, staying along Hwy 1, for a ride of about 6.2 miles, or continue by turning left on the Class II roadway. Pass a school, a residential neighborhood, and then reach the Shell Beach resort district (4.2).

Turn left on Beachcomber (4.8). Ride down the hill to lovely South Palisades Park, then take the concrete path to the right (photo p25), emerging at Indio and Searidge. Take Indio to the gated Bluffs community (5.8). An access road leads down to a small parking lot on the left and the paved Shell Beach Bluff Trail. This spectacular though hilly trail atop the bluffs has beautiful vegetation and amazing views down the coast to Pismo Beach and to San Luis Bay. It is not very wide and best experienced on foot. Bicyclists are allowed to cycle through the Bluffs gate and on the community road, which is less hilly with similar views. Turn around at the cul de sac (6.3). Option: An old road (best for wider tires) leads up a steep hill (e-bike edge!) to a panoramic view bench (see photo) along a level ridge to Cave Landing Rd in about 0.3 miles. This is the parking area for Pirates Cove nude beach. Either return to Indio Dr, and left up El Portal (6.8) to Shell Beach Rd to extend your ride into Avila Beach (see AV1), or retrace your route through the park, return to Shell Beach Road, and follow SR 1 back to your starting point near the Pismo Beach pier (11.7). Extend the ride by ducking down the same residential streets to the coast as in the outbound ride.

Future Plans: The Pismo Beach Bicycle and Pedestrian Master Plan (2010) calls for many more Class I trails and Class II lanes, including a Class I trail running parallel to SR 1 replacing the current Class II route in Ride PB3, and possibly connecting to the Bob Jones Trail. Another Class I trail would hug the coastline throughout the entire city limits, but don't hold your breath for that anytime soon. For the entire master plan do a web search for the document.

Carrizo Plain National Monument— California's Serengeti

The 250,000-acre Carrizo Plain National Monument, adjacent to the southwest corner of the San Joaquin Valley, preserves a large swath of the natural ecosystems containing desert grassland, saltbush and alkali scrub, wetlands, and in the higher elevations, juniper oak woodlands. The area provides important habitat for endangered and sensitive species, such as the majestic California condor that was introduced in the nearby mountains but is rarely actually seen over the plain, as well as the San Joaquin kit fox, giant kangaroo rat, and San Joaquin antelope ground squirrel. The re-introduced pronghorn antelope and Tule elk can sometimes be seen grazing in this largest remaining natural grassland in California, especially in the early morning and late afternoon.

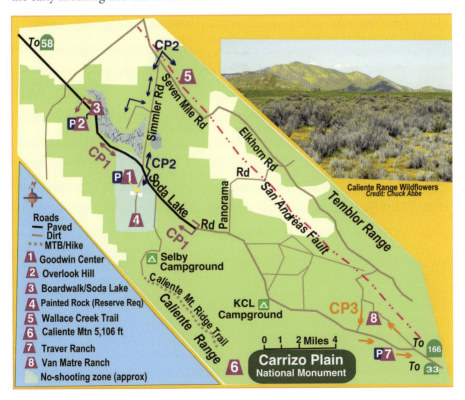

Caliente Range Wildflowers
Credit: Chuck Abbe

Carrizo Plain is an internal drainage basin, and during December through April water can fill the 3,000-acre Soda Lake if it has rained sufficiently, attracting shore birds en route along the Pacific Flyway. In the dryer seasons, and even in the winter in dry years, the lakebed becomes a rare alkali wetland containing salt-tolerant plants, and its salt crystals glisten in the sun across the valley. Birds of prey are common all year.

The east side of the park straddles the San Andreas Fault, with evidence of past seismic events on display in the form of ridges and ravines. The fact that the land in the monument moved 30 feet closer to San Francisco one day in 1857 is a sobering reminder of what is yet to come, and an interpretive trail at Wallace Creek recounts the land's seismic importance. The Temblor Mountains rise up to 4,332 feet to the northeast of the monument, while the Caliente Range lies to the southwest, including 5,106-foot Caliente Mountain, the highest point in San Luis Obispo County, and site of a popular hike within the park.

Evidence of Native American activity from 4,000 years ago is displayed in the paintings on the sandstone rock formation called Painted Rock, one of the best examples of rock art in the world. It can be visited seasonally via reservation. The monument was the site of cultivated agriculture and ranching since the late 1800s, and although now the focus is on ecosystem and species preservation, livestock grazing and hunting is allowed.

The best season to visit the Carrizo Plain is spring in wetter years, when Soda Lake is full of water and a dazzling display of wildflowers carpets the grasslands and up into the Temblor Range. Although timing varies year to year, the bloom of yellow, gold, purple and pink flowers is typically seen from mid-March to mid-April, with the peak times usually in early to mid-April. During drier years there may be no wildflowers at all, and perhaps not even grasses.

Many of the dirt roads in the park turn to mud during and after wet periods (mostly December through March), which limits your exploration to the paved park road, along which are many of the park's most popular features. The well-maintained unpaved section of Soda Lake Road is typically passable as well. In December through May, the Goodwin Education Center is open Thursdays through Sundays, 9:00–4:00.

Access: *Those with larger RV's will not appreciate the drive.* From US 101 in Santa Margarita take SR58 40 miles east; or from I-5 in Buttonwillow take SR58 16 miles west to McKittrick, then 27 miles farther west. Take Soda Lake Rd south to the monument. Address, Goodwin Ctr: 17495 Soda Lake Rd, California Valley. Several primitive campgrounds with toilets are on site, but no food or potable water are available.

Carrizo Plain Road & MTB Routes   CP1, 2, and 3

Cycling is a good way to see portions of the monument. Bikes are allowed on all public dirt roads but are banned from all foot trails except for the trail along Caliente Ridge. On the map, we have identified three options for easier rides.

CP1 ⭐ When conditions are wet, the paved park road is the only choice. A 16 to 21-mile out and back route covers many of the highlights of the park. Although the speed limit on the park road is 55 mph with no shoulders, traffic on it is typically sporadic except during wildflower season weekends. Start at the Overlook Hill parking lot and ride south past Soda Lake, with the option of cycling to the Goodwin Center conditions permitting.

Boardwalk along Soda Lake in dry season

CP2 ⭐ When drier conditions prevail, we prefer cycling the unpaved Simmler Road that takes you between two portions of Soda Lake and up about 350 feet in elevation to the eastern hills and the Wallace Creek seismic zone for a moderate-difficulty round-trip ride of about 17 miles. For an easier 14-mile ride skip the hill climb and ride to a spot along the north side of Soda Lake as shown on the map. At your option add a 6 mile round trip to the Goodwin Center. The other main park route, Selby Road, is much hillier (e-bike edge).

CP3 ⭐ A 10-mile loop on dirt roads with some small hills takes you past preserved homesteads of the 1920s and '30s, including the Van Matre Ranch site where geologists have discovered well-preserved stream channels that were offset by the San Andreas Fault.

Further Info: For Carrizo's Bureau of Land Management (BLM) website, that also has links to a wildflower report, navigate from blm.gov; BLM Bakersfield: 661.391.6000; Goodwin Education Center: 805.475.2131. Painted Rock reservations: recreation.gov

Cycling along Simmler Road (CP2)

2. Santa Barbara County

Santa Barbara County shares its northern boundary with San Luis Obispo County and its eastern boundary with Ventura County, while the Pacific Ocean surrounds the county to the south and west. The north-south coastline suddenly curves more east-west at Point Conception, creating what is known as the Southern California Bight, which extends to near Ensenada, Mexico, impacting the region's climate. Point Conception is a notoriously windy spot with frequent rough seas and the site of many a shipwreck over the centuries.

Santa Barbara County is 3,789 square miles in size, of which 2,737 square miles is land and 1,052 square miles is water. The county includes four of the islands of Channel Islands National Park (San Miguel, Santa Rosa, Santa Barbara, and Santa Cruz), while Anacapa Island is in Ventura County. The mountainous interior that forms such a beautifully dramatic backdrop to the coastal plains is mostly the domain of Los Padres National Forest. The county's mountain ranges include the Santa Ynez Range outside of Santa Barbara in the south, and the Sierra Madre and San Rafael Mountains in the northeast, where the highest point of 6,820 feet is found at the summit of Big Pine Mountain.

Only 432,000 people call Santa Barbara County home, which compares to the population of Long Beach. Most of the population lives along the US 101 corridor, on rolling plains backed by coastal mountains, from Santa Maria at the north end to Carpinteria near Santa Barbara at the south. Northern Santa Barbara County is prime wine country, centered around the town of Los Olivos near the Danish village of Solvang.

Vandenberg Air Force Base occupies much of the coast in the north of the county, and there is limited public access to the wild coastline from Point Conception to the north county line, which makes the Amtrak route that hugs the coast through that stretch that much more exciting—a journey back in time to what the coast looked like before it was massively developed. In fact, the Amtrak route through much of Ventura and Santa Barbara County is along the coast, with stops that access many of the rides featured in this book. Amtrak's Pacific Surfliner train between San Diego and San Luis Obispo stops in Carpinteria, Santa Barbara, Goleta, and Surf station near Lompoc, providing access to our rides. Trains depart throughout the day, and take about 2 to 3 hours from LA's Union Station. The Coast Starlight train that connects Los Angeles and Seattle stops only at Santa Barbara within the county.

SANTA BARBARA COUNTY

The bike rides presented in Santa Barbara County include a jaunt along a river levee in Santa Maria (SAM1), an exciting wine tour in the Solvang-Los Olivos area (SO1), a flowery ride to the beach from Lompoc (LOM1), and several fabulous scenic excursions in the Santa Barbara–Goleta region (SB1, SB2 and options). Santa Barbara, with its distinctive Spanish architecture and resorts, is the most popular destination in the county. See the Santa Barbara County map for general locations of the featured rides, except for the Santa Maria ride that is shown on the San Luis Obispo County map. Although the county comes up short with regards to extended Class I trails, it does have a bike-friendly attitude with many designated bike routes and striped lanes that you can try in addition to our featured rides, and some new trails are being built in Santa Barbara at this writing. See trafficsolutions.info for maps.

Climate Data for Santa Barbara (Source: NOAA 1981 to 2010 normals)													
Month	Jan	Feb	Mar	Apr	May	Jun	Jul	Aug	Sep	Oct	Nov	Dec	Totals
Average High °F	64.7	65.4	66.1	69.0	69.6	71.2	74.7	76.0	75.1	72.8	68.9	64.7	69.9
Average Low °F	46.4	48.1	49.8	51.8	54.6	57.5	60.4	60.4	59.6	56.2	50.3	46.7	53.5
Precipitation, inches	4.14	4.68	3.59	0.77	0.35	0.09	0.01	0.03	0.29	0.52	1.48	2.63	18.58

Santa Maria

Santa Maria, the county's largest city with a population of over 106,000, is situated just south of the SLO County line and the wide Santa Maria River. The Santa Maria Valley was once a very prolific oil-producing area, but most oil production is now south of town in the Orcutt Oil Field in Solomon Hills, not readily visible from the populated areas. Agriculture is the main industry in the valley, especially grapes for the wine industry in the surrounding Santa Barbara and San Luis Obispo wine country. Strawberries are another big cash crop, and a fresh strawberry pie is the desert of choice to accompany a fabulous Santa Maria–style tri-tip barbeque dinner. The tri-tip cut was invented here and has become synonymous with California barbeque. Tri-tip is sirloin rubbed with salt, pepper, and other spices, then either cooked whole on a rotisserie or grilled on red oak. Side dishes are typically pinquito beans, salad, and garlic bread. Well-reviewed local BBQ places that serve tri-tip include Shaw's Steakhouse, 714 S. Broadway; El Pollo Norteno, 1954 S Broadway; Swiss, 516 N Bway. Nipomo: Rancho Nipomo BBQ, 108 Cuyama Ln; Jocko's, 125 N. Thompson.

While Santa Maria is not a top-notch easy-scenic-cycling destination, you may want to stop here to sample the regional cuisine and work it off with a 7.2-mile up and back ride (two times perhaps?) along the Santa Maria River Trail (SAM1), described below. For information on designated bike routes through town see the site cityofsantamaria.org and select Visitors-Maps-City Bikeway Map.

Santa Maria River Trail   SAM1

Distance: 3.6 miles each way.
Route & Bike: Easy, flat. Packed fine gravel, suitable for most bikes, hybrid or thicker tire preferred.
Camp 'n Ride: The campground near the trail closed. Besides an Elks Lodge the closest camping is in the Pismo Beach area.

SANTA BARBARA COUNTY

Access: From Hwy 101, exit North Broadway and find a parking lot on the east side of 101 along Broadway. Or, go west on Broadway, then north on Preisker Lane to the end. Restrooms are at Preisker Park, 2 blocks south of the trail. Other entrances are at the intersection of Seaward Drive and Carlotti Drive and the Suey Crossing trailhead (Donavon exit off 101, east to Suey Crossing, then north).

Santa Maria River Trail (SAM1)

The Ride: This level trail sits above the wide open flood plain of the river, enabling some nice vistas of the San Rafael Mountains to the east, and interesting eroded river topography. Don't expect to see water in the river, though, since it is dry most of the time and any flow tends to be far across toward the north bank. The trail runs between Suey Crossing Road to the east and North Blosser Road at the city limits to the west. Another rougher unofficial 3.5-mile stretch continues west through the agricultural zone to Bonita School Road. That is county land and the trail may be extended to Guadalupe in the future.

Los Flores Ranch MTB SAM2 ⭐

Los Flores Ranch Park is a city-run open space park about 8 miles south of town in the scenic Solomon Hills. The 2.8 square mile park, on former oil company property, contains about 8 miles of trails open to mountain biking. Many of the trails are on old degraded roads, and they range from very easy to challenging in difficulty. From Hwy 101 exit east on Clark Ave and south (right) on Dominion Rd to the park entrance. A $3 entry fee is charged to non-residents. For further info and a map see cityofsantamaria.org/LosFloresRanchPark.

Santa Barbara Wine Country

Located about an hour northwest of Santa Barbara, the bucolic Santa Ynez Valley is a popular destination, home to numerous wineries and the oh-so-cute Danish village of Solvang that was founded by Danish teachers in 1911 and now lures tourists by the thousands. The valley has the highest concentration of wineries in Santa Barbara County, with Chardonnay and Rhône varietals the most prominent planted grapes. The quaint town of Los Olivos is the center of the region, filled with tasting rooms, and is the jumping off point for the famous Foxen Wine Trail to the north.

The verdant valley is framed by the Purisima Hills and San Rafael Mountains to the north and the Santa Ynez Mountains to the south. This area is one of the most popular places to cycle in Southern California, although riding here is predominantly on-road. While many well-seasoned riders cycle the Foxen Wine Trail, we suggest cycling our easier route and touring the Foxen route by car. You can also select bits and pieces of the ride to suit your ability, perhaps just transporting your bikes between the towns and pedaling around the quaint business districts.

Riding Sideways with Danish, Wine & Windmills   SO1

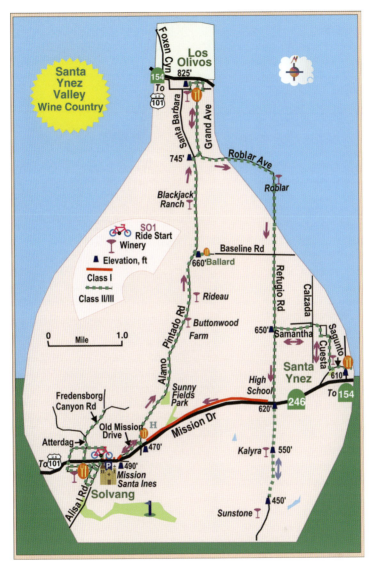

The Old West towns of Santa Ynez and Los Olivos, charmingly preserved with a Victorian architectural overlay, are accessible from Solvang via Class I and Class II routes, enabling a delightful excursion. Families may want to stick to the 2-mile hilly Class I trail between Solvang and Santa Ynez and the parks of Solvang, although road-savvy teens should be able to handle the Class II roadway sections, and the Class III rural residential sections. Adjust your route to suit the needs and ability of your own group. You can visit wineries, take the kids to horse farms, pick apples, joust at windmills, have a wonderful outdoor lunch, or pig out at a Scandinavian smorgasbord all along this scenic ride. Want the ideal romantic biking getaway? A stay at a Los Olivos B&B with wine tasting and fine dining just steps away could be topped off with an exhilarating bike tour.

The region was the setting for the 2004 film *Sideways,* starring Paul Giamatti and Thomas Hayden Church, whose characters go wine tasting and gallivanting. The Solvang Visitor's Information Center has maps to the film's location shoots, which included Sanford Winery, Days Inn, and Hitching Post II in Buellton, Solvang Restaurant in Solvang, Kalyra Winery in Santa Ynez, and in Los Olivos the Blackjack Ranch, Firestone and Fess Parker Wineries as well as the Los Olivos Café and Wine Merchant. Of these locations, the restaurants in Solvang and Los Olivos and the Kalyra and Blackjack Ranch Wineries are along our tour.

Tunes: The jazzy soundtrack to *Sideways* by Rolfe Kent; Red Red Wine by UB40

Eats: Local dish: medisterpølse with æbleskiver. Try a smorgasbord in Solvang or a café in Santa Ynez or Los Olivos.

Distance: About 21 miles. Options for much shorter rides. Time: 3 hours for full ride.

Route & Bike: Paved; any bike. Moderate difficulty with easier options. Class I, II and III, with some rural residential streets not on bike routes. Topography varies from flat to rolling hills and some gradual inclines. The main townsites are fairly level, especially Solvang and Los Olivos. Gradual incline of about 350 feet along Alama Pintado Rd from SR 246 up to Los Olivos; the return should be easier. See map for elevations. E-bike edge.

Seasons: All. Best on sunny uncrowded spring weekday, or fall day at peak foliage.

Alisal Road, Solvang (top) and Blackjack Ranch Winery, as featured in "Sideways," along Alamo Pintado Rd (bottom).

Facilities: Restrooms and water in parks en route.

Knocks & Hazards: Street crossings: Use extra caution crossing Mission Dr at Alisal. Some riding alongside traffic in bike lanes and some rural residential streets without bike lanes. Potential mountain lion country. Rattlesnakes.

Warning: Biking while intoxicated is illegal. Use moderation at the wineries.

Rent 'n Ride: In Solvang, Wheel Fun Rentals, 475 First St, 805.688.0091; Dr. J's Bicycle Shop, 1693 Mission Dr, 688.6263 (Regular and E-bikes); Pedego E-Bikes (also hybrids), 2948 San Marcos Ave, Los Olivios, 691.3045.

Camp 'n Ride: Flying Flags RV Resort, 180 Ave Of The Flags, Buellton, 877.783.5247, just west of US 101, Mission Dr exit. Cachuma Lake Recreation Area, tents and RV's with hookups. Info: countyofsb.org/parks/. From US 101 take Mission Dr 8.6 miles east to SR 154 east/south for 6.4 miles.

Bike 'n Brunch: Restaurants in the central districts of Solvang, Santa Ynez, Los Olivos, and Ballard. See ride description.

City code, bike riding on sidewalks: In Solvang no bike riding on sidewalk in "central business district." Impacts our ride at segment along Mission Dr between Alisal Rd and Pine St. If you ride it, be courteous to peds to avoid the very rare citation.

Events: June: Olive Festival: jazzandolivefestival.org; Danish Days is in September in Solvang, solvangdanishdays.org; Solvang Farmers' Market is Wednesday afternoon in summer. Cycling events: Solvang Century (March); Solvang Prelude (November).

Further Info: Solvang Visitor Information Center, 1639 Copenhagen, 800.468.6765, solvangUSA.com; Kalyra Winery, 343 N Refugio Rd, Santa Ynez, open daily, 805.693.8864, kalyrawinery.com; Sunstone Winery, 125 Refugio Rd, Santa Ynez, open daily, 800.313.9463, sunstonewinery.com; Quicksilver Miniature Horse Ranch, 1555 Alamo Pintado Rd, tours by appointment, 805.686.4002. Other wineries along route: roblarwinery.com; blackjackranch.com. For comprehensive area winery and vineyard information: sbcountywines.com.

Access: From Santa Barbara and Goleta, US 101 heads west along the Pacific Coast, and then turns inland at Gaviota State Park. The first town encountered about 10 miles up the grade is Buellton. Exit here and head east (right) on Mission Drive (Hwy 246) for 3 miles to Solvang. Turn right at the Mission Santa Inés, 1740 Mission Drive, after the light at Alisal Road. The mission itself is worth a visit. Parking is free here and throughout downtown Solvang.

The Ride: From the west ped/bike entrance to the mission property, explore the adjacent downtown core of Solvang with its quaint squares, parks, shops, restaurants, and windmills. Your ride through downtown will amount to less than a mile, or up to 5 miles if you explore along the surrounding roadways. It is a mellow atmosphere for riding except for SR 246, but be extra careful of parked cars pulling out and doors opening, and do not ride on the sidewalks. If you venture north of Mission Drive you can ride up Atterdag Road a few blocks to check out the Old Danish Church (Bethania Lutheran) at Laurel Avenue. Locals like to pedal a few blocks farther to Fredensborg Canyon Road, turning right on this delightful, mostly flat country lane, and in 1.3 miles come to historic Wulff's Windmill, the oldest in town, at address 1245.

When you are finished touring Solvang, return to the traffic light at Alisal Road and SR 246, where our valley tour begins (mile 0). In general, the tour begins by heading east along busy Mission Drive (SR 246) to the first major intersection at Alamo Pintado Road, but we prefer to avoid the highway. Very carefully cross SR246 at the light at Alisal Road, then courteously cycle to the right along the sidewalk. To comply with local ordinance, you'll need to walk your bike on the sidewalk between Alisal and Pine Street, but law enformcement told me cyclists are rarely if ever cited here. After Pine, the sidewalk is lined by a wooden fence and curves to the left and onto the cul de sac of Old Mission Drive (0.3). Follow it to the stop sign at Alamo Pintado Road (0.6). At this intersection are options for coffee, donuts, pizza, and also natural foods at New Frontiers Marketplace where you can pick up your picnic supplies. Turn left on Class II Alamo Pintado. The road has a speed limit of 35-45 mph and only moderate traffic, but be careful since motorists have a tendancy to speed through here. This is a beautiful road indeed, taking you past vineyards and wineries, orchards and pumpkin patches in season, horse farms, and vistas of the surrounding hills. Some of the attractions include the unique Sunny Fields Park in a Danish style (1.2), Apple Lane Farm (U-pick) (2.0), Buttonwood Farm winery and vineyard (2.4) (at #1500), the elegant Rideau Vineyard (2.8), and Quicksilver Ranch (2.9) that raises miniature horses (at #1555, tours by reservation). At mile 3.3 is Baseline Road. To the right along a quiet Class II bikeway is a short optional diversion to the tiny town of Ballard. Delightful Bob's Well Bread bakery and al fresco café is on the left across from the Ballard Inn (upscale dinner only). Continuing up Alamo Pintado Road, pass Honea Vineyards (4.0) and Blackjack Ranch Vineyards (4.2), which was featured in *Sideways*.

At mile 4.6, Alamo Pintado Road and the Dan Henry Bike Route continues to the right, while Santa Barbara Road is straight ahead. Follow the bike route to the right, then merge to the left onto Grand Avenue (4.65). Follow Class II Grand Avenue into lovely Los Olivos. After Hollister Street (5.4) is the Los Olivos Wine Merchant Café, on the left, as seen in *Sideways*.

The center of town is at Alamo Pintado Avenue, with a delightful general store and the Panino café, perfect for a reasonable al fresco lunch treat. There are several wine tasting rooms about town as well. Pedal up and down the quaint streets, then return to the center of town at Grand Avenue (approx. 6.6). Go back the way you came down Grand Avenue. Once you reach the intersection of Alamo Pintado Road, this is a decision point (7.3). You can return the same way by turning right here, following the bike route, down Alamo Pintado Road to Old Mission Road to Alisal Road for a total ride of about 12.5 miles.

Otherwise, continue on our featured route to visit Santa Ynez. It is not quite as fabulous as Los Olivos, but is worth seeing. At this intersection continue straight onto Roblar Avenue, which soon curves to the left. Turn right onto Refugio Road (8.4). Roblar Winery (that offers expensive appetizer/wine pairings) is on the left. Pedal south through the picturesque valley along the shoulder that is sometimes designated as a bike lane. Pass Baseline Road (9.4), then at mile 10.5 turn left onto Samantha Road. You are now pedaling in the residential districts of Santa Ynez.

When Samantha Road ends (11.0), turn left onto Calzada, then make a quick right onto Cimarron Drive. Follow it until it ends at Willow Drive (11.3), and do a left right jog onto Cuesta Street, heading south. Pedal down this wide street until it ends at a park (11.8), and turn left. You will soon be in the midst of the center of Santa Ynez on Sagunto Street, which includes the historic Santa Ynez Inn, and several dining options including another Panino. Sagunto Street ends at Meadowvale Road (12.3). We suggest doing a bit of exploring around town. Then, either retrace your route back to Refugio (14.1), turning left to return to SR 246 (15.1); or, take Edison or Meadowvale south a few blocks to SR 246 (lovely Gainey Vineyard is 0.5 mile east/left from here), and turn right on the wide shoulder next to fast moving vehicles, to Refugio.

Another option presents itself at Refugio, adding 3.4 miles of riding and some elevation gain on the return. If you want more exercise and a *Sideways* experience, you can cross SR 246 and cycle down the hill along Refugio for 1 mile to the funky Kalyra Winery, a nice place for a picnic with a great view of the valley. For even more riding, continue south down the hill another 0.7 mile and turn right to reach Sunstone Vineyards & Winery, built into the hillside in Provençal French style. Return up the long hill (e-bike edge). Cross SR 246, and turn left (west) onto its shoulder.

If you do not visit the above wineries down Refugio, just head west on the shoulder of SR 246. Watch for a Class I trail that starts in front of the high school (15.2). After a couple of residential street crossings, the trail dives down a hill (watch your speed) and separates nicely from the busy highway, as you ride among oak woodlands next to a riparian ecosystem. After some more rolling hills, it ends, dumping you back on the shoulder of SR 246 (16.8). Beyond the small bridge you can make your way onto the sidewalk, turning right up Alamo Pintado (17.0). Cross Alamo Pintado at the first stop sign and onto Old Mission Road where you came from earlier.

At the end of the road (17.4), ride west along Mission to be legal or risk the sidewalk if you prefer to be safer, and cross Mission at the light at Alisal Road (17.6). Ride back east on Mission Drive on the road (or safer but semi-illegal sidewalk) to return to the Mission Santa Ines parking lot (18.0). Add to this total your mileage through Solvang (about 1–5 miles for 19–23 miles total) and the optional winery tour on Refugio south of SR 246 (about 3.4 miles) for up to 26.4 miles total.

Lompoc

Lompoc, the City of Art and Flowers, is known for its murals on its downtown buildings (centered around Ocean Boulevard and H Streets), and the surrounding fields of cultivated flowers that bloom mostly in spring and summer. Its population of nearly 43,000 supports many businesses, making it a practical place to base your exploration of the area. Lompoc is about a 45-minute drive from the Santa Ynez Valley or the Santa Barbara area. Topography is generally flat within the town, making for easy cycling to get from point A to B. Bike route signs direct cyclists onto the Class II streets and even a couple of Class I trails that run for a few blocks. Lompoc's River Park on SR 246 just east of Cabrillo Hwy (SR 1) has bike-in campsites and RV spaces.

Lompoc to Surf Beach Road Ride   LOM1

The most popular bike ride in the Lompoc area is the Class II trip on Ocean Boulevard through the Lompoc Valley for 8-9 miles to Ocean Beach County Park or Surf Beach. Cycling to Ocean Beach is a virtually flat ride along a 55-mph two-lane road with wide bike lane shoulders. The ride out through the Lompoc Valley is fairly uninteresting except when the cultivated flowers are blooming. Beware that the area can bake in summer, especially inland. Ride LOM1 starts at V Street (0.0).

When the roadway begins to ascend a hill, turn right (7.3) onto an access road to Ocean Beach that, after crossing the railroad tracks, is barely wide enough for two vehicles, but is very scenic. An observation pavilion (8.3) overlooks the wide, beautiful delta of the Santa Ynez River, so bring your binoculars for bird watching. A paved path leads under the Amtrak tracks to the beach here, which is closed when the snowy plover nests between March and September.

A more popular beach is reached by riding up the 50-foot hill that you just avoided on Ocean Boulevard (9.3). At the summit, traffic is directed away from the Vandenberg Air Force Base property into a parking lot (10.5) with the automated Amtrak "Surf" train station and access to the beautiful sandy beach where you can walk for miles along undisturbed coastline below the base. Portions of Surf Beach also are subject to the snowy plover closure. Although the waves look inviting, a sign warns of a history of fatal shark attacks here. Both beaches have restroom facilities. Return to V St for a 19 mile ride. For those in great shape who would like a big adventure, you can take the Pacific Surfliner Amtrak train that runs between San Luis Obispo and San Diego and get off at Surf Station to explore the region.

Lompoc flower field

Surf Beach

Option: For an epic adventure, cycle all the way to Jalama Beach County Park, an isolated spot along the undeveloped coastline with campground and café/store famous for Jalama Burgers. Although it is an advanced ride for only the fittest of cyclists, if a friend drops you off at the summit of narrow and winding Jalama Road about 5 miles down the road from Hwy 1 (and picks you up at the beach) it is mainly a scenic downhill affair in a valley through undeveloped hilly ranchland about 9 miles farther to the beach. E-bike!

Santa Barbara—Goleta

The City of Santa Barbara is a popular weekend getaway from the Los Angeles area, located about 2 hours to the northwest. This city of Spanish colonial architecture and dramatic coastline is backed by the 4,000-foot Santa Ynez mountains, which turn a deep green color in the winter and spring. The downtown area is resplendent in shops, galleries, restaurants, and entertainment venues. Adjacent to the northwest is Goleta, a bucolic coastal suburb, home of University of California at Santa Barbara (UCSB).

Santa Barbara's beach trail (SB1) tends to be overly crowded, and is not very long, but if you hit it at the right time it can be a sublime ride. Options are presented to extend SB1 west to Goleta/UCSB on a mix of route types (e-bike edge). Or head southeast to Carpinteria on a Class II route, or as far as Ventura via ride VE4, perhaps taking Amtrak back. You can also opt to cycle inland on flat Class II State Street to visit the beautiful and partially redeveloped Spanish-themed downtown area. Some of the most scenic easy riding, and less crowded than downtown Santa Barbara, is around the UCSB campus and its coastal bluffs, with options to extend onto a creekside Class I paved trail and two ocean bluff MTB parks (SB2).

Some other highlights, such as the hillside neighborhoods and the Mission Santa Barbara are reachable via Class II routes as well. If you are in good shape and can tackle hills and longer rides, pick up a bike map at a local bike shop, or check it out online at trafficsolutions.info. Our Santa Barbara area map depicts the general routes of some of these rides.

Santa Barbara Waterfront and Beyond   SB1 ⭐

Cabrillo Beachway is a 3-mile Class I promenade that could have been a top ride if it were not so short and a multi-user trail to boot, and if it crossed over to the beach side sooner than it does. It is forever crowded with pedestrians and surreys that create continuous obstacles on busy days, and is over with before you know it. But, if you are able to ride the trail on an uncrowded sunny winter weekday, you may just achieve that elusive fabulous experience on this trail. The views are amazing; a wide sandy beach backed by tall palms, sailboats bobbing in the ocean, fishing boats in the marina, the Channel Islands in the background, and as you look to the east, the ever-present Santa Ynez mountains. If you like people watching, this trail is for you. If you like to eat, you are also in luck, with too many dining choices and al fresco patios to mention. For a workout try Options 1 or 2 to continue on Class 1/II/III routes through interesting neighborhoods to worthwhile destinations. E-bikers check out the hilly scenic Mountain Drive Loop ride: cyclecalcoast.com/rides/santabarbara.

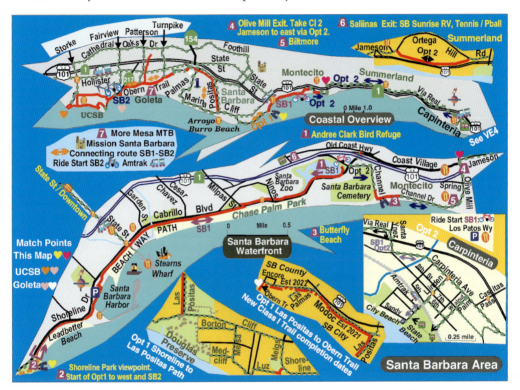

Tunes: Walk on the Ocean by Toad the Wet Sprocket; Barbara Ann by The Beach Boys; Confirmation by Charlie Parker
Eats: Seafood lunch on the pier, or an al fresco patio meal along State Street, which became a ped/bike promenade during the 2020-21 pandemic and may still be.

Distance: 6 to 7 miles out and back + options. Time: 1 hour plus view stops.
Route & Bike: Easy. Main ride is on paved Class I trail and in parking lots. Any bike. Flat with one optional but worthwhile hill. E-bike edge for Options.
Seasons: All. Best on sunny uncrowded off-season weekday.
Facilities: Restrooms and water in parks along route.
Knocks & Hazards: Clueless peds and rental surreys can make trail unpleasant during peak periods. Short distance. Some lurkers. Busy signaled street crossing. Speed limit: As posted.
Rent 'n Ride: Wheel Fun, 805.966.2282: 23 Cabrillo, 24 Mason, 29 State (e-bikes); SB Bikes To-Go, 736 Carpinteria, 628.2444; Open Air Bicycles, 1303 State, 962.7000; E-Bikery, 506 State, 869.2574. Shops: Hazard's Cyclesport, 110 Anacapa, 966.3787; Bici Centro (used, u-fix), 434 Olive; Fastrack, 118 W Canon Perdido, 884.0210;

Velo Pro Cyclery, 15 Hitchcock Way, 963.7775.

City of Santa Barbara Bike Spot (membership required—commuter bike parking, tools, shower, etc), 1219 Anacapa St in Granada Garage Lot 6.

Camp 'n Ride: Sunrise RV Park, 515 S Salinas, 805.966.9954, 1.1 miles from east SB1 trailhead via Old Coast Hwy, under 101. El Capitan, Refugio, and Gaviota State Park campgrounds are on the coast northwest of town—not in riding distance to our rides, but the scenic 2-mile paved oceanfront Aniso Trail between El Capitan and Refugio runs along the bluffs. Carpinteria State Beach (RV hookups, tents, bike-in sites) is 13 miles south, per Option 2. Coastal state parks require reservations far in advance for weekends and summer.

Bike 'n Brunch: Numerous restaurants are along the route or in close riding distance.

Further Info: Santa Barbara Bicycle Coalition: sbbike.org; bike advocacy and tours: bike-santabarbara.org. General info including dining and the numerous festivals held in Santa Barbara: santabarbara.com. Natural History Museum: sbnature.org.

Access: Northbound: Exit US 101 at Cabrillo Boulevard and head west. Make the first right onto Los Patos Way and find free parking here, as well as a couple of outdoor cafés. The trailhead is less than 0.1 mile up Los Patos Way on the left. Finding the exit southbound on US 101 is tricky the first time around. It is best to enter "1 Los Patos Way" on your GPS and follow it. When you see a left exit for Hot Springs Road, an exit that says only "Exit 95" appears suddenly on the right, around a bend, which feeds into Los Patos Lane. There is a low-clearance (12'4") bridge at the exit so it is not for tall RV's. Alternatively you can take the Hot Springs/Cabrillo left exit (94B), and turn right onto Cabrillo Boulevard, then right on Los Patos.

The Ride: Begin at the Andre Clark Bird refuge. First, spend some time watching the bird life in the lovely lake and the surrounding reeds, then set off westward on the Cabrillo Beachway path. The trail begins quietly next to the lake, then emerges between a residential development and busy Cabrillo Boulevard at 0.7 mile, across which are the volleyball courts of East Beach and the blue Pacific. Cross Ninos Drive (0.8) near the Santa Barbara Zoo, and then cross Cabrillo Boulevard at the signal near Milpas Street (1.0). The trail now runs along the beach side of Cabrillo Boulevard among the palm trees

Cabrillo Beachway (SB1)

of Chase Palm Park with a view of Stearns Wharf in the distance. At Anacapa Street, Santa Barbara FisHouse offers brunch with an ocean view (2.0). Wheel Fun bike rentals is near Helena Street. Cross the entrance to Stearns Wharf (2.2) with its five touristy seafood restaurants, the best-reviewed being Santa Barbara Shellfish Co., and the Ty Warner Sea Center, an interactive museum that is an extension of the Santa

Barbara Museum of Natural History. Check out the bronze dolphin statue at the wharf entrance.

> **Sidetrip:** To the right at this point is State Street, the main drag of Santa Barbara, where you will find every kind of dining and shopping option your heart desires along a bike friendly Class II route. In two blocks pass the Amtrak station, dip under Hwy 1, and pass Haley St, where in 2020-21 State St became a car-free promenade through and then left on Victoria St for a block. Make sure to check out the new Paseo Nuevo complex.

After another few minutes of riding along the beach, the trail reaches Santa Barbara Harbor (2.5), a busy marina filled with pleasure boats and commercial fishing vessels. Here is yet another dining opportunity with several waterfront restaurants to choose from including Breakwater and Salty at the Beach. The trail winds through parking lots for a while and emerges at Leadbetter Beach (3.0). This is the end of Cabrillo Beachway, but if you ride through the Leadbetter parking lot, a Class I trail begins adjacent to Shoreline Drive (3.2). Ride up the gradual hill to Shoreline Park, a very pretty spot (3.5). You'll have to walk your bike or lock it up here since bike riding is not allowed on the paths, but be sure to take in perhaps the best vista spot in town, back toward the waterfront, the city, and the mountain backdrop. From here you can continue for 0.5 mile on bike lanes along Shoreline Drive next to the park and turn around at the end of the park. You can also continue onward, as described in Option 1.

Option 1: Santa Barbara Coast Route to UCSB SB2 ⭐ *12.7 miles each way. Moderate.*
Extending SB1 west along the Coast Route involves a variety of route types, some hills (e-bike edge) and busy roads. Mile 0 is at Shoreline Park, at the end of the Class I trail near the viewpoint. At mile 1.1 the road curves to the right and becomes Meigs Road. [See map for a shortcut through La Mesa Park to a neighborhood and the Douglas Preserve to the Las Positas path to avoid busy Cliff Dr.] Reach Cliff Drive (1.4), with several restaurants nearby, and turn left on the hilly artery. Near the bottom of a hill is a roundabout for Los Positas Rd (2.4), with a new (2021) Class I path on its west side, which continues our route. Or, continue down the hill 0.25 mile to Arroyo Burro Beach County Park, which is a worthwhile diversion to check out the lovely beach and the beachside Boathouse at Hendry's Beach restaurant for brunch. From there a Class II route becomes Marina along cliffside estates, then scenic Las Palmas to Modoc. Our route on the Los Positas path rises 100 ft, passing Elings Park and reaches Modoc Rd. At the junction with Modoc Road (4.0) you can either turn right and follow the Class II Cross Town Route for a loop back to downtown, or continue to the left on the bike path (2021 or 2) to the trailhead for the Goleta/UCSB ride (SB2), described as follows:

At mile 6.0, along Modoc Road across from the second intersection with Encore Drive, is a Class I trail to the left (see the map on page 69). This leads to Nogal Drive (6.3). Jog right/left on Nogal onto Nueces Drive, left on Arroyo Drive (6.8), and pedal down to the end of the block and the trailhead of the Class I Coast Route (7.0). This is the Obern Trail described in Ride SB2–Option 3, a suburban trail next to neighborhoods, following a stream channel lined with riparian vegetation. It intersects the Maria Ignacio Class I Trail (8.9), and then parallels Hwy 217 (9.9).

Turn left onto Sandspit Road (10.4) to cross over an inlet, and then reach the Goleta Beach County Park and Goleta Pier. Find restrooms here. The trail continues to the right on the landward side of the parking lot and leads to a scenic stretch up a small hill along the dunes with some great ocean vistas. This scenic 0.5-mile stretch and the Class I trail ends at Lagoon Road across from the UCSB campus (11.1). You can continue cycling through the UCSB campus and mountain bikers can enjoy some fabulous trails atop the ocean bluffs (ride SB2).

Option 2: Coast Route South ⭐ *10.3+ miles each way. Moderate. Mostly flat.*
The Coast Route continues south from our SB1 trailhead (mile 0). It is mostly a Class II route with about 1 mile of Class I paths thrown in. The best part of the route is near the beginning when it is near the ocean in Montecito, but it soon turns inland, running mostly parallel to the inland side of the 101 Freeway. However, it passes quaint inviting downtown sections of Montecito, Summerland, and Carpinteria, ending at the beach in that charming town. From the trailhead at Los Patos Drive, very carefully cross unsignaled Cabrillo Blvd and follow Channel Dr around to the right, circling the Santa Barbara Cemetery. At road's end enter the trip's highlight, a stunning 0.3-mile Class I trail on an oceanfront bluff surrounded by flowering landscape that attracts butterflies and views up and down the coast. Once the path begins to descend to a busy beach park you may want to turn around, unless you are headed to that popular beach.

If you are intending to ride the south coastal route continue onto the beachfront road that is packed with vehicles coming and going on busy beach days. We typically ride in the center of the lane to avoid being hit by doors opening or cars leaving suddenly. This section of Channel Drive curves inland around the Biltmore Four Seasons resort and becomes Olive Mill (mile 1.2). This ends the most scenic stretch and is a nice turnaround point. Brunch at the Biltmore anyone? Bring a frock! (and some bucks).

The Coastal Route crosses Highway 101 and leads to the Class II Jameson Lane on the right. To the left at this point is the toney Montecito business district along Coast Village Drive if you want to check it out for eats or perhaps watch for locals like Oprah. Turn right (east) on Jameson Lane and follow this Class II route parallel to the 101 Freeway. When Jameson curves sharply to the left (3.2), continue straight ahead onto Ortega Hill Drive and bear right onto a Class I trail that parallels Highway 101 and leads to the town of Summerland (3.7). Turn right to rejoin Ortega Hill Drive that becomes Lillie Avenue and cycle through about 0.7-mile of the town, which has several interesting restaurants to choose from. Next, pass some agricultural land.

At mile 6.8, Padaro Lane intersects for a second time and crosses under US 101, leading to the Santa Claus Lane tourist area if you want to make a short side trip over there. It is now more of a New England fishing village than the North Pole, since the landmark giant Santa Claus has retired to Oxnard. There are a couple of restaurants here, including Padaro Beach Grill, with a nice patio. Return the way you came, as there is no outlet other than to 101 South.

On the Coast Route, pass neighborhoods of Carpinteria (7.5), and then turn right when Via Real Ends at Santa Ynez Avenue (8.5). The Coast Route crosses over US 101, then turns left onto Carpinteria Avenue (8.7), where you'll find a choice of restaurants in the downtown core starting at Holly Avenue (9.0). Turn right on Linden Avenue, which is the main drag of this appealing low-key beachside community. Pedal past the restaurants and cross the railroad tracks (9.5). The unmanned Amtrak station platform is to the right. Follow Linden to a public beach park and turn around. Notice the RV's off to the east, which are in Carpinteria State Beach. To get there, head east on 6th Street then right on Palm Avenue to access the park entrance (10.3). Fees are charged for vehicles and camping but not for bike/ped entry. A Camp 'n Ride from there to the Santa Barbara waterfront is about 26 miles round trip. The park offers some good wildlife viewing opportunities, including riparian woodland, a tide pool area, and a harbor seal haulout and rookery. Return the same way for a 20.6 mile ride, or continue southward:

Return to the Coast Route by turning right on Carpinteria Ave (10.7). Someday a path will connect to the Rincon Trail. Until then, turn left on Bailard Ave, over US 101 (11.9), then right on Class II Via Real to CA 150/Rincon Rd (13.1). Turn left, then right on Class III Rincon Hill Rd (13.4), down the hill (e-bike edge), becoming Bates Rd, under 101, to the entrance to the Rincon Trail on the left (14.2). The very scenic but noisy 3.6-mile path is next to the ocean side of the 101 freeway, leading to a connection to Old Rincon Highway (17.8). See Ventura ride VE4 for a description of this path and connection to the paths to Ventura and Ojai (VE1,2,3). The next Amtrak station after Carpinteria is in downtown Ventura (27.5).

UC Santa Barbara and its Fabulous Coastal Trails SB2 ⭐

The University of California at Santa Barbara (UCSB) is located in a magnificent setting along dramatic coastal bluffs. The campus itself is an attractive public university, the highlight of which is a beautiful oxbow-shaped lake called the UCSB Lagoon, where sea and shore birds thrive. The campus is very bike friendly, with crisscrossing paths that meet at roundabouts and tunnel under roadways. The Coast Route in fact goes through the center of the campus. The 22,000 students flood into the adjacent town of Isla Vista where you may see more young people on bikes than in cars, including students transporting their surfboards to the beach.

Isla Vista has multitudes of eateries to choose from to give you a great Bike 'n Brunch option. The highlight of riding here, however, is the presence of coastal bluff trails that extend both east and west from Isla Vista. Most of these are smooth packed dirt and better for a hybrid or mountain bike, but there are a few on the UCSB campus that are paved. You can also extend the ride to the west along beautiful bluff-top mountain bike paths. On a sunny warm day, a pedal around the UCSB paths can be heavenly.

To add more miles to your ride, pedal up the Class I Obern Trail that leads to the east from this ride's Goleta Beach Park trailhead along a riparian drainage in residential and equestrian neighborhoods in the broad alluvial plain of Goleta, with an option to hop off for some bluff-top mountain biking. You can also connect to SB1 via designated Class II and Class III bike routes.

Tunes: To the Sea by Jack Johnson; Be Good to Your School by The Beach Boys; Teach Your Children by Kathy Mattea et al (1994).
Eats: Ahi Sandwich at Beachside Café, Goleta Beach Park.

Distance: 8.1 miles + options. Time: 1 hour.
Route & Bike: Easy. Mostly Class I; some easy Class III through Isla Vista. Hybrid or mountain bike gives the best options. Also option for road bike. Mostly flat with some short steep hills on the UCSB coastal trails.

Seasons: All. Best on sunny uncrowded off-season weekend when classes not in session.

Facilities: Restrooms and water at Goleta Beach County Park and around UCSB (including east of Stadium Road along trail).

Knocks & Hazards: Coastal Fog. Campus trails crazy during class changes, especially roundabouts. Street riding through busy Isla Vista. Some steep hills along coastal trails and some deep sand in places. Rattlesnakes. Obern Trail: Clueless peds/dog walkers and possible lurkers. Some low-traffic residential street riding.

Rent 'n Ride: Isla Vista Bicycle Boutique, 880 Embarc. Del Mar, 805.968.3338. Shops: Bicycle Bob's, 320 S Kellogg, 682.4699; Varsity Bikes, 6547 Pardall, 968.4914

Camp 'n Ride: None close by. See SB1.

Bike 'n Brunch: Student cafés on campus and restaurants in Isla Vista: Buddha Bowls for bread bowl meals, 901 Embarcadero Del Mar; Freebird's World Burrito, 879 Embarc. Del Norte; Woodstock's Pizza, 928 Embarc. Del Norte. Also nearby are Vietnamese, Indian, and more taco shops and pizza. Get sandwiches to go and a local feeling at the Isla Vista Co-op, 6575 Seville Rd. Pardall Road is the main east-west downtown street. Near the Goleta Pier is the popular Beachside Café.

Further Info: ucsb.edu; santabarbara.com/dining/; see also SB1.

Access: Exit from US 101, west of Santa Barbara, onto SR 217 southbound and follow the signs to Goleta Beach County Park. Free parking is available here. Alternatively, park on the street in Isla Vista as allowed, and begin from there.

The Ride: From the parking lot, find the Class I Coast Route trail and pedal westward, up a gradual hill and be treated to a fabulous view down the Goleta coastline and out to the Channel Islands. The trail brings you to Lagoon Road across from the UC Santa Barbara campus in 0.4 mile. Carefully cross the road and continue on the paved path through UCSB, following any signs for "Coast Route." When in doubt stick to what seems like the principal bike path. At the first bike roundabout go to the right, then follow the path as it bends left around the Chemistry building (mile 0.6), and after some more jogs around Phelps Hall (0.8), heads due west. It passes through a tunnel under Ocean Road (1.0), then next to the main athletic fields and gymnasium, and across Stadium Road (1.3) to another bike roundabout. For those restricted to pavement, head south on the Class I trail across El Colegio by crossing at the light, and see Option 1.

From the bike roundabout our main tour continues straight/west on the Class I trail parallel to El Colegio Road. Carefully cross entrance drives to student housing complexes, and reach Slough Road at the end of the Class I trail (2.3). Storke Road to the right leads in 0.75 mile to a large new commercial center with lots of dining options. Carefully turn left onto our recommended route down the degraded pavement of Slough Road. There is no bike lane, but the road is lightly traveled because it is a dead end with no beach or trailhead parking. As the road begins to curve left in only about 0.2 mile, a trailhead on the right among several trees leads to some scenic mountain biking (see Option 2).

Enjoy a scenic ride along Devereux Slough with views out to sand bars and the open ocean. The accessible portion of the road ends at a gate (3.0). Past the gate a paved road leads to the left, but take the right fork on a bluff-top trail that is mixed pavement and dirt. This degraded coastal sage ecosystem is in the process of being restored, as described by interpretive signs along the way. It merges back to the end of the paved road (3.2), and continues to the right on a gravel road. Follow it straight,

Bluff trail near Coal Oil Point

bearing right to the access area for Coal Oil Point, a popular surfing spot (3.3). There are bike racks and a porta-potty here.

Turn around, and ride east along the bluffs on a nicely compacted, wide gravel path. This pathway provides fabulous vistas up and down the coastline. The path connects to Class III Del Playa Drive in Isla Vista (3.4). You also have the option to continue on a packed dirt path that leads on the ocean side of the houses, ending at a park with a volleyball court, at which time you can return to the street. Del Playa Drive houses the lucky students who get to live near the beach, and it can be party central. We rode this area on infamous Halloween weekend, so we may have a skewed view of the amount of partying and police activity that goes on here.

Turn left on Embarcadero Road (4.7) to go into the center of Isla Vista with its parks and restaurants. Bear right and ride up Embarcadero del Norte. The popular Isla Vista Food Co-op is across the park on Seville. Our route continues past Anisqoyo Park to Pardall Road, which is the center of activity with the most choices of places to eat (4.8). Turn left or right to explore, but head to the east toward campus to continue onward. Connect to the Class I trail at the end of the street (about 5.0). For the shorter way back through campus, go through Pardall Tunnel under Ocean Road and follow the bike paths due east with one jog at the library to the starting point.

Otherwise, instead of going through the tunnel, turn right on the Class I path and head south. The path reaches oceanfront bluffs (5.3) and turns eastward (to the left). Here you have a choice of a paved path on the left, or a nicely graded gravel path closer to the bluffs. They converge above the beautiful UCSB Lagoon (5.6). We recommend carefully gliding down the hill along the paved path to reach the point between the beach and the lagoon. Watch for sandy areas on the trail at the bottom. For the easiest way back from here, turn left to ride along the lagoon.

Or, for some dramatic ocean vistas, cycle up the hill on the most obvious paved path in front of you that then curves around to the right, getting closer to the ocean. An optional detour on the left atop the hill takes you on a scenic dirt singletrack trail above the lagoon. Continue onward and enjoy the myriad of bluff-top trails with awesome views above Campus Point. This is a dead end, with the only option for a loop being a bike-carry down a long staircase leading to the end of Lagoon Road (6.1). Therefore, cycle back the way you came to the point between the beach and lagoon.

Rather than going back up the hill, turn right onto the wide path along the scenic lake that is frequented by a plethora of birds (6.5). As you cycle around its perimeter, you will come to an interpretive sign describing the birdlife at the north end near campus buildings (6.9). We watched plenty of pelicans, great white egrets, cormorants, and many others including a swan. Our ride continues on a scenic route around the lagoon on a paved road signed "Authorized Vehicles Only" and ends up a small hill in a campus parking lot (7.3).

Take the access road (Channel Islands Road) to the right to Lagoon Road, and turn left onto the roadway that parallels a bluff-top park (7.4). After a bike crossing sign, turn right onto the Class I trail (7.7), enjoying the great ocean vistas as you coast down the path to the park and your starting point at the beach park (8.1). At this point you have cycled only about 8 miles plus options, so you may still need to work off that burrito you ate in Isla Vista. See Option 3 for the Class I Obern Trail that heads to the east for 4.3 miles, plus some more optional bluff-top mountain bike riding.

Option 1: UCSB on paved surfaces only *Variable distance. Easy, any bike.*

For those on road bikes requiring pavement who prefer not to try the packed dirt trails along the bluffs, spend your time exploring Isla Vista and UCSB instead by looking at the map and keeping to the red and green-labeled paths. From mile 1.3 at Stadium Road, cross Colegio and head south on the Class I trail between UCSB and Isla Vista. When you come to Pardall Tunnel to UCSB on the left, you have the option of exploring to the right on Pardall Road and through the town of Isla Vista. Return to this spot and continue toward the ocean, then turn left on the paved trail that runs on the bluffs next to Manzanita Village. As the path reaches a trail junction at the east end of the bluff, either cruise down the hill to the UCSB Lagoon and follow the rest of ride SB2 from there, or, turn to the left staying on top of the bluff and go around the buildings. Find your way to an east-west path just past the Theater and Dance building and turn right. Continue east to make your way back to Lagoon Road and your starting point.

Option 2: Ocean Bluffs and Butterflies Too *3–4 miles. Easy to moderate MTB.*

A beautiful oceanfront park with a 1-mile long ocean bluff trail and eucalyptus trees full of wintering monarch butterflies is located just west of the UCSB property. It is a bit hillier than the rest of SB2 (high-low difference of around 80 feet), but the riding is still novice level on the single and doubletrack paths. The property is a combination of open space land referred to as Elwood Mesa and Santa Barbara Shores Park, a Goleta city park.

From SB2, once you turn left down Slough Road from Colegio Road, look for a trailhead among some trees on the right in less than 0.25 mile as Slough Road bends to the left. This dirt path leads down to a bridge over the slough (elevation 7 feet here). Continue west (left) on an access road for about 0.5 mile as it curves to the left and heads to the sea, leading to a row of eucalyptus trees. Make your way to the Bluffs Overlook Trail. You can follow this path west for about a mile along the scenic bluffs, a popular sunset ride among locals. Be careful when next to the 60- to 80-foot high bluffs. The path curves to the right when it reaches the property boundary at the Sandpiper Golf Course.

Another path on the property parallels the Bluffs Trail across the property, and others run through the thick eucalyptus grove at the north end of the property up against the residential zone. A path between the end of Santa Barbara Shores Drive and popular Elwood Beach bisects the center of the property. Other entrances from the adjacent neighborhoods are at the end of Canyon Green, Elmwood Beach Dr and Coronado, as well as from Hollister. New dirt and paved paths adjacent to the north of the Slough Rd trailhead around a wetland area make a good extension, as shown on the map.

Option 3: Goleta's Obern Trail ⭐ *8.6 miles total (plus MTB option). Easy, any bike.*
From Goleta Beach Park, pedal back across the access bridge and onto the signed Obern Trail on the right. You are in for 3 miles of easy pedaling along Atascadero Creek. The scenery is mostly pleasant riparian vistas with some residential and a golf course. Cross Patterson Avenue in a crosswalk (1.4). See Option 3A for a coastal MTB and beach excursion from here.

Reach a junction with the Marie Ignacio Trail on the left (1.5). At your option you can follow it northward, crossing under Hollister Avenue in 0.7 mile, where the delicious Woody's BBQ is in a shopping center to the east. The path continues under US 101 (1.2), and to residential areas beyond. At mile 2.7 along the Obern Trail is the Turnpike Road turnoff. This connector leads north to Class II Turnpike Road that also crosses US 101 (1.0), where you will find an In-N-Out Burger and two hotels. Both of these optional routes also intersect the regional Class II Cross Town and North Goleta bike routes.

Near the end of the Obern Trail (3.4) cyclists are directed through a quiet residential area along Arroyo Road, then right onto Nueces Drive, and across Nogal Drive, back onto a Class I trail past an equestrian training center. The trail ends at Modoc Road near Encore Dr in about 30 minutes (4.3). Modoc Rd is part of the Coast Route (Goleta to Santa Barbara, see SB1) and Cross Town Route. *A class I path is planned along Modoc to Las Positas and south to Cliff.* Return the way you came via the Coast Route (8.6).

Option 3A: More Mesa MTB ⭐ *1 mile round trip to trailheads and 2–3 mile novice MTB*
Although not quite as scenic as Santa Barbara Shores (Option 2), More Mesa oceanfront open space park is also worthwhile to add some fun mileage to your ride. From the Patterson Avenue crossing, turn right (south) and ride on this rural road that curves to the left to become Shoreline Drive. At 0.3 mile, after a horse farm, is the first trail entrance on the left. Another follows when the road makes a right angle turn to become Orchid Drive (0.4) and another on the left around mile 0.5. The latter makes the best entrance to the main part of the network of single and doubletrack trails across More Mesa. A staircase down to the beach is on the far (east) side of the bluffs. The beach to the west (right) of the staircase is clothing optional, but intermittent police crackdowns have been reported. Unfortunately a portion of this park will probably be developed in the future. For furthur info on this park and updates see www.moremesa.org.

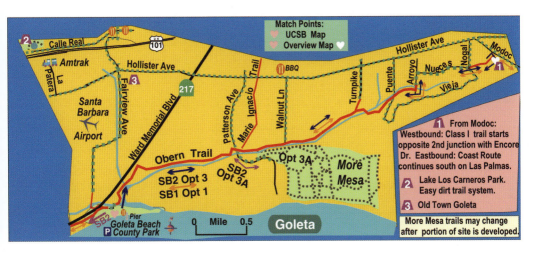

3. Ventura County

Ventura County (population 840,000) is thought of as being divided into East and West County. East County contains affluent suburbs such as Thousand Oaks and Simi Valley adjacent to LA's San Fernando Valley. We have no featured rides there, but if in Simi Valley check out the Arroyo Simi rail trail that runs about 7.8 miles from Tierra Rejada Rd and Stargaze Pl to Yosemite Ave and Damon St. It is mostly paved with some crushed stone areas and has some nice mountain views, a good way to get across town. See rsrpd.org.

West County contains the coastal plain that includes Camarillo, Oxnard, Ventura, and the Ojai Valley. The northern portion of the county consists of rugged mountainous terrain with with little population, the highest point being 8,831-foot Mt. Pinos. The county has a total area of 2,208 square miles, of which 1,845 square miles is land and 363 square miles is water. Anacapa Island (of Channel Islands National Park) and the military-run San Nicolas Island are within its boundaries. Our featured Ventura County rides are in the West County areas of Ventura and Ojai.

The city of Ventura (population 110,000) is the county seat and an interesting city to visit. It is resplendent in bike trails that are included in this chapter. Oxnard, with a population of over 200,000, is the largest city in the county, but is less interesting than adjoining Ventura, except along the waterfront area of Channel Islands Harbor. Although not highlighted in this chapter, you can pedal around the Channel Islands Harbor area on Class II roads.

Oxnard sits at the edge of the Oxnard Plain, one of the most fertile agricultural areas in the world, and is known as the strawberry capital of California. A strawberry festival held in May features all kinds of interesting food items made from strawberries. Oxnard also has a military element, with the Port Hueneme and Point Mugu naval bases located adjacent to its south.

Highway 1 leads south out of Oxnard along the spectacular coastline to Malibu and Santa Monica, while the US 101 Freeway continues inland to the East County area. US 101 also continues northwest to neighboring Santa Barbara County. To the north over the mountains is Kern County. LA's Metrolink commuter rail system extends only as far as East Ventura/Oxnard, while Amtrak services the downtown Ventura station near our bike routes.

As in most of Southern California, the coastal cities, such as Ventura, boast moderate temperatures tempered by the cool Pacific year round, while inland cities, such as Ojai, tend to be warmer in summer and experience cooler nights in winter.

Climate Data for Ventura (Source, NOAA 1900 to 2013 normals)													
Month	Jan	Feb	Mar	Apr	May	Jun	Jul	Aug	Sep	Oct	Nov	Dec	Totals
Average High °F	66.9	65.3	68.2	68.0	67.7	70.9	73.0	74.3	74.3	73.7	71.2	69.9	70.3
Average Low °F	45.0	43.2	45.8	47.0	48.7	53.0	55.1	54.3	52.8	51.6	48.1	45.1	49.1
Precipitation, inches	3.05	3.26	2.55	0.98	0.23	0.04	0.01	0.02	0.22	0.49	1.46	2.37	14.67

Climate Data for Ojai (Source, NOAA 1948 to 2005 normals)													
Month	Jan	Feb	Mar	Apr	May	Jun	Jul	Aug	Sep	Oct	Nov	Dec	Totals
Average High °F	66.6	68.5	70.3	74.5	77.3	82.9	89.9	90.7	88.1	81.7	73.7	67.7	77.7
Average Low °F	36.7	38.9	40.6	43.9	48.0	51.4	55.4	55.5	53.4	47.7	41.2	36.6	45.8
Precipitation, inches	4.93	5.13	3.44	1.48	0.43	0.06	0.02	0.04	0.30	0.56	2.16	2.95	21.50

Ventura

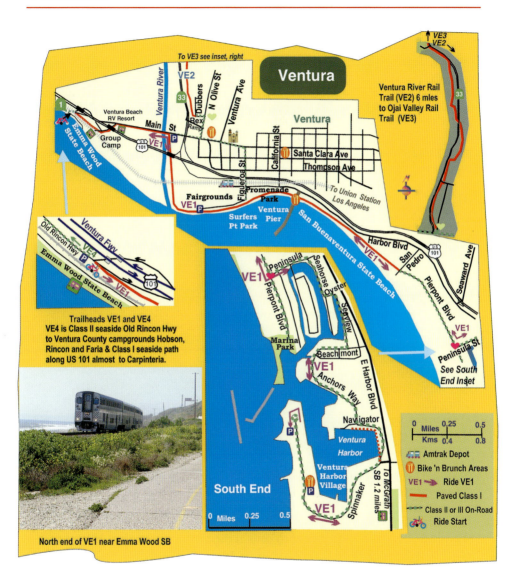

North end of VE1 near Emma Wood SB

Located about 25 miles south of Santa Barbara along the spectacular Pacific coastline lies the city of Ventura, whose official title is San Buenaventura, named for the Mission San Buenaventura, built by Father Junipero Serra in 1782. The actual mission building remains as a tourist attraction in the charming downtown district, which is built on a hillside, its streets lined with antique shops, galleries, and restaurants. Another landmark is the City Hall, a fine example of early twentieth-century neo-classical architecture with terra cotta ornamentation.

Ventura is known for its good surfing beaches, and a paved beachfront promenade provides a nice off-road pedal, with an option to dart off into the adjacent downtown area for some dining or shopping. Ventura Harbor is bustling with activity and is the gateway to Channel Islands National Park. Boat trips are offered to visit the islands, including day trips to Anacapa Island for a very scenic easy hike. Ventura has numerous oceanfront campgrounds adjacent to bike routes, making it one of the best (and busiest) Camp 'n Ride destinations in Southern California.

This is a fabulous area to come to for some easy scenic riding with decent mileage options. Oceanfront cycling involves a mix of Class I promenades and some Class II and Class III cycling through neighborhoods (ride VE1). Cyclists can also ride for miles on an oceanfront frontage road and bike path to the north (VE4), or cycle a fine rail trail, 15 miles inland through the Ojai Valley to Ojai (VE2 and VE3).

Ojai is a smallish resort town of Old West and Spanish colonial architecture beautifully situated beneath the Santa Ynez Mountains. It is a popular getaway for Angelinos who visit its resorts and spas, and is a draw for artists, musicians, and outdoors enthusiasts. Our fabulous Ojai ride (VE3) includes a tour of the lovely and compact downtown district.

Ventura Oceanfront and Harbor Tour VE1

A Class I trail system extends from the US 101 overpass near the entrance to Emma Wood State Park for 4 miles along the Ventura waterfront, and a bike route continues for another 4 miles on Class II and III streets through the Ventura Harbor area. Along the way the rider can experience dramatic ocean vistas, a verdant river delta, a vibrant beach scene, yacht-y neighborhoods, and exciting places to stop for a meal.

We usually start in the free day-use parking area next to Emma Wood State Park. The stunning vistas across the ocean to the Channel Islands and up the dramatic coastline to Santa Barbara compensate for

VE1 near Ventura River delta

the shortcomings of the trail itself, which can be in disrepair and crowded in places. At trails end in the Ventura Harbor district, a nice sequence of Class II and III bike routes bring you to a fabulous Bike 'n Brunch oasis at the entrance to Ventura Harbor for a great 16-mile round-trip cruise. For a truly memorable day, combine your ride with a boat excursion out to Channel Islands National Park.

Tunes: Ventura Highway by America; Ventura by Lucinda Williams; I Have Found Me A Home by Jimmy Buffet; Southern Cross by Crosby Stills & Nash
Eats: Al fresco meal at the Ventura Harbor Village complex or a fish lunch on the Ventura Pier.

Distance: 16.2 miles + options. Time: 2 hours
Route & Bike: Easy to moderate due to distance. Class I (Omer Rains Coastal Bike Trail), II, and III. Paved route option for Class I only. Any bike.
Seasons: All. Best on sunny uncrowded off-season weekday with minimal fog or wind.

Facilities: Restrooms in parks and commercial facilities along route, starting 2 miles southeast of trailhead.

Knocks & Hazards: Can be foggy and/or windy. Paved beach promenade can be packed with trail users of all types. Since the Great Depression, the north Ventura area has been popular with vagrants, especially along the Ventura River. The wilderness park area at Emma Wood State Park was once called Hobo Haven. It's best to ride the northwest portion with a companion, as well as any portion of the trail when not in heavy use. The south half of the trail involves street riding, either on Class II lanes, or Class III streets through quiet neighborhoods. Be extra careful, especially at all street crossings. The bike lanes on Spinnaker Drive are narrow.

Rent 'n Ride: Ventura Bike Depot, 239 W Main St, 805.652.1114; Wheel Fun Rentals, 805.650.7770, multiple locations along trail including the pier, Crowne Plaza Hotel on the Promenade, Ventura State Beach Picnic Area, Marriott on Harbor Blvd, Four Points Sheraton on Schooner. Shops: Open Air Bicycles, 2386 E Main St, 653.1100; Matt's Cycling Center, 2427 E Harbor Blvd, 477.0933.

Camp 'n Ride: Along Old Rincon Hwy north of trailhead are Ventura County beachfront campgrounds Faria Beach & Hobson Beach (tent & RV, some full hookups), and Rincon Parkway (self contained RV only, no hookups). For information see countyofventura.org. Near the trailhead are Emma Wood State Beach for self-contained RV's (beachfront camping next to noisy railroad tracks, no facilities) and the park's group camp area for tents and RV's (no hookups), 805.968.1033. Ventura Beach RV Resort (RV's and tents) is also near trailhead, 805.643.9137. South of Ventura Harbor, 1.2 miles on Harbor Blvd is McGrath State Beach: Tents and RV's (size limit, developed, no hookups, subject to closure). See also ride VE3.

Bike 'n Brunch: Restaurants near pier, downtown, and at Ventura Harbor Village at trail's end.

City code, bike riding on sidewalks: Permitted except for the downtown business district, defined as Ventura Ave to the west including the western sidewalk, Ash St to the east including the eastern sidewalk, Poli St to the north including the northern sidewalk, and Harbor Blvd to the south including the southern sidewalk.

Further Info: San Buenaventura State Beach: www.parks.ca.gov/?page_id=600; Emma Wood State Beach: www.parks.ca.gov/?page_id=604; City of Ventura: cityofventura.net; venturaharbor.com; Channel Islands National Park: www.nps.gov/chis/; other: venturaharborvillage.com; ventura.com; venturacountyfair.org.

Access: North trailhead: From US 101 in Ventura heading north out of town, take the Hwy 1—State Beaches exit. After you drive under the freeway, watch for the bike path trailhead on the left. Just beyond it on the left is free day-use parking used by surfers. Park here, or if it is full, continue to the bottom of the hill to a large day-use parking area along Old Rincon Hwy on the left. Or, you can park in the harbor area in any of the neighborhoods along the route. Other options include parking at San Buenaventura State Beach or near the Ventura Pier for a fee.

Rail 'n Ride: Amtrak's Surfliner and Coast Starlight stop at the station on Harbor Blvd. From the station take Harbor east (left if looking toward the ocean) to Figueroa Street. Turn right to reach the beach pathway, or left to reach the downtown pedestrian mall in two blocks.

The Ride: Start pedaling down the Class I trail with a sign indicating that this path was the first one adopted by Caltrans, with the assistance of Channel Islands Bicycle Club. The path is paved but fairly rough, so watch for bumps. It begins with sufficient elevation to enable great views out over the Ventura River delta and the ocean that is dotted with the islands of Channel Islands National Park. Santa Barbara Island is the largest, while Anacapa Island, the most visited island due to frequent boat tours, is closer, smaller, and more jagged. The US 101 Freeway is above you on the left, and active railroad tracks and the long and narrow Emma Wood State Beach campground are below you on the right. Campers staying there typically carry their bikes across the railroad tracks at several locations to reach the trail. Expect a few dips as the trail gradually works its way to sea level.

VE1 Waterfront promenade heading towards pier.

After 1 mile reach the group camp area of Emma Wood State Park, which has a different entrance than the main campground. The path crosses under the 101 Freeway (mile 1.3) then parallels the group camp access road to Main Street (1.4). Curve to the right, adjacent to Main Street, as you pass Ventura Beach RV Resort, then cross a long bridge over the Ventura River. Pause to look north toward the Ojai Valley and south to the river delta, which bustles with bird life. The trail curves to the right after the bridge (1.8). If you want to check out downtown Ventura, or take the Ventura River Trail (ride VE2) that connects to the Ojai Valley Trail (ride VE3), head down Main Street in the bike lane (see Option 1). Otherwise, continue on our waterfront trail toward the ocean. It crosses under US 101 again, then passes an active, signaled on-grade railroad crossing.

Reach the beachfront at the Ventura River delta (2.3). You may see dozens of pelicans or other sea or shore birds atop the sandbar. Start cycling along the beachfront promenade, which has been nicely rebuilt in this first section. On windy days the kite surfers will be jumping the waves. This multi-use promenade is sometimes packed with pedestrians, as would be expected. The first part of the promenade is between the ocean and Shoreline Drive, with the Ventura County Fairgrounds beyond. Pass Surfers Point Park (2.7), then at Promenade Park at mile 2.9 is a connector to Figueroa Avenue. That street leads to the center of downtown Ventura in 0.3 mile. Continue along the oceanfront Promenade, past the Crowne Plaza Hotel (3.1), and cross under the Ventura Pier (3.3), which contains the Beach House Fish seafood restaurant and taco stand. The next stretch is less crowded and very scenic as you near the main part of San Buenaventura State Beach (4.0). The Class I Omer Rains Trail ends at the park entrance off of San Pedro Street (4.3). This is an optional turnaround point for an 8.6-mile all Class I cycle.

To continue, carefully cross San Pedro Street and pedal straight ahead down the bike lane along Pierpont Boulevard. When you reach Peninsula Street this is a decision point (5.0). Pierpont becomes the spine of a peninsula that ends at scenic Marina Park in another 0.4 mile, another potential turnaround point. Our main ride continues to the left (east) down Peninsula Street.

Turn right on Seahorse Avenue (5.2). You may notice large masts behind the houses, as the houses in this harbor neighborhood have their own docks. Jog to the left down Oyster Street, then right down Seaview Avenue. Turn right when you reach

Beachmont Street (5.9). As it rounds the bend across from Marina Park it becomes Anchors Way, passing Harbortown Point Resort and Water's Edge restaurant with a great sunset view. A few pedals farther the new Portside Ventura Harbor residential community has a promenade, park, and restaurants to explore.

The road ends at Navigator Drive in front of the large Ventura West Marina. Either turn left on Navigator Drive or cut through the marina parking lot, find the paved path along the water, and head to the left to the point where Navigator Drive ends at Spinnaker Drive (7.0). Turn right into the bike lane of this divided 4-lane harbor access road. It passes several marinas, and we tend to cut through the parking lots and sightsee along the way. As the road bends to the left and then to the right, prepare to be wowed with Bike 'n Brunch opportunities starting around mile 7.4.

Ventura Harbor Village is a great destination with all kinds of shops and international restaurants to choose from. This is one of the main destinations in Ventura, and it can get crowded. At this point you are on a narrow peninsula, with ocean beaches to the west and the harborfront commercial establishments to the east. After mile 7.7, the harbor side is lined with marinas, yacht clubs, Island Packer Cruises (tours of the Channel Islands), and Channel Islands National Park Headquarters and Visitor's Center (worth a stop). Harbor Cove Beach is along the ocean, from where there is a beautiful view up the coast to Santa Barbara. Harbor Cove Café on the bay side is a quiet alternative to the busy Ventura Harbor Village. The road ends with a turn-around at mile 8.1. Return the same way.

Option 1: Cycle into Downtown or Connect to the Ventura River Trail (VE2) and Ojai Valley Trail (VE3)

A few blocks of city street riding followed by about 6 miles on a rail trail connect the Ventura Beach and Harbor ride to the Ojai Valley Trail (VE3). At mile 1.8, at the east side of the bridge over the Ventura River where the bike trail heads toward the ocean, continue east in the bike lane along Main Street. To head up the Ventura River rail trail, turn left in less than 0.2 mile onto North Olive Street, then after passing the entrance to Highway 33 make the first left at Rex Street and find the trailhead at the corner of Dubbers Street (VE2). Otherwise, Main Street leads into downtown Ventura, which is worth exploring for its restaurants, shops and historic buildings such as City Hall and Mission San Buenaventura.

Reach the main part of downtown with the mission and Figueroa Street pedestrian mall in about 0.5 mile from the point where you left VE1. Beyond there the diagonal style of parked cars begins which is so dangerous for cyclists, however, it corresponds to the area with the best selection of restaurants. Therefore, consider walking your bike (riding not allowed) along those sidewalks as you browse the offerings.

Ventura River Rail Trail VE2

Details: 12 miles roundtrip, 1–1.5 hours, paved Class I rail trail.

See Option 1 of Ride VE1 for directions to south trailhead. The rail trail roughly follows SR 33 and Ventura Avenue, passing through a myriad of industrial properties that some may find interesting. The highlight is several unique sculptures that have been installed along the route. The trail crosses under SR 33 in 3.2 miles, passes a mix of agricultural and industrial land, then becomes more rural, agricultural, and scenic around mile 4.7. It ends at mile 5.6 at Casitas Vista Road, across which is the trailhead to the Ojai Valley Trail (VE3).

The Ojai Valley Trail VE3

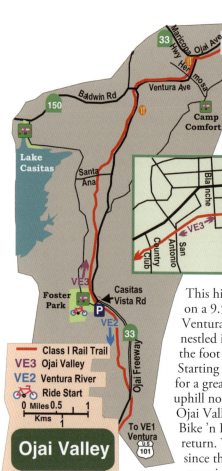

This highly regarded rail trail leads the rider on a 9.5-mile journey that roughly follows the Ventura River to the popular resort town of Ojai, nestled in the horse country of the Ojai Valley at the foot of the impressive Santa Ynez Mountains. Starting at the south trailhead at Foster Park allows for a great day of cycling, with a gradual steady uphill northbound ride along the former Ventura and Ojai Valley Rail line, wonderful opportunities for a Bike 'n Brunch in Ojai, and an easy cruise on the return. You can also try a Spa 'n Ride experience, since there are some twenty day spas in Ojai. If it promises to be a hot day, you will be glad to get the uphill portion out of the way first (e-bike edge). However, if you are staying in Ojai, the uphill climb on the return of about 500 feet in 9 miles is not all that strenuous. The gradual slope continues mostly for the first 6 miles heading north along the river, and then levels out for the last 3 toward Ojai. The paved trail is mainly in good shape and offers its share of impressive vistas, mostly in the northbound direction, which conveniently is the uphill direction where you will be going much slower. You have the option of a 19-mile round trip beginning at Foster Park, or a 30+ mile round trip if you follow the rail trail from Ventura. Ride VE2 between Ventura and Foster Park is predominantly through an uninteresting industrial area and we recommend that segment only if you want to tack on the extra mileage.

Tunes: The Valley Road by the Nitty Gritty Dirt Band with Bruce Hornsby; Equestrienne by Natalie Merchant; Brandenburg Concerto No. 5 in D Major by Bach.
Eats: California-style lunch al fresco in an Ojai café.

Distance: About 20 miles total. Time: 2 hrs. Option to link to Ventura River Trail (VE2), Ventura Oceanfront (VE1); and Rincon route to Santa Barbara (VE4).

Route & Bike: Moderate due to distance and gradual uphill northbound (e-bike edge). Paved Class I; any bike that can handle some trail bumps. Topo: 235 ft elevation at south Foster Park trailhead; gradual slope to 800 ft at north trailhead.

Seasons: All. Best on sunny spring day.

Knocks & Hazards: Numerous street crossings along the route, mostly easy. Ojai can be much hotter than on the coast, especially in summer. Watch for bumps in trail and control downhill speed southbound. Don't leave valuables in car at trailheads. Some mountain lion habitat; rattlesnakes. Flash flood possible near creek.

Facilities: Find restrooms and water at Foster Park, fast food joints along the way across Hwy 33, Vons market at mile 7.8, and Libbey Park near trail's end.

Camp 'n Ride: Two Ventura County Parks welcome tents and RV's including some full hookup sites. Foster County Park is at the trailhead. Camp Comfort County Park along San Antonio Creek is 7.3 miles north along the trail, then 0.7 mile down the hill along Hermosa Road. Reservations: venturaparks.org. Several campgrounds are located in Ventura (see ride VE1) and at Lake Casitas.

Rent 'n Ride: The Mob Shop, 110 W Ojai Ave, 805.978.5193; Bicycles of Ojai, 108 Canada St, 805.646.7736. Ojai Valley Inn downtown, 800.422.6524.

Bike 'n Brunch: In Ojai try a chile relleno on Agave Maria's patio, 106 S Montgomery, or popular pizza al fresco at Ojai Pizza Co, 331 E Ojai Ave. Vegans can try Hip Vegan at 928 E Ojai Ave. Other casual or fast food spots are found along the trail.

Spa 'n Ride: Day spa near our route: Body Essentials, 236 W Ojai Ave, 805.646.7600.

City code, bike riding on sidewalks: Allowed only if part of a marked bike route.

Further Info: See ojaivisitors.com for special Ojai events such as June's Ojai Classical Music and Lavender Festivals. City of Ojai: ojaicity.org; ojaichamber.org. Trails sites: venturacountytrails.org; abandonedrails.com/Ojai Branch.

Access: From US 101 at the northwest end of Ventura take Highway 33 toward Ojai. For the south trailhead, exit at Casitas Vista Road and follow signs to Foster County Park (right on Ventura, right on Casitas Vista under the freeway overpass). Parking fee is $2–$4 at the park. Many park beneath the freeway overpass to avoid the fee. From downtown Ojai, the trail is 2 blocks south of East Ojai Avenue. Take the trail through Libbey Park, or head down a side street such as Fox Street to intersect the trail, and head west (right). Rail 'n Ride: See ride VE1.

The Ride: Begin cycling northward from the trailhead on Casitas Vista Road at Foster County Park. The trail passes Foster Park and veers away from the Ojai Freeway, which has become the 2-lane Ventura Avenue. The pathway passes under power lines (mile 0.75) and runs between the river drainage and rural residential backyards, then returns next to Ventura Avenue to pass by a mobile home park (1.4). One of the best sections follows, as the path returns to the riverside area and enters dense oak woodland. At about mile 2.0, it crosses a new (2012) bridge over San Antonio Creek near its confluence with the Ventura River. The prior low-water culvert crossing was frequently closed due to high water in winter and spring, and the structure had inhibited the migration of the endangered southern steelhead.

Reach the community of Oak View (2.7) and begin a series of street crossings at Prospect Street (3.1), Mahoney Avenue (3.4), and then Santa Ana Boulevard, where the trail continues kitty-corner across Monte Via (3.5). It crosses Valley Road (3.6),

Ojai Valley Trail (VE3)

then heads out of the community for a more scenic stretch. It returns to the side of Ventura Avenue (4.3), crosses Barbara Street in a residential area (4.6), then Wiley Street (4.7), and then the signaled Woodland Avenue (5.3). Across Ventura Avenue between miles 5.4 and 5.8 are several fast food restaurants and a coffee house.

The rail trail next crosses another signaled intersection at Baldwin Road (SR 150) (5.9), then Tico Road (6.1), Loma Drive (6.4), followed by another very pleasant stretch, still near the highway, but with wide open pastureland to the north, along with mountain vistas. It crosses Hermosa Street (7.4), where the Camp Comfort county campground is located down the hill to the right. After a stretch between residential properties and a golf course, it reaches a shopping center with a Vons supermarket and breakfast/lunch favorite, Home Kitchen (7.8). The trail skirts the parking lot and then turns right to cross Highway 33 with a traffic signal, as it continues toward the center of Ojai.

The path passes a country club, then reaches Country Club Drive (8.4) and San Antonio (8.5). Once the street crossings come close together, starting at South Blanche Street at mile 8.7, you can detour two blocks to the left to reach Ojai Boulevard, the main drag of Ojai, which is lined with shops, restaurants, galleries, and spas. After crossing Signal Street you can also make your way on paths through pretty Libbey Park (around mile 8.9) for a more scenic detour into town. Libbey Park's public tennis facility, along with the many private tennis clubs, is indicative of why Ojai is considered to be one of the country's top tennis towns.

The rail trail passes Montgomery Street (9.0), the tennis courts of the Ojai Valley Athletic Club, Fox Street (9.1), and then Bryant Street (9.3). It continues across the street but just dead-ends at a golf course (9.5). Enjoy a Bike 'n Brunch or some other pursuits in town, and then happily cruise down the trail (even watching your speed in places) to your starting point.

Rincon Coastal Cruise VE4

Details: Class II road ride: 15 miles round trip, 1.5 hours, easy. Class I path: 7.2 miles round trip, easy. Combined: 22.2 miles round trip, 2-2.5 hours, moderate.

Old Rincon Highway runs parallel to US 101 for 7.5 miles between "Coast Highway" interchanges at the VE1 trailhead in the south, almost to Mussel Shoals in the north. This popular cycle route with wide shoulders passes beach accesses, private homes, and RV campgrounds (see VE1). The scenic paved 3.6-mile Rincon Bike Trail continues north on the ocean side of 101, ending at surfers' favorite Rincon Point. A waist-high decorative wall separates the path from the freeway, making the north-bound ride against traffic unsettling. Riding southbound is typically more enjoyable.

The Ride: From the VE1 trailhead, ride down the grade to the coastal highway at the beach, where Emma Wood State Park campground is to the left (0.5). Straight ahead is day use beach parking. Be careful as cars tend to speed along "The Rincon." Beach-front homes block much of the ocean view for a while (1.7 through 4.0), then Faria County Park campground appears (food stand). Next is the Rincon Parkway county campground, with RV's parked along the road adjacent to the beach for 1.5 miles, followed by Hobson County Park campground (5.8). The roadway passes under the 101 with interchanges for both directions (6.3, 6.6). Take the next left under the 101 (7.1) and reach Mobil Pier Rd. Turn right, to the trailhead parking for Rincon Trail (7.3). Follow the trail, that daylights at Mussel Shoals, with a waterfront dining option at Cliff House Inn (8.1). Cross the freeway ramps in the crosswalk, and re-enter the trail. A freeway undercrossing to the community of La Conchita (no services) is at mile 9.0, and a very scenic stretch follows as the trail gets closer to the ocean and the coastline curves to the west (9.9). The trail then reaches a path to the Rincon State Beach parking lot, and ends at Rincon Point Rd (10.8). Across the street is an access road/parking lot for Rincon County Beach, worth exploring (11.1). Both of the beach parks have restrooms and water. A path may one day connect to Carpinteria Ave. Until then a hilly road route (e-bike edge) goes under 101 to Bates Rd to Rincon Hill Rd, left on Rincon Rd to Via Real or Carpinteria Ave. See SB1 Opt 2.

4. Los Angeles County

The size of Delaware and Rhode Island combined, and more populous than 42 states at over 10 million, Los Angeles County is the center of all things Southern California. Although most of the population lives on the wide coastal plain, the county includes two islands (Santa Catalina and San Clemente), mountains as tall as 10,000 feet (Mt. San Antonio aka "Mt. Baldy") that in winter are snow-covered, several rivers (Los Angeles, San Gabriel, Rio Hondo, and Santa Clara) and the western edge of the Mojave Desert in Antelope Valley.

There are 88 incorporated cities, the largest of which are Los Angeles with around 3.9 million, the second largest in the United States after New York, and Long Beach with around 468,000. The county sprawls out into population centers such as the San Gabriel Valley and the Pomona Valley to the east, the San Fernando Valley section of Los Angeles to the north, and up into the Santa Clarita and Antelope Valleys. Air quality can be an issue, especially as one heads east into the mountain-rimmed valleys. When the Santa Ana winds blow, however, the same particulates are blown toward the coast.

Hollywood is a district of Los Angeles and also a generic term for the region's movie production industry, where the majority of American movies and TV shows are produced. Filming is done in studios mostly in the Burbank, Hollywood, and Culver City areas, as well as at locations throughout the region. Universal Studios near Burbank offers a theme-park style tour. Popular museums include the new expansive Getty Museum in West Los Angeles and the Romanesque Getty Villa museum in Pacific Palisades. Los Angeles County Museum of Art (LACMA) attracts major international exhibits, and the Norton Simon in Pasadena has a diverse collection. La Brea Tar Pits near LACMA displays remnants of the region's Pleistocene past.

All kinds of entertainment venues are scattered throughout Los Angeles and surrounding burbs that host sporting events, concerts, plays, ballet, opera, and dance. The Rose Bowl in Pasadena is a venerable sports venue and the New Years Day Tournament of Roses Parade is a national tradition. Downtown Los Angeles is an attraction in itself. Just get off a train at Union Station and walk to El Pueblo de Los Angeles State Historic Park and its Olvera Street Mexican marketplace, the Chinatown district, or the Museum of Contemporary Art (MOCA) and The Geffen Contemporary at MOCA. On Sunday mornings cycling here may be pleasant.

Some like to ogle famous neighborhoods such as Beverly Hills, Pacific Palisades, and Malibu, though cycling through them is not the best way to do that. As a matter of fact, the experience of being able to safely cycle to LA County's attractions is more the exception than the rule, so those routes that fit our criteria become that much more precious here.

As cyclists, we appreciate that a 22-mile bike trail extends along the flat portion of the public beaches of Los Angeles County. This is a fabulous scenic trail, one of the best anywhere, and the premier trail of this book (rides LA1 and 2). Another great trail ride tours the coast around the more industrial city of Long Beach, just north of the Orange County border (LO1 and 2). Those two rides alone keep us happy whenever we are in the Los Angeles area, and are rides that can be enjoyed repeatedly.

Los Angeles does not have a lot of scenic bike trails for a city of that size, but we enjoy cycling at several other locales, including a section of Griffith Park (LA4) and in the Sepulveda Basin in the San Fernando Valley (LA5). Cycling around Los Angeles Harbor and the beautiful San Pedro coastline is also stimulating, even if it is mostly on-road riding (LA3). In the south county the San Gabriel River Trail can provide a good ride from the ocean at Long Beach up to El Dorado Park and beyond (SGR1), while the Whittier Narrows area is a nice oasis along the river in the San Gabriel Valley (SGR2), and the views from the upper section in the San Gabriel Mountain foothills near the Santa Fe Dam can be spectacular on a clear day (SGR3). The West Fork San Gabriel Trail is a fabulous easy mountain escape on a gradual streamside paved path (SGR4). Puddingstone Reservoir near LA County's fairgrounds "Fairplex," has a variety of trails around it that enable a fun scenic loop (LA10). Some routes on low-traffic roadways include a ride near Pasadena's Rose Bowl in Arroyo Seco (PA1 and 2) and a jaunt around San Marino to combine with a visit to the beautiful Huntington Gardens (PA3). Finally, a fun Bike 'n Brunch adventure awaits on lovely Catalina Island (CAT1). Several other notable rides are mentioned in the "Encore" section on page 368, including Santa Clarita's extensive network of Class I trails (LA9), reachable via Metrolink trains.

Other regional trails on our county map are described but not featured due to space limitations, including the south sections of the LA River Trail (someday to be joined with the north section), and the connected Rio Hondo Trail, collectively known as LARIO. Many enjoy riding these trails, however they are not very scenic and have had problems with crime and debris. Parts of the San Gabriel River and Coyote Creek Trails also have their issues.

Los Angeles County Bicycle Coalition (LACBC) is a membership-based nonprofit organization that works to build a better, more bikeable Los Angeles County through advocacy, education, and outreach: la-bike.org. CicLAvia organizes popular car-free street events periodically around LA County. See ciclavia.org.

See also: LA County's Bicycle Facilities Plan: dpw.lacounty.gov/pdd/bike/masterplan.cfm. LA Bike Paths: Check for updates and new trails: www.labikepaths.com. LA Area Bike Clubs: lawheelmen.org. South Bay Area: southbaywheelmen.org; meetup.com/southbaycruisers/; San Fernando Valley: sfvbc.org. LA bike news and blog: bikinginla.com.

Climate Data for Burbank (Source: Weather.com)												
Month	Jan	Feb	Mar	Apr	May	Jun	Jul	Aug	Sep	Oct	Nov	Dec	Totals
Average High °F	68	68	70	73	76	81	87	88	86	80	73	67	76.4
Average Low °F	42	44	46	50	55	59	62	62	60	54	46	41	51.8
Precipitation, inches	3.53	4.62	2.97	1.11	0.35	0.11	0.02	0.07	0.23	0.97	1.07	2.40	17.45

Climate Data for Long Beach (Source NOAA)												
Month	Jan	Feb	Mar	Apr	May	Jun	Jul	Aug	Sep	Oct	Nov	Dec	Totals
Average High °F	68.0	68.5	68.9	72.7	74.0	78.3	82.9	84.6	83.1	78.9	73.4	68.8	75.2
Average Low °F	46.0	48.1	50.4	53.2	57.8	61.3	64.6	65.6	63.7	58.3	50.1	45.3	55.4
Precipitation, inches	2.95	3.01	2.43	0.60	0.23	0.08	0.02	0.10	0.24	0.40	1.12	1.76	12.94

Los Angeles and the Beach Cities

The Los Angeles city limits snake around the coastal area encompassing such districts as Pacific Palisades, Venice Beach, portions of Marina Del Rey, and Playa Del Rey. Filling in are the cities of Santa Monica to the north and El Segundo, Manhattan Beach, Hermosa Beach, Redondo Beach, and Torrance to the south. Linking them all is a fabulous bike trail, the most storied in the land.

LA's Santa Monica and South Bay Beach Trails
LA1 and LA2

There's no denying it—LA's Santa Monica/South Bay Trail is the ultimate easy scenic Bike 'n Brunch ride. The flat coastal trail completed in the 1980s along miles of public beaches is one of the most fabulously successful and renowned bike trails in the world. It now bears the official title Marvin Braude Bike Trail, named for a long-time Los Angeles city councilman instrumental in getting it built. Best known for the stretch through Venice that has been seen in so many movies and TV shows, the trail passes through many incarnations along its 21.4-mile route from Will Rogers State Beach in Pacific Palisades near Malibu at the north end to Torrance County Beach just past Redondo Beach at the south end.

The Beach Blanket Bingo scene in LA is so well ingrained into pop culture that one feels like a spectator in one of the world's most enduring cultural phenomena; surfers, skaters, bikers, strollers, bodybuilders—all can be seen along the route. As a bike ride it has it all. Experience mile after mile of flat paved bike trail, awesome people-watching (even if there may be too many at times), beautiful and changing coastal scenery, and so many choices for your Bike 'n Brunch that you will have a hard time deciding where to eat. It certainly is a fun, fabulous ride, worth making a special trip for.

The trail can be considered to be divided into three sections. The Santa Monica Trail extends from Will Rogers State Beach in Pacific Palisades 6.1 miles to the south past Santa Monica to Venice (ride LA1). A 2.8-mile connector trail consists of a series of Class II bike lanes and trails around Marina Del Rey. It leads to the South Bay Trail at Playa Del Rey near Los Angeles International Airport, then continues along the

LOS ANGELES COUNTY

beach through several beach cities 12.5 miles to Torrance County Beach (LA2). The total length is a staggering 21.4 miles of fabulousness each way, or 42.8 miles round trip. Easy riders may consider doing only half of the trail at a time, or better yet, doing a shuttle and cycling the entire path in one day.

Tunes: I Love LA by Randy Newman; California Girls by the Beach Boys; California Gurls by Katy Perry; Gidget TV Theme; Coming Into Los Angeles by Arlo Guthrie; Counting Airplanes by Train; Redondo Beach by Morrissey.

Eats: Gourmet salad al fresco at Fig Tree Café in Venice.

Distance/time, one way: Up to 21.4 miles and 3 hours total of all segments.

Route & Bike: Easy to strenuous depending on distance and winds. E-bikes mitigate both. Paved, mostly Class I, with some Class II; any bike. Flat with a few small rolling hills near El Segundo on the South Bay Trail.

Seasons: All. Best on sunny uncrowded off-season weekday. On crowded days better in morning, although mornings are also the most likely times for overcast conditions.

Facilities: Restrooms and water in parks and commercial establishments along route.

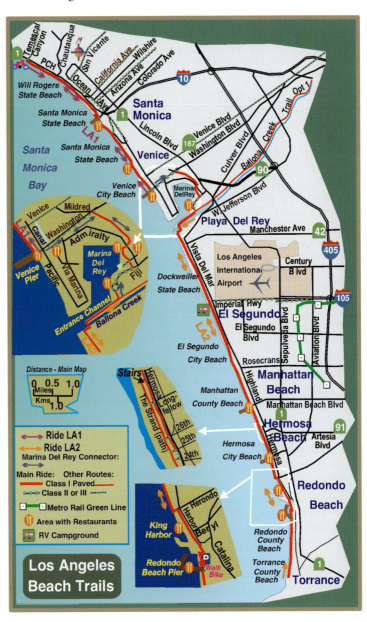

Los Angeles Beach Trails

Knocks & Hazards: Depending on when you ride, the number of people on the trail can be daunting; it's best where bike/peds are separated. It's generally a safe ride, but it can't hurt to ride with a friend, especially from LAX to the north. The coast can be foggy and overcast, such as on summer mornings or during May Gray and June Gloom periods. Wind can make riding difficult at times. Marina Del Rey Connector has Class II bike lanes next to parked cars on busy Washington Blvd; consider sidewalk or alt route shown on map thru MDR. Beware of strict rule enforcement to avoid fines: Obey speed limits and notices to walk bikes at Redondo Beach Pier, and during peak times at Manhattan and Hermosa Beach Piers.

Rent 'n Ride: Santa Monica: Perry's along beach. SM Beach Bike Rentals, 1428 4th, 310.428.5337; Sea Mist, 1619 OceanFront, 395.7076; Venice Beach Rentals, 3100 OceanFront, 823.6730; Venice Bike & Skates, 21 Washington, 301.4011; Spokes 'n Stuff, 327 Wash, 439.7276; Boardwalk Skate & Surf, 401 Ocean Front, 450.6634. MDR: Daniel's Rentals, 13737 Fiji, 980.4045; LA E-bike, 108 Catamaran, 424.272.1153. Manh'nBeach E-bike, 3616 Highland, 213.986.7635. Hermosa Cyclery, 20 13th, 374.7816; Jeffers, 39 14th, 372.9492. Redondo: Marina Bike, 505 N Harbor, 318.2453; Pedego E-bikes, 701 S PCH, 316.6309.

Camp 'n Ride: Dockweiler RV Park in Playa Del Rey is on the bike trail! The front row of this big RV parking lot with hookups has awesome ocean views, except when a berm is up in winter. Planes taking off from adjacent LAX are noisy. Operated by LA County. Reserve at reservations.lacounty.gov. Closed January.

Bike 'n Brunch: Find food along the trail in Santa Monica, Venice Beach, Marina del Rey, and the beach cities starting at Manhattan Beach. See the ride description.

Further Info: lacity.org; smgov.net (Santa Monica); elsegundo.org; citymb.info; (Manhattan Beach); hermosabch.org; redondo.org; ci.torrance.ca.us; californiabeaches.com; visitmarinadelrey.com

Access: Although you can start anywhere along the route, we begin our fabulous riding adventure at the north end of ride LA1. Will Rogers State Beach is located at the end of Temescal Canyon Road across Pacific Coast Highway in Pacific Palisades. Someday the trail may extend another 3 miles northwest toward Malibu ending near the Getty Villa Museum, but not in the near future. Take I-10 west until it ends on Pacific Coast Highway (PCH). Follow PCH north until the Temescal Canyon Road signal and either turn left into the pay parking lot, or right for free on-street parking, which may be hard to come by during busy beach days. The bike trail begins on the bluff across from the entrance to the park, and heads south (to the left). To start at other parts of LA1 or LA2, just stay near the coast and look for parking, since the trail will always be nearby.

Santa Monica Trail (North segment)   LA1

Details: 6.1 miles each way. Easy to moderate due to distance and wind.

The bike trail heads southward along a small bluff between the beach parking lot and this beautiful Pacific Ocean beach along Santa Monica Bay. The view on your return heading north is more dramatic with the Santa Monica Mountains behind Malibu forming the backdrop to Santa Monica Bay as the coast curves westward. Looking south, the view is of the buildings of Santa Monica, the Santa Monica Pier and its amusement park, a power plant in the far distance, and the South Bay coastline curv-

LOS ANGELES COUNTY

Trail heads north near Santa Monica Pier

ing around to the tip of the Palos Verdes Peninsula.

On clear days Catalina Island will look especially large from this angle, to the west of Palos Verdes. After a delightful stretch on the bluff with seasonal wildflowers on an iceplant greenbelt between you and the crashing waves, the trail drops down to the wide Santa Monica State Beach (mile 1.1). On weekends expect the volleyball nets to be full and plenty of surfers out catching the waves. The tall cliffs of Santa Monica come into view on your left. Fabulous Palisades Park runs the entire length of these bluffs, worth checking out at another time, better suited for a walk. Signs direct peds onto a separate adjoining path from here to Venice.

The trail curves closer to the beach to go around a row of private homes and a resort that line the west side of PCH. Back on the Beach Café here is a popular spot for lunch (2.1). The Santa Monica Municipal Pier is a bustling attraction with restaurants including Bubba Gumps and more casual eateries, an amusement park complete with roller coaster, and a small aquarium (3.1). Pedestrians who disobey the "bikes only" trail rule can make riding through this area a challenge on peak days. The trail runs through a tunnel beneath the pier, then emerges onto another beach and runs past the Ocean Park section of Santa Monica. If you want to learn how to surf, the beach off of Crescent Bay Park at the end of Bay Street (3.5) frequently offers good novice-level breaks and instruction is available at popular gosurfla.com. Cha Cha Chicken on Ocean a block up on Pico or Bay is a fun spot.

The excitement builds as you reach Venice Municipal Beach and the bustling bohemian beach scene of Venice. The bike trail veers toward the ocean around a parking lot as Ocean Front Walk (no cycling) leads straight ahead (4.4). The bike trail winds sinuously through this area, and even though it remains bikes-only, it can be crowded.

Venice is a noteworthy place for a detour, and you can walk your bike down Ocean Front Walk and get a bite to eat in one of the many cafés, shop for crafts, or even get pierced or tattooed here while taking in the urban street scene. We like the Fig Tree Café halfway up the Walk for an al fresco lunch. Or, from the bike trail, turn inland across the parking lot (4.6) and cycle up Rose Avenue to brunch fave Rose Café and Market at #220.

Trail winds through bustling Venice area

The trail veers away from the street scene (5.2) and passes the Venice Recreation Center, skateboard park, and the famous Muscle Beach. Next, ride along some very interesting modern beachfront homes as the Venice Pier comes into view (5.6). When you reach a "Bikes Dismount" sign at the pier, this signals the end of the Santa Monica Trail portion (6.1). You can turn around here for a 12.2-mile round trip, continue along the beach for another mile if a planned trail extension has been completed, or continue on to LA2 via the connector route described below.

There are lots of restaurants here and up Washington Blvd. You can also lock your bike and walk up Washington one block to the entrance to the Venice Canals Walkway (no bikes). The canals were the result of a 1905 planned community, and have an interesting history, including annexation by Los Angeles in 1925, neglect and deterioration, a 1950s Beat Poet hangout, an oil boom, and revitalization. Presently, a few of the canals remain, and are lined with homes.

Marina Del Rey (MDR) Connector

Details: 2.8 miles, 25 minutes each way. Easy.

From Venice Pier (mile 0), head northeast along Washington Blvd in Class II bike lanes. Anticipate car doors opening that can be a hazard to cyclists, buses pulling over and busy intersections. You may want to opt for the south sidewalk. At Pacific Ave consider taking an alternate scenic route to the right as shown on the map to see more of MDR, LA's main private yacht harbor and district. Otherwise, cross the bridge over the Grand Canal. Across the street (0.15) are the entrance to the Venice Canal walking paths, and al fresco Baja Cantina and Siamese Garden. Cross busy Via Marina and pass more restaurants. At the signal for Mildred Avenue our bike trail is on the right (0.8). It passes a wetland and greenbelt area, then crosses Admiralty Way at a signal (1. 6). It cuts through a marina parking lot and crosses Bali Way to begin a new delightful waterfront promenade with restaurants. At Mindanau Way consider checking out Burton Chase Park to the right beyond a new Trader Joe's for harbor views and concerts. Find restaurants and a Ralph's market on adjacent Admiralty Way. At trail's end turn right into the bike lane of Fiji Way after checking for typically light traffic (2.2). The nautical-themed Fisherman's Village appears as you pedal around the bend. This is another great place for your Bike 'n Brunch on patios overlooking the marina, including an El Torito, Sapori (Italian), and several casual choices (2.6). The road ends in a loop, which completes our connector route (2.8).

South Bay Trail   LA2

Details: 12.5 miles, 1.5 hours, each way. Easy to moderate due to distance and wind.

At the end of Fiji Way, find the bike trail that begins from the loop and continues to the southeast (mile 0). When it reaches the intersection with the Ballona Creek Trail (that continues to Culver City, see Option 1), turn right (toward the ocean) onto the South Bay Bike Trail. Ride along an interesting narrow strip of land with the tidal portion of Ballona Creek on the left, and the Entrance Channel to Marina Del Rey on the right. Note the faded remains of murals once painted by various rowing crew teams along the concrete-lined Ballona Creek.

The trail crosses a wide bike/ped bridge over Ballona Creek, a great place to stop and take in the views (0.8). On clear winter days the snow-covered San Gabriel Mountains may be visible to the northeast beyond the creek. Watch for seals, pelicans, and the other usual nautical suspects in the Entrance Channel. This bridge makes another nice turnaround point for a 19.4-mile round trip ride if you started from the LA1 trailhead.

The trail bends toward the ocean as you reach a scenic stretch along Dockweiller State Beach in Playa Del Rey. Cruise along the beach past volleyball nets in front of beachfront homes. Look for a path that leads to Culver and cyclists' favorite Tanner's Coffee for food and drink. When the homes end (1.8), that signals the beginning of the Los Angeles International Airport (LAX) property above on the bluff. If you enjoy watching planes take off over you at various heights, you are in luck, as they take off on parallel runways virtually non-stop, day and night. After a rise in the trail to a lifeguard headquarters, you will see RV's on the left. This is the RV Park at Dockweiller State Beach, one of the best RV Camp 'n Ride locations anywhere (3.6).

The trail rises gently to a small bluff that contains a food concession and affords nice views out along the coast, the Palos Verdes Peninsula to the south, and the Santa Monica Mountains to the north. The landward side of the trail becomes industrial for a stretch starting around mile 5 as you pass Hyperion Sewage Treatment Plant, the main plant for the LA area, and the Scattergood steam power plant. The City of El Segundo's beach appears on the sea side, with a sign indicating that it is a non-smoking zone. A hang glider concession provides an interesting stop if you care to watch them in action.

The appearance of waterfront homes landward from the trail (5.5) signifies that you have reached the city of Manhattan Beach. The beach and trail begin to get busier here. Manhattan Beach is very bike friendly, with the bike trail designated as bike-only and signs banning pedestrians from the trail, except as the bike trail crosses in front of the municipal pier, with a walk-bike signal (7.0). The circa 1920s pier, the oldest concrete pier on the West Coast, has the Roundhouse Marine Studies Lab and Aquarium at its tip. Choose from restaurants near the pier, perhaps brunch at viewy Strand House, fish lunch at Rock 'n Fish, Tacolicious on Manhattan Ave, or Uncle Bill's Pancake House up the hill at 13th & Highland. A nice greenbelt separates the trail from the homes, and the view of the ocean is excellent here. It is also interesting to look at the multi-million dollar homes of all different architectural styles that line the trail. The beach is volleyball-central, with nets everywhere.

Trail approaching RV campground at Dockweiler State Beach, showing winter sand berm in place.

In Hermosa Beach (8.0) the bikes-only path continues next to Hermosa Ave behind beachfront homes until 24th Street. However, you can walk your bike down stairs at 35th St, or ride at Longfellow, near 28th, 26th, 25th or 24th Streets to the beachfront multi-use Millennium Walkway. Bikes are allowed here but not favored, and peds have the right-of-way. On crowded days you will face a virtual obstacle course of cyclists, skateboarders, skaters, and peds. The speed limit on both paths is 8 mph.

As you near the Hermosa Beach Pier (8.7), red lights will flash during peak use times, signifying that you must walk your bike. Even though we did not see a single person walking their bikes here, we have read horror stories on blogs about the police giving out expensive tickets, so you may not want to risk it. Or, you can dart into an adjacent alley and ride until you emerge onto the bustling Pier Avenue, which is "The" place to be on weekends as the street is crowded with beachgoers and is lined with eateries with outdoor patios, such as the popular Silvio's Brazilian BBQ. Or, try the rooftop ocean-view deck at Hennessey's Tavern. Pier Avenue is also the entrance to the Hermosa Beach Pier. Either return to the beach trail here, or pedal a couple more blocks in the alley to avoid this crowded area.

The trail bends away from the beach at Herondo St, and becomes a Class IV cycle track next to Harbor Drive in Redondo Beach (9.4). Make sure to obey traffic rules and signs in Redondo Beach where police are known to ticket cyclists. Nifty bike signals were installed at several parking lot entrance crossings to restaurants in the Port Royal Marina area, which include Bluewater Grill, Joe's Crab Shack, Cheesecake Factory, and Ruby's diner. After Captain Kidd's restaurant, the bike trail takes you on an interesting sojourn through the Kings Harbor waterfront development at the Redondo Beach pier, another magnificent Bike 'n Brunch opportunity with Kincaids, Pier Seafood, Redondo Beach Crab House, Shrimp Lover, and Tony's seafood restaurants, an El Torito, and Samba for Brazilian champagne brunch.

Don't fret as the trail takes you through the parking garage, since you will get a great birdseye view of the waterfront from inside. Watch for crossing pedestrians and vehicles in this segment. Then, STOP! at the "Walk Bikes" sign and make sure to dismount. If you look up to the left, you will see a glass window and a "Police" sign with officers on radios looking down at you. Here we did not see a single bicyclist riding, and have heard stories of people getting tickets even when the place was completely deserted.

Bear slightly to the left after the sign to continue on the bike route, and after a short distance past the pier area is a "Resume Bike Riding" sign. Not only can you get back on your bike, you will also enjoy perhaps the best part of the South Bay Trail from here (around mile 10.5) to its end at mile 12.5. On the landward side the landscaped bank in front of the homes along Redondo Beach's Esplanade gets progressively steeper so that you do not even see them after a while, and the ocean inches closer to the trail. Meanwhile, pedestrians are segregated onto a separate trail through Redondo Beach, although many do wander onto the bike trail. The coastline of the Palos Verdes Peninsula nears as the trail comes to an abrupt end at Torrance County Beach.

Those wishing further exploration can walk their bikes up one of the steep ramps and continue riding on the hilly roads around the Palos Verdes Peninsula, a popular route for road cyclists. Otherwise turn around here. The view and lighting on the return will be different. The Malibu coastline curves to the west, offering a dramatic backdrop. Also in your northward view will be the power plant and tall buildings of West Los Angeles in the distance.

Option 1: Ballona Creek Trail

A 7-mile paved Class I trail follows the channelized Ballona Creek from the point described in the Santa Monica Beach/South Bay Beach trail at Playa del Rey to Syd Kronenthal Park at National Boulevard in east Culver City. It is a way to get to the beach for those living or working in the Culver City area, or a commuting trail in reverse, and offers some wildlife viewing along the way at Ballona Wetlands. Unfortunately, like many inner city bike trails, you may have to pass a gauntlet of thugs along the way. In recent years daytime assaults have occurred west of Sawtelle Boulevard, especially under the I-405 and SR 90 overpasses. Because of the potential danger, we do not recommend this path unless you ride with a large group and during daylight only. The community is attempting to improve the trail and make it safer. For detailed information on the trail and its access points see ballonacreek.org/bike-path/. Another path from Culver City to Santa Monica follows the Exposition rail line, mainly of interest to commuters.

San Pedro

A narrow finger of the city of Los Angeles dips down to San Pedro Bay and is the home of the Port of Los Angeles in the San Pedro district, located at the south end of I-110, the Harbor Freeway.

San Pedro and LA Harbor Tour LA3

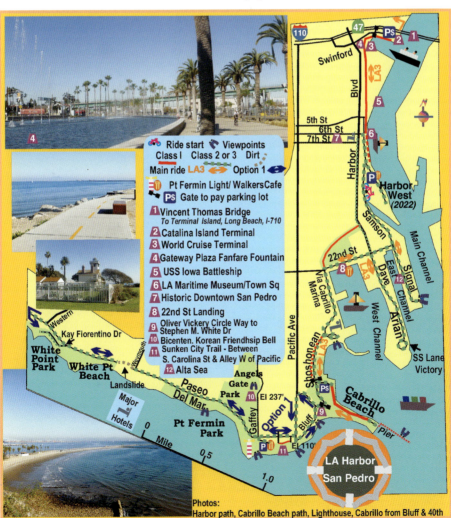

Photos:
Harbor path, Cabrillo Beach path, Lighthouse, Cabrillo from Bluff & 40th

The Port of Los Angeles, busiest in the Western Hemisphere, is a sight to behold with cranes and cargo as far as the eye can see. The western end of the port in the San Pedro district is open to the public, with new harborfront promenades, plenty of dining options and connecting trails to scenic ocean beaches, making it a cyclist's delight.

Since the 1960s the centerpiece of this district was Ports O' Call Village, a 15-acre New England style fishing village with a wide variety of restaurants. It is now being redeveloped into Harbor West with an ETA of 2022, expected to contain restaurants, an amphitheater, a brewery, parks and waterfront promenades for peds and bikes. Construction may alter our biking routes in the meantime. Between this property and the Cruise Ship Terminal to the north, a beautiful promenade enables a delightful pedal next to the harbor facilities, and upgraded Class II lanes provide a nice connection through fingers of the port and to the beaches of San Pedro.

Replicas of the Red Cars of the Pacific Electric Railroad, as described in the PET-Route 66 ride, ran weekends along Harbor Blvd next to the port, but redevelopment shut it down in 2015 and its future is uncertain. The exciting new AltaSea facility, a state of the art oceanographic research facility fostering sustainability of the world's oceans, is being built at time of writing. The 400,000 sf campus, situated along the East Channel, has an auditorium and exhibits for the public to visit. See altasea.org.

Other attractions along the route are the battleship USS *Iowa*, the Merchant Marine vessel SS *Lane Victory*, the LA Maritime Museum depicting LA's history in relation to ocean activities, the dancing musical Gateway Plaza Fanfare Fountain, Cabrillo Beach and Aquarium, and Point Fermin Lighthouse. Our route takes you on a wide promenade, a beachfront Class I trail, and Class II and III bike routes with some sidewalk options. The main ride is mostly flat, while Option 1 leads up to the bluffs above the scenic San Pedro coast (e-bike edge). On clear days views include the huge port facilities backed by the San Gabriel and Santa Ana Mountains, the rocky San Pedro coast, and the open Pacific out to Catalina Island that looks especially close from here.

Tunes: If I Had a Boat by Lyle Lovett; Under the Bridge by Red Hot Chili Peppers
Eats: Fish Lunch at San Pedro Fish Market (Slated to move to Catalina terminal).

Distance: 11 miles + option. Time: 1.5 hours
Route & Bike: Easy. Paved Class I, II, and III routes for any bike. Mostly flat with an option for hilly add-on. E-bike edge: Ride up the hills in Option 1 for fabulous ocean vistas, steep grades up to Angels Gate Park or down to White Point Beach.
Seasons: All. Best on mild sunny day.
Facilities: Restrooms and water at Harbor West (2022); beach parks along the route.
Knocks & Hazards: Riding on Class II lanes with traffic, and some Class III roads with no bike lanes. Street crossings. Cross any railroad tracks as close to a right angle as possible, or walk bike. Possible lurkers at San Pedro parks and beaches. Redevelopment of Ports O' Call to Harbor West and elsewhere creates construction detours.
Camp 'n Ride: Closest: Long Beach. **Rent 'n Ride:** bikeshare.metro.net.
Bike Shop: The Bike Palace, 1600 S Pacific Ave, 310.832.1966.
Bike 'n Brunch: Main Ride: Harbor West (2022); 22nd St Landing seafood, outdoor patio and weekend brunch. Option 1: Walkers Café near Point Fermin Lighthouse is a popular greasy spoon and motorcyclists' hangout.
City code, bike riding on sidewalks (City of LA/San Pedro) Allowed per state rules.
Further Info: portoflosangeles.org; LA City Parks (Cabrillo Beach): laparks.org; County Parks (White Point and Royal Palm Beaches): beaches.lacounty.gov.
Other: sanpedro.com; lanevictory.org; lamaritimemuseum.org; altasea.org.

Access: From I-405 take the Harbor (110) Freeway south until it ends at Gaffey St. Turn left on Gaffey and then left on 6th Street. Follow 6th across Harbor to Samson Way, turn right and follow signs to lot for Harbor West or restaurants until then.

The Ride: Head north from the lot (Harbor West by 2022) on a path if available, or else the Harbor Blvd bike lane. Pass San Pedro Marina. In about 0.25 mile is 6th St, gateway to historic downtown San Pedro to the left, and to the right the LA Maritime Museum, new Town Square (0.4), and a paved pathway. It continues past 5th Street and becomes a wide, delightful harborfront promenade parallel to the former Red Car tracks, with only one additional street crossing at 1st Street (0.7). As the towering Vincent Thomas Bridge nears, reach the Gateway Plaza Fanfare Fountain, featuring synchronized musical water shows (1.0).

The promenade curves to the right, parallel to Swinford Street, that leads to the parking lot for Catalina Cruises, crossing the entrance to the USS *Iowa* and cruise ship parking area. The path ends next to a heliport (1.4), so turn around and make your way back on the path to Samson at 6th (2.4). Follow Samson past Harbor West (2.6–2.8). Cross 22nd Street (3.3) and continue down Signal along this finger of the harbor, past the AltaSea facility. Turn left before the end of the pier to a great viewpoint across to the Coast Guard base and Outer Harbor (3.7).

Cyclists on promenade near cruise ship terminal

Return to 22nd, turn left, then left on Class II Dave Arian Way (4.3). Cycle down this finger of the harbor past the expansive Cabrillo Marina, enjoying vistas out to sea, and visit the SS *Lane Victory* if you wish (fee). Return to 22nd (5.8). If you are near the end of your endurance level or are starving for a fish lunch, turn right on 22nd and left on Samson to return to restaurants (for a total 6.6-mile ride). Otherwise, turn left on 22nd to continue, riding between 22nd Street Park and Cabrillo Marina. The 22nd Street Landing has a popular restaurant for your fish lunch. Ascend a small hill on the Class II road or sidewalk. At your option explore 22nd Street Park to the right. Otherwise, turn left on Via Cabrillo Marina (6.2), and cruise to road's end past the Double Tree Hilton, another al fresco dining option (6.8).

Head back through the parking lot along the west side of Via Cabrillo Marina so that you can access a left (west) turn onto Shoshonean Road (6.9). This Class III sharrow route with sidewalk promenade leads past a salt marsh into Cabrillo Beach Park (7.3). Cycle past the gate, through the parking lot to the left, and just south of the boat launch area you'll find the beginning of a bike/ped path along the beach (7.4). When this scenic path turns to the east along a narrow spit (7.6), the protected harbor is to the northeast, and the open ocean surf is to the south. Before swimming here, check publichealth.lacounty.gov/beach/ for water quality, which can be an issue. The path ends in a parking lot for the pier (7.8). Ride through the lot and to the end of the pier (8.2). Our route turns around from here and returns to Harbor West (11.0).

Option 1: Point Fermin/Sunken City ⭐ *5–7 miles extra round trip, moderate, e-bike edge*
Explore farther along the beautiful San Pedro coastline via this hilly ride. From Cabrillo Beach, exit south via Oliver Vickery Circle Way, then turn right on Stephen M. White Dr, up a hefty hill to Class II Pacific Ave. Turn left on Pacific to its end at a scenic Catalina Isle ocean viewpoint (0.6). On the return ride you can take one-way Bluff Place to the left from the end of Pacific to return to Cabrillo Beach, but beware of the 15% downhill grade. Go back up Pacific and make the first left on Class II residential Shephard St. Turn left in the first alley to access the gravel Sunken City Trail, with great views of the ruins of a cliffside neighborhood that fell into the sea from landslides starting in 1929 (No public access). Go right up South Carolina St and left on Shephard, which curves right and becomes beautiful Paseo Del Mar along ocean bluffs at Pt. Fermin Park.

At Gaffey St is a landmark lighthouse and blufftop promenade (0.9) and Walker's Cafe across the street. Angels Gate Park is to the right here. The Bicentennial Korean Friendship Bell is up the hill on Gaffey, with pano ocean views. Continue on blufftop Paseo Del Mar past Wilders Addition Park (1.5), until the road ends at Weymouth Ave (2.1). Beyond is the site of a 2011 landslide. You can skirt the fenced-off area on a decomposed granite path (2.4). Reach Royal Beach Park (2.6). Descend to the beach at White Point Park and explore tide pools, then return up a steep 135 foot climb (3.6). Scenic Paseo Del Mar ends at Western Ave. The upscale neighborhood ahead (no ocean views) isn't gated for a while, so you can ride up and back (5.0). Return via Paseo Del Mar the same way, with the option of taking Bluff Place down the steep hill as discussed (~7.0 miles total).

Long Beach

Long Beach has come a long way since the 1980s with a remarkable downtown revitalization and installation of a plethora of bike infrastructure. Awarded Silver status as a bike-friendly community by the League of American Cyclists, Long Beach has set its sights on becoming the most bike-friendly city in the US.

Shoreline Marine Village attracts gobs of tourists, April's Long Beach Grand Prix is an institution, and the *Queen Mary* and the Aquarium of the Pacific have become staples of the LA-area tourism industry. The Long Beach Arena—painted with huge whale murals by Wyland—and adjacent Long Beach Convention Center is one of the main commercial draws in the region.

The THUMS oil rig islands in San Pedro Bay, disguised as tropical resorts with landscaping and waterfalls, were built in the 1960s by a consortium of oil companies, each named for a fallen NASA astronaut. If you see these in a TV show that's supposed to take place in Miami, like *Dexter,* you'll know better.

The massive New Gerald Desmond Bridge connecting Ocean Blvd downtown to Terminal Island contains the Mark Bixby Bicycle Path, for some hi-flying cycle fun.

Just southwest of downtown is the Port of Long Beach, the nation's second busiest container port next to its twin, the larger Port of Los Angeles. You can take a whale-watching tour during the winter grey whale migration season from downtown's Rainbow Harbor, or jump on a Catalina Express boat for a full day or weekend's journey back and forth to Catalina Island (free on your birthday, plus island freebies).

Our favorite part of Long Beach is at its southeast corner where the Belmont Shore neighborhood is located, featuring a mile-long strip of restaurants, shops, and galleries along 2nd Street, and the adjacent Italian-themed Naples Island, home of a wonderful holiday festival set up along its canals. See ride LO2 for a tour of that sector. To the south is the laid back beach city of Seal Beach and the start of the epic 38-mile San Gabriel River Trail. See the Orange County chapter for rides farther south in Huntington Beach, accessible via a short ride on high-speed PCH from Seal Beach.

LOS ANGELES COUNTY 93

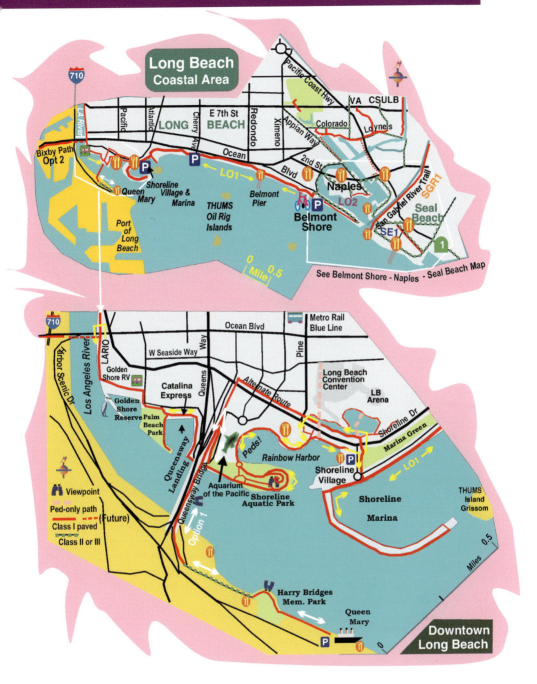

The Long Beach World Class Waterfront LO1

A top notch 3.2-mile Class I scenic bike trail runs along the beach from Belmont Shore to downtown Long Beach, and continues on to the Los Angeles River/Rio Hondo bike trail (LARIO). Ancillary paths explore most of the fascinating revitalized Long Beach waterfront. Your tour includes miles of beach, views of bobbing boats, the THUMS oil islands, developed waterfront facilities with tempting restaurants, the Aquarium of the Pacific, and the *Queen Mary*. Options connect you to interesting points to the southeast.

Tunes: Sea Cruise by John Fogerty; Shipbuilding by Elvis Costello; Jump by Van Halen
Eats: Seared Ahi at Tokyo Wako's Teppanyaki

Distance: 14 miles + options. Time: 1.5–2 hours.
Route & Bike: Easy. Paved Class I for any bike. Up and back route, enables shortening of ride distance. Options for some easy Class II and III. Flat except for optional bridge. Separate ped path along entire 3.2 mile beach segment from ride start.
Seasons: All. Best on sunny uncrowded off-season weekday with little fog or wind.
Facilities: Restrooms and water in parks and commercial establishments along route.
Knocks & Hazards: Clueless peds downtown, surrey bikes, crowded near Aquarium, Long Beach industrial aroma. Urban ride: Possible lurkers, especially near Cherry Ave parking lot. Speed limit 15 mph on some trails; 5 mph around pedestrians.
Rent 'n Ride: Wheel Fun Rentals at Shoreline Village, 562.951.3857, or near *Queen Mary*, 562.435.7676; Alfredo's Beach Club at Belmont Pier, 562.314.8778; Pedal Movement offers to the public bike rentals, bike parking, air, and a bike repair shop, 1st St Transit Mall, 223 East 1st St, 562.436.2453. For LB Bike Share stations see longbeachbikeshare.com.
Camp 'n Ride: Golden Shore RV Park (west end of trail), 101 Golden Shore, 562.435.4646. Nice RV park but usually full.
Bike 'n Brunch: This trail has beaucoup restaurants to offer, mostly in the area of Shoreline Village and west, right along the trail. On the Belmont Shore (east) end the popular trailside Belmont Brewing Company patio is next to the Belmont Pier. Otherwise make your way north a few blocks to busy but sharrowed 2nd Street for great neighborhood restaurant selections. For a boaty splurge, try brunch on the *Queen Mary* or on a Naples gondola.
City code, bike riding on sidewalks: Not allowed in business districts, over bridges, ped underpasses, and next to various institutions like schools, churches, senior housing, and other specific areas as signed. Speed limit on allowed sidewalks is 15 mph; 5 mph when peds present.
Further Info: Bike Advocacy: longbeach.gov/goactivelb/. City site: longbeach.gov. Other: queenmary.com; shorelinevillage.com; aquariumofpacific.org; Grand Prix (April): gplb.com; Gay Pride (May): longbeachpride.com; newgdbridge.com; Charity ride and bike festival in May: touroflongbeach.com (the site of enCYCLEpedia's 1st Edition launch in 2014).

Access: Stage from anywhere along the route. We like to start in the Belmont Shore area. From Orange County, take I-405 north to Westminster Blvd west about 6.3 miles (it becomes 2nd St). Turn left after the 2nd bridge on Bayshore, then bear left on 54th Pl. The Class I Trailhead is across Ocean Ave. Park for free on street or in pay beach lots. From I-405 southbound exit Lakeview south, take PCH (Hwy 1) southwest from the traffic circle, then right on 2nd St, and continue as above.

To start at Shoreline Village follow Ocean Ave west to Shoreline Drive downtown and turn left. LA Metro Rail's Blue Line train ends at 1st St in downtown Long Beach, just a few blocks from the trail. It carries bikes, except when overly crowded. Boaters can hop right on to LO1 from the Shoreline or Rainbow Harbor marinas. See www.longbeach.gov/park/marine/.

The Ride: Begin cycling on a 17-foot wide concrete bike path along the wide beach, while a parallel pedestrian path greatly reduces bike/ped interactions. The path runs 3.1 miles from 54th Place to downtown Long Beach. At mile 1, pass by the public Belmont Plaza Pool. The Belmont Pier in front of you has restrooms, Buoy's restaurant at its end, and Belmont Brewing Co. with its popular patio at its base. The path continues along the beach past downtown waterfront homes and hotels. It traverses the Cherry Avenue parking area (2.0), and emerges next to the large Long Beach Marina (3.2).

Across from Carnival and Spruce Goose Dome, Queen Mary

The expansive Long Beach Convention Center and Arena with its Wyland whale murals comes into view on the right. Continue pedaling through Marina Green Park next to the bobbing boats and reach Shoreline Village (3.6), a popular destination with lots of waterfront

Shoreline Trail's parallel ped path keeps clueless ped factor to minimum. Electronic sign shows use stats. Cruise ship and Queen Mary in background.

restaurants for your Bike 'n Brunch, including the landmark Parker's Lighthouse, The Yard House, and Tequila Jack's. Pedal onward to the peninsula breakwater, and turn left onto the outer path, reaching the tip of it (4.3) that overlooks the entrance to the marina and Island Grissom, a close-in oil island. Take in great views of the yachts in the harbor and of the *Queen Mary* across the channel as well.

Return to Shoreline Village, but turn left at a roundabout onto a bike path that crosses Shoreline Dr at a light (5.0). Ride either way to explore the pretty Rainbow Lagoons next to the Hyatt Regency and Long Beach Convention Center (~5.8), then cross Shoreline again at the same spot. To shorten the ride return the way you came for a trip of about 10 miles. Our tour continues to the Golden Shores area, adding another 4 miles, plus another 2 miles to visit the *Queen Mary*.

Find a path on the south side of Shoreline Dr that leads west, under the elevated walkway to the Convention Center, and past a tempting row of restaurants, many with patios (Q Smokehouse BBQ, Tokyo Waco, Gladstones seafood, PF Chang's, Outback, Chili's, and Hooters). Next, pedal slowly along Rainbow Harbor with its docked tour boats. Stay near the waterfront as you come to the fabulous Aquarium of the Pacific. This area may be so crowded with peds you may want to walk your bike for a short distance. Just beyond at mile 6.4 is Shoreline Park, where a path loops around the small peninsula between the river channel and harbor, around a lighthouse that can be ridden to via a gradual hill. City and harbor views from the knoll where the lighthouse sits are awesome, from downtown to Shoreline Village, the *Queen Mary*, and the Port of Long Beach. Note: Check the map for an alternate return path along the north side of Shoreline Dr past the outlet mall that avoids this busy area.

The trail next crosses under the Queensway Bridge (6.9). Option 1 takes you over the bridge to the *Queen Mary* and back from this point. Our main route winds along the developed waterfront, past Queensway Landing where the Catalina Express boats leave for Catalina Island (7.1). Pedal north, around Golden Shores Preserve, a restored marshland with eel grass, mudflats, and open water areas—a small mitigation effort to help compensate for all of the wetlands that were destroyed at the mouth of the Los Angeles River during the construction of the port facilities.

The trail runs next to Golden Shore RV Resort on the right (7.5), your Camp 'n Ride option. At mile 7.7 reach the Los Angeles River bike trail (LARIO) that runs north 29 miles along this river channel and the Rio Hondo all the way to the Whittier Narrows area (see SGR2). You can explore it a bit, perhaps riding under Ocean Boulevard and past Golden Park (8.2), but we don't recommend venturing too far north on this non-scenic path that goes past some of the worst Long Beach neighborhoods farther up. Instead, turn around and return the same way. If you retrace your route to the Belmont Shore trailhead but stay on the most direct route, you will have ridden about 14 miles. From there consider doing ride LO2.

Option 1: Queensway Bridge and the *Queen Mary* *2.5 miles round trip, easy.*
A wide, separated bike path crosses the east side of the Queensway Bridge allowing access to the *Queen Mary* and great vistas en route. From the waterfront trail at the east side of the bridge, cross Golden Shore and find a bike path that parallels the bridge structure, heading north. This path loops around and becomes a wide separated path next to the bridge roadway. Although you'll need to cycle up an incline to get to the apex of the bridge, it is well worth the effort for the fabulous vistas back toward the city, *Queen Mary,* and out to the ocean. The path descends to a stop sign across from the Maya resort hotel. Continue straight ahead on Queensway Drive, following the bike route sign to get you past the Maya resort and The Reef restaurant (brunch splurge).

Just beyond is Harry Bridges Memorial Park with waterfront paths that you can pedal along and take in the amazing views across the water toward Long Beach with mountains beyond on clear days. The path empties into the large parking lots for the *Queen Mary.* Brunch anyone? The Spruce Goose geodesic dome, once the home of Howard Hughes' iconic airplane, is now the terminal for Carnival cruise passengers. Watch for a new Class I path from near the *Queen Mary* heading south along South Harbor Scenic Dr.

Option 2: Mark Bixby Mem. Bike Path on south side of New GD Bridge to Terminal Isle has overlooks to take in the amazing vistas. Access is pending construction of a new LA River bike/pd bridge parallel to Ocean Blvd connecting to downtown bike paths.

Belmont Shore and Naples Island LO2

Tunes: O Solo Mio by Mario Lanza; Felicita by Al Bano & Romina Power
Eats: BBQ at Naples Rib Company (or brunch on that gondola!)

Distance: 5.4 miles total
Route & bike: Easy, flat. Class II and III plus optional narrow sidewalk paths (speed limit 15; 5 if peds present). Any bike.
Knocks & Hazards: On-road riding. Naples sidewalk paths are narrow and can be unrideable when crowded with peds.
Bike 'n Brunch: Several restaurants are along 2nd St in Naples, although the Italian restaurants are more upscale and open for dinner only. Also Irish pubs, sushi, and The Small Café popular for breakfast/lunch. Naples Rib Co. has great ribs, open weekends for lunch. Belmont Shore to the west on 2nd St offers many more options.

LOS ANGELES COUNTY

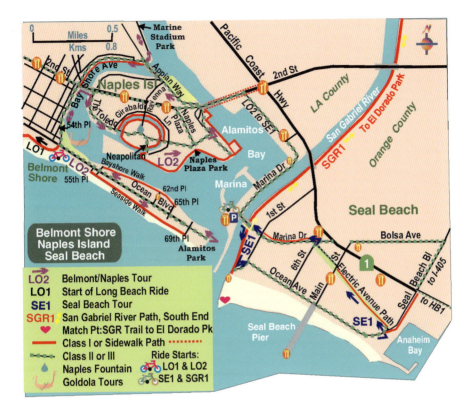

Access: Same ride start as LO1.

The Ride: Although the off-road paths are narrow and better for walking, and some of the roadways are crowded with parked and moving vehicles, this is such a delightful sector of Long Beach to explore by bike that it makes it all worthwhile.

Ocean Boulevard continues to the east from the trailhead onto a peninsula. Ride along this narrow strip of land between Alamitos Bay and the open ocean. When the densely packed oceanfront style houses start, narrow paved trails run behind them, along both the beach and bay sides. Bikes are not banned from these (at time of writing), so you can ride to the right up the ocean side along East Seaside Walk to 69th Place, but they are considered to be "sidewalks."

When the path ends, get back onto Ocean Boulevard and turn right. Alamitos Park at the end of the road overlooks the entrance to Alamitos Bay, the parallel San Gabriel River outlet, and Seal Beach beyond (1.1). Turn around, and ride the road or find the very narrow East Bayshore Walk entrance at 65th Place on the right, which runs along Alamitos Bay across from Naples Island.

Upon your return to your starting point (2.2), there are several concessions along Alamitos Bay. Gondola Getaway offers romantic tours of the Naples Canals and can handle small or large groups. Reservations at 562.433.9595. You can also rent kayaks from Kayaks on the Water, 562.434.0999.

The remainder of LO2 entails mostly on-street, low-traffic riding. Turn right on 54th Place to follow the contour of Alamitos Bay, merging with Bay Shore Avenue. The beach along here is a popular hangout for locals. I learned to windsurf in this bay, which has good breezes and protected flat water. Bay Shore is a narrow Class III with sharrows road with parked cars and lots of slow-moving traffic along the several blocks involved. You can also just transport your bikes to Naples and skip this street altogether, or use the sidewalk.

Reach the light at 2nd Street, the main drag of Belmont Shore to the left, with multitudes of restaurants yours for the sampling and unique new green sharrow lanes on the roadway to get you there. Our ride continues by heading right in the bike lane across the level bridge to Naples Island, where, never fear, there are restaurants as well.

Naples' residential streets that wind through the island are fun for cycling, and there are also narrow waterside sidewalk paths where bikes are allowed, but are more suited for pedestrians. If you plan to cycle the paths, try to choose an off-peak time and ride slowly and courteously. Naples Island is fairly small, so you can cycle around it easily, exploring up and down the maze of streets. Getting lost is part of the fun, like in Venice. You can always make your way back to 2nd Street to get your bearings.

Make the first right onto The Toledo, the main street that traverses the entire island. The first bridge you come to (3.0) leads over Rio Alto Canal. This circular canal creates a smaller island within the main island. You can lock your bike somewhere along the canal if you wish, and stroll along the canal-side path, taking about 30 minutes to come full circle. Or, you can cycle it, very slowly, using ramps to cross three streets along the way. During the winter holidays most of the houses along the canal exhibit elaborate light displays, and a stroll along the canals during that time is one of the best holiday activities anywhere. The early December boat parade consisting of decorated gondolas and small boats on the canals is a crowded seasonal highlight.

Continue along The Toledo to the very Italian central square with the Naples Fountain. As The Toledo curves to the left, you can continue to its terminus at Appian Way (3.6). If you'd like a pleasant waterfront cruise to Appian Way instead, head straight onto Neapolitan Lane East, and cross another bridge over the canal to the narrow waterfront paved path on the right. Take it slowly, and give pedestrians, that may be abundant, the right of way. Enjoy the beautiful landscaping, boats in the bay, and interesting homes that line the path.

On Appian Way, head back to the northwest past the marina. You can use the road or try the waterside paths if still allowed. The tall 2nd Street highway bridge that you see ahead of you is your connection to cycling points south, including Seal Beach and Huntington Beach (Option 1). The entrance ramp that you share with vehicles comes up on your left before the bridge at mile 4. Otherwise, continue under the bridge along East Appian Way, past Marine Park, and across a low bridge, which takes you off of Naples Island (4.3).

Ride LO2 continues to the west down Bayshore Avenue on street or sidewalk. First, however, check out Marine Stadium and park, a State Historic Site. This extension of Alamitos

Narrow pathways line the canals of Naples Island

Bay was dredged in 1925 to create the Stadium and extended for the 1932 Olympics' rowing events. It is presently the site of speed boat races and is open for water skiing, and rowing in off hours. There are picnic tables, restrooms, and a Wednesday late-afternoon farmers' market at the north end. A fee is charged to park here, but bike-in is free. You can get into the park just across the bridge via the parking lot on the right. Then, ride along the access road for the length of the park. The official entrance is on the right just before Nieto Ave. See the map on page 93 for the bike path heading east from here to Loynes St and across PCH, eventually near Cal State Long Beach.

LO2 returns to Bay Shore Ave. Turn right on the road or sidewalk path that runs a a couple of blocks (6.0). Follow Bay Shore across 2nd St to your starting point (7.2).

Option 1: South to Seal Beach, San Gabriel River Trail, and Connection to Huntington Beach Trail ★ *Moderate, Class II and III*

To head south toward Seal Beach and the San Gabriel River Trail, cycle up the entrance ramp to the 2nd Street Bridge, heading east. Across the bridge are lots of interesting restaurants to choose from in all directions. Make the first right on Marina Dr, in a protected bike lane built in conjunction with the new commercial district. Extensive Alamitos Bay Marina is to the right. As you round the bend you are now between the entrance channel to Alamitos Bay and the channelized San Gabriel River. After crossing the bridge over the channel you are in Seal Beach and Orange County.

San Gabriel River Trail in Seal Beach

Seal Beach

This laid-back all-California beach town is a tight-knit community with a great beach for surfing or body boarding. Actually situated just over the border in Orange County, it is linked to LA County because of its interconnection with the Long Beach rides. Main Street extends from PCH to the classic wooden pier, and is lined with a wide variety of restaurants, including the long established Walt's Wharf and the original Charo Chicken, with its delectable lemon butter sauce. Many other choices line Pacific Coast Highway (PCH, or SR1). At time of writing there is no restaurant on the pier. Although the city limits extend inland past I-405, the portion of interest to visitors is that which lies between PCH and the ocean.

Seal Beach is a fun town to cycle around in, but it is not all that big. To get some real exercise and earn whatever meal you decide on, the San Gabriel River Trail (SGRT) is at your disposal. You can pedal up the channelized waterway to the foothills of the San Gabriel Mountains, 39 miles away. Our suggested route, however, drops you off at an expansive park where you can cool down and enjoy a huge selection of dining options in a modern adjacent complex (ride SGR1). Other sections of the SGRT are explored later on as well. Seal Beach is the link between the Long Beach rides (LO1 and LO2) and the Huntington Beach ride (HB1) to the south in Orange County.

Seal Beach Ramble SE1

Cycling around Seal Beach is flat and easy, although it is mostly on-road. Riding through the compact beach district can be done freeform, or follow this suggested route that encompasses the beach area and the pier, a short rail trail, and downtown.

Tunes: Summer Breeze by Seals & Crofts; La Playa by Linda Mirada
Eats: Mama or Papa Charo meal at the original Charo Chicken on Main near PCH.

Distance: 7 miles. Time: 45 minutes. Map: Page 97.
Route & Bike: Easy, flat. Paved, any bike. Class II and III through town plus short Class I. E-bike edge: Extend on San Gabriel River Trail or to adjacent cities.
Seasons: All. Best on sunny uncrowded off-season weekday.
Facilities: Restrooms and water at beach parks, pier area, and Mary Wilson Library along Electric Avenue path.
Knocks & Hazards: On-road cycling (speed limit 25 mph on city streets). Ride is a short distance.
Rent 'n Ride: Main Street Cyclery, 317 Main St, 562.430.3903. See also rides LO1 and HB1.
Camp 'n Ride: None in town. See LO1 and HB1.
Bike 'n Brunch: Restaurants along Main Street between the pier and PCH, on PCH, and along Alamitos Bay Marina in Long Beach.

Access: You can find plenty of free parking around the town. To link with other rides, the trailhead chosen is in the parking lot for Long Beach Alamitos Bay Marina. Follow the directions to LO1, however after crossing PCH and before ascending the 2nd Street bridge over Alamitos Bay, turn left onto Marina Drive and follow it all the way around the bend until just before it bends to cross the river. Turn right here and find free parking in the marina complex parking lot, where allowed. Another way to get to Seal Beach is to exit Seal Beach Blvd southbound from I-405 and take it until it ends in town, which is along the SE1 route. See the Belmont Shore/Naples/Seal Beach map.

The Ride: Cross the bridge over the river to the left to enter Seal Beach in Orange County. Notice the Class I San Gabriel River Trail on both sides of the road across the bridge. To the left is ride SGR1 to El Dorado Park. Turn right to begin ride SE1. Cruise down the Class I trail until it ends at a beach facility with River's End Café and restrooms (mile 0.4). You can gaze eastward across the wide beach to the Seal Beach Pier. Take the beach access road to Ocean Avenue and turn right.

After several residential blocks reach the Seal Beach Pier and Eisenhower Park at the foot of Main Street (1.0). The beautiful wooden pier is worth exploring (on foot), out to its tip. Main Street has a huge array of restaurants from taco shops to the venerable Walt's Wharf, an Irish pub, and more. Our route continues along Ocean Avenue. There are several opportunities to jog to the right and get to the beach walkway that is behind homes here.

When the road curves to the left it becomes Seal Beach Boulevard (1.5). The wetlands of Anaheim Bay beyond create a natural boundary to the southeast. Anaheim Bay forms the entrance to the upscale Huntington Harbor maritime community. It is also the home of Seal Beach Naval Weapons Station, and don't be surprised to see a rather large naval vessel docked here. To continue southeast across the bay to Huntington Beach (HB1), see Option 1. SE1 heads left on Electric Ave or the narrow trail on its greenbelt median. The pleasant 0.5-mile long rail trail crosses several streets, including Main St, which brings you to another selection of restaurants (2.0). To the right are a couple of coffee houses and Charo Chicken. To the left are the others mentioned previously. The path continues past the small Red Car (Pacific Electric Railway) museum and the Mary Wilson Library and ends at 6th St (2.2). Turn right, then make a quick left into the bike lane of Marina Dr.

Follow Marina Drive back to the intersection with the SGRT (2.6). Although Charo Chicken is delicious, the lemon butter sauce is probably not on your diet, so you'd better turn right up the SGRT and work some of it off. Try going up past the power plants, turning around before the 7th Street overcrossing, for a 7-mile total ride. Or, continue onward as described in ride SGR1.

Option 1: Route South to Huntington Beach ★ (See Orange County chapter) 3.6 miles. From the corner of Seal Beach Boulevard and Hwy 1, turn right and ride in the bike lane next to fast-moving traffic, over the long bridge that crosses Anaheim Bay and the entrance channel to Huntington Harbor. Across the bridge is the community of Sunset Beach. Coast Highway through Sunset Beach is lined with interesting restaurants, including established old-salt seafood places. Make a right in 1.6 miles onto Anderson (the Water Tower B&B is a landmark here) that takes you to Pacific Street. Turn left and pedal another 1.2 miles on the 15 mph street or greenbelt walkway to the trailhead for the fabulous Huntington Beach ride, HB1. To reach the restaurants detour down any of the side streets en route that connect to Hwy 1.

The San Gabriel River Trail (SGRT)

This 38-mile long paved trail starts from the base of the San Gabriel Mountains at Azusa in the San Gabriel Valley and follows the San Gabriel River all the way to the ocean between Long Beach and Seal Beach, dividing Los Angeles and Orange County at that point. It provides a wonderful opportunity for cyclists who want to do that epic ride without having to deal with automobile traffic. Along the way it passes a multitude of parks, some areas where the river bottom is natural and beautiful, and in the northerly directions, great mountain views on clear days. In a perfect world, it would be cycling heaven, and many people do actually regard it that way. In our easy scenic safe cycling world, however, we do not enjoy the areas of poor pavement, unappealing scenery, ne're-do-wells who smash bottles on the trail and the threat of being bashed by thugs who want your bike, mostly in the upper-middle sections around El Monte, but just about anywhere when you get away from the coast.

So, while racers and endurance riders may venture out, hopefully in groups, to tackle the entire trail, we have selected three sections to ride along the trail that we feel are the most scenic, easy, and relatively safe compared to other parts. These are the lower section from the Seal Beach oceanfront to Long Beach's Eldorado Park (ride SGR1); the scenic Whittier Narrows Recreation Area, which is adjacent to the SGRT trail and provides an option to take a spin along that section (SGR2); and the best part, the upper extent of the trail around the Santa Fe Dam Recreation Area up against the San Gabriel Mountains, which provides a great cycling stretch and equally appealing mountain views on clear days (SGR3). For those who would like to ride along other sections as well, a summary of the entire trail is presented below. See the LA/Orange County Ride Locator map for a schematic of the entire trail.

LOS ANGELES COUNTY

Distance: Mile 0 to Mile 6.7: Seal Beach to Eldorado Park

See ride SGR1 for a detailed description of this segment, ending at Carson Street. Mile 0: The beach at Seal Beach; 0.8: Pacific Coast Highway undercrossing (U/C); 1.6: 2nd St U/C; 2.6: Garden Grove Fwy (SR 22)/7th St U/C, then access to Edison Park; 3.5: I-405 Freeway U/C; 4.1: Junction with Coyote Creek Trail (straight ahead). *Bike bridge to the left carries the SGRT*; 4.8: Willow Street U/C (El Dorado Park's golf course on left across river); 5.2: Spring St U/C. Main part of El Dorado Park on the right; 5.8: Wardlow Road U/C, another entrance to El Dorado Park; 6.7: Carson Street—exit to Long Beach Towne Center (many newer restaurants). End of SGR1.

The following sections are not covered in our rides:

Mile 6.7: Carson St U/C; 7.0: Begin Rynerson Park; 7.7: Del Amo Blvd U/C; 8.3: Liberty Park at 195th St; 8.6: South St U/C, Auto Mall; 9.1: 183rd St U/C (caution: narrow tunnel); 9.7: Artesia Blvd U/C; 9.9: 91 Freeway U/C; 10.7: Alondra Blvd U/C; 11.7: Rosecrans Ave U/C; 12.5: I-105 Fwy U/C; 12.8: Imperial Hwy U/C; 13.4: Railroad U/C; 13.5: Firestone Blvd U/C; 13.8: Begin natural river bottom/Wilderness Park (restrooms), which is a nice section of trail; 14.5: Florence Ave U/C; 14.8: I-5 U/C, Santa Fe Springs Park; 15.3: Telegraph Rd U/C; 15.7: Trail moves close to I-605; 16.3: Trail moves away from I-605 at railroad U/C; 16.6: Slauson Ave and railroad U/C's; 17.3: Washington Blvd U/C; 17.4: Begin retention basins; 18.8: Whittier Blvd U/C, end retention basins; 19.5: Railroad U/C; 19.6: Beverly Blvd U/C.

The following section is in the area of ride SGR2:

Mile 20.2: San Gabriel River Pkwy U/C, trail crosses over on the highway bridge to the opposite bank; 20.8: Pico Rivera Golf Course; 21.1: Switchback up to top of Whittier Narrow Dam; 21.3: Four Corners Intersection, Rio Hondo Trail to left, SGRT to right, and access to Whittier Narrows Natural Area & Recreation Area (SGR2) straight ahead; 22.6: Peck Rd U/C, end of wilderness area. End of our suggested SGR2.

The following sections are not covered in our rides:

Mile 22.9: Pomona Fwy (SR 60) U/C; 23.3: Confluence with San Jose Creek; 24.6: Ball fields; 25.0: Valley Blvd U/C; 25.1: Railroad U/C; 25.2: Confluence with Walnut Creek; 25.6: I-10 undercrossing; 26.5: Ramona Blvd U/C; 27.0: Begin area of large ponds and gravel pits across I-605 to the east; 27.5: Lower Azusa Rd, gravel pits to the west; 28.0–28.4: Alongside large pond associated with sand & gravel ops; 28.4: I-605 U/C, industrial zone; 29.1: Live Oak Ave U/C; 29.6: Arrow Hwy, at grade crossing, base of Santa Fe Dam—trail goes to the left at the base of the dam; 30.0: Trail switchbacks right, climbs to top of dam; 30.2: Trail reaches top of dam.

SGR3 covers from here to the end of the trail. See that ride for a detailed description. SGRT continues east around the dam, overlooking Santa Fe Dam Recreation Area and mountains to the north, and LA megalopolis in other directions. Great San Gabriel Mountain views from here onward when clear. Mile 32.5: Bottom of dam on east side—follow bike route signs to the left; 34.1: Railroad and Foothill Freeway (I-210) U/C's; 34.6: Huntington Dr U/C; 34.9: Trailhead/restrooms; 35.1: Ped/bike bridge to Encanto Park; 37.2: Junction with trail to parking lot of San Gabriel Canyon Rd/Azusa; 37.3: Enter San Gabriel Canyon, bridges to new housing development; 38.0: End of trail alongside San Gabriel Canyon Rd.

Seal Beach to El Dorado Park SGR1 ⭐3

Details: About 14 to 17 miles total, easy, paved, for any bike

The lower portion of the SGRT offers an opportunity to get a good workout on a Class I trail. The scenic factor is best closer to the coast, and deteriorates as you proceed inland, along with the safety factor, as evidenced by daylight assaults on solo male cyclists in 2012 near Eldorado Park and 2020 north of Hwy 22. The park is a good destination with restrooms, and is a popular family outing with paved trails throughout, and families may want to skip the trail and just ride around the park. A large shopping center adjacent to it provides excellent Bike 'n Brunch options.

From the parking area described as the ride start of SE1, cross the bridge over the San Gabriel River and turn left onto the Class I trail alongside it. Pass some residential development then cross under PCH in 0.6 mile, and pass under 2nd Street (1.4). On a popular beach day, you may see people recreating in this tidal portion of the river in their Sea-Doo's. A large steam power plant follows on the right. Its discharge makes the water at Seal Beach near the river outlet warmer than normal, attracting stingrays, which you will need to be mindful of if you swim there.

The industrial zone ends as the trail crosses under East 7th Street (2.4) and adjacent College Park Drive. Pass by Edison Park and view College Park across the river, both accessible via College Park Drive. Next are some high-tension lines and commercial nurseries before reaching I-405 (3.2) at the I-605 interchange. The tidal portion of the river ends around mile 3.6, beyond which is a concrete spillway. The San Gabriel River Trail, and our route, crosses the channel over a ped/bike bridge at mile 3.9, while the Coyote Creek Trail continues straight ahead, following a concrete-lined channel between neighborhoods for 12 miles, passing Del Amo and Don Knabe Park with facilities and a lake, a popular park to stage from. After crossing under CA 91 and I-5 it ends on Foster Rd in Santa Fe Springs. A bike route directs you to Norwalk Metrolink station in 1.5 miles. Whittier Greenway Trail is reachable via bike routes in about 4 miles (see LA11 on page 368).

As we continue north along the San Gabriel River Trail, El Dorado Golf Course is on the left.

San Gabriel River Trail in Seal Beach

After SGRT crosses under E Willow St (4.6), it reaches El Dorado Park. The path traverses the western edge of the park and reaches a trail junction at mile 4.9 prior to Spring Street. At your option you can turn right to explore a lake and walk through the pretty Nature Center (add 0.6 mile). Otherwise, continue under Spring Street, and veer right at a trail junction (5.1), then right at a "T." Begin a loop eastward around the park, bending north to run parallel to the 605 Freeway, and then west before reaching Wardlow Road (6.0). You will see the park's main lake to the south from this area, which you can visit from here. Continue west, crossing the Wardlow park entrance roads (6.2), then cross another park road (6.5) to return to the river trail. Turn right to go under Wardlow Road, and then once again veer right to get to a trail through this portion of the park. Cross a park road, and make a right at a "T" (6.7). This trail brings you to the middle of the park and a lake with paddleboat rentals. Bear left at a fork (7.0), cycle between two lakes, and reach a parking lot (7.2). Ride through the lot to the one-way park road and turn left (7.2). The road heads north, and then west, next to the upper lake.

On your right is a modern big box shopping center, the Long Beach Towne Center. At a junction, where the Long Beach Police Academy is straight ahead (7.6), going to the right will not take you into the shopping center since it is completely fenced off from the park. So, go to the left instead.

There are other more minor trails through El Dorado Park that you can explore to increase your mileage. Our route just covers the west side of the park as we continue south. Before reaching a large parking area, you can veer off to the left onto a path to avoid the lot (7.9). Next, reach the same junction where you entered this portion of the park and turn right, retracing your route.

Once you reach the SGRT you have two options: To reach Long Beach Towne Center, turn right and then veer right again before Carson Street to find a way into the Center, which is near the Wal-Mart gas station. The Center has theatres, courtyards, stores, and restaurants, including a TGI Friday, NY Pizza, Lucille's Smokehouse Barbecue, Islands, and various fast food places. Add about 2.5 miles round trip to explore the Center. Otherwise, turn left to return to your ride start. First cycle under Wardlow Road (8.2). You can either just follow the SGRT all the way back, or take the park trails to the left along the west side of the park. If you explore the park, your total mileage will be about 14.5. E-bike edge for headwinds on the return.

Whittier Narrows Recreation Area   SGR2

Distance: 8 miles, easy.

Whittier Narrows Recreation Area is a 1,492-acre Los Angeles County park located in the city of South El Monte, spanning both sides of the Pomona (60) Freeway at Rosemead Boulevard and Santa Anita Avenue. The centerpiece of the park is Legg Lake, split into three separate sections, that is open for boating and fishing. A multitude of recreation activities are offered through this large park, and on weekends expect large crowds of happy families enjoying the facilities in the urban oasis, utilizing a Wheel Fun bike rental near the Santa Anita Ave parking lot, 805.252.5894.

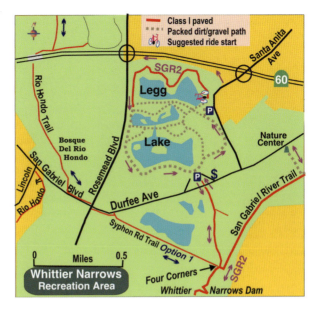

Pleasant scenic bike trails meander through the Legg Lake area of the park, which are asphalt at the north end and unpaved smooth compacted dirt suitable for most bikes everywhere else. The setting is the most beautiful in winter when snow-covered San Gabriel Mountains form the backdrop, however be mindful of severe rain events that may result in river flow. South of Durfee Avenue is the Whittier Narrows Recreation Area that contains a mix of disturbed land as well as restored habitat. A Nature Center off Durfee Avenue contains displays and offers environmental education to the community, accessible via a path from the SGRT. Some of the dirt trails in the Nature Center area are hike-only, but a paved path through it connects the Recreation Area to the San Gabriel River Trail at the Four Corners Intersection.

Another trail links to a connection to the Rio Hondo trail that leads to the section of the Recreation Area north of the 60 Freeway and beyond, through urban territory. Once on the San Gabriel River Trail, you can ride "forever" in either direction. Along this section of the SGRT there have been more assault incidents reported to the north in the El Monte/Valley Boulevard area than toward the south in Whittier in the past, but I cannot predict what will happen in the future. It is best to ride with a friend, in daylight hours, and be mindful of lurkers mostly in the brush and underpasses. There may also be rattlesnakes and coyotes.

To access the ride from the Pomona Freeway (60) in South El Monte, exit on Santa Anita/Tyler Avenue and drive south. Look for a large free parking lot on the right in about 0.3 mile. If that lot is full there is another lot farther along. Turn right on Durfee in another 0.4 mile, and 0.2 mile to the lot on the right ($6 weekends). Or turn left at Durfee to park at the Nature Center or the new Discovery Center if built.

Ride into the park to the west from the parking area on any of the trails. Most of the concessions are situated here, open mostly on weekends, including a refreshment stand and "fun" style bike and boat rentals. Go to the right, and find a paved path that circles around the north end of Legg Lake. The best views are from the west side of the lake that may take in lots of ducks, water, and mountains, along with tall power lines. Explore the rest of the area around the lakes later on, free form, on the main trails that circle around them, and other trails that run between them. When you reach the south end of the park and curve to the left parallel to Durfee Avenue, look for the large pay parking lot (about 1.7 miles). Cut through the lot and find a walkway about mid-way that leads to Durfee Avenue.

SGRT in Whittier Narrows Recreation Area with San Gabriel Mountains backdrop

Across the street is a signed paved path through the Nature Area. About 40 species of birds live in the park, and around 300 varieties have been spotted in this area. When you come to a junction at a small drainage canal, veer to the right (2.0). Ride along some more and reach a trail junction, known as the "Four Corners" (2.3). The paths left and straight ahead are the SGRT, while the path to the right along Syphon Road leads to the Rio Hondo path and the north end of Whittier Narrows Recreation Area. Turn left on the SGRT, and enjoy some great mountain vistas in this direction as the path becomes elevated along adjacent channels. When it descends, look for a path that crosses the small channel to the left (3.3).

Take this path, curve immediately to the left, then watch for the first trails to the right. Either one takes you to the Nature Center, which is worth checking out, when open (3.6). The Center hosts bird walks, hayrides, lectures, and school tours. Return to the SGRT and turn right (3.8). Ride back to the Four Corners area (4.8). Turn left onto the SGRT and cycle up the switchbacks to the top of the dam (5.0). At your option ride south on the SGRT for a bit farther to increase your mileage, then return. Either way, return to the Four Corners (5.2). As you head north on the SGRT, the Rio Hondo is to the left as described below.

Our main route continues straight back into the Nature Area. At the same junction near the canal (5.6), bear left and reach Durfee Avenue (5.7) as before. Cross the road and ride through the parking lot, then turn right on the same path that runs to the south then to the east of the lakes. Return to your start (6.3) and at your option explore more of the trails around the lake (7.5).

Option 1: Rio Hondo Trail ★ *6 to 16 miles round trip. Easy to moderate.*
From the Four Corners, the trail that goes to the northwest is the Rio Hondo Trail along the Old Syphon Road path at first. It heads straight toward Durfee Avenue, passing a wooded area and crossing over a small bridge along the way (0.7). The trail curves left alongside the road to reach the intersection with Rosemead Blvd. It continues kitty-corner across the road, along what is now San Gabriel Blvd, then turns north (right) before the bridge over the Rio Hondo channel (1.0). [Note that the Rio Hondo Trail southbound continues from the other side of the bridge, to the left. It joins the Los Angeles River Trail [becoming LARIO - ride with friends] and ends in downtown Long Beach along the waterfront. Do a 53 mile loop via Seal Beach]. Ride along the right bank in this nice area of thick riparian vegetation in a park called Bosque del Rio Hondo (Forest of the Deep River), or as locals refer to it, Marrano Beach ("Pig Beach"). The thick brush combined with lots of graffiti indicates this is a "ride with a friend" zone.

The trail follows the Rio Hondo under the Pomona (60) Freeway, and curves to the right next to it (1.8). The Rio Hondo Trail curves to the left (2.0). If you prefer, you can just do a loop around this northern portion of the Recreation Area on lightly traveled roads or paths, and return to the Four Corners for an option total of 6 miles. Otherwise, turn north up the Rio Hondo Trail. After leaving the Recreation Area (2.7), the riding is still pleasant, between a golf course and planted nurseries, however the beautiful natural channel becomes lined with concrete, and the viewscape soon consists of industrial and commercial buildings (3.2).

Pass under Garvey Avenue (3.5), Rosemead Boulevard (3.6), and then ride next to a residential neighborhood, looking out at a channel and industrial neighborhood on the west bank. Next cross under I-10 and reach Fletcher Park (4.8), pass under Valley Boulevard (5.3) where fast food is on the right, before reaching El Monte Airport (5.8), where you can take a rest stop to watch the aero action. A residential area is across the river here.

Cross under Lower Azusa Road (6.6), and through a mixed-use area, under Santa Anita Ave (fast food to the right behind Sam's Club) (6.9). The path reaches a Rio Hondo retention basin. One branch crosses over the dam to the left, runs between the basin and Arcadia Golf Course, then ends at Live Oak Ave. The other branch goes along the right side of the basin and ends at the Peck Road Water Conservation Park (8.0) in a scenic area with nice mountain views over the water. Return to Four Corners for an approximate 16-mile add-on.

Further Info: parks.lacounty.gov; Park Headquarters: 626.575.5526; naturalareafriends.net; sangabrielriverdiscoverycenter.org; Corps of Engineers: www.usace.army.mil

San Gabriel River—Santa Fe Dam Recreation Area SGR3

The upper end of the San Gabriel River Trail is the most scenic, situated at the foot of Angeles National Forest and the San Gabriel Mountains. Take in spectacular San Gabriel mountain scenery on clear days, especially after a winter storm when they are the most snow-covered, while riding next to the flowing river. The area

San Gabriel River Trail at Santa Fe Dam Recreation Area

between the Santa Fe Dam and trail's end provides a nice escape from the sprawling urban industrial zone below it. The huge Santa Fe Dam, a flood control structure, is 4.5 miles wide and topped by a section of the SGRT. Santa Fe Dam Recreation Area behind the dam is an 836-acre facility containing a 70-acre lake with year-round fishing and non-motorized watercraft usage, and a summer-only 5-acre chlorinated swim beach and water play area. The property contains a host of protected native plants and animals, and The Nature Center is operated and staffed by volunteers of the San Gabriel Mountains Regional Conservancy, offering some opportunities for walking tours and interpretive programs. Dirt mountain bike trails cross the park, providing an option for more fun and scenic riding for the novice mountain biker.

Tunes: Down by the Riverbed by Los Lobos; Ballad of Easy Rider by The Byrds; Brasileira, Tout Simplement by Nazare Pereira.
Eats: Picnic at the lake.

Distance: 18.3 miles (options to shorten or lengthen). Time: ±2 hours
Route & Bike: Easy to moderate. Paved Class I regional trail, paved trails and roads in park; any bike. Also optional dirt trails (hybrid or mountain bike). Gradual slope to the north, plus incline from both sides up to top of dam. See map for elevations. As the ride is described, the elevation gain is about 350 feet, or about 400 feet if a ride onto the dam is included. For an Arrow Highway ride start add another 80 feet.
Seasons: All. Best on sunny mild winter weekend when mountains are snow-covered.
Facilities: Restrooms and water at Encanto Park and Santa Fe Rec Area.
Knocks & Hazards: Fast-moving cyclists (keep to the right). A few clueless peds, more so on the trails in the Santa Fe Dam Rec Area. Possible lurkers and gang activity, although less than that reported downstream. A few park road crossings. Rattlesnakes. Potential for mountain lions and black bears, especially closer to mountains. Can be hot and smoggy, especially from summer into fall. Stay away from lowlands during major storms and extensive runoff.
Rent 'n Ride: Wheel Fun Rentals in Santa Fe Rec Area near the lake (mostly "funmobiles" for riding around the lake), 626.334.6555.
Camp 'n Ride/Bike 'n Brunch: Nothing in immediate vicinity. See LA10 for camping. Picnic in Santa Fe Dam Recreation Area. Restaurants to the east in Azusa.
Further Info: LA County Parks: parks.lacounty.gov/wps/portal/dpr.

Access: There are several options to access this section of the SGRT. Our preferred ride start is at Encanto Park, a popular meeting place for groups to leave their vehicles, since this active family-oriented park seems the safest free alternative, and starts you out near the middle of this ride. From the 210 Freeway, exit on Irwindale Avenue. Go north on Irwindale to Foothill and turn left, over the river, then right on Encanto

Parkway. Encanto Park is on the left, just past the bike bridge over the river. Another option is the Azusa free lot near the upper end of the trail, but that requires an all-uphill return. From I-210 exit Azusa Avenue (Hwy 39) and head north about 6 miles to the free public parking area on the left, at the mouth of the canyon. You can also park near the bottom of the trail, enabling a downhill return ride.

Parking inside Santa Fe Dam Recreation Area is $10 (free winter weekdays), but is a great staging area with facilities like picnic tables, restrooms, and bike and boat rentals. From I-210 take Irwindale south to Arrow Highway and turn right. There is free parking along Arrow Highway in this area. The trail runs across the top of the dam, then down into the park. If you park at Arrow Highway you will need to cycle on the fairly steep vehicle access road onto the dam, and then down the other side into the park. There is no fee for bike entry. Otherwise just drive in, pay the fee, and have the option of whether or not to ride onto the dam. It is easy to find the SGRT, with obvious Bike Route signs that direct you onto that trail.

The Ride: From Encanto Park, ride south down Encanto Parkway on the road or sidewalk, then cross the road to access the bike/ped bridge over the wide San Gabriel River drainage that has a natural riparian stream bottom in this area. Reach a junction with the SGRT on the other side (0.3). Watch for fast moving bikes! We recommend starting off heading left (north) which is uphill. On a clear day the scenery will include foothills and the taller peaks of the San Gabriel Mountains beyond. The more snow-covered they are, the more spectacular the view. The northbound direction toward the mountains is more scenic, and is also the slower, uphill direction so you can enjoy the vistas. The grade is very gradual and not difficult except perhaps for one short fairly steep hill.

Besides mountain views and the riparian swatch created by the river drainage, there are some sand and gravel operations, which are not unpleasant to look at, including a gravel pit filled with water. The trail eventually draws closer to San Gabriel Canyon Road (Hwy 39) at around mile 2.2. The parking lot to the right is the Azusa public lot, accessed via a spur trail (2.4). The trail runs next to the highway as it enters San Gabriel Canyon. Although you are next to a road, the view down to the river becomes more striking as you can see the flowing water in its natural state. Alas, a new residential subdivision was constructed across the river and several new bridges access it, creating street crossings that are rare for the SGRT (2.7). The trail abruptly ends at a rest stop (no restrooms) (3.0).

Turn around and enjoy your downhill cruise through the canyon. Watch your speed, although a headwind might aid in that department. Reach the bike/ped bridge you started from (5.8). A return to your car here will accomplish a 6.1-mile ride. Any further riding will require an uphill return, as follows:

Reach another popular staging area with a free paved parking lot (6.0) that seems more remote than the others. It is accessed off Foothill Boulevard, just east of the river. Cross under Foothill (6.4) and then I-210 (6.9), where we noted a drop structure (waterfall) on the river below, and lots of graffiti everywhere. Emerge onto a very scenic stretch of trail through a beautiful coastal sage ecosystem. A dirt trail to the right at a fork (7.3) indicates the start of mountain bike trails through the Santa Fe Recreation Area. Our route keeps to the left on a paved trail that widens and heads straight toward the southeast. Reach an obvious junction (7.9), where the Bike Route sign points to the left. The Nature Center, open occasionally, is to the left here at this intersection. If you just want to continue on the SGRT to the dam, go left past the Nature Center, then right, following the trail as it takes you gradually up to the top of the dam.

Our suggested route makes a detour to explore the beautiful park. Head straight on the paved road, which leads to the north side of the park's scenic lake (8.3). You can do a freeform exploration of the park on the paved concrete paths next to the lake. This will be a slow moving casual cruise to be courteous to peds and to avoid the surreys and other fun-mobiles rented by Wheel Fun Rentals here. Although there are lots of novice-level dirt paths available in the vicinity, our route stays on the paved paths, encircling the lake clockwise halfway to the south

Scenic Santa Fe Dam Recreation Area

past the sandy beach, a great place to photograph sand, water, palms, and snow when conditions are right (8.8). Continue on whatever park paths you like. A Renaissance Faire may block the end of your paved path (9.1). MTB's can detour around it on a dirt path and encircle the lake, but our route returns the same way, through the park.

Ride along parallel and below the dam to the northeast, then reach the park entrance/exit road (10.1). If you've encircled the lake on a mountain bike you can find yourself back at the park entrance road as well. You can ride up the fairly steep vehicle exit, but our route will continue onward to rejoin the SGRT (10.4). Here is a decision point. If you've started at Encanto Park and can only handle a 13.5-mile ride (remembering the return 2.5-miles of the ride is a gradual uphill), turn left on the SGRT and retrace the route back to the Encanto Park. Otherwise, it is worthwhile to experience a spin atop the dam. Turn right and ride up the gradual incline to the top of this large flood control structure. Carefully cross the vehicle entry road at the fee kiosk (10.9) and continue along the dam. The wide trail follows the dam, gradually bending to the right, overlooking the lake and the rest of the rec area, and the San Gabriel Mountains beyond. From this vantage you can also see in the other direction the industrial zones of the San Gabriel Valley, power lines, and on a clear day the LA skyline will be visible in the distance to the west.

Once you've ridden along the dam for a while, judge how far of a ride you'd like to do and turn around as you wish. The return ride is even more scenic with a better view of the San Gabriel Mountains, and even the San Bernardino range on a clear day, although there are power lines in the mix. The SGRT continues atop the dam until our mile 12.5. We'll turn around at the point that the trail descends steeply down the face of the dam to Arrow Highway, then continues south across Arrow Highway.

Side note: If you continue south on the SGRT, it passes an industrial area, however, in about a mile it looks out over a large water-filled gravel pit that affords some nice views. On the return there can be great mountain views on clear days.

Return the same way you came back across the dam, reaching the park entry kiosk (14.8). Glide down along the top of the dam, and turn left, following the Bike Route sign (15.5). Turn to the left toward the Nature Center, then a make right behind it to continue along the SGRT (15.8). Cross back under I-210 (16.8), reach the bike/ped bridge over the river (18.0), then cross the river and return to Encanto Park (18.3).

West Fork San Gabriel River
SGR4 ⭐

Details: Up to 6.5 miles each way; Easy. Option for strenuous. Paved, any bike.
Facilities: Near trailhead and campground. Bring ample water. No food nearby.
Elevation: 1,590 ft to 2,040 ft at camp.
Hazards: Isolated (bring tubes, etc.).

No cellular. Bear and cougar country, rattlesnakes, poison oak, falling rocks, flash floods.

West Fork National Bikeway is a gem of a trail in the San Gabriel mountains above the SGRT. From I-210 drive about 11 miles north on CA 39, past the end of the SGRT, Morris and San Gabriel Reservoirs, to the junction with East Fork Road. Keep left here, and in another 1.5 miles cross a bridge over the river, then park in the lot on the left (requires $5 Adventure Pass, buy in Azusa). It can fill on weekends. Cycle back across the bridge, and start riding on the service road labeled "Cogswell Dam" to the right that runs along the south bank of the river. It is closed to all vehicles, except parks or utility vehicles and those with special permits. At the onset are popular swimming holes backed with graffiti-covered canyon walls, but farther along the people diminish and it becomes very peaceful. Enjoy the gentle uphill grade through the forested canyon, with cascades of water coming down the sides of some of the cliffs en route. The canyon narrows around mile 3. Glenn Trail Camp is at mile 6.5. Camping is allowed here with a permit. To continue beyond the camp requires a very steep climb of 350 feet in less than half a mile to reach scenic Cogswell Reservoir and dam and beyond. Return the same way. The ride can be done all year, but avoid winter storms. The surrounding mountains are spectacular when snow-covered, though it rarely snows at this level.
Further info: calwild.org/west-fork-national-scenic-bikeway/

San Fernando Valley

This world-famous region known as "The Valley" lies over the Hollywood Hills from the main part of the city of Los Angeles, and is home to many of the major motion picture studios, as well as the Universal Studios Hollywood attraction. It can get pretty hot here in summer and fall, but on a clear winter day, cycling on some of the trails can be an enjoyable experience. The backdrop to your ride can incorporate the Santa Susanna Mountains to the north, the San Gabriel and Verdugo Mountains to the east, and the Santa Monica Mountains to the south. The trails here are not destination rides, but there are several worthwhile cycles that are popular with locals.

The highlight is the Sepulveda Basin area, which offers a lot of scenic value and a welcome respite from the dense urban environment, thanks to its function as a giant floodplain (ride LA5). See page 368 for the Orange Line Busway bike path that follows a dedicated busway from Burbank west to Encino and Canoga Park, with an extension along an elbow north to Chatsworth (LA6). This trail is described as an option to extend the scenic Sepulveda Basin ride. At the east end it connects to the short but popular Chandler Bikeway (LA7). LA's Griffith Park touches the east end of the valley, another beautiful urban oasis that is mostly spread out in the Hollywood Hills, but contains a much flatter area where most of the park's main attractions, such as the LA Zoo, are located. A pleasant ride through the park incorporates a loop using a path along the LA River (LA4), with the option of extending the ride farther downstream. E-bikers can tackle a car-free route in the hills, shown on the map.

Griffith Park and LA River Loop LA4

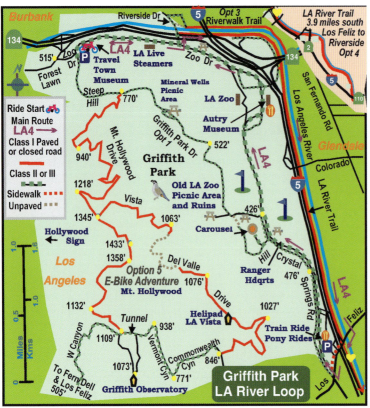

Seen in so many TV shows and movies, Griffith Park encompasses 4,310 acres, making it the tenth largest municipal park in the United States, and the second largest in California after Mission Trails Regional Park in San Diego (rides SD12 and 13). The park was named for Griffith J. Griffith, a mining magnate of Welsh origin, who donated the land at the turn of the twentieth century amidst controversy, as he had shot and severely injured his wife. It is situated at the eastern extent of the Santa Monica Mountains, which separate Hollywood from the San Fernando Valley, and is laced with hilly hiking and equestrian trails popular with local individuals and groups.

Some of LA's most popular attractions are here, including the Hollywood sign, the Greek Theatre outdoor concert venue, and the Griffith Observatory, the location of a key scene in James Dean's *Rebel Without a Cause,* and now home of LA's newly renovated planetarium. The most visited and accessible part of the park is its northeast corner, located southwest of the junction of the Ventura Freeway (SR134) and the Golden State Freeway (I-5). This is also the flattest part of the park, and the most conducive to easy cycling on its Class II and III park roadways with a speed limit of 25 mph. Found here are the LA Zoo and Botanical Gardens, several public golf courses, an ornate carousel, the Autry Western Heritage Center and Museum and entertainment venue, and Travel Town Museum of transportation.

The channelized Los Angeles River makes a right angle bend from east-west to north-south here, surrounding the park with its Class I pathway. Although it suffers from loud freeway noise and potential for lurkers, it provides a good scenic option to extend the riding experience away from vehicle traffic. Revegetation efforts have turned the LA River through these parts into a very scenic waterway with lots of shore birds to gaze at, including great blue heron. The LA River trail continues south beyond our suggested ride as well (Option 4), and someday will extend all the way to the ocean at Long Beach.

Tunes: At the Zoo by Simon & Garfunkel; 2+0+1+2=Cinco by Quetzal; Saturday in the Park by Chicago, Finally Free by Stitched Up Heart

Eats: Light lunch at Autry Museum Café, BBQ Pork Sandwich at Pecos Bill's BBQ, or picnic in the the park.

Distance: 9.8 mile loop. Time: 1 hour riding.

Route & Bike: Easy. Fairly flat with minor grades and option for short steep hill. Paved Class I river path and Class II and III park roadway, any bike. E-bike edge: Try hilly rides of various degrees as described in Options and shown on the map.

Seasons: All. Best on sunny uncrowded mild winter or spring day. We prefer the isolated river trail on weekends (more company for safety). Park roads have more cars with park goers on weekends and commuters avoiding freeways on weekdays.

Facilities: Restrooms and water throughout the park.

Knocks & Hazards: Park riding is on-road. LA River trail is isolated with potential for lurkers. Ride with a friend. Some hills on main route. Coyotes, rattlesnakes and potential for mountain lion in park, moreso in interior hills. Summer heat.

Rent 'n Ride: Spokes 'N Stuff, 4730 Crystal Springs Dr, (Ranger Headquarters Parking Lot), 323.662.6573.

Camp 'n Ride: None nearby. See Sepulveda Basin.

Bike 'n Brunch: Autry Café at the museum and food concessions at pony ride facility and inside the zoo. A few blocks north on Riverside Drive (1551 Victory Blvd in Glendale) is Pecos Bill BBQ restaurant, 818.241.2750.

Further Info: www.laparks.org/dos/parks/griffithpk. LA Zoo: lazoo.org; Autry Museum: theautry.org; Travel Town Museum: traveltown.org; LA Live Steamers Museum: lals.org; bike.lacity.org/plan-your-trip/bicycle-maps/

Access: Griffith Park lies just west of the Golden State Freeway (I-5), roughly between the Ventura Freeway (SR 134) on the north and Los Feliz Boulevard on the south. Freeway off-ramps leading to the park from I-5 are Los Feliz Boulevard, Griffith Park and Zoo Drive. Approaching the park on SR 134 eastbound, take either the Forest Lawn Drive or Victory Boulevard off ramps. From SR 134 westbound, take Zoo Drive or Forest Lawn Drive. After exiting the freeways, follow the signs into the park. Our suggested starting point is the Travel Town Museum at the west end of Zoo Drive, just east of Forest Lawn Drive exit. There is a lot of free parking throughout the park, and since the ride is basically a loop, you can start anywhere along the route.

The Ride: Start from the parking lot of the Travel Town Museum, which displays railroad history as it pertains to the development of the Southwest, particularly the Los Angeles area. They restore, operate, and interpret historic railroad equipment. Turn right onto Zoo Drive, and glide down a gradual hill, riding between the park on your right and the 134 Freeway on the left. Reach the Los Angeles Live Steamers Railroad Museum, where you can ride 7½" gauge model trains from 11 a.m. to 3 p.m. most Sundays, or check out their model train displays (mile 0.5).

At Riverside Drive turn left (1.0), ride across the bridge over the 134 Freeway, and make an immediate right onto the Class I Los Angeles River Trail. Although there are giant power transmission lines above and a freeway nearby, concentrate on the tranquil riparian vegetation that has been reintroduced in the channel, and the Verdugo Hills and San Gabriel Mountains beyond the Glendale skyline. Cross under the I-5 Freeway (1.3). The interesting yellow building across the river is the Dreamworks Animation facility. The trail bends to the right, as does the LA River. At this point you are riding between soccer fields of Griffith Park, and there is a rare trail exit here. Verdugo Wash flows in from the east as you cross under the 134 Freeway (2.0).

Farther south the trail runs between the loud I-5 Golden State Freeway and the river channel (2.25), although the trail is below the freeway, which numbs the noise

LA River Trail runs under power lines along river. Riparian vegetation in river attracts shorebirds

a bit. The skyline of downtown Los Angeles gradually comes into view. The farther along you go, the more isolated you are from the park, so take this into account before choosing to ride here. The trail passes under the Colorado Street Freeway Extension (no access) (2.8), and subsequently reaches Los Feliz Boulevard, where there is a ramp leading up to the street on the right (4.2). Ride along the sidewalk to the right, very carefully cross an I-5 entrance ramp, cycle across the I-5 overpass, and carefully cross two more unsignaled access roads to the I-5 Freeway, before reaching Crystal Springs Road (4.5).

Turn right into Griffith Park here, as Crystal Springs Road splits into north and southbound sections. The northbound route is flatter and lower in elevation, which is why we ride in this direction. The Class III road is a bit crowded between the entrance and the first attraction on the right, which is a popular family-oriented concession with a miniature train ride and pony ride (4.8). There is also a food concession that offers a lot of choices. A very scenic section follows, as it becomes a wide Class II roadway surrounded by forest with mountains in the distance, which creates a welcome, though temporary, escape from the metropolis.

Cross a freeway access road (5.1) as the roadway ascends a gradual hill, then descends to another busy part of the park with the Ranger Headquarters, a bike rental concession, and a picnic area (5.8). We recommend ascending a small hill on the road to the left (Fire Road), turning right toward the parking lot for the ornate carousel (5.9). Take in nice views of the merry-go-round and the mountains beyond. You can also explore some more paved paths in this area (6.4). Return the same way down the hill to the left (6.5). However, if you are in great shape and want a workout, consider following Griffith Park Drive over steep hill and dale to your starting point (Option 1) and even connecting to the ultra hilly La La Land e-bike adventure (Option 5).

Our route returns down the hill toward the ranger station, then turns left on Crystal Springs Road (6.6). Ride a pleasant stretch between golf courses, then follow the main road as it snakes to the right and then the left. Pause at the magic spot directly between the entrance to the LA Zoo and the impressive Autry Western Heritage Center and Museum (7.9)—a great place for photos. The LA Zoo and Botanical Gardens contain 1,100 mammal, bird and reptile species including rare and endangered animals displayed in interesting surroundings. The Autry Center is a history museum dedicated to exploring and sharing the stories, experiences, and perceptions of the

Pleasant cycling along Crystal Springs Road in Griffith Park

diverse peoples of the American West, including celebrations of the contributions of women and the LGBT community. Admission is required to both, but the Autry's Café is accessible without museum admission.

Reach Zoo Drive, which goes to the right over I-5 and to the park's soccer fields, and also straight ahead, which is our route (8.0). The road bends to the left, around the huge zoo parking lot, and continues along a pleasant Class III stretch through the woods, parallel to, but not next to the 134 Freeway. Reach Riverside Drive where you accessed the LA River trail previously (8.8). At this point you may want to consider checking out the new Glendale river trail across the river (Option 3), or having a Pecos Bill BBQ sandwich a few blocks up on Victory Boulevard. Our main route continues straight, ascending the gradual hill back to your starting point at the Travel Town Museum parking lot (9.8).

Option 1: Hill Ride *About 9.2 miles total, moderate to strenuous, e-bike edge* Cycle Griffith Park Dr between the Ranger Headquarters and Travel Town on the return, but be prepared for a steep half-mile grade at the midpoint. Access Option 5.

Option 2: Park Only *8.2 miles total, moderate* The easiest cycling route staying within the park is up and back along Zoo Drive and Crystal Springs Drive with only one grade.

Option 3: Glendale Riverwalk North across the LA River in Glendale, the Glendale Narrows Riverwalk is a 1-mile multi-use trail, park, and equestrian facility extending from Betty Davis Park (east of Riverside Drive), running east under I-5, and beyond Dreamworks Animation, ending at Verdugo Wash. An LA River bike bridge is planned.

Option 4: The Rest of the Upper Los Angeles River Trail *8 miles round trip, easy* Instead of taking the Los Feliz turnoff you can explore the rest of the Upper LA River trail along its west bank. This stretch of trail offers some great birdwatching, but is best ridden with a friend and during the day. Cross the bike bridge over Los Feliz (0.0), and reach the heron gates of Rattlesnake Park via the south side of Fletcher Dr (1.3). Other parks en route are Marsh Park (2.3), Elysian Valley Gateway Park (2.8), Steelhead Park (3.8), and Egret Park (3.9) near Elysian Park. The trail ends at Riverside Dr and Figueroa Street next to the point where I-5 crosses the LA River and meets SR110 (4.0).

The LA River Trail will eventually continue through downtown and join the existing LARIO trail to Long Beach Harbor. It will also extend to the northwest from Griffith Park to Sepulveda Basin. Several isolated sections are already complete, the longest being Radford 1.5 miles to Coldwater Canyon, but with no good road crossings yet.

Option 5: La La Land E-Bike Adventure *7-10 miles, strenuous or moderate with e-bike* Two car-free roads lead into the park's Mt. Hollywood highlands as shown on the map with elevations to gauge difficulty. Mt. Hollywood Dr starts off of Griffith Park Dr, and provides iconic vistas including the Hollywood sign near the top. Up and back is ~7 miles. Watch downhill speed, with sharp curves, bad pavement, and obstacles. Vista Del Valle intersects it, circling the mountain to the east, with a 0.25 mile unpaved section. Park roads connect those two roads near Griffith Observatory. A loop is ~10 very hilly miles. You can also access the area from Los Feliz to Fern Dell in the south.

Sepulveda Dam Recreation Area Loops LA5

Just northwest of the busy US 101/I-405 interchange between Encino and Van Nuys lies the remote-feeling Sepulveda Dam Recreation Area, a flood control basin that also encompasses parks and golf courses. It is a very popular recreation facility for the million people that live in the vicinity, and can get overly crowded on weekends. On less crowded days, cycling on several loops through the area can provide a welcome respite from the urban surroundings. Cycling is mostly on paved Class I trails except for an optional 0.3-mile stretch along White Oak Boulevard. The loops also connect to the cross-valley Orange Line Busway bike path that runs west from Burbank to Canoga Park, then north to Chatsworth. The main and more scenic ride is along the loops to the east of Balboa Boulevard. Pass by a pretty lake, a wildlife refuge, the LA River, and several golf courses. The optional west side trails run between public recreation facilities and residential areas.

Tunes: San Fernando Valley by Johnny Mercer and the Berries; Valley Girl by Frank & Moon Unit Zappa; Lost You in the Valley by Marc Cohn; La Bamba Rebelde by Las Cafeteras; New Divide by Linkin Park
Eats: Park picnic or Chicken Sosaties at Springbok Grill.

Distance: 5.3 miles + options. Time: 45 minutes
Route & Bike: Easy. Flat except for dip under roadway. Paved Class I Trail with limited road crossings. Option 1 has Class II section. Any bike.
Seasons: All. Best on sunny uncrowded mild weekday with clean air.
Facilities: Restrooms and water in the park.
Knocks & Hazards: Clueless peds (remember to be courteous of them though, especially children). Possible lurkers. Summer heat/smog. Bloggers report flat tires from goathead thorns on trail, mostly in late summer and fall. We had no problem in November but we recommend flat-resistant tires/spare tubes. Potential for flooding.

Rent 'n Ride: Wheel Fun Balboa Lake: 6300 Balboa Blvd, Van Nuys, 818.212.4263.
Camp 'n Ride: Balboa RV Park, 7740 Balboa Blvd, Van Nuys, is about 3.5 miles north, 818.785.0949.
Bike 'n Brunch: For something unique, Spring Bok Bar and Grill serves South African food with a large beer selection, 16153 Victory Blvd, west of Woodley, 818.988.9786. Woodley Lakes Golf Course had a restaurant (check status), 818.780.6886. Our guilty pleasure is Versailles Cuban food, which is 1 mile south on Balboa then 0.5 mile west to 17410 Ventura. Best to drive to apres ride.

Left: Versailles' garlic chicken. Right: Balboa Lake

Access: From US 101 take the Balboa Blvd exit northbound. There is parking just north of Burbank Blvd on the left. From I-405 take Victory Blvd westbound and turn left on Balboa to find the same parking lot, on the right before Burbank Blvd. If this is full you can try other lots around the park since this is a loop ride. By bike-carrying Metro bus: Line #154 (Burbank and Woodley); Line #164 (Victory and Woodley).

The Ride: From the parking area, go north on the path that veers to the left, and then right, next to the LA River and under Balboa Boulevard. Upon emerging on the other side, turn south (left) down the pleasant pathway (mile 0.2). It will reach Burbank Boulevard and head to the left next to the north side of the road (0.7). The nicely treed trail bends around parallel to Burbank Boulevard, adjacent to golf courses. It winds through the Balboa Golf Course parking lot where you can access a clubhouse that serves food and drink and has restrooms (0.9). Pass the terminus of Havenhurst Avenue (1.3) and then the entry road to the Hjelte Sports Center on the right (1.7), while riding next to Encino Golf Course on the left. A slight uphill grade brings you to a bridge over the Los Angeles River in a scenic area that includes a view of the Sepulveda Dam (2.2).

At Woodley Avenue (2.3) is an offshoot paved path that leads 0.4 mile along the south side of Burbank Avenue to the top of the dam. The area between Woodley Avenue and the dam is the Sepulveda Basin Wildlife Reserve, with its willow, cottonwood, and sycamore trees and an understory of mulefat, sage, and mugwort. Besides waterfowl, there is abundant bird life in this habitat. The dirt paths through this area are for hikers only.

The main bike path continues northward in a scenic stretch on the west side of Woodley, past the model airplane area and some open fields, with Woodley Avenue Park visible across the road. Sepulveda Japanese Garden in Woodley Avenue Park is a nice diversion. Reach a paved path adjacent to the entrance to Woodley Lakes Golf Course on the left (3.4), 0.1 mile before reaching Victory Boulevard. Ride to the west (left) here. The path and access road curve around to the left to reach Anthony C. Beilenson Park and the popular Balboa Lake (4.1). This 27-acre lake is filled with reclaimed water from the Tillman Water Reclamation Plant and is the main attraction of the park. Expect crowds on weekends, but on weekdays it is a good place to park and stage from. Water and restrooms available. The path around the immediate lake perimeter is ped-only. A highlight of this area is the cherry trees that blossom in the spring. As the path bends around the south end of the lake there are some nice vistas of the lake and its abundant waterfowl, and Santa Susanna Mountains beyond.

An urban oasis: Sepulveda Dam Recreation Area

After crossing a creek past the southwest end of the lake, bear left at a trail junction and head toward the LA River (4.9). Take the path under Balboa Boulevard and emerge on the other side. To complete a 5.3-mile ride, head south along the roadside path a short distance to your starting point. Otherwise, utilize the map and extend the ride on the paths as shown.

To add a few miles on a scenic trail, ride down and back along the LA River as shown on the map, or do another loop by repeating one of the trails to the north or south. Option 1 describes the loop that runs to the west of Balboa Boulevard.

Option 1: West Loop *4.3 miles, easy, mostly flat.* From the starting parking lot head south on the path parallel to west side of Balboa Blvd, and curve right along Burbank Blvd (0.5) as you encircle Balboa Sports Center. The path bends right prior to reaching a residential area (0.7) and heads north. It then bends west next to the terminus of Oxnard St, now part of the Orange Line Busway Bike Path (1.2). It runs on the north side of Oxnard next to a wash and passes the Encino Velodrome. The actual Orange Line Busway curves around to the west adjacent to the trail along this stretch (1.8). Reach White Oak Ave (2.0). Turn right into the bike lane, and cross the LA River bridge (2.3).

A paved path continues to the right on the north side of the bridge. The path curves right as it reaches busy Victory Boulevard (2.4). Pass by an off-leash dog park, an Army National Guard training center (2.9) and some vacant land and commercial buildings before reaching Balboa Boulevard (3.4). From here, turn right onto the path adjacent to the west side of Balboa to return to your starting point (3.9 miles total), or cross the road in the crosswalk and take the paths on the east side of the road, then cross back under Balboa Boulevard to your starting point (4.3).

Option 2: Orange Line Busway addition.   See ride LA6 in "Encore" page 368.

East LA County Puddingstone Reservoir Loop LA10

This urban oasis with mountain backdrop has something for everyone, and when the mountains are snow-covered the viewscape is even prettier. Paved paths and roads lead around the reservoir and Brackett Airport, while MTB'ers can try novice and intermediate trails in Bonelli Regional Park. Non-bikers can stroll, swim or boat, and Bonelli Bluffs makes a great Camp 'n Ride. Adjacent are classic LA features Raging Waters water park and the county fairgrounds, aka Fairplex, whose fair is in September.

South shore path

Road on dam

Distance and Route : 7.2 mile loop on Class I and low traffic Class II and III. [MTB's can shorten to 5 miles (see map) or try 9.4 mile hilly Bonelli Trail loop.] E-bike edge for hills especially in RV park.
Facilities: Restrooms and water in parks.
Knocks & Hazards: Coyotes, rattlesnakes, rare cougar. Avoid winter storms, summer smog. Mild hills, some vehicles on roads.
Bike Shop: Incycle, 501 W Arrow Hwy, near SR 57, San Dimas, 909.592.2181.
Bike 'n Brunch: Norm's Hanger at ride start, breakfast/lunch. Runway view patio. Bonelli Bluffs RV camp store, upper loop.
Camp 'n Ride: Bonelli Bluffs RV is in middle of the ride. Best sites are in upper loops but easiest bike route goes through lower Unit F. Parking for campers is available near trail, 909.599.8355. Also, Fairplex KOA, 2200 N White, Pomona, 593.8915.
Access: Take the Fairplex exit north from I-10, just east of SR 57. See the map for directions to Bonelli Bluffs, Bonelli Park (fee) and our ride start at Brackett Field. There is typically free parking available at the lot near Norm's at the end of McKinley.
The Ride: Ride past the gate on the closed road next to the airport. It leads into the Bonelli Bluffs property (0.5). [The dirt path here goes to wetlands and the north end of Bonelli Park.] Cycle through the Unit F camp loop to a closed road/trailhead (0.8). Pedal or walk up a small hill and enjoy great lake views. Glide down the path past Bonelli Park facilities. Cross the park road to a "T" (1.6). Either path forms a 2 mile paved loop. Go right, enjoying a scenic pedal along the lake. At a "Y" near the picnic area (2.2) go left. [MTB's can go right, through the swim beach lot to a novice dirt trail along the lake, keeping right at forks.] At the next path junction bear right, up a hill, under a road, then parallel an access road. Reach the dam (3.1) and ride over its flat 1-way low-traffic roadway with great vistas. Descend to Puddingstone Dr (3.8). Cycle right, up a hill, enter Bonelli Park (4.0), and pedal its waterfront promenade. Exit the park via the group lots to Puddingstone, (5.1). [MTB's find dirt route from last waterfront lot per map]. Ride to Fairplex (6.2). Turn right on its Class I path. Cycle (under planes landing) to McKinley (6.7). Turn right to ride start (7.2).

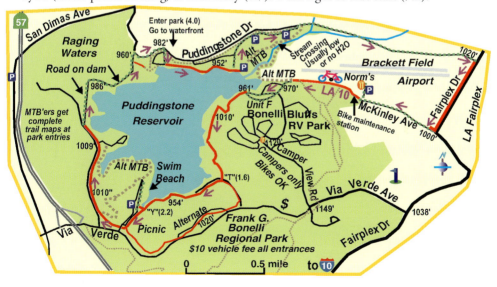

Pasadena and San Marino

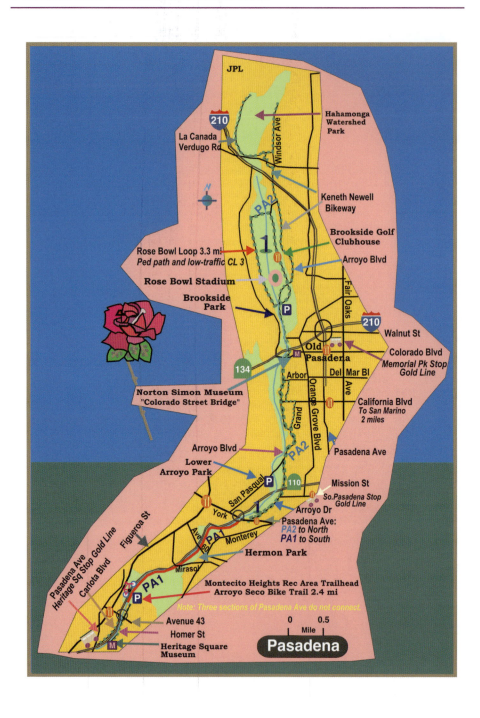

LOS ANGELES COUNTY

Colorado Street Bridge with its Beaux Arts arches, over Arroyo Seco

Pasadena is an older city known as the place where America starts its New Year with the Rose Bowl football game and the amazing Tournament of Roses parade. The weather has an uncanny habit of being absolutely beautiful on New Years Day in Pasadena regardless of what happens before or after, making Pasadena seem like an ideal place to be. The Rose Bowl stadium is situated in the very scenic Arroyo Seco Canyon that winds southward, located west and down the hill from Old Pasadena, a downtown district of hip restaurants and nightspots.

South of the stadium, the beautiful wooded canyon is lined with hiking-only trails for several miles. Scenic cycling is confined to the roadways in Pasadena, and there is a pleasant Class III bikeway along the edge of the arroyo through town. Although Pasadena has no Class I trails, you can literally do loops around the Rose Bowl on a 3-mile low-traffic bike route. Sidewalk cycling is allowed, an option if streets seem too dangerous to ride on. A Class I trail is found just south of town, but the Arroyo Seco Bike Trail in a concrete-lined section of the arroyo is less than 2.5-miles long.

To include this city that is so important to Southern California, and that has one of the best city songs to boot, we have put together some combination ideas to make the most of your day of cycling. LA's Metro Rail trains can also be used to transport you between points of interest. Nearby toney San Marino with its fabulous Huntington Library and Gardens is also a must-see place, however cycling around town involves very hilly Class III residential streets.

Tunes: Little Old Lady from Pasadena by Jan and Dean; Love Is A Rose by Linda Ronstadt; Pasadena by Al Jolson

City code, bike riding on sidewalks: Pasadena and South Pasadena: No riding in front of schools, churches, other places of public assembly except where allowed by sign. In both cities plus LA bikers must be courteous to peds. In San Marino cycling is allowed except when signed otherwise.

Rent 'n Ride: Incycle Bicycles, 175 S Fair Oaks Avenue, 626.577.0440; Around the Cycle, 1270 Lincoln Ave, 765.6601. Shops: Trek, 323 S Arroyo Pkwy, 377.4114; Pasadena Cyclery, 1670 E. Walnut, 795.2866; Empire Bike Shop, 546 N. Fair Oaks Ave, 578.9350.

Further Info: See cityofpasadena.net/transportation/complete-streets/#bicycling/ for planned buffered bike lanes and cycletracks in Pasadena.

Arroyo Seco Bike Trail & Heritage Square   PA1

Just south of Pasadena is the Arroyo Seco Bike Trail, which is actually in South Pasadena and Los Angeles. It follows a portion of the route of the Cycle-Way, a "bicycle freeway" constructed of green-painted wooden planks that ran about 9 miles from the Hotel Green in Pasadena to the Plaza in Los Angeles for a toll of 10 cents. It operated from around 1880 to the early 1900s, but like most cool things of yesteryear in Los Angeles, the advent of the motorcar also put an end to the bicycle as a principal mode of travel and the Cycle-Way was no more. The current version of the Cycle-Way consists of a 2.4-mile Class I trail along the east bank of the concrete-lined Arroyo Seco channel. It is mostly tree-shaded by oaks and sycamores, including a nice leafy separation from the adjacent 110 Freeway that reduces its impact. Some portions are closed during and after rain events that cause stream flow and flooding of the trail.

The trail passes several parks that you can explore and also stage from as described in "Access." Heading south are occasional views of the LA skyline, and views of the local mountains in the other direction. Although not a destination trail because of its short distance and lack of fabulousness, you can combine a jaunt on the trail with a visit to a historic district to the south, or take a more ambitious road ride north through the valley to the Rose Bowl (ride PA2).

Distance: 5.8 miles + option to combine with PA2. Time: 45 minutes
Route & Bike: Easy. Flat/gradual slope. South end of trail (Montecito Rec Center): 415 feet elevation. North end of trail near York: 540 feet. Paved Class I and short Class III with option for extended Class III.
Seasons: All. Best on sunny mild day when Heritage Square Museum is open.
Facilities: Restrooms and water in parks along route.
Knocks & Hazards: On Class I trail, clueless peds, possible lurkers, graffiti, broken glass. Optional rides: Elsewhere, on-street riding, mostly no bike lanes. Rattlesnakes. Mountain lions (less so this far south in arroyo).
Bike 'n Brunch: None along Arroyo Seco Trail, but some nearby. From Ave 43, west one block to Figueroa are several fast food franchises including Subway. At north end of trail, a few blocks east at 266 Monterey is Charlie's Coffee House. In the other direction on York are several fast food places a couple of blocks west.
Further Info: Check before going: heritagesquare.org

Access: Parking for the Class I trail is found at Montecito Heights Recreation Center, 4545 Homer Street. Exit SR 110 (Arroyo Seco Parkway) at 43rd Street and go east, then turn left on Homer to the center. Other trailheads are at Hermon Park, 5566 Via Marisol; Sycamore Grove Park, 4702 N Figueroa St; and Ernest Debs Park, 4235 Monterey Rd.

Rail 'n Ride: Metro Rail Gold Line's Heritage Square/Arroyo stop is on the corner of Pasadena Ave and French St. To get to the ride start from the station, cross Pasadena and ride up Carlotta Boulevard to 43rd, passing the El Alisol historic house. Turn right on 43rd to cross the 110 Freeway and reach Homer Street. Ride to the left to reach the Montecito Rec Center trailhead, or to the right to reach Heritage Square Museum.

The Ride: For a worthwhile excursion that combines exercise with a cultural experience, start at the Montecito Rec Center and ride north up the trail to its end. The trail ends before the York Avenue Bridge, at the San Pasqual Stables. If you don't mind on-road riding and some hills, consider doing ride PA2 to continue farther north through a more scenic stretch. After you are done, ride back down the trail to ride start, then continue south on Homer Street for about 0.5 mile until it ends at the Heritage Square Museum.

Heritage Square contains eight preserved historic Victorian structures from the 1800s that were saved from demolition and transported here. The museum purveys the story of the first one hundred years of California statehood, and period-dressed docents lead tours when it is open on Friday to Sunday and holiday Monday afternoons (fee). There are other historic buildings in this area, including the stone Lummis Home, El Alisol, on the corner of 43rd and Carlotta. If you cycle in the morning you can reach Heritage Square by the time it opens in the afternoon.

Arroyo Seco Road Ride and the Rose Bowl PA2

The Kenneth Newell Bikeway is a Class III (with some Class II) route designated by the city through its most scenic area along the Arroyo Seco. In general, the most interesting vistas are northbound, when a tall art deco bridge and public buildings, the Rose Bowl, and the surrounding foothills come into view.

Distance: 12 to 16 miles. Time: 1 to 2 hours
Route & Bike: Moderate. Mostly Class III roadway with slow-moving traffic; for any bike. Topography varies from flat to moderate hill climbs. More level along the arroyo edge and around the Rose Bowl. Arroyo Drive at San Pasqual: 670 feet; Arroyo Blvd at California: 734 feet; Rose Bowl: 780 feet; Arroyo Blvd east of (beyond) Rose Bowl: 970 feet. Downtown (Memorial Park Gold Line stop): 875 feet. North end of bikeway: 1,100 feet. E-bike edge.
Seasons: All. Best on sunny, mild uncrowded weekday.
Facilities: Restrooms and water in Brookside Park.
Knocks & Hazards: Riding with traffic. Rattlesnakes. Mountain lions. One was photographed in upper end of Arroyo Seco near JPL in 2008. Golf ball hazard around Rose Bowl Loop. Summer heat and smog.
Bike 'n Brunch: Brookside Restaurant at the golf course, along the Rose Bowl recreation trail northeast of the stadium is popular for breakfast and lunch. If you ride up the hill or take the Gold Line into downtown Pasadena, there are countless choices in the Old Pasadena district. South Pasadena city center is a Gold Line stop, and is 0.5 mile east on Mission St from Arroyo Dr just south of the 110 Freeway. Heirloom Café at Meridian Ave is popular with cyclists.
Further Info: rosebowlstadium.com; Dining in Old Pasadena: oldpasadena.org.

Access: Either do this ride as an extension of PA1, or park along the route. Lower Arroyo Park has a parking lot along San Pasqual Avenue. From the 110 Freeway, exit York and go west then north on San Pasqual to the lot on the right just before the bridge. Brookside Park just south of the Rose Bowl also has free parking.

The Ride: From the north end of the Arroyo Seco Trail (PA1) turn right on an access road that leads to Marmion Way/Arroyo Verde (mile 0). Turn left and ride to Pasadena Avenue, then turn right. Bear left at the first opportunity onto Arroyo Drive (0.4) and follow it past Arroyo Seco Golf Course and over the 110 Freeway (0.9). Reach Arroyo Seco Park on the other side, which is another potential staging point. Parking is along San Pasqual Avenue. Arroyo Drive merges with Arroyo Boulevard at San Pasqual Ave (1.4). Arroyo Boulevard emerges at the edge of the canyon at mile 1.75 in this very beautiful section of Pasadena. At around mile 1.8, the signed Kenneth Newell Bikeway veers to the right onto Grand Avenue, and you can go that way if you like to see some Pasadena neighborhoods, although it is much hillier.

Otherwise, continue winding your way along the edge of the pretty canyon above Lower Arroyo Park, as the official bikeway rejoins the road at Arbor Street (2.7). See Option 1 for a route to Old Pasadena from here. Ahead is the historic concrete-arched "Colorado Street Bridge" (1913, retrofitted 1993) towering overhead with its Beaux Arts arches. Pass under the bridge (3.0) and then look up to the right at the Spanish Revival building atop the hill. The Richard H. Chambers U.S. Court of Appeals Building was originally a hotel, then a multi-use federal building and has undergone renovation as a historic structure. The next massive bridge up ahead carries the Ventura Freeway, and the view of the mountains through the bridge is classic. The familiar-looking Rose Bowl stadium next comes into view. First ride past Brookside Park (large parking lot, tennis, aquatic center, restrooms, Kidspace Children's Museum).

The Rose Bowl Loop is a separated pedestrian path along roadways that runs 3.3 miles around the Rose Bowl and Brookside Golf Course. It intersects Arroyo Boulevard at Seco Street (4.0), and goes along the side of each street that is closest to the Rose Bowl or golf course. Cyclists are expected to ride clockwise on the adjacent low-traffic roadways, just outside of the delineators. You can also ride another 3.3 miles north from the Rose Bowl on the designated bikeway, although it gets much hillier. To do that, follow the Kenneth Newell Bikeway signs that continue along Arroyo Boulevard through neighborhoods to the east of the Rose Bowl. You can also take the Rose Bowl Loop to its northeast corner, and ride up the hill on Rosemont to meet up with Arroyo Boulevard there. The route crosses over I-210, and becomes Windsor Avenue. A Jack-In-The-Box is on the left.

Follow the bike route signs that will lead you on a series of jogs (take the first left on Weimer/right on Yucca/left on Woodbury/right on Arroyo) to La Canada Verdugo Road. At that point turn left to follow the road to its end past the Hahamonga Watershed Park near athletic fields just south of the NASA Jet Propulsion Laboratories (JPL). Or, continue straight from Arroyo and La Canada Verdugo, down Arwin Street, then left on Windsor Avenue to the end of the east arm of the bike route in the park as well.

Option 1: Rail 'n Ride/Old Pasadena Metro Rail's Gold Line stops near the south end of the Arroyo Seco Bike Trail, and also in downtown Pasadena, where the best Bike 'n Brunch options are found in the Old Pasadena district. It also continues on to the San Marino/Huntington Gardens area as described in PA3. From the Memorial Park station near Old Pasadena, restaurants start about a block south, and are concentrated in the blocks defined by Holly (N), Arroyo Parkway (E), Green (S), and Pasadena (W). Explore the interesting alleys, sidewalk cafés, galleries, and shops in this district. Street riding is not the greatest downtown, but at time of writing sidewalk riding is still allowed.

To cycle from Arroyo Blvd to Old Pasadena, take Arbor St east to Orange Grove Blvd. Turn left, then right on Del Mar Blvd. Across the 210 Freeway turn left on Class II Pasadena Ave and reach the district in a few blocks. You can also use Metro Rail to do a one-way mostly downhill trip by taking the train to Old Pasadena (Memorial Park stop), making your way downhill to Arroyo Seco, heading south on the Class III and Class I route, and taking the train back to your home station from the Heritage Square stop. The only problem with that plan is that the best vistas are in the other direction.

San Marino and The Huntington PA3

Distance: 5 miles, moderate, paved, any bike. E-bike edge.

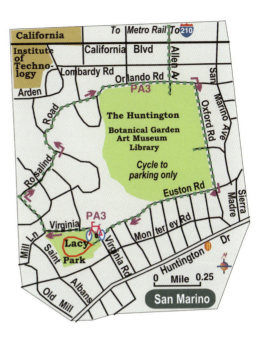

San Marino is known for The Huntington—a 120-acre botanical garden, art museum, library containing rare volumes, tea garden and café; huntington.org. Ride PA3 is a hilly route that passes the city's stately mansions and follows the perimeter of The Huntington property. East from Pasadena take I-210 to the Sierra Madre exit, southbound. Turn right at Huntington Dr, right on Virginia Rd and park near lovely Lacy Park ($4 admission weekends). Cycle north on Virginia, then right on Rosalind, and follow the route shown on the map. Via Metro Rail Gold Line get off at Allen Ave and cycle south 1.4 miles on the Class III road or sidewalk to join the loop at The Huntington's Orlando Rd entrance. For food, detour south on Oxford to Huntington Dr. Across the road restaurants offer sushi, Chinese, seafood, coffee, ice cream, etc. Add miles by cycling flatter but less interesting neighborhoods south of Huntington Dr.

Catalina Island

Santa Catalina (aka "Catalina") Island is located about 22 miles from the mainland, the landmark that the sun sets behind for millions watching from the LA/Orange County coast. The southern-most of the Channel Islands, it is 22 miles in length and contains two towns, the small unincorporated Two Harbors in the north and the main town of Avalon to the south, separated by a rugged Catalina Conservancy-run wilderness area where a herd of buffalo roams. Catalina is the main destination for mainland boaters who moor at the two towns, although the vast majority arrive by passenger ferry at the Cabrillo Mole in Avalon. Catalina Express boats leave from ports along our rides in San Pedro/LA Harbor (LA3) (also with limited service to Two Harbors), downtown Long Beach (LO1), and Dana Point (DP1). Catalina Flyer catamarans depart from Newport Beach (NB1). Crossings take between 70 and 90 minutes and cost $30–$40 (+ $3.50 per bike) each way. Avalon, which is also a frequent port of call for the LA-Mexico cruise ships, has the feel of a Mediterranean village with its curved harbor filled with pleasure craft, a shoreline promenade lined with restaurants, shops and parks, and its landmark casino/museum/ballroom, all backed by steep hills. Avalon is the site of our easy scenic bike ride, but more adventurous mountain bikers may consider cycling between Avalon and Two Harbors on very hilly dirt roads and trails. Membership in Catalina Conservancy is required for cycling outside of the two towns.

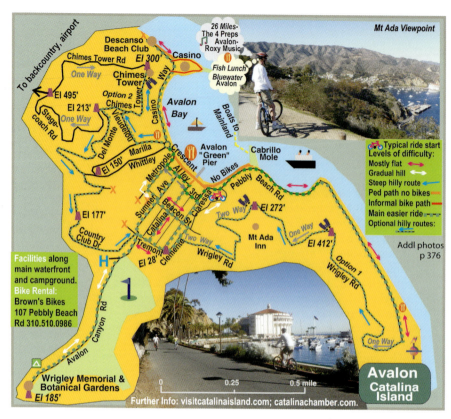

Avalon—A Mediterranean Island Village CAT1

Details: 5–8.5 miles + options. Easy with e-bike edge options. Paved, any bike.

The Ride: From the Crescent promenade (no bikes) cycle along oceanfront Pebbly Beach Rd to Buffalo Nickel restaurant at the heliport (1.0). Watch for some service vehicles and tourists in golf carts. An industrial stretch follows to road's end at the power plant (1.3). Turn around to ride start (2.6), or try the Option up the hill to the right. Cycle through town and from the promenade at Metropole (3.1) Casino Way leads along the waterfront to the historic Casino (3.5). Pedal around the small peninsula, then continue on St. Catherine Way along the coast to the entrance to Descanso Beach Club (3.75), where you can rent a beach cabana or enjoy the café. Return to explore downtown (5.5). Most restaurants are along the seaside promenade and adjacent streets. Ride the gradual but very noticeable grade up Avalon Canyon Road from Tremont St to the impressive Wrigley Monument & Botanical Garden ($7) (6.75). En route pass a golf course in a canyon with a variety of trees and birds, and Hermit Gulch bike/ped campground (restrooms). Return to your ride start (8.5).

Options (strenuous): The 1-mile 400-ft climb up Mt Ada via one-way Wrigley Rd from the end of Pebbly Beach Rd is doable in lo-gear or e-bike with reward of great harbor vistas. Watch your speed on the 1-mile downhill on the two-way road section from Mt. Ada Inn. On the northwest side of town follow the steep two-way route to Chimes Tower for a scenic viewpoint. See the map for other options here. Or pay to transport your bike to Airport in the Sky for a generally downhill ride (with some uphills) on dirt roads back to town. For even more adventure, ride across the island on the hilly dirt roads and trails.

5. Orange County

Los Angeles County melds into Orange County (OC) in a seamless mass of humanity linked together by freeways whose first name is always "The." The majority of the people live in a wide alluvial basin that is fronted by sandy beaches and backed by coastal mountains, though the basin gives way to coastal hills toward the south end of the county. For us, the best feature of OC, besides Disneyland and California Adventure, is the fabulous scenic cycling available year round, especially along the coast. *OC's overview map is combined with Los Angeles on page 80.*

Starting from the Los Angeles County border at Long Beach, one can experience scenic cycling all the way down the coast, and most of it is along Class I bike trails. After an optional connection through Seal Beach, our first fabulous bike ride is found in Huntington Beach (ride HB1), where a delightful 8-mile bike trail runs adjacent to the beach. A connection on side streets leads to Newport Beach and both a great beachfront ride (NB1) and a memorable pedal around a large wetlands wildlife preserve (NB2). More scenic side street cycling through Corona Del Mar leads to another fabulous, though short, beachfront trail at Crystal Cove State Park (NB3), with an optional novice (or advanced) mountain bike trek inland (NB4).

The next stretch involves the narrow curvy roads of spectacular but bike-unfriendly Laguna Beach. We recommend transporting your bike through Laguna, and perhaps taking a stroll on the bluff-top Heisler Park Trail just north of downtown, followed by a walk along the beach boardwalk and through the charming village. You can also attempt a couple of acceptable rides we have put together (LB1 and 2) if you prefer to tour it on two wheels. In Dana Point, Salt Creek Beach has a short but spectacular beach path with hilly connections inland (SV2).

Dana Point Harbor is the next fabulous cycling destination (DP1), with disjointed but fun riding available around the harbor, Doheny State Beach, and up to the Spanish village of San Juan Capistrano (SJ1). A Class I path leads to the San Clemente beach trail (SC1), with the option of pedaling farther south along the coast through Camp Pendleton Marine Base to Oceanside in San Diego County (SC3). You can also use rail service to take you back as far north as San Juan Capistrano, or even to Irvine or Tustin to connect back to Newport Beach.

If it's foggy or crowded on the beach trails you can find plenty of cycling opportunities inland. The Santa Ana River tumbles out of the San Bernardino Mountains and once created huge floods across the county until it was dammed and channelized. A bike trail now runs along most of its length (SAR1, 2, and 3), similar to the San Gabriel River Trail in Los Angeles County, connecting to the Huntington Beach trail. A separate section of the Santa Ana River trail runs through Riverside and San Bernardino Counties (R1).

Numerous OC wilderness mountain bike parks offer novices some nice scenic options (NB4, TU2, CH1, OR2, SV4, 5, 6, 8, and 11, F1 and 2). Many pretty local parks contain enough paved trails to keep a young family happy for an afternoon (HB2, FV1, IR2, OR2). Irvine has bike paths throughout; IR1 connects to Newport Beach and to the foothills as part of a Mountains to the Sea Trail (TU1). Aliso Creek Trail in Saddleback Valley (SV1) is yet another scenic regional path. Most cities have some sort of bike trails, but we concentrated on the longer more scenic ones. So, strap on your Mickey Mouse helmet, saddle up, and enjoy the rides!

Climate Data for Newport Beach (NOAA 1981 to 2010 normals)												
Month	Jan	Feb	Mar	Apr	May	Jun	Jul	Aug	Sep	Oct	Nov	Dec	Totals
Average High °F	64	64	64	66	66	68	71	73	73	71	66	64	67.5
Average Low °F	48	50	51	54	57	60	63	64	63	59	52	48	55.8
Precipitation, inches	2.60	2.54	2.25	0.70	0.18	0.08	0.02	0.09	0.30	0.28	1.02	1.59	11.65

Climate Data for Anaheim (Source: The Weather Channel)													
Month	Jan	Feb	Mar	Apr	May	Jun	Jul	Aug	Sep	Oct	Nov	Dec	Totals
Average High °F	71	71	73	76	78	81	87	89	87	82	76	70	78.4
Average Low °F	48	48	51	53	57	61	65	65	63	58	52	47	55.7
Precipitation, inches	2.86	3.08	1.90	0.80	0.28	0.10	0.03	0.01	0.25	0.72	1.38	2.02	13.43

Huntington Beach

Huntington Beach exploded in population during the 1960s and 1970s and now is home to about 190,000 people, the largest Orange County beach city. The main downtown and entertainment area surrounds Main Street and the municipal pier. The city is known for its year-round consistent surf break that has earned it the nickname "Surf City, USA." A top-notch beach trail extends along the entire length of the city's coastline (HB1), connecting with the Santa Ana River Regional Trail (SAR1), and linking to the Newport Beach rides to the south (NB1 and 2). HB Central Park located 2 miles inland is popular with birdwatchers and families to bike around (HB2).

Surf City Beach Trail   HB1

Remember that Jan & Dean song, "Surf City"? Plan to be humming it while pedaling this fabulous ride along the surfers' paradise that is Huntington Beach. This 8.5-mile long beach trail offers the best of easy riding—long flat stretches of paved trail, interesting views of the ocean surf and scores of surfers, a pier, and plenty of Bike 'n Brunch opportunities. While the surrounding terrain is flatter and the trail farther from the water when compared with the Santa Monica/South Bay ride, it offers plenty of its own rewards, especially when some elevation is achieved along Bluff Park north of the pier. On an uncrowded day, you can open up and cruise for miles with minimal inter-

ruption. On a crowded day, well, there are still some stretches that are not overrun with beach goers. You can combine the ride with a bird-watching stroll through the adjacent Bolsa Chica Ecological Reserve, and you can also take advantage of ride extensions in three directions.

Tunes: Surf City by Jan & Dean; Surf Beat by Dick Dale; Good Vibrations by The Beach Boys; Pacific Coast Highway by Nils.

Eats: Waterfront breakfast or lunch at Sandy's or Duke's at the pier, or picnic on the beach.

Distance: 17 miles round trip + options. Time: 2 hours.

Route & Bike: Easy to moderate based on distance and wind. Flat except for a small incline onto bluffs north of the pier. Paved Class I beach trail mostly in good condition with some bumps and blowing sand. Any bike will do, although a hybrid or fatter tire is your best bet. Many fast-moving road bikers cycle along Pacific Coast Highway (PCH, Hwy 1) due to peds and the 5 mph speed limit in congested areas of the trail. E-bike edge: Combine with other rides, and beat coastal headwinds.

Seasons: All. May be closed during occasional winter flooding events in the lowlands around the Bolsa Chica area in the north. Best on sunny off-season weekday with minimal wind. During busy days, mornings are best before crowds accumulate.

Facilities: Restrooms and water in parks along route.

Knocks & Hazards: Road noise from PCH. On busy beach days (or any day) watch for inattentive people running across the trail from the parking lot to the beach. The beach is also lined with fire pits and on-shore breezes blow the smoke onto the trail. The pits are used mostly on summer evenings, but can be used during the day as well. Wind blows sand onto trail. Bikes/peds are not segregated. Low speed limit or dismount required at crowded areas near the pier at peak times. Rattlesnakes in optional Bolsa Chica Reserve hike.

Rent 'n Ride: Check near pier and trail for Zack's 714.536.0215 and Jack's 536.8328. Ray's Rentals, 24 Main, 374.8600; HB Cycles, 19729 Beach, 594.3844; Pedego E-Bikes, 301 5th, 465.2782; Bolt E-Bikes, 311 5th, 949.235.4274; EV Rideables, 220 Walnut, 800.470.8939; Wheel Fun, 21351 PCH, 714.536.4863. Bike shops: Jax, 401 Main St, 969.8684; Huntington Beach Bicycle Co, 328 Main, 842.4222

Camp 'n Ride (RV parks with hookups): Bolsa Chica State Beach's beachfront parking lot sites give those with a rear window a nice view of the surf. The City of Huntington Beach's Sunset Vista located next to the pier, open October through May only, reserve at sunsetvistacamping.huntingtonbeachca.gov. Waterfront RV Park, located on east side of PCH at Newland Ave across from the City Beach and next to power plant, 714.536.8316.

Bike 'n Brunch: The only beachfront restaurants along the trail are Sandy's or Duke's at the base of the pier and something new (2022) at the end. Snack bars that sell burgers in peak season are also scattered around the city and state parks along the trails.

If you venture off the trail, options abound. To the north is the community of Sunset Beach with numerous options along PCH. Huntington Beach's Main Street begins at the pier, and is lined with interesting international restaurants, many with outdoor patios. Hilton's Waterfront Beach Resort and the Hyatt Regency on PCH between Huntington St and Beach Blvd offer breakfast buffets and Sunday brunch with ocean views. Additional restaurants can be found in Newport Beach to the south.

City code, bike riding on sidewalks: Prohibited in business district, adjacent to schools, churches, recreational centers, playgrounds, pier or pier plaza. No locking bike onto pier.

Further Info: City: www.huntingtonbeachca.gov; Dining: surfcityusa.com.

Events: Taste of Huntington Beach in May; tastehb.com

Access the trail from any point from Sunset Beach, all through Huntington Beach, to Newport Beach. A connection from NB1 is described in that ride. To reach the north trailhead, make your way to PCH in Sunset Beach. The trailhead is in the cul de sac at the end of Warner Avenue, just west of Hwy 1. From I-405, take the Warner exit in Huntington Beach and follow it west 5.7 miles to the trailhead. Free parking, which may be hard to come by at peak times, is available in the Sunset Beach neighborhood north of the trailhead. Pay parking lots are also available in the state and city beaches along the trail. The south ends of Brookhurst Street and Magnolia Street have free on-street parking within an easy ride of park entrances across PCH.

The Ride: From the north trailhead begin your beach cruise. You may want to ride against the wind first to gauge the distance you would like to ride. An ocean beach is on your right, with the sight of beautiful crashing waves across a wide, sandy beach. Two oil platforms are close to shore, with several more in the distance, and Catalina Island can be seen beyond on clear days. Beach parking lots are on your left. This creates problems for riders on busy days because of all the people crossing the trail to get to the beach, many of whom do not watch for bikes first. Hence, the more off-peak you do this ride, the better.

Behind the parking areas is the busy PCH, beyond which is the Bolsa Chica Ecological Reserve, a great place for a walk (no bikes) with your binoculars and camera to view multitudes of sea and shore birds. We particularly enjoy watching pelicans dive for fish here. A free parking area for the reserve is located across PCH from the signaled north entrance to Bolsa Chica State Beach (mile 1.5). Another trailhead is at the visitor's center on Warner near PCH. See bolsachica.org for further info and a map showing the 3 miles of trail available.

The bike trail continues past the park's RV campground at mile 1.8 and additional beach parking areas, crosses over Tidal Inlet Channel which is the ocean's connection with the Bolsa Chica wetlands (2.5), and continues to the entrance to the very popular Dog Beach, which is across from the signal at Seapoint (2.9). You will climb gradually up to Bluff-top Park, a highlight of the trail (3.3). Look to the left across PCH at an oil production area. This is what the park you are now riding through looked like until the 1980s. From your perch on the bluffs you have a great view of the crashing waves that on many days will have scores of surfers competing for the best breakers, with the Huntington Beach Pier beyond. The posted speed limit here is 5 mph when pedestrians are present, or 10 mph otherwise. The path descends back to the beach (4.8).

The path curves around some condos before entering the vicinity of the pier (5.2). Flashing lights instruct bikers to dismount when the area gets overly crowded. Zack's stand serves food and rents bikes and other fun items, and is open more frequently than the other similar stands along the city and state beaches. The pier is the terminus of Huntington Beach's Main Street. If you make your way up to Main Street, you will find all kinds of interesting restaurants including a stretch lined with sidewalk cafés. Beachfront restaurants Sandy's and Duke's are situated at the foot of the pier and possibly a new seafood restaurant at the end to replace closed Ruby's by 2022.

From atop the pier (no bikes) you can take a closer look at surfers catching the waves, and there may even be a competition going on. South of the pier, a building to the left of the trail contains several restaurants, while beach volleyball nets are on the right. Farther along after the lifeguard headquarters you may see RV's parked in a lot on the left past the pier during fall through spring (5.6). This is city-operated Sunset Vista campground. Next, pass Hilton's Waterfront Beach Resort and the Hyatt Regency. The City Beach meets Huntington State Beach at PCH and Beach Boulevard, which serves as the entrance to both (6.3).

The trail along Huntington State Beach is not quite as scenic as the trails along Bolsa Chica and Huntington City beaches. The beach is wider, and the ocean appears as but a narrow slit behind it, while on the left beyond the beach parking lots and PCH are a mobile home park, an RV Park Campground at Newland Street (6.8), a large power plant, and the third largest sewage treatment plant west of the Mississippi. At mile 8 Brookhurst Street is across PCH. Consider an optional detour to the Talbert Marsh Trail up Brookhurst on the right, a good place to watch sea and shore birds. It ends at the Santa Ana River Trail, and you can take that back under PCH to rejoin the beach trail.

Next, cross a small bridge where you can ride to the end of a jetty (8.2). A fenced area protects a least tern preserve here. The second, larger bridge crosses the Santa Ana River (8.4). Just before the bridge, another trail veers off to the right, then circles down underneath the bridge. This is the 30-mile long paved Santa Ana River Class I Trail (See SAR1, 2, and 3). The bridge over the outflow of the river is only slightly elevated, but it does afford some nice views down the river to the breaking waves. The end of the Huntington Beach ride is the midpoint of the bridge, about 8.5 miles from the start, for a 17 mile round trip ride. Across the bridge are the city of Newport Beach and a 1.7-mile Class II trail connection to the Newport Balboa Bike Trail (Option 1).

Option 1: Connect to Newport Balboa Bike Trail ⭐ *Map P133; 1.7 miles each way, easy*

You can keep going south to the Newport Beach oceanfront promenade (NB1), Balboa Island, the Back Bay Wildlife Refuge (NB2), Corona Del Mar and Crystal Cove State Park (NB3 and 4). The HB1 bike trail ends on a sidewalk along PCH where bikes are allowed, or use the bike lane on the roadway. A commercial district with restaurants begins here and extends along PCH through most of Newport Beach. Make a right at the first light onto Orange St (0.3 miles). A small park with restrooms is at this corner. Turn left on Seashore Drive onto the two-way bike lane. This lane goes on until mile 1.6, with peek views of the ocean at each street crossing. There are no stop signs, so bikes can move along continuously. It can be dangerous at busy periods such as weekends when there are lots of cars and bikes going in all directions, not necessarily staying in the correct lane. An alley behind the homes is an option to avoid this mess, but is slower going. Turn right on 36th St to reach the northern entrance to the Newport Balboa Bike Trail (NB1) (1.7).

Huntington Beach Central Park   HB2

Distance: 4 miles, easy

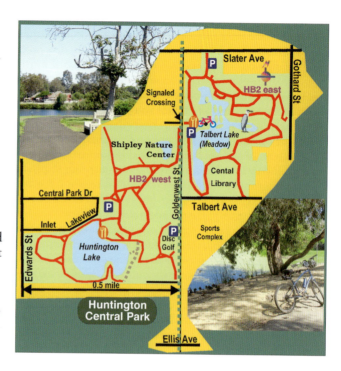

This pleasant park is a good location for a family outing on their two-wheelers, or for a casual Bike 'n Brunch when a long distance ride is not important. The park contains east and west sections divided by Goldenwest Street. The east section is prettier, with denser vegetation and paths meandering around Talbert Lake and meadows. However, that lake can dry up during draught periods. On the west side, Huntington Lake is kept full of water year round and stocked with fish. Huntington Beach Central Library on Talbert east of Goldenwest contains the largest collection of children's books west of the Mississippi.

The park is popular with birders, due to great habitat consisting of a variety of landscape zones. It is a stop along the Pacific Flyway for migrating birds and home to numerous resident birds. Shipley Nature Center in the park does bird counts. See shipleynature.org/birding/ for a typical species list, counts, and other info. If you park at the lot at Goldenwest Street and Rio Vista Drive, you have access to the Park Bench al fresco café, open for breakfast and lunch with a varied menu for humans and their pooches! Then pedal the park at your leisure, taking a loop around the perimeter and perhaps darting into the interior trails as well. To get to the west section of the park, cross Goldenwest with the light at Rio Vista, and find the path that goes to the left parallel to the road. It curves to the right into this expansive park that is mostly lawns with some trees. A paved trail loops around the center of the park.

At the southwest side of the park is pretty Huntington Lake, and Kathy May's Lakeview Cafe serving breakfast and lunch on a delightful outdoor patio is on its north shore. You can get in about 4 miles of riding in the park. To connect with HB1, a 3-mile (from Talbert) mostly Class II route begins south on Goldenwest for 1.25 miles, then right on Summit Drive until the end at Seapoint Street, and then left to ride to

The pond and meadow in the east section are great for bird watching.

Coast Highway and HB1. See huntingtonbeachca.gov; click "Visitors" and "Parks." Access: From I-405 take the Slater Avenue exit west to Goldenwest, then left. Prior to the light at Rio Vista get into the left turn lane to go into the parking lot. If that lot is full there are other lots that you can find by driving around the park perimeter.

Newport Beach

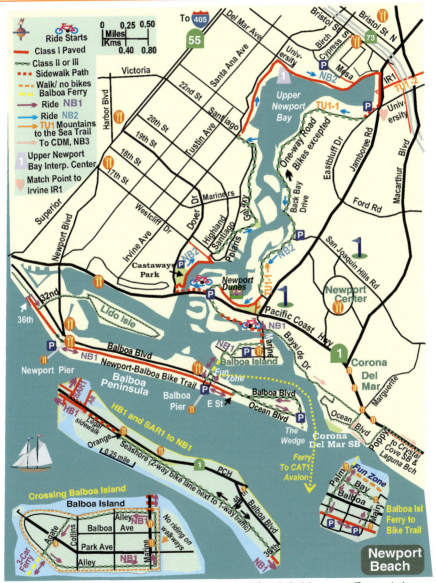

Newport Beach is a wealthy conservative city in The OC. Newport Center is its downtown, with high-rise office buildings surrounding the beautiful Fashion Island outdoor shopping mall, a worthwhile après ride destination. The Pacific coastline here runs mainly northwest-southeast, so one goes south or southwest to go to the beach. The Balboa Peninsula juts out from the northwest end of town and curves southeastward, protecting Newport Harbor, the largest private boat harbor in the West where so many waterfront mansions have docks in front to park their megayachts.

Several islands were created from harbor dredgings, which now contain tightly packed

The Newport-Balboa Bike Trail runs along the beach next to oceanfront homes

communities of expensive homes. Balboa Island is a popular destination, with a main street lined with shops and restaurants and pedestrian-only walkways surrounding it. A short bridge connects the island to the mainland at the end of Jamboree Road. A 3-car ferry connects the other side of Balboa Island to the peninsula, saving a long cumbersome drive and dealing with traffic and parking nightmares at peak beach times. While cars may have substantial waits to use the ferry during busy times, bikes can usually hop right on. The ferry lands at the Balboa Fun Zone, a mini amusement park in which the kids may enjoy spending some time. A short 3 blocks across the peninsula are miles of wide sandy ocean beaches, two piers, and lots of restaurants centered around them. A paved oceanfront promenade known as the Newport-Balboa Bike Trail runs for 3 miles along the peninsula. Ride NB1 encompasses Balboa Island, the ferry ride, and the beach promenade, for a total ride of 9.5 miles.

The Back Bay is a colloquial term for the inland delta of Upper Newport Bay created by San Diego Creek that is adjacent to Newport Harbor. The Back Bay is one of the last remaining examples of a coastal wetland estuary ecosystem in Southern California, as most of the others have fallen victim to development or flood control projects. The countless bird species and the huge flocks using the Pacific Flyway that stop here are testament to the importance of the bay. It is one of the best bird watching areas in North America, where up to 35,000 birds can be seen here at one time during the spring and fall migrations. Endangered or threatened birds include brown pelican, light-footed clapper rail, California least tern, peregrine falcon, Savannah sparrow, and black rail. The grasslands and coastal sage scrub of the surrounding bluffs provides habitat for the threatened California gnatcatcher, San Diego cactus wren, and burrowing owl.

Much of the surrounding land was designated as Orange County's Upper Newport Bay Regional Park. It is a popular place for ecology field trips, kayak tours, walking, and biking. You are definitely in an urban wilderness, surrounded by development, and in the flight path of busy John Wayne International Airport (SNA). But, in between planes, you can find quiet places to meditate on the complexities of nature. The 10.3-mile Back Bay Loop ride (ride NB2) encircles the preserve via Class I, II, and III segments. The route passes some new bluff-top parks along its west side, which does add some hills, but also spectacular vistas of the bay and out to the ocean.

Rides NB1 and NB2 can be cycled in combination for a 21.4-mile half-day adventure, or split up into segments. A 0.8-mile Class II/III route connects the two rides. You can also just do portions of either of the rides. Connections are available to the

Huntington Beach (HB1) and Santa Ana River trails (SAR1) to the northwest, the San Diego Creek (IR1) and Mountains to the Sea (TU1) trails to the east, and the Crystal Cove trails (NB3 and 4) to the southeast after a Class III pedal through beautiful Corona Del Mar.

Rent 'n Ride: Ray's Rentals, 601 E Balboa, 949.220.7245; Seaside Bike Rentals, 105 Main, 270.6911; Balboa Beach and Bicycle, 204 Washington, 220.4884; Sports Rents, 329 Marine, 600.9941; West Newport Velo, 6000 W Coast Hwy, 612.8389; PedegoE-Bikes, NewportPier, 723.0043; Newport Bch Rentals, 309 Palm, 630.5600.

Camp 'n Ride: Newport Dunes Resort, ideally located along Back Bay Dr, 800.765.7661. See also the Huntington Beach (HB1) and Crystal Cove (NB3) rides.

Bike 'n Brunch: The beach area has a plethora of restaurants, mostly near the piers and the ferry landing. Balboa Island has lots of choices along Marine Avenue. Along the Back Bay Loop there is the Back Bay Bistro at Newport Dunes with a nice patio. A Subway and Starbucks (popular with cyclists) is at Bayside Drive and PCH. Or take a 0.8-mile detour to Bristol Street for fast food and other restaurants. See the ride descriptions for more details.

City code, bike riding on sidewalks: Prohibited except when indicated otherwise. Sidewalks in our rides are legal, but Poppy to NB3 is questionable. See city's bike map.

Further Info: City: newportbeachca.gov; Ferry info: balboaislandferry.com; Restaurants: newportbeachdining.com.

Access: From I-405 in Irvine, take the Jamboree Road exit and head southwest (if you are southbound on I-405 turn right, if northbound, turn left). Your starting point will depend on how much of the two connected rides you wish to do. If you are doing the whole thing, then park at any of the trailheads mentioned below.

In 2.5 miles you will have a view of the Back Bay area and reach Eastbluff North. If you are only doing the Back Bay Loop (NB2) you can turn right and park along the road, then do the loop clockwise. The next trailheads for NB2 are farther along Jamboree. Turn right at the light at San Joaquin Hills Road and find parking at the end of the road. Or, turn right at the light at Back Bay Drive and look for parking along the road near the Hilton and Newport Dunes resorts.

For the optimal, central trailhead to do both rides (and to reach our mile 0 of NB2), continue on Jamboree, reaching Pacific Coast Highway (PCH) in 5.2 miles. Turn right on PCH and descend the hill, then turn right at the first light onto Bayside Dr. Find parking along the road. Cycle NB2 in the clockwise direction. To do only the Balboa Island/Ocean ride (NB1), continue on Jamboree past PCH. At the first light (Bayside) turn left and find free parking along the road. Don't park in the Bayside Center to the right (Pavillions Grocery, Bayside Restaurant) since they tow. Or, cross the bridge onto Balboa Island straight ahead and find free on-street parking there. The ferry terminal is to the right from the bridge, at the south end of Agate Street.

Balboa Island and the Newport Ocean Beaches   NB1

Tunes: Beach Baby by First Class; Someday by Sugar Ray; Secrets of the Sea by Billy Bragg & Wilco

Eats: Chile Cheese Omelet al fresco at Charlie's Chile or Fish Lunch! at the Crab Cooker

Distance, round trip: 9.5 miles + options. Time: 1.5 hours

Route & Bike: Easy, flat. Paved. Mostly Class I; some easy Class II and III. Any bike. E-bike edge: Coastal headwinds. Lots of opportunity to combine with other rides.

Seasons: All. Best on sunny uncrowded off-season weekday with minimal wind and no fog. On peak days best in morning before beach crowds arrive.

Facilities: Water, restrooms in beach parks and on Balboa Island side of ferry crossing.

Knocks & Hazards: Beach promenade can be very crowded to the point of unrideable in places. Walk-bike zone and parking lot riding near Newport Pier. Clueless peds on trail. Street crossings and bike lanes next to traffic on Balboa Island. Slow (8 mph) speed limit on promenade.

The ride starts on the west (right) sidewalk on the north end of the bridge to Balboa Island. You can ride on the sidewalk paths over the bridge, but bikes are unfortunately not allowed on the scenic perimeter trail around Balboa Island. We typically duck into the alley to the right just past the south end of the bridge to avoid cycling through the crowded commercial district that begins immediately (and we use the corresponding alleys across the island on the return). Carefully make your way down the alley and then onto side streets as you head west, and then south, ending up on Agate Street. Navigate down Agate Street past the cars waiting to get on the ferry.

At the ferry terminal (mile 0.8), walk your bike down the ramp on either side of the boat, and sit on the bench, holding your bike. The three cars will load in the middle. An attendant comes around and collects the fares ($1.50 adult with bike in 2021) and can give change. The ferry ride is short but sweet. Watch the bevy of boats darting about from junkers to multi-million dollar wonders. Across the bay are the ferry docks at the Balboa Fun Zone, complete with Ferris wheel and bumper cars. You are now on the Balboa Peninsula, a thin strip of sand with Newport Bay on one side and the open Pacific on the other. For geology buffs, this area straddles the Newport-Inglewood earthquake fault and has high liquefaction potential.

The Balboa Island to Balboa Peninsula 3-car ferry.

From the ferry, ride straight down Palm Street, cross Balboa Boulevard at the light, then continue one block until the paved Class I bike path crosses (1.0). The speed limit is 8 mph, and the trail is not especially wide for the amount of use it gets. It can be impossibly crowded at peak times, especially near the piers, so is recommended during off-peak times. Watch for children darting across the trail and numerous oblivious pedestrians. In contrast, in the off-season, especially on sunny weekdays, the riding can be sublime. From this point, pedal eastward (left) and reach the Balboa Pier area in two blocks where there is a large parking lot, an option for a place to park to skip the ferry portion. Summer weekends can be a zoo here, though, with parking lot gridlock common. The beach is wide and sandy, with the hills of Newport your backdrop, and on clear winter days, snow-covered mountains to the north.

As you cross Main Street, look to the left and notice the commercial district including the popular eat/drink spot Cabo Cantina on the corner. To the right is the Balboa

Pier, which has a Ruby's diner at the end of it. Peninsula Park at the base of the pier has restrooms and a playground. The trail runs adjacent to beachfront houses and the wide sandy beach with the ocean off in the distance. This portion of the trail is a tad less crowded than the section to the west. When you reach E Street (1.5) you can turn around if you are only doing the Class I trail that ends just beyond here. Our ride continues by turning down E Street, then turning right on Balboa Boulevard. Bear right on G Street and left on the lightly traveled Ocean Boulevard.

As an even lower-traffic option, take the alley behind Ocean Boulevard (East Ocean Front). Either way, oceanfront homes block your view. When the road T's at Channel Road (2.2), turn right and ride until the sand starts at West Jetty View Park, where there is a water fountain. As you face the ocean to the south, the busy entrance channel to Newport Beach Harbor is on the left, and beyond is Corona Del Mar State Beach. To the right farther along is The Wedge, an area next to the jetty with a notoriously large surf break popular with body surfers and body boarders, allowed at different times by local ordinance.

Return back down Channel Road, but continue on it until it curves to the left and becomes Balboa Boulevard. Follow it back to E Street (mile 3.3), and turn left to return to the Class I bike trail. Turn right, and follow it back past the Balboa Pier to where you entered on Palm Street (3.8). Keep going along the trail. It passes beachfront homes on the right, with the ocean beach on the left. Check out Newport Elementary School, with its playing field on the beach (4.8). Can you imagine going to school here? When you reach the Newport Pier area, signs warn you to walk your bike, and you should obey (5.4). Charlie's Chile is a popular breakfast spot on the right. A restaurant is typically open at the end of the pier, and there are lots of restaurants along the trail, and down side streets that cross over to the harbor side. The funky Crab Cooker is eternally popular (from the pier, go to Balboa Blvd, then left 1 block).

Families beware, after the pier you must cycle through a busy parking lot to continue on the oceanfront trail. The beach path tends to be the most crowded from here until its western end, as it is the easiest accessible, with lots of popular beaches along the way. Enjoy views up the coast over the beach up toward Huntington Beach. The Class I trail ends at 36th Street (6.1). Our ride NB1 turns around here. The connection to the Huntington Beach Ride.(see Option 1 below) begins down 36th Street. Turn around and head back east along the oceanfront trail. The views in this direction down the coast encompass the hills of Newport Coast down to Laguna Beach. Consider touring Lido Isle on the return (Option 2).

Option 1: North Connection to Surf City Ride (HB1) ⭐ *1.7 miles each way*. At the northwest end of the beach path turn right on 36th and left on Seashore Dr to continue north to HB1 and SAR1. A 2-way bike lane runs along the west side of Seashore Drive. This path can be unpleasant, since oncoming bikes may be diverted into your lane by improperly parked cars or other hazards, sending you off into traffic lanes. It is a low-speed side street, so with some caution you should be fine. At Orange Street, turn right and make your way to the sidepath that runs along the southwest side of PCH to the left. The trail crosses over the mouth of the Santa Ana River. The midpoint of the bridge is the southern end point of HB1. The start of the Santa Ana River Bike Trail (SAR1) is across the bridge, as described in rides SAR1 and HB1.

Option 2: Lido Isle ⭐ *3.3 miles total*
At 32nd Street cycle across the peninsula and pedal the perimeter of Lido Island, a popular low-traffic ride around that exclusive enclave, then return to this point.

Follow the Class I beach trail all the way back to Main Street at the Balboa Pier (8.6). Turn left onto Main Street and pedal through the Balboa commercial district, crossing Balboa Avenue at the light. You can either make the next left onto Bay Avenue, or ride to the next block, then walk your bike through the Balboa Fun Zone if you want to get in on the fun, including arcades, a Ferris wheel, bumper cars, and the like. You can also rent a boat along here to explore the harbor. Both routes lead to Palm Street in 2 blocks, and the ferry dock for the Balboa Island Ferry (8.8).

Enjoy another ferry crossing, and carefully make your way down side streets and alleyways (but not the waterfront walkways) across Balboa Island as shown on the map inset, or explore other streets to see more of the island. Return to your starting point across the bridge for a total ride of 9.5 miles. At this point, you've barely worked off your clam chowder, so you should really continue on to the Back Bay Wildlife Refuge.

Option 3: Connect to Ride NB2, the Back Bay Wildlife Loop *0.8 mile each way.*
From the north end of the Balboa Island bridge, ride west on the south sidewalk bike path along Bayside Drive for 0.6 mile, then cross over at Harbor Island Drive to the bike lane on the north side. Reach PCH (0.8). Starbucks and Subway are on the right. Carefully cross at the light. This point is mile 0 if you are doing the entire Back Bay Loop (ride NB2). That ride continues on the sidewalk along PCH to the west. For an easy, flat, sampling of the wildlife refuge ride, try Option 4 instead of doing the NB2 loop.

Option 4: East Side of the Back Bay *8 miles round trip.*
See ride NB2 for more details on the features along the route. From PCH (mile 0) continue down Bayside Drive. After passing a mobile home park look for a paved trail on the right (0.2) with a sign indicating that it is closed at night. This trail passes behind Newport Dunes RV Resort and ends at Back Bay Drive (0.9). Turn left, and reach the entrance to the one-way road through the wildlife refuge (1.2). Then, pedal along that road next to the wetlands for as long as you desire, keeping in mind there may be an onshore breeze on your return.

The path winds around the side of the huge tidal wetland. Check out the interpretive signs and exhibits that have been installed along the route. The view of the wetlands and the surrounding bluffs changes around every bend. There are also hiking trails along the way that bring you into the brush or out closer to the marsh. The first half-mile follows a tidal channel and leads to the end of San Joaquin Hills Road, where there is ample parking along the road (1.7). At mile 2.2 is a large parking lot with porta-potties (sometimes), then at mile 3.8 the delightful flat trail betrays you with a steep climb to reach Eastbluff Drive at mile 4. You are rewarded with a great view across Upper Newport Bay from here. This is the end of the park road and an optional turnaround point or you can, of course, opt to turn around before climbing the hill.

Option 5: Connect to Corona Del Mar and Crystal Cove State Park
3.7 miles each way. Easy with a couple of hills. Class II and III roadways.
Bayshore Drive, which crosses Jamboree Road between PCH and Balboa Island, is also your gateway to Corona Del Mar and Crystal Cove State Park (Ride NB3) to the south. Head south along Bayshore Drive until it ends on Marguerite Avenue in about 1.5 miles. Turn right to reach the bluff-side coastline at Ocean Avenue (1.8). Be extra careful of car doors opening along here. Explore by turning right, and noting the entrance down to Corona Del Mar State Beach, which is worth exploring. A bluff-top park at the end of Ocean Boulevard is a favorite sunset watching spot, and offers a panoramic view over Newport Harbor (2.0).

Turn around and ride back down Ocean Boulevard along the bluffs until it ends at Poppy Street (2.6). Straight ahead is a walking trail leading down to an interesting rocky shoreline and pretty Little Corona Beach. Ride along Poppy Avenue to the northeast until you reach PCH (2.9). To the left down PCH is downtown Corona Del Mar with its shops, restaurants, and supermarket. To continue the ride, turn right and ride on the shoulder of PCH. There is also a sidewalk, handy for the return even if not totally legal. After passing a residential area and a golf course, watch for a trail entrance on the right. This is beautiful Crystal Cove State Park (3.7). See that ride (NB3) for details.

Back Bay Wildlife Refuge Loop   NB2

Tunes: Free Bird by Lynyrd Skynyrd; Bluebird by Buffalo Springfield; Birdland by Weather Report
Eats: Weekend Brunch at Back Bay Bistro

Distance: 10.3-mile loop. Option for 5.4-mile up and back. Time: 1 to 1.5 hours
Route & Bike: Moderate due to hills and headwinds. Paved, any bike. Mostly Class I, some easy Class II and III. Flat on east side of bay except for steep hill leading up to Eastbluff in northeast corner. West side has steep hill leading up the bluff from Dover, and rolling hills north of there. E-bike edge for hills and headwinds.
Seasons: All. Best on sunny uncrowded off-season weekday with minimal wind. In summer it is much less crowded than beach routes.
Facilities: Restrooms and water at Upper Newport Bay Muth Interpretive Center (closed Mondays and holidays). Detours to Bob Henry Park (past Castaways Park on Dover) and end of Harbor Island Dr. Sometimes port-a-potties along east path.
Knocks & Hazards: Clueless peds on trail, mostly on east side, not as bad as the beach trails. Sporadic slow moving vehicles on east side. Hills. East side subject to flooding, mudslides, and closures during and after strong winter storms.
Further Info: Back Bay: ocparks.com/parks/newport; newportbay.org; Birding: SeaAndSageAudubon.org; Park officials: 949.223.2290, unbic@ocparks.com. Kayaking: newportaquaticcenter.com, southwindkayaks.com.

The Ride: A loop around the entire Back Bay is possible via a combination of the Class I trails, "legal" sidewalks, and Class III residential surface streets. This route is of moderate difficulty because of several hills. To keep to the optimal side on the various sidewalks and remain closest to the bay, it's best to do this ride in the clockwise direction, and follow the blue Back Bay Loop signs printed on the pavement. This is one of our favorite rides, combining great scenery with a good workout.

Castaways Park offers over a half mile of coastal panoramas.

From the corner of Bayside Drive and Coast Highway (mile 0), ride west along the north sidewalk of PCH over the level bridge where you can stop for a vista of the Back Bay to the north and Newport Bay to the south. Take the first right on Dover Drive where you continue riding along the sidewalk. Look for a paved trail rising steeply up to the right (0.5) to the bluffs of Castaways Park. Signs instruct downhill riders in the other direction to walk their bikes for safety, and you may opt to walk up the short hill as well. For a gradual climb, follow the bike lane to the parking for Castaways Park.

Atop the bluff, curve to the right and reach a fabulous viewpoint that overlooks the Back Bay, Newport Center, Newport Harbor, and across the Balboa Peninsula to the ocean. A statue of a contemporary soldier adorns the park, a tribute to the First Battalion First Marine Division of Camp Pendleton and their heroic exploits since World War II. Also find benches, a water fountain, and a live display of some of the native plants found in this restored coastal scrub habitat. Enjoy a spectacular half-mile ride northward along the bluff, experiencing the million dollar views of the homes to the left. After the trail curves inland (1.2), take the first fork to the right that leads to the intersection of Polaris and Santiago. Go straight onto Santiago, taking it to the northeast through this upscale Newport Beach neighborhood until Galaxy Drive and turn right (1.7). Check out a great view of another section of the Back Bay at Galaxy View Park (2.0), which has a water fountain and view benches. Continue on Galaxy Drive until it turns and ends on Santiago (3.0).

Turn right, glide down the short hill, then right again onto the Irvine Avenue sidewalk that joins the "Brown Trail" bike path. Follow the paved Class I path parallel to Irvine Avenue over some rolling hills. Dirt pedestrian paths fan out to the right through the coastal scrub along the bluff. You can lock your bike and take a pleasant stroll here to stretch your legs. The path then curves to the right, next to a disconnected block of University Drive, and the entrance to the informative Muth Interpretive Center built in a unique earth-sheltered architecture style. It has full service restrooms when open (closed Mondays and major holidays) (4.4). Continue downhill to a scenic wooden bayfront boardwalk, then along additional paved bayside trails. The 1.2-mile stretch from here to Jamboree Boulevard is a good choice for a family ride because it is less crowded, there are no cars, and it goes through a beautiful nature preserve. It also features an adjacent equestrian path.

After the wooden boardwalk ends, note the first paved trail junction on the left. This leads to an optional route to get some food, and also an alternate place to park in a residential neighborhood and stage the ride. To park here, check the map to see how to take Birch Street to Mesa Drive. To ride to the restaurants, arrive at Mesa Drive from the main trail, and ride to Cypress Street. Turn right and ride to the end of the street and through a bike/ped passage that leads to the restaurants along Bristol Street South. Find El Pollo Loco, Foster Freeze, Burger King and Carl's Jr. to the left, and Kitayama Japanese (lunch weekdays) to the right. Return the same way to the trail.

Our main trail next curves to the right at Jamboree Road (5.6). Follow the curvature of the bay to the south, past a junction with the San Diego Creek Trail (IR1) (5.8), which is part of the Mountains to the Sea regional trail (TU1). A short detour on this trail, which goes under Jamboree Road, will take you along a nice riparian ecosystem that is usually great for bird watching, while farther along the trail continues to the University of California Irvine (UCI), William Mason Regional Park, and all through Irvine, enabling many miles of Class I suburban riding. See Irvine rides IR2 and IR3.

After passing the San Diego Creek Trail junction, our Back Bay Loop ascends a small hill as it nears Eastbluff Drive. The sidewalk continues up Eastbluff to another great viewpoint (6.2) with interpretive signs and benches. Turn right onto the one-way bike lane on Back Bay Drive. Be extra careful gliding down this steep hill, as one-way vehicle and bike traffic is traveling in the opposite direction. Vehicles are allowed on Back Bay Drive, but the speed limit is 15 mph, and not many make the journey in deference to the hordes of runners, walkers, and cyclists that use this path regularly.

It is a one-way road for cars in the northbound direction, and bikes share the road with cars for this portion. Bike and ped lanes are painted for southbound travelers. As would be expected, not everyone rides or walks where they are supposed to, so ride defensively.

During the busy summer months, we enjoy these wide paths compared to the crowded narrower beach paths. The next 3 miles are along the wildlife refuge, offering fantastic bird-watching opportunities. You may unfortunately experience an on-shore headwind along this stretch as well. The interpretive display and elevated walkway at Big Canyon Inlet is a good spot to bird-watch. Sometimes porta-potties are set up here. The intersection of San Joaquin Hills Road is next, which is another good place to park. After a few twists and turns, the south entrance to the Back Bay road is reached (9.1). On the right is the access road to the Back Bay Science Center, a place to learn about estuarine ecology of Newport Bay and ocean ecology, and how to promote natural resource conservation and stewardship throughout the watershed. See backbaysciencecenter.org for information on events and tours. Along its access road is the trailhead display platform for the Mountains to the Sea Trail that extends 22 miles inland through Irvine and Tustin to Irvine Regional Park. See that ride description in the Tustin section (TU1).

Pedal along Back Bay Drive past Newport Dunes resort (9.4). The café near the boat launch is a great place to stop for an al fresco meal. Take the bike path to the right, adjacent to the Newport Dunes entrance road. A short distance ahead on the trail, a paved path on the left ascends to Back Bay View Park atop the bluff. This preserved coastal sage ecosystem has a couple of benches and water fountain with a view of Newport Dunes and the bay beyond. If you are doing the entire ride you may want to skip this extra exertion. The Back Bay Loop trail continues around behind Newport Dunes. This section closes at dusk. Turn left onto Bayside Drive or its legal sidewalk (10.1) to your starting point at PCH (10.3). To connect back to the Balboa Island/Newport Ocean Beaches ride (NB1), cross PCH and ride in the bike lane, being careful to avoid any doors opening from the parked cars. At a stoplight for a pedestrian crossing you can begin riding on the sidewalk trail, reaching the bridge to Balboa Island in 0.8 mile.

The bike trail runs along the base of the bluffs in the beautiful Back Bay area. Cars are allowed 1-way, 15 mph.

Option 1: Ride the East Portion of the Back Bay ⭐ *5.4 miles total, easy.*
Just ride the flat portion of the east side of the Back Bay between Newport Dunes and the bottom of the hill up to Eastbluff Drive. Park along Back Bay Drive near Newport Dunes as allowed or along the road at the bottom of San Joaquin Hills Drive.

Bike 'n Boat Options: A great place to launch a hand-carried boat is at the east end of Sapphire Street on Balboa Island, where a public dock is available. Hand-carried boats can also be launched from any of the public beaches, or for a fee at Newport Dunes Resort. Many types of boat rentals are available at the Balboa Fun Zone. Kayak rentals for the Back Bay are available off of Bayside Drive just west of PCH. High-speed passenger ferries leave from the Fun Zone to Catalina Island, a great day or overnight adventure. See the Catalina Island section at the end of the Los Angeles County chapter.

Crystal Cove State Park

Once the only undeveloped stretch of coast in south Orange County, since the 1990s the northeast side of PCH between Newport Beach and Laguna Beach is now completely carpeted with multi million-dollar homes, timeshares, and golf courses. Luckily, the seaward side remains as Crystal Cove State Park, along with a section in the San Joaquin Hills to the east of PCH. The park consists of coastal bluffs and a beautiful beach below that extends for 3.2 miles. Spring wildflowers enhance the appeal of the bluffs' coastal scrub ecosystem. The Crystal Cove Promenade along PCH provides some dining options and a Trader Joe's grocery store that can supply a picnic for your ride. The state park also contains a group of historic early twentieth-century cottages, used in the movie *Beaches,* among others, which have been restored and are available for overnight stays. A beachfront restaurant in the district makes a great Bike 'n Brunch spot. The 2.7-mile ocean bluffs trail (NB3) is paved and the inland canyon trails (NB4) are popular with mountain bikers of all levels, including novices.

Distance, round trip: Coast/ocean bluffs: 5.4 miles. Inland trails: 6 miles (options for more advanced mountain biking). PCH Connector: 0.6 mile. Total easy to moderate combo ride: 12 miles.

Seasons: All. Best on sunny uncrowded off-season weekday.

Fees and rules: $15 fee in park lots. $5/hr in Los Trancos (historic dist) lot and others weekdays Oct-Apr. No fee to bike in. Leashed dogs allowed only on paved multi-use trail on coast section but not on beach or mountain bike trails. For complete info see crystalcovestatepark.com and www.parks.ca.gov/?page_id=644.

Rent 'n Ride: See NB1 and LB2.

Camp 'n Ride: Moro RV/tent campground is situated at the southeast end of Crystal Cove State Park on the inland side of PCH, with great ocean views and a highway undercrossing to the beach (but does not connect to the coastal bike trail NB3). It does have direct access to the inland mountain bike trails (NB4). Three primitive hike/mountain bike-in camps are located at the inland section of the park (permit/reservation required). See also HB1, DP1, SC1. Newport Dunes RV Resort is 3.5 miles to the northwest (NB2). The restored historic Crystal Cove cottages are available for rent along the beach within the park, crystalcove.org.

Bike 'n Brunch: See ride description for eats along the coastal bluffs trail including Crystal Cove Shake Shack and Beachcomber. Crystal Cove Promenade is across PCH from Reef Point park entrance; contains Trader Joe's grocery and a variety of restaurants, many with patios, including Starbucks, Z Pizza, Javier's, Bear Flag Fish Co (with Taco Tuesday), Bluefin Sushi, and Pressed Juicery.

Further Info: Ranger Station for general park information and to speak to a park supervisor: 949.494.3539; Interpretive line for field trips, volunteer information, and public programs: 949.497.7647.

Access: Located along PCH (Hwy 1) between Corona Del Mar and Laguna Beach. Park in any of the Crystal Cove State Park lots along PCH (fee), or find free street parking in Corona Del Mar to the north and ride along PCH to the north trail access. Advanced mountain bikers can park for free at the end of Ridge Park Road east off Newport Coast Drive as shown on the map. Our ride begins from the pay beach lot farthest to the south. To get to the area, exit I-405 onto Highway 133 westbound until it ends at PCH in Laguna Beach. Make a right, drive through north Laguna Beach, then make a left into the Reef Point entrance to the park, across from Crystal Cove Promenade. You can also follow MacArthur Boulevard from I-405 near John Wayne Airport to PCH, turn left and drive past downtown Corona Del Mar to find street parking there or to the various park entrances.

Coastal Bluffs Trail NB3

Tunes: The Wind Beneath My Wings (from *Beaches*) by Bette Midler; Crystal by Fleetwood Mac; The Last Resort by the Eagles.

Eats: Crab Cake Benedict at the Beachcomber on the beach. Or beach picnic with supplies from Trader Joe's or Crystal Cove Shake Shack to-go.

Distance, round trip: 5.4 miles. Time: 45 minutes.

Route & Bike: Easy. Paved Class I, any bike. Small rolling hills with a couple of short, steep sections and gradual grades down between PCH and the bluffs.

Facilities: Restrooms with water are located next to the parking lots.

Knocks & Hazards: Traffic noise from PCH, crowds on weekends, but not nearly as bad as the nearby beach boardwalks. Clueless peds. Short trail, only 2.7 miles. Comingle with cars at Shake Shack turnoff. Path crosses several park access roads. Rattlesnakes.

The Ride: Find the paved trail that runs next to the ocean side of the parking lot. Head northwest. Enjoy the rich coastal sage scrub ecosystem and listen to the birds flitting about while gazing out over the ocean in the distance. Shield your eyes from the development to the right and concentrate on the sound of the surf and not of the adjacent 6-lane high-

Bluffs Trail (NB3) above, Moro Campground vista (NB4), below.

way, a far cry from the 2-lane PCH of old. Take detours on trails leading to bluff-top viewpoints, but avoid descending down the steep trails to the beach until you intend to go there for your walk or picnic. About 1 mile along the trail, you will emerge into the small parking lot for Ruby's Shake Shack, formerly a Date Shake Shack that for decades was the only landmark along this stretch of PCH, and is now part of the Ruby's Diner chain. To its credit, Ruby's kept its style and also offers a date shake here.

A little farther along are stairs leading down, and then a trail leading to the Crystal Cove Historic District, which is worth exploring, or even stopping for a meal at the seaside Beachcomber Café. Return to the trail and continue riding as the trail parallels the access road to the Historic District, then crosses it (1.3). Pass three more parking lots at mile 1.5, 1.7, and 2.1, and then a trail junction (2.3). The trail to the right leads to PCH and Corona del Mar. Continue to the left instead.

The pavement curves toward the ocean upon reaching the fenced-off exclusive Pelican Hill Golf Course, and descends a gradual hill to the bluff-top (2.5). Turn to the right behind some fencing protecting you from golf balls, and follow the trail to its end at a nice beach viewpoint from which you can see the coastline of the state park property to the southeast and the Corona Del Mar and Newport Beach coastline to the northwest (2.7). This is a good picnic spot. Return the same way. You can combine your ride with a walk along the beach (up to 3 miles each way). It is also a popular scuba diving beach in the protected ocean reserve.

Connector to El Moro Canyon MTB Trails

The ocean and inland sections of the park are not connected by a bike trail. Therefore, to extend your ride with a mountain biking option, you can either drive to the El Moro Visitor Center, or ride your bike 0.3 mile along a wide bike lane next to the very busy and high-speed PCH. Due to the riding on the hilly highway, this segment is only for experienced riders wearing a helmet and riding a dependable bike with good brakes. Turn right onto PCH from the Reef Point parking area where you started, ride down a moderate hill, and make a left at the first light to the southeast, which also accesses an elementary school. *There is no crosswalk or ped signal at this intersection to cross PCH, only a left-turn lane. Some ride against traffic.* Ride up the hill to the visitor's center to get your bearings and pick up a trail map.

El Moro Canyon Mountain Bike   NB4 ⭐

Tunes: Out in the Country by Three Dog Night; The Mountains Win Again by Blues Traveler
Eats: Picnic in the day use area or at the beach.

Distance, round trip: 6 miles + advanced MTB options. Time: 1 hour 15 minutes.
Route & bike: Doubletrack packed dirt with some rocks for MTB. Moderate difficulty. Upper end of novice skill level. Not technical. Optional trails up the sides of the canyon are for more advanced riders. See the map for the trails with elevations. Moro Canyon has one long hill near the beginning and several shorter hills. Elevation rises from about 125 feet at the visitor's center to 590 feet at trail end, however a downhill is encountered near the beginning of the ride, so that your return will end with a final uphill. E-bikes: Not allowed per the park website.
Facilities: Restroom with water located at the Moro Canyon Visitor's Center.
Knocks & Hazards: Dirt trails may be closed during/after rain due to mud. Rattlesnakes. Mountain lions (infrequent). Poison oak in riparian valley. Hills.

The Ride: El Moro Canyon, the inland section of Crystal Cove State Park, contains lovely coastal chaparral with a network of trails popular with mountain bikers. From the visitor's center head downhill through the parking lot to the gated El Moro Canyon Trail on the left. You can ride about 3 miles each way on non-technical, though fairly hilly, double track through a pleasant canyon.

Trail in Crystal Cove State Park

Although the trail used to traverse a rich riparian habitat, most of the sycamore trees that once shaded the canyon trail burned in the 1993 Laguna Beach fire. Novices should remain on the El Moro Canyon Trail, while more advanced riders can explore the other more challenging trails leading up to the ridges as shown on the map. All route names are nicely posted on maps at key trail junctions throughout the park. The upper trails also connect to Laguna Coast Wilderness Park to the east, and to a trailhead in the Newport Coast development at the end of Ridge Park Road to the west.

Laguna Beach

The jewel of Orange County is nestled in coastal hills that hug a magnificent coastline resplendent in rocky coves and sandy beaches backed by bluffs holding multi-million dollar abodes. Laguna Beach is situated along PCH between Newport Beach to the northwest and Dana Point to the southeast, and is at the end of Hwy 133 southwest from I-5 or I-405 in Irvine. The delightful downtown district borders the beach and spills over onto Main Beach and its boardwalk. North of the beach is spectacular Heisler Park, the location of one of the most scenic coastal strolls in Southern California, and overlooked by the very popular Las Brisas restaurant and its ultra-scenic patio. The park is accessed from Cliff Drive, just northwest up a hill from the junction of Hwy 133 (Broadway) and Hwy 1. Combine a stroll through that park with a walk on a path down the hill to Main Beach and all along the sand, best at lower tides, then explore the adjacent downtown area on foot as well.

While in town you can relax in the solitude of a quiet cove, hike in the surrounding hilly greenbelts, visit an art gallery, shop for unique items or antiques, and of course have a bite or two to eat. Artists flock to Laguna to paint the beautiful flowering vegetation backed by a viewscape of sea and land that is reminiscent of the Amalfi Coast of Italy. In fact, artists have been coming to Laguna since the late 1800s, giving it a reputation as an artists' colony, which is evidenced by the popular Sawdust Festival and the Pageant of the Masters, an open air production with orchestra where living paintings are displayed on stage.

Unfortunately Laguna Beach is not a wonderful easy-cycling destination. County-controlled PCH is a terror to ride on, with high-speed traffic, parked cars, and few bike lanes. The other entrance to town, sinuous and busy Laguna Canyon Road, is almost as bad. Side streets parallel to PCH are a preferable alternative through much of the town, but those roads are also busy and narrow, with parked car hazards. Two rides have been identified, one a hilly jaunt along a spectacular view ridge in a greenbelt (LB1), and the other along side streets through the main part of town (LB2).

For info on Laguna's restaurants see visitlagunabeach.com. Cliff Restaurant in Laguna Village on PCH at Legion has an awesome blufftop patio. Hotel Laguna at PCH near Park also has a great casual oceanfront patio. Most are in the downtown core, along Ride LB2. No food available near ride LB1. Laguna Beach Cyclery, 240 Thalia, 949.494.1522 (rentals). Electric Cyclery, 1200 N Coast Hwy, 715.2345.

Top O' Laguna   LB1

Details: 5 miles, strenuous (steep hills, e-bike edge!). Paved Class I, II, III, any geared bike. MTB'ing option.

One of the most scenic areas of Laguna Beach is the mile-long asphalt fire road along the 850-foot elevation ridgeline through the greenbelt between the Arch Beach Heights and Top of the World neighborhoods. Laguna Beach and the Pacific coastline with Catalina Island floating out at sea are on display to the west, while the verdant valley of Aliso Creek and Aliso and Wood Canyons Wilderness Park (SV3 and 4), the Saddleback Valley, and the surrounding mountain ranges are to the north and east. To reach the trailhead drive up steep Nyes Place north-

Side trail off fire road past goats eating fire break.

Dramatic view of Laguna Beach from fire road

east from PCH until it changes to Balboa Avenue and ends at Del Mar Avenue in Arch Beach Heights near Moulton Meadows Park (restrooms). Begin the ride by maneuvering around the fire road gate at the corner of Balboa and Del Mar.

You may encounter large herds of penned-in goats up here. They are eating a firebreak, trying to prevent a repeat of the 1993 Laguna Beach fire disaster. Cycle over the scenic rolling hills, perhaps detouring on side trails to vista points. Watch for peds with their dogs. The end of the road is greeted by a very steep uphill, leading to a private road with no access (0.9). A new 900-foot public trail to the west of the houses starts as crushed granite but soon becomes a very steep signed "walk-your bike" affair consisting of concrete steps adjacent to a ramp to facilitate the journey down, and then back up. It is still much better than what it replaced.

Follow the path to reach Top of the World (1.0), turn left and then bend to the right on Alta Laguna Boulevard. Ride through this hilltop community to Alta Laguna Park (restrooms) (2.2) and enjoy the great vistas. For the best view go back to Alta Laguna Boulevard, turn right and take the wide dirt trail a short distance past the end of the road to the Aliso and Wood Canyons trailhead station. From this area enjoy an amazing panorama from Laguna Canyon and Laguna Coast Wilderness Park to Laguna Beach and the ocean beyond.

You can take the trails down to Aliso and Wood Canyons Park (SV4), but just remember you have to come back up. You can also lock up your bike and walk up the obvious short trail to the viewpoint for an even better view. Return the same way you came, for a ride total of about 4.3 miles, which will seem like twice that because of the hills. In Arch Beach Heights you can do some exploring on the roads and trails at the summit of the neighborhood, perhaps resulting in a 5+ mile ride. To reach Alta Laguna Park by car, take Park Avenue from downtown all the way up the hill to Alta Laguna Boulevard and turn left.

Laguna Village to Crescent Bay   LB2

Details: 8.3 miles, moderate. Class II and III, paved for any geared bike with good brakes E-bike edge: Several hills en route.

This ride guides you along some of the more bike-friendly streets in the city. Refer to the map and choose your own route based on your goals for the day. Just make sure to avoid riding on PCH. This ride description starts from Cliff Drive and PCH, heading northwest. The first part of Cliff Drive is the most crowded as it passes Heisler Park, with cars frequently coming and going from the metered spots. At the northwest end of Cliff Drive, the road turns into Circle Drive, after

View from Crescent Bay Point Park in North Laguna

Cliff turns right to rejoin PCH. At the far end of Circle Drive is a concrete stairway with 22 steps between homes (1.0). It's well worth the bike carry through the passageway to access the Crescent Bay area. Crescent Bay Point Park, around the bend to the left, is one of the most beautiful spots on the SoCal Coast. It juts out into the sea overlooking rock islands that are frequently full of barking sea lions, sea and shore birds, and perhaps scuba divers in the water exploring the marine preserve. You may luck out and see the blows of grey whales migrating past during December through April. The view back toward Laguna Beach of Crescent Bay Beach and the city framed by the coastal hills is also memorable.

Returning the same way down Cliff Drive is the most scenic option, however if you would prefer to see another area and perhaps cycle with less interruptions, return via the streets to the northeast of PCH as shown on the map. Those roads comprise an actual bike route with signs and sharrows or bike lanes. To connect to that route, pedal up Crescent Bay Drive to PCH and ride to the right to access the signal at Cliff (1.4). Cajon is across the street. Cross PCH, ride up the hill on Cajon to Hillcrest and turn right onto the bike route. Hillcrest ends at High Drive near Boat Canyon Park, with the Boat Canyon shopping center below, accessible by a steep driveway (grocery, pizza, burgers). Turn right on High Drive (1.9) and left on Cypress Drive. Continue on Cypress to Astor Street (2.3).

The starting point of the ride is to the right down Astor Street, so you can complete the loop now and end there. Otherwise, follow Cypress around to the left and turn right on Rosa Bonheur Drive to reach Cliff Drive (2.5). Meanwhile, if you had chosen to go back on Cliff Drive on the ocean side, cross PCH and veer to the right to continue on Cliff Drive, meeting up with Rosa Bonheur Drive. Next, carefully negotiate the short steep hill down North Beach Street. A jog to the right then left on Broadway (Highway 133) will allow you to continue on Beach Street through town, giving you the option of exploring any of the downtown streets. Leave downtown from Forest Avenue by turning southeast on the new sharrow bike route of Glenneyre (approx. 3.0). Ride up a small hill to Park Avenue. For a less-traveled route, turn left on Park and then right on Catalina Street to cycle through the Laguna neighborhoods. Be extra careful at all street crossings. When you get to Thalia Street (3.6), jog right/left to continue on Catalina.

Turn left on Cress St (3.9) and follow it past Bluebird Park at Bluebird Canyon Dr. (4.2). Follow Bluebird Canyon Drive straight ahead up into the scenic canyon. Turn around upon reaching Rancho Laguna Road (4.7) to avoid a hill climb. Otherwise, bear right on Rancho Laguna that turns into Morningside and runs along the base of the steep Laguna Beach Greenbelt. Turn left on Regatta (5.2). Follow it around as it leads into Bluebird Canyon Drive and winds its way down to where you had veered off on Rancho Laguna (5.8). Turn right to continue on Bluebird Canyon and ride back down the gradual hill. Pass Bluebird Park as the road becomes Cress again (6.3).

Turn right on Temple Terrace toward the large St. Catherine of Siena Church. Turn left down Oak Street (6.5). Turn right on Wilson and follow it across town, jogging left/right at Anita Street (6.8) and right/left at Thalia. Pass Nick Carman Park, and turn right when Wilson ends at El Bosque (7.1) and veer right. From El Bosque turn left on Camino Del Mar, then left to return to Catalina Street. Follow Catalina back to Park (7.4), turn left, then right on Glenneyre. Make the first right on Mermaid, then left on 2nd Street, with an optional stop at the outdoor Dawson Cole sculpture garden, then reach Forest (7.7). Follow Forest, which may be backed up from the stop sign where 3rd Street comes in from the right. Turn left in front of the civic buildings and reach Broadway (7.9). Go left, then veer right up the Cliff Drive hill, and follow Cliff all the way back to PCH, which is your starting reference point (8.3).

Dana Point

Dana Point is named for Richard Henry Dana, an 1800s Massachusetts lawyer, writer, and anti-slavery politician whose book, *Two Years Before the Mast,* is a diary of his experiences as a seaman on the sailing ship *Pilgrim* that explored the California coast. The original town was comprised of the Lantern District, with streets named for the colored lanterns that ships in the natural harbor would hang to indicate their fares. Present day Dana Point is a conglomeration of districts that has struggled to attain an identity of its own, and is best known for its huge private yacht marina that was built in the 1960s and obliterated the famous but dangerous Killer Dana surf break immortalized in songs such as the Beach Boys' "Surfin' USA."

The picturesque harbor is backed by rugged 200-foot sandstone cliffs, which are capped with parks, residences, and restaurants. Excursions leave from the east side of the harbor for whale watching, deep sea fishing, and Catalina Island crossings, while the December holiday boat parade is a locals' favorite. A whale festival is held in early March and Doheny Blues Festival is in May. The main Dana Point business district is not along the bike routes, and consists of the parallel Highway 1 and Del Prado located up the hill from the harbor, but with no ocean views.

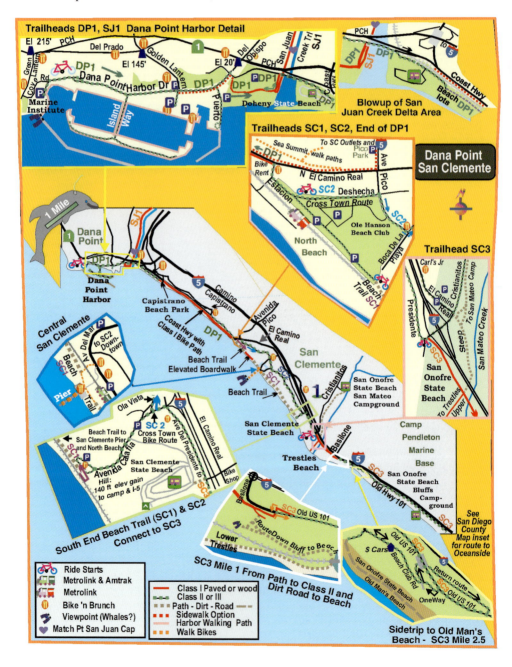

Dana Point Cruise   DP1 ⭐

Dana Point Harbor has a fabulous system of paved walking trails conducive to long strolls. Bikes are allowed on them as well unless signed otherwise, but they are typically crowded with peds. The harbor's Class II roadways are better for leisurely bike rides, and pass many dining options. Doheny State Beach provides an ocean playground with a short Class I path and long narrow oceanfront parking lots to ride through. A separated Class I path along the coast highway now continues into San Clemente.

Tunes: Killer Dana by the Chantays; Surfer Joe by The Surfaris; Surfin' USA by The Beach Boys; Calypso by John Denver.
Eats: Fish lunch or Sunday brunch at one of the marina restaurants.

Distance: 13–15 miles. Time: 1.5–2 hours of flat coastal riding.
Route & Bike: Easy to moderate depending on distance. Paved Class I and II, with sidewalk options. Any bike. E-bike edge: Coastal headwinds; combine with SJ1.
Seasons: All. Best on sunny uncrowded off-season weekday with little wind or fog.
Facilities: Restrooms and water in beach parks and commercial establishments.
Knocks & Hazards: Class II & III with traffic around harbor and Doheny linear lots. Busy street crossings. Clueless peds on Class I's. Ocean blocked by homes along most of the route betw Dana Point and San Clemente. Possible lurkers in parks.
Rent 'n Ride: Wheel Fun, Doheny Beach; Pedego E-Bikes, 34186 PCH, 949.481.2044; Shops: Cycleogical, 34102 La Plaza, 542.4777; EZ Green E-Bikes, 34193 Golden Lnt
Camp 'n Ride: Doheny State Beach: Tents and RV's, no hookups; dump station and water in main park's lot. Beachfront sites reserve well in advance.
Bike 'n Brunch: Find lots to eat in Dana Point Harbor, accessed by turning south on Golden Lantern. To the left is the Dana Wharf section where you can find seafood, deli, a diner and Wind 'n Sea with a Sunday al fresco buffet brunch. To the right is Mariners Village with El Torito (Sunday buffet brunch), Harpoon Henry's (Sunday al fresco brunch), Harbor Grill, The Brig diner, Coffee Importers with a patio along the harbor pathway, Beach Harbor Pizza and lots of shops as well. Several restaurants on the landward side of Dana Point Harbor Drive at Golden Lantern. Seasonal cafe on Doheny Beach. PCH/Del Prado through Dana Point are lined with restaurants, including fast food, though not directly on our bike route.
City code, bike riding on sidewalks: Defer to state law. Prohibited in several parks, including the parks along the south end of the San Juan Creek Trail (SJ1), but is allowed at Heritage Bay and Lantern Parks in the headlands above the harbor.
Further Info: City: danapoint.org; Harbor: www.danapointharbor.com; ocdph.com.
Note: Harbor revitalization project pending. Harborside trails may be widened.

Access: From I-5, take the Beach Cities—Highway 1 exit and head west. Turn left at the second light onto Dana Point Harbor Drive. The first light along the harbor drive is for Doheny State Beach (to the left, parking $3/hr). This is a good bet if some in your group want to hang on the beach rather than ride. The second light at Golden Lantern is the gateway to most of the restaurants in the harbor area, to both the left and right. Parking is free here. Our ride description starts at the very end of Dana Point Harbor Drive, in one of the free parking lots there, about 3.5 miles from Coast Highway.

Rail 'n Ride: Get off at San Juan Capistrano and access this ride via SJ1, or San Clemente's North Station (Metrolink) at the south end of this ride.

The Ride: The Ocean Institute at the end of Dana Point Harbor Drive contains exhibits and hosts an annual whale festival in early March, which is the peak of the grey whale migration off the coast here. Sidewalks along the harbor lead to a great viewpoint of the high bluff landform called Dana Point and the crashing surf. Benches here make it a good place for an impromptu picnic. You can also explore on the rocky beach here below the cliffs, or stroll along the outer jetty if it is open, based on surf conditions. We recommend riding on the Class II bike lanes around the harbor along Dana Point Harbor Drive rather than the crowded narrow harbor walkways. Be extra careful at all road crossings.

San Juan Creek Delta - DP1 meets SJ1

Cycle away from the Ocean Institute along Dana Point Harbor Drive. At mile 0.7 take the Island Way Bridge to the harbor island. There are no bike lanes on this low speed limit road, so if you do not want to ride in traffic, either use the sidewalk or skip this segment. On the island, a statue of the city's namesake, Richard Henry Dana,

Above: Doheny State Beach at Mile 4.8.
Below: Class I path between Dana Pt & San Clemente

greets you. From this point cycling to the left leads to a view of the marina entrance. The road to the right ends at a yacht club facility with a view over a protected bay popular with SUP's and small sailboats, and the Ocean Institute beyond. Return over the bridge and turn right on Dana Point Harbor Dr (2.8). The first traffic light (Golden Lantern) is your gateway to most of your Bike 'n Brunch options in both directions.

At the next light a road leads to a great viewpoint over Doheny Beach. DP1 turns at the following light into the entrance to Doheny State Beach (3.4). Stay on the sidewalk and follow the Class I trail to the right that leads to the beach. During busy periods this short promenade can be somewhat of a zoo, shared by strollers, bikers, and lots of children. Bike rentals and refreshments are available at a concession. In a few minutes enjoy a view of the San Juan Creek delta, which at lower tides can attract thousands of sea and shore birds (3.7). Two trails lead off to the left at this point. The first one that parallels the parking lot is your way to continue DP1 along the coast. The second trail along the river delta leads to San Juan Capistrano, as described in ride SJ1.

Continuing along our coastal route, follow the short trail to the park road. Turn right to cross the bridge, then make an immediate right (4.0) and pedal past the Doheny State Beach campground entrance. After the campground, ride parallel to the beach through the long, narrow parking lots used by beachgoers, including day use RV'ers. This oceanfront section is a ride highlight. Adjacent railroad tracks and Coast Highway form a barrier between the beach park and several restaurants across Coast Highway. These can be accessed via a pedestrian bridge near Olamendi's Mexican restaurant. Many also use that bridge to take advantage of free parking along Coast Highway. The parking lots end at a cul de sac (4.8), followed by a short paved path that leads past more beach area before reaching Palisades Drive/Beach Road. To the right is Capistrano Beach Park, another staging option (restrooms, parking $1/hr). Turning around at this beach park will give you a fairly easy 10-mile ride.

To continue on, carefully cross the active railroad tracks at a right angle, and reach Coast Highway. You can turn left and ride along the roadway to access the restaurants mentioned previously. Otherwise, turn right onto the two-way bike path separated by a concrete barrier along Coast Highway. Steep precarious cliffs tower over the highway to the north, while railroad tracks, a row of beach houses, and views of the ocean where there are vacant lots can be seen to the south. Ride single file and keep to the right as many cyclists ride this path full throttle. Take the trail to the first traffic light where the barrier ends at Camino Capistrano (6.6). Turning around here gives you a 13.2-mile ride. If you turn left at Camino Capistrano there is a small shopping center with a couple of cafés including good pizza. Otherwise, continue into San Clemente.

The coast highway is N. El Camino Real in San Clemente, and the multi-use path becomes a two-way bikeway, separate ped path, and landscaped median. Enjoy a 0.3-mile ocean vista before it disappears behind houses. Inland, ocean-view walking paths in the Sea Summit development extend to an outlet mall, but there's no bike access from the coast path. Upon reaching a ped plaza at the first light (Avenida Estacion, 7.5), turn right toward the San Clemente Metrolink Station at North Beach. Beach Hut Deli here (2021) has outdoor seating, as does Moulin (up Calle Deshecha, then right on Pico, the start of ride SC2). Other restaurants are nearby along El Camino Real. San Clemente Beach Trail (SC1) starts at the south end of the parking lot (7.6).

San Juan Capistrano

San Juan Capistrano takes you back to the time of Father Junipera Serra, who built one of his beautiful missions in what is now the center of this suburban town of 36,000. Although the majority of its famous swallows now prefer to return from Goya, Argentina, to other locales such as Chino Hills in the spring, the recently renovated compound is definitely worth a visit. The compact downtown district is comprised of similar Spanish architecture that creates a welcome respite from the surrounding suburban sprawl. The nicely refurbished 1895 Santa Fe Railroad depot, complete with restaurants, provides easy access to the major Southern California passenger rail routes.

Just across the tracks lies the charming Los Rios Historic District, containing 31 structures along Los Rios Street. It is reported to be the oldest continuing neighborhood in California, including three adobe homes built in 1794 for mission families, and numerous single-wall board and batten homes erected between 1887 and 1910. It is a delightful place to cycle back to yesteryear, and dine at the well-reviewed restaurants in historic houses. Saturday morning walking tours introduce participants to the town's history and architecture; see the kiosk near the train tracks. To the east in the main equestrian district the new Reata Park celebrates the historic citrus culture.

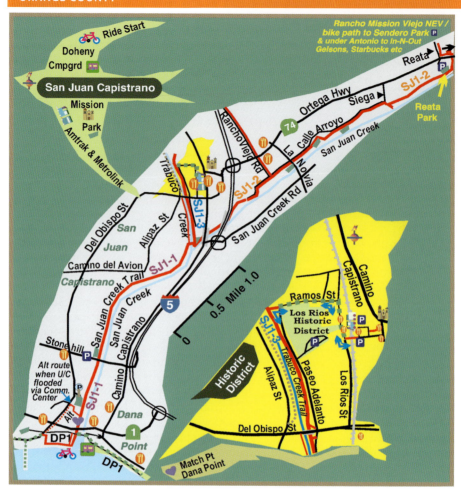

Cycling with the Swallows SJ1

San Juan and Trabuco Creeks flow through town, each channelized and lined with Class I bike trails connecting to the beach 3 miles away at Dana Point, making a nice combo ride with DP1. The path continues east under I-5 to pleasant neighborhoods next to San Juan Creek's natural riparian zone and horse country. The surrounding hills frame the town eloquently, especially when winter rains turn them green, while faraway mountains add an extra layer to the backdrop of your vistas as you cycle.

Tunes: When the Swallows Come Back to Capistrano by The Five Satins; Chestnut Mare by The Birds; Take the "A" Train by Lionel Hampton; Yo Canto by Los Lobos.
Eats: Al fresco meal at the San Juan Capistrano Depot or Los Rios District

Distance: Up to 14 miles plus options. Time: 1.5 - 2 hours.
Route & Bike: Easy to moderate depending on ocean breezes. Paved, any bike. Mostly Class I, flat except for dips under roadways. Some easy Class III through historic district. E-bike edge: Headwinds heading to ocean. Combine with DP1, SC1.
Seasons: All. Best on sunny mild day with minimal wind.
Facilities: Restrooms and water in most parks along route and Capistrano Depot.

ORANGE COUNTY   155

Knocks & Hazards: Clueless peds. Possible lurkers. Hwy 1 undercrossing subject to flooding. Stiff winds coming off the ocean may make the return ride more difficult. Wilder area east of I-5 has potential of mountain lions and rattlesnakes, and poison oak off the trail. Cycling with slow-moving sporadic traffic in historic districts.
Rent 'n Ride: See DP1. Shop: Buy My Bikes, 32302 Cam Capistrano, 949.493.5611.
Camp 'n Ride: Doheny State Beach. See Dana Point.
Bike 'n Brunch: Options in Dana Point, downtown San Juan Capistrano, Los Rios District, and east of I-5 up Rancho Viejo Rd sidewalk path. See ride description.
City code, bike riding on sidewalks: San Juan Cap: Not restricted. Dana Point: See DP1.
Further Info: City site: sanjuancapistrano.org; Del Rio walking tour info and more: sanjuancapistrano.net.

Access: This ride can be an extension of the Dana Point ride. From I-5 take the Highway 1 Beach Cities exit. Follow it to Dana Point Harbor Drive and turn left, then left into the state park ($15/day or $3/hour). Go to the east end of the parking lot (before bridge). Find the bike trail that runs along San Juan Creek. To drive directly to San Juan Capistrano, from I-5 take the Ortega Hwy exit west. Turn right at the next light to stay on Ortega Hwy. At Cam Capistrano (the Mission is at the corner) turn left, then right to get to the Depot area, and the large free parking lot. Also park free in Dana Point Harbor (see DP1), along Stonehill where SJ1-1 crosses, on Coast Hwy west of Palisades, or along SJ1-2 east of I-5 via Ortego Hwy on Calle Arroyo or in Reata Park.

The ride is split into 3 segments. Segment SJ1-1 is the San Juan Creek Trail from DP1 at the ocean to the confluence with Trabuco Creek (2.4 miles each way). Segment SJ1-2 is from that confluence northeast along San Juan Creek under I-5 out to horse country (3.4 miles), and Segment SJ1-3 is from the same confluence up and into the historic districts of San Juan Capistrano (1.2 miles).

San Juan Creek From the Ocean SJ1-1 3

The trail starts by going north under the Hwy 1 (PCH) bridge that is closed during flood or very high tide events. See the map for an alternate route via the Del Obispo sidewalk to the Community Center. As you ride north along with skaters, joggers, and walkers, the rolling south county terrain and 5,687-foot Santiago Peak (aka Saddleback Mountain) makes a nice backdrop, although the surrounding scenery is mostly residential on the west side of the creek and commercial/light industrial on the east. The trail crosses under Stonehill Drive (0.9) with access to it, passes Creekside Park, and bends gradually to the northeast (1.7). It then bends back to the north at the confluence with Trabuco Creek (2.4) where there is a bike/ped bridge. Cross the bridge to Descanso Park, that has restrooms and water.

San Juan Creek to Horse Country SJ1-2 4

From Descanso Park the main trail curves to the right, then bends left to rejoin the levee along San Juan Creek. It dips under railroad tracks, then approaches Camino Capistrano. A ramp to the left leads up to the street and shopping centers with casual restaurants, a TJ's and a Vons. The path dips under that road (2.6) then under I-5, emerging into the more natural riparian area near San Juan Creek. It empties into the end of Paseo Tirador (3.2), then continues to the right at Calle Arroyo, past Ortega Stables, and runs parallel to that road that soon intersects with Rancho Viejo Rd. Option: A Class I path runs about 3.5 miles next to hilly Rancho Viejo Rd almost to Avery Parkway. Restaurants are two blocks away on both sides of Ortega Hwy.

Scenic riparian Class I trail east of I-5

The main route next to Calle Arroyo passes some appealing Spanish-influenced office buildings, and then goes by Cook Park where there are restrooms. Carefully cross La Novia Avenue (3.8), then look for the continuation of the trail on the right as it descends into the pretty riparian habitat and away from the road. Side trails lead to the various residential streets. The trail eventually returns next to the road near Via Sonora (4.3). It runs beside a popular park (with restrooms) between Via Cordova (4.5) and Via Estenaga (4.8), followed by Mission Trails Stables. Reach Avenida Siega (5.0). The trail continues to the right, leading to interesting Reata Park (5.5-5.8) with historical plantings, orchards, picnic tables and restrooms. Option: Continue under Ortega Hwy then east on the "NEV" path past Sendero Park, under Antonio and up a steep hill to a shopping center (Gelson's, In-N-Out, Starbucks etc). Return the same way past Descanso Park to the ped/bike bridge, but don't cross it (9.1).

Historic San Juan Capistrano SJ1-3

Head north from the east side of the ped/bike bridge on the asphalt East Trabuco Creek Trail. Just before the first undercrossing at Del Obispo Street (9.6), you can make your way to the right and carefully cross the railroad tracks to reach the popular breakfast/lunch spot called Mollie's Famous Café on the right, a more reasonable option compared to what is to come. Otherwise, follow the trail under Del Obispo and look for the spur trail that accesses the Los Rios Historic District on the right (9.9). *FYI—the Trabuco Creek trail just ends in a neighborhood around the bend.* Cycle down Ramos Street, then right on Los Rios Street (10.1) to reach the area of concentrated restaurants and shops housed in historic buildings. Delightful dining options in order of appearance include the Ramos House Café for a gourmet brunch splurge, the quaint Tea House for your afternoon tea experience, Hummingbird House Café, a very popular lunch place (Greek), and Hidden House Coffee. A park with historical displays is also worth exploring.

Los Rios Historic District

Just across the tracks to the left via the scenic ped/bike crossing (10.2) is the beautifully restored Capistrano Depot complex with a lovely patio restaurant (Trevor's) for your al fresco meal. Take the second left into the parking lot entrance. Just as you are entering the parking lot, look to the right for a bike/ped pathway (Arquello Way) between the commercial buildings. This passageway daylights on San Juan's main street, Camino Capistrano, at the intersection with Ortega Highway. The Mission San Juan Capistrano is at the northwest corner of this intersection. We suggest walking your bike over to it and locking it up to visit the mission (10.3). You can also stroll to the east along the main street, where you will find lots of restaurants, including a Starbucks, Hennessey's Tavern, and El Adobe Mexican, one of Tricky Dick's favorites when his San Clemente estate was the Western White House. Return via the Los Rios district to East Trabuco Creek Trail (10.7), turn left, and this time when you reach the bike/ped bridge take it to the right over the creek (11.5).

Take the San Juan Creek Trail (SJ1-1) back to your starting point at Doheny State Beach (14.0). Options: Shorten the ride by leaving out any of the segments. Lengthen by combining with the Dana Point (DP1) and San Clemente (SC1 or 2) rides.

San Clemente

The southernmost city in Orange County was founded in 1925 by real estate developer Ole Hanson. He named it San Clemente after a city in Spain, and also influenced a city design requirement that buildings include a Spanish aspect to them, which is reflected in the Spanish architecture of the downtown area and of many homes. Today the "Spanish Village By the Sea" contains about 65,000 people and extends from the coast up and over the hills in a continuous sprawl. The city straddles the San Diego County line, and is bordered by the Camp Pendleton Marine Base to the south, Dana Point and San Juan Capistrano to the north, and is the only city in Orange County that is closer to San Diego than Los Angeles.

San Clemente's surfing culture continues to thrive with its local surfboard fabricators, surfing magazine headquarters, famous surfers in residence, and a championship surfing team at the high school. The San Clemente area coast enjoys some of the best breaks in SoCal, and the wide sandy beaches are ever popular with all sorts of beachgoers. Beaches include, from north to south, Poche, North Beach, 204, The Pier, T-Street, Beach House, The Hole, Lasuen, Lost Winds, Riviera, State Park, North Gate, and the famous and natural Trestles, which is technically just south of the city line. The beautiful municipal pier is the center of the city's beach activities and contains restaurants on and adjacent to it. The downtown district is about 0.4 mile up the hill from the pier along Avenida Del Mar, at an elevation between about 150 and 225 feet. The city is fairly hilly, except for the actual beach strip, where the train tracks transport Amtrak and Metrolink lines through one the most scenic stretches of rail in SoCal.

San Clemente does not have any extended bike trails, but makes a great destination to enjoy the beaches and variety of restaurants. El Camino Real is the main business route through the city and passes through the downtown business district, connecting with the north end of Avenida Del Mar, but it is not safe to ride on. Instead, the city has constructed a signed bike route through residential streets, which is a fairly hilly and sometimes confusing affair that is described here as SC2. It has also built a beautiful beach-front trail (SC1) with a mostly smooth packed sand and gravel surface in which bikes are allowed, but it was designed for a casual ride at best. Cyclists are required to walk bikes next to the main beach in summer. A new multi-use coastal path connects the Beach Trail to the rides to Dana Point (DP1) and San Juan Capistrano (SJ1) to the north. You can also do an SC1-SC2 loop, or connect with SC3, the ride that leads past prime surf beaches through San Onofre State Park to Camp Pendleton and Oceanside in San Diego County. Metrolink rail stops in San Juan Capistrano, San Clemente, and Oceanside create great options for one-way rides. *Map: Page 150.*

Seasons: All. Best on sunny uncrowded off-season weekday.

Rent 'n Ride: Bicycles San Clemente, Metrolink Station, 1900 N El Camino Real, 949.492.5737; San Clemente E-Bike and Rentals, 2345 S El Camino Real, 444.6421. BikeShop: Jax Bicycle Center, 1421 N El Camino Real, 492.5911.

Camp 'n Ride: San Clemente State Beach, a bluff-top beachfront park (full or no hookups with dump station) close to the south end of both SC1 and SC2, or about 1 mile on a Class II road to the SC3 trailhead. The inland San Mateo Campground of San Onofre State Park (partial or no hookups with dump station) requires a hilly cycle of two miles on a Class II road or dirt path to get to the pathway to Trestles Beach and the SC3 route. The campgrounds fill most weekends and all summer despite their high fees. San Onofre State Park's Bluffs campground (no hookups, with dump station, usually open summer only) is located along the long linear parking lot of the state park along the SC3 route. About half of the sites have ocean views. See also Dana Point and Oceanside.

Bike 'n Brunch: Fisherman's on the pier open for lunch and dinner everyday, breakfast weekends, peak times. Snack bar at end of pier. Several restaurants across the street. Beach Hut Deli and Moulin French Cafe at the north end of SC1/SC2. Several restaurants along El Camino Real in that area as well. Multitudes of restaurants via a detour up to the downtown area along Del Mar. See also ride descriptions.

City code, bike riding on sidewalks: Refer to state law, with exceptions. Riding is prohibited on the municipal pier, accesses to the pier, service roads, and beach access roads. Also, there are some restrictions regarding the Beach Trail as posted on the trail, including walk bike for the 1/4 mile south of the pier in summer.

Further info: State beaches: San Clemente: www.parks.ca.gov/?page_id=646; San Onofre: www.parks.ca.gov/?page_id=647; San Onofre Foundation (preserving Trestles Beach and the parks): sanoparks.org; Local Surfrider chapter: southoc.surfrider.org; Camp Pendleton: See www.pendleton.marines.mil/Base-Access/Recreational-Bicycling/ for lastest permit requirments to pass thru. Base Access Control Branch: 760.763.7604; Local cycling news/Camp Pendleton bike trail closures: bikesd.org.

San Clemente Beach Bike 'n Hike SC1 ⭐2 Summer ⭐4 Winter weekday

The San Clemente Beach Trail extends 2.3 miles from North Beach at El Camino Real (Coast Highway) near the Metrolink Station south to Avenida Calafia, reaching the municipal pier near its midpoint, a worthwhile destination. This is a beautiful seaside vista trail that runs at the base of the cliffs along the beach next to the active passenger rail tracks. It provides an easy way to get across town without riding through the hilly, confusing maze of streets and affords breathtaking views of the adjacent San Clemente beaches, some of the region's finest. Although at time of writing bikes are allowed, the trail is not very bike friendly,

San Clemente's beach trail runs parallel to the beach and train tracks.

and is only suitable for casual, slow riding. Despite all of its shortcomings, however, the vistas and access to great restaurants make the trail worthwhile as a bike and hike. It is constructed of compacted sand and dirt, with some exceptions.

Tunes: Surfer Girl by The Beach Boys; Hotel California by the Gipsy Kings
Eats: Fish lunch on the deck of Fisherman's on the pier.

Distance: 4.6 miles up and back, Time: 1 hour including walking.
Route & Bike: Easy and flat except for one raised boardwalk. Packed sand for hybrid or mountain bike, packed gravel, concrete sidewalk.
Facilities: Restrooms and water in the beach parks.
Knocks & Hazards: Short distance. Clueless peds. Narrow trail in places. Walk bike required near pier and where signed, including first 0.25 mile south of pier in summer. Speed limit 10 mph.

Access: Rides SC1 and/or SC2 can be a continuation of the Dana Point ride (DP1) from the north, the San Onofre/Camp Pendleton ride to the south (SC3), or they can be done on their own: From I-5 exit on Pico and take it southbound past El Camino Real, then turn right for the Metrolink depot/beach trail parking lot. This is the north trailhead. Or for free parking, try a neighborhood along the SC2 route. Throughout San Clemente, parking is available in pay lots or metered street parking close to the beach, or free street parking farther from the beach. See map on page 150.

The Ride: From the north trailhead, begin on a nice wide stretch of packed dirt trail with great ocean views. A 0.25-mile elevated fiberglass boardwalk (rebuilt in 2021) enables even more spectacular vistas. Farther along, some very narrow sections will inevitably lead to pedestrian-bike conflicts, but hopefully will not result in a ban of bikes some day. Dismount is required in the pier area. Fisherman's restaurant on the pier has breakfast feasts on weekends and a dramatic dining patio that hangs out over the beach, a perfect spot for a fish lunch. A second section of the restaurant across the pier (restrooms here) is a more casual oyster bar. The pier is a great place to walk to watch the waves, look for sea mammals and surfing land mammals, and gaze back at the hilly town of Spanish Colonial influence. Additional restaurants are located across the street from the pier. South of the pier the trail becomes a wide, compressed sand surface (not good for road bikes) for about 0.25 mile that requires dismount June to Labor Day.

The trail crosses the active railroad tracks (pay attention to any signals) and encounters a few narrow bridges that may require dismount if crowded or signed. It continues to Avenida Calafia and San Clemente State Beach (restrooms). From the beach, you can ride up the 0.4 mile hill (150 foot elevation gain; e-bike edge) of Ave Calafia, past the State Beach campground entrance atop the bluff, to continue on a coastal bike route southward. Turn right on Class II Avenida del Presidente (ie Nixon) and reach the trailhead for ride SC3 to the surf beaches, Camp Pendleton and Oceanside in about 1 mile. Or, to loop back through town on the city's (hilly; e-bike edge) designated bike route (ride SC2), turn left on Ola Vista before reaching the top of the hill.

Bike Route Through San Clemente   SC2

Distance: 6.2 miles up and back. Moderate with hills (e-bike edge), paved, for any bike

Access is the same as ride SC1. From the Metrolink station area, follow the green Bike Route sign along Calle Deshecha, take a right on Pico and a quick left on Boca de la Playa. Keep right through the roundabout, and bear right onto Sacramento then bear left to stay on Sacramento. Turn right on Avenida Florencia (0.4), then ride up the hill and turn left on Avenida Pelayo, and right on Calle Puente (0.7). Ride past the pretty Max Berg Plaza Park (restrooms), then continue past several dips and rises and cross streets to Avenida Palizada (1.2).

Turn right, then left on Calle Seville (1.3). In two blocks Seville crosses Avenida Del Mar, the main street of San Clemente, with lots of restaurants and a sizeable Sunday morning farmers' market starting a block up the hill to the left. Down the hill 0.25 mile to the right are the municipal pier and the beach trail. Seville meets Ola Vista in three blocks (1.6). Turn right to follow Ola Vista, which becomes a bike route with sharrows, and then Class II with bike lanes, ending at Avenida Calafia near San Clemente State Park (3.1). The vehicle entrance to the park and campground is to the right, down the hill, and then the first left back up a steep hill.

To continue heading south toward San Onofre or Camp Pendleton, or to use the easier, less hilly bike entrance to the State Park, turn left on Calafia then right on Class II Avenida Del Presidente past the San Clemente Inn, which contains Adele's restaurant. A path into the state park is 0.3 mile on the right across from the Avenida San Luis Rey I-5 overpass. Several restaurants are across I-5 on the El Camino Real frontage road. The trailhead for SC3 is about 1 mile down Del Presidente, around the bend on the right just before the I-5 on-ramp.

Surfin' USA! San Onofre State Beach and Camp Pendleton to Oceanside   SC3 ⭐

The south border of San Clemente where this ride starts is within San Diego County, but because the most scenic section of the ride is the north end near San Clemente, it has been included here. The best part of this ride is the first couple of miles, beginning with a Class I cycle following the surfers to the famous "Uppers" Trestles Beach, and then a MTB option to cycle down to beautiful "Lowers" Trestles Beach. Beyond that the cycling is mostly for cycling's sake except for a couple of scenic coastal stretches. The first 7 miles of this ride is along Class I, II, and III routes including the access road of long and narrow San Onofre State Beach, but after that

Vista of Lower Trestles Beach from path.

the riding is on the property of the huge Camp Pendleton Marine Base, the only reason that the coastal LA and San Diego metro areas have not melded together along the coast. A permit is required from Las Pulgas Rd south.

Highlights along the route include beautiful coastal bluffs and fields of seasonal wildflowers dipping down toward the ocean, and a glimpse into

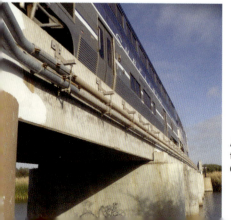

An Amtrak Pacific Surfliner whizzes over the rebuilt trestles at the famed Trestles surfing beach south of San Clemente

the intricate coastal desert sage ecosystem that once carpeted the coast. However, for the most part, ocean views are obscured by the bluffs and hills, the Class I off-road stretches are eclipsed by Class II or III cycling, and I-5 and railroad noise is a factor for much of the trail. For those wishing to continue farther south, cycling through the Marine Base is not always allowed. Several ride options are presented, and if you try it on a sunny weekend day (the most likely days that the base will be open to cyclists) with little wind, you may really enjoy it. Hearty cyclists can do the strenuous 42-mile round trip through Camp Pendleton to the quaint Oceanside Harbor for a Bike 'n Brunch. Or, you can always arrange for a shuttle; the Oceanside Harbor area has just enough shops and places to stroll to keep the non-riders in the group busy while the driver waits for you. Another option is to utilize a Metrolink or Amtrak train in one direction between the Oceanside and San Clemente or San Juan Capistrano stations to extend the ride. See San Clemente "Further Info" for Pendleton pre-registration.

Tunes: Catch a Wave by The Beach Boys; The Marine's Hymn by U.S. Marine Band; Blue Train by Dolly Parton, Linda Ronstadt & Emmylou Harris.
Eats: Beach Picnic in San Onofre State Park; Fish and Chips in Oceanside Harbor.

Distance: 17 to 42 miles. Time: 2 to 6 hours. Best on sunny wind-less weekend day.
Route & Bike: Moderate to strenuous depending on distance. Paved mostly Class I, some Class II and III. Class III through Marine Base when open to the public. Any bike okay, but rough pavement in places is more amenable to hybrid, and mountain bike opens up more options to get to the beach. Rolling hills, some short steep hills. SC3's route is on the Dana Point, Oceanside, and San Diego County maps. E-bike edge: Hills near start, Old Pacific Hwy, and Pendleton roads. E-MTB to Lowers.
Facilities: Restrooms and water in San Onofre State Park and Oceanside Harbor.
Knocks & Hazards: Rolling hills and some poor pavement, leading to Class II riding next to traffic. The ride through San Onofre State Beach is with slow-moving park traffic. Camp Pendleton is south of the park. If the base is closed for security or other reasons the state beach is your turn-around point, and to get to San Diego you must ride up to 17 miles along I-5, exiting at each off-ramp to avoid conflicts with traffic (or, take the train). The marine base always closes at dusk to cyclists. Even when the base is open to cyclists there may be military vehicles and activity close to the trail that can be exciting or unsettling, including exercises involving helicopters, tanks, and troupe movement. The permit process to ride through the base has become more arduous in recent years. The roads at the south end of Camp Pendleton are busy with little or no bike lanes. Harbor Drive to Oceanside is also crowded. Watch for rattlesnakes on trail especially in the brushy areas.
Bike 'n Brunch: Carl's Jr. and Cafe del Sol near the Christianitos exit, or head north on San Clemente's El Camino Real for more options. Those making it all the way to Oceanside Harbor can choose from ten waterfront restaurants. See the Oceanside ride in San Diego County. Or have a picnic at a scenic spot in San Onofre State Park.

Access: Start your ride with the surfers. Take the Cristianitos exit off I-5 at the south end of San Clemente. Just east of the freeway are options to park in the state park pay lot, or along the street, obeying parking signs, near (but not in) the Carl's Jr. restaurant lot. Follow the surfers, many with boards attached to their bikes, who are heading toward the legendary Trestles Beach down a paved trail on the left, just west of the southbound on-ramp to I-5. Rail 'n Ride: From the Metrolink station at North Beach take either the SC1 or SC2 rides to Calafia, go to the top of the hill and turn right on El Presidente, reaching the trailhead in about 1 mile on the right just after the road makes a sharp left toward the freeway. See map on page 150.

The Ride: Carefully glide down the paved path, swerving out of the way of the surfboards, and take a detour at the bottom of the hill on the trail to the beach to watch the waves and the surfers in the Trestles Beach Preserve, a natural area bisected by train tracks passing over the beach on new concrete trestles that replaced the old wooden ones. Return to the main route and turn right, cycling on the extremely wide Old Highway 101 as it goes over an old bridge over San Mateo Creek. This was the main road to San Diego before the days of I-5, and this section is now delightfully closed to cars. Climb to the top of a gradual hill where there is a fork in the road (~1.0).

The narrow left fork continues on our main route. For now, take the wider path to the right, then a quick right on a dirt road past a lifeguard building, to a fabulous viewpoint of Lower Trestles Beach. A bench makes this a great picnic spot. To get down to the beach, ride on the dirt road leading south along the bluff. It descends a fairly substantial hill and curves under the train tracks. Then ride to the right as far as the sand is compacted, about 0.25 mile's worth, and check out all the bikes with surfboard racks parked along the beach. There are porta-potties here.

Returning to the main trail, turn right and merge onto a wide shoulder of Old Hwy 101. This road has light but brisk vehicle traffic, so keep to the right. Bike lane improvements are planned. After 1.3 miles (about 2.5 miles into the ride) is the entrance to San Onofre Surf Beach. At your option, cycle down the one-way access road on the right, past the entry kiosk (bikes free) to the long dirt beachfront parking lot. The "Old Man's" break here is a historic draw for longboarders and is popular with novice surfers. The mellow beach is adjacent to defunct San Onofre nuclear plant. To exit, follow the road to the left under Hwy 101, that bends back to 101.

Back on the road, arrive at the entrance to San Onofre State Beach at about 3.8 miles into the ride. (No fee for bikes to enter; $15 per vehicle, another option to stage from if there are non-riders in your gaggle.) The road through the park is also the former Highway 101, now used as camping and beach access, with park facilities such as restrooms available. Bluffs obscure a view of the ocean through about half of the park, but you can lock your bike and hike down to the 3 miles of beach (referred to as "Trails") on the regularly spaced trails for a great Bike 'n Beach experience.

At mile 7, the last parking lot leads to Beach Trail 6, that can be ridden if not prohibited by signs. Down at the beach is lifeguard tower 6, and to the left about 1,000-2,000 ft is the site of SoCal's former premier clothing optional beach from 1973 until recently when the state banned nudity at this remote spot. Check "Friends of San Onofre" on line to see the current status.

The most scenic stretch of trail is just south of San Onofre State Beach in Camp Pendleton.

Meanwhile, back at the parking lot, ride past the gate and onto a bike trail. The next segment is the highlight of the ride, along another stretch of abandoned Hwy 101, but this time on Camp Pendleton property, so prepare for just about anything. This fabulous trail segment sports great views across a bluff to the sea. You will be disappointed when the trail turns all too soon to the east (left) at mile 8.8, through a tunnel under I-5. A sign warns to watch for military vehicles, like tanks, yikes! This is a possible turnaround point for a total ride of about 17.5 miles. The trail continues around a bend (bear right, don't go over the overpass) and onto another stretch of abandoned road that is also used by the marines as a practice runway, and is closed to bikes at those times. The road ends at a free parking lot (notorious for vehicle break-ins) accessed from the Las Pulgas Road exit from I-5 at mile 10.4. Turn around here for a 21-mile round trip ride.

Those in good shape that wish more adventure can ride the bike route along Camp Pendleton Marine Base roads. You must wear a helmet, carry the ID you pre-registered with, and not deviate from the bike route. Traffic is mostly light, except near the south end of the base at Oceanside, which can be very busy. Terrain is flat to rolling hills, plus a couple of steep hills. Turn left on Las Pulgas Road, and pass the guardhouse, stopping to check in. Keep right, then turn right at Stewart Mesa Rd (11.0), which is scenic with desert flora, but hilly. Turn right on Vandegrift Boulevard at mile 18. The south entrance guardhouse is at mile 19.5.

The road then crosses under I-5 (this is the most tricky area traffic-wise) and becomes Harbor Drive that leads to the picturesque Oceanside Harbor with its ten harborside restaurants at mile 21. This ride is 42 miles round-trip from the San Clemente trailhead, or about 19 miles round trip south from the Las Pulgas lot. From the south end of Oceanside Harbor you can connect with the San Luis Rey River Trail and The Strand along Oceanside's beach (ride OC1), or continue on a Class II ride through San Diego's coastal cities as far as San Diego (ride SDC1). Use Metrolink, Coaster, or Amtrak trains in one direction to shorten the distance. See OC1 for a map to the station.

Santa Ana River Trail

The 96-mile long Santa Ana River, the longest in Southern California, drains a watershed of 2,650 square miles encompassing portions of four counties from as high as 9,300 feet elevation in the San Bernardino and San Gabriel Mountains to the coastal plain of Orange County and the Pacific Ocean. Flow is from rainfall and snowmelt, predominantly in winter and spring, while discharge from groundwater, sewage treatment plants, and irrigation and urban runoff keep the river flowing somewhat during the dry seasons. The river is impounded at several locations, the most famous being Big Bear Lake created by the damming of the Bear Creek tributary. It flows through the narrow Santa Ana Canyon and is next impounded by Seven Oaks Dam. It continues southward in concrete channels through the San Bernardino area, but opens up into a natural drainage from the city of Riverside up until Prado Dam at the Santa Ana Mountains where the 91 Freeway enters Orange County. Settling basins in Anaheim ensure the water stays around long enough to recharge Orange County's groundwater aquifer, and what is left flows down a concrete channel, usually in a trickle, to the ocean at Huntington Beach, where it meets a tidal section at the outflow.

Someday, a 110-mile bike trail will extend from Big Bear Lake all the way to the ocean. For now, three main sections of trail are completed. The Lower Trail spans about 30 miles through Orange and Riverside Counties from the ocean to near Prado Dam along the 91 Freeway in Corona. It passes through the cities of Huntington Beach, Costa Mesa, Santa Ana, Orange, Anaheim, and Yorba Linda, and skirts Fountain Valley. The next reach, from Prado Dam through Corona, past I-15 and Norco is on the drawing board, and riders must use surface streets.

The Middle Trail currently extends from the Hidden Valley Nature Center in Riverside just east of Norco, through the cities of Riverside and Colton to the southwest corner of San Bernardino just northeast of the I-10 and I-215 Freeway interchange. Future plans call for extending the trail through San Bernardino and Redlands. The Upper Trail in San Bernardino National Forest is a fairly technical mountain bike trail beyond Seven Oaks Dam through Santa Ana Canyon that is beyond the scope of this book.

We have recommended three portions of the Lower Trail that we find to be the most interesting. Ride SAR1 begins at the Surf City Huntington Beach trail (HB1) near the ocean and extends roughly 5–6 miles through Costa Mesa and adjacent natural areas with options to explore some nearby attractions and/or combine with a beach ride. Ride SAR2 is a 7.7-mile reach that includes portions of Orange, Santa Ana, and Anaheim, including Angels Stadium and the Honda Center. Ride SAR3 continues in Anaheim Hills from where SAR2 leaves off, and extends about 10 miles all the way eastward along the river through Anaheim and Yorba Linda to the current trail's terminus at the Green River Golf Club near the 91 Freeway. There is a gap of about 5–6 miles between SAR1 and SAR2 through central Santa Ana. This segment is not as interesting and has some safety concerns, so is not part of our featured rides. However, for those who would like to do it, it is described as Option 3 of ride SAR1, including a map. Since the Middle Trail through Riverside–San Bernardino is not connected to the lower trail at this time, that trail is described as a separate entity (R1) in the Inland Empire chapter.

Costa Mesa and Fountain Valley

Although Costa Mesa is another city melded into the sprawl of central Orange County, the city of 113,000 is the home of several of the county's most lauded attractions. The Segerstrom Center for the Arts contains two major architecturally unique venues and several theatres on landscaped grounds filled with sculptures (see scfta.org). A fabulous landscape garden entitled "California Scenario" aka "Noguchi Garden" occupies an entire courtyard between 3200 Park Center Dr and 611 Anton Boulevard. This district is located just north of I-405 on Bristol Street, and to the right on Anton Boulevard. An elevated walkway leads across Bristol Street between the park in front of the Westin hotel, site of the region's largest annual Christmas tree, and South Coast Plaza, a world-renowned shopping mall that generates a billion dollars worth of sales annually, and offers a choice of restaurants as well. Its Crystal Court building is most unique with a dramatic atrium (see southcoastplaza.com).

The Orange County Fair in July is one of the largest in the state, attracting top name entertainment. The rest of the time it is the site of a gigantic weekend outdoor marketplace. The Santa Ana River Trail runs along the western boundary of the city between Huntington Beach to the south and Fountain Valley and Santa Ana to the north. A 2.5-mile Class II route enables a visit via the back way to the mall and adjacent arts district, as described in SAR1, Option 1. Another optional Class II route leads in about 1.7 mile to Mile Square Park and ride FV1, which is the principal attraction in Fountain Valley, a bedroom community of about 57,000 wedged in between several other Orange County cities. For further info on Costa Mesa see costamesaca.gov (city site) and travelcostamesa.com (tourism). Fountain Valley's site is fountainvalley.org.

Santa Ana River Trail—Costa Mesa Area SAR1

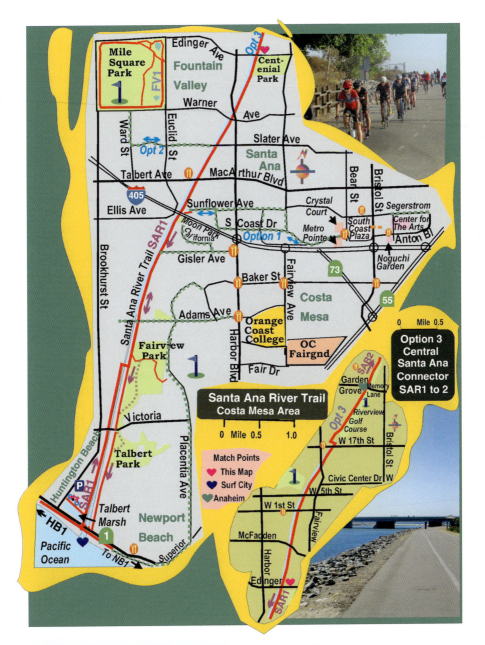

The lower end of the SART is a winner because it can be combined with a fabulous beach ride, portions of the channel are typically filled with tidal water, bird watching can be fantastic, on a clear day the San Gabriel Mountains frame the scene to the north, and it is relatively safe. On the downside on a day with strong on-shore winds the return down the channel can be brutal, so it's important to gauge this when you set out. Earlier in the day is typically better for the wind factor. Those with fat tires can detour into a wildlife preserve, and all can detour on 2-mile Class II routes to the shopping and entertainment district or Mile Square Park.

Tunes: Take Me To the River by The Talking Heads; The Sea Refuses No River by Pete Townsend.
Eats: Double-Double at In-N-Out Burger via Gisler.

Distance: 14.5 miles total + options. Time: 1.5+ hours.
Route & Bike: Easy except when very windy. Flat Class I paved trail with option for packed dirt side trail on return. Any bike. Hybrid or MTB better for wildlife preserve. E-bike edge: May be strong headwinds returning to the ocean.
Seasons: All. Best on sunny uncrowded weekday with minimal wind.
Facilities: Restrooms and water along beach trail and in Fairview Park.
Knocks & Hazards: Clueless peds. Possible lurkers, crime, more toward Santa Ana. Can be strong headwind returning to ocean. Trail is not especially scenic except for mountain backdrop on clear days.
Rent/Camp 'n Ride: See Huntington Beach and Newport Beach.
Bike 'n Brunch: Finding restaurants requires a detour off trail as described in ride, or ride south to Newport Beach from the ocean trailhead for more selections along PCH.
City code, bike riding on sidewalks: Defer to state law.
Further Info: Talbert Regional Park: ocparks.com/parks/talbert; Fairview (City Park): costamesaca.gov/fairviewpark/; Detailed SART info, pics: santa-ana-river-trail.com; SART conditions: trailsafetypatrol.com.

Access: 1) Park along the southern end of Brookhurst Street where allowed and make your way down the sidewalk to the Talbert Marsh Trail that goes to the east to join the SART; 2) Park in the State Beach ($15 fee) at the end of Brookhurst or Magnolia Streets and start from the beach trail; 3) Park at the end of Magnolia as permitted and enter the Beach Trail from there, heading east to join the SART; or 4) Park at Fairview Park in Costa Mesa and enter the SART from there.

The Ride begins at the Surf City Beach Trail (ride HB1), where a connector trail hooks around and goes under PCH to begin the SART. Another Class I connector starts near the end of Brookhurst Street and heads east past the Talbert Marsh to join it. "Mile 0" is painted onto the pavement here. SART heads north past an industrial area along the lined channel that is tidal at this point. A parallel path leads north from the southeast side of the PCH bridge with access to Talbert Regional Park. In 1.4 miles the trail crosses under Victoria/Hamilton Street, and at mile 2.3 is a ped/bike bridge that directs you to the east bank of the river where the main trail continues to the left. Access is available across a secondary channel to Fairmont Park and Talbert Regional Park via a bike bridge (2.6) that we'll opt to explore on the way back down the river. The parks are located off Placentia Avenue in Costa Mesa, another trail access point. The trail passes under Adams Avenue (3.1), then next to Mesa Verde Country Club (3.5–4.2) while nurseries under power lines are across the river.

ORANGE COUNTY

Lower Santa Ana River Trail looking north toward bike bridge and San Gabriel Mountain backdrop

A trail entry is at the end of Gisler Avenue. A 1-mile detour down that Class II street to Harbor Boulevard will bring you to some eats including In-N-Out to the left and El Pollo Loco to the right. Along the SART from Gisler to a point just before crossing under I-405, the west bank passes an Orange County Sanitation District Sewage Treatment Plant, while the east bank passes a nice suburban residential neighborhood, where there is another trailhead at Moon Park (4.7) (By car, take Harbor Boulevard south from I-405, turn right on Gisler Avenue, right on Gibraltar /California Street to the park).

Once reaching I-405 (4.8), you can turn around here for a ride of about 10 miles, continue along the SART, or consider the following option:

Option 1. South Coast Plaza/Arts District via Class II Roads ⭐ *5 miles round trip, easy*
On the north side of I-405 look for a path between the freeway and office buildings, and make your way to the right to the end of Sunflower Avenue. Head east on Sunflower, turning right on Hyland Avenue, and then left on South Coast Drive. Follow South Coast all the way around, past the Metro Pointe shopping center (restaurants). At Bear Street is the Crystal Court shopping center to the left and South Coast Plaza straight ahead. The Costa Mesa entertainment district is across Bristol Street from South Coast Plaza. A ride from the ocean to this district and back will be about 15 miles.

Moving onward from I-405, after passing a light industrial/commercial district, cross under Talbert Avenue/MacArthur Boulevard (5.2). If it's lunchtime you can detour to reach the Costco shopping center on the west side of the river in Fountain Valley, where you can try one of the many international casual eateries in the center. The bridge has no bike lanes but it does offer sidewalks. Back on the east bank of the SART, continue through the commercial/light industrial district that lines both sides of the river, passing under Segerstrom Ave (5.8).

Option 2: To Mile Square Park ⭐ *3.4 miles round trip to park, plus ride FV1 mileage, easy*
From the Segerstrom underpass ascend to the westbound lane of Segerstrom and ride over the bridge, as the road becomes Slater Avenue in Fountain Valley. This is a Class II route with occasional sidewalks. Continue to Ward Street (about 1.2 miles from the SART) and turn right on that Class II route for another 0.5 mile to Mile Square Park across Warner Avenue. See the Mile Square Park ride that follows (ride FV1).

Continue under Warner Avenue (6.2) and Harbor Boulevard (6.4) to just prior to the Edinger Avenue underpass (7.2). The large Centennial Regional Park in Santa Ana is on the right here, south of and accessed from Edinger, which is another potential starting point. This is the end of SAR1. At your option you can continue northbound via Option 3.

On the return ride you have the option of taking a detour into Fairview Park and Talbert Regional Park on the delightful dirt trails if you have the appropriate bike (hybrid or thicker tire preferred). After passing back under Adams Avenue look for a bike bridge over the secondary channel to the east (left going downstream). Across the bridge jog to the left then right, onto a paved path that curves around to the right and reaches an interestingly designed restroom facility in Costa Mesa's Fairview Park.

Take the dirt trail to the south that parallels the SART through Talbert Park, a park that is replicating an "ecological staircase" of a salt marsh, fresh-water wetlands, grasslands, and woodlands. The main path winds through the park and rejoins the SART downstream before the Victoria underpass. Another section of the park lies south of Victoria. You can also spend some time exploring other trails in both adjoining parks. The SART continues on the east bank from here all the way past a Corps of Engineers salt marsh restoration project, reaching the end of the trail at Coast Highway. To return to the starting point on the west bank, cross the highway bridge to the right on the roadway or sidewalk. Another option for more mileage is to backtrack on the SART all the way up to the bike bridge that will take you to the west bank of the river.

> **Option 3: Continue onward through Santa Ana to SAR2** *3.7 miles each way, easy*
> Be forewarned that between Edinger and 17th Street is the trail section that has experienced the most frequent assaults on trail users in the past. Thugs threw old bikes in the paths of cyclists with seemingly valuable bikes, and bike-jacked them, sometimes assaulting the rider in the process. This even happened in daylight hours. Although the local police made arrests, this is still the turf of youth gangs, so it is best to ride in groups through here and preferably during daylight hours, and to check with local authorities and the SART websites for recent activities.
>
> Pass under Edinger, then McFadden Avenue (7.9), next to high-density residential areas, under West 1st Street (8.5), West 5th Street (8.8), North Fairview Street (9.4) and West 17th Street (9.7). Just beyond, another bike/ped bridge takes you back to the west bank, reaching Edna Park, another trailhead (9.9). By car, from Edinger take Fairview Avenue North then right on Edna Drive to the park at the river. North of here the concrete channel changes into the Riverview Golf Course. Cross under West Memory Lane (city of Orange) (10.9) and the SR 22 Freeway (11.3). At this point The Outlets at Orange, a complex of entertainment venues, outlet stores, and restaurants is a block to the west, behind the commercial buildings next to the trail. The bridge at Memory Lane is the point at which this ride option overlaps with ride SAR2.

Mile Square Park in Fountain Valley   FV1

Distance: 4 to 8 miles, freeform, easy, flat, paved

Mile Square Regional Park is, as the name indicates, nearly a square mile in size and contains three regulation golf courses, three soccer fields, three baseball and three softball diamonds, an archery range, a nature area, two fishing lakes, bike and paddle boat concessions, a tennis center, and many picnic areas with picnic shelters. Paved paths parallel the perimeter roadways; about 1 mile each along Edinger Avenue to the north, Euclid Street to the east, Warner Avenue to the south and Brookhurst Street to the west. Cycling next to the busy streets is not wonderful, but in places the paths meander away from the road and into the park. The most scenic cycling is in the eastern portion, where there is a pretty lake and lots of paved paths going hither and thither so that you can do loops using the paths and park roadways.

On clear days you can see Saddleback Mountain to the east and the San Gabriel Mountains to the north. The bike rental concession ensures that on weekends surrey bicycles will dominate the paths. On weekdays contend with lots of strollers, many with pooches, and not many bikes. Numerous international restaurants are situated off each corner of the park and at Heil and Brookhurst. The two golf courses in the western half of the park also have restaurants. For a map and info see ocparks.com/parks/mile.

Access: From I-405 exit on Warner and go east about 0.5 mile to Brookhurst. Turn left and go about 0.5 mile north to Heil Avenue, where there is free parking at the Fountain Valley Recreation Center within the park. There is also free on-road parking on Edinger, Euclid, and Warner as signed. This park was also described as Option 2 from ride SAR1, the Santa Ana River Trail in the Costa Mesa area, and is shown on that map.

Anaheim and Santa Ana

The two largest cities of Orange County are Anaheim, with about 347,000 people and Santa Ana with about 335,000. Anaheim is the more well known name thanks to the twin Magic Kingdom amusement parks of Disneyland and California Adventure, with the dining and entertainment complex of Downtown Disney. Angels Stadium is the home of the Los Angeles Angels pro baseball team, and former home of the pro football Rams (now in LA) while the Honda Center, aka "The Pond" is home to the Mighty Ducks pro hockey franchise and center of the mega ocV!be development project. The Anaheim Convention Center is a major business attraction and revenue generator. Anaheim Hills at the northern end of Anaheim is the more upscale sector of the city.

Santa Ana is the seat of Orange County. City highlights include the Bowers Museum, The Saint Joseph Ballet, art galleries, art schools, historic buildings, and the Santa Ana Zoo. The city is 78 percent Hispanic and Spanish is spoken widely, so you can save lots of money by just visiting here and making believe you are in Mexico or perhaps Spain. Santa Ana has a historic district dotted with art deco buildings, bordered by Ross to French Streets and First to Civic Center Streets. The downtown district comprises the municipal buildings at the north end around Civic Center Drive and the retail section at the south end, featuring Artists Village whose hub is the 2nd Street Promenade between Broadway and Sycamore. Find great restaurants, art galleries in the Santora Building, and fun festivals celebrating film or various Latin holidays. Presently there is no bike route between the train depot, located near I-5 at Grand Avenue, or the SART, and this district.

The Santa Ana River Trail extends through both Anaheim and Santa Ana, which is the main ride offered by both cities. For locals this is a good recreation resource, however use caution because of occasional gang activity and assaults along the trail, especially in Santa Ana as mentioned in SAR1, Option 3. For that reason if you are picking and choosing sections of the trail to ride, central Santa Ana is not the best. We typically will ride from the Anaheim Stadium vicinity and north (SAR 2 and 3), or from Costa Mesa and south (SAR1). For those who like to ride long distances and need to ride through central Santa Ana, it is best to ride with a friend and during the daytime. The trail is not close to Artists Village of Santa Ana, or Disneyland in Anaheim but it is next to Honda Center, a few blocks from Anaheim Stadium and alongside the impressive ARTIC transportation center. Anaheim established a Class II/III bike route from ARTIC to the Disneyland vicinity along Douglass, Cerritos, and other boulevards.

Santa Ana River Trail—Anaheim Area   SAR2

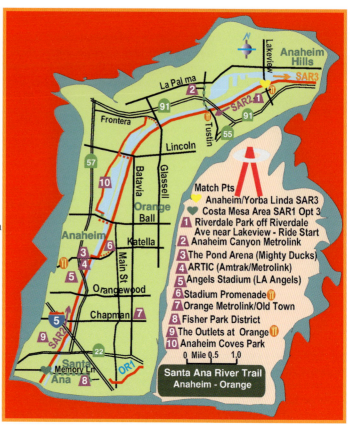

On a clear day, the towering San Gabriel Mountains can make anything look picturesque, from high tension lines to industrial buildings, and large barren concrete culverts they call rivers in these parts. As such, riding north from the Angels Stadium area can be quite rewarding both physically and aesthetically. The distinctive stadium with it's giant haloed "A" is interesting to look at, as is the Honda Center arena, home of the Mighty Ducks hockey team. The impressive glass Anaheim Regional Transportation Intermodal Center (ARTIC) is a good place to start our rides, whether arriving by rail or by car.

Anaheim's reach of the Santa Ana River is where the huge Orange County groundwater aquifer is recharged, and the detention berms in the river and adjacent ponds keep the water from flowing past too quickly so that it can percolate into the sandy soil below. It's all part of a big recycling system, since in the dry season most of the water is treated effluent from sewage plants. The SART actually spends the majority of the time in this reach in the city of Orange, when it is on the east side of the river from Katella north to Tustin Avenue, and on the west side of the river south of Orangewood. Orange has other featured trails, however, and the city is included in its own section. Wherever you start, it is a great ride with no interruptions. SAR2 connects with the Anaheim—Yorba Linda SART ride (SAR3), so for a longer adventure you can combine the two.

Tunes: Disney Girls by the Beach Boys; Calling All Angels by Jane Siberry; Los Rios by Incendio, One Black Sheep by Mat Kearney ("Amtrak...south to California").
Eats: Pesto Chicken & Hummus on Lazy Dog Café patio (Katella east of trail).

Distance: This section is up to 15.4 miles round trip, with options to combine with other sections of the SART. Time: 1.5–2 hours.

ORANGE COUNTY

Route & Bike: Easy to moderate depending on distance and wind (e-bike edge for that). Paved Class I continuous trail. Any bike. Flat with inclines to dip under roadways.
Seasons: All. Best on any sunny mild day.
Facilities: Restroom/water: On trail north of Katella, Anaheim Coves, Riverdale Park.
Knocks & Hazards: Homeless encampments come and go, especially between Ball Rd and Katella along trail. Some clueless peds. Speeding bikes.
Rent 'n Ride: None in Anaheim or Orange near the trail. See Orange rides.
Camp 'n Ride: Orangeland RV Park, 1600 Stuck Ave, Orange, 714.633.0404. Other RV Parks in Anaheim closer to Disneyland, but not near the ride.
Bike 'n Brunch: Restaurants on Lakeview, north of trail. Subway, Circle K at Tustin. Promenade east of trail on Katella (in Orange) has Kings Fish House, Lazy Dog Café, Tilted Kilt, Prime Cut Café, Which Which, Starbucks. JT Schmid's restaurant and Brewery on Katella near ARTIC.
City code, bike riding on sidewalks: Anaheim: Allowed; defer to state law. Orange (across river from ARTIC): Bikes okay on sidewalks except in commercial zones.
Further Info: SART: santaanarivertrail.org; City of Anaheim: anaheim.net; Disneyland: disneyland.disney.go.com; Los Angeles Angels Baseball: losangeles.angels.mlb.com

Access: Our ride start is from the upstream location in Anaheim Hills. Take the 91 Fwy east from the 57 or 55 Freeways to Lakeview Ave, northbound. Turn left on Riverdale Ave to Riverdale Park on the right. See also ARTIC in Rail 'n Ride.

Rail 'n Ride: The impressive glass structure of ARTIC services Metrolink and Amtrak trains and regional OCTA and local ART buses equipped with bike racks. Inside are some Grab'n Go food concessions. Bike lockers and racks are available for commuters. Access the SART from the east side of ARTIC. ARTIC is incorporated into the ocV!be mega-multiuse development, including a riverside park, opening during 2024-2028. See ocVibe.com. From CA 57 exit Katella and go east a short distance to ARTIC at 2626 E Katella Ave, Anaheim. Until Vibe construction starts parking lot A has free parking and SART access, but parking will change. Another Metrolink stop near this SART segment is Anaheim Canyon: From that unmanned station ride east through the business park to Tustin Avenue, turn right, then cycle about 1 mile south over the river to meet the SART. Transfer in Orange to get back to ARTIC.

The Ride: From Riverdale Park head west (left facing the river), where the river typically has impounded water for recharge in it. A newer residential area is on the inland side. Cross under the 91 Fwy (1.0) and Tustin Ave (1.1) (Subway, Circle K). Anaheim Canyon Metrolink station is 1 mile north on Tustin Ave. The trail now runs between the river and Riverdale Ave, in the city of Orange. Cross under the Metrolink tracks (1.5) and Glassell Street (2.1) as the river and trail bend to the south with diversion structures impounding water throughout this reach. Pass a sand and gravel plant (2.5), then more residential development once you cross under Lincoln (2.9).

> **Option 1: Anaheim Coves** ⭐ Explore this nature park on the west side of the river. It contains a 2.5-mile linear paved path with interpretive signs, restrooms and water. Access it via south sidewalks along Lincoln, Ball or Glassell to Frontera.

Along the SART by mile 3.5 the trail runs next to an industrial zone. Cross under Ball Road (4.3). Farther along are restrooms (5.0), and then Katella Avenue (5.1). Ride up the ramp to street level. SART continues to the right on a wide path over the bridge to Anaheim and its Honda Center and ARTIC transportation hub. However for the best food options carefully detour down the sidewalk 0.5 mile to the left, and enter the Stadium Promenade complex when you see a Starbucks. At time of writing the direct entrance from the SART is blocked off. After crossing the bridge carefully make a hairpin turn back under the bridge (5.3). At various times the areas under the bridges here can be heavily populated. The glass ARTIC facility will appear on the right, a possible option for grabbing some grub.

Next ride under the 57 Fwy (5.8) and enjoy a great view of Angels Stadium. Cross under Orangewood Avenue (6.1) where there are access ramps if you would like to see the LA Angels in action, or perhaps attend an RV show in the parking lot. At this point you've seen the highlights, so turn around at will. If you continue, at mile 6.5 the river water cascades, and at 6.7 the SART ducks under Chapman Avenue (in Orange again), where there are also ramps to ascend and visit a Waba Grill, Jack in the Box, Pita Grill, Urban Cactus Grill and Lee's Sandwiches. Next, cross under I-5. Before crossing under the 22 (Garden Grove) Freeway, you are a block away from another mega entertainment and dining complex called The Outlets (formerly The Block) at Orange, down The City Way to the west. After crossing under the 22 and passing some modern office buildings, reach West Life Drive (7.7). This is a good turnaround point unless you are going all the way to the ocean. See SAR1 Option 3 for a description of that route.

ARTIC accesses the SART. Arrive by car, rail, or bus. Angels Stadium's "Big A" is in the background.

Across this bridge to the east are Memory Lane and the upscale Santa Ana neighborhood of Fisher Park. Someday there may be a connection between this neighborhood and the end of the Santiago Creek Trail (OR1) described in the Orange section, however, the Fisher Park residents appear to be fighting this "missing link." If it is completed, you could not only reach the Santiago Creek Trail, but also easily ride to Old Towne Orange and potentially use Metrolink from the Orange station to get to the Anaheim Canyon station. Check santiagogreenway.org for updates. There would still be the issue of a long spooky tunnel under I-5 though, even if lighting were to be installed.

Upon returning to the Riverdale Park ride start, you can also ride east on the SART, in our favorite segment of the trail. See ride SAR3 that follows.

Santa Ana River Trail—Anaheim to Yorba Linda SAR3

The northern end of the lower SART extends between Green River Road west of Prado Dam and heads west, providing a nice pedal through some relatively safe areas, passing several parks with welcome amenities, as well as easy detours for your Bike 'n Brunch. On a clear day, views of surrounding mountain ranges can be stimulating, more so if you can shield out the imposing 91 Freeway that runs parallel across the river, or sometimes directly up against the trail. The river bottom contains retention structures downstream toward central Anaheim, and a more scenic natural bottom farther upstream through Anaheim Hills and Yorba Linda moving toward the dam. You'll see all kinds of cyclists, casual strollers, mothers with kids, people with dogs, and lightning fast racers or groups getting a great off-street workout. Our favorite place to stage from for this portion of trail is the free lot west of Yorba Regional Park in Anaheim, which is west of the midpoint of this 10-mile trail section.

Tunes: Let the River Run by Carly Simon; (Cross the) Heartland by Pat Metheny Group.
Eats: Real Tacoz along trail NE of Yorba Linda Blvd bridge.

Distance: About 21 miles round trip. Time: 2 to 2.5 hours.
Route & Bike: Easy to moderate depending on distance or wind. Paved Class I trail, a regular bike highway. Any bike. Mostly flat except for small hills to cross bridges. E-bike edge: Fight headwinds and go farther, combine with SAR2.
Seasons: All. Best on any mild sunny day.
Facilities: Restrooms and water in Yorba and possibly Featherly Regional Parks.
Knocks & Hazards: Clueless peds plus speeding cyclists can make a dangerous combination, but usually trail users are courteous. Possible lurkers. Rattlesnakes and potential for mountain lions farther east. Stay out of channel during high flow. Avoid heat/smog of summer.
Rent 'n Ride: Wheel Fun in Yorba Regional Park. Bike Shop: Rock 'n Road Cyclery, 5701 Santa Ana Canyon Road, at Imperial Hwy, Anaheim Hills, 714.998.2453.
Camp 'n Ride: Canyon RV Park is a private park within Featherly Regional Park, near the east end of the trail, a great place to start the ride, 24001 Santa Ana Canyon Rd, Anaheim, 714.637.0210.
Bike 'n Brunch: See ride description for restaurants along route.
City code, bike riding on sidewalks, Anaheim and Yorba Linda: Allowed except when signed otherwise. Yield to peds and give audible signal when passing.
Further Info: SART: santaanarivertrail.org; City of Anaheim: anaheim.net; City of Yorba Linda: www.ci.yorba-linda.ca.us

Access: From the Riverside (91) Freeway westbound, exit Yorba Linda Blvd and go right (north) to La Palma. Turn left and go 1.6 miles past Yorba Regional Park to the free parking lot on the left at Huxford Lane. From the 91 eastbound, exit on Imperial Highway. Turn left (north) to La Palma. Turn right and travel about 1 mile to the parking lot on the right after Fairmont Blvd. Then, just cycle toward the river to reach the trail, and cycle in either direction, or enjoy a cycle through the adjacent county park.

Distance: West through Anaheim—6.0 miles round trip

Heading west, enjoy a pleasant ride for a mile before reaching a bike/ped bridge that takes you over the river, just before Imperial Highway. Prior to crossing the river check out an interestingly decorated rest area (no facilities). Lots of restaurants are a short ride on the Imperial Hwy sidewalk to the right at La Palma. Find In-N-Out, Starbucks, Keno diner, Thai, Indian, pizza, Viet, seafood, etc. Once across the river, the trail ducks under Imperial Highway then runs next to some nursery plantings. Although it draws closer to the 91, it is a very pleasant stretch between the river and the planted trees with lots of birds. A diversion structure directs water into an adjacent channel around mile 2, as the trail is now between the river and a residential neighborhood. Another structure creates a bit of a waterfall, followed by the Lakeview Ave overpass (mile 2.9). Take the east sidewalk south for Chinese, Japanese, Italian, Subway, or donuts. At mile 3.0 is Riverdale Park (restrooms). This is the turnaround point for the SAR3 segment, but you can of course go as far as you want. See SAR2 for the segment starting here. Our route retraces our steps to the ride start (6.0). To get in more riding continue east on the trail.

Distance: East through Yorba Linda—14.8 miles round trip plus options

The first stretch of trail heading east from the trailhead is very scenic, passing between the lush treed landscape of Yorba Regional Park and the riparian vegetation of the Santa Ana River. Impoundments on the river attract a plethora of shore birds. There is also a more serene parallel, packed dirt trail inside the park that you can take instead in either direction. At mile 1.3 is a turnoff leading to the left to La Palma Avenue. This is your ticket to a route to some restaurants via the Yorba Linda Boulevard bridge over the river (Option 1).

River trail ride SAR3 in Yorba Linda.

Option 1: Bike 'n Big Box Brunch ★ *2.8 miles round trip* Although it is not a bike-friendly thoroughfare, Yorba Linda Blvd does have sidewalks on the bridge. Go left on the Savi Ranch Pkwy sidewalk, and follow it past the Costco, crossing to the other side to continue to El Torito, Wahoo's Fish Taco, and various fast food at the big box center. Upon returning over the Yorba Linda Blvd bridge, turn right onto the SART, which is now next to La Palma Avenue. The distance from the SART turnoff to Wahoo's is about 1.5 miles out, 1.3 miles return.

After crossing under Yorba Linda Blvd, the main SART veers to the left up a hill (while the path straight ahead turns to dirt, so a MTB can go that way) (1.6). The main path runs next to La Palma Avenue, above the river, which is now a very appealing wide riparian zone with a stream of water running through it. A commercial center along the route at the Yorba Linda border has a taco shop (2.1). The trail follows the river around a bend to the right, while La Palma Avenue and business parks are in the other direction. SART next bends to the left, between the river and a residential neighborhood district (3.4). At mile 4.4 is the Gypsum Canyon Road bridge over the river, with a wide separated bike lane for the SART. The paved trail also continues under the bridge and along the north side of the river for another mile. Mountain bikers can go that route and double back through parkland in the river channel (but stay out of there during high water), returning to the west side of the Gypsum Canyon Bridge.

Crossing the Gypsum Canyon Bridge can be quite scenic, with views up and down the river, surrounding hills and mountains, and perhaps even a passing Metrolink train beyond La Palma Avenue. Look for a bike trail ramp on the south side of the bridge (4.7) that leads around and under it, passing the entrance to Canyon RV Park. The trail is next wedged between the river and the noisy 91 Freeway. It currently ends at the end of Green River Road near Green River Golf Club (7.4). A couple of fast food restaurants are about 0.5 mile up the road from the trailhead. There is parking along Green River Rd, a popular staging spot for folks who do the epic ride to the ocean and back. In the future, when Prado Dam reconstruction is completed, the trail is expected to extend to the segment that recommences in Norco/Riverside (R1) as featured in the Inland Empire chapter. An isolated 1 mile section was built west of CA 71 in 2020.

The SART crosses the river on the Gypsum Canyon Road Bridge. The Metrolink train is en route from the Anaheim Canyon station to Corona and Riverside.

Yorba Linda

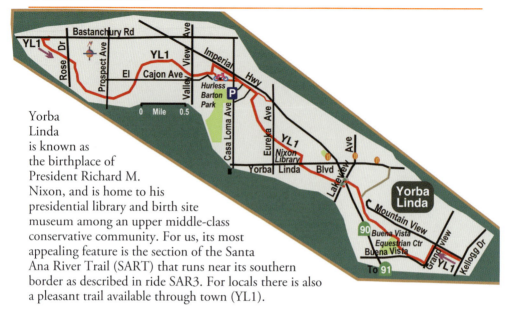

Yorba Linda is known as the birthplace of President Richard M. Nixon, and is home to his presidential library and birth site museum among an upper middle-class conservative community. For us, its most appealing feature is the section of the Santa Ana River Trail (SART) that runs near its southern border as described in ride SAR3. For locals there is also a pleasant trail available through town (YL1).

Yorba Linda Recreation Trail YL1

Details: 8 miles total, paved, Class I, easy, any bike. Also known as: El Cajon Trail

A typical trail section, with the highlight—a view of Nixon's Army One chopper

The 4-mile long paved Class I Yorba Linda Recreation Trail (YL1) at the center of the city cuts through equestrians' backyards and passes the Nixon Library. Find access to the trail and restrooms at Hurless Barton Park and Buena Vista Equestrian Center, or start at the Nixon Library. From the Riverside Freeway (SR91) take Imperial Hwy (SR90) north for 3.7 miles and turn left onto Casa Loma Avenue, then find Hurless Barton Park on the right. The trail is mostly level, with a parallel equestrian trail next to a white fence. At Lakeview Avenue the trail crosses over Imperial Highway on a sidewalk in one direction and a bike lane in the other. Expect both signaled and unsignaled street crossings en route. A sidewalk detour east along Yorba Linda Boulevard from the vicinity of the library leads to restaurants such as Mimi's Café. Someday the trail may connect to the SART at Fairmont Blvd. For a map of Yorba Linda's bike routes and trails see yorbalindaca.gov.

Irvine

Irvine, the master of master-planned communities, boasts 63+ miles of Class I bike trails and is rated bronze for bike-friendliness by the League of American Bicyclists. James Irvine and partners purchased 120,000 acres in 1864 to create the Irvine Ranch. The land encompassed portions of what are now Laguna Beach, Newport Beach, and several other cities, while Irvine was incorporated in 1971 with 14,231 people and now is home to over 270,000.

   Irvine is a center of commerce and high-tech industry, home of the renowned University of California at Irvine, and popular with people of Asian descent who make up 46 percent of the populace. It has also been ranked the safest city (for violent crime) of over 100,000 population in the U.S. many times, so for a family outing this statistically safer excursion may appeal.

   Although scenery is mostly unspectacular through sprawling suburbia, routes through the greenbelts and parklands along re-vegetated San Diego Creek can be quite pleasant indeed, with vistas to the surrounding mountain ranges both near and far. The landlocked city is close enough to the ocean to benefit from sea breezes, and an easy connection to Newport Beach allows residents access to the bays and beaches on a fairly flat route (IR1, NB1 and 2). Most of Irvine is perched on a deliciously flat, wide plain, however a new scenic Class I ride takes you up into the southern hills and open space lands of the Shady Canyon and Turtle Rock subdivisions (IR2). If you prefer an easier family excursion, pretty William Mason Regional Park has loops of trails for you to explore. The new Great Park in East Irvine has lots of bike paths and connects to a network of Irvine's paths forming a fabulous, though hilly loop with lots of options (IR3). The advantage of being encircled by suburbia is that it is easy to accomplish a delightful Bike 'n Brunch with many options. So, whether you live here or in the surrounding area, are in town on business or staying here as a base to explore the Orange County region, make sure to check out Irvine's bike trails.

Location and access: Irvine is located at the southern confluence of the I-405 and I-5 Freeways in central Orange County, about halfway between San Diego and Los Angeles. Orange County's John Wayne Airport (SNA) is in unincorporated land adjacent to the city with its entrance off MacArthur Blvd south of I-405.

Rail 'n Ride: Irvine Station at 15215 Barranca Parkway within the Irvine Spectrum office and entertainment district services Amtrak and Metrolink. From I-5, exit at Alton Parkway. Go east on Alton and turn left (north) on Ada. When arriving with your bike by train you can cycle to the east end of IR1 by taking Ada to Class II Barranca Parkway to the west (right), over I-5, left on Pacifica, and look for the trailhead on the right at Spectrum. The trail takes you under the 133 Freeway. If that undercrossing is not available, cross 133 via Alton Parkway and join the trail where Alton crosses over it. You can cruise all the way to Newport Beach, or just ride around Irvine. The Tustin Metrolink (no Amtrak) station is at 2975 Edinger Ave (see map for TU1). From I-5, exit at Jamboree Rd southbound to Edinger. Head west (right) on Edinger to the first traffic signal and turn right into the station. When arriving by train, you can join the bike trails described here by cycling east 0.25 mile on busy Class II Edinger, under Jamboree. Just beyond at Peters Canyon Wash ramps lead down to the bike path that is part of the Mountains to the Sea Trail (TU1), which runs south to join the San Diego Creek Trail (IR1). Take that east to the Irvine station, or south to the Newport Back Bay (NB2). Heading north on TU1 leads to the IR3 trails, or Peters Canyon Park (TU2) and Irvine Regional Park (OR2). Finally, a planned pathway across the tracks from the Irvine station will connect to Marine Way and a future path along the road to the Great Park District and Ride IR3. Sound confusing? There's just too many options, which is a wonderful thing. Check the maps and plan your own routes.

Rent 'n Ride: For UC Irvine only: ZotWheels bike share: parking.uci.edu/zotwheels; Groove E-Bikes, 4622 Barranca Pkwy, 949.274.7944; Trails End Cycling Ctr, 17145 Von Karman near Alton, 863.1982; A Road Bike 4U, Main St & Red Hill Ave, 752.2080. Shops: Jax Bicycle Center, 14210 Culver Dr, (near I-5), 733.1212; Rock 'n Road Cyclery, 6282 Irvine Blvd (near Sand Canyon, north of I-5), 733.2453; Irvine Bicycles, 6604 Irvine Center Dr, 453.9999.

Camp 'n Ride: Newport Dunes RV Resort is within riding distance of the San Diego Creek Trail (see NB1 and 2).

City code, bike riding on sidewalks: Permitted except when signed otherwise. Yield to/give audible signal to peds. Allowed in playground, park, or school only when permitted by supervisor of facility.

Further Info: City of Irvine: cityofirvine.org. Contains maps of bikeways and complete lists of restaurants available at each shopping center, parks, and entertainment venues; the Great Park (check for construction progress): ocgp.org

San Diego Creek Trail   IR1 ⭐

Irvine's bicycle highway to the sea, the Class I San Diego Creek trail, runs for nearly 10 miles from the Irvine Spectrum office and entertainment district all the way through the heart of Irvine to the Back Bay of Newport Beach. It also serves those who are already in Newport Beach that want to get in some less-crowded Class I mileage on those muscled bike legs. Along its route it connects with several other trails and provides access to shopping centers full of restaurants. Although there are a few blips along the way, this is a great choice for those who want to get an off-road workout in the relatively safe community of Irvine. It is also a useful commuter trail for getting to destinations around the city, including schools and the number one employer, UC Irvine.

The route is mostly flat as it follows the creek drainage, except where it drops down under several major roadways, including some that may be flooded during periods of high runoff. Because of these short relatively steep hills on this concrete trail, and the presence of many fellow trail users, make sure to wear your helmet on this seemingly benign trail. It is indeed through suburbia, but for most of the way the creek has riparian vegetation and water flowing in it, in addition to the tidal zone near its outlet to the Back Bay. Therefore, bird watching can be pretty rewarding. You may see a ferruginous hawk setting on a fence post, or a great blue heron down in the streambed.

Typical scene along east-west segment of San Diego Creek Trail

Civilization is visible along most of the path, including condos, medical and office ings or shopping centers, but many parks as well. The southern segment next to University Dr is more wide open and scenic. As you ride northeastward from the Back Back Bay on a clear day enjoy the distant vistas of the San Gabriel Mountains, which are especially beautiful when snow-covered, and then after the trail veers to the southeast, the closer-in Santa Ana Mountains form the backdrop, including the distinctive Saddleback. A new section of path tunnels under I-405 and leads to the large Los Olivos aprartment village.

Tunes: Many Rivers to Cross by Jimmy Cliff; The Suburbs by Arcade Fire
Eats: Chicken meal at El Pollo Loco, trail at Jeffery.

Distance: 9.5 miles each way. Time 45 minutes to 1.5 hours each way.
Route & Bike: Easy to moderate depending on distance and headwind. Paved Class I, any bike. Flat with dips under roadways. E-bike edge: Headwinds toward bay.
Seasons: All. Best on sunny, mild, uncrowded, winter or spring weekday with snow in the mountains.
Facilities: Restrooms and water at parks along route.
Knocks & Hazards: Clueless peds/strollers/dog walkers especially in Woodbridge section. Fast moving road bikers (keep to the right). Several low-traffic street crossings. Road undercrossings may be flooded during high runoff. Short steep hills to dip under roadways. Possible strong headwinds heading toward Back Bay. Some potential for rattlesnakes and rare mountain lion. Poison oak along wilder segments.
Bike 'n Brunch: Lots of choices on the eastern half of the trail (see ride description).

Access: To do the entire trail from the Back Bay, take Jamboree Road south from I-405, past MacArthur Blvd and the Route 74 San Joaquin Transportation Corridor toll road. Turn right on Eastbluff where there is on-street parking. Ride back down the sidewalk toward Jamboree, curving to the left. This is part of the Newport Back Bay ride (NB2). Reach a "Y" (mile 0) and go to the left onto the San Diego Creek Trail that bends around to the right next to the creek under Jamboree Road. Otherwise find parking in any of Irvine's parks along the route. An example is Windrow Park. From I-405 take Jeffery Road north to Alton Boulevard west, and East Yale Loop North to the park entrance on the right, just after crossing San Diego Creek. Or Irvine Community Park accessed from Harvard heading south from Barranca is another good staging spot. Access by rail was described previously.

The Ride: From the trailhead at the junction with NB2, follow the Class I trail next to the tidal portion of San Diego Creek, passing a residential area, then a wooden bridge (2.25) and a trail junction. The trail to the right leads to Bonita Creek Park, and then Bison Avenue in 1.4 miles. IR1 continues straight ahead under the SR 74 toll road and the MacArthur Boulevard overpasses. It draws nearer to University Drive, and the signal at California Avenue to the right allows the first access to UCI (0.8). The next access is via Campus Drive, but our trail route dips underneath it (1.4). Across the creek here is the bike-unfriendly San Joaquin Marsh and Wildlife Sanctuary whose entrance is off Campus Drive.

IR1 pulls away from University Drive and reaches another trail junction on the right, behind Bethel Korean Church (1.7). This trail leads to University Drive across which is William Mason Park (IR2 and 3). IR1 continues along the marshy creek channel, heading north, with Michelson Water Reclamation Plant across the creek to the west, and now Harvard Drive and the San Joaquin Country Club golf course to the east (2.0).

Cross under Michelson Drive (2.7), passing Boomers funpark, then cross under I-405 (2.9), reaching another trail junction on the right (3.0). This Class I "Freeway Trail" runs adjacent to I-405 extending to Jeffrey Road (IR2) and then to Sand Canyon. Our IR1 route continues north under Coronado (3.2) and Main Street, where there is a shopping center with coffee and restaurants to the right, and a Boudin SF a block to the left. Westpark neighborhoods are to the right here, and at the next trail junction (3.6) a path leads to the right to San Marco Park, off Harvard Avenue, another potential staging spot. As you cross under Alton Parkway, the Irvine civic buildings will be on the right (3.9).

The trail next curves to the right as we reach the confluence of Peters Canyon Wash and San Diego Creek (4.2). To your right is the large Civic Center Park with playing fields, tennis courts, and restrooms. Cross the creek to the left on the bike/ped bridge (4.3). Notice the giant airplane hangers (world's largest wooden structures) to the north at the closed Tustin Marine Base, and The District center across Jamboree with scores of restaurants. To the left is the Peters Canyon Trail, part of the Mountains to the Sea Trail (TU1) that IR1 has been a part of so far. IR1 now splits off and continues to the right instead. The trail runs alongside San Diego Creek roughly parallel to Barranca Pkwy, in a reach that is narrower and concrete lined, with little vegetation. It swoops down to cross under Harvard Avenue (4.6) and then Paseo Westpark.

Across the creek from here is a center with a Sprouts market, Olive Garden and Chili's, while on our side is a large Target shopping center with numerous interesting casual eateries, some with outdoor patios, and all accessible via a spur trail to the west (5.2). The main trail makes a deep dip to cross under Culver Drive (5.3), down

ORANGE COUNTY   181

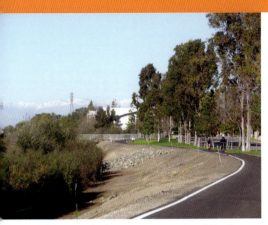

Looking north along San Diego Creek Trail toward San Gabriel Mountains

to a spot that may flood in high runoff situations. Up the sidewalk to the northeast along Culver are an Islands burgers and Mimi's Café. The Class I trail continues along the creek, which has widened with greener, more vegetated banks. Cross under West Yale Loop (5.5).

At this location along Barranca to the northeast is a strip center with several casual restaurants. The next crossing is via a crosswalk at Lake Rd next to a car wash (5.8). Woodbridge Village Shopping Center on the east side of Lake Road offers coffee, tea, pizza, yogurt and a Grocery Outlet. The trail returns to the creek, and reaches a bike/ped bridge to Woodbridge Community Park and South Lake, one of Woodbridge's two lakes. Along the San Diego Creek trail, Creek Road is the next street crossing via a crosswalk, next to a Del Taco (6.2). Medical buildings line the north side of the trail until the East Yale Loop undercrossing that leads to Windrow Park, a potential staging point (6.7). A tunnel (do not proceed when flooded) takes cyclists under Jeffrey Road and up to the sidewalk on its east side (7.0). Turn left (back toward the creek) to carry on. Cross the bridge and turn left to continue on the trail. Or, if you need refreshment, the centers on both sides of Jeffrey at Alton contain a variety of establishments including Ralph's and Gelson's markets and several restaurants including El Pollo Loco and Pick up Stix. The creek trail continues onward, under Valley Oak Drive (8.0) then Sand Canyon Avenue, where the streambed widens.

From this point to the end is perhaps the most scenic and peaceful as the riparian vegetation increases and it feels separate from civilization. It curves away from the creek (8.5) and reaches a trail junction on the right that leads to Alton Pkwy and Kaiser and Hoag Hospitals. Reach the Laguna Canyon Rd undercrossing (8.7). If you plan to continue into the Irvine Spectrum area, take the ramp to the road surface and switch to the north bank of the trail either here or at the next crossing, Alton Pkwy (9.0). The south bank trail ends at the 133 Fwy (9.4), while the north bank trail tunnels under 133 and ends at a T at Spectrum (9.5). It continues right, over a bridge, then left for 1 mile under I-405 to the Los Olivos community and dining options. Or, the Irvine Spectrum complex with mega restaurant choices is to the right down Class II Pacifica (10.2), while the Irvine train station is to the left as described previously.

Option 1: Newport Back Bay/Beaches
The southern trailhead is along the Newport Beach Back Bay Trail (NB2). When you come up to the trail from under Jamboree Road, go to the right toward Eastbluff to combine with that loop, with the option of using connecting streets at the south end of the bay to reach the ocean (NB1).

Option 2: Combine with Shady Canyon/Turtle Rock Loop and/or William Mason Park
At mile 1.7 (in back of Bethel Church), a spur trail leads to University Dr near Harvard. After crossing both University and Harvard, take the sidewalk along University to the east, and to the right, into William Mason Park (IR2 Option 1). You can also visit University Center, or ride portions or all of the Shady Canyon/Turtle Rock loop (IR2).

Shady Canyon & Turtle Rock Loop IR2

Shady Canyon Trail vista.

The best Class I ride in Irvine is also the hilliest, but well worth it—a ride to work up to. Just put your bike in its lowest gears and you'll be glad you agreed to do this moderate workout. You'll cruise through some nicely preserved coastal sage habitat in the Irvine Open Space area, gaze at panoramic mountain vistas (on clear days), gain entrance to an exclusive gated community of multi-million dollar homes in Shady Canyon, enjoy the beautiful Turtle Rock community's greenbelt trails, and pass lakes, golf courses, a riparian open space park, and some restaurants, all on a series of Class I paved trails that forms a rewarding loop. When we rode it the signage was pretty much non-existent, so pay close attention to the directions. Watch for birds along the way including California quail, roadrunner, and ferruginous hawks.

Tunes: Turtle Rock by Béla Fleck and the Flecktones; Happy Together by The Turtles
Eats: Wild Salmon Lite Burrito at Sharkey's (near trailhead)

Distance: 8–9 miles. Time: 1–1.5 hours
Route & Bike: Moderate. Paved, any bike. Mostly Class I, a couple blocks on Class II. Hilly with a few flat sections. Definite e-bike edge for the hills.
Seasons: All. Best on sunny, mild, uncrowded weekday.
Facilities: Restrooms and water at all trailheads and Turtle Rock Community Park. Several water fountains along route.
Knocks & Hazards: Clueless peds. Several street crossings, the busy ones are signaled. Uphills and downhills (watch speed). Rattlesnakes. Potential for mountain lion.
Bike 'n Brunch: Near the trailhead is Quail Hill Shopping Center with an impressive selection of casual international restaurants, and a few more at Parkview Center (mile 2). The only other dining options are at University Center, which requires a detour through William Mason Park as described.

Access: From I-405 in the south Irvine area, take the Sand Canyon/Shady Canyon exit south toward Shady Canyon. The free Quail Hill trailhead parking area is ahead on the right.

The Ride: From the Quail Hill lot, go back out to Shady Canyon and turn left onto the Class I trail that runs alongside it. Cross over the fire station access road. At a trail junction with a posted circular map (mile 0.3), go to the left on the paved path, toward "Jeffrey Road." Although the next stretch is adjacent to the San Diego Freeway (I-405), you can concentrate on the vacant overgrazed hills to the left that are pretty in the springtime. Access to the bike/ped overpass to Jeffrey Road and ride IR1 appears at mile 1.3. Our main route next begins a gradual ascent to the left adjacent to University Drive. At the light at Strawberry Farm Road (1.9) you have the option to cross University and access Parkview Center with a Zion specialty market, a Subway, and casual Asian eateries. The next light is Ridgeline and the trail appears to end with no signage, but it does actually continue (2.2).

Cross Ridgeline and turn left on its wide sidewalk, then look for an obvious concrete trail that leads into the riparian wilderness of William R. Mason Regional Park (2.3). This very pleasant segment through a wooded area runs parallel to, but out of sight of, University Drive. Bear left at the junctions that start at mile 2.8, including Bobcat Junction (3.1). At this point you can choose to explore the developed portion of William Mason Park by turning right (see Option 1 below). Otherwise, keep left and enter the Turtle Rock development's greenbelt. It winds through a very pleasant park-like stretch between homes.

Cross Rockview Drive (3.4) and look for the continuation of the trail to the right. It curves to the left to parallel Campus Drive (3.5). Aim for the tunnel under Turtle Rock Drive (3.6) and continue through the greenbelt on the most obvious trail as it winds around and through another tunnel under Sycamore Creek (3.9). It then curves to the right before reaching Turtle Rock Drive, then veers away from it, and crosses Sycamore Creek again. The path arrives at Turtle Rock and Starcrest (4.2). Cross Starcrest and begin a long gradual climb on the sidewalk along Turtle Rock Drive. Reach the top of the hill at Ridgeline (4.8). Cross Ridgeline and turn right, following the Turtle Rock Trail alongside of it up a small incline. It veers off to the left, and winds its way down the hill, reaching Ralph C. Bren Memorial Park (5.1), then emerges at Turtle Rock with Sunnyhill across the street (5.4). To reach this point from Ridgeline you could have also taken the Class II bike lane down Turtle Rock.

The Shady Canyon Trail includes some welcome open space areas.

Proceed down Class II Sunnyhill toward Turtle Rock Park (restrooms, water, picnic). Reach Shady Canyon (5.5). Cross Sunnyhill to go left onto the sidewalk into the Shady Canyon development, following the signs for the Shady Canyon Public Trail. It is a private gated community, but the public can enter via this paved trail. The trail to the right across the road leads in 0.5 mile to Bonner Canyon parking/staging area (restrooms/water) and beyond.

IR2 bears left without crossing Shady Canyon Rd. It runs roughly parallel to it, but traverses a nicely intact coastal sage ecosystem. Enjoy pano views of a lake and golf course below as you cycle the rolling hills, taking in a vista atop the final hill across Saddleback Valley to Saddleback Mountain. Cruise carefully down the hill. When you see the Quail Hill Park athletic fields, get ready to turn left to your staging area (7.7).

Option 1: Wm Mason Park ⭐ The beautiful 345-acre developed section of this park is located west of Culver and south of University where the vehicle entrance is located (fee). Access it from IR1 as described in that ride, or from IR2 mentioned above: After bearing right at Bobcat Junction, bear right at Rattlesnake Junction to reach the University sidewalk. Go left, cross Culver at the light, go slightly left, then right onto an ample path along the edge of the park that crosses the access road. Narrower paths meander throughout the park, around the lake and under shade trees. It's less crowded on weekdays. A trail exit to Harvard entices a Bike 'n Brunch trip to University Center with its many al fresco dining options, but don't park there as they tow.

OC Great Park - Jeffrey Open Space Loop IR3

Northeast Irvine has seen massive development of late in and around the former Marine Corps Air Station El Toro, now Orange County Great Park and associated neighborhoods. Bicycling infrastructure is incorporated into the development, resulting in a fabulous 12-mile loop ride encompassing the new areas and the impressive Jeffrey Open Space Trail, with options to shorten or lengthen the ride.

1. Orange County Great Park
2. Cypress Village Trail
3. Portola Springs Park
4. Bosque Trails
5. Peters Cyn/Mts to Sea Tr
6. Peters Cyn/East Branch

Great Park - Jeffrey Loop
NE Irvine

Details: 12.5 miles +/- options, 60-90 minutes, easy+ to moderate (e-bike edge for hills). All Class I paved except 0.8 mile Class II. Elevation: 230 ft at start to 500 ft at Portola high point. Restrooms in parks. **Access:** I-405 or I-5: Exit Sand Cyn NB. Right on Marine Way, left on Ridge Valley to Lot 1.

The Ride: From Lot 1 (free), explore OC Great Park via its bike paths. It is a work in progress with athletic fields, a Visitors Center, and a giant tethered orange helium balloon that provides a 400-foot birds eye area view (fee). Return to Lot 1 (~1.5 mles), then go left on the Ridge Valley sidepath. Turn right onto Class II Marine Way and reach Sand Canyon (2.1), turning right into the bike lane. Cross at the Night Mist light (2.4) and go left down the Sand Canyon sidepath. Veer right onto the Cypress Village Path (2.6). Pedal through the pleasant greenbelt, and round a bend to meet the Jeffrey Open Space Trail (3.7). Along the way it widens into parkland with restrooms, and features artsy plaques depicting the area's agricultural history. Tunnels or bridges cross all roadways, and side paths lead to intersections or neighborhoods. Several international dining options are at Trabuco (4.1). At Bryan/Longmeadow (4.6) is a shortcut back to Sand Canyon via the sidepath along Longmeadow. IR3 via the Jeffrey path continues over Irvine Blvd (5.2) and ends at Portola. IR3 bends right on the Portola Sidepath (Option - to the left is lovely Hicks Cyn Trail, see map for loops). Cross Sand Canyon (7.0), Ridge Valley (7.9), and up a gradual grade past Portola Spgs Rd (8.4). After passing under a bike/ped bridge, the bike trail on the right continues our IR3 route (8.7). (The bridge leads to a 0.5 mile path through vacant land to Tomato Spgs Rd. Portola Spgs Park is to the right here, or off Portola.) Ride the path downhill through Round Cyn Open Space to a light at Portola Spgs & Modjeska (9.1). Take the Modjeska sidepath to Irvine Blvd (9.7). Cross to its far sidepath and go right. A path into Bosque parkland of the Great Park (10.2) starts just before Bosque Rd, and follows a sinuous route downhill through three bike tunnels, ending at the Great Park/Bosque roundabout (11.5). Follow the bike path across Great Park Blvd into the park, and take any path back to Lot 1 (12.5).

Tustin

Tustin is a middle-class suburban community of about 81,000 people located between Irvine to its south and east, Santa Ana to its west, and Orange (and unincorporated North Tustin) to its north. It was founded by Columbus Tustin, a carriage maker from Northern California in the 1870s. The city has preserved its history in Old Town Tustin, located along Main Street (between Williams St and Newport Ave) and intersecting El Camino Real, where buildings from the late 1800s and early 1900s are situated. See website tustinca.org/833/Tustin-History/ for details. As for cycling, our main interest in Tustin is the section of the Mountains to the Sea Trail that runs through the town (TU1), and Peters Canyon Regional Park (TU2), which is a part of TU1. There is also a convenient Metrolink station in Tustin that can be used to get to the Tustin and Irvine rides, and even Newport Beach though it is farther afield. From TU1, a Class II route along Bryan Avenue leads 1.8 miles west to Red Hill, leaving about 0.5 mile on sidewalks to reach Main Street and Old Town. Sidewalk cycling is allowed in Tustin as long as cyclists yield right of way to peds.

The Mountains to the Sea Trail TU1

This ambitious project of the Irvine Ranch Land Reserve joins together mostly Class I trails extending from the Back Bay in Newport Beach, past neighborhoods in Irvine and Tustin, through Peters Canyon Regional Park to Irvine Regional Park, while more skilled mountain bikers can continue on to the Weir Canyon Loop. The paved portion extends from the Back Bay to the southern entrance to Peters Canyon Regional Park. Mountain bikers can continue through the park on a wide fire road trail. Others can bypass the park by staying on Class II roads with sidewalk options as shown on the map, rejoining

ORANGE COUNTY

TU1 at the north end of Peters Canyon Park at Canyon View Ave, then riding into beautiful Irvine Regional Park. From there you can even link up to the Santiago Creek Trail and ride all the way to downtown Orange, perhaps using Metrolink to return to Tustin. Because this trail incorporates portions of other rides, see those ride descriptions for more detail and map sections. These include Newport Beach Back Bay (NB2), Irvine's San Diego Creek (IR1), Tustin's Peters Canyon Park (TU2), and Orange's Irvine Regional Park/Santiago Oaks Park (OR2). The connecting Class I trails are next to residential neighborhoods and channelized drainages, some sections more scenic than others. Portions of the paved trail are referred to as the Peters Canyon Trail as well, since it parallels Peters Canyon Wash. At time of writing there is a small detour in Irvine around a wash and across active train tracks until a right of way can be obtained to go under the tracks. Although the trail perhaps spends more time in Irvine, Tustin has done the best job to date of marking the trail with "Mountains to the Sea" signs, and we therefore have "awarded" the trail to Tustin.

Typical trail segment, Mountains to the Sea Trail through Tustin.

Tunes: Ain't No Mountain High Enough by Diana Ross; One Headlight by The Wallflowers

Eats: Sweet Potato Hash at Snooze, El Camino Real across Jamboree, or lunch on the patio of Lazy Dog Cafe, Jamboree between Bryan and Irvine Blvd.

Distance: 19 miles each way. Time: 1.5 to 2 hours each way. All year.

Route & Bike: Easy to strenuous depending on distance. Paved Class I with some road crossings. Any bike except for Peters Canyon Park MTB trail. Mostly flat, gradual incline heading north. Steeper hills through Peters Cnyn and trail's end. E-bikes not allowed on Peters Canyon dirt trails. E-bike edge on hilly alternate route.

Facilities: Restrooms and water in parks along route.

Knocks & Hazards: Clueless peds. Street crossings. Trail disjointed in places. Possible rattlesnakes. Mountain lions possible in urban/wilderness interface farther east. Can be hot in summer.

Rent 'n Ride/Camp 'n Ride: See other rides encompassed by this ride.

Bike 'n Brunch: The Marketplace supercenter has over 30 restaurants, from fast food to popular sit-down chain restaurants offering a variety of cuisines. Access from TU1 is 1-2 blocks to the west on El Camino Real, Bryan Avenue or Irvine Blvd. See ride IR1 for others.

Further Info: www.americantrails.org/national-recreation-trails/featured?state=california

ORANGE COUNTY

The ride summary below describes the route as it currently exists, starting from the "Sea" end, with links to other rides. See the Los Angeles/Orange County Ride Locator Map for a general overview of the trail location, and other maps as indicated in the following:

Along the Newport Back Bay Trail TU1-1   (See Newport Beach map, ride NB2)

Mile 0: Back Bay Drive at Shellmaker Road, south entrance to Back Bay. Park along the road in front of Newport Dunes as allowed. Cycle along Back Bay Drive past San Joaquin Hills Road (mile 0.5). There is free parking if you stage from there (west off Jamboree). Continue winding around on the trail and come to the bottom of a sizable hill (2.7). Climb the hill and reach Eastbluff Drive (2.9). An observation area and bench is at the top of the hill. Bear left down the Eastbluff sidewalk, then left again on the sidewalk along Jamboree (3.2).

Along the San Diego Creek Trail TU1-2   (See Irvine map, ride IR1)

Take the San Diego Creek trail to the left before the bridge, and cycle under the bridge. Ride along San Diego Creek in this pretty riparian corridor. Cross under I-405 (6.25). Reach Civic Center Park (restrooms, free parking) (7.5). The trail curves to the right following the channel at the confluence with Peters Canyon Wash. It crosses San Diego Creek via a bike bridge to the left (7.7). Across the bridge, the trail going to the left is our current route that follows Peters Canyon Wash, while the path to the right is the continuation of the San Diego Creek Trail (IR1) that we will now leave.

Peters Canyon Trail (Paved) Between IR1 and Peters Canyon Park   TU1-3

(See Mountains to the Sea map)

Our route heads left from the bridge, then makes a hard right to follow the contour of Peters Canyon Wash. Those large buildings to the left are airplane hangers, the largest wooden structures in the world, located at the closed Tustin Marine Corps Air Station and site of a future county park. The trail dips under Barranca (8.0). The District with its many restaurants is a few blocks west via sidewalk. The bike path next dips under Warner (8.5). The trail used to end here requiring a detour east to Harvard (which you can still do), but as of 2021 Tustin has completed the trail along the channel, dipping under Moffett and Edinger, avoiding those road crossings. Until a railroad crossing is built in 2022 or later the trail veers right before the tracks on Tustin's side of the Walnut Trail behind an apartment complex, and daylights at Harvard (9.9). The Walnut Trail continues across Harvard into Irvine as described in Option 1.

Option 1: Irvine's Walnut Trail
This trail follows power lines and railroad tracks east for about 3.2 miles across town to the Sand Canyon Avenue path, which goes north to Ride IR3 and south 1.6 miles where it veers right before I-405 and leads to a bike bridge over the freeway to the Shady Canyon Loop (IR2), or right to Jeffrey Road and Ride IR1.

TU1 continues to the left. Stay on the same side of Harvard and carefully walk your bike across the active train tracks, then hop on the path to the left. It follows Como Channel to Peters Canyon Wash, and makes a hard right (10.2). If the trail has been completed under the train tracks since this was written, this description will once again be accurate from this point on. Continue along the trail next to the concrete channel that passes the large Harvard Athletic Park, then dips under Walnut (10.6) and then I-5 (11.2), an undercrossing that seems especially susceptible to flooding. Next cross under El Camino Real (11.5) and Bryan Avenue (11.7). Here is a decision point. To continue on the trail to Peters Canyon, go under the roadway, then make a hard right back to the bridge and cross over the creek and the 261 Toll Road on the wide pathway. You will notice a large shopping center ahead to the left, which is The Market Place, a mega center with all kinds of restaurant and shopping options (see Bike 'n Brunch). The TU1 Class I path continues via a turn to the right next to the SR 261 Toll Road (11.8).

> **Option 2: Peters Canyon Trail East Branch (Paved)**
> If you don't need to go all the way to Peters Canyon Regional Park, just continue past Bryan along the creek rather than going up and over the bridge. The trail gets more scenic with greener surroundings and mountain views, passing the Hicks Canyon trailhead (to IR3) and ending in 1.7 miles at Portola Pkwy. Either turn around at Portola, or you can meet up with TU1 again by riding west (left) down Class 2 Portola or its sidewalk until it meets Jamboree Rd, then finding TU1 kitty-corner across that intersection.

Continuing on our main route, cycle north next to the freeway along a nicely treed promenade that tunnels under Irvine Boulevard. To the left at this point along Irvine Boulevard is the Irvine Ranch Historical Park that preserves original buildings used by the Irvine Ranch, which was once the world leader in Valencia oranges. It is now the headquarters of Orange County Parks. Several interesting restaurants at The Market Place are also situated in this area. The trail then bends to the left away from the freeway between newer high density housing units, twisting and turning before reaching Jamboree Road next to the Historical Park (12.9). It bends to the right and parallels Jamboree, crosses a couple of roads, then loops through Valencia Park (13.4) and tunnels under Jamboree and up to the other side. It crosses Champion Way (13.8) and reaches Tustin's Citrus Ranch Park (restrooms and water) (14.0). You can cut through the park, or follow TU1 alongside Jamboree. TU1 turns left alongside Portola Pkwy.

Follow the path between Portola and the Citrus Ranch Park to Tustin Ranch Road. (14.4). Cross at the signal to the trail on the other side that goes right, next to Tustin Ranch Road. From here to the trail's end is perhaps the nicest part of the route, through woodlands with hills beyond. The route then turns left next to Pioneer Way (14.6). Cross Pioneer Road at the signal (14.7), then cycle, finally away from roads, next to Cedar Grove Park (restrooms and water). The paved trail ducks behind a school and emerges adjacent to the south side of Peters Canyon Road (15.1).

For those wishing to continue to Irvine Park but wanting to skip the steep dirt path through Peters Canyon Park, make your way onto Peters Canyon Rd and head right. Go left on Class II Pioneer, then left onto the west sidewalk of Jamboree.

Otherwise, the path crosses Silverado, and continues into parkland (15.4). A junction to the right leads down a paved path to the south trailheads of Peters Canyon Regional Park (porta-potties) (15.7). This is another turnaround point.

Peters Canyon Regional Park   TU1-4   (See Peters Canyon Regional Park map, ride TU2 MTB) All e-bikes prohibited on OC Parks dirt trails.

The route follows the main, novice but hilly mountain bike trail, a fire road, through the park, exiting at Canyon View Avenue and Jamboree (17.5).

To Irvine Regional Park TU1-5 (See Orange Parks Area map, ride OR2)

From Canyon View, a Class I trail along the west side of Jamboree climbs a gradual incline and passes an Albertsons shopping center, crosses Chapman Ave/Santiago Canyon Rd (18.0), then follows Jamboree across East Santiago Canyon Rd (18.3) to a trailhead for the upper end of the Santiago Creek MTB trail (OR2) that leads to Santiago Oaks Regional Park for mountain bikers and a connection to the paved Santiago Creek Trail to Old Towne Orange (OR1). The official Mountains to the Sea Trail continues via a hilly intermediate-level mountain bike ride to the popular 4-mile long Weir Canyon Loop Trail in Anaheim Hills. This is definitely not an easy novice ride, however. Our easy riding version of the Mountains to the Sea Trail continues around to the right to the entrance to Irvine Regional Park (18.6). The beautiful park is worth exploring and there is no charge to bike in. E-bikes stick to paved paths and roads.

> **Option 3: Orange and the Train**
> Santiago Canyon Road west of Jamboree is a Class II route that joins up with the Class I portion of the Santiago Creek Trail in about 3 miles (see ride OR1). You can follow that back to central Orange and go downtown to the Metrolink Station, then take the train two stops to Tustin to get back to near your ride start. Or, get off at Irvine for a longer ride (see IR1).

Peters Canyon Regional Park MTB TU2

Distance: 4–5 miles MTB, moderate
No e-bikes allowed on OC Parks dirt trails.

The pleasant Peters Canyon Wilderness Park in Tustin and Orange contains 354 acres of coastal sage scrub, grassland, riparian, and freshwater marsh habitats. Peters Canyon Creek and the Upper Peters Canyon Reservoir are lined with sycamores, willows, and black cottonwoods. This is an excellent place for bird watching, with resident and migrating waterfowl in the waterways, while the coastal sage habitat is home to gnatcatcher, cactus wren, California quail, and rufous-crowned sparrow. Raptors include Cooper's, red-shouldered and red-tail hawks in addition to the ravens, crows, and turkey vultures. Critters include mule deer, bobcat, coyote, raccoon, and opossum. A mountain lion can potentially roam through here as well. Reptiles can include rattlesnakes so watch for them on the trail.

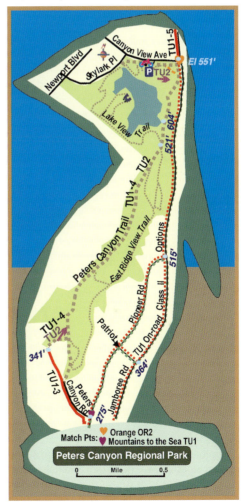

The 2-mile long Peters Canyon Trail, which is a segment of the Mountains to the Sea Trail (TU1–4), is basically a fire road open to MTB's, hikers, and equestrians. Although novice skill level, it is hilly, with a gain of 200 feet elevation from south to north, which makes it moderate in difficulty. Side trails are hillier, steeper, and have some more advanced terrain on single and double track trails, however

Great vistas from the Lake View Trail

the elevation gained offers rewards in the form of vistas of the countryside. Taking the hilly Lake View loop combined with the main trail yields a scenic ride of about 5 miles. Find a restroom at the north trailhead and porta-potty at the south trailhead. For information and trail conditions check ocparks.com/peterscanyon/, or call 714.973.6611 or 714.973.6612. Trails typically close during and after rain events.

To access the north trailhead (Orange) from I-5 take Jamboree Road north for 5.2 miles to Canyon View Avenue and turn left to reach the park entrance on the left. From SR 55 (Costa Mesa Freeway) take Chapman Avenue east 2.3 miles, then right on Canyon View 2 miles to the park entrance. Address is 8548 E Canyon View Ave, Orange. Parking is $3 ($5 weekends) in a self-pay station. For the south trailhead (Tustin) from I-5 take Jamboree northbound and turn left on Tustin Ranch Road in 3 miles, then make quick rights on Pioneer Way and Pioneer Road, and left to park in Cedar Grove Park. Hop on the paved path behind it and go right to the TU2 trailhead at the end of Peters Canyon Road to the park.

Orange

Orange was once a center of the citrus industry like many other cities in the region, and now holds its own within the suburban sprawl of Orange County. Because it preserved its early 1900s houses rather than tearing them down like most other cities did, Orange is now home to the largest historic district in California. Old Towne Orange contains a square mile filled with 1,300 historic buildings, the second largest number in California, representing various early California residential and architectural styles. The center of town is Plaza Square Park with its circa 1937 fountain, and the surrounding traffic circle joins Chapman Avenue and Glassell Streets, named for the two founders of the city. The antique capital of Orange County has 60 antique shops and fun places to eat such as the friendly old timey Watson Drugs & Soda Fountain, the location of movie scenes in films such as *That Thing You Do!* Adjacent to downtown is Chapman University, and a Metrolink station provides yet another option for accessing this locale. We have constructed a ride (OR1) to incorporate Old Towne with the Class I Santiago Creek Bike Trail.

The Santiago Creek basin gets wilder and more beautiful as it continues to the northeast part of Orange and runs through adjoining Santiago Oaks and Irvine Regional Parks, all connected by the MTB portion of the Santiago Creek Trail. This is one of the most scenic areas of Orange County with large sections of land preserved as parkland. Santiago Oaks Park is centered around the meandering Santiago Creek, set in rolling foothills containing oak and sycamore trees and a variety of wildlife. The tall Villa Park Dam, a flood control structure, is the gateway to the park, a good portion of which was burned in the 2007 Windy Ridge Fire, but is recovering nicely. Irvine Regional Park is an Orange County landmark, established in 1897 when James Irvine donated the land for the county's first park. It is perhaps the most beautiful of the county parks, with heritage oaks and sycamores, green lawns and lakes, surrounded by foothills, the riparian strip of Santiago Creek, and views of the Santa Ana Mountains beyond. Families flock to the park to enjoy features such as the Orange County Zoo, a miniature train ride, a fishing lake with paddleboat rentals, seasonal food concessions, picnic grounds, and several miles of scenic paved paths perfect for an easy cycle. Our ride, OR2, is mostly on a MTB trail that connects the two parks with an option to continue via ride OR1.

City code, bike riding on sidewalks: Prohibited in business districts unless designated as a bicycle route. On other sidewalks yield to peds.

Old Towne Orange and the Santiago Creek Trail   OR1

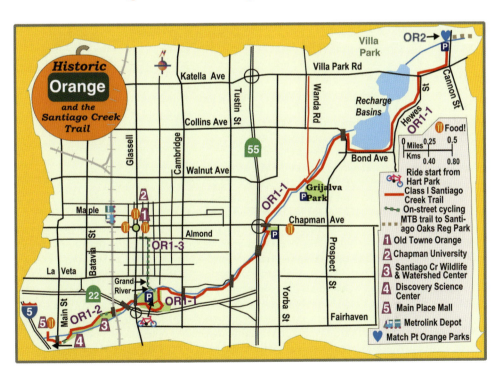

Cycling around busy Old Towne is not the greatest experience, and riding on the downtown sidewalks is not an option here, so for your downtown exploration you should probably just lock and stroll. However, you can combine your visit to Old Towne with a spin on one of Orange County's newest paved Class I trails, the Santiago Creek Trail that extends close to 7 virtually uninterrupted miles from I-5 in Santa Ana through Orange to upscale Villa Park to the northeast. The trail is mostly in a narrow greenbelt through residential areas, however, where the creekbed is full of vegetation and when water is flowing through it, there is a very pleasant milieu to gaze at. At times the surrounding hills and even the Santa Ana and San Gabriel Mountains are visible, and several parks at its southwest end provide a leafy cruise. Also at the southwest side in Santa Ana are Main Place Mall and the Discovery Science Center, a hands-on museum that is fun for all ages. At the northeast end, the trail skirts a giant retention basin that impounds Santiago Creek. It resembles a reservoir, but is a facility to replenish Orange County's groundwater aquifer. The paved portion of Santiago Creek Trail ends along Cannon Street, and continues as a MTB trail across the road. That path leads to Santiago Oaks and Irvine Regional Parks as described in Ride OR2.

Tunes: That Thing You Do! by The Wonders; Old Days by Chicago
Eats: Cuban Roast Pork at Felix Café

Distance: Up to 15.4 miles. Time: Up to 2 hours
Route & Bike: Easy to moderate, based on distance. Paved Class I for any bike. Flat in west, gradual inclines and a couple of small hills in east.
Seasons: All. Best on sunny mild day.
Facilities: Restrooms and water at parks along route.
Knocks & Hazards: Some clueless peds. Possible lurkers, more toward the Santa Ana end; best to ride with a friend. Flooding may impact portions of the trail. Side trip into Old Towne is on-street riding on residential streets with several intersections.
Bike Shop: Orange Cycle, 210 South Glassell, 714.532.6838.
Camp 'n Ride: None found near ride. See Anaheim.
Bike 'n Brunch: Try Felix Café for Cuban food al fresco on the central plaza, Watson's Drug and Fountain for old-timey fun, or the popular Gabbi's Mexican Kitchen. The Filling Station has all day breakfast, popular with nearby Chapman University students. Ruby's unique train-themed diner is at the Metrolink station. There are several restaurants at Main Place Mall, and also via a detour east on Chapman Avenue when the trail crosses that road.

Historic Old Town Orange is a great Metrolink Bike 'n Brunch destination and this meal at Felix Cuban restaurant in the central square can be your reward.

Access: From the Costa Mesa (55) Freeway just north of the 22 Freeway, take the Chapman Westbound exit. Turn left at Shaffer Street and take it south past La Veta into Hart Park. Another option is to park in the Old Towne district, which is straight ahead on Chapman to the obvious central plaza. From the 57 Freeway take Chapman eastbound. To get to Hart Park from downtown, go east two blocks on Chapman and turn right on Grand Avenue and follow it past La Veta, then turn left onto River Street into the park. Rail 'n Ride: Via Metrolink, when you exit the train, go to the right and then walk your bike down the sidewalk a couple of blocks to see the sights and make your way to the central plaza. Or, if you prefer to ride, go left from the train, and right on Maple, and cycle for two blocks to Glassell. Turn right to get to the central plaza.

The Ride: From the east side of the Hart Park lot, find the paved trail and choose your options. Facing the park from downtown, you can go to the right (west) through the more leafy segment in Santa Ana, or to the left (east) that starts off leafy but then opens up to more regional vistas. This direction has more of a noticeable incline, uphill on the outward ride. Or, you can always start by riding into Old Towne first. We will describe the ride by starting to the east first to get the elevation gain over with.

East to Villa Park OR1-1

Distance: 10.2 miles round trip, moderate

Santiago Creek Trail heading north out of town

Head east (left) along the trail. It runs past residential areas but the creek is very pretty. Although channelized, it has a natural bottom and vegetation along the sides. Cross under Class II Cambridge Street (mile 0.3), Rock Creek Drive (0.8), busy Tustin Street (0.9), then start the newest trail section. Go through a long semi-creepy underpass under the Costa Mesa (55) Freeway (1.2), then pass a doggie park and take a bike bridge over the creek. At busy Chapman Ave (1.6), find restaurants starting a block to the right with breakfast fave Broken Yolk and all kinds of choices farther along. The trail continues under Chapman. The view opens up and the pretty vegetated creek continues until the bridge to Grijalva Community Park, where the channel turns to the more typical concrete culvert (2.25). Last we rode it, the Bike Route Sign pointed straight ahead. That just leads away from the creek between homes to Collins Avenue and then an extension continues to Villa Park Road. Our route continues across the bridge to Grijalva Park, and then a quick left onto the channelside path. It follows the channel past new residential areas. The Orange County Water District has proposed tearing out the concrete channel bottom through here to increase groundwater recharge to the underlying aquifer, which may disrupt trail use someday.

The path then tunnels under Collins Avenue (3.0) and emerges between Prospect Street and the large Santiago retention basin. There are views of it along Prospect, but around the bend when the path bends left to follow Bond Avenue (3.2) a wall blocks any view so that your view is of the road and the local hills beyond. The path bends left again at Hewes Street (3.7), still around the edge of the basin. At the Rancho Santiago signal (4.3) a Bike Route sign points up that hill, but our path continues along the edge of the basin, and leads to busy Villa Park Road (4.6). The path crosses the road with the signal and goes to the right, passing the entrance to a private school, then bending left at Cannon Street (4.9). The path ends at the side of Santiago Creek in a gravel parking lot entered from the west (left) side of the road (5.1). Return the same way to Hart Park (10.2), or consider the following options. Mountain bikers can continue on, via Option 1 below, while road bikers can try an interesting way back using Option 2 (e-bike edge).

Option 1: Mountain Bike Trails

A dirt trail connects to Santiago Oaks and Irvine Regional Parks. To find it from the end of the paved trail along Cannon Street, cross the road and ride across the bridge and up the hill to the north as shown on the map. The trail runs against the fence behind the first neighborhood encountered. It is a fairly level, packed dirt trail that skirts the neighborhood above the creek and reaches Santiago Oaks Regional Park in about 1.3 miles. The riding in the park itself is a bit more difficult. See ride OR2. No e-bikes.

Option 2: Road Biker Options and Return Using Metrolink

Upon reaching the light at Cannon Street and Santiago Canyon Road, road bikers can cross Santiago Canyon Road and cycle the Class II route to the left. *Stick to pavement along here due to goathead thorns.* Cycle up the hill for about 3 miles to get to Irvine Regional Park, a worthwhile destination (see OR2). From there you can return the same way, or join the Mountains to the Sea Trail, TU1. Take Class II Jamboree south until the paved trail resumes at Portola. Reach the Tustin Metrolink station (west via Edinger) and take the train two stops north to Orange.

West Through Santa Ana OR1–2

Distance: 3.2 miles round trip, easy.

From the same starting point at Hart Park, the trail curves around the ball fields and makes a couple of sharp turns to go under Glassell Street, one of the main streets of Orange (mile 0.4). It crosses over the creek and goes left, under the Garden Grove (SR 22) Freeway and into a pretty area occupied by the Santiago Creek Wildlife and Watershed Center, which is worth a visit. They also have restrooms when open (0.8). The route may detour along the park road but resumes again, leading through an especially wooded section of the creek. It crosses its only roadway at Lawson Way, a park entrance road, with a traffic signal (1.1). It then crosses a bike bridge (1.3), leads through a park (with restrooms) then empties into a cul de sac. Follow that street a short distance to the continuation of the trail on the right (1.4). It dips under Main Street and leads to an entrance to the Discovery Science Center (1.5). At a junction, where the left branch ends under I-5 at a tunnel rimmed with graffiti (not recommended), either turn around, or go to the right as the trail ends across from Main Place Mall (1.6) where there are lots of places to find some grub including a Mongolian BBQ and Baja Fresh. Once again, return to Hart Park (3.2). A sidenote: Orange residents would like to see the passage under I-5 lit and made safer, and a link constructed through Santa Ana's upscale Fisher Park neighborhood on the other side of the freeway to the Santa Ana River Trail. See ride SAR2 (Anaheim) for further info.

Historic Old Towne District OR1-3

Distance: About 2.0 miles round trip, easy

Back at Hart Park, a route is suggested to get to Old Towne through the historic residential district, but you can experiment and find the best way. Leaving the parking lot, look for a big One Way Do Not Enter sign, and go through there, carefully walking your bike the few feet through the entrance to be legal of course. This is River Way. We suggest making the first right from River Way onto Grand Street. Although the first street crossing at La Veta Avenue (0.2) is not signaled/stop signed and extra caution is required, the remaining cross streets have stop signs. Try turning left on Almond Avenue (0.6) and riding two blocks to Glassell Street. From here those comfortable with riding with traffic can continue to cycle. For the rest of you we suggest dismounting and walking your bike up the sidewalk (riding on sidewalks is not allowed) taking in the sights of Old Towne and reaching the central Plaza in 1 block (0.8). Explore the Old Towne area, on foot or by bike, and return to Hart Park the same way.

Santiago Oaks MTB and Irvine Regional Park   OR2

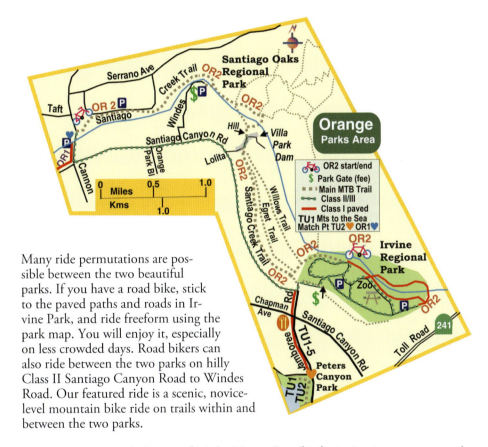

Many ride permutations are possible between the two beautiful parks. If you have a road bike, stick to the paved paths and roads in Irvine Park, and ride freeform using the park map. You will enjoy it, especially on less crowded days. Road bikers can also ride between the two parks on hilly Class II Santiago Canyon Road to Windes Road. Our featured ride is a scenic, novice-level mountain bike ride on trails within and between the two parks.

Tunes: Dream A Little Dream of Me by Mama Cass (birds singing in sycamore trees); Another Park Another Sunday by The Doobie Brothers
Eats: Picnic in Irvine Park

Distance: 10 to 12 miles. Time: 2 hours
Route & Bike: Easy to moderate. Mostly off-road level doubletrack dirt trails with some singletrack and some areas with loose rocks. Hybrid or preferably MTB. Options for road bike as described. Flat with one very steep hill halfway and a few short steep hills in Santiago Oaks Park. Mostly novice MTB skills with a couple of sections that some may opt to walk. No e-bikes allowed on OC Parks dirt paths.
Seasons: All. Best on any sunny mild day.
Facilities: Restrooms and water in the main part of both parks but nothing in between along the trails.

Knocks & Hazards: Rattlesnakes, starting in spring—watch for sticks along trail! Mountain lions have been seen here. Ticks. Poison oak. Route may be cut in half on rare occasions when water is flowing out of Villa Park Dam. Dirt trails may be closed during and after rain events. Novices may not appreciate a couple of tricky areas, although the park rates these trails as "Easy."

Rent 'n Ride: Wheel Fun Rental at Irvine Park (mostly "fun bikes" for paved park roads).

Camp 'n Ride/Bike 'n Brunch: Nothing close to parks. A food concession is in Irvine Park, and a shopping center with a couple of restaurants is at Jamboree and Chapman near Irvine Park accessible via a Class I trail (Part of Ride TU1).

Further Info: See the websites for trail conditions and a park trail map, or pick up a map as you enter the park. Irvine Regional Park: ocparks.com/irvinepark/, ocparks.com/oczoo, irvineparkrailroad.com. Address: 1 Irvine Park Road, Orange. Phone: 714.973.6835 or 714.973.3173. Santiago Oaks Regional Park: ocparks.com/parks/santiago/. Address 2145 N Windes Drive, Orange. Phone 714.973.6620. Email: santiagooaks@ocparks.com. Similar vehicle fees.

Access: Irvine Regional Park is located at the northern end of Jamboree Road. Take it all the way north from I-5. From the 55 Freeway exit Chapman eastbound, take it to Jamboree and turn left to the park. You can also use the 241 Toll Road and exit Santiago Canyon Road, taking it west, then north on Jamboree. GPS should get you to the correct place. For Santiago Oaks Regional Park, from near the end of Jamboree head west on Santiago Canyon Road. Note that Santiago Canyon Road makes a jog at Jamboree, so that when traveling west you need to turn right on Jamboree then a quick left to continue on Santiago Canyon, whereas straight ahead is Chapman Avenue here. After a couple of miles turn right on Windes Road to the park. Vehicle entry fee in OC Regional Parks is $3 weekday/$5 weekend /$7 holiday. There are a couple of free parking options west of Santiago Oaks Park. One is the small trailhead parking lot at the northeast end of OR1 (see the map for that ride). A less isolated spot is in an upscale neighborhood: Continue north on Cannon across the bridge, turn right on Serrano, right on McKinley that bends to the left to become Mabery. The Santiago Creek MTB trail runs adjacent to the road here.

The Ride: Starting from Irvine Park gives non-riders in your party the most options for exploration while you are gone. If you are doing this ride as a continuation of OR1, use that map and ride the route in reverse. From any of the lots in Irvine Park ride to the north toward Santiago Creek. Begin on the paved trail and head west (left) until you come to a junction with Santiago Creek Trail (mile 0). Follow that level dirt trail around the perimeter of the park, which curves around to the left, or south, heading toward the Irvine Park entrance road. You will pass three trails on the right, Willows, Egret, and Santiago Creek (0.6). They are all very nice, level trails that head northwest through the wide scenic floodplain, and all meet up in front of the Villa Park Dam (1.9). Ride to the right, up to the top of the rocky structure that is an extension of the dam, and come to a junction. If you'd prefer to get back to the roadways, turn left on Lolita Street, which leads to Santiago Canyon Road.

To proceed with our route, turn right on the paved roadway, then continue straight, back onto the dirt Santiago Creek Trail, with the impressive main Villa Park Dam structure on the right. Next comes the trickiest part of this ride—a long, steep hill of dirt and rocks that leads straight down to the bottom of the dam spillway and into a wide parking lot area (where parking is prohibited). Make sure your brakes are in good working order, or carefully walk it. At the bottom of the hill there is an option (2.2). Straight across the large dirt lot is the Pony Trail that leads into Santiago Oaks Park, crossing over the creek farther along. A slightly easier route is to the right, following the Santiago Creek Trail. It crosses Santiago Creek straight away when there is no water in it, which is most of the time. Signs warn to keep out when flowing. The trail runs roughly parallel to the creek as you head into the main part of the park, which becomes more lush and shady. The trail crosses the creek

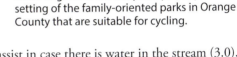

Irvine Regional Park has perhaps the prettiest setting of the family-oriented parks in Orange County that are suitable for cycling.

again, with elevated stepping-stones to assist in case there is water in the stream (3.0). This leads to the main part of the park with restroom facilities and an orange grove, a possible turn around point.

If you are continuing along the Santiago Creek Trail, however, do not cross the stream here. Instead, take the fork to the right on the Towhee Trail. The Santiago Creek Trail ascends a staircase here so you'll need to detour around it. Ride up the Towhee Trail, bear left at the first fork and reach the junction of the Wilderness and Ladybug Trails. Both are rated Easy but Wilderness Trail involves more climbing. Taking Ladybug to the left leads back to the Santiago Creek Trail at the top of the stairs (3.1), and now bends to the right. Follow Santiago Creek Trail to the junction with the other end of the Wilderness Trail and bear left (3.3).

Easy and scenic mountain bike trails between Irvine and Santiago Oaks Regional Parks

The next stretch is more intermediate in skill level, with short steep hills, curves, and single track. There is no way around it, however, so walk your bike carefully if you need to, or turn around. It leads down to the park boundary and onto a welcome wide flat dirt trail between the creek, which has impounded water at this point, and a neighborhood of new large homes. The remaining trail ride to Cannon Street is easy on mostly level doubletrack between the riparian basin and the neighborhood. The trail runs alongside East Mabury Avenue where there is free street parking, a potential staging area (3.9–4.4). It then veers away from the street and continues behind homes until reaching Cannon Street (4.6). At this point you can consider Options 1 or 2 (below), or return the same way, perhaps choosing another of the trails on the Irvine Park side of Villa Park Dam.

Once back to your starting point in Irvine Park (9.2), enjoy some delightful riding on the paved trails throughout the park. Use the park map and ride freeform on the trails and roads at your whim. The most scenic paths line both sides of Santiago Creek, and also wind through the center of the park, although most families seem to ride on the park roads (Speed Limit 10) on surreys and other fun-style bikes available from the on-site Wheel Fun rentals. There are also unpaved mountain bike trails around the perimeter of the park, including the end of the Santiago Creek Trail. Your total ride mileage could add up to around 12 miles.

Option 1: Take the Roadway Back to Irvine Park

If you have had enough of trail riding, you can take Class II roadways back to your ride start and also cut off about 0.7 mile distance. Very carefully cross busy Cannon Street when safe, turn left, ride over the bridge and along the adjacent Class I trail (OR1) to the corner of Santiago Canyon Road. Go left on Class II Santiago Canyon (4.9), pass Windes Drive (that leads back to Santiago Oaks Park) (5.9), and ride up the gradual incline. You will pass the campus of Santiago Canyon College (7.4) and reach Jamboree (7.8). Turn left. The obvious trailhead at the first bend leads to the Santiago Creek Trail where you passed previously. Or, stay on the park road or parallel dirt trail to get back into the park. Once you reach your starting point you will have ridden about 8.5 miles. Cruise around Irvine Park freeform as described earlier.

Option 2: Link to ride OR1

Once at Cannon Street you can ride on the paved portion of Santiago Creek Trail all the way to Old Towne Orange, where there is a Metrolink station. If you are really adventurous you can take the train two stops to the south and get off at the Tustin station, then follow the Mountains to the Sea Trail (TU1) back uphill (the key word here) to Irvine Park.

Fullerton

Fullerton in north Orange County was originally founded as a railroad town, and it retains its heritage with a downtown core highlighted by its historic Santa Fe Depot that is still used as a convenient Metrolink and Amtrak station, while the 1923–1972 Orange County Depot for the Union Pacific Railroad now houses a Spaghetti Factory restaurant. The surrounding revitalized district to the north and west of the depots centers around Harbor Boulevard and Commonwealth Avenue, and bustles with dining and entertainment venues.

The city coined SOCO "South of Commonwealth" as an attempt to further enhance the downtown area. It has attracted its share of eating and drinking establishments to the district. Other highlights are the Spanish-themed circa 1922 Villa Del Sol complex at Harbor and Wilshire, which is a great place for your Bike 'n Brunch, and the Fullerton Museum Center at Pomona and Wilshire and adjacent Downtown Plaza with its spring to fall Thursday afternoon market. Fullerton College, a two-year community college, is the oldest of its kind in the state and is located on the northeast corner of the downtown district along Chapman Avenue, together with the Plummer Auditorium venue of striking Spanish Colonial architecture.

Besides being the home town of rock great Jackson Browne and the original site of the Fender guitar company, Fullerton was more recently the center of Orange County's punk rock scene, producing groups like Social Distortion. Other rock groups such

as No Doubt and The Offspring are from the Fullerton-Anaheim area. To approximately 135,000 people, Fullerton is home and the city is doing its part to provide recreation trails for its residents. The trails are mostly unpaved, so that those with a mountain bike will get the most benefit out of riding around the trails in this city.

Rail Trails, Hills 'n Brunch F1 and F2

Most of Fullerton's trails are of the dirt variety, including some in mountain bike parks within the city. Two are flat unpaved rail trails, and they can be combined to create an easy loop, with an optional detour to downtown for a good variety of meal choices (F1). Along the way the more adventurous can venture off into the mountain bike parks, some of which are used to create the Fullerton Loop, a popular trail used by locals along a fairly confusing route on a myriad of trails (F2). It is longer and much hillier than the rail trail loop, but provides more spectacular vistas. The scenery along the trails is pleasant, with greenbelts, a few parks, and lots of suburban backyards of some of the nicer Fullerton neighborhoods. The Fullerton Loop trail ventures out into some rare remaining open space in the Coyote Hills next to residential neighborhoods. Although not a destination ride on its own, the combination of touring the downtown with cycling through some of the nicest parts of the city makes it a worthwhile excursion, especially with its accessibility by train.

Tunes: I'm Alive by Jackson Browne; California (Hustle & Flow) by Social Distortion; Don't Speak by No Doubt

Eats: Stuffed French Toast at Rialto Café

Route & Bike: Mostly Class I unpaved paths or packed dirt and gravel, best for MTB's. The main rail trails are bridle paths with soft surface. Some easy Class II & III paved roads. Many street crossings. Gradual grades closer to downtown and steeper hills along the perimeter on F2. Downtown elevation: 165 ft. Juanita Cooke Trailhead: 205 ft. Laguna Lake, northeast end: 320 ft. Max elevation in the hills (F2): 530 feet. E-bike edge: Class 1 & 2 helpful on hills, especially F2.

Seasons: All. Best on any mild sunny day.

Facilities: Restrooms and water in Laguna Lake Park. Downtown, try Downtown Plaza on Wilshire between Harbor and Pomona.

Knocks & Hazards: Clueless peds. Some paths shared with equestrians. Short, steep hill in ride F1. Ride F2 has many hills of various lengths. Street riding, especially with downtown option and many road crossings on trail. Rattlesnakes more likely in open space (ride F2). Summer heat and smog. Trails can be very muddy after rain.

Bike Shops: East West Bikes, 206 N Harbor, 714.525.2200; Fullerton Bicycles, 424 E Commonwealth, 879.8310; Jax Bicycle Center, 2520 E Chapman, 441.1100.

Bike 'n Brunch: Numerous choices downtown, centered around Harbor Blvd between Santa Fe Ave to the south and Chapman Ave to the north. Rialto Café has good breakfasts all day, 108 W Wilshire. Wahoo's Fish Taco is at Chapman. Brownstone Café and Café Hidalgo in the historic Villa del Sol Courtyard at 305 N Harbor are both popular, with outdoor patios. Check out menus along Commonwealth, or succumb to the reliable Old Spaghetti Factory at the Depot. If you choose not to venture downtown, across from the Berkeley Ave trailhead is a Ralph's Supermarket shopping center with several casual eateries with outdoor patios.

City code, bike riding on sidewalks: Allowed. Defer to state law.

Further Info: City site: cityoffullerton.com. Has visitor info including SOCO and restaurant guide as well as trail maps.

Access: Fullerton is surrounded by freeways on three sides. SR 57 is to the east, SR 91 is to the south and I-5 is to the west. Take the 5 or the 91 Freeways to the Harbor Boulevard exit, northbound, and pass a myriad of shopping malls. The downtown area is 1 mile north of the 91 near the railroad tracks between Truslow and Chapman. Continue about 0.4 mile north on Harbor from Chapman to North Berkeley and turn left. Look for the Juanita Cooke trailhead straight ahead when the road bends to the right. Find parking to the left, at the courthouse. The trail runs behind the parking lot. Laguna Lake Park is another staging option, as shown on the map. Rail 'n Ride: Both Amtrak and Metrolink trains stop at the downtown depot, so you can come for the day with your bike to tour the town and get in a nice ride as a bonus. Rather than riding along busy Harbor Blvd to the trailhead, we recommend taking secondary streets as described in F1.

Rail Trail MTB Loop with Downtown Option   F1

Details: 6–7.5 miles. Time: 1 hour. Easy, not technical. Mostly flat. Gradual rail trail grades with a couple of short steep hills.

The Ride: Pedal north from the trailhead on the Juanita Cooke Greenbelt. Carefully cross Valley View Drive and look for a sign here depicting the route of the Fullerton Loop ride (F2), which is an optional longer ride. The trail passes through a nicely landscaped greenbelt corridor between homes. Cross Richman Avenue (mile 0.6) and then reach a trailhead for Hiltscher Trail (0.8), which makes for a very pleasant optional out and back detour through a riparian corridor. The second trail down to the park is much more gradual. Farther along the rail trail, beware of a short steep hill that leads to busy Bastanchury Road (1.1). Those with questionable brakes or bike riding skills should walk down this short hill. Carefully cross the busy road with the signal. The trail is interrupted here, so you need to cycle up Morelia Avenue. At the end of the street make a right/left jog on West Laguna Road back onto the trail (1.3) that soon crosses above railroad tracks (1.6). Consider Option 1 from this point.

Option 1: Brea Dam

You can ride to Laguna Lake as described below and return to this spot, then explore the Brea Dam area to the east, a loop route that returns you to the Juanita Cooke Trail. The lake and the dam area are two of the highlights of this trail network. Glide down the gradual trail that starts from just south of the bridge and reach the unused train tracks, then go to the right, following the route described in ride F2 starting at its mile 8.8. The route through the Brea Dam area has a few hills to contend with.

After more cycling northward in the greenbelt of nice Fullerton neighborhoods, watch for a view of a lake and a connector to the left (2.25). Use the crosswalk to cross Lakeside Drive and begin cycling on the Bud Turner Trail along the south side of the lake at Laguna Lake Park. This is the highlight of the ride, with benches and picnic tables under shady trees, a great place to stop and watch the waterfowl on the lake. The trail continues along the lake's entire shoreline and enters the park's parking lot (2.6), which is another potential staging point. The public restroom and water available here are the only facilities on this route. It passes through the south end of the park, the riding stables, a nice wooded area, and then reaches Laguna Road (3.0). Ride to the right a short distance on the trail next to Laguna Road and reach Euclid Street. Cross Laguna Road and come to the continuation of the Bud Turner Trail that runs along the east side of Euclid.

Cycle south next to Euclid, crossing Paseo Dorado (3.7) and Bastanchury Road, with a signal (3.9). At mile 4.1 reach Valencia Mesa Drive, considered a connecting bike route. Turn left at the light and follow this street until mile 4.7 when you reach a bridge over the Juanita Cooke Greenbelt. A dirt path leads from the northeast side

Laguna Lake Park is the refreshing highlight of the Fullerton rides

of the bridge down to the Juanita Cooke trail. Once back on the trail, turn left to return to the trailhead (5.6). From the trailhead, note the Ralph's center across the street that has several casual dining options with a central outdoor table area.

Option 2: Historic Downtown Fullerton

From the trailhead area you can either end the ride and load your bike back onto your vehicle, or cycle to downtown and SOCO. The bike route is not wonderful, but you can take side streets to reach the central depot area. From the trailhead, go right on Berkeley and turn right down the first alley, very carefully crossing a couple of residential streets where cross traffic does not have a stop sign. When the alley ends at Malvern Avenue (5.9) turn right, and then left on Highland (6.1). You may prefer to ride the sidewalks of Highland, at least until the bike lane starts farther down. Cross Chapman Avenue at the light and continue to the next light at Commonwealth (6.4). Most of the downtown core including the train depot is to the left (east) from here a couple of blocks, at Harbor. You may want to make your way down the next alley or the following street (Santa Fe) instead of riding on Commonwealth, or you can walk your bike down the sidewalk along Commonwealth. The downtown option would make your total ride about 7.5 miles, not including the other options.

The Fullerton MTB Loop with Downtown Option F2

Details: 11.4–13 miles. Time: 1.5–2 hours. Moderate. Combination of flat stretches with some very steep hills. Advanced novice MTB level. *Note: Locals request this loop be ridden clockwise as described.*

The Ride: This loop is a favorite of local mountain bikers, but many hills, especially in the outlying greenbelt section, make it anything but easy. However, the upland section offers the best scenery with great vistas from the tops of those same hills. Begin the ride from the same trailhead as F1, pedaling up the mulch-covered Juanita Cooke Greenbelt. Turn left in 0.75 mile onto the Hiltsher Trail (the furthest option is the least steep). Go gradually downhill through this delightful park on a packed dirt trail with some sandy spots, while riparian vegetation and trees block out most of the surrounding neighborhoods. Carefully cross unsignaled Richman Knoll (a quiet street), then busier Euclid Street (1.7) with a crossing signal. After a brief cycle along the trail, struggle up the short steep hill to the right toward the houses rather than the easy way out down the concrete drainage to the left. Cross Fern Drive at the top of the hill (1.8) and ride straight ahead onto Valley View Drive, coasting gradually downhill through this pleasant residential neighborhood to the street's terminus.

Turn right on Bastanchury, and a quick left on Warburton (2.3) (recommend for safety using sidewalks and signal), and then a quick right (2.4) onto a dirt trail to the right of the inactive railroad tracks. Cross Parks Road (2.6), then cross the tracks and enter a dirt trail (Parks Trail) that parallels Parks Road. It goes on through Edward White Park (2.9), then crosses very busy Rosecrans Avenue (3.2). Cycle through Virgil "Gus" Grissom Park on the paved Bridle Trail, pass more backyards, cross Camino Rey (3.6) and follow the unpaved path, which soon turns to the left. Cross Parks Road again (3.8) and enter West Coyote Hills Tree Park. Stay to the right down a steep hill, and then bear left on the trail that approaches Coyote Hills Drive (4.0). The trail turns to the left away from the road at mile 4.2 and cuts between homes to reach Rosecrans Avenue.

Turn right onto the dual sidewalk/unpaved Rosecrans Trail. The trail crosses Gilbert Street (4.6) and Sunny Ridge Place (4.9) and ends at the Fire Hall (5.0). The Castlewood Trail takes off to the right here. It travels through open space scrubland, but

The Fullerton Loop trail gets pretty hilly but affords great vistas along the northern open space.

encircles a residential area, never staying too far from it. Travel to the north and around to the east here over steep hills, reaching Gilbert Drive (near Chantilly Drive) at mile 6.3. Carefully cross Gilbert Drive and continue on Castlewood Trail that now parallels Castlewood Drive but remains in the open space. At mile 6.5, where Parks Drive intersects Castlewood in the adjacent residential area, turn left onto the Nora Kuttner Recreation Trail, and follow it up and over a substantial hill to the east with great vistas at the summit, adjacent to the residential area, ending at the bottom of the downhill at Euclid Street (7.3), to the south of Sunny Hills Church.

Make your way on the sidewalk along the left side of busy Euclid, and cross the street at the signal at Laguna Street. Across the street turn left onto the Bud Turner Trail into Laguna Lake Park (7.4). Follow the lower trail along the picket fence north to Laguna Lake (restrooms at the parking lot) where the trail runs along its southeast shore. Watch for a crosswalk across Lakeside Drive (8.2).

Cross onto the Juanita Cook Greenbelt Trail and turn right. Option 1: To return via the shortest route, follow this trail back to your starting point for a ride of about 9 miles. Along the way, when the trail seems to end at a residential street (West Laguna), jog right then left down Morelia to its end where the Class I trail continues across busy Bastanchury.

Our main route continues to tour the Brea Dam area. After crossing above the railroad tracks (8.8), note the nice gradual trail on the left that leads back down to the tracks. Head east (right) on the singletrack packed dirt path surrounded by gravel next to the tracks and pass under Harbor Boulevard (8.9), then watch for a steep narrow path that curves up to the right and reaches the side of a road. It ends atop the small hill, so look for the continuation of the trail across the road (9.0). It drops steadily downhill, adjacent to the Fullerton Municipal Golf Course, partially shielded from wayward golf balls by netting. An S-curve to the right takes you through tunnels under Bastanchury Road into the Brea Dam Recreational Area.

Take the trail to the right, in the southerly direction, through a pleasant riparian area, with the Brea Dam visible ahead that is used for flood control (9.9). Turn right and ride up the hill next to the dam, reaching the parking lot for the Leonard Andrews Tennis Center (10.0). Make your way along the sidewalks in the medical center so that you end up heading west (left) and crossing Harbor at the light. Ride west on Valencia Mesa Drive or its north sidewalk, past Sunny Crest Drive and medical facilities. The sidewalk leads into a dirt path that descends a short incline to the right to the Juanita Cook Greenbelt Trail (10.4). Turn left and follow that back to the original trailhead for a total ride of about 11.4 miles. Option 2: From here you have the option of exploring downtown Fullerton as described in F1 for a total of about 13 miles.

Chino Hills State Park

This jewel of a park in the middle of the megalopolis between Brea and Chino Hills is now open daily except during extreme winds and 48 hours after 1/4 inch of rain. The fields of oats, coastal sage ecosystem, and stately oaks once provided a spectacular resemblance of the California of old, and a beautiful template for recreation via bike or hike. Since the 2008 Freeway Complex Fire burned 95 percent of the park, its fields have returned in a hurry, but many of the trees are now charred remains, so goes the story of Southern California. Park info: parks.ca.gov/?page_id=648.

Chino Hills is indeed a hilly park, with elevation ranging from 500 to 1,500 feet and a ridge dividing its east and west sides. Therefore, novice mountain bikers need to choose one end or the other to avoid a steep uphill and downhill. Each side has its own entry stations. The most popular trail in the park for cycling is the Telegraph Canyon Trail on the west end, which is suitable for novice mountain bikers but not for beginners because of hills and some rocky areas and stream crossings. A novice trail on the east side of the park is the Aliso Canyon Trail (not related to SV3). Critters of concern in the park include the usual SoCal rattlesnakes and cougars.

Telegraph Canyon MTB Trail CH1

Details: 12 miles MTB, moderate. E-bike edge for hill. Check park site for latest rules.

Access: From the 57 Freeway north of the 91 in the Brea area, take the Lambert Avenue exit eastbound. Follow Lambert, which changes to Carbon Canyon Road (SR 142) after Valencia. At about 2.4 miles is Carbon Canyon Regional Park on the right. This is a good place to park ($3/$5/$7). The next driveway along Carbon Canyon is Chino Hills State Park Discovery

The popular Telegraph Canyon Trail

Center, another option ($5). If you choose the Regional Park, drive all the way to the eastern most parking lot and look for the signs pointing toward the Telegraph Canyon Trail. You'll cycle on a path, then through the Discovery Center parking lot and continue to the trailhead on its east side. The Discovery Center and the Regional Park are the only options for water and restroom near the trail.

The Ride: The Telegraph Canyon Trail consists of a doubletrack fire road that rises gently throughout its length from the west edge of the park over the top of a 1,500-foot ridge, then down steeply to the east side. Our ride extends 6 miles and 840 feet in gradual elevation gain. The trail is packed dirt with some sand and gravel. In about 2.5 miles you'll encounter a water crossing and a rocky stretch. There are 5 or 6 very shallow seasonal water crossings along the route. At around mile 5 is a picnic area, while more hill climbing leads to the Four Corners intersection at mile 6.0, where there is an awning over a couple of picnic benches. Turn around here for a 12-mile ride. Others may wish to turn around much sooner depending on ability. Watch your speed on the return because of some loose gravel, curves, and other trail users including equestrians. This popular trail can get pretty busy. Several more advanced trails join the main trail for those who possess the skills and condition to tackle them.

The Saddleback Valley

South of Irvine the sprawl continues into the Saddleback Valley. The good schools and low crime rate make it another desirable place for families to settle. The area is bike-friendly, with Class II bike lanes found commonplace, as well as some Class I trails thrown in amongst the relatively new development. Local mountain bikers have access to some good dirt at several local parks. The valley's namesake, Saddleback Mountain, or Old Saddleback, is actually comprised of the two tallest mountains in the Santa Ana Mountains, Santiago Peak at 5,689 feet and Modjeska Peak at 5,496 feet, and the ridge between them that together resembles a saddle when viewed from the west. The mountains can also be seen from other vantages of the Los Angeles metro area and serves as a southern landmark, forming part of the boundary between Orange and

Riverside Counties. Cities considered to be in the Saddleback Valley include Mission Viejo, Ladera Ranch, Rancho Santa Margarita, Lake Forest, Laguna Hills, Aliso Viejo, and portions of Laguna Niguel. These are mostly bedroom communities, however business parks here serve as employment centers. The area is fairly hilly, which impacts the selection of rides, although plenty of trails were constructed along creeks where the elevation change is much more gradual.

Rides in this area include the 15-mile Aliso Creek Trail (SV1), a hilly route from that trail to Salt Creek Beach (SV2), and an easy connection to a mixed road and MTB ride through popular Aliso & Wood Canyons Wilderness Park (SV3 and 4). Meanwhile, the upper end of SV1 connects to the not-so-easy MTB trails at Whiting Ranch Wilderness Park (SV5 and 6). The Trabuco Canyon/Rancho Santa Margarita area, closer to Saddleback Mountain, includes a ride through O'Neill Regional Park (SV7), a popular mountain bike ride from there through Trabuco Canyon (SV8), a newer, parallel paved trail higher up in the valley (SV9), and a loop combining the previous 3 rides (SV10). Caspers Wilderness Park, accessible from Ortega Highway near San Juan Capistrano, is a great Camp 'n Ride spot with some pleasant road riding in the park and trailheads for MTB trails (SV11).

Aliso Creek National Recreation Trail   SV1

In October 2012, the Aliso Creek Regional Riding and Hiking Trail was recognized by the U.S. Secretary of the Interior as an exemplary local and regional trail as part of America's national system of trails. The 15-mile asphalt paved Class I trail is used for bicycling, hiking, bird watching, and horseback riding. It is almost a Mountains to the Sea trail, traversing the sprawling south Orange County cities/communities of Foothill Ranch in the foothills of the Santa Ana Mountains through Mission Viejo, Lake Forest, Laguna Hills, Aliso Viejo, and Laguna Niguel, ending near the boundary of Laguna Beach. It mostly follows the riparian corridor along Aliso Creek that passes six schools, two community churches, two skate parks, and ten community parks.

The sometimes-fabulous trail runs mostly parallel to the creek, but alas stops short of following the creek to its delta at Aliso Beach in South Laguna Beach because of private property issues. Instead, an alternate route enables cyclists willing to tackle a few significant Laguna Niguel hills to reach Salt Creek Beach farther south in Dana Point (SV2). However you may prefer to skip the hills and drive there, or somewhere closer to there to ride to it. The northern end of the Aliso Creek Trail is its most wild and scenic section, while there are many pleasant riparian stretches farther south through suburbia. Several choices are also available for your Bike 'n Brunch en route. Because of the elevation gain of nearly 1,000 feet heading northeast, SV1 is described, and recommended, as starting from the southwest end. Or better yet, have someone drop you off at the top!

Tunes: God Willin' and the Creek Don't Rise by Ray LaMontagne and the Pariah Dogs; Bitter Creek by The Eagles; Born to Be Wild by Steppenwolf
Eats: Burger and (one) beer at Cook's Corner

Distance: Up to 13 miles each way + options. Time: Up to 2 hours each way. Downhill return is quicker.
Route & Bike: Easy to strenuous depending on distance traveled. Paved Class I with only a couple of signaled road crossings. Most of the route is smooth blacktop or concrete. Some parallel dirt paths. Any bike. Gradual grade uphill to the northeast

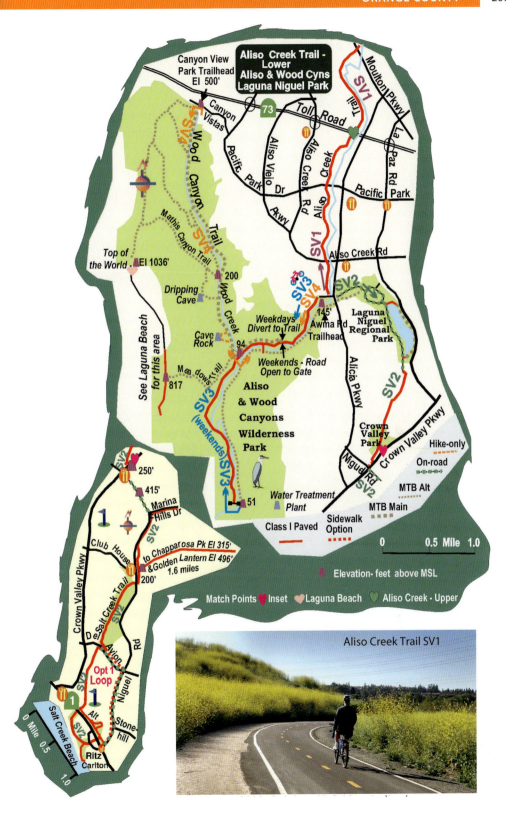

with a few steep sections. Low: 145 feet (Awma Road trailhead). High: 1,100 feet (at Cook's Corner). Steepest pitch is found in the last few miles to the northeast. E-bike edge: Due to the length of the trail and the steady grade especially near the north end, an e-bike could be what the doctor ordered. Class 1 and 2 allowed.

Seasons: All. Best on sunny mild weekday.

Facilities: Porta-potties & water at Aliso & Wood Canyons trailhead, Sheep Hills Park and McFadden House. Restrooms & water at Laguna Niguel Regional Park, Woodfield Park, Aliso Viejo Community Park, El Toro Park, and Heroes Park.

Knocks & Hazards: Clueless peds with dogs and baby strollers. Street crossings in Laguna Hills. Several undercrossings and in-channel sections may be flooded during rainy periods including I-5 with no easy detour. Rattlesnakes. Mountains lions at the northeast end of the trail near Whiting Ranch Park have been seen, mostly at dawn or dusk.

Bike Shops:
Performance Bicycle, 24721 Alicia Pkwy, Laguna Hills, 707.0344; Rock 'n Road Cyclery, 27281 La Paz, Laguna Niguel, 360.8045; Pure Ride Cycles, 24844 Muirlands, Lake Forest, 581.8900; Dicks Sporting Goods, 24821 Alicia, Laguna Hills, 472.8180; Jax Bicycle Center, 27190 Alicia Pkwy, Laguna Niguel, 364.5771.

Camp 'n Ride: None identified along trail. O'Neill Regional Park is closest (see ride SV7). Also see Crystal Cove, Dana Point, San Clemente, Newport Beach, and Huntington Beach rides.

Aliso Creek Trail Upper Section

1. Springdale Park
2. Aliso Viejo Community Park
3. Creekside Park
4. Sheep Hills Park
5. Juan Avila Adobe Monument Trail to Clarington Park
6. Sycamore Park
   Access restaurants at Alicia Pkwy
7. El Toro Park
8. Lake Forest Golf & Practice Center
9. Heroes Park
10. Cherry Park
11. McFadden Ranch House & Interpretive Center
12. Cook's Corner. Live Oak Cyn Rd to O'Neill Park

Paved Class I — Match Point - Aliso Creek (lower)
0   0.5   Mile   1.0

Bike 'n Brunch: See the ride description for locations of places to eat, including a Whole Foods and others near the south trailhead, fast food and a Denny's near Sycamore Park, international cafes near Heroes park, fast food at Trabuco and El Toro Road, and Cook's Corner at the northeast end of the trail.

Further Info: www.americantrails.org/NRTDatabase/trailDetail.php?recordID=3758.

Access: For the south (Awma Road) trailhead take Alicia Parkway off of I-5, heading south for about 5 miles. About 100 yards south of Aliso Creek Road turn right on Awma Road. Parking is in a self-pay lot ($3) or along Awma Road if you can find a free spot there. Check the map for parks and other potential staging spots along the trail. The Cook's Corner lot at the north end is for restaurant patrons only. Cycling south from there involves riding on the shoulder of busy El Toro Road for a few hundred yards. The left (east) branch diverges from the shoulder of El Toro, and then tunnels underneath it, while the right (west) branch starts beyond Ridgeline.

The Ride: The Aliso Creek Trail starts along Awma Road just over the small bridge. When riding from the parking area back to Alicia Parkway it is on the left. However your first opportunity for food (Souplantation, IHOP, Whole Foods) is via sidewalk east on Alicia and right on Aliso Creek. Early in the ride the trail passes a stream impoundment that creates a waterfall below it and a pond above it frequented by shorebirds. Similar milieus are repeated along the stream's length. The first overpass is Aliso Creek Rd (0.25), then Hillview Park. Next cycle past Aliso Niguel High School (0.5). The Chet Holifield Federal Building to the right is shaped like a stepped pyramid silhouette that resembles a ziggurat, an ancient Mesopotamian temple.

The trail dips under Pacific Park Drive. A large regional shopping center to the right here has a Starbucks, Coco's, Pickup Stix, and several others. Next reach Woodfield Park's baseball fields (1.6), another potential staging area with free parking, restrooms and water. Up ahead is the SR 73 Toll Road undercrossing (2.0), followed by Aliso Viejo Community Park and Aliso Viejo Middle School (2.2). When the trail curves to the right and over the creek, bear left at the fork (2.7). Cross under Moulton Parkway (3.0) to Sheep Hills Park, which has porta-potties. You can cycle the loop around the park and turn around for a 6-mile ride, or continue onward.

Follow the trail to the right that reaches the south side of Laguna Hills Dr (3.3) and starts a gradual incline. Cross Indian Hills Lane and pass Laguna Hills High School (3.5). Very carefully cross Paseo de Valencia (3.9) with the light and turn left on the trail adjacent to it. Cross Beckenham Street, Kensington Drive (4.3) and then curve to the right away from the road (4.5) through a greenbelt adjacent to residential areas.

At a four-way junction (4.7), continue straight ahead. The trail to the right crosses the creek and rises steeply to go to Clarington Park. The main route continues climbing gradually uphill toward the I-5 Freeway (4.9). A sign discussing Juan Avila and the former Spanish ranchos in this area is at the top of the small hill that overlooks a scenic oxbow with sandstone cliffs in the stream below. The trail curves to the right and runs downhill, adjacent to the freeway. A tunnel takes you under I-5 (5.0), a passageway susceptible to flooding. The main trail runs along the west side of the channel between the creek and older homes, while a bridge provides an option to cycle through adjacent Sycamore Park, which has a water fountain at the playground.

From the park you can ride east down Charlinda Drive to reach a commercial center along Alicia Parkway with a Target store, and restaurants including Denny's, Five Guys Burgers, Del Taco, and Subway. The main trail is soon sandwiched between housing tracts (5.4), then ducks under Los Alisos Boulevard (5.6) to El Toro Park.

This is another staging option, which you can access by crossing a bike/ped bridge if you need restrooms or water located near the tennis courts. Otherwise, stay on the right side of the channel. This section of trail is within the channelized creek itself, and is usually closed during rain events, at which time you will have to take an alternate route onto the sidewalks along adjacent Los Alisos Boulevard. Steep ramps into the channels are signed "Walk Your Bike."

Continue under Muirlands Boulevard (6.0) while still parallel to Los Alisos Boulevard. The trail curves around the Lake Forest Golf and Practice Center to duck under a railroad crossing next to the creek (6.5), and then bisects Heroes Park, another potential staging spot with free parking, facilities, and a vehicle entrance off of Jeronimo Road just west of Los Alisos Boulevard. You can detour to your choice of several restaurants including several international choices and a Sonic Drive-In at the corner of Jeronimo and Los Alisos. Cross under Jeronimo (6.75) then take the bridge to the west bank of the channel that ends the concrete channel segment (6.9). The suburban riparian greenbelt becomes more freeform and wild. Pass a nice trailside rest area with a water fountain. Cherry Park is across Cherry Avenue at this point (water but no restrooms). Before the Trabuco Road undercrossing (7.6), take the bike bridge to the right to continue on the main trail under that roadway.

If you would like a restaurant break, go straight instead of taking the bridge and follow the path to the left up to roadway level. Paths on both sides of Trabuco Road reach El Toro Road 0.4 mile to the west, across which are several casual restaurants. The main trail north of Trabuco Road traverses some more suburban riparian greenbelt and reaches Sundowners Park, equipped with a water fountain (8.6).

The trail next tunnels under El Toro (8.7) and continues between El Toro and the stream, becoming a wide sidewalk path parallel to the 6-lane roadway. It dips down under Normandale Drive (9.6) and morphs into a wide asphalt pathway. It then goes under Portola Parkway/Santa Margarita Parkway (10.1). Find coffee to the left. The path becomes lined with eucalyptus trees through this area, while above you now is Saddleback Church, Rick Warren's religious-right mega-compound, and at mile 10.8 you cross under the mega bridge to it, as Marguerite Parkway is to the right. Keep right at a junction just before going under the looming toll road (11.0). The left fork leads to the hilly Edison MTB Trail to Whiting Ranch Wilderness Park.

As you emerge from under the bridge the view opens up to the surrounding mountains and you are among a beautiful riparian area with El Toro Road now far above you, creating perhaps the most scenic stretch of the trail, with a mix of prickly pear cactus on the hillsides above and the sycamores and oaks in the riparian corridor below. The pitch of the incline also increases in spurts from here to the end of the trail. Cross under Glenn Ranch

Aliso Creek Trail becomes hillier and more scenic toward the north end

Road where the dirt Alisco-Serrano Riding and Hiking Trail intersects (12.1), also leading to Whiting Ranch Park.

After the trail intersects the access road for McFadden Ranch House and Interpretive Center (outhouse and water), turn right through a tunnel under El Toro Road (12.6), pointing to "Live Oak Trail." Turn left on the other side. It dumps you onto a bikeable shoulder of fast-moving El Toro Road (12.9). This is an optional turnaround point unless you want to go to Cook's Corner. If so, carefully cycle to Live Oak Canyon Road (13.1). Be wary of cars careening full speed around this corner. Across the street is the motorcyclists' mecca Cook's Corner restaurant and bar, and the end of this route. On the return, choose your poison; either cross El Toro Road at the unsignaled crossing and cycle about 0.4 mile past Ridgeline to where the trail daylights on the right, or make your way back the way you came, perhaps walking your bike the short distance to rejoin the trail, and take the tunnel back to the other side.

Option 1: Laguna Niguel Connections
From the Awma Road trailhead, connect to Laguna Niguel Regional Park and the pathway to Crown Valley Road, with a hilly option to get to Salt Creek Beach at the Ritz Carlton in Dana Point. See ride SV2. Or, ride in Aliso Wood Canyons, SV3 & 4.

Laguna Niguel Regional Park and Salt Creek Corridor to the Beach SV2

Laguna Niguel Regional Park is popular with families and fishermen that utilize the stocked Sulphur Creek Reservoir. It is also a pleasant place to cycle through, especially as an extension to the lower section of the Aliso Creek Trail (SV1). Salt Creek Regional Park at the beach is a spectacular spot shared with waterfront McMansions and the Ritz Carlton Laguna Niguel. Surfers enjoy the big waves that break here. In between the two park areas is a very hilly route that will make you earn your Bike 'n Brunch.

Salt Creek Beach Park and bike path backed by Ritz Carlton.

Tunes: Puttin' on the Ritz by Fred Astaire or Taco; Wipeout by the Surfari's.
Eats: Picnic in the park or beach; Souvlaki at Tastes of Greece, Crown Valley and Niguel.

Distance: 5.4–14 miles. Time: 45 minutes to 2 hours

Route & Bike: Easy to moderate Class I paved with dirt options; park roads, Class II and III roads. Small hills in park; larger hills after Crown Valley: E-bike edge!

Seasons: All. Best on sunny, uncrowded, off-season weekday.

Facilities: Restrooms and water in Laguna parks at both ends of trail.

Knocks & Hazards: Some riding with vehicles in park and on Class II roads. Salt Creek Trail is hilly. Rattlesnakes. Coyotes. Small chance of mountain lion.

Camp 'n Ride: None along route. See Dana Point, Crystal Cove, San Clemente.

Bike 'n Brunch: Casual restaurants near ride start on Aliso Crk Rd, mid-route at Crown Valley and near end at PCH. Less casual restaurants at the Ritz (bring spare duds).

City code, bike riding on sidewalks: Laguna Niguel, Dana Point: Bikes allowed on sidewalks per state law except where posted otherwise.

Further Info: Laguna Niguel Park: ocparks.com/parks/lagunan; Salt Creek Park: ocparks.com/beaches/salt; Cities: cityoflagunaniguel.org; danapoint.org.

Access: Use SV1, SV3, or SV4 trailheads. From Awma Rd, ride south (right) on the Alicia Pkwy sidewalk to the crossing signal. The trail ahead is hilly singletrack; novices should ride to the left to a bike/ped park entrance. To drive to this park from I-5 take the La Paz Rd exit, south 4 miles, past Aliso Creek Rd, to entrance on right ($3-$10). To just cycle near the beach (Option 1) take Crown Valley to PCH, left 3/4 mile to Ritz Carlton Dr on right. Left into Salt Creek Beach parking lot ($1/hr). Ride down the hill to the beach trail or under PCH to lovely Sea Terrace Park.

The Ride: Assuming you started from the Alicia Pkwy entrance, pedal through the park, turning right at the fork past the tennis courts. The road rises up to the level of the dam and levels off (mile 1.0). If you have fat tires, check out the hard-packed dirt road that starts on the opposite side of the dam. Access it by turning left before the dam, and then ascend the sidewalk path to lake level. This level road extends for about 0.75 mile along the pleasant lakeside and provides a close-up view of sea and shore birds, such as white pelicans. It connects back to the paved park roadway at the end of the lake via a bridge. To continue farther along the bikeway, pedal westward either on a path or on the adjacent park road past the cul de sac (1.6). The Class I trail leads through a narrow canyon along chanelized Sulfur Creek, passes a water treatment plant, then reaches Laguna Niguel YMCA (2.3) and Sulfur Creek Park, ending at Crown Valley Parkway (2.7). This is a potential turnaround point.

If you have desires on reaching the beach, turn right at Crown Valley onto the bike lane or sidewalk and reach Niguel Road (2.8). At this intersection find several casual restaurant choices including Greek, fish tacos, Japanese, and Subway. Carefully cross Niguel and then Crown Valley, and head up the steep hill along Niguel Rd in the bike lane or sidewalk. Cross La Hermosa Avenue (3.2) and a couple of minor residential access roads and reach Marina Hills Drive (3.5). A Class I trail begins a short way up the right (south) side of Marina Hills Drive. Turn right on it to parallel Niguel Road down the hill. The Salt Creek Trail intersects when you see a large open space area in front of you (4.3). The left branch goes up the hill to Chapparosa Park and Street of the Golden Lantern in about 1.6 miles. Meanwhile Club House Drive intersects Niguel Road to the west, and a shopping plaza contains several restauants. At the trail junction, go right, downhill on Salt Creek Trail, and carefully turn right and through a tunnel under Niguel Road (4.5). Bear right, then left onto the asphalt paved path to continue.

Enjoy more downhill riding through refreshing Salt Corridor Regional Park, while homes are up on the ridges. Once you reach Camino del Avion (5.6) the trail bends left, and then through an undercrossing. It runs through the greenbelt behind condos for a while, then golf holes from Monarch Beach Golf Links appear, indicating you are near the beach. The trail goes under Pacific Coast Hwy (PCH) (6.7) and then runs between the exclusive Ritz Cove estates and the golf course, all the while taking in panoramic ocean views by this point. The trail ends at beautiful Salt Creek Beach Park (7.0) with a lawn and picnic tables, and access to a great beach below that is shared with the adjacent Ritz Carlton. A bonus paved oceanfront path runs below the Ritz around the point. A Beach Hut Deli sandwich shop is at Niguel Rd and PCH. Return the same way, or take Niguel Road, which is partially Class II or Crown Valley Parkway, which is all Class II, but with more steady fast-moving traffic. All options involve a moderately strenuous journey because of the hills involved.

Option 1. Salt Creek Beach and Park Corridor
Loop, 4 mi: From Salt Creek Beach lot, ride under PCH, around Sea Terrace Park trails, left on Niguel sidewalk, left on Del Avion, after Ritz Pt enter Salt Creek Trail, then back to beach.

Aliso and Wood Canyons Wilderness Park

Approximately 30 miles of designated trails wander through this 3,900 acres of wilderness and natural open space land. The property was owned by the Acajchemem tribe, Don Juan Avila, Louis Moulton, The Mission Viejo Company, and now by OC Parks. The park is a wildlife sanctuary that protects mature oak, sycamore, and elderberry trees and many endangered plants and animals. Two streams flow through the park, including the lower end of Aliso Creek that can be quite impressive during major rainfall events. At many areas of the park, a wilderness feel is achieved, although development can be seen atop some of the ridges. Those in top shape can even make their way to the ocean via the park. Very steep mountain bike trails climb over 600 feet to the summit of the Laguna Beach ridges, and riders can then coast down to the beach on residential streets. Most of us, however, will be content to ride in the scenic valley and drive to the beach later. On weekends when the paved utility road is open to the public, you have the option of taking a fabulous 6.8-mile round trip paved ride, perhaps one of the most scenic in the region with its tall ridges, stream valley, and cool ocean breezes wafting up the canyon. Someday if a right-of-way through Ben Brown's Golf Course and The Ranch resort is worked out, you will be able to follow Aliso Creek all the way to its delta at Aliso Beach in South Laguna, but that is a big "if."

Tunes: Songs from the Wood by Jethro Tull; Ladies of the Canyon by Joni Mitchell
Eats: Picnic in the park, or restaurant meal 0.5 mile from trailhead via sidewalk

Seasons: All. Best on sunny uncrowded spring weekday with dry trail conditions.
Facilities: Porta-potties are located at the main park entrance, Wood Canyon gate, and in Canyon View Park, which also has a water fountain. Restrooms with water on the Laguna Beach ridgetop at Alta Laguna Park and Moulton Meadows Park.
Knocks & Hazards: The park may be closed for at least 3 days after a significant rain event or during red flag fire alerts. Check ocparks.com or call the OC Parks office for current trail conditions at 949.923.2200, or the local park ranger at 949.923.2299. Watch for rattlesnakes. Potential for rare mountain lion. Poison oak.
Further Info: See SV1 for map & nearby amenities. Park site: ocparks.com/parks/aliso.

Access: Trailhead parking is the same as described for the Aliso Creek Trail. From 1-5 take Alicia Blvd south for about 5 miles. The entrance is at 28373 Alicia Pkwy, 100 yards south of Aliso Creek Road, on the right down the Aliso Water Management Agency (Awma) Road. Parking is in a self-pay lot ($3) or on the adjacent side street. Another entry with free street parking is Canyon View Park at the upper end of the Wood Canyon trail. Follow the same instructions, but from Alicia after crossing under the 73 Toll Road, turn right on Pacific Park and in 2 miles turn left on Canyon Vistas to the park. Access from this trailhead involves some fairly steep hill climbing on the return.

Weekend Aliso Canyon Road Ride SV3

Distance: 6.8 miles round trip. Time: 30–45 minutes.
Route & Bike: Rolling hills, more easy downhill in, moderate uphill out (e-bike edge). Class I paved road for all bikes.

Water District road through Aliso Canyon is open weekends at time of writing.

On weekends when access is available past the 0.8-mile point of the road, take advantage of cycling on this exceptionally beautiful road through Aliso Canyon. It is very popular with cyclists and hikers but the road is wide enough for all. At mile 1.5 is the turnoff to the Wood Canyon Trail for mountain bikers. Continue your pleasant cruise down the paved road, as the tall coastal sage scrub hillsides close in as you head south, always next to the wide riparian zone created by Aliso Creek. Watch for great blue heron, prairie falcon, several varieties of woodpecker and other birds that frequent the riparian ecosystem, as well as those indigenous to the dryer sage ecosystems such as the California quail, thrasher, and brown towhee. Turn around at the gate that is near the water treatment plant (3.4). Ocean breezes tend to blow up the canyon in the afternoon, assisting you on the return, which is gradually uphill. Road bikers can combine the ride with the Aliso Creek Trail (ride SV1) or the cruise through Laguna Niguel Park with an option for a hilly ride to the beach (ride SV2). Mountain bikers can combine the ride with a cycle through Wood Canyon (ride SV4).

Mountain Bike Ride in Wood Canyon SV4

Distance: About 10 miles round trip. Time: 1–2 hours.
Route & Bike: Easy to moderate; novice MTB. Mostly easy, gradual hills with some steeper hills toward the north end of Wood Canyon. Short distance on paved road but mostly packed dirt and gravel doubletrack. Some sand. Hybrid or mountain bike. At current writing all e-bikes are banned from OC Parks' unpaved paths.

From the Awma Road parking area take the paved road past the gate down the gradual hill through the beautiful riparian valley. At mile 0.8 on weekdays, all must exit onto the adjacent singletrack trail as explained by signs. This is a wide, novice-level trail that

Wood Canyon Trail, Aliso & Wood Canyons Wilderness Park

descends a gradual grade. On weekends (at time of writing) you may stay on the paved road instead, which most do. After about 1.5 miles on weekdays all must turn right at a gate onto the Wood Canyon doubletrack trail. Picnic tables and a porta-potty are available here. On weekends the paved park road is open as described in ride SV3. Novice mountain bikers can ride 3.3 additional miles each way via the Wood Canyon Trail in the valley. While not totally flat, it is not difficult and gradually uphill on the way in, making the return trip a cinch. There are a couple of short steep hills that require extra caution.

You can take a couple of short diversions along the way early on as marked along the trail, first to Cave Rock that actually resembles a reclining elephant (no bikes, lock bikes and walk), and Dripping Cave, rumored to be a hiding place for stagecoach bandits. Bikes are allowed to ride up to it. Since this area hasn't burned in recent years there are still nice sycamores and oaks in the riparian valley providing shade along much of the route, while the remainder is exposed semi-desert terrain.

More advanced riders will want to play in the network of hillside trails, as shown on the map. One can even ascend a 600-foot high hill and reach the hilltop neighborhoods of Laguna Beach, with the option of coasting down to the beach. The upper end of the Wood Canyon trail connects to a paved uphill trending path through Canyon View Park, another staging spot, with a water fountain and porta-potty.

A nice easy doubletrack path starts across from the bike/ped light at Alicia and runs adjacent to the east side of Aliso Creek. A concrete stream crossing at 1 mile from the main trailhead enables an alternative route for your return.

Whiting Ranch Wilderness Park MTB   SV5, SV6

Details: 3–10 miles. MTB, moderate to strenuous. No e-bikes.

Limestone Canyon and Whiting Ranch Wilderness Park preserves approximately 4,300 acres of oak woodland canyons, grassy hills, steep slopes coated with coastal sage scrub and chaparral, and riparian vegetation along the intermittent Borrego, Serrano, and Aliso Creeks. About 90 percent of the park burned during the Santiago Fire of 2007, and the vegetation is in the recovery process. Scenic rock formations including Red Rock Canyon are one of the main draws of the park, which is located in the foothills of the Santa Ana Mountains around the communities of Foothill Ranch and Portola Hills in central Orange County. The park has been known to contain an abundance of wildlife, including mountain lions, one of which killed one mountain biker and mauled another in 2004. Once a cattle ranch, remnants of those operations are still present. The Limestone Canyon portion of the park is only open to guided hikes.

Unfortunately the only truly novice easy trail is the one-way Borrego Canyon Trail into the park (SV5), so you either have to walk it back or continue on a loop on much more difficult trails. A moderate ride is Raptor Road and Serrano Cow Trail (SV6, 3.1 miles) accessed from the Glenn Ranch Road Trailhead parking area, or via a 3.5-mile ride on the Alisco-Serrano Trail next to that road from the Aliso Creek Trail (SV1). Check ocparks.com/whitingranch/ for a park map and current trail conditions, or call the OC Parks office at 949.923.2200, or the local park ranger at 949.923.2245.

Trabuco Canyon Area

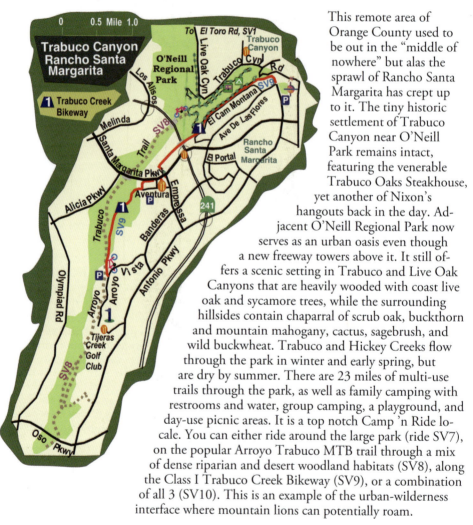

This remote area of Orange County used to be out in the "middle of nowhere" but alas the sprawl of Rancho Santa Margarita has crept up to it. The tiny historic settlement of Trabuco Canyon near O'Neill Park remains intact, featuring the venerable Trabuco Oaks Steakhouse, yet another of Nixon's hangouts back in the day. Adjacent O'Neill Regional Park now serves as an urban oasis even though a new freeway towers above it. It still offers a scenic setting in Trabuco and Live Oak Canyons that are heavily wooded with coast live oak and sycamore trees, while the surrounding hillsides contain chaparral of scrub oak, buckthorn and mountain mahogany, cactus, sagebrush, and wild buckwheat. Trabuco and Hickey Creeks flow through the park in winter and early spring, but are dry by summer. There are 23 miles of multi-use trails through the park, as well as family camping with restrooms and water, group camping, a playground, and day-use picnic areas. It is a top notch Camp 'n Ride locale. You can either ride around the large park (ride SV7), on the popular Arroyo Trabuco MTB trail through a mix of dense riparian and desert woodland habitats (SV8), along the Class I Trabuco Creek Bikeway (SV9), or a combination of all 3 (SV10). This is an example of the urban-wilderness interface where mountain lions can potentially roam.

Tunes: Morning Dance by Spyro Gyra; Celestial Soda Pop by Ray Lynch; Take it Easy by Jackson Browne
Eats: Picnic in O'Neill Park or In-N-Out Burger, KFC, etc along SV9

Seasons: All year. Best on sunny, uncrowded, off-season spring weekday.
Facilities: Restrooms and water at O'Neill Park.
Camp 'n Ride: Camping in the park for tents/RV's (no hookups). For camping reservations go to the park's website or call 800.600.1600.

Bike 'n Brunch: TJ's Cantina at the Tijeras Creek Golf Course accessible from SV8 and SV9 has Sunday brunch. Casual and fast food restaurants near midpoint of SV9. Apres ride drive to Rose Canyon Cantina's leafy patio in Trabuco Canyon.
Further info and trail conditions: Check ocparks.com/oneillpark or call 949.923.2260.

O'Neil Park Ramble SV7

Distance: Up to a few easy miles.
Route & Bike: On paved park roads shared with vehicles, for any bike. Easy to moderate due to optional hill.
Knocks & Hazards: Mountain lion, bear, and rattlesnake country.

From I-5 take El Toro Rd north/east to Live Oak Canyon Rd (Cook's Corner). Turn right and drive 3 miles to the park entrance at 30892 Trabuco Canyon Rd, Trabuco Canyon. Vehicle fee is $3–$7. The paved park roads make for a pleasant scenic cycle popular with families. Pedal around the Oak Grove day use area, out to the equestrian campsite, past the campgrounds and through the lush forested west area adjacent to Live Oak Canyon Road. You can also ride up the steep hill to the east "Mesa" side of the park and ride along the mile-long park road or adjacent wide dirt trail, or join the paved Trabuco Creek Bikeway (SV9) that borders both the park and suburbia above the canyon.

Arroyo Trabuco MTB Trail SV8

Distance: 10–11 miles. Time: 1.5–2 hours.
Route & Bike: Single and doubletrack MTB with varied terrain. Several stream crossings that may be difficult or impossible during high water. Moderate. Rated upper end of novice level. E-bikes not allowed on unpaved paths in O'Neill Park.
Knocks & Hazards: Mountain lion and rattlesnake country, as well as ticks and plentiful poison oak near stream. Also potential for bears. Dirt trails closed during and 3 days after rain storms. Sign warns of unexploded ordnances.
Access: See SV7. The trailhead is at the west end of the Oak Grove picnic area, west of the park offices. Some start at Cox Sports Park off Crown Valley and head north.
The Ride: Regarded as one of the best easy MTB trails in Orange County, this trail descends for six miles to the south, mostly parallel to Trabuco Creek as it flows seasonally toward Oso Parkway in Mission Viejo. The trail is mainly fire road, but there is some twisting singletrack (watch for oncoming bikers!), wet stream crossings in season, and sandy and rocky sections.

Follow the fire road as it leads toward the massive overpass of SR 241, the Foothill Transporta-

Arroyo Trabuco Trail emerges from creekside

tion Corridor Toll Road (0.25). Next pass under the Santa Margarita Parkway bridge (1.2), which is accessible via a side trail. Although these overpasses detract from the wilderness experience, a lot of the native trees and shrubs that you see were planted as mitigation for them. The trail descends and crosses the stream channel (1.9) that may require a water crossing in the wet season.

Consequently our route ascends the other side of the arroyo toward a subdivision, meeting up with an access point on Arroyo Vista (2.7), which is another potential staging point with free on-street parking. You will also notice a parallel paved trail that ascends to the roadway, which is ride SV9. You can exit onto Arroya Vista and ride to the right to reach the clubhouse for Tijeras Creek Golf Course, where TJ's Cantina has a Sunday brunch buffet (so bring a collared shirt just in case that's your plan). Alternately, Arroyo Vista can be accessed via breaks in the fencing when the trail gets close to the roadway again farther along. The trail eventually veers away from the subdivision (3.5) and heads back down via a fairly steep hill to the creekside below the golf course.

A vista point overlooking the creek and the valley a little way down the hill is a good turnaround point for a 7-mile ride. However, the next section of the trail is very scenic, along the floodplain among oaks, sycamores, and meadow. Once past the golf course (4.6) and before crossing under power lines, there is a trail junction to the left (east) (5.0). The Tijeras Spur Trail leads to Antonio Parkway, which is another staging point. You may want to turn around there, because at time of writing storm damage has wiped out portions of the trail between there and the Oso Parkway overpass (5.5), where the trail crosses the creek several times. If the trail has been repaired you can continue onward. There is access to Oso Pkwy from the trail, but no parking on it. It continues all the way past Crown Valley Pkwy near O'Neill Drive. Cox Sports Park here is a popular staging point and a shopping center has food available. A Class I trail starts to the west on Crown Valley leading 2 miles south to Trabuco Creek Rd.

Trabuco Creek Bikeway SV9 4

Distance: 8.4 miles up and back. Time: 1–1.5 hours
Route & Bike: Paved Class I with several road crossings at the midpoint. Any bike. Moderate difficulty due to inclines. Gradual uphill to north: Arroyo Vista (south trailhead): Elevation 770 ft; Aventura (middle trailhead): 867 ft; first entrance to O'Neill Park at Danta: 976 ft; end of trail at Antonio: 1,163 ft. (e-bike edge).
Facilities: Restroom and water inside O'Neill Park and Trabuco Mesa Park at trail north end but none at south end.
Knocks & Hazards: Two road crossings. Rattlesnakes. Mountain lions. 'Ordnance' sign.

Access: If you are not staying at O'Neill Park, we recommend starting at the Arroyo Vista south trailhead and going uphill first. From I-5 in Laguna Hills, exit Alicia Parkway and take it until it ends at Santa Margarita Pkwy. Turn right and cross the bridge over the canyon with the Arroyo Trabuco (SV8) route far below. Take the second right at signaled Avenida Empressa, then right at Banderas, right on Arroyo Vista and find the obvious trailhead at the junction of Paraiso. Street parking is available here. For the Aventura (middle) trailhead, after crossing the bridge on Santa Margarita Pkwy, make the first right on Calle Corta, then right on Aventura, and find street parking. The trail passes at the end of Aventura. From the SR 241 Toll Road, exit Santa Margarita Pkwy, go south and turn left on Empressa or Calle Corta, and follow instructions as above.

The Ride: From the Arroyo Vista trailhead, a dirt trail goes to the left and a paved trail leads down to the right. Both meet up with the Arroyo Trabuco MTB trail, eventually making their way down to the creek in both directions. Our Class I trail continues north on the paved trail. The dirt trail junction encountered to the left early on is the SV8 MTB trail. Although modern residential development is visible to the right, the view riding northward on the paved trail is spectacular with Saddleback Mountain forming the backdrop, vacant hills with seasonal wildflowers farther along to the right, and the lush riparian valley of Trabuco Creek down to the left. Reach the end of this portion of the trail (mile 1.4) at a "T" junction next to the end of Aventura and a Christian school. This is another potential staging area with plenty of street parking.

Trabuco Creek Bikeway heading north toward the Santa Ana Mountains

To continue, take the trail to the left that leads down to a sidewalk along Santa Margarita Parkway (1.8). Carefully cross the entrances to a commercial center, where there are several dining options including a KFC and some independent eateries in the strip mall. Cross Empressa Parkway with the light, then cross Santa Margarita. Another dining option is an In-N-Out Burger to the right past the Ford dealership, accessed via the Santa Margarita Pkwy sidewalk. Our route continues up the short block of Empressa to the resumption of the Class I trail that is straight ahead between buildings (2.0). At the "T" junction, turn right, and cycle along the paved path and then across a bike bridge over the SR 241 Toll Road (2.4). The trail continues behind a church and then runs parallel to El Camino Montana between O'Neill Park and a residential community.

Just before the intersection with Danta is a bike/ped entrance to O'Neill Park with convenient restrooms (2.8). We suggest continuing on the paved path along Montana and returning through the park. The trail keeps chugging along up the gradual incline. Another entrance to the park is farther along the trail across from the intersection of Ensilado. Our path bends away from Montana (3.7), and runs between the bluff-top O'Neill Park and more suburban homes.

As the trail bends around to the right behind the homes (4.1), several dirt trails go off to the left and connect to Trabuco Canyon Road. We don't recommend riding on that road, especially to the left, where it descends steeply with moderate traffic and leads to the settlement of Trabuco Canyon and the main part of the park. The road inside the park is a better option.

Meanwhile, our paved path continues to bend around and ends at the northern end of Antonio Parkway at Avenida de Las Flores (4.2). At that corner is the large Trabuco Mesa Park with restrooms and free street parking. Return the same way, taking an alternate route by ducking into the first entrance into O'Neill Park, where you can ride either on the low-traffic park road or the parallel wide dirt trail (no e-bikes) that follows the rim of the canyon, which is the most scenic option, but also tends to have the most peds along it that stroll in from the adjacent neighborhood. To get to the main part of O'Neill Park requires descending a steep hill on the park road that drops 100 feet, and riding across the concrete crossing over Trabuco Creek.

Combination MTB and Class I Loop SV10

Do ride SV8 southbound on the mountain bike, but return via ride SV9 on the paved Trabuco Creek Bikeway starting from where the trails intersect near Arroyo Vista. Near ride SV9's north end take the park road back down into the valley to your starting point, cycling around the park roads in the valley as you wish (SV7). Distance depends on how far you go on SV8 past Arroyo Vista, but expect about a 10-mile ride of moderate difficulty.

Caspers Wilderness Park MTB SV11

Details: 4 miles paved road and variable miles MTB (no e-bikes), easy to strenuous.

This 8,000-acre protected wilderness preserve, the largest in Orange County, is nestled amid river terraces and sandstone canyons of the western coastal Santa Ana Mountains, with beautiful vistas up toward Saddleback Mountain. The park contains fertile valleys and groves of native coastal live oak and California sycamore. At 7 miles up Ortega Highway (CA 74) from I-5 at San Juan Capistrano, it is truly isolated from the sprawl of Orange County, with virtually no civilization in sight from within the park. That will probably change as the sprawl expands eastward. Springtime can bring wildflower blooms and several running streams, while strong winter storms can turn San Juan Creek into a raging torrent, cutting off most of the park that is accessed via a low water crossing bridge. Many species of birds and animals live in the park, including deer, rabbits, bobcats, coyotes, and mountain lions, responsible for two attacks on children in 1986 (who survived). *Pets are still not allowed in the park* because of that.

Caspers contains an interesting nature center with viewing platform, playground, picnic area, and campgrounds. It is a great Camp 'n Ride park for MTB'ers of various levels. The best novice path is the 2-mile Bell Canyon Trail that begins from the far end of the park road. Intermediate MTB'ers can make it a 5 mile loop via the Oso and East Ridge Trails, with a 600 foot elevation gain and great vistas. Or just pedal around the pretty campground gravel loop roads and other park features. Road bikers can cycle a few miles on the hilly and scenic park road, but we don't recommend cycling dangerous Ortega Highway. For park info and map see ocparks.com/parks/ronald/ or call 949.923.2210 or 923.2207. Entry fee is $3 weekdays, $5 weekends per car.

The easy San Juan Creek Trail runs parallel to Ortega Highway. It offers some great vistas toward Saddleback Mountain but also has a few unpleasant rocky sections.

6. San Diego County

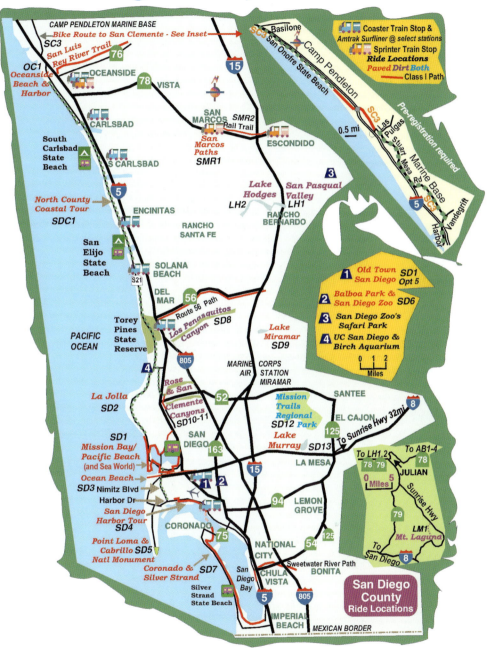

One of the best year-round climates in the world, a beautiful 70-mile coastline extending into inland bays, and an abundance of scenic easy bike trails make San Diego County heaven on two wheels. The county's 3.3 million people live mostly in the western portion of its 4,526 square miles that extend from the ocean inland over hills, mesas, and small to medium mountains up to 6,500 feet elevation, to the vast Colorado Desert at its eastern border with Imperial County. The desert at the foot of the eastern slope of the Laguna Mountains provides the greatest contrast to the coastal and mountain communities, but is included in The Deserts chapter instead, in the Anza-Borrego section.

To the north along the coast, the county borders San Clemente in Orange County, separated by Camp Pendleton Marine Base. A popular road ride connects Oceanside to San Clemente through the base (Orange County, SC3). Oceanside is a featured cycling destination, with a rewarding combination ride along a river, harbor, and beach (OC1). A scenic coastal road ride south from there towards San Diego can be combined with a return via Coaster train (SDC1).

Farther east the northern border is shared with Riverside County, from its Temecula wine country to the Santa Rosa Mountains north of Anza-Borrego State Park. To the south is Mexico, including Tijuana and the Baja Peninsula. Imperial County borders to the east.

Novice mountain bikers have some awesome options for a fun and scenic escape, the best being at Lake Hodges near Escondido (LH1 and 2). Several other locales are also worthwhile (SD8, 10–12). A great day trip to the Laguna Mountains (LM1) combines an easy dirt ride, a hike on the Pacific Crest Trail overlooking the Colorado Desert, and pie in historic Julian.

The county's main cycling attractions are found in the City of San Diego and its immediate suburbs, with its world famous destinations such as the San Diego Zoo, Old Town, and Sea World. Countless miles of scenic Class I biking, mostly with views of the ocean, bays or reservoirs, create some of the best easy scenic rides in SoCal (SD1–7, 9, 13).

Getting here: San Diego International Airport (SAN) or Lindbergh Field is close to both downtown and Mission Bay; www.san.org, 619.400.2404. The county is well serviced by rail and bike-carrying buses, as described in the introductory chapter. Drivers can take I-5 south from the LA/Orange County areas, I-15 south from the Inland Empire (Riverside/San Bernardino), or I-8 west from Phoenix and Yuma, Arizona, to get to the San Diego area. See the individual rides for further directions.

Climate Data for San Diego (Source NOAA 1981 to 2010 normals)													
Month	Jan	Feb	Mar	Apr	May	Jun	Jul	Aug	Sep	Oct	Nov	Dec	Totals
Average High °F	65.1	65.0	65.6	67.5	68.5	70.8	74.6	76.4	75.9	72.8	69.0	64.7	69.7
Average Low °F	49.0	50.7	53.2	55.9	59.4	62.0	65.4	66.7	65.2	60.6	53.6	48.4	57.5
Precipitation, inches	0.98	2.27	1.81	0.78	0.12	0.07	0.03	0.02	0.15	0.57	1.00	1.53	10.33

Oceanside

The beach city of Oceanside is at the north end of coastal San Diego County, bordering Camp Pendleton Marine Base. Mission Avenue is the main drag, with lots of restaurants along it and Tremont Streets a few blocks from the long municipal pier. The 1.3-mile Strand roadway and boardwalk runs along Oceanside's beautiful sandy beaches, centered around the pier. Although vehicles are allowed on most of The Strand, it also has separate lanes for bikes. Oceanside Harbor is a public marina for private boats accessible from The Strand by an easy 0.4-mile Class II/III route. It is a very popular place to dine out, stroll, and cycle on its Class III bike route.

To get up some speed and escape from vehicle traffic, you can pedal up the Class I San Luis Rey River Trail for up to 9 miles each way along a scenic riparian route with

SAN DIEGO COUNTY

mountain backdrop. It makes a great workout trail with virtually no interruptions, mostly courteous trail users, and no speed limit. Our route takes you about 6 miles along the trail (and an option to do the entire 9-mile trail) with a short side trip to the Mission San Luis Rey de Francia, the largest mission in California.

The San Luis Rey River Trail can be easily accessed at a point halfway between The Strand and the harbor. So, take your pick of ride options, or ride them all as described in our suggested route, and enjoy the variety and the beauty of it all. Oceanside is one of three San Diego County cities given a silver "Bicycle Friendly" rating by The League of American Bicyclists, and we consider it to be a fabulous scenic biking destination. Oceanside is easy to get to as well. Not only is it at the crossroads of I-5 between LA and San Diego, and the 78 Freeway that leads to I-15 in Escondido, it is also a passenger rail center. See the Orange County chapter for a connecting ride that combines roads and trails north through Camp Pendleton to San Clemente (SC3), and this chapter for a Class II ride south along the coast (SDC1).

Oceanside Tour:
Your Mission—Boats, Beaches, and Birds OC1

Tunes: Take My Breath Away (from "Top Gun") by Berlin; Walk Don't Run by The Ventures; Reach the Beach by The Fixx
Eats: Oyster Po' Boy Sandwich from Tin Fish at the pier

Distance: Up to 20 miles. Time: Up to 3 hours
Route & Bike: Easy to moderate difficulty depending on distance and headwinds on river trail. The Class I paved path has a few dips under roads and short steep hill at south trailhead. The Strand and street connections to it are Class II with short steep hills leading to the beach. Oceanside Harbor is Class III with some sidewalk along the beach. E-bike edge on hills, fighting headwinds on river trail, and increasing distance such as riding entire river trail or combining with adjacent rides (SC3, SDC1). Any bike. Fat tired cruiser if you try riding on the sand.
Seasons: All. Best on sunny, clear, uncrowded, off-season weekday with no fog and minimal wind.
Facilities: Restrooms and water at Harbor, Strand, M Buchanan Park on river trail.
Knocks & Hazards: Clueless peds, especially on The Strand, although they have a separate sidewalk north of the pier. Summer weekends and holidays are worst. Cycling with slow-moving traffic along The Strand and Harbor. Street crossings, and bike lanes next to traffic on Pacific Street. Possible lurkers along the river trail, including some homeless. Also watch for rattlesnakes on trail, and there is the potential for a mountain lion. Keep right in deference to fast cyclists.
Rent 'n Ride: City of Oceanside: Beach cruisers $5/day, byo helmet, M–Th & alt Fri, 300 N. Coast Hwy, 760.435.5041. Wheel Fun under pier rents a variety of bikes. Shop/Rent: Mostly E-Bikes, 203 Wisconsin, 442.266.8137. Shops: SoCal Bike, 2028 S. Coast Hwy, 760.710.1478; Alan's Bike Shop, 805 South Coast Hwy, 760.722.3377; Omega Bicycle, 459 College Blvd, near north end of river trail, 760.631.2834. Bike lockers at transit station, see bikelink.org.
Camp 'n Ride: Oceanside Harbor, Lot 11B and Lot 12 (Sep 15-May 15) smaller self contained RV's (no popouts) ($30-$35, no reserv's,) dump station but no utilities. Two RV parks are a mile from The Strand: Oceanside RV, 1510 S Coast Hwy, 760.722.4404, and Paradise by the Sea RV, 1537 S Coast Hwy, 760.439.1376. Guajome Regional Park, 3000 Guajome Lake Rd, 9 miles inland, off SR76 has tent and RV sites (hookups), 724.4489, sdcounty.ca.gov/parks/Camping/guajome.html. An unpaved 0.4-mile trail connects the park to the paved San Luis Rey River trail's northeast trailhead at Santa Fe Ave via a highway underpass, or connect via SR 76. See Option 1A. Ride 5.5-miles to San Luis Rey Mission or 10 miles to the beach.

SAN DIEGO COUNTY 225

Also consider camping at North Carlsbad State Beach for a Class II ride to Oceanside (SDC1), or San Clemente and San Onofre State Parks in Orange County for a ride through Camp Pendleton to Oceanside (Ride SC3 - see for permit info).

Bike 'n Brunch: At the main harbor complex are Joe's Crab Shack, Harbor Fish & Chips, Stratford on the Harbor, Rockin' Baja Coastal Cantina, Lighthouse Oyster Bar & Grill, Nautical Bean, Sushi Harbor, and others. Farther along North Harbor Drive is Oceanside Broiler. At the end of Oceanside Pier is a Ruby's diner. Below the pier is Tin Fish, a fresh fish grill take-out. Up the hill in town along Mission and Tremont are many choices, and the popular upscale 333 Pacific Restaurant on Pacific Street has good ocean views. Northeast on the river trail, find fast food 0.3-mile north on Douglas Drive or south on College Blvd. See the ride description for other options.

City code, bike riding on sidewalks: Prohibited on docks, fingers or walkways in the harbor; Municipal Pier, its ramps or Plaza; or where fronting upon any commercial business unless signs permit it. Cycling along The Strand road itself is allowed, just not in the amphitheater and other ped areas.

Further Info: City of Oceanside: www.ci.oceanside.ca.us/. The Mission: sanluisrey.org; Other/dining: visitoceanside.org.

Access: Choose from numerous places to start this ride. Keep in mind that on-shore winds tend to blow up the river valley, sometimes starting in late morning, and intensifying in the afternoon. Therefore, starting at the east end of the river trail may make the ride easier. However, you can start in the marina in the morning, get your exercise before the winds pick up, and then return to do the fun parts such as cycling along the harbor and beach, and of course, do a Bike 'n Brunch. To get to the main harbor parking lot from I-5, exit at Harbor Drive/Camp Pendleton. From the southbound exit, cross Harbor Drive to North Coast Hwy. From the northbound exit, go under the freeway and turn left on North Coast Hwy. Turn right on Monterey and left on San Luis Rey Drive, which curves around and reaches the free parking lot. A bike/ped tunnel under the tracks leads to Harbor Drive and the main dining area of the marina. There is also parking downtown, along The Strand, and in neighborhoods. Along the San Luis Rey River Trail parking is available at Mance Buchanan Park, Douglas Drive (downriver of underpass), Foussat Road, Benet Road, and at trail's end at Santa Fe Road and Hwy 76.

Rail 'n Ride: The Oceanside train station is at 195 Tremont Street. From I-5 exit Mission southbound, pass Coast Hwy, and turn left on Cleveland to the station. Bikes northbound on Pacific St turn right on Oceanside Blvd and left onto a rail trail to the station. Bikes southbound on Pacific turn left up Tyson. Amtrak goes north to Los Angeles and beyond and south to San Diego. Metrolink goes north through the Los Angeles and Inland Empire areas. San Diego's Coaster goes south to San Diego and the Sprinter line goes east to Escondido. If arriving by train, follow the green line painted on Cleveland northbound to Class I San Luis Rey River Trail at Neptune, or ride down to The Strand via Pier View to Pacific, then to Surfrider or Seagaze. Heading south down the coast, start off on the rail trail next to Track 2 to Oceanside Blvd.

The Ride: Our suggested route is broken down into three parts that represent each segment's character. The ongoing mileage noted reflects the complete ride. Options to each section are also presented, and the mileage associated with each option can be added to the total. OC1-1 begins in the harbor, turns up the Class I San Luis Rey River Trail from Pacific Street to Douglas Street, detours to visit the mission, and returns to Pacific Street. Those wanting more distance can ride the entire trail. OC1-2 continues to The Strand for a ride along the beach with an optional trip into downtown and the pier, and then returns to the harbor. OC1-3 is a jaunt on the roadway through the harbor.

Oceanside Harbor Start and San Luis Rey River Trail OC1-1

Distance: 13 miles + options, easy to moderate.

From the main harbor parking lot, go through the ped/bike tunnel toward Joe's Crab Shack and turn left onto Harbor Drive. Ride around the curve to the right and up the incline, overlooking the scenic restaurant area, to the Pacific Street Bridge (mile 0.2). Straight ahead is Harbor Beach, which you can explore later in the ride. Our route turns left to cross the flat bridge in the wide bike lane. You can stop and take in the vista of the San Luis Rey River delta, typically filled with a wide variety of sea and shore birds. Look for a trailhead on the left past the bridge. The paved Class I San Luis Rey River trail dips down steeply under the railroad tracks. To the right is a trail junction (watch for fast moving bikes!), which just extends a couple of blocks into neighborhoods. Ride OC1-1 goes to the left, parallel to the wide river delta with great bird watching opportunities, and drops under the Coast Highway and I-5 overpasses before emerging next to SR 76 (0.8).

The route soon pulls away from the highway as it continues on a levee above the river but within the riparian vegetation, then climbs up higher above it with more expansive views of the surroundings, which include development in the hills above the valley and mountain views in the distance (1.9). Reach the first cross street, Benet Road (2.7), with Oceanside Municipal Airport to the right. After ducking under that roadway, the trail continues adjacent to Alex Road, reaching access to another trailhead off of Foussat Road (3.4), then crosses under the street. It gets close to a residential area at mile 4.9, then circles around it. After passing a school and some residences, it reaches Douglas Street (5.7). Some fast food restaurants including a Carl's Jr. are a few blocks north (left) on Douglas. This is a potential turnaround point for an 11.4-mile ride, however, our suggested route pays a visit to the Mission San Luis Rey De Francia.

Turn to the right in the Class II bike lane (or as we prefer, the nice sidewalk) along Douglas. Continue to the signal at El Camino Real (6.3). Turn left at this busy intersection by carefully crossing El Camino Real and then Douglas using the pedestrian signals. Ride down a short industrial block of El Camino Real and past the 50-year old San Luis Rey Restaurant and Bakery (6.5). The outdoor tables may be too tempting to pass up for a nice Mexican repast, and if you go inside beware the display of goodies! From there carefully cross the street and into a bike/ped entrance for the mission. The left fork leads directly to the mission (6.7). You can return to the river trail the same way via the sidewalk or bike lane along the east side of Douglas, or return on residential streets with no bike lanes or sidewalks via Peyri Drive to the right, bearing left on Pala Lane back to Douglas (7.5). Return to the river trail. Our route goes left and returns to the trailhead on Pacific Street (12.9).

> Option 1: Continue on the San Luis Rey River Trail   *6.8 miles total, easy*
> For additional mileage on the Class I river trail beyond Douglas Drive, turn right onto the trail if you have visited the mission. Or, if you did not go to the mission, just continue along the trail under Douglas (mile 0). It continues through a scenic stretch along the berm where the wide swatch of riparian vegetation has grown high enough to mask

The San Luis Rey River Trail is mostly atop a levee

the surrounding residential and commercial districts. Around mile 1.7, just before College Boulevard, is a bike entrance to Mance Buchanan Park. The ample parking and the only restrooms along the trail make this park one of the best staging points. The main park entrance is off College Boulevard.

Either continue on the trail under the road, or detour southeast on Class II College Boulevard for 0.4 mile up a hill for a variety of chain restaurants at Mission Marketplace including Subway, McDonalds, El Pollo Loco, plus pizza, Hawaiian, and Mexican offerings. Denny's and Carl's Jr are just across Highway 76. The trail carries on between the river basin and a residential neighborhood, then makes a sharp turn to the right and ends temporarily at Andrew Jackson Street (2.3). In the future the trail may be extended to avoid this detour.

Watch! for passing cars and then turn left, then bend to the right to Tyler Street and look for the continuation of the Class I trail on the left, indicated by a large Bike Trail sign (2.5). The trail drops down to the right, then curves around the perimeter of the neighborhood next to more riparian vegetation (watch for snakes here), and ends at the intersection of North Santa Fe Avenue and Highway 76, where there is a small parking lot and ample street parking (3.4). Road bikers can turn around here, for a total segment mileage of 6.8 miles round trip added to your main ride total.

Option 1A: Guajome Park *Up to 5 miles, easy, MTB*

Those with mountain bikes can take a rough, wide equestrian trail to the left of the highway that leads to a highway undercrossing, emerging at lovely Guajome Regional Park. Over 4 miles of novice-level multi-use trails (a choice of flat or hilly) lead to two lakes, a campground, and restrooms. This excursion to and around the park adds another 2 to 5 miles to your ride total. As another potential staging spot, the fee is $3 to park inside or free in surrounding neighborhoods. By vehicle, follow the signs to the entrance off Gaujome Lake Road rather than GPS that will probably direct you to Santa Fe Road instead.

The Beach! OC1-2

Distance: 4.1 miles plus options, easy.

Upon returning from the San Luis Rey River Trail (12.9), carefully cross Pacific Street and turn left into the bike lane, then turn right down Breakwater Way (13.1), reaching The Strand along the long public beach to the left, with the pier in the distance (13.2). The roadway is open to vehicles, designated one way heading northwest toward Breakwater Way. Bikes can travel both ways in the bike lane on the west side of the road, although most cyclists heading northwest stick to the east side of the roadway in the same direction as the vehicle traffic. Needless to say, this situation can be fairly precarious on a very busy beach day with confused cyclists traveling every which way, so ride courteously and defensively. We think it's worth it though, because the beach is just so beautiful. At least a separate sidewalk for pedestrians helps the situation.

Option 1: Downtown Oceanside ⭐2 *Variable mileage, easy.*

Surfrider Way (13.4) is your chance to cycle up the hill to visit downtown and the pier. Once atop the hill turn right on Pacific Street to Pier View Way, and take a stroll on the pier if you fancy, but cycling is not allowed on it. Left on Pier View Way takes you on a bike/ped trail under the train tracks to the most interesting part of downtown with a concentration of restaurants and shops along Tremont Street between Pier View and Mission Avenue to the right. Movie buffs take note of the blue house on the northeast corner of Pacific Street and Seagaze (the other access from The Strand to downtown, south of the pier) where key *Top Gun* scenes were filmed.

Surfrider is also where cars enter to drive northwest on The Strand. However, as you continue along The Strand southeast of here, the road is blocked off to vehicles in the vicinity of the pier. Since there is a separation of peds and bikes, there is no "Walk Bikes" sign here, which makes for a nice stretch. Under the pier are a Wheel Fun bike rental concession and the Tin Fish restaurant take-out stand (13.7). Upon reaching Seagaze Drive (13.9) vehicles once again have access but this time it is designated as one way to the southeast. There is a 2-way bike lane on the west side of the road (photo) and the ocean vistas are beautiful, but it is a messy situation with the bikes and peds all next to 15 mph traffic. If it's a busy day we tend to ride on the landward sidewalk when northbound. The Strand ends at Wisconsin Avenue, with a parking lot and restrooms on the corner (14.4). Turn around here. At low tide when the sand is firm, those with thick tires may want to just ride back on the beach.

Option 2: Coast Ride ⭐3

From the southeast end of The Strand at Wisconsin Avenue, continue on Class II/III bike routes along the coast to Carlsbad and beyond. See the Oceanside map for the route south out of town and the San Diego Coast Tour (SDC1) maps for the rest.

Return the way you came via The Strand to Pacific Street, crossing over the bridge to the harbor (15.9). This time, turn left, toward the beach, and explore the beach here, which features beach parks and a primitive RV camping area. Return up the incline to the bridge (16.9), then go back down the incline to your starting point near the restaurant area (17.0).

Oceanside Harbor OC1-3 ⭐2

Distance: 2.5 miles total, easy

To explore more of the harbor, continue cycling along Harbor Drive. After it curves to the left, and Harbor Drive continues up a hill, note that this is the point at which the ride through Camp Pendleton to San Clemente connects (SC3). Our route stays in the harbor area (17.1), riding along what is now North Harbor Drive. After passing Oceanside Broiler seafood restaurant, the road curves again to the right (17.3), and then curves left a few times to go around another picturesque arm of the marina.

The route ends along the beach at Oceanside Marina Suites (18.2). Return to your starting point in front of Joe's Crab Shack, and then back to your car in the main parking lot (19.5).

Oceanside Harbor for your Bike 'n Brunch

The North San Diego County Coast SDC1

Details: Variable miles on road, moderate. E-bike edge: Headwinds; some hills along Coast Hwy, steeper on some side roads, and brutal south of Del Mar.

Perhaps the most popular cycling route in San Diego County is along Coast Highway between Oceanside and Del Mar. On weekends, hordes of Lycra-clad cyclists zip up and down the roadway, enjoying the dramatic ocean vistas and refreshing breezes. The route varies from ocean bluff-top to beachfront to beach town, with each city exuding its own unique character, offering countless dining opportunities. It is perfect for a Rail 'n Ride, since the Coaster line stops at Oceanside, Carlsbad, South Carlsbad, Encinitas, and Solana Beach, enabling a one-way ride to cover more ground. We ride in the southbound direction for the superior vistas on the ocean side.

Sculpted arches on Solana Beach's nice rail trail through town. A welcome break from cycling on the coast highway.

This is not the typical type of ride featured in this book, because it is mostly in bike lanes next to a busy highway, suitable for experienced cyclists only. However, it is such a popular activity in these parts that it is mentioned for those who feel comfortable with this type of riding. Several detours are available to take you off of the Coast Highway, although the routes may encompass hillier terrain than the main road. Note that bikes are prohibited from riding on sidewalks in Carlsbad and in the business districts of Oceanside and Encinitas, however there are usually sharrows or Class II bike lanes through these stretches.

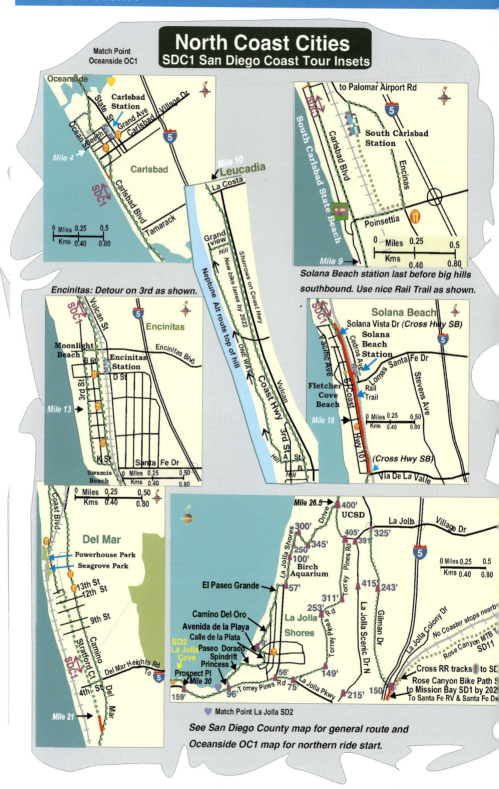

SAN DIEGO COUNTY

A typical stretch of Class II roadway on the Coast Highway, with the best views heading south

In Solana Beach, a nice rail trail runs parallel to the east side of Coast Hwy. It is a piece of the proposed rail trail that may someday run between Oceanside and San Diego. Mile 0 of ride SDC1 is the south side of the Pacific St bridge in Oceanside. See the San Diego County map for the general route, the Oceanside map for the ride start, and North Coast Cities maps for detail of the cities it passes through. The route becomes very hilly south of Del Mar as it reaches Torrey Pines State Reserve, and descends steeply into La Jolla Shores, connecting with the La Jolla ride, SD2. Two state park campgrounds are perched on the ocean bluffs in Carlsbad (South Carlsbad State Beach) and Cardiff-By-The-Sea (San Elijo State Beach).

See the book's website to download a complete description of this ride, including alternate routes and new developments such as Leucadia's re-configuring of Coast Hwy.

San Marcos

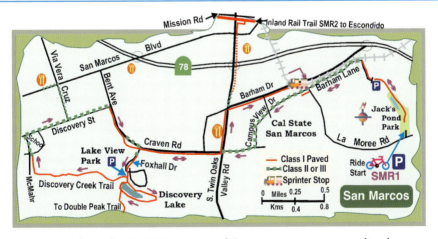

San Marcos lies along the SR 78 Freeway and Sprinter commuter train line between Vista and Escondido in a pleasant populated valley surrounded by small mountains about 8 miles inland from the north San Diego County coast. Cal State San Marcos is a fairly new and expanding university in town. The city plan calls for 72 miles of recreational trails throughout the city, of which 63 are already constructed. Many paths are wide sidewalks along existing roadways.

South San Marcos Tour SMR1

The most popular easy scenic trails in San Marcos are along Discovery Creek and Discovery Lake. The trail around the lake is only 0.8-mile long and the trail along the creek is 1 mile next to neighborhoods, allowing a 3-mile Class I ride. A continuation of the trail along the creek to South Lake is planned, which will enable a more substantial easy trail ride in the 8-mile range. Other pleasant areas around town are Jack's Pond, for a short 1-mile total ride to view the pond, stream, and a pretty barn, and the new Cal State San Marcos campus. We have combined these features with a ride that is mostly on Class I trails, with some Class II riding, most of which has sidewalk options. A convenient Sprinter light rail stop provides a nice Rail 'n Ride option to tour the town, and there are also nice Bike 'n Brunch options to enhance your visit. A strenuous mountain bike (or hiking) trail leads from Discovery Lake, gaining about 850 feet in 2.5 miles to Double Peak, where there are fabulous views of the area.

Tune: Down in the Valley by The Head and the Heart
Eats: Grilled chicken salad or burger at Players Sports Bar

Distance: 9–11 miles. Time: 1–2 hours
Route & Bike: Moderate due to hills. Paved Class I and II, any bike. Rolling hills, nothing too steep. E-bike edge due to hills and/or to combine with SMR2.
Seasons: All. Best on sunny mild weekday.
Facilities: Restrooms and water at Jacks Pond (La Moree Road lot) and Lakeview Park.
Knocks & Hazards: Park trails may be crowded with peds on weekends. Hilly terrain. Rattlesnakes possible in the natural park areas, also the rare mountain lion. Several unsignaled street crossings and bike lanes next to traffic. Speed limit as posted on park trails. Use extra caution on sidewalks when hills are involved to anticipate obstacles. Can be hot in summer.
Bike Shop: Trek Superstore, 1617 Capalina Rd, 760.599.9735.
Camp 'n Ride: See Oceanside and Lake Hodges rides.
Bike 'n Brunch: Several choices available in shopping center along route or detour into town.
City code, bike riding on sidewalks: Defer to state law. Speed limit 15 mph on trails, 5 mph around peds.
Further Info: City trail maps: san-marcos.net/Home/ShowDocument?id=1474

Access: Our route begins at Jack's Pond Park. From Hwy 78 exit Twin Oaks Valley Road, southbound. Turn left at Barham Drive, then right at La Moree Road. Proceed about 1.1 miles, up the hill to the south, then bend to the left, reaching the entrance to Jack's Pond Park on the left, where there is a parking lot and restrooms. The Discovery Lake area is the highlight of the ride, and if you prefer a ride of under 5 miles that is your best option, so instead of turning on Barham Drive, follow Twin Oaks Valley Road south to Craven Road and turn right, then left on Foxhall Drive up the hill to the park. Rail 'n Ride: Take the Sprinter light rail line from Oceanside or Escondido and get off at the Cal State San Marcos stop. Ride south on La Moree Road toward the University, and meet our route at the first junction, which is Barham Lane (as opposed to Barham Drive) on the left and College View on the right. SMR1 ends with a right turn on La Moree from Barham Drive near the train station.

The Ride: From the Jacks Pond parking lot make your way north onto the obvious paved trail that skirts around the pond. It is pleasant, though houses are also very visible nearby. After a gradual downhill, reach a small park (mile 0.5) with only a few parking places and locked restrooms. Cross the residential street to a Class I trail alongside Shelley Street. At mile 0.75 the trail ends when the street bends to the

Cycling around pretty Discovery Lake

left and becomes Barham Lane. Use the bike lane or sidewalk to traverse the general downhill trajectory between newer neighborhoods and the Sprinter train tracks, ending at La Moree Drive (1.2). Very carefully cross the unsignaled intersection. Note the Sprinter station to the right, which is where the ride will start if you arrive by train. Ride west down the Class III stretch of Campus View Drive in the Cal State San Marcos property. Campus View Drive soon improves to a Class II roadway. Be very careful of comings and goings of vehicles from the parking lots along the way. Cross Campus Way with the signal (1.6). The route becomes more scenic as it gains elevation gradually, with views over the valley and campus.

Reach Craven Road, which ends as a cul de sac on the main part of the campus on the left (1.9). Turn right on Craven Road down a gradual hill in the bike lane. If the pretty tree-shaded sidewalks are not crowded with students, it presents a nice option. Reach Twin Oaks Valley Road (2.2). Cross with the light and onto the bike lane or sidewalk. If you need refreshments or supplies, there is a shopping center just down to the right on Twin Oaks Valley Road, which is described later in the ride.

Cycle along Craven Road past two health complexes, then descend the hill to Foxhall Drive (2.8). Carefully cross Craven to go left (south) on Foxhall. After a short climb up Foxhall, look for the entrance to a trail (2.9) that parallels the road to the left and climbs to the top of the hill. Cross the residential street at trail's end (3.0) and enter Lakeview Park, another potential staging spot with free parking in and around the park.

Take the trail straight ahead that descends to Discovery Lake, and bear to the left (3.2). There are two parallel paths, one paved and the other packed dirt. The next 0.75 mile is the highlight of the ride, so savor it. Ride slowly around the pretty lake, which is surrounded by maturing non-native plantings and is popular with ducks.

Reach the dam, and a trail junction (3.8). The trail that rises steeply to the left leads to a trailhead for the dirt trails that climb up to Double Peak Regional Park, a potential hike for you. The section of trail atop the dam and spillway bridge is the best place to photograph the lake in the afternoon. Once back atop the hill in Lakeview Park, look for a trail off to the left near a signboard, which may have trail maps stocked in it (3.9). Descend the short steep hill to the level of Discovery Creek. The parallel paved and equestrian trails pass through a pleasant riparian valley surrounded by suburban neighborhoods and power lines with views to the Cerro de las Posas Mountains to the south. Carefully cross Applewood Drive (4.2) and Via Vera Cruz (4.5), both unsignaled residential streets. The path bends around to the right next to Macmahr Road and ends at La Noche Drive across from Discovery Elementary School (4.8). You can return the same way for a 9.6-mile ride, or continue on our route, which includes options for your Bike 'n Brunch.

Pass the elementary school by riding down Macmahr Road one block to Discovery Street (5.0). Turn right and ride in the bike lane or sidewalk. Your first option for dining choices is to the left up Via Vera Cruz (5.3). There is a short share-the-road stretch that leads to a wider section of road. At San Marcos Boulevard (both Class II and sidewalks) "Restaurant Row" is to the left, with a coffee house, pub, Thai, Buffalo Wild Wings, Mexican restaurants, IHOP, Rubio's and a few others. Return the same way to Discovery Street. We won't add this 1-mile or so to our ride totals, however, in favor of a more bike friendly route to another area.

From Discovery Street, continue east to the end of the road at Craven Road and turn right onto the Class I trail along the right side (5.7). Ascend the gradual hill. When the path veers away from the road and ascends a steep hill, you may want to hop into the bike lane for that short stretch that leads up to Foxhall Drive, where you turned previously (6.1). You can get back on the sidewalk trail after Foxhall as you continue along Craven Road down the hill, returning to Twin Oaks Valley Road (6.8), but don't cross the road. Cross Craven Road in the crosswalk, and ride down the wide sidewalk path past the health center to Ralph's shopping center on the left for a convenient Bike 'n Brunch opportunity. There is a Player's Sports Grill and casual restaurants including Subway, Vietnamese, sushi, BBQ, tacos and Starbucks. For more selections you can make your way down Twin Oaks across the SR78 Freeway to a center with an Old Spaghetti Factory and sushi and pizza restaurants.

From the corner of Twin Oaks Valley and Barham Drive (Discovery is to the left here), cross Twin Oaks Valley via the crosswalk and ride onto the Class I trail on the right side of Barham Drive (7.1). Follow this path under the Sprinter train tracks (7.6), and turn right on La Moree Road (7.7). Find access to the Sprinter Station here. Then carefully turn left onto Barham Lane (7.8). You can also ride 1.1 mile up La Moree to your ride start to change it up, but that route is hillier with more traffic. Continue up the hill along Barham Lane and around the bend onto Shelley Street. Ride either on the street or cross over to the Class I path, returning to the small park (8.5). Ride on the trail to the left of the park, past Jack's Pond, up the gradual hill to the barns at the main section of the park (9.1).

Inland Rail Trail SMR2

Distance: Up to 24 miles round trip, easy to moderate. E-bike edge to combine SMR1.

This paved rail-with-trail will someday run 21 miles from Escondido to Oceanside. As of 2021 it extends from Escondido Transit Center (north side of Valley Pkwy at Quince St), 11.5 miles through San Marcos to Civic Center Dr in Vista (last mile by late 2021). The next 2 miles to N Melrose awaits funding, while the final 7 miles to Wisconsin Ave in Oceanside is a future project. The utilitarian path crosses many streets, running next to the active Sprinter line tracks and parallel roads, including Mission Rd most of the way. The closest connection to ride SMR1 is about 0.8 mile from Barham Dr, north on Twin Oaks Valley Rd over SR78, onto a parallel access path from the northeast corner of San Marcos Blvd. From there to 2021 trail's end is 6 miles west and 6 miles east. The trail also connects to the 4.5-mile Escondido Creek Bike Path, which is not especially scenic and mainly of interest to locals.

Lake Hodges Area

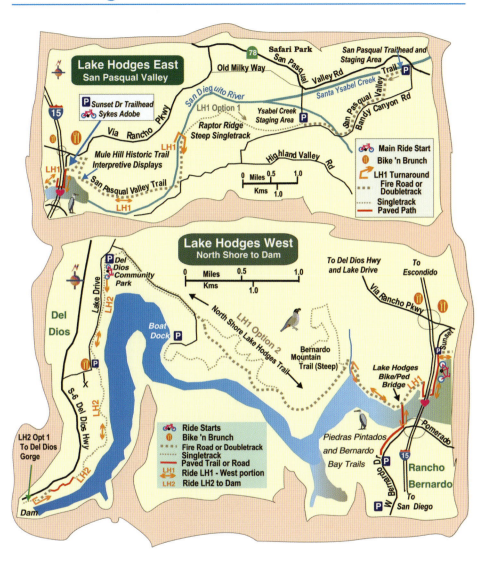

The planned 55-mile Coast to Crest Trail from Del Mar to Volcan Mountain north of Julian already has some completed sections, including an area centered around Lake Hodges, located at the I-15 Freeway between Rancho Bernardo and Escondido. The trail lies within San Dieguito River Park, a joint jurisdiction with San Diego County and several cities along its path. The reservoir was created by the damming of the San Dieguito River in 1918, and has subsequently become a major bird stopover point along the Pacific Flyway, and a popular spot for birders.

Lake Hodges is a beautiful, almost fjord-like lake that fills a winding valley. Its size changes dramatically based on the water level at the dam, most of the time not reaching eastward to the area around I-15. The surrounding hillsides preserve some of the last remaining coastal sage scrub ecosystem in SoCal, home of the endangered California gnatcatcher. Unfortunately much of this area burned in the devastating 2007 Witch Creek wildfire, although some gnatcatcher habitat was spared. Gone are many of the beautiful oaks that once graced the area though, not to mention 21 homes destroyed in Del Dios near the west shore.

The 8.2-mile North Shore Lake Hodges trail is open to mountain bikes, hikers, and equestrians. The David Keitzer Lake Hodges Bicycle Pedestrian Bridge connects to the 3.8-mile Piedras Pintadas and Bernardo Bay trails on the southeast shore, which are mostly hilly singletrack and better for hiking. At a length of 990 feet, the bike/ped bridge is the longest concrete stress ribbon bridge in the world. Additional trails extend out in both directions from the North Trail, as described in the various ride options.

The easiest ride involves a combination of portions of the North Trail and the Mule Hill/San Pasqual Valley Trail, centered around I-15 (LH1). Wide doubletrack with only minor hills enables a long ride without too much exertion that can be combined with a ride over the stress ribbon bike bridge. Fun novice singletrack runs along the far west end of Lake Hodges to its dam (LH2). In between is a moderately strenuous route up and down hills along the north shore of the lake.

Tunes: Little Bird by Annie Lennox; Hummingbird by B.B King & John Mayer; Muddy Water by Keb' Mo'; Closer to the Edge by 30 Seconds to Mars

Eats: Margarita and carnitas at Hernandez Hideaway

Fjord-like Lake Hodges

Lake Hodges and the stress ribbon bike/ped bridge

The scenic and easy dirt trail in the San Pasqual Valley

Seasons: All. Best on sunny mild weekday. Spring can bring wildflowers.

Facilities: Restrooms and water only at Rancho Bernardo Community Park, Lake Hodges Boat Launch area and Westfield Mall. Porta-potties at Sikes Adobe (Sunrise trailhead), on north side of ribbon bridge and across from Hernandez Hideaway restaurant.

Knocks & Hazards: Clueless peds. Equestrians on trails. Rattlesnakes; possible cougar. Small stream crossing on North Trail. Light park road traffic. Inclines and hills of various steepness, some very rocky. Can be very hot in summer. No water along trail. Best to ride with friends: Though serial rapist/murderer from 2009 is in jail, there was a bikejacking of solo male (shot in the hand) under I-15 bridge in 2019.

Camp 'n Ride: Closest well-reviewed campground is Escondido RV Resort, 6.5 miles north on I-15 to El Norte Parkway east, 1740 Seven Oakes Rd, Escondido, 866.477.6153.

Bike 'n Brunch: North of Sunrise Drive across Via Rancho Parkway is the Westfield North County Fair mall, with Red Robin, BJ's Pizza & Brewhouse, Cheesecake Factory, On the Border Mexican Grill, Black Angus, Romano's Macaroni Grill, Sarku Japan, and Panera Bread. A few fast-food options are located west along Via Rancho just past the freeway overpass. Along the west end of the trail in Del Dios is the Hernandez Hideaway Mexican restaurant (weekend brunch).

Further Info: www.sandiego.gov/reservoirs-lakes/hodges-reservoir/

Attraction: San Diego Zoo Safari Park (formerly Wild Animal Park) is about 6 miles northeast from the Via Rancho exit off I-15. Follow the signs.

Access: Central Trailhead: The Sunrise Drive trailhead accesses the east end of the North Lake Trail and Mule Hill/San Pasqual Valley Trails and is easiest to find. From I-15, exit on Via Rancho Parkway, east. Turn right at Sunrise at the first light. Note: to the left is Westfield North County Fair mall, with Bike 'n Brunch options there and west of the freeway. At the end of Sunrise is the parking lot and trailhead, near the Sikes Adobe farmhouse, built in 1870. It is one of the oldest buildings in San Diego County and is open to the public (fee). It was partially burned in the 2007 fire and reconstructed.

South Trailhead: The next I-15 exit to the south is Pomerado Road/West Bernardo Drive. Head west from the exit and find trailhead parking along the south side of the road halfway up the hill as signed, at the unpaved Bernardo Bay Natural Area lot at the top of the hill on the right, or the Rancho Bernardo Community Park farther down West Bernardo Drive (water and restrooms). The half-mile long Class I paved West Bernardo bike trail, built partially cantilevered next to West Bernardo Drive, connects the two parking areas with the bike/ped bridge to the north shore as well. There is a substantial grade from the bridge up to the parks along the trail.

North/West Trailheads: Two trailheads along the north shore are located in the small community of Del Dios to the west. From the Via Rancho Parkway exit, head west and follow it about 3 miles until Lake Drive, just before Del Dios Highway. Turn left, and then in about 0.8 mile turn left to park in the Del Dios Community Park's lot. Another parking area is located about 1.2 miles farther south on Lake Drive at Rancho Drive, across from Hernandez Hideaway restaurant, a popular place for a margarita or weekend Mexican brunch. You can also stage from the boat rental concession lot by taking the park road east from the community park, although it is only open periodically.

East Trailhead: On San Pasqual Valley Rd just west of Bandy Canyon Rd. See Option 1.

The East Lake Hodges Wetlands MTB LH1

Our pick for the best novice-level ride starts from Sunrise Drive, goes east between agricultural and riparian areas, and leads to an optional hilly singletrack trail where you can turn around. It then returns to explore a bit of Lake Hodges west of I-15 and the nifty bike/ped ribbon bridge. Although not quite as scenic as an all Lake Hodges ride, it is no slouch with local 2,000-foot mountains framing the backdrop as you ride east. The best part is that it is all easy, scenic riding where you can get a nice steady workout without dealing with trail obstacles found elsewhere on the Lake Hodges trails that novices may find intimidating. Intermediate mountain bikers may opt to start at the same Sunrise trailhead, but instead of going east, just go west under I-15 and do the North Shore Trail, described as Option 2.

Distance: About 11 total miles + option. Time: 2 hours.
Route & bike: Easy. Packed dirt doubletrack novice level MTB. Sections near I-15 on pavement. Flat and small hills. Continuing east up Raptor Ridge on the single track or going west along the North Shore trail is much more difficult. E-MTB edge.
Seasons: All. Best on sunny mild weekday. Spring can bring wildflowers.
Facilities: Porta-potties at main trailhead and on north side of ribbon bridge.

The Ride: From the Sunrise Drive trailhead, take the path that heads east past the Sikes Adobe historical house where there is a porta-potty. The first segment is the 1.25-mile Mule Hill Historical Trail that is open to bicyclists, hikers, and equestrians. The packed dirt trail runs next to wetlands, along the back of the fenced off Hodges Golf Improvement Center and then reaches the side of Via Rancho Parkway for a short distance, long enough to see the On the Border Mexican restaurant across the street. It veers south along an existing dirt farm road, and terminates at interpretive stations describing skirmishes of the Mexican-American War of 1846, the flooded town of Bernardo, and the old San Diego to Yuma Road. The trail climbs a small hill and becomes the San Pasqual Valley Agricultural Preserve Trail after that point.

This ride includes only the first two miles of this 8.75-mile-long trail, but those with more honed MTB skills have the option to continue onward. The path heads east past agricultural fields, and since the trail exists because of cooperation from the farmers, it is very important that you do not wander off trail and disturb the premises. Be warned that at times the trail may be closed during pesticide spraying on the adjacent fields. At about mile 2.5 into the ride is an organic asparagus, gourd, and squash farm on your left, followed by a low-flow crossing of the floodplain and the San Dieguito River, and then the Highland Valley-Old Coach Staging Area parking lot. The trail turns left at this point, and continues north along a dirt road around the base of a small mountain adjacent to the river. At around mile 3.5 arrive at a picnic area with an information kiosk. This is the turnaround point for the easy ride. Those with intermediate and above mountain bike skills can continue, as described in Option 1.

Option 1: Remaining 6.75 miles of San Pasqual Valley Agricultural Preserve Trail
13.5 miles round trip additional; Strenuous (e-MTB edge) (or easy option from east end)
Beyond the kiosk, the Raptor Ridge portion of the trail narrows to singletrack as it climbs 400 feet over 3,400 feet distance through beautiful oak woodland. Be alert for cyclists and hikers coming from the other direction. Your reward is a panoramic vista of the area from the summit. Descend the hill into the agricultural valley, reaching the staging area at Ysabel Creek Rd and Bandy Canyon Rd, with interpretive signs about San Diego County agriculture. Farther along the trail is cantilevered on the Bandy Canyon

Rd Bridge over Santa Maria Creek. The trail runs next to Bandy Canyon Rd, passes Verger Dairy and ag fields, then turns left next to an orange grove. When you reach Santa Ysabel Creek the trail turns to the right (east) again, through a short but sweet riparian area where springtime brings wildflowers and orange blossom scent.

Trail's end comes soon, at the trailhead staging area along San Pasqual Valley Rd (Hwy 78) just west of Bandy Canyon Rd, 3 miles east of the San Diego Zoo Safari Park. The trail through this ag area presents an option for a pleasant cycle when visiting Safari Park or heading east. A continuation of the trail is planned through the gorge across Hwy 78 to Boden Canyon and Cleveland National Forest.

The return ride to the Sunset Drive trailhead trends slightly downhill (7.0). Once reaching the cul de sac where your car is parked, turn left onto the paved path that runs south parallel to I-15. Although noisy I-15 is above you to the west, there is a beautiful vista to the east toward the wetlands of Lake Hodges and surrounding mountains. The path curves around under I-15 (7.5), then back up to the north shore of the lake and the North Lake Trail, where it turns into a wide and level compacted dirt and gravel path (7.6). Reach the ribbon bridge (7.9), and take a spin back and forth on it to take in the great views of the lake and to experience this unique structure (8.3). The wide path continues above the north shore of the lake with good views of sea and shore birds that are taking advantage of whatever water may be standing in the lake at its shallower end. When the path turns inland toward a row of sycamores in a riparian area and reaches a trail junction (8.9), easy riders may want to just turn around here and return to the trailhead (10.8).

Option 2: North Shore Trail *Variable mileage, moderate, advanced novice MTB.*
This trail can be ridden on its own from several of the trailheads, or as a continuation of LH1, as described. Those who want some adventure can continue onward and cross the stream (9.0). It is usually an easy crossing, perhaps with a board bridge or low water with a firm bottom, but higher water may be problematic. The trail then begins a steady and rocky climb but soon levels off again, enabling even better vistas of the sinuous lake basin from up above. At mile 9.5 a short spur trail leads off to the left to a great viewpoint over the lake—worth a stop. This is a potential turnaround point for a 12-mile moderate ride. Otherwise, return to the trail and continue on to the left (west) (9.6).

At mile 10 there is a fork in the trail. More advanced mountain bikers choose the right fork that leads to some singletrack, while others should keep to the main trail that begins to descend to the left to the lakeshore (10.2), then leads to the parking lot of the boat launch area and concessions (open Wednesday, Saturday, and Sunday in fishing season). Turn right on the park road (10.9) and ride on it or the adjacent path until reaching Lake Drive and Del Dios Community Park (12.0), and the start of ride LH2. Returning to Sunrise Drive from this point would result in a 17-mile ride. The ride from Sunrise Drive to this point, without first riding the trails to the east, is 10 miles round trip.

Dam Sweet MTB   LH2

The trail along the west side of the lake consists mostly of rolling singletrack with fabulous views of Lake Hodges.

Distance: About 7 miles round trip. Time: 1 hour.
Route & Bike: Easy to moderate sections as described. Mostly dirt singletrack with some gravel doubletrack, fire road, and paved road. MTB, suitable for advanced novice level and above. Small rolling hills with one substantial singletrack hill in the southwest end. E-MTB edge.
Facilities: Porta-potty in the parking area across from Hernandez Hideaway.

The Ride: Starting from the south end of Del Dios Community Park follow the obvious trail that runs south past oak groves, between the quaint community of Del Dios and Lake Hodges, which is full of water at this end that is closer to the dam. The paths branch out in places, with the upper path closer to the road typically easier to manage, but you can change

Typical singletrack on west side of lake near the dam

it up on the return. Enjoy views of the almost fjord-like lake with its steep hillsides surrounding it. The trails daylight in a parking lot across from the Hernandez Hideaway restaurant. Past the restaurant Lake Drive is closed to the general public, and Rancho Drive connects back to Del Dios Highway. Our trail continues from the south end of the parking lot, making its way above the lakeshore. It is a fairly rough singletrack trail at times, except for a section of new smooth pathway lined with a railing where you can pause for great lake views. You can make your way down to the beach area on offshoot trails, but our route goes generally upslope instead.

After more ups and downs, the main trail begins a steady climb, which many of you will walk up. At the top of the hill is a paved road, a very scenic stretch high above the lake leading to the left past a City of San Diego-owned house structure. The road then turns to gravel, and as you near the Lake Hodges Dam, you are thrown off that road, for security purposes no doubt, and back onto a singletrack that goes uphill, above and beyond the dam. Turn around after you reach a good vantage point for some photos (better lighting in the morning) of the dam and the Del Dios Gorge beyond. More advanced mountain bikers can continue onward with Option 1.

Option 1: Del Dios Gorge *4–7.8 miles roundtrip, intermediate MTB, moderate to strenuous, e-MTB edge*

From the dam you can continue another 2 miles on the scenic Del Dios Gorge Trail, perhaps stopping at the new Rattlesnake Overlook. This trail runs parallel to Del Dios Highway and is rated "easy" by the park agency, but has some switchbacks and is even more challenging than the North Shore trail, with grades leading down to a new steel truss foot bridge over the drainage. The Del Dios trail connects with the 1.9-mile Santa Fe Valley Trail that dead-ends and is rated "moderate." Return the same way. You may consider a shuttle for this ride, starting at the trailheads at I-15 or Del Dios and ending down-gradient at the west end of the Del Dios Canyon Trail. The trailhead for doing these trails alone is off the Del Dios Highway west of the dam. Take the first left after the dam, just before Calle Ambiente, to reach trailhead parking near Bing Crosby Boulevard.

… SAN DIEGO COUNTY   241

San Diego

Visitors flock to San Diego to visit the world-famous San Diego Zoo and its Safari Park, Sea World, Balboa Park with its many museums and theatres in historic buildings, historic Old Town or Liberty Station, or just to take in some sunshine and beach time. The U.S. Navy is king here, and bases, shipyards, and support facilities are a major cog in the local economy. Being on the Mexican border, there is a significant Latin influence both culturally and gastronomically. Expect to find many excellent Mexican restaurants during your visit, from the mostly touristy places at Old Town, to the more basic cafés in other neighborhoods.

California's second largest city of 1.5 million people has constructed bike trails, lanes, and routes to connect most parts of the city and surrounding areas. We have recommended several fabulous flat and scenic rides here, each next to a bay and the open ocean, and some options for hillier rides. The Mission Bay & Pacific Beach ride (SD1) is a wonderful cycling loop, mostly through public parkland. Connecting rides to beautiful La Jolla (SD2), eclectic Ocean Beach (SD3), and Historic Old Town (SD1 Option 5) make for enjoyable adventures.

The Coronado/Silver Strand Peninsula ride straddles San Diego Bay with an option to encircle the bay on the Bayhore Bikeway and explore the waterfront districts of Coronado, Imperial Beach, Chula Vista and San Diego, returning on a bike/ped ferry (SD7), while getting a glimpse into the Navy's dominant presence here. Balboa Park is a fascinating place to explore by bike, with options to incorporate it into your downtown ride and explore the adjacent Hillcrest neighborhood as well (SD6). And, no visit to San Diego would be complete without a trip to Cabrillo National Monument at Point Loma (SD5). Also within San Diego city limits are several reservoirs and open space areas for an enjoyable escape, on both paved and dirt trails.

City Code, bike riding on sidewalks: Riding on sidewalks may become relevant in most of the city of San Diego rides. Except in front of commercial establishments, riding on sidewalks in most other cases is allowed, including over bridges. Also on Ocean Front Walk and Bayside Walk (SD1) only disabled persons are allowed to ride anything besides a conventional (or tandem) 2-wheeled bike.

Mission Bay & Ocean Front Walk   SD1 ⭐

Mission Bay was formerly an area of mudflats that was dredged in the mid-twentieth century to create a 4,600-acre urban recreation paradise in the middle of San Diego. Now surrounded mainly by public parkland, flat recreation trails encircle a good portion of the bay, connected by a few Class II bike lanes and Class III side streets. As you cycle along scenic Mission Bay, enjoy the sights of sailboats, sand, and skylines, along with plenty of people watching. Two wildlife refuges along the route provide great bird watching and harken back to what Mission Bay used to be before it was dredged; a paradise for shorebirds. To add even more excitement to your fabulous ride, Ocean Front Walk is a popular 3-mile rideable concrete boardwalk akin to the fabled trails in Los Angeles. While pedaling along the ocean, take in the crashing surf, beachfront homes, surfside restaurants, and plenty of sun worshipers. The ocean and bay trails are connected by two short blocks along surface streets. A plethora of interesting restaurants provide top-notch Bike 'n Brunch opportunities, especially in the areas of Mission Beach and Pacific Beach.

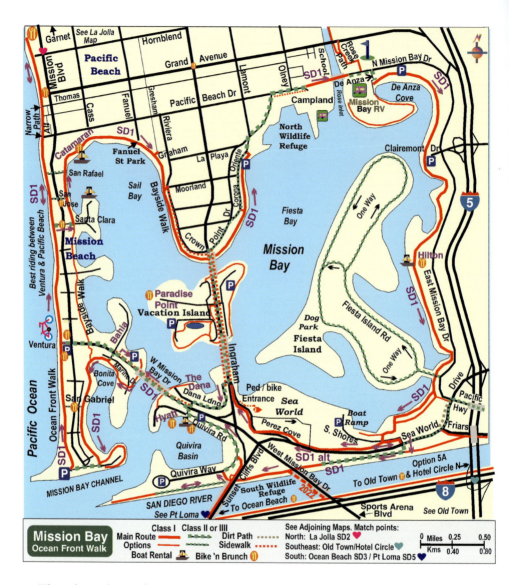

The ride can be so pleasant on an uncrowded winter weekday, you won't even notice that you've cycled 19 flat miles if you complete the entire loop described. If you prefer to people-watch and negotiate through a formidable human obstacle course, try the oceanfront boardwalk on a busy day such as a summer weekend or during college spring break. For those wishing to do a shorter ride, the most fabulous areas are the 4-mile Bayside Walk trail that follows the west and north shores of Mission Bay, and the 3-mile Ocean Front Walk that runs between Mission Beach and Pacific Beach.

So many options are available that you can do the ride freeform using the map and can combine it with several other rides in the area. An easy detour to Ocean Beach (ride SD3) provides another area of great Bike 'n Brunch options, while a connection to an MTS Trolley (light rail) stop opens up other options for spending the day on two wheels while leaving the horseless carriage behind.

Tunes: The Best Place by Best Coast; Sea and Sand by The Who; Por Un Amor by Linda Ronstadt; Pacific Coast Party by Smashmouth
Eats: Any place with an outdoor patio along Ocean Front Walk. Or, Carnitas Hash on Barefoot Bar & Grill's patio, Vacation Island.

Distance: ±19 miles + options. Time: 2 hours.
Route & Bike: Easy to moderate. Paved, any bike. Mostly Class I, some easy Class II and III. Flat except for one arched bridge. E-bike edge when combined with SD2.
Seasons: All. Best on sunny, uncrowded, off-season weekday. On crowded days, morning is best.
Facilities: Restrooms and water in parks along route, and along Ocean Front Walk.
Knocks & Hazards: Clueless peds and uncontrolled children on bikes. Possible lurkers, mostly at river sections, Vacation Island, or parks. Street crossings and bike lanes next to traffic. Crowded conditions can make many sections unpleasant, especially portions of Ocean Front Walk. Rattlesnakes possible near brushy areas. Speed limit: 8 mph on trails through parks, Ocean Front Walk, and Bay Side Walk.
Rent 'n Ride: Mission/Pacific Beach: Ray's, 3221 & 3830 Mission Blvd, 858.488.7297; Cheap Rentals, 3689 Mission Blvd, 858.488.9070; Pacific Beach Bike Shop, 1815 Garnet, 858.201.9959; Pacific Beach Bikes, 910 Grand, 858.220.6187; Boardwalk Electric Rides, 4150 Mission Blvd, 858.345.0203. Rent at resorts along paths including Hilton, Catamaran, and Paradise Point.
Camp 'n Ride: In the northeastern corner of Mission Bay route: Mission Bay RV Resort accepts newer self-contained RV's only, 2727 De Anza Rd, 877.219.6800; Campland on the Bay has more resort facilities; accepts RVs or tents, 2211 Pacific Beach Dr, 800.422.9386. Its closure date keeps getting delayed indefinitely by the city.
Bike 'n Brunch: Numerous restaurant choices as described in The Ride.

Access: From I-5 southbound, exit Sea World Drive, head west, then right on West Mission Bay Dr. From I-5 northbound take I-8 west, follow signs to Sea World, then exit to West Mission Bay Dr. That road ends at Mission Blvd, across which it becomes Ventura Place. Several free public parking lots are located here, north and south of the Belmont Park roller coaster. Free parking can also be found all along the route in parks and neighborhoods. On crowded beach days choose places away from the beach.

The Ride: Ocean Front Walk extends 3 miles along the beach from S Mission Bay Park and the Mission Bay entrance channel, through the communities of Mission Beach and Pacific Beach, ending at Law St to the north. SD1 starts (0.0) at its midpoint, at the end of Ventura Pl, and ends here coming up from the south end. Ride north on the wide, uncrowded stretch between homes and the beautiful beach for about a mile, far and away the best part of this path. At Pacific Beach Dr the path narrows and trailside patio restaurants begin, starting with World Famous. On busy days you may want to detour to the alley called Strandway that runs parallel to the trail to avoid the narrow crowded stretch, through Thomas St. Ocean view restaurants in this area include Waterbar, coffee houses, bars and local diners from basic through upscale, through Felspar. Numerous restaurants and fast food joints are also situated along sharrowed Mission Blvd, which runs north-south, halfway between the ocean and the bay. The largest concentration of restaurants is along Garnet Ave, which ends at the pier, and Grand Ave, four blocks to its south. Some new trailside patio restaurant/bars are also located just south of our starting point at the main beach area.

Crystal Pier (1.7) is lined with circa 1936 cottage acommodations. Stroll on it, but no biking. North of the pier past some park-like paths is a scenic blufftop stretch with great vistas of the beach and the coastline that leads to trail's end at Law Street (2.2), our turnaround point, and also the jump-off point for the La Jolla Loop ride (SD2). Turn around and ride back down Ocean Front Walk to an appropriate cross

The north end of Ocean Front Walk gains elevation enabling great vistas. Point Loma can be seen beyond Crystal Pier.

street. Using Santa Clara Place (3.6) gives you a traffic light to cross Mission Boulevard at the Old Mission Beach District with its tempting and popular al fresco cafés, including Olive restaurant and bakery. Bayside Walk crosses just past the last building. Beyond is parking, boat rentals, and restrooms. As shown on the map, other good streets to cross to the bay side with stop signs for Mission Blvd traffic are San Rafael, and San Jose where breakfast/lunch fave The Mission restaurant is located.

Upon reaching Bayside Walk (3.7), turn left onto this paved path and begin your ride along the bay. The route is much less crowded than Ocean Front Walk, though on peak days it has its fair share of trail users. It heads north then curves sublimely to the east along the bay past waterfront homes and luxury condos, while small sailboats dart back and forth across Sail Bay. Catamaran Resort (4.2) has a boat/bike rental concession, patio restaurant, and beach chair/tables open to the public. The playground at Fanuel Street Park (4.7) may produce some child-like obstacles, so slow down there. The wide trail curves south then east as it passes underneath the Ingraham Road Bridge (5.7) (to Vacation Island), then to the northeast, as views of the San Diego skyline and Sea World become prominent to the south and southeast. The trail continues into Crown Point Shores Park (6.0), which can be hopping on weekends, so beware of uncontrolled darting children. You may want to turn around after riding through this park to complete an all-fabulous ride (recommended for families with young children), or continue on with your loop ride.

Option 1: Using The Bay Bridges

The best part of the ride is the western half, so if you want to cut the ride short, make your way up to the bridge to Vacation Island, and continue over the second bridge to West Mission Bay Drive, as shown on the map. The bridges have both bike lanes and separated ped paths to choose from, and afford great vistas of the Mission Bay area. Acrophobes may not appreciate the south bridge. See also Option 3: Vacation Island.

Upon exiting the bike trail at the Crown Shores Park parking lot, turn right on Corona Oriente Road (6.5), and ride up the small hill, turning right onto lightly trafficked Crown Point Drive (6.7), and right onto Pacific Beach Drive (7.1). The Northern/Kendall-Forst Mission Bay Marsh Reserve is visible along this stretch, with interpretive signs at viewing platforms that you can stop to read and do some bird watching. Pass Olney Street and Campland on the Bay RV resort (7.4). Go straight onto a Class I path behind Mission Bay High to Mike Gotch Memorial

Bridge over Rose Inlet for bikes/peds, leading to the end of N Mission Bay Dr. Note the Rose Creek Trail to the left. As of 2021 it follows the creek past rides SD10,11 to La Jolla Colony Dr at Gillman Dr, which is a hilly Class II route to La Jolla. (e-bike edge). Our SD1 route continues straight on North Mission Bay Drive.

Take the first right onto De Anza (8.0), where Mission Bay RV Resort is on the right. Head left at the end of the short street onto the bike trail through De Anza Cove Park. The next portion of the bike trail wanders through Mission Bay Park along the eastern shores of Mission Bay. It is pleasant, but because of the traffic noise from I-5, and the crowds in the parks overflowing onto the paths, it is not as nice as Bayside Walk at the west end. Many cyclists opt to tangle with the cars on the parallel sharrowed East Mission Bay Drive instead of the 8 mph path. After crossing a park road (9.8) pass the Hilton resort (and bike/boat rental), and then reach the crossing with the Fiesta Island access road (10.8).

The Mike Gotch Memorial Bridge over Rose Inlet made a fabulous ride even more wonderful when it opened in 2012.

Option 2 Fiesta Island Cyclists love to cruise this pile of dredged sand in the middle of the bay. The scenic 5-mile route around the perimeter (with a cutoff to shorten route) is a one-way 25 mph sharrowed road. A large off-leash dog park is at its southwest corner.

After continuing past Fiesta Island Road, watch for two parallel paved paths on the right. The first, a newer wide promenade, runs directly along the bay through South Shores Park. The second, preferred by cyclists, is narrower and slightly higher, providing a better vista.

Note Pacific Highway to the left across Sea World Drive, which is a Class II route to Old Town (Option 5b). Farther along Sea World Drive is Friars Road, accessed either from the bike lane or the dirt path that runs parallel to the road. The closest MTS Trolley stop is a mile down the Class IV cycletrack alongside Friars Road (see Option 5 notes).

The two paths join near a large gazebo (11.3). Continue south on a wide concrete path that bends to the west. At the next junction turn onto the asphalt path to the left (11.5) rather than continuing on the concrete path that leads to the public boat launching area (and restrooms). The asphalt path daylights at the South Shores Park access road (11.6). Cross it to reach the bike trail along the south side of the road.

Decision point: *To the right:* This path that runs past Sea World is a slightly shorter and easier route that gives you the option of visiting Sea World by bike, or to cut across Mission Bay to the north using bridges and potentially shorten your ride. *To the left:* SD1 trip mileage follows this option that is mostly along the San Diego River South Wildlife Refuge. The two roadway bridges (one by 2022) provide access to the south side of the river and options to ride on a Class I trail to Ocean Beach, Old Town, or Hotel Circle. They also lead to Class II Nimitz Blvd that ends at San Diego Harbor (SD4) and its connecting rides.

Sea World Path: Turn right on the sidewalk trail (separated for bikes/peds) that runs between busy Sea World Drive and the Sea World parking areas. After crossing the Sea World access road at the signal, the trail curves around toward the north. If you plan to visit Sea World, watch for the crosswalk and Pedestrian Entry signs on the northwest side of the property, where you can ride your bike in, saving the $16 parking fee. Bike racks and lockers are provided near the admission entrance. Otherwise, reach the signaled crossing of Ingraham Street. The bridge to your right has a bike lane or separated sidewalk to Vacation Island: *See Option 1: Take in the great vista from the top of the bridge. You can reach the north Mission Bay trail section after crossing Vacation Island.* Our SD1 route crosses Ingraham at the signal and bears to the left, following sharrowed Dana Landing Rd past The Dana resort, then daylights at a signal at the base of the West Mission Bay Bridge to the right. This is where the San Diego River option rejoins our route.

North Mission Bay trail with the San Diego skyline beyond

San Diego River Path: From the decision point (11.6) turn left and follow the sidewalk next to the park access road to the traffic signal at Sea World Dr (11.8). Cross it and turn right onto an old, little-used dead-end road that parallels the San Diego River channel, portions of which form the South Wildlife Refuge. The next mile or so can be a great place to watch sea and shore birds such as great blue herons, sanderlings, terns, and snowy egrets. Car access ends as the road passes under the Mission Bay Dr Bridge (12.6). A bike path over the new bridge is expected by 2022, with possible detours until then. Next is the Sunset Cliffs Bridge (12.9). After crossing under the bridge, note a trail to the right that connects back up to the bridge deck (13.0). It accesses a protected bike path on the level bridge's west side, enabling an easy ride across to the Ocean Beach Bike Path on the south side of the river. See Options 4, 5, and 6 and ride SD3.

Meanwhile, on the main route, after passing (for now) a cutoff trail to Quivira Way, continue on the jetty path up to the fence to catch a glimpse of the ocean waves (13.7). At times you may see feral cats lounging in the sun along the rocks here. Look to the north across the Mission Bay entrance channel and notice the park. That is your next destination. Backtrack to the Quivira Way cutoff to the left, then turn right on Quivira Way (14.4) and ride in its bike lane. Carry on along Quivira until an opportunity to turn right to a signal (15.2). To the left here are a few restaurants and ahead is the Hyatt. Cross West Mission Bay Drive. You have now met up with the Sea World route option, which comes in from Dana Landing Road straight ahead. Turn left (west) at the light and ride across the bridge in the bike lane or sidewalk. The sidewalk at the high point of the bridge is a good spot to stop and take in a Mission Bay panorama.

SAN DIEGO COUNTY

Ocean Front Walk

If you are tired and just want to end the ride, proceed along Mission Bay Drive to your starting point for a 16.3 mile total ride. Otherwise, for a fabulous finale, go to Bonita Cove Park across the street. You can get there by turning left at the light onto South Marine Drive (15.9) (Bahia Hotel is on your right). However, we avoid the street crossing by cutting through the park on the right and finding a paved trail back under the bridge that leads around Mariner's Basin along the bay.

In Bonita Cove Park find the trail that runs southward along the west shore of Mariners Basin, with great bay views to the left and homes to the right. Once you reach an access road next to the jetty (San Diego Place) (17.4), turn left, continuing on the trail, and pedal around the very scenic waterfront park (17.8), then head west down Jetty Drive into the western beach parking lot. Look for the signed entrance to Ocean Front Walk on the right (18.0), and cycle north on this narrow but uncrowded section of boardwalk trail to your starting point (19.0).

Option 3: Vacation Island

From the north or south sides of Mission Bay, try this easy side trip. From the north make your way to the Ingraham Bridge from the bike lane of Crown Point Drive. You can connect to it from the Crown Point Park trail using Corona Oriente. The bridge has bike lanes, but the protected sidewalks on both sides keep you away from traffic. It starts out level, then descends fairly steeply to the island. At the signaled intersection turn right (west) to access Paradise Point Resort. There are no bike trails along the Paradise Point Resort portion of the island, however it presents a nice Bike 'n Brunch opportunity and offers bike and boat rentals. We especially enjoy al fresco breakfast at Barefoot Bar & Grill that feels so tropical.

Sail Bay from Ingraham bridge to Vacation Isle

As shown on the map, bike trails run along the remainder of the island's shoreline with great bay views in every direction, and continue underneath the bridges on both the north and south ends. To find the trails, turn either right or left instead of entering the resort property. You can also find the trails from the parking lots on the east side of the island. A pleasant park in the southwest quadrant has nice meandering trails, a lake for model boaters, and restrooms. You can also use Vacation Island to cut your Mission Bay loop in half by using both the north and the south bridges (see Option 1).

Option 4: Ocean Beach   4–10 miles, easy.

Connect to the Ocean Beach bike ride (SD3), a great Bike 'n Brunch, by cycling across the Sunset Cliffs Bridge and turning right on the paved Class I Ocean Beach Bike Path.

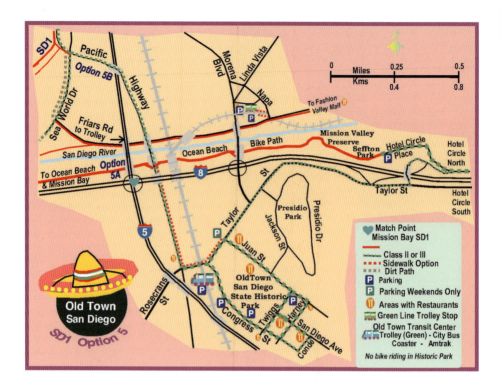

Option 5: Hotel Circle Stay 'n Ride & Old Town San Diego Side Trips
Variable miles, easy.

Option 5A: Hotel Circle to Old Town and/or West Mission Bay

Ocean Beach Bike Path runs 3.7 miles from the western terminus of Hotel Circle Place (at the west end of Hotel Circle North) along the south shore of the San Diego River all the way to the ocean. The Hotel Circle area has a huge variety of accommodations, many of which are more affordable than those in other parts of town. The closer you are to the west end of Hotel Circle North or better yet Hotel Circle Place, the easier the connection to the path will be, with less street riding. Hotel Circle South lies across the I-8 Freeway, however there is a freeway crossover at the west end of the district, making a trail ride from a hotel there possible as well.

Just west of Hotel Circle Place is the 51-acre Mission Valley Preserve, home to many rare and endangered plants and birds, so bring your binoculars and/or camera. Farther along, past the underpass to Morena Boulevard are ramps leading up to both lanes of Class II Pacific Highway. The east side of Mission Bay is 1.1 miles to the right (north) at this point. To get to Old Town, go left (south) for 0.4 mile, under the I-8 Freeway to the Old Town Transportation Depot beyond Taylor Street. This is your gateway to rail and bus travel in the region including the Trolley, Coaster, and Amtrak trains. Locally, the Trolley or Coaster can take you and your bikes downtown to the Santa Fe Depot area to access the rides at San Diego Harbor (SD4), Coronado (via ferry) (SD7), Balboa Park (SD6) or Point Loma (SD5) (via bus connections or uphill ride on street).

This is also the gateway (to the east of the depot) to Old Town San Diego State Historic Park, which has been restored to its former glory with museums, displays, and fun restaurants. Signs at the entrances prohibit bike riding in the actual park. The adjacent Old Town commercial district to its southeast mimics Old Town's Spanish architectural theme and is one of the most popular dining districts in the city. Presidio Park to the east is the site of California's first Euro-American settlement (1769), but as the name "Presidio" implies, the main part of the park is on the top of a hill, accessed via a winding narrow road.

The Ocean Beach Bike Path continues west along the San Diego River all the way to Ocean Beach. Connect to the west side of the Mission Bay ride by cycling north in the separated lane on the west side of the Sunset Cliffs Bridge (the second bridge after the I-5 under-crossing), which is 2 miles from Old Town. Or, from the same bridge, take Class II Nimitz Boulevard south to explore San Diego Harbor (see Option 6).

Old Town San Diego State Historic Park

Option 5B: East Mission Bay to Old Town

You can also ride from the east side of Mission Bay (where the RV parks are located) to Old Town by taking Class II/III Pacific Highway for 1.5 miles. At Taylor Street jog to the left on a sidewalk to cross the tracks (look both ways on these very active tracks) and reach the entrance to Old Town at Congress Street or Juan Street farther along. Pacific Highway is also the route to get from the Hotel Circle area by either road or trail to the east side of Mission Bay, as shown on the Old Town map.

Some notes on Option 5 routes:

- The Ocean Beach Bike Path in the area of the I-5 overpass and east is notorious for transients and homeless encampments that come and go depending on police activity. The unlit path is definitely not the place to ride in the dark and best not to ride alone.

- On Pacific Highway, the bike lane disappears along the bridge over I-5, replaced by sharrows on the roadway and a sign warning motorists of your presence along this short but curved stretch. The direction toward Old Town seems narrower and less safe, so if you are doing a loop consider using this route in the direction toward Mission Bay where the bend in the road to the left provides more visibility.

- Although it is tempting to take the Class I bike path next to Friars Road rather than busy Pacific Hwy, it does not lead to Old Town, but is a bike route to the Mission Valley malls. It also provides a mostly Class IV route to an MTS Trolley stop (Green Line), the closest one to Mission Bay. Take it either one stop south to Old Town, or continue to downtown and connect to other rides. To find Friars Road from the Mission Bay loop, take the dirt path or bike lane along Sea World Dr south from the Pacific Hwy interchange to the light at Friars Rd. Go east for 1.4 miles along the Friars Rd path, cross with the light at Napa St, and make your way down the walkway next to the tracks to the Trolley stop on the left. To drive there, the stop is accessed from Morena Blvd, north from the I-8 exit. From the Trolley station you can also cycle to Old Town by passing through the parking lot to Morena Boulevard and taking it southbound, however there are no bike lanes, narrow raised sidewalks shared with peds over the bridges, and freeway entrance crossings.

- If you prefer to take roadways between Hotel Circle and Old Town and/or Mission Bay, Hotel Circle South is a Class III route with sharrows, and the continuation west along busy Taylor Street is a Class II route. Within Old Town, Juan Street is a bike route and Congress Street has sharrows in traffic lanes. Old Town is mostly a slow-moving traffic area dominated by peds and cars. The roads through Presidio Park are hilly and are shared with vehicles, with no bike lanes. E-bike edge.

Option 6: South Connector To connect to rides to the south (SD4 though SD7) and access the Santa Fe train depot, cross the Sunset Cliffs Bridge and cycle the 2.25-mile Class II bike lane along busy Nimitz Blvd that connects to Harbor Drive where the Harbor Tour route (SD4) is across the road. There is a movement underfoot to construct a Class IV bikeway along Nimitz, though the new bike lanes may have taken its place. To avoid the dangerous street crossover at Sunset Cliffs and Nimitz, continue along the bike path or lane down Sunset Cliffs and cross Sunset Cliffs at the Point Loma Blvd signal, then follow Point Loma Blvd to Nimitz and turn right. The Nimitz/I-8/Sunset Cliffs intersection is a known concern for cyclists' safety, so hopefully that will be mitigated someday. As mentioned in Option 5, a mostly Class I option involves cycling to a Trolley stop near Friars Road and taking the Trolley green line south to downtown.

Option 7: To La Jolla Ride SD2
Ride the 10-mile La Jolla Loop ride from north end of Ocean Front Walk (e-bike edge).

La Jolla Loop SD2

La Jolla's meaning has been disputed, but one interpretation from the Spanish for "la joya" that translates to "jewel" accurately describes this fabulous district within the city of San Diego. Eons of wave action pounding on its surrounding sandstone cliffs has created a dramatic quintessential California-style coastline occupied by California sea lions, harbor seals, pelicans, and scores of other sea and shore birds. Grey whales migrate along the coast in winter, while strollers parade down the scenic walkways that line the perimeter parks of La Jolla Cove. San Diego's most expensive address offers the general public an enjoyable destination with countless dining options, art galleries, and shops.

While cycling through the crowded downtown area is wrought with hazards from the comings and going of vehicles, there are enough cyclists cruising the bike routes that at least the motorists are mostly cognizant of them, and we have found the majority of drivers to be courteous here. On weekends the sidewalks are way too crowded to take advantage of San Diego's lenient cycling guidelines, but you may find some opportunity on weekdays to be able to cruise along away from traffic here and there.

While La Jolla extends up into some very hilly country, our loop has only minor hills and connects with the fabulous Mission Bay/Pacific Beach ride (SD1) to the south. We suggest riding northbound along the inland route that takes you to the east end of La Jolla Cove, which is frequently labeled the UC San Diego bike route, while the coastal route is labeled the La Jolla Cove bike route heading north. Returning via the coastal route from the west end of La Jolla is labeled the Pacific Beach bike route in the southbound direction. It mostly passes multi-million dollar homes, with a couple of oceanfront parks including a quarter-mile stretch of beach along the way. Of the two routes, the inland route is quieter, seems safer, and is a tad hillier, while the coastal route is more scenic and exciting but has more potential impact from vehicle traffic.

SAN DIEGO COUNTY   251

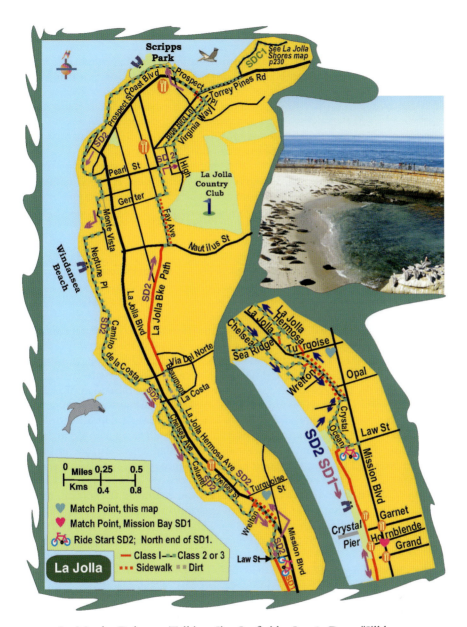

Tunes: La Mer by Debussy; Tell 'em I'm Surfin' by Jan & Dean "I'll be out at Windansea"; Life's Been Good by Joe Walsh; San Diego Serenade by Tom Waits.
Eats: Seared ahi soba noodle salad on the rooftop, George's at the Cove on Prospect St.

Distance: 9.5 miles. Time: 1–1.5 hours
Route & Bike: Moderate. Class III, II, and short Class I trail. Paved, any bike. Varies from flat to gradual grades and short steep hills. Substantial e-bike edge.
Seasons: All. Best on sunny, uncrowded, off-season weekday.
Facilities: Restrooms and water in Ellen Browning Scripps Park at La Jolla Cove.

Knocks & Hazards: This is mostly an on-road ride, with numerous street crossings, through residential and commercial areas, cycling near vehicles, so keep that in mind. Several short hills in both the inland and coastal routes. Crowded La Jolla waterfront parks require walking bike for about 0.5 mile to see the scenic bluffs.

Rent 'n Ride/Camp 'n Ride: Pedego E-Bikes, 5702 La Jolla Blvd, 858.291.8845. See also SD1 rentals. Mission Bay RV and Campland on the Bay are 5 miles away from trailhead via SD1, making for an approximate 20-mile total excursion.

Bike 'n Brunch: Wide variety of places to eat in La Jolla, or along the north part of Ocean Front Walk, 0.5 mile south of the trailhead.

Access: We begin this ride at the north end of Ocean Front Walk, at the corner of Law Street and Ocean Boulevard, enabling an extension of SD1. See directions and map for that ride. To do this ride on its own, find parking in the neighborhoods along the route. To drive to downtown La Jolla from I-5 take La Jolla Village Drive west to Torrey Pines Road. Turn left (south) then turn right on Prospect Place into town.

The Ride: From the north end of Ocean Front Walk at Law Street, follow Ocean Blvd straight ahead, bending away from the coast up a small hill. Bear left on Crystal Drive, then right on Loring St to reach La Jolla Blvd. Continue to the right to Mission Blvd and cross La Jolla Blvd at the crosswalk, then proceed to the left down the wide bike lane along La Jolla Blvd (mile 0.3). At mile 0.57 reach Wrelton St. Our coastal return route daylights across La Jolla Blvd on Wrelton. If you are doing the coastal route in both directions access it here, or wait for the light at Sea Ridge. Otherwise continue on our inland route to Turquoise St. Cross Turquoise at the crosswalk and continue straight ahead onto the short path to the dead end of La Jolla Hermosa Ave (0.7), a pleasant, wide Class II residential boulevard with ample bike lane and light traffic.

The road ends at Camino De La Costa (1.6). Here you can either continue straight ahead on a wide dirt path (that leads to a paved alley then back to dirt) or jog to the right, then left on quiet Beaumont Street, and left on Via Del Norte. As the dirt path meets Via Del Norte on the left, the paved Fay Avenue Path or "La Jolla Bike Path" goes to the right (2.0). This pleasant path is a rail trail between leafy backyards, has its own bridge over Palomar Avenue (2.3), and offers some vistas all the way out to the ocean in places. Next reach a fork. Our path unfortunately is the one that ascends the hill, which is also the highlight of the trail with even better vistas. The path ends at Nautilus Street (2.7) where you go to the right up the hill a short distance to the traffic signal and turn left onto Fay Avenue. At this point you are starting to get into the business district of La Jolla and traffic increases. Turn right on Genter Street (3.0), left on Girard Avenue, and right on Pearl Street (3.3). Turn left on High Avenue and right on Virginia Way, which ascends a hill and is signed as a Bike Route. (Alt route: Left on Virginia and right on Blue Bird

The beaches and walkways of La Jolla bustle on this sunny winter day

Lane, an alley, but less hilly route). Turn left near road's end on Prospect Place (3.9), then carefully descend a short steep hill to cross Torrey Pines Road with the signal.

Cruise down Prospect Place. At mile 4.2 is a junction. Prospect continues to the left and leads to the downtown district with all of its offerings. The road to the right descends steeply, leading to the bluff-side parks where you will be thrilled with all of the wildlife in view at any particular time. The first point of interest is the adjacent bluffs typically populated with a gazillion sea and shore birds starring the ubiquitous pelicans, then an area that you will smell where the California sea lions haul out and entertain on the rocks below.

We suggest walking your bike along the bluff-side sidewalk that rims the wide green lawns of Ellen Browning Scripps Park, or securely locking your bike somewhere and finishing your La Jolla exploration on foot. The path returns to Ocean Blvd at mile 4.7. At mile 4.9 is the popular spot where the harbor seals haul out in a sandy crescent beach framed by a short accessible breakwater. The coastline turns to the south, and Ocean Boulevard reaches a one-way (south-bound) section (5.2). Be leery of parked cars on both sides here. We tend to "take a lane" in situations like this.

Windansea Beach is a highlight of the loop ride to La Jolla from Mission Bay

The bike route bears right on Olivetas (5.6), then bears right again rather than ascending Pearl Street, and reaches Marine Street (5.75). Turn right, then left on Monte Vista, across Sea Lane, then right down Fern Glen (6.0) to Neptune. The highlight of this ride segment occurs when you reach beautiful Windansea Beach, a favorite sunset and surfer-watching spot. Be careful to avoid the parked cars coming and going until you pass Bonair Street (6.4), after which the no-parking zone along Neptune enables a delightful seaside cruise. Neptune ends and you must cycle to the left up the hill and head inland on Palomar Avenue (6.7). Make the first right on Camino De La Costa and follow it past oceanfront homes to a viewpoint (7.3) where the road curves left, then right again behind more homes.

Turn right when you reach Chelsea Avenue (7.6). The easiest, flattest route is to just stay on Chelsea Avenue/Street until Wrelton. Otherwise, to tackle more coastal hills, turn right on Dolphin. When Dolphin curves around to rejoin Chelsea, turn right (7.9). Turn right on Forward St, then left on Calumet Ave, passing Calumet Park (8.2), providing a nice blufftop break from the homes. Curve to the left onto Sea Ridge Dr. At the roundabout with Chelsea St (8.6) go to the right despite the "No Outlet" sign. Follow Chelsea until it rounds a bend to the left and becomes Wrelton Drive. Bikes/peds only can continue on to La Jolla Boulevard (8.9). Ride to the right in the bike lane or sidewalk until you reach Loring Street (9.2), which should look familiar. Follow the signs for Ocean Front Walk at this point. Turn right on Loring, a quick left on Crystal, then down the hill to Ocean Boulevard around to the left, and to the north end of Ocean Front Walk and ride SD1 at Law Street (9.5).

Ocean Beach SD3

This ride is an easy add-on to your Mission Bay ride (as Option 4), or can be done on its own. From the beautiful Class I trail along the estuary of the San Diego River, to the sandy beaches of Ocean Beach, its laid back throwback surfy but antiquey downtown district, and the fabulous coastline of Sunset Cliffs Natural Park, the Ocean Beach (aka "O.B.") neighborhood of San Diego is not to be missed. Besides the Class I river trail, riding is mostly on quiet residential streets, plus some optional cycling in the business district. There are so many people on bikes here that most motorists are used to them.

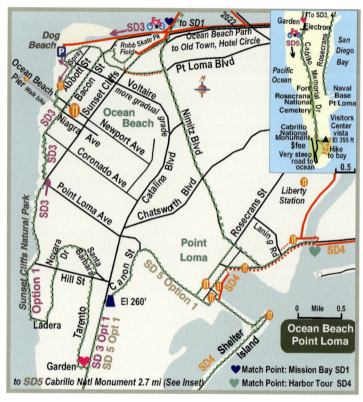

Tunes: Spring Vacation by The Beach Boys; Soul Limbo by Booker T and the MGs; Like the Sea by Alicia Keys

Eats: Lobster omelet or mango pancakes at Walking on Water Café on the pier, or see if a Hodad's burger on Newport is as good as CNN raved.

Distance: 4–10 miles + option. Time: 1–2 hours

Route & Bike: Easy to moderate depending on distance. Class I, II, and III, any bike. Flat in the north, hillier in the south, but nothing too steep.

Seasons: All. Best on sunny, uncrowded, off-season weekday.

Facilities: Restrooms and water at Ocean Beach Park.

Knocks & Hazards: Clueless peds and possible lurkers on Class I trail. Riding with traffic through intersections and near parked cars. Bike route south of town may be tricky to follow.

Rent 'n Ride/Camp 'n Ride: Shop: Bernie's, 1911 Cable, 619.224.7084. See ride SD1.

Bike 'n Brunch: Restaurants along beach on Abbott and throughout downtown district centered around Newport Avenue and Voltaire Street near the beach. Also try the café near the end of the pier (walk bike on pier).

Further Info: oceanbeachsandiego.com.

Access: By bike, ride south over the Sunset Cliffs Bridge from the Mission Bay ride (SD1). From Hotel Circle ride 3 miles west on the Ocean Beach Bike Path. The closest San Diego Trolley and Coaster stops are at the Old Town depot: From there ride on Class II Pacific Hwy north 0.4 mile to the bike path, and then west 3 miles. See SD1, Option 5 for further info on this path. By car, take I-8 west until it ends at Nimitz Blvd/Sunset Cliffs Blvd and follow Sunset Cliffs west to West Point Loma Blvd. Turn right to get to the popular Dog Beach and terminus of the Ocean Beach Bike Path. For downtown OB, continue on Sunset Cliffs, then right on Newport Avenue. Or to reach beautiful Sunset Cliffs Natural Park stay on Sunset Cliffs Blvd.

Ocean Beach Bike Path along the delta of the San Diego River

The Ride: This beachy cruise starts as Option 4 from the Mission Bay ride (SD1), so if you are doing it independently and arriving to O.B. by car, adjust as necessary from your actual starting point using the map. From the north side of the San Diego River (mile 0), cycle south across the Sunset Cliffs Bridge and turn right (west) on the paved Class I Ocean Beach Bike Path (0.4). Follow it toward the ocean, cycling carefully along on the buckled pavement. On the left is mostly public parkland including a skateboard park, while to the right is a beautiful river delta with some paths through the sand in prime bird watching country. You'll notice a directional sign about halfway to the ocean (1.2) that points to the left toward Ocean Beach Business District—1 mile. If you are starving, that is the quickest way to get some grub. The route is down sharrowed Bacon Street, with slow moving traffic, leading past several restaurants to the main drag, Newport Avenue. The Ocean Beach Bike Path ends at the dog beach at Ocean Beach Park (2.0). You can enjoy some beach time here, and there are new restrooms. Turn around here for a 4-mile ride, or continue onward to explore the really cool town and/or the beautiful coastal bluffs farther south.

Cycle to the left through the beach parking lot, then ride away from the beach at its far end, up Brighton Avenue, then right on Abbott Street (2.4). This is the beginning of the commercial district of Ocean Beach. In a couple of blocks are a few water-view cafés, and one of the main beach hangouts to the north of the pier. Abbott curves to the left and becomes Newport Avenue, an impressive street with buildings straight out of the 1950s and '60s that now house antique shops, restaurants, cafés, and shops. On Wednesday afternoons two blocks are closed off for a Farmers' Market. You can also find dining options on several of the side streets off of Newport, up to Sunset Cliffs Boulevard. Be very careful on Newport, since the cars park diagonally so give them a wide berth. Or better yet, just walk your bike down the sidewalk to explore.

Upon reaching Sunset Cliffs, you can turn to the right and then go right on Niagra Avenue (3.6), returning to Bacon Street (4.0). The O.B. Municipal Pier is straight ahead. The 1,971-foot long structure is the longest concrete pier on the West Coast, however bike riding is not allowed on it. A nice cafe is near its end. The shortest return route from Niagra and Bacon is to take Bacon all the way back to the Ocean Beach Bike Path and return to the other side of the bridge for a 6.5-mile round trip. Or return the way you came using the Class I path in its entirety. To see more of the spectacular coast, turn south on Bacon.

Ride with traffic along Bacon until the road curves to the left and becomes Coronado (4.5). Begin a series of jogs down alleys and side streets to take you through this coastal residential area while avoiding the busiest roads for the most part. Bike Route signs help direct you through many of the turns, but not all, so use your common sense to stay as close to the ocean bluffs as possible but avoiding dead ends. The first alley takes you past Ocean Front Street and to the end of Del Mar Avenue, where a bluff-top park with a couple of benches lets you share the million-dollar views with the adjacent homes (4.6).

After several more jogs down alleys and streets, you will eventually run out of alleys and end up on Sunset Cliffs Boulevard at Point Loma Avenue (5.4). From here the beautiful Sunset Cliffs Natural Park is just a short block away to the right (southwest). You can ride with the traffic or on the sidewalk, reaching the signed bluff-top park. A solid dirt path connects to the first couple of parking lots (5.75). You can stop here and enjoy the spectacular vista, then return in a similar manner, including using Bacon Street to reach the Ocean Beach Bike Path, for a ride of about 10 miles. But, alas, this is fabulous San Diego so you have even more options, as described in Option 1 below.

Option 1: Point Loma and Cabrillo National Monument *20 extra miles, strenuous*

South of Ocean Beach is some very beautiful coastline with bluffs reminiscent of Monterey. The bike riding is not the greatest along the busy ocean road, but many do it. Reach the Sunset Cliffs Natural Park as described previously (5.8), but ride with traffic along the spectacular coastal route. You can join the Point Loma ride (SD5) by ascending the steep hillside to Catalina Blvd. From the south end of Sunset Cliffs Blvd bear left on Ladera (7.4) up the steep hill to Cornish. Cross Hill Street (8.3) then bear right each time on Novara (8.6), Santa Barbara (9.0) and Tarento (9.4). Turn left when Tarento ends at Garden to meet up with Catalina (10.9). The tough climb is rewarded with awesome views along the way. Continue to Cabrillo National Monument to the south (15.7). Return the same way, for a total of about 30 miles, or do a loop by following the optional route suggested in the Point Loma ride (Catalina to Cañon St, down the hill, left on Rosecrans St, then left on Class II Nimitz Blvd; about 28 miles total ride). You can also follow Catalina north until it veers left to become Voltaire St. Follow it into OB, and turn right on Bacon to the OB Bike Path. Note: The Voltaire to Catalina route is a much more gradual climb than from Sunset Cliffs Blvd up Ladera and Hill. Significant e-bike edge on these hills.

San Diego Downtown & Harbor Tour SD4

This tour is a feast for the senses. It takes in the bustling San Diego Harbor area with its gobs of attractions like the U.S.S. *Midway* aircraft carrier and the San Diego Maritime Museum featuring the tall sailing ship, *Star of India*. It offers fabulous Bike 'n Brunch opportunities in complexes such as Seaport Village or the new Liberty Station converted Navy base, gives you a birds-eye view of jets taking off and landing at San Diego's Airport, and a glimpse into the extensive naval and coast guard operations that are an important component of the character of the city. Wend your way around waterfront parks next to marinas and down promenades past grand structures such as the Convention Center, San Diego Padres' Petco Park baseball stadium, and the new Hilton and Marriott Hotels. Cruise down the downtown rail trail next to the red trolleys. Finally, explore Harbor and Shelter Islands for more bayside mileage.

San Diego Harbor and the city skyline from the bike trail

A cross town bike route on Class IV cyclepaths (see the map) also enables a jaunt up to Balboa Park that houses the San Diego Zoo, where you can try Ride SD6.

Despite all its wonderful attributes, this ride suffers from the deficiencies noted in "Knocks & Hazards," most notably the crowded sidewalks along the harbor, the banning of bikes on the scenic sidewalks on both islands, the absence of a good path through Seaport Village, and the disjointed nature of the trail. Still, if you want to tour the San Diego Harbor area and love to bike, this is a great way to do it.

Tunes: Harbor Lights by Boz Scaggs; Sail on Sailor by The Beach Boys; Trains & Boats & Planes by Dionne Warwick; Jet Airliner by Steve Miller Band
Eats: A delightful meal on a waterfront Seaport Village patio

Distance: 16 miles + options. Time: 2 hours
Route & Bike: Easy to moderate, depending on distance. Paved Class I, optional Class II and III. Mostly flat, any bike. E-bike edge: combine with hilly SD5 or 6.
Seasons: All. Best on sunny, uncrowded, off-season weekday.
Facilities: Restrooms and water in parks and commercial establishments along route.
Knocks & Hazards: Clueless peds in many areas. Some tourist areas along the central waterfront may be too crowded to ride some days. Urban ride, many homeless along route. Street crossings. Walk bike 0.5 mile through Seaport Village (or detour). Harbor and Shelter Island tours have Class III routes without bike lanes. Obey posted speed limit on trails. Jet fuel fumes may waft over from airport.
Rent 'n Ride: Pedego E-Bikes, 900 Bayfront, downtown, 800.604.7187. Wheel Fun Rentals, 619.342.7244 has locations at Holiday Inn (1355 N Harbor Dr) and Marriott Hotel (333 W Harbor Dr). Check for any bike share operations.
Camp 'n Ride: Nothing downtown. See Mission Bay (SD1) and Coronado (SD7).
Bike 'n Brunch: See ride description for multitude of choices.

Access: Start anywhere along this out and back route. Our start in front of the ferry landing at Broadway and Harbor reflects the option of combining this ride with the Coronado ride (SD7). To get here, take I-5 to the Hawthorn Street/Airport exit and head west to Harbor Drive. Broadway is about 10 blocks south of here, and you can park wherever you can in the public lots along the waterfront. If you are doing the entire ride, Shelter Island at the west end of the ride has a lot of free parking. Take Harbor Drive west past Nimitz Boulevard to Scott Street, turn left, then left on Shelter Island. Find free parking at the waterfront park. Rail 'n Ride: The main Santa Fe Depot (Amtrak, Coaster, Trolley) is two blocks inland from the harbor on Broadway.

The Ride: Begin at the terminal for the ferry to Coronado so that it can be combined with SD7. This area has most of the attractions that were described in the introduction. The *Midway* and Seaport Village are to the south, and the San Diego Maritime Museum is to the north.

Heading north and west: The first part is by far the most crowded, where you will have to navigate a tourist-filled sidewalk, especially if a cruise ship is docked at the B Street Terminal, or worse if it is loading. An option in this district is to jostle with cars by riding in the continuous parking lots. It is a very interesting stretch with tall masts of the sailing ships, and if you are patient you can take a photo of a jet as it appears to land over a tall ship at the airport just to the north. The crowds thin out a bit as you continue on. The path gets a little wider, but expect lots of human obstacles along the way. It curves around the very scenic waterfront as it turns to the west, and when it passes Laurel Street it becomes the North Harbor Drive Bike Path (mile 1.0). Just before the U.S. Coast Guard facility is a good place to watch the planes take off and land at the airport across Harbor Drive.

The next stretch is the least interesting, as you cross over the entrance to (1.5), then ride next to, the rental car facilities of the airport. After the Port of San Diego Harbor Police building is the entrance road to Harbor Island (2.0). Cross the street at the light here, and ride in front of the Sheraton Hotel. At the fork that comes quickly, turn left if you want to explore Harbor Island, or right to skip it.

> **Option 1:** ⭐ Since bikes are prohibited on Harbor Island's scenic waterfront promenade, your ride will be among cars on a 4-lane road that runs both ways from the harbor entrance road (or the inland sidewalk). The reward is fantastic views back toward the San Diego skyline, perhaps during a Sunday brunch splurge at Tom Ham's Lighthouse near the west end. Add about 3.25 miles to the mileage total if you explore the island.

Back on the Class I trail along Harbor Drive, continue into Spanish Landing Park (2.1–2.9). This is a very nice stretch of mostly Class I riding, with wide waterfront sidewalks overlooking Harbor Island and the San Diego skyline beyond. The bike route detours into several pay parking lots along the way, when the sidewalk narrows at these locations. After the last parking lot, you will see the Harbor Drive Bridge over a channel into the former Navy training center. It has a nice wide sidewalk along its

A nice uncrowded section of the harbor trail ride near Spanish Landing Park

south side, a safe route (3.0). Option: Ride under the bridge to the bike/ped Nimitz Bridge parallel to the north. Cross it and observe the U.S.S. *Recruit*, a model of a battleship once used for training. Paved paths along the inlet lead north through parks, adjacent to which is the Liberty Station complex, a converted Navy base with restaurants, shops, museums, and a popular Public Market. Return to the *Recruit* and turn right. Pass restaurants, go left on the east sidewalk of Laning St, and cross Harbor to its south sidewalk, meeting up with the main ride (3.5). Ride to the right.

Some may prefer taking the bike lane along Harbor, turning left on sharrowed Scott St, then left on Shelter Island. We stick to the sidewalk, then near Scott St we cut through the parking lot upon sighting the Fisherman's Landing building. You can then pedal along the Fisherman's Landing harborfront promenade, past the popular Point Loma Seafoods restaurant. A new path next to new condos leaves the harbor and daylights at Shelter Island Dr, just west of the Shelter Island welcome monument in the middle of the road (4.4). Several restaurants may tempt you in this area. Carefully cross the street, turn left, and comingle with slow-moving traffic for a few blocks to reach Shelter Island (4.8).

At the island entrance are the Bali Hai restaurant on the left, and Humphrey's By the Bay on the right, a great outdoor concert venue. Shelter Island Park lines the east side of the island, with gobs of free parking. Although you can't ride on the scenic sidewalks, you can cycle through the parking lots, or down the 2-lane road. Shelter Island is not as busy as Harbor Island. At the south end are nice restrooms and great views of the Point Loma Peninsula (6.0). Return the same way, staying on the right side of Harbor Drive or on the sidewalk, then into Spanish Landing Park. Reach the ride starting point at the ferry terminal (12.0), and continue to the south.

Heading South: Two parallel paths lead southward from the ferry landing, soon passing the fascinating *Midway* aircraft carrier museum (12.1). Next, detour right to see WWII-era sculptures "Embracing Peace" and Bob Hope entertaining the troupes. Farther along in Seaport Village, a no-bicycles sign on the path indicates you cannot ride your bike along its seaside promenade (12.5). You can bypass it by riding in alleys and parking lots behind it. This famously popular conglomeration of restaurants and shops is a great place for your Bike 'n Brunch, and it is worth walking your bike through here to experience it. Choose from several bay view patio restaurants en route.

About three-quarters of the way through the complex (12.6), you can hop on your bike and explore the scenic peninsula occupied by Embarcadero Marina Park North (13.1), with great views of the marina, San Diego skyline, and the Coronado Bridge. You will still need to dismount for the remaining block or so of Seaport Village when you circle back. The best part of the trail follows as you get back on your bike and ride along a very wide path between million dollar yachts in the marina and the San Diego Convention Center (13.4).

At the south end of the marina is the peninsular Embarcadero Marina Park South that you can cycle around (13.5–14.2). Near its entrance on the left is the Convention Center dock of the Coronado Ferry, followed by Joe's Crab Shack. Next ride on the wide waterfront promenade beside the beautiful new Marriott, and end on the seaside promenade of San Diego Bayfront Park (14.5), built on the former Campbell Shipyard site in conjunction with the 30-story 1,190-room Hilton San Diego Bayfront Hotel. On the return, skip the peninsular parks and ride in the parking lots behind Seaport Village, for a total ride of about 16 miles. Or, for your return route, explore more downtown districts like the Gaslamp Quarter via the Martin Luther King rail trail, and end up with about the same mileage (Option 2).

Option 2: Martin Luther King Promenade ⭐2 *1.1 miles each way, easy*

This rail-with-trail runs next to the very busy commuter tracks through downtown San Diego. The red Trolley light rail trains make their way along the adjacent tracks. The trail runs between the main Santa Fe Depot train station and Petco Park stadium to the south, passing some impressive newer downtown developments such as the Convention Center, as well as the entrance to the historic Gaslamp Quarter, a cornucopia of restaurants, shops, and entertainment venues housed in refurbished Victorian buildings that comprises the centerpiece of the San Diego nighttime scene.

San Diego's distinctive red Trolley runs next to the MLK Rail Trail through downtown

Although the MLK is a newer Class I trail, it requires numerous street crossings, where trail users are supposed to detour across train tracks to the nearest crosswalk, which is only a few steps away, but always a pain. Still, the sights and sounds of this downtown corridor make it worth the excursion.

Starting from the harbor-side trails at the south end, go inland through the park north of the Hilton Bayside toward Petco Park. The path begins across Harbor Drive at Park Boulevard, just north of the pedestrian-only bridge to the stadium. It heads north parallel to the train tracks. At 5th Avenue on the right is the arched entry to the Gaslamp Quarter, and the sidewalk cafés that line the streets may be too tempting to pass up. At G Street and Kettner Boulevard the trail appears to end, with no obvious directional sign in place. To continue, turn left on G, then cut to the right on a promenade between two apartment buildings. The trail emerges to the right of parking areas, then reaches its end at West Broadway across from the Santa Fe Depot.

To find the path heading south, from the south end of the Santa Fe Depot, the path starts on the south side of West Broadway across from the large parking lot, just to the right (west) of the train tracks. Follow it about 1/8 mile until it reaches a roadway (G Street) and turn left, then right onto the trail at Kettner. Besides the street crossings, another detraction is other trail users, including the homeless pushing shopping carts, or even worse, groups of clueless conventioneer peds with nametags.

Point Loma Peninsula & Cabrillo National Monument SD5

Details: 5.4 miles on paved roads, easy, any bike. See map inset page 254.

One of the most spectacular areas of San Diego is the Point Loma Peninsula that juts out to the south from the Mission Bay area. Its northern two-thirds contains neighborhoods that house about 50,000 people, including the fabulous Ocean Beach area (ride SD3) that is also accessible from the Mission Bay ride (SD1). Its southern third contains the Naval Base Point Loma, Fort Rosecrans National Cemetery, and Cabrillo National Monument at its tip. The monument commemorates "where California began" when Portuguese navigator João Rodrigues Cabrilho landed here in 1542. The first permanent settlement did not take hold until over 200 years later, at Presidio Park near Old Town. The main, upper portion of Cabrillo National Monument overlooks the open Pacific Ocean to the west, a prime spot for watching the winter (December through early April) gray whale migration. To the east is an amazing panorama of the San Diego area, including San Diego Bay with its military and tour boats, Coronado

Cabrillo National Monument, looking south at US Coast Guard station and Mexico's Coronado Isles. See p8 for city and bay panorama to the east.

Island and the Silver Strand (SD7), Downtown San Diego (SD4, 6), and the mountains beyond. This is a great place to get a feel for the lay of the land. The lower portion of the monument near sea level provides access to tide pools and a more up close visit with the surrounding ocean.

The eastern bay section can be reached by a hiking trail, and the western ocean section by a steep park roadway that is popular with the most fit of cyclists who tackle the 400-foot climb. There are no easy bike trails, but you can do a scenic Class II ride. From the Visitor's Center ride through the parking lots out toward the park exit (mile 0.3). Ride along the spine of the peninsula, past the Rosecrans National Cemetery on both sides (0.6–1.5) with inspiring views sloping down toward the sea and city. Next pass the buildings of the naval base. The bike lanes end past the naval base at Electron Drive (2.7). Turn around (or start here) for an easy 5.4-mile Class II ride. Admission to the monument is $10 per vehicle or $5 per cyclist, so make sure to take your receipt when you cycle out of the park. As shown on the map (p 254) you can combine this ride with a hilly transition to the harbor (SD5 Opt 1) or Ocean Beach (SD3 Opt 1) (e-bike edge).

Balboa Park and Hillcrest SD6

San Diego's 1,200-acre Balboa Park was constructed just east of downtown for the 1915–16 Panama-California Exposition and expanded for the 1935 California Pacific International Exposition. Many of the historic buildings remain, some of which house its 15 museums and the several performing arts venues including the Old Globe Theatre. The central area of the park is reminiscent of a medieval European city, a must-see. The adjacent world-renowned San Diego Zoo was one of the first to feature animals displayed in natural looking surroundings, and remains one of the most popular attractions in California. Roads and paths for biking and hiking wind through the park, and most of its roadways have bike lanes or sharrows.

The park is hilly but you can stay away from most of the hills if you follow our suggested routes. The off-road pathways are both paved and dirt, and the city has numbered them to correspond to their difficulty with regard to hills. Ride past Old World buildings, gorgeous floral gardens, impressive fountains, an artists' marketplace, and landscaped lawns. The park can get very crowded on weekends and holidays, and if your schedule is limited to weekends you can minimize the impact by arriving Sunday morning when street and sidewalk traffic is lighter before the hordes of park-goers arrive "after church." Since the majority of the attractions are concentrated in one area, walking is a good way to tour most of the park's highlights, and the clueless ped index can be off the charts, but on a non-crowded day biking is a great way to see more of the park. You can always come back to the central area along El Prado and stroll later after you've seen what there is to see by bike.

You can ride to the park from downtown (see map page 257). A Class IV cycletrack along Beech Street connects to the cycletracks along 4th and 5th Avenues (complete by 2022, Class II options until then). E-bikers can mitigate the 200 foot elevation gain.

Cycle into the adjacent hip Hillcrest neighborhood for your Bike 'n Brunch. Although not the best place to ride, Hillcrest is full of inviting restaurants and cafés and is the hub of San Diego's vibrant LGBT community.

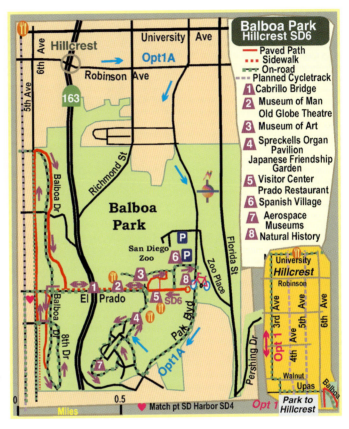

Tunes: Galileo by The Indigo Girls; Balboa Park by Bruce Springsteen; San Diego Zoo by The 6ths; Parranda by Al DiMeola

Eats: Lox-N-Latke Benny at Snooze in Hillcrest or, in Balboa Park, tea & light Japanese lunch al fresco at the Tea Pavilion or Shrimp Cobb Salad on The Prado's patio.

Distance: 5.1–6.1 miles. Time: 1–1.5 hours plus stops

Route & Bike: Easy from park. Strenuous from downtown (e-bike edge). Paved Class I, II, and III on paths, sidewalks, parking lots, and roads. Most of the time there is an option to choose paved paths or sidewalks instead of roads. Main park area/Hillcrest slopes gently to the north. Topography slopes more steeply downward from the main part of the park to the east and south.

Seasons: All. Best on sunny, uncrowded morning.

Facilities: Restrooms and water in the park along route.

Knocks & Hazards: Urban park with lurkers and some crime in various sections: Bloggers have posted warnings of restrooms in remote sections of the park. Cycling next to traffic and through intersections and parking lots. Be careful at every type of junction, and stay away from parked cars whose doors can swing open. Very crowded on sunny weekends and holidays, when finding parking may be an issue and the walkways may be impossibly crowded with peds. Even on weekdays there will be plenty of peds on walkways, as this is a major San Diego attraction.

Rent 'n Ride: Check for new concessions or bike share. Closest rentals at this writing are downtown (Ride SD4). Shop: Uptown Bicycles, 2665 5th Ave, 619.795.7222.

Camp 'n Ride: See Mission Bay and Coronado rides.

Bike 'n Brunch: The Prado in the House of Hospitality is the premier Balboa Park restaurant with indoor & outdoor dining; expensive but has happy hour 4–6 p.m.

and/or lounge menu. Tea Pavilion at Japanese Friendship Garden has seating in the pavilion or outdoors overlooking the garden and serves tea and light Japanese fare. Check for choices in Fleet Science Center and many of the other museums and attractions that may have snack bars or cafés. Or you can try a picnic in the park. If you end up downtown your choices are endless from the Gaslamp Quarter to Little Italy to Seaport Village. Closer to the park if you ride to the Hillcrest district, choose from breakfast/lunch at Snooze, 3940 5th Ave, Hash House A Go-Go, 3628 5th Ave, and many others.

Plaza de Panama

Further Info: balboapark.org has extensive park information including trail and route maps in case you want to tackle some more difficult trails in more remote sections of the park. The Balboa Park app is helpful as well.

Access: Southbound on I-5 take the 10th Ave exit. Turn left on A St then left on Park Blvd. Follow the signs to Balboa Park and turn left on Village Place to the first parking lots. Northbound on I-5 take the Pershing Dr/B St exit to Pershing Dr. Take Pershing and then turn left on Florida Dr. Turn left on Zoo Place and left on Park Blvd, then right on Village Place. Ride start is from Village Place between the first parking lots. These lots are frequently full, so you may need to park along Park Blvd or in other lots accessed via Presidents Way. Adjust the ride start accordingly. There are sidewalks along busy Park Blvd. Via transit, from the downtown America Plaza trolley stop east of Santa Fe Depot take the Orange or Blue lines east to the City College stop, then transfer to the Route 7 bus in the La Mesa direction and get off near the zoo. See sdmts.com for specific route planning and schedules.

The Ride: From ride start on Village Place continue south through the parking lot (parallel to Park Blvd) to reach the Bea Evenson Fountain and the east end of El Prado's pedestrian promenade. A small sign posted says "no skateboards, bikes, etc" probably due to the kids terrorizing pedestrians with their BMX bikes, so you may want to walk it through the fountain plaza on a busy day. Amble west (right) past the Fleet Science Center, Natural History Museum, Zoro Garden, Model Railroad Museum, Lily Pond and the Botanical Building to its north (mile 0.25) along this dramatic stretch that will make you think you are in Spain. Continue to the Plaza de Panama Fountain, a unique park landmark surrounded by a traffic roundabout in front of the Museum of Art (0.3). Vehicle traffic is allowed from here onward, but you can escape to the adjacent covered pathway along the Museum of Man, whose California Building with its three-stage California Tower is one of the most photographed historic buildings in the state. Pass the Sculpture Garden, north of which is the Old Globe Theatre and arched entry gates.

After the St. Francis Chapel comes the Cabrillo Bridge over the SR 163 Freeway in the gorge below (0.5). Ride on its wide sidewalk, or on the road if the sidewalk is too crowded then turn left onto Balboa Drive (0.8) or an adjacent paved path. The road forms a one-way loop with parked cars along it, around grassy parkland, and heads south, gradually downhill, to a viewpoint over downtown San Diego then curves left, and back up the hill to the north, becoming 8th Drive. The paved path dips down to the gorge northbound so you may want to stick to the road here. After looping around, continue straight (west) onto Juniper Road (1.6), then turn right on the nice sidewalk path along 6th Avenue. Ride along the edge of the park and reach the north end of Balboa Drive (2.5) and cross it.

Cycling over the Cabrillo Bridge toward the main part of Balboa Park

Here is a decision point. To include a visit to Hillcrest (Option 1), cross 6th Avenue to Upas Street and ride west, then north on 3rd. Otherwise, ride along the paved path to the right on Balboa. It winds through park lawns and palm trees, and when we rode it on a weekday afternoon, there were homeless people sleeping all over the lawns. The path rolls along some small hills, and passes "Redwood Circle," which you can spin around. There are a couple of trail junctions but keep in mind that you are going south, parallel to Balboa Drive and heading for El Prado (3.2).

Turn left on El Prado and retrace your route over the bridge. Reach the Plaza de Panama Fountain, and turn right in the grand square onto Pan American Road East (3.6). Pass the El Cid statue and the toney Prado restaurant, as well as the Casa del Rey Moro Garden. The road bends to the west (right) in front of the magnificent outdoor Spreckels Organ Pavilion, a place to watch for concert events. Bear right on the narrower Pan American Road West (3.75) (sign says "Authorized Vehicles Only," so there is just tram traffic) and pass the House of Pacific Relations/International Cottages that hosts open houses and international festivals, and then the Mary Hitchcock Puppet Theatre, before arriving at a central parking lot in front of the Automotive Museum (4.0).

Turn right before the museum where another sign says "Authorized Vehicles Only," then cycle to the right again in front of the Air and Space Museum, on a narrow access road (Speed Limit 15 mph). Cycle counter-clockwise on the road around the back of the museum, taking in views of downtown and the Coronado Bridge. Bear right through another parking lot area, then curve left around the Starlight Musical Theatre venue below, look for the Hall of Champions Sports Museum to the left, and ride up the road to its left, emerging back into the central parking lot in front of the Automotive Museum. Turn right at the parking lot (4.4), then continue north on Pan American Road East, past the Japanese Friendship Garden and its tea house on the right, and return to the Plaza de Panama Fountain (4.8). Turn right back into the El Prado promenade, but then turn left onto Village Place (5.0).

Note a junction to the left that is an access road that runs above the zoo (listen to the birds and monkeys) to the Old Globe Theatre plaza area that you may want to check out if you missed it before. Otherwise, curve to the right toward one of the most interesting park attractions, the Spanish Village Art Center complex on the left. Its art galleries housed in historic Spanish tile-roofed buildings and flagstone patio with seasonal blooms are worth seeing. The ride start is just beyond (5.1). From here, the Balboa Park Carousel and the San Diego Zoo are through the parking lot to the north.

> Option 1: Hillcrest Bike 'n Brunch *2–4 miles extra, easy, on-road* This option adds 1 or 2 city-cycling miles on streets with sidewalk options and a further option (1A) that leads to more sections of the park. The designated Class III bike route to Hillcrest starts at the north end of Balboa Drive at 6th Avenue as described in the main ride (mile 2.5). Cross 6th Ave to reach Upas Street, westbound. Turn right on 3rd Ave, which then jogs left/right. Continue up 3rd Ave to University Ave (3.1). The center of the Hillcrest District, as indicated by the arched "Hillcrest" sign over the road, is at University and 5th Avenue, which is two blocks to the east (right). You may want to lock your bike extra securely and stroll around. *New cycletracks along 4th & 5th Ave's may alter the route.*
>
> When you are done exploring, the way to minimize street riding is to return to the same point at 6th Ave and Balboa and continue into the park on the paved path to the left next to Balboa Drive. If you don't mind street riding with moderate traffic you can do this optional loop to add a bit more mileage and variety (Option 1A): From University Ave head south on 6th Ave to Robinson Ave and turn left (3.3). Follow Robinson east over the Hwy 163 overpass, make a hard right onto the sidewalk of Park Boulevard (4.0) and follow that road or sidewalk south, into the park, past the huge Zoo parking lot and Village Place (5.0). Turn right on Presidents Way (5.5), and take it across to the far end of the Pan American Plaza parking lot (6.0). Then, continue as in the main ride by taking the road to the right in front of the Automotive Museum (mile 4.0 in the main ride), for a total ride of about 7.1 miles.

Coronado & The Bayshore Bikeway SD7

The City of Coronado is near the northern end of a peninsula that is in the middle of San Diego Bay. Although a separate city, it is combined with San Diego due to the connectivity of the rides. Coronado is accessed either from the south from Imperial Beach along the 10-mile sandy Silver Strand isthmus, or from the downtown San Diego area via the towering Coronado Bridge. Coronado was established in 1885 as a resort town, and the Hotel Del Coronado was constructed soon after in 1888. You've seen that unique hotel, referred to as the Hotel Del, many times in movies and TV shows, including the 1959 Marilyn Monroe classic *Some Like it Hot,* where the "Seminole Ritz" was supposed to be located in Florida. Several other major hotel resorts have appeared over the years as well as smaller boutique hotels, and scores of restaurants serve the locals and gobs of visitors that flock here.

Coronado Beach, regarded as one of the best in the U.S., is a major draw. The North Island Naval Air Station occupies the northwest end of the peninsula, and the Naval Amphibious Base Coronado south of town is the home of the Navy SEALs, which explains why this community of about 25,000 includes so many retired navy personnel. Home prices now average around $1.8 million, making it one of the most expensive markets in the country. The Silver Strand contains both off-limits military beach lands, and also Silver Strand State Beach that the public can enjoy.

For cyclists, the Class I trail that runs along the west side of San Diego Bay with amazing views of the San Diego skyline, the mouth-watering waterfront restaurants, the Hotel Del and cute downtown district, the scenic sprint down a rail trail along the Silver Strand to the State Beach and beyond, and an optional ferry ride combined with a cycle along San Diego Harbor, make Coronado a fabulous cycling destination.

SAN DIEGO COUNTY 267

Tunes: Navy Blue by Diane Renay; Ride Like the Wind by Christopher Cross; I Wanna Be Loved By You by Marilyn Monroe

Eats: I've enjoyed a couple of birthday lunches on Peohe's bay view patio near ferry landing. Or Calamari Relleno with Jalapeño White Sauce at Miguel's Cocina in town.

Distance: 16 miles + options. Time: 1.5–2 hours

Route & Bike: Easy to moderate. Paved Class I, with some easy Class II and III, any bike. Optional dirt paths. Flat. Good directional signs. E-bike edge for headwinds.

Seasons: All. Best on sunny, uncrowded weekday. Saturdays fast bike clubs dominate.

Facilities: Restrooms and water in parks en route.

Knocks & Hazards: Wind, traffic noise along Silver Strand. In tourist area near ferry landing and Hotel Del path: 8 mph speed, clueless peds. Golf balls on Glorietta.

Rent 'n Ride: Near ferry at 1201 1st St: Holland's Bikes & Beyond, 619.435.7180, and Bike & Kayak Tours, 858.454.1010. Rays-Coronado Marriott, 619.655.1062. Holland's (downtown), 977 Orange, 619.435.3153. Action Rentals at Loews Coronado Resort next to Silver Strand SP, 619.424.4466. Wheel Fun Rentals, 1019 C St, 619.342.7244. See also ride SD4.

Camp 'n Ride: Silver Strand State Beach has a beachfront lot for self-contained RV's with water & electric hookups and a dump station. The new Costa Vista (Sun RV Resorts) is located at the west end of E Street along Bayshore Bikeway south of National City Marina and Sweetwater Bikeway. Provides access to the southern Main St trailhead or round the bay ride.

Bike 'n Brunch: A multitude of options near the Ferry Landing, in downtown Coronado, and at other locales mentioned in the ride description.

City code, bicycle riding on sidewalks: Prohibited in business districts and as signed elsewhere. Walking bikes on sidewalk is okay.

Further Info: coronadovisitorcenter.com; fws.gov/refuge/san_diego_bay/; sandag.org

Access the ride by taking I-5 south from downtown San Diego to the Coronado Bridge/SR 75 exit west. Cross the toll-free bridge (no bikes except on buses) into Coronado. SR 75 turns into 4th Street. Turn right on Orange Avenue, which ends at 1st Street. The passenger-ferry terminal is one block south. Look along side streets for free on-street parking, or in free lots in the nearby parks. By bike, take the ferry across to Coronado from Broadway Pier in San Diego. Ferry fare is $5 (no extra for bike).

Rail 'n Ride: Get off at the Santa Fe Depot (Coaster, Amtrak, or Trolley) and ride two blocks west to the terminal for the ferry to Coronado.

The Ride: Begin at the Coronado Ferry Landing. The area has great Bike 'n Brunch options, with a seaside complex of restaurants and shops to explore. Peohe's and Il Fornaio have fabulous waterfront patios. The passenger and bicycle ferry to the downtown San Diego harbor area replaced the vehicle ferry that was discontinued after the Coronado Bridge was built in 1969. Find the obvious concrete bike trail that heads south along the bay. Except for possible crowds, that thin out as you go, this is a terrific stretch, with magnificent views across San Diego Bay to downtown, the Coronado Bridge, and all the excitement of marine traffic. Photography lighting is best later in the afternoon when the sun illuminates the San Diego skyline.

The Coronado waterfront approaching the Coronado Bridge

The trail soon passes the Coronado Island Marriott Resort, then enters Tidelands Park (mile 0.7), with lawns, a playground, and restrooms. It continues along the bay, jogs to the right to cross under the Coronado Bridge (1.0), and then runs along a fenced-in stretch between the Coronado Golf Course and the access road to the bridge. It turns left onto a sidewalk trail as it reaches Glorietta Boulevard (1.4), then dumps you onto that wide, pleasant boulevard with light automobile traffic at 5th Street. Carefully cross the street to the north side to ride with traffic in the ultra-wide bike lane, past well-kept stately homes on your right and the golf course on your left. Glorietta follows the golf course southward, then bends around to the north, with views of the marina behind the golf course. Watch for wayward golf balls here.

As Glorietta Boulevard bends to the west and San Luis Rey intersects (2.4), look for a sidewalk bike trail that begins along the south side of Glorietta Boulevard. This begins the Silver Strand Bikeway, a rail trail that extends 10 miles to Chula Vista. It is part of the Bayshore Bikeway, a bike route that encircles San Diego Bay (see Option 2). We suggest riding either all or a portion of the Silver Strand, formerly a rail bed originally built by the Coronado Railroad Company, then part of Southern Pacific who abandoned the right of way in 1977. It first passes the Coronado Tennis Center. The trail is now along Pomona Avenue. On your left are boats bobbing in picturesque Glorietta Bay at Coronado Yacht Club and Glorietta Bay Marina. You can even rent a boat at the marina. As you round the first bend you'll notice the historic 1887 on the Bluewater Boathouse seafood restaurant.

When Pomona Avenue intersects with Orange Avenue, our route follows a very scenic 1-mile detour to see the Hotel Del Coronado and the ocean, and to find some great dining options. Cross Pomona Avenue at the light, then cross Orange Avenue at the signaled crosswalk. Ride down the sidewalk to the left, then to the right along Avenida del Sol as the Hotel Del Coronado property is on the right. Just before the cul de sac, a short but extremely sweet multi-use trail begins on the right (3.0). It runs along a beautiful ocean beach with the Hotel Del on the right. Their famed Sunday brunch is close to $100. Or just have a fine luncheon. The trail ends at Rh Dana Place (3.4). To the left is a continuation of the

The short, crowded trail in front of the Hotel Del Coronado is a highlight of the ride

beautiful beach along Ocean Boulevard. Unfortunately local residents blocked a plan to extend the promenade along the beach, afraid of it turning into Pacific Beach. Across Orange Ave are several restaurant choices, including popular Miguel's Cocina. Our route returns the same way via the Hotel Del scenic trail. You can also take a shortcut down Orange Avenue instead.

Back on the Silver Strand trail heading south, high-rise condos appear on the right. To the left is a delightful view of the marina and across the bay to the San Diego skyline. The view diminishes as you pass several civic buildings, and reappears beyond Glorietta Bay Park (with restrooms) (4.6), and then is lost again behind the off-limits U.S. Navy Amphibious Base, which requires you to cross several of its signaled entrances. Your view improves at the end of the base, where you skirt the fenced Least Tern Preserve on the bay side (5.3). An unpaved trail that is open to bikes, entitled

Bridge to Discovery, parallels the paved trail through this area, which contains viewing platforms with interpretive signs that overlook the bay and preserve.

To the west here across Hwy 75 are sand dunes that, until you reach Silver Strand State Park, are on military property that is closed to the public. Although your senses may be disturbed by the adjacent four lane highway that parallels the Bikeway, look across at the dunes and at times see the open ocean, which may be chock full of sailboats on windy days. Out to sea are San Diego's Point Loma Peninsula to the northwest, the coastline of Baja California, Mexico curving around to the southwest, and its Coronado Islands in the foreground.

Across the bay to the northeast are the San Diego skyline and the Coronado Bridge, to the east are Naval shipyards, Chula Vista with Tecate Peak beyond, and to the southeast is Imperial Beach at the head of the bay. The sand dunes were created by wind, and this can be a very windy peninsula. You may want to do a test by riding in the opposite direction to gauge what your return ride will be like before going too much farther (e-bike edge). Pass Fiddlers Cove Marina and RV Park for military personnel (6.5), and the Silver Strand military housing development.

Long wide open stretches make the Silver Strand Bikeway a great trail for a scenic workout

Silver Strand State Beach begins just past this development (7.4). Those with mountain bikes should turn left into a paved parking area/access road immediately after the development ends. Proceed to a trailhead and onto a gravel and sand bike trail. Those with road bikes can use a signed entrance 0.3 mile farther south via a paved path through a break in the fence that leads to restrooms. The flat mountain bike trail runs east through a field of coastal sage to reach the shore of San Diego Bay, which is unfenced here, and a highlight of our ride (7.6). The trail bends to the right and provides a short, lovely bayside pedal. It turns back to the southwest and becomes paved as it follows Crown Cove (8.0), meets the paved park entry path at the restrooms, then winds along the bay through the park (8.5). Another dining option is available if you continue on the park bike trail until it ends at the entrance to Loews Coronado Resort, which contains several restaurants and offers a weekend breakfast buffet. The water on the bay side of the peninsula is warmer and calmer than the ocean side, providing an option for swimming.

Three pedestrian tunnels connect the bay side with the ocean side of the park. Walk your bike through the third, or southern-most tunnel which leads to the beachfront parking lots. Explore up and down this beautiful stretch of ocean beach by riding through the parking lots. This is a great place to lock your bike and take in a beach walk or a picnic. At the ocean side of the middle pedestrian tunnel is the main park facility that contains showers, restrooms, phones, and a refreshment stand, open seasonally. At the north end of the park is a popular parking lot style beachfront RV campground with electric and water hookups. Return via any of the tunnels and make your way back to the Silver Strand Bikeway (about 9.5). Return to the ride start without repeating the Hotel Del detour for a total ride of about 16 miles. Or, continue south from here, as described in Options 1 and 2 (e-bike edge).

Option 1: Complete the Rail Trail *Distance including Option 1: 21– 27 miles*

From Silver Strand State Beach, return to the Bikeway (approx. mile 9.5) and continue southward. The trail passes the Coronado Cays development and emerges next to scenic salt marshes (11.2). The southern end of San Diego Bay has been preserved as part of the San Diego National Wildlife Refuge. An estimated 90 percent of submerged lands, intertidal mudflats, salt marshes, and eel grass beds were eliminated by dredging in San Diego Bay. The 3,940-acre South Bay Refuge preserves and restores the remaining 10 percent of this habitat that is necessary for the survival of the bay's thousands of migrating and resident shorebirds and waterfowl, including many endangered species. This is a beautiful stretch of trail with great bird watching opportunities. The trail turns eastward away from the road (12.7), and the remaining 2.1 trail miles run between the mudflats at the head of the bay and a residential area (13.0-13.8). Option 1A   Before the first homes is a path labeled "Ecoroute" leading to a Class II/III signed route to the interesting Imperial Beach waterfront district and Tijuana River Wildlife Refuge. *See map inset for details.*

Our SD7 path passes the north ends of 7th, 8th, 12th and 13th Streets, location of popular cyclists' meeting place of Trident Coffee and 2Wheels Bicycle Boutique. SD7 continues next to mudflats and salt mining activity, crossing a couple of low, restored railroad bridges, ending at Main St and Frontage Rd near Swiss Park in Chula Vista, just west of I-5 (14.8). A paved path here leads south to Palm Dr in 0.75 mile. For the best riding and most scenic option, return the same way on the Silver Strand trail for a total ride of about 27 miles. Or, to do a loop, continue around the bay via Option 2 and take the ferry back.

Option 2: Bayshore Bikeway—East Bay   *Status: sandag.org/bayshorebikeway*

Complete the 26-mile loop around San Diego Bay by following the Bayshore Bikeway signs through Chula Vista, National City and San Diego, utilizing the Coronado ferry to return from downtown San Diego. You can also shorten the distance by hopping on the Trolley train's Blue Line at several locales. As of 2021 projects are still ongoing to complete the circuit. Until then, expect a mixture of Class I, II and III bike routes. The current Class II section through industrial zones in south San Diego is best done on weekends with less worker traffic. And, due to the urban nature of the segments from Imperial Beach through south San Diego, it is best to ride with a friend.

Upon exiting the Bikeway (0.0) head left, following Bayshore Bikeway signs along low-traffic Frontage Road, or when the Class I path is built here use that. Curve left onto Stella St, down a small hill to Bay Blvd. Turn right, and reach Palomar St (0.8), where your first Trolley stop is up the hill past I-5. A Class I path begins along the west side of Bay Blvd. It separates from Bay Blvd and becomes isolated when the road climbs a hill to meet L St. Turn left onto the Class II Marina Pkwy/J St sidepath (2.1) instead of the path straight ahead that just leads to H St and a Trolley stop. *A Class I path is planned to start to the left here, parallel to Marina Pkwy, through the redeveloping Chula Vista Marina District, meeting the existing path at E St.* As Marina Pkwy bends to the right you can opt to go left on Marina Way and explore a nice marina-side park. Continue on Marina Pkwy to Sandpiper Way and turn left onto the left sidepath. Pass the popular Galley restaurant and a neat wind sculpture. Follow the sidepath along the marina through lovely Bayside Park (restrooms). Ride to the end of a concrete pier, taking in views across the bay and to downtown San Diego. The park path bends to the right and emerges at the end of G St. Take G St to the northeast, then follow Bikeway signs to the left down Marina Pkwy and to the right down F St/Lagoon Dr to Bay Blvd. Go left on Bay Blvd via the sidewalk or bike lane, to E St (4.1). To the left is the new Costa Vista RV Resort and the Living Coast Discovery Center (enviro ed, $16). To the right across I-5 is a Trolley stop and lots of restaurants. Zorba's Greek buffet is 0.7 mile away at D and Broadway. *Chula Vista's massive waterfront redevelopment will include an extension of E Street to a new hotel complex and the new Harbor Park that will have waterfront paths.*

Carefully cross to the west side of Bay Blvd to a Class I path that skirts the edge of Sweetwater Marsh Wildlife Refuge, weaves its way under freeway overpasses, crosses Sweetwater River, and intersects the north side of Class I Sweetwater Bikeway (5.0). From here the continuation of Bayshore Bikeway to National City's Pier 32 Marina is 0.4 mile to the right (west) and Plaza Bonita Center is 2.3 miles to the east (Opt 2A). Emerge from the path onto 32nd St, with the al fresco Waterfront Grill on the left. The sidepath to the right along Marina Way leads to a small historic railcar park. The Bayshore Bikeway route continues west on 32nd, taking the next right onto Class II Tidelands Ave near the Port of San Diego, which tends to have lots of big rigs parked alongside it. At 1/4 mile past 19th St take the crosswalk to the west side to a Class IV cycletrack, becoming a Class I path and emerging along Harbor Dr. At 8th St next to Naval Base San Diego the path crosses to the east side of Harbor Dr with a light, then currently ends at San Diego's 32nd St (7.8). A Class I path is planned to continue to Park Blvd downtown, but has not begun as of this writing in early 2021.

Class II riding along Harbor Dr through industrial San Diego follows. Ride past giant shipyard cranes, a Chevron facility, and under the Coronado Bridge approach (no bikes on bridge). Conditions of roads and Class II lanes vary from good to bad, and sometimes you'll pass parked cars. At Park Blvd and Petco Park (10.1), you've met the south end of SD4. You can cycle the MLK Rail Trail to the right, or go left, across Harbor at the light onto Park to a path to the waterfront and a bayside path to Coronado ferry stops at the Convention Center or Broadway Pier (11.4). If you took the Trolley Blue Line, get off at 12th & Imperial. Cross the tracks at 5th Ave, then double back to Park for a final waterfront ride; or get off at America Plaza near Santa Fe Depot.

Option 2A: Sweetwater Bikeway *2.3 miles each way, easy +Options. Caution: Isolated*
Class I Sweetwater River Bikeway follows the north bank of the channelized river next to westbound lanes of noisy South Bay Freeway (SR 54), with scattered commercial areas beyond. The channel is sloped and graded, but the portion closest to the ocean has tidal water in it, while riparian vegetation is found farther upstream. It crosses under eastbound lanes of the 54 Freeway (mile 1.5), then I-805 (2.0), emerging in a park along Plaza Bonita Rd opposite Plaza Bonita Mall, with restaurants (2.3). Option: The trail now continues next to Plaza Bonita Rd, tunnels under it, then turns hard right to reach Bonita Rd. At that turn begins a series of pretty dirt paths that pass through Bonita (restaurants) and reaches scenic Sweetwater Summit Park and RV campground atop a significant hill (9.0). It makes for a nice Camp 'n Ride.

Option 3: Combine with the San Diego Harbor Tour Ride
If you have completed the loop around the bay, you will need to take the ped/bike ferry back from downtown San Diego as described in Option 2. However, if you are in Coronado and want a fun adventure, take this hourly ferry from the Coronado Ferry Landing across to the Broadway Pier or Convention Center in downtown San Diego. Ride along the scenic, interesting, but often-crowded sidewalk pathways to the north and south from here, with options to ride on the MLK rail trail through downtown to the Gaslamp Quarter, or to Balboa Park, the Point Loma Peninsula, and more. See the San Diego Harbor Tour ride (SD4) for details.

Los Peñasquitos Canyon Preserve MTB SD8

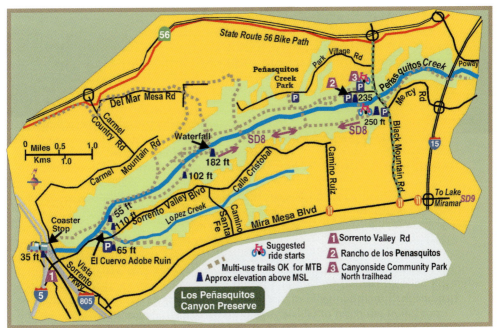

The 3,700-acre Los Peñasquitos Canyon Preserve is rich in ecological diversity; a delightful riparian strip of live oak, sycamore, willow, and grasslands along Peñasquitos Creek complete with small waterfalls and surrounding hillsides of coastal sage scrub habitat. The preserve extends from past the I-15 Freeway in the northeast to the I-5 and I-805 interchange to the southwest. Although mostly surrounded by development, the visitor is frequently ensconced solely by the serenity of this Southern California parkland. A historic adobe ranch house built in 1823 and expanded in the 1860s by the recipients of the first Mexican land grant in San Diego County, Rancho de los Peñasquitos, is at the northeast end of the park. The building and site comprise a National Historic and Archaeological District, and weekend tours are offered. The ruins of the El Cuervo Adobe are at the southwest end of the park.

The preserve can be entered from either end. The surrounding habitat seems to be more preserved at the northeast end, and more disturbed at the southwest end from overgrazing. Parallel trails run the length of the canyon with several stream crossings connecting them along the way, some more practical than others for cyclists. The south trail is the original, a fire road running closest to the creek mostly through the riparian habitat. The north trail is more exposed but also skirts some wetlands. A nice 6 or 7-mile ride involves a cycle from the northeast trailheads to the waterfalls. Numerous other rides are possible in this fabulous novice-level mountain biking park, with up to 13-mile rides possible.

For a funfilled day, cycle here in the morning, load your bikes and drive to lunch along Mira Mesa Blvd, then drive to nearby scenic Lake Miramar (SD9), riding around it once or possibly twice, depending on the lunch calories you consumed.

Tunes: Waterfall by Electric Light Orchestra; Wildfire by Michael Murphy
Eats: Picnic at the waterfall

Distance: About 7 miles round trip for the South Trail, 6 miles for North Trail. Time: 1–1.5 hours. Longer and shorter options available.

Route & Bike: Easy to moderate sections as described. MTB. No bikes on singletrack as signed. Class 1 and 2 e-bikes allowed; e-bike edge for hills. Surface varies from smooth packed dirt to sand, gravel, rocks, and seasonal mud with escape routes to avoid it. Extreme novices may have difficulty with some of the surfaces. Some areas are flat, others have gradual grades and small hills. Elevation gain of about 200 feet from west to east end of south trail. Our ride from the northeast trailhead encounters an elevation gain of about 70 feet on the return.

Seasons: All. Best on sunny, mild, weekday after dry spell. Spring brings wildflowers.

Facilities: Porta-potties at trailheads. Bring sufficient water.

Knocks & Hazards: Trails can get crowded. Rattlesnakes in season. Mountain lion country (child attacked in 2019). Ticks may carry tularemia here. Poison oak. Low lying portions of trails have muddy sections in winter. Trails closed during rainy periods and 1 to 2 sunny days after rain stops. Trailhead break-ins. Some of the stream crossings may not be feasible depending on water level in creek.

Bike 'n Brunch: None near trail. Take the ample bike lane on hilly Black Mountain Road south 1.5 miles to restaurants at Mira Mesa Blvd.

Further Info: Friends of Los Peñasquitos Canyon Preserve: penasquitos.org. San Diego County Parks: sdparks.org. County park rangers (most responsive to calls): 858.484.7504. City park rangers (also have jurisdiction in this park): 858.538.8066. A park host resides at the trailhead at Black Mountain Road and Mercy Street. See mountainlion.org/portalprotectstaysafe.php for info about mountain lion safety. The one attack occurred midday near the waterfall when a cougar attacked a child in a group, but thankfully the father was able to fight off the animal in time. Though that was a rare incident, be alert.

Access: Northeast end: From I-15 exit Mercy Road westbound and drive to Black Mountain Rd. Options are: 1) Directly across Black Mountain Rd is the main preserve parking area and equestrian staging area with a live-in park host ($3 fee); this is the trailhead for our south trail ride. 2) Turn right from Mercy Rd on Black Mountain and make the first left into Canyonside Community Park. Drive past the ball fields to the free parking lot. A sign en route to the ranch house stream crossing (to the south trail) describes the trail system. The north trail begins near the northwest corner of the lot. Another free lot farther along is for visitors to the historic Los Peñasquitos Ranch House. From CA56 you can exit on Black Mountain southbound to the park.

Southwest end: From I-5 exit Sorrento Valley Rd or from I-805 exit Vista Sorrento Parkway. From either road, head north and then turn right (east) on Sorrento Valley Blvd. In about 1.5 miles when you see an open space area, look for the preserve entrance on the right, where there is a large free parking lot equipped with a porta-potty. This lot is more isolated than the northeast lots. Head north on the trail with the option of exploring the dead-end Lopez Canyon Trail. The main trail goes to the left under the roadway, and then requires going up and over a pretty steep 65-foot hill to get down to the streamside. There are also other entry points and parking as shown on the map. Rail 'n Ride: The Sorrento Valley Coaster station is just west of I-5. From the station, ride south 0.1 mile on Sorrento Valley Rd and east 1.2 miles up the gradual hill on Sorrento Valley Blvd to the southwest trailhead.

The Ride: South Trail: From the pay lot across from Mercy Rd, head west on the wide double track trail. Come to the ranch house crossing, which is one of the better crossings with an actual small bridge to assist. Take this across to visit the historic Rancho or to cycle on the north trail. Otherwise continue on the south trail that is sometimes near the stream with its riparian vegetation, and also goes through grassy meadows.

The road surface condition varies as you proceed, from smooth compacted dirt and gravel to some rocky areas, and some muddy areas where alternate routes are available on adjacent higher ground. Subsequent optional stream crossings are not quite as good as the first. Stop and listen to the sounds of acorn woodpeckers in the trees. At about 3 miles, the road ascends a hill and at the summit are bike racks and hitching posts, where you can lock up and walk down a short path to the "waterfall," a place where the creek tumbles down between rocks in a lovely rocky canyon. This is a good destination and turnaround point for a 7-mile round trip ride. As you can see from the vantage point atop the hill if you continue, you will be going down the other side of the slope and farther down canyon, so gauge your energy if you'd like a longer ride.

North Trail Option: From the ballfield lot's northwest corner take the wide compact gravel path that is below homes and above wetlands. It drops down (0.5) closer to the creek, away from civilization, and becomes rocky or sandy in spots. Watch for a path (~2.7) signed "Waterfall" that leads left to the park's cascade (3.0). Return the same way, or from the prior junction go left to explore more of the park.

Spring greenery along north trail en route to waterfall.

Lake Miramar Loop SD9

There is something very satisfying about a paved loop trail around a lake, and the mostly flat, 5-mile Lake Miramar loop is a very popular place for locals to jog, walk, skate, or bike. Auto traffic is allowed along two-thirds of the trail, but it is of the sporadic slow-moving park goer variety, with the same speed limit (15 mph) as bikes. Novice mountain bike trails are also available to extend the riding. The viewscape in some areas is to the west over the developed coastal plain, and on the clearest of days, all the way out to the ocean.

Popular loop ride around the fingers of Lake Miramar

The trail follows the fingers of the lake that is lined with pine, eucalyptus, and mixed deciduous trees, various palms, reeds and grasses, while the surrounding hills preserve a more natural coastal sage scrub ecosystem. This variation of ecosystems attracts a litany of Southern California birds, from shore birds around the lake to those that live in the brush. Aqueducts from the Colorado River and Northern California provide the reservoir's water that is treated in the large adjacent plant for domestic use. Fishing is allowed in the lake but not swimming. Make sure to have your vehicle out of the park's lots before they lock the gates at the posted time that varies by season, and typically is around sunset.

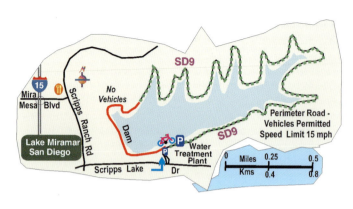

Tunes: Roundabout by Yes
Hold On by Tom Waits
Hard Sun by Eddie Veder
Eats: Picnic by the lake

Distance: 5-mile loop. Time: 45 minutes.
Route & Bike: Easy. Either Class I or Class I/III paved roadway with limited traffic depending on day. Any bike. Optional adjacent mountain bike trails. Flat with some gentle inclines.

Cycling across the dam

Seasons: All. Best any sunny, mild day.
Knocks & Hazards: Avoid hot summer days, clueless peds (though the road is wide), some vehicles, and snakes (including rattlesnakes) that like to lie on the roadway in warmer months.
Further Info: sandiego.gov/reservoirs-lakes/miramar-reservoir/ Phone 619.465.3474.

Access: From I-15 in the Scripps Ranch area, exit on Mira Mesa Blvd eastbound, turn right on Scripps Ranch Blvd and left on Scripps Lake Drive to the reservoir entrance on the left.

The Ride: Just park, hop on your bike, and ride around the loop! Either ride counter-clockwise to coincide with the mile markers, or ride clockwise to be closer to the lake. It is a very pleasant, mostly level ride that goes in and out of the fingers of the lake. Signs request that trail users keep far to the right except to pass. Good luck with that! Although cars are allowed, the western mile segment of the trail that includes the dam is bike/ped only. As the trail nears the dam, there is a chain link fence first on both sides, and then along the dam itself on the lake side. This is where the vistas open up over the northern portion of San Diego, and just about out to sea. Before you know it you are back at your vehicle after this easy ride, so why not take another lap? Novice mountain bikers may enjoy riding on the parallel dirt trail.

Marian Bear Memorial Park SD10 and Rose Canyon SD11 Riparian MTB Adventures ⭐2

Details: 5–7 miles each park, easy novice MTB; portions of SD10 advanced novice

These two long and narrow open space parks provide an opportunity for a fun and easy mountain bike adventure close to central San Diego. As shown on the San Diego County map, they are situated roughly between I-5 and I-805, separated by the 52 Freeway. Marian Bear Memorial Park (SD10) is more lush and scenic, while Rose Canyon Open Space (SD11) is easier to ride and navigate.

Access: Both parks can be accessed from the north end of Santa Fe Road. From I-5 southbound take the Garnet/Balboa exit that leads into Mission Bay Drive. Turn left on Damon and left on Santa Fe to its end. North on I-5, exit on Garnet, then cross Garnet to Santa Fe Road. Santa Fe ends 2.25 miles north of Garnet, and the Class I paved Rose Canyon Bike Path continues 1.1 miles from there, connecting to La Jolla Colony Drive. (The path will also run south to N. Mission Bay Dr by late 2021). Near the end of Santa Fe Rd is Santa Fe RV Park that makes a good Camp 'n Ride home base for these rides. Park as close to the end of Santa Fe Road as allowed. This is the best trailhead for SD11, but a better option for SD10 if you're not doing a Camp 'n Ride is the following: From the 52 Freeway, exit Regents Rd or Genesee Ave and go south to the free parking lots that provide direct access to the main trail. For trail maps see sandiego.gov/parks-and-recreation/; also posted on our website.

The Ride: From the end of Santa Fe Road, cycle up the Rose Canyon Bike Path. For Marian Bear Park, look for a gate and trail down to the train tracks. CAREFULLY cross the very active rail tracks at the 258 marker, go back to the right on the dirt road, and circle left riding across the stream to join the trail network. This park contains 467 acres in San Clemente Canyon and preserves a vibrant riparian ecosystem filled with sycamores, oaks, and willows. Novices may have some difficulty in places depending on the trails they end up on, but one can always walk those sections. Officially MTB's are allowed only on maintenance roads, which are the easiest paths through

A Pleasant cycle in the urban oasis of Rose Canyon

the canyon, roughly parallel to the stream. Stream crossings may be fairly dry in summer to sometimes impassable in winter, but mostly somewhere in between. The main trail ends just south of the I-805 Freeway, and your ride will be about 6.5 miles round trip.

For Rose Canyon Open Space (SD11), cycle the entire length of the Rose Canyon Bike Path to La Jolla Colony Drive. Ride on the sidewalk to the right, and look for a dirt path that veers off down an incline toward the railroad tracks. CAREFULLY cross the active tracks at the 257 marker and cruise down the incline to the obvious wide path. The route to the right leads down to the stream area with some bridges to aid in crossing through the thick riparian zone. You may be turned back sooner or later by high water in areas that do not have bridges to assist.

The route to the left eventually brings you to busy Genesee Avenue. We recommend turning around at this point for a ride of just under 5 miles, but if you want more riding, cycle to the left up the Genesee sidewalk, then cross Genesee at the light that services the University High School entrance. Parking is allowed there when school is out. A rougher trail to the left of the high school entrance leads down next to the stream and the train tracks.

Mission Trails Regional Park— Mountain and Road Bike Combo SD12

Mission Trails Regional Park is a wonderful cross section of coastal California, including riparian woodland along the San Diego River, coastal scrub, oak woodland, and desert chaparral. Located just 12 miles northeast of downtown, mountain bikers of all levels appreciate this 6,100-acre park, one of the largest urban parks in the U.S. An impressive visitor's center overlooks the beautiful wildlands and serves as a starting point. Looking down at Mission Gorge there is no evidence of civilization, pretty amazing for being in the middle of the San Diego metro area. Your ride consists of a scenic riverside paved Class I trail along 2 miles of the San Diego River through a narrow

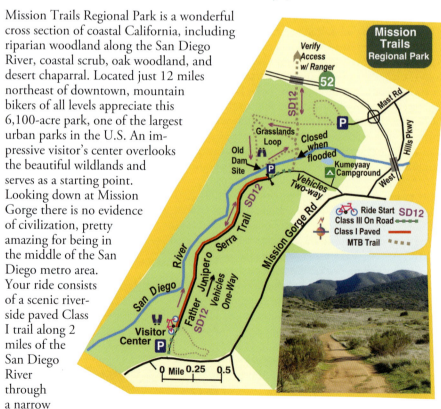

gorge, and 4+ miles of novice mountain bike trail, with many more miles available as options at more advanced levels. The western portion of the park has more steep and technical terrain, whereas the eastern part consists of rolling grasslands with some easy doubletrack near Oak Canyon.

Tunes: Happy Trails by Roy Rogers & Dale Evans; In-A-Gadda-Da-Vida by Iron Butterfly
Eats: Picnic at the Old Dam Site.

Distance: 4 miles (paved trail only) to 8 miles (paved trail plus mountain biking). Time: 1–1.5 hours.
Route & Bike: Moderate, due to rolling hills. Paved Class I and II for any bike. Optional 4 miles doubletrack sand and gravel for MTB. Allowed Class 1 & 2 e-bikes will help with the main hill and e-MTB's will open up more options.
Seasons: All. Best on sunny, mild, uncrowded winter weekday.
Facilities: Restrooms and water at visitor's center; restrooms at Old Dam Site.
Knocks & Hazards: Class I shared with peds. Mountain bike portion closed when San Diego River floods because of low bridge. Rattlesnakes, most active April–June. This is mountain lion habitat but they are rarely seen. Active coyotes. Watch speed on hills. Speed limit 10 mph on Class I trail. Can be hot in summer. Problem with trailhead break-ins at all lots, so do not leave valuables in car.
Camp 'n Ride: Kumeyaay Lake Campground is within the park. Tents & RV's but no hookups, open weekends. Picnic on weekdays. Bathrooms and showers on site.
Rent 'n Ride/Bike 'n Brunch: No rentals in park vicinity. Outside the east entrance on Mission Gorge Rd are a few restaurants accessible via sidewalk, and many more about 2 miles east.
Further Info: Check for trail conditions and camp reservations at www.mtrp.org.

Access: From I-8 east of San Diego take Mission Gorge Road northeast for 4.2 miles. After passing Jackson Drive, turn left into the park and access the visitor's center for trail information and maps. Do not park inside the gate of the visitor's center if you will be returning after closing time. There is on-street parking outside the gate. Many people park at the north end of the park as well. No fees.

The Ride: Begin from near the visitor's center on the paved park road, Father Junipero Serra Trail, that is divided into two lanes by a high curb. The right side is one way for vehicles heading north, with speed limit 15 mph and many speed bumps. The left side of the road is designated two-way for bikes and pedestrians, with a speed limit of 10 mph, and no speed bumps. It begins with a steady descent to a level just above the San Diego River, which is mostly a large stream at this point. Since it drains a watershed of 440 square miles it is rarely dry. The rich riparian habitat next to the river supports abundant bird life, and several interpretive signs along the way explain many of the natural and cultural features of the area. Hiking trails emanate from both sides of the road along the way, and the Oak Grove Loop near the visitor's center allows bikes.

The Class I trail climbs gradually above the river and curves a bit to give even more perspective to this beautiful natural valley.

The paved though hilly Father Junipera Serra Road through the beautiful canyon has a separated bike lane

It ends in about 1.8 miles at the parking area for the Old Mission Dam, a rock and concrete structure that once dammed the river. You can detour to the parking lot and walk your bike down to the dam, or continue on the park road.

In about 0.3 mile on the left is the obvious gated trailhead for Grasslands Crossing, which is mountain bike territory. Cruise down the incline to the shallow bridge over the San Diego River (closed during high water), through beautiful riparian habitat along a gravel path, then up the other side to emerge in hilly grasslands. Civilization rears its ugly head at this time with the 52 Freeway slicing through the viewscape, and various communication towers and power lines also in view. It is still a pleasant area, with about 2 miles of hilly non-technical double track trails to pedal.

The prettiest area is that closest to the hills to the west. When we rode it, civilization disappeared and we witnessed coyotes engaged in what seemed like a territory dispute. The trail map indicates where bikes are allowed, and signs also reinforce the designation of the hike-only trails. Make sure to stop at the overlook for the Old Mission Dam. A doubletrack fire road also extends under SR 52, up a gradual incline into a scrubby, civilization-free valley. Despite the notation on the park map of "No Access North of Hwy 52," the rangers told us that it's fine to ride there unless there are signs prohibiting it. The trails lead toward military property, however, so stay down in the valley and avoid anything that looks like a military installation. We rode up a couple of miles into the valley. Return the same way.

Lake Murray   SD13

Details: 6.4 miles out and back, easy, paved, Class I, any bike.

The Lake Murray reservoir is part of the huge Mission Trails Regional Park, although in a separate section of the park southeast of ride SD12. A wide, flat paved Class I trail runs for 3.2 miles next to the lake, but does not complete the loop as the south end is off limits. This is a very popular trail with local joggers, families, and casual cyclists, so go on off-peak times to avoid an obstacle course, and obey the 10 mph speed limit. The lake is very park-like and pleasant, surrounded by a coastal sage ecosystem. Spring wildflower blooms can be splendid, as seen in this April photo. See the map for nearby places to eat.

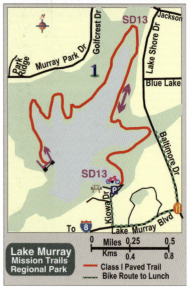

Access: From I-8 east of San Diego exit on Lake Murray Drive North and in about a half-mile turn left on Kiowa Drive to the parking lot. The gates close at sunset. No fees. Further Info: mtrp.org/lake-murray/. Phone 619.465.3474.

Laguna Mountains

One of our favorite areas in Southern California is Laguna Mountain Recreation Area in Cleveland National Forest, south of the quaint town of Julian in the Peninsular Range Mountains east of San Diego that reach up to 6,400 feet elevation. The Pacific Crest Trail (PCT) hugs the rim of a steep 4,000-foot high escarpment overlooking the vast Colorado Desert of Anza-Borrego State Park and the Salton Sea beyond, which lies below sea level. This is a wonderful place to watch the sunrise and take spectacular day hikes. Although the scenic PCT and rim-side trails are off limits to bikes, there are enough trails open to MTB's to make the area one of the premier MTB destinations for San Diegans. It is a great day or weekend trip from San Diego as you can combine a fun MTB ride, any number of amazingly scenic hikes, and an après ride excursion to the beautiful old timey town of Julian, famous for its apple pies.

Laguna Mountain MTB 'n Hike   LM1

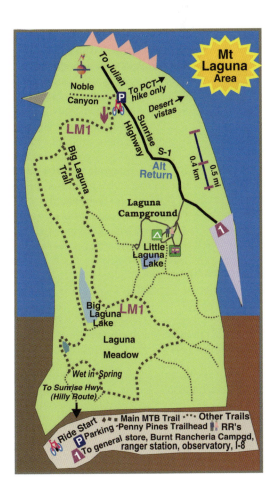

The mountain bike trail described here does not offer panoramic vistas except via a short optional return ride along Sunrise Highway. However, it does provide an exhilarating journey through the vanilla/butterscotch-scented Jeffrey and ponderosa pine forests with black oaks, sprawling meadows, and pretty ephemeral lakes that typically fill with water by early winter and dry up by midsummer.

In April and May, wildflowers such as lavender mountain phacelia, bright baby blue eyes, and yellow violets can be abundant. Bird sightings may include Steller's jay, mountain bluebird, chickadees, finches, various hawks and woodpeckers, and even golden eagle. Animals are your typical forest dwellers such as squirrel, raccoon, or deer. You may also see a coyote or an elusive bobcat. You probably won't see a cougar, but one might just see you. In summer, cattle graze the meadows, which detracts from the wilderness experience. When winter snows are deep enough, the Laguna Meadow area is the prime cross-country ski area of San Diego County. Thankfully this area was spared from the huge Cedar Fire of 2003 but you will see evidence of it just to the north. After riding you can lock up your bike and hike one of the easy desert-view trails to experience the amazing contrast of ecosystems. End the day with a drive to the lovely town of Julian.

Tunes: Mountain Dance by Dave Grusin; Apple Scruffs by George Harrison.
Eats: Picnic by the lake; apple pie in Julian.

Distance: 7–11 miles. Time: 2+ hours.
Route & Bike: Moderate. Singletrack hardpacked dirt MTB trails. Some rocky areas. Southwest portion can be wet/muddy. MTB skill level: Mostly advanced novice. Hill between trailhead and flat meadow (e-bike edge). Trail elev 5,400–5,600 feet.
Season: April–November, or warm winter day when no snow. Best in late April–May when wildflowers are blooming and lakes are full, or sunny, brisk, late-October day during peak fall foliage when southwest area is dryer.
Knocks & Hazards: Active mountain lion country (best not to ride alone), rattlesnakes, wildfire hazard. Cold/snowy winter storms, and can be hot in summer with sudden thunderstorms. High altitude. Cattle grazing in summer. Hunting areas nearby, but not on trail—consult a forest ranger for details. During wet periods like springtime, southwest area can be soggy.
Facilities/Camp 'n Ride: Water, restrooms at Laguna Campground. Possible water at Penny Pines trailhead. Laguna and Burnt Rancheria Campgrounds are operated by the National Forest Service. Reserve at 1.877.444.6777, 518.885.3639, recreation.gov. Laguna Campground provides direct access to the Big Laguna mountain bike trail while Burnt Rancheria accesses great desert-view hike-only trails. Water spigot at both camp entrances but no hookups or dump stations. For RV's under 30 feet, larger RV's check Julian area.

Access this area via a 1-hour drive from San Diego by taking I-8 about 45 miles east, past Alpine. After the freeway climbs to Laguna Summit at 4,055 feet elevation, exit on S-1, the Sunrise Highway, northbound. This curvy but solid road climbs to over 6,000 feet elevation. Look for an information station and store 6 miles from I-8 (milepost 19.1) where you can learn about the highlights of the area including trails, and buy the required Adventure Pass for parking. The Penny Pines parking area is the trailhead for the ride, a couple of miles north of Laguna Campground (about 14.3 miles from I-8) at mile marker 27.3. Read the signboards here about the Penny Pines project for the reforestation of the area. Parking Fees: National Forest Service Adventure Pass: $5/day, $30/year, or use federal parks pass.

The Ride: Start cycling on the Noble Canyon Trail, accessed from the west side of the road. After 0.1 mile, turn left onto the Big Laguna Trail. Note that trail nomenclature in this area can be confusing because trail names and offshoots are mostly either Big Laguna or Big Laguna Spur. Follow the trail up a hill through a thick pine forest. You may feel the altitude a bit here, but the climbing is soon over with. As the trail bends to the south and expansive Laguna Meadow begins to come into view at mile 1, a trail junction to the right is labeled Big Laguna Trail to Sunset Trail. This is the more fun and adventurous option to enjoy the downhill stretch into the meadow (west option).

The trail straight ahead (east option) is shorter but with more rocks and roots to contend with. During the wet spring season, you may want to stick with this drier option. It continues downhill to Big Laguna Lake (2.1) where we love to picnic on the large lakeside boulders. It then bends around to the left past Little Laguna Lake (3.0) and a spur extends to Laguna Campground (3.4). Return the same way for a 6.8-mile ride, or continue through the campground and turn left onto scenic Sunrise Highway for a much easier 5-mile loop ride. See the west option for more detail on Sunrise Highway.

If conditions permit, take the trail to the right (west option—Big Laguna to Sunset Trail) and cruise down the sweet sandy singletrack into the meadow, reaching the ephemeral Big Laguna Lake (2.3). If the terrain is very dry, you may be able to cross over the meadow on the south side of the lake to shorten your ride. Otherwise, continue on the trail that curves to the right, and around a berm atop a small pretty pond (3.2). Cross a stream that drains the meadow, which can either be dry or have a bit of water flowing through it. On the other side of the stream the trail continues but is grassy and bumpy. Keep hugging the perimeter of the meadow, staying out of fenced areas.

Big Laguna Trail approaching Big Laguna Lake

During the wet season things may get pretty soggy in these parts. At one point you may have to carry your bikes across a 3-foot wide concrete berm for about 12 feet to avoid the muck. In general, keep following the perimeter of the meadow and Big Laguna Trail signs, rather than going off in other directions as the Big Laguna Trail also does. You will eventually start heading north again, across another shallow seasonal stream, through the forest, over some rocky areas, and a potpourri of trail conditions including soft meadow.

When you come to a junction marked by a small arched bridge on the right (around mile 6), this is a decision point. You can continue straight on the trail, across a meadow, and head left to reach the path along the east side of Big Laguna Lake and over the hill to the Penny Pines trailhead for a 9-mile ride. Or, you can take the trail to the right to head toward Laguna Campground where there are facilities and a shorter, very scenic on-road option for your return. This trail gives you some nice easy single track, passes Little Laguna Lake, turns right after leaving the forest, and leads along the Laguna Campground fence to the left, entering between Sites 14 and 15 of Meadow Loop (6.5).

From the campground, either return to the Big Laguna Lake area via a path from the group camp area to the north, and return to Penny Pines that way for a ride of about 10.5 miles, or make your way to Sunrise Highway for a much quicker and easier return for an 8-mile ride. The road is shared with sporadic traffic, but it is only a 10-minute cycle back to the trailhead along one of its most scenic stretches. There are a couple of small hills, as well as pullouts to stop and take in the amazing views down into the desert below. Despite the sporadic traffic, keep to the right and ride single file because vehicles can appear suddenly.

Après Ride Hike: After returning to your car, load your bike and drive to one of the following trailheads, then walk eastward to take in the breathtaking views of the desert below to the east. Garnet Peak is a wonderful 2.4-mile round trip hike with 500-foot elevation gain to the summit. Park on the shoulder of Sunrise Highway at mile 27.8. The view encompasses the amazing contrast of the Anza-Borrego Desert below to the forest and chaparral at the higher elevations. For an easier stroll, Kwaaymii Point is a 1-mile round trip walk along the cliff-hugging Old Sunrise Highway roadbed. Park at Pioneer Mail trailhead at mile 29.3 or the Kwaaymii Point trailhead down Kwaaymii Place at mile 30.3. The PCT intersects both of these trails, following the ridge and providing spectacular vistas. Or, just walk east from the Penny Pines trailhead, following the sign to Garnet Peak, 2.2 miles north from there on the PCT. Enjoy the fabulous desert vista from the chaparral-covered ridge while marveling at how well this area has recovered from the 2003 fire.

Après Ride Pie: To get to Julian, drive north on beautiful Sunrise Highway about 10 miles from Penny Pines, then turn right on Highway 79 for 6 miles. The old gold-mining town, now a tourist destination with a potpourri of restaurants, shops, and B&B's, is fun to explore. Famous for its local apple pies, Julian's pie apples now come mostly from Washington. On our most recent trips there, Apple Alley made an excellent caramel pecan apple pie! You can also get on your bikes and explore this small town and some of the back roads around it, or take a ride on a horse and buggy. Return to San Diego via Highway 79 south to I-8 west.

View from Sunrise Hwy (near LM1) of Anza-Borrego State Park thousands of feet below. Your optional return along the roadway will yield spectacular vistas.

7. Kern County and the San Joaquin Valley

Imagine a vast valley of sprawling grasslands with a million Tule elk and pronghorn antelope roaming and grazing, while predators such as grizzly bears and mountain lions thrive on the bounteous game. Countless shore and sea birds gather around the biologically diverse wetlands and the lakes created by runoff from the winter rains and spring snowmelt from the surrounding mountains. Spring also brings an explosion of wildflowers across the plain, coloring the hills like an Impressionist painting.

That is what the Central Valley of California was like before the mid-1800s, when the land was planted and developed and the rivers were diverted for irrigation and channelized for flood control, turning it into one of the most productive agricultural areas in the world. Sadly, the development drained the lakes and the Tule elk were hunted to near extinction. The few remaining wetlands are now only preserved in a handful of wildlife refuges.

The San Joaquin Valley is the portion of California's Central Valley that is south of the Sacramento River delta. The valley has also become a huge oil producer that is prone to frequent air quality issues from automobiles, agricultural chemicals, and industry. The area is not a major tourist draw, although it serves as the gateway to surrounding mountain destinations such as Lake Isabella to the south, and Sequoia, Kings Canyon, and Yosemite National Parks farther north.

Southern California is typically considered to contain only Kern County and its largest city of Bakersfield at the southern end of the valley, where a rainshadow effect creates a semi-desert environment. For residents, there is a fabulous Class I recreation trail along the Kern River at Bakersfield, and Carrizo Plain National Monument just to the southwest of the valley gives us a glimpse of what the area was once like. See San Luis Obispo County for that ride.

Climate Data for Bakersfield							(Source WRCC Normals 1961–1990)						
Month	Jan	Feb	Mar	Apr	May	Jun	Jul	Aug	Sep	Oct	Nov	Dec	Totals
Average High °F	56.9	63.9	68.9	75.9	84.6	92.4	98.5	96.6	90.1	80.7	66.8	56.5	77.7
Average Low °F	38.6	42.6	45.8	50.1	57.3	64.0	69.6	68.5	63.5	54.8	44.7	38.3	53.2
Precipitation, inches	0.86	1.06	1.04	0.57	0.20	0.10	0.01	0.09	0.17	0.29	0.70	0.63	5.72

Bakersfield

Bakersfield is the major city in the southern San Joaquin Valley, located about 110 miles from both Fresno to the north and Los Angeles to the south. The city's population is about 369,000 in a metro area of around 840,000. The area is a major oil and gas producer as well as an agricultural center. Oil was discovered around 1900, and the hills to the northeast of town are still blanketed with wells, while oil refineries are mostly closer to downtown, north of the Kern River near the 99 Freeway.

Although not renowned as a vacation destination, there are some places of interest in the city, and it is known for its Basque restaurants. It was also the center of the Bakersfield Sound of country music, born of depression-era refugees from the Oklahoma dust bowl and featuring artists such as Merle Haggard and the Strangers and Buck

Owens and the Buckaroos. They performed in local honkytonks in the 1950s and '60s and their down-to-earth barroom songs with piercing electric guitars influenced other artists that became the harbingers of country rock. Buck Owens' Crystal Palace restaurant and museum captures the feeling of that era.

The Kern River Parkway and Bakersfield BA1

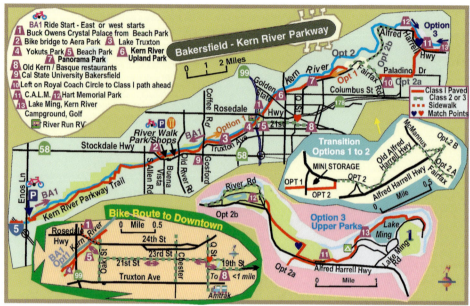

The 165-mile long Kern River flows south out of the southern Sierra Nevada Mountains near Mount Whitney in two forks that join prior to entering the Lake Isabella reservoir. It then flows west, through dramatic Kern Canyon, which is popular with fishermen and whitewater rafters. Once it reaches the San Joaquin Valley the pitch lessens and the river flows gently through Bakersfield. Historically the river drained into a series of sloughs and lakes with no outlet to the ocean except for periods of extremely high water when Tulare Lake would overflow into the SanJoaquin River. In its current incarnation, diversions for irrigation and groundwater recharge ensure that it rarely flows far enough to feed into the now mostly dry lakebeds, and in dryer years it barely even flows through Bakersfield.

The paved Kern River Parkway Trail is an important recreation resource for the southern San Joaquin Valley. It stretches over 20 miles from Bakersfield's industrial facilities in the east, past California State University at Bakersfield (CSUB) and the adjacent River Walk Park and shopping complex, to more remote riparian countryside en route to the vicinity of I-5 to the west. We prefer the western 10 miles between CSUB and I-5, which offers some good wildlife viewing opportunities including roadrunner, egret, quail, coyote, San Joaquin kit fox, and even the occasional bobcat and mountain lion. For your Bike 'n Brunch there are lots of options at the River Walk trailhead.

If you have multiple days to spend here you may want to also try Option 1, the eastern half of the trail, which is more urban and industrial in nature but still provides some pleasant riding through parks along the Kern River. Perhaps the nicest, but separate section of trail to the northeast is a 4.4-mile path (Option 3) through Hart Memorial Park and Lake Ming connected to the main trail via a hilly Class I/II/III route (Option 2). Hart Park is the most prolific birding spot in the region, and Lake Ming is the site of wintering bald eagles and a large population of great egrets. This area is part of the 1,012-acre complex referred to as Kern River County Park.

Tunes: Kern River by Merle Haggard; Down to the River by Buck Owens; Far Away Eyes by Rolling Stones; Act Naturally by Ringo Starr and Buck Owens; Streets of Bakersfield by Dwight Yoakum with Buck Owens

Eats: Encore Steak Sandwich at Crystal Palace.

Distance: 21 miles up and back + options up to 36 additional miles.
   Time: 1.5–2 hours
Route & Bike: Easy to moderate. Paved, Class I, for any bike. Flat except for hills associated with options (e-bike edge).
Seasons: All. Avoid summer heat and smog. Best on sunny mild day in spring or fall.
Facilities: Restrooms and water in major parks along route and several water fountains along trail, but no facilities in western 6–7 miles except possible porta-potty at west trailhead.
Knocks & Hazards: Clueless peds closer to town. Trail gets industrial and more urban in the optional eastern segment (east of SR 99). Lurkers may be present, especially on east trail between Hwy 204 and Manor St, but trail is patrolled by police and is heavily used on weekends. Nighttime use is not recommended there. Emergency call boxes are installed along the route. Intense heat common in summer. Bakersfield has the worst air quality in the U.S. (similar to Los Angeles) so those with sensitive lungs should check the air quality status on line. Tule fog in winter. Rattlesnakes and mountain lions have been seen on trail, especially in the rural western segment. Rafting in Kern River rapids can be dangerous; fatalities are common.
Rent 'n Ride: Finish Line, 8850 Stockdale Hwy (At CSU), 661.833.6268. Renters can park there and have direct access to trail. Bike Shop: Riverbend Bikes, 2437 Oak St (near Beach Park, end of Oak St near trail), 661.380.7269.
Camp 'n Ride: Kern River Campground (County Park) on river near Lake Ming, along upper trail. Tents and RV's, no hookups, 50 sites, no reservations. See county site kerncounty.com/government/parks/. Bakersfield River Run RV Park (3715 Burr St, 661.377.3600) is across the river from trail (some cross when dry) near 99 Fwy, 2.5 miles away via Truxton and Mohawk (sidewalks or bike lanes available). Other RV parks found around town are at unfeasible riding distances from trail.
Bike 'n Brunch: At our trailhead the Shops at River Walk contains Panera Bread, PF Chang's, BJ's Pizza and Brew, California Pizza Kitchen, Yard House, Eureka!, and others. For some local country music flavor, Buck Owens' Crystal Palace has a restaurant serving lunch or Sunday brunch (reserve: 661.328.7500), as well as a museum, store, and concert hall, located about 0.4 mile from the trail. East of Beach Park, go under the overpass, then look for a connecting path to the end of Oak St. Ride up Oak St and onto the right sidewalk of Rosedale Hwy, over the bridge, then right to 2800 Buck Owens Blvd. This is along the east portion of the trail (Option 1), about 6 miles east of the main trailhead, just past the 99 Freeway. The famous Basque restaurants are about 2.8 miles east of the trail, mostly clustered in Old Town Kern at Baker St near 19th St. From the trail (Option 1, see map inset) at Beach Park take Class II 21st St. east for 1.6 miles, right on Q St. 2 blocks, and left on 19th St. for about 1 mile to the area. Locals' favorites include Wool Growers at Baker & 19th, Narducci's at Baker & 21st, Pyrenees at Kern and Sumner, and Luigi's (Italian) at King & 19th.

City code, bike riding on sidewalks: Unless otherwise posted it is prohibited only in the central traffic district (bounded by F, 25th, Q and 15th Streets), and Old Town Kern (bounded by Hwy 178, Truxtun, Q St, and Beale). This will only impact your route if you ride to the downtown restaurant district.
Further Info: City of Bakersfield: bakersfieldcity.us
Local advocacy group: bikebakersfield.org; Local tourism: vistibakersfield.com
News: Bakersfieldmagazine.com. Real Time Air Quality (RAAN): valleyair.org
Cal State Bakersfield: csub.edu.

Access: Stage from either the park or the Shops at River Walk, which is the site of your most convenient Bike 'n Brunch options. From SR 99 exit onto Stockdale Highway, westbound for about 4.2 miles, past CSUB and Calloway Drive. The restaurants and shopping center appear first, followed by the park at around mile 5. From I-5 take Stockdale Highway east about 12 miles, just past the Kern River overpass to the park on the left. Cycle north to the adjacent river trail from any of the parking areas.

The trail's western terminus and trailhead is near I-5. This is a popular though more isolated trailhead, and probably not a great idea if you are en-route and have a car full of "valuables." From I-5 exit onto Enos Lane (SR 43) northbound. After crossing the Kern River, watch for the obvious developed trailhead parking lot on the right, about 0.9 mile from I-5. Since your food options are near River Walk and the city, you will have to make that big decision of whether you'd rather have your meal mid way or at the end of your ride. Rail 'n Ride: There is an Amtrak station in downtown Bakersfield, and Class II routes can join the trail in 2.5 miles. However, the San Joaquin route only goes north from there toward Sacramento or the Bay Area. From the station go left on Truxtun, right on Q and left on 21st to Beach Park, which is along the eastern trail section.

The Ride: From the River Walk area head west (left) along the paved path. Our mile 0 is the junction with the ped/bike bridge over the river that leads to Aera Park. Our route continues west under Stockdale Highway and between suburban neighborhoods and the river. The natural riparian habitat attracts lots of wildlife, and an early

Typical view of west side of Kern River Trail

morning or late afternoon ride can be rewarding for birdwatchers. The trail passes through River Oaks Park before going under Allen Road (mile 1.0). Residential development remains to the north of the river, but to the south is now agricultural.

As the trail begins a series of jogs to the left and right to follow the natural course of the river channel (2.4), civilization gradually disappears and the remainder of the trail is through the important riparian wetland that slices through this agricultural region. Near the end it crosses a canal (8.2). Make sure to follow the Bike Route signs through this area rather than going off on side trails. It then curves to the right and over the Kern River, reaching the Enos Lane parking area at around mile 8.6. Return the same way.

After passing the original bike/ped bridge starting point, continue through a nice shady zone along The Park at River Walk. Cross under Old River Road and behind the university buildings. If you turn around at the end of the university property as the trail bends to the left, about 1.9 miles from the ped/bike bridge, you will have ridden about 21 miles. Upon your return to the starting area perhaps take a cycle through the park to see the lakes and pavilion, or bridge over to Aera Park.

Option 1: Kern River Parkway Trail to the East ⭐ *Up to 23 miles round trip (about 40 miles if combined with main ride), easy to moderate on paved Class I for any bike.*
From the bike/ped bridge (mile 0) cycle to the east, under Old River Road, past the CSUB buildings (1.9), and veer to the left. The trail next runs parallel to and then curves under Coffee Road (2.5). It then runs parallel to Truxton Avenue, leading to Truxton Lake, a good place to watch waterfowl (3.3), followed by a city park with volleyball courts and playgrounds (3.8). Across the river to the north are oil refineries. Veer to the left, then to the right under Mohawk Street (4.1) along more parkland. The trail crosses under railroad tracks (4.8) and around the bend reaches Yokuts Park that features a disc golf course and access to the river that frequently has water in it at this point during wet years (5.4). Next cross under the noisy SR 99 Freeway (5.7) and reach Beach Park, another possible river access point (5.9). The next undercrossing is Rosedale Highway, SR 178 (6.0). See Bike 'n Brunch for your connections to the downtown Basque restaurants and Crystal Palace from this area.

The trail runs next to a canal for a while behind a residential district and ducks under Golden State Avenue (SR 204) (7.1). You'll notice an impoundment in the Kern River (7.2), and to the right is the home field of the minor league baseball team Bakersfield Blaze. Cross under Chester Avenue (7.9) and pass a wide floodplain. Continue next to a canal, then cross under Manor Street (8.7). The hillsides to the north of here have been covered with oil wells since the early twentieth century. Cycle across the canal and through a canyon with Panorama Park atop the bluffs to the south. The path crosses the canal (10.1) in an oil production area, and then crosses back (11.0). I find this portion of the eastern segment more interesting and scenic than off-putting. It is a good turnaround point, as the trail just ends in 0.5 mile, running through an oil production area to a street in front of a mini storage facility (11.5).

Overview of the east side of Kern River Trail from Panorama Park showing the oilfield-covered hills

Option 2: Connection to the Upper Trail ⭐
Two options are available to continue on to the Upper Trail (Option 3), however they require navigation of hills and riding on the shoulder of roadways next to traffic. Those who prefer relatively flat Class I trails may want to transport their bikes to the upper trail and stage from one of the parks instead of cycling there. Others who are up for it can consider doing a loop using both Options 2a and 2b. Option 2b is a better bet for the return leg because it is an all-downhill cruise on a wide shoulder with nice vistas and good visibility from vehicles. Option 2a on the return leg encounters a substantial uphill heading west from CALM, while the downhill on Fairfax Road has only a narrow shoulder and can be a high-speed ride with traffic.

Option 2a: Connection to Upper Trail via Class I & II/III Route ⭐
6.5 miles each way, moderate to strenuous. e-bike edge.
Upon emerging onto China Grade Loop (mile 0), cross the road and take the path to the right that curves around Derrel's Mini Storage (0.3). Cross the next road to get onto Old Alfred Harrell Highway, and follow it to the right to McMannus Road (1.2). Turn

right and ride under the Alfred Harrell Highway overpass onto what is now Fairfax Road, up the long hill on a not-so-great road with narrow shoulders and fast traffic, to Royal Coach Circle (2.6). Turn left and look for the signed bike path to the left of the entrance to a gated community (2.7).

Follow the path around the perimeter of the community to the right and over the hill, reaching Paladino Drive and running parallel to it (3.9). The path breaks off from Paladino Drive and turns left (4.5), then heads to the north on what locals call the Rattlesnake Trail through some hilly open space, eventually turning right and running parallel to Alfred Harrell Highway (6.0). As the path curves to the left and ends (6.5), cross the road to reach the parking lot for the California Living Museum (CALM), worth a stop for its zoo and exhibits. The Upper Trail continues from both the north and south ends of the parking lot. Go to the south (right) first, and then return to Hart Park with the option of taking Option 2b back.

Option 2b: Connection to Upper Trail via Alfred Harrell Highway
4.25 miles each way, Class II, moderate. e-bike edge.
Upon emerging onto China Grade Loop (0.0), cross the road and take the path to the right of Derrel's Mini Storage (0.3). Cross the road to get onto Old Alfred Harrell Highway, and follow it to McMannus Road (1.2). Turn right and follow it under Alfred Harrell Highway (1.4). Turn left onto the shoulder of the entrance ramp, and cycle on the shoulder of Alfred Harrell Highway, a scenic road with views of the hills off to the north, up the long gradual hill. Turn left into Hart Memorial Park on River Road (3.3), following it to the right, and then veer right on Lake Road (3.4) and ride along the lake, then bear left on Park Road (4.0). Cross River Road to reach Kiddyland Drive (4.1), and look for the start of the Class I Upper Trail on the left (4.25). To return this way, when riding southwest on Alfred Harrell Highway, exit on Fairfax Road and turn right to return the same way to the lower trail.

Option 3: The Upper Trail *4.4 miles each way, Class I paved, easy with some small hills.*
Perhaps the most pleasant segment of the Kern River Trail is the section that connects riverside and lakeside parkland features at the northeast extent of the Bakersfield area and provides an excellent Camp 'n Ride opportunity for tenters. On warm weekends the locals are out recreating here in force, cooling off in the river and lakes or picnicking. The west end of the trail is at Hart Memorial Park, just south of Park Road along Kiddyland Drive, running parallel to the Kern River, as described in Option 2b. Generic bike route signs direct the way. It continues southeast through Kern River County Park, then curves to the right to run parallel to Alfred Harrell Highway (1.4) and past the California Living Museum (CALM). The trail crosses River Road and enters the very popular Kern River Campground (2.7), then leads to the north shore of pretty Lake Ming (3.0), which begins a scenic lakeside section. It reaches and runs next to Lake Ming Road (3.9), ending at the Kern River Golf Course (4.4). Find restrooms at the public parks. Turn around here. For an extra workout do an out-and-back ride up the hilly paved Class I Rattlesnake Trail accessed from across Alfred Harrell Highway at the entrance to CALM.

Lake Ming with bike trail on opposite bank

8. The Inland Empire of Riverside and San Bernardino Counties

Riverside and San Bernardino Counties extend from the hills of San Diego, Orange and Los Angeles Counties to the west, all the way to the Colorado River at the Nevada and Arizona borders to the east. San Bernardino County covers 20,100 square miles, which is the largest in area in the U.S., while Riverside County encompasses 7,303 square miles. Western Riverside and San Bernardino Counties make up what is known as the Inland Empire (aka the "IE"), a population center of 4 million people with cities including Corona and the county seat of Riverside in Riverside County and Ontario and the county seat of San Bernardino in San Bernardino County.

The IE, once an agricultural area dominated by the citrus industry, is now a mix of fast-growing suburban sprawl, industrial complexes, and some remaining agricultural areas with pig, dairy, and horse farms in areas such as Norco and Chino. The area resides mostly in a valley, surrounded by the tall San Gabriel and San Bernardino Mountains to the north and northeast, the equally tall San Jacinto range to the east, and smaller mountains and hills to the south.

The topography creates beautiful backdrops on clear days, especially when the mountains are snow-covered in the winter. However, the smog generated in the LA Basin becomes trapped by those same mountains and creates some of the worst air pollution in the country, especially in the summer and fall. The situation has improved drastically since vehicle emissions standards set by the state were enacted, however you still would not want to cycle in most of the IE on a day when pollution levels are elevated.

The San Jacinto Mountains help ensure that Palm Springs and the vast deserts to the east remain relatively free of the IE's air pollution, and most of the precipitation that falls there. Annual rainfall in San Bernardino is 16 inches and 10.3 inches in Riverside, versus Palm Springs that gets only 2 to 4 inches. Since the desert and its large parks sometimes span multiple counties, the eastern desert portions of Riverside, San Bernardino, and even San Diego Counties are contained in a separate chapter, entitled "The Deserts." In that chapter, the Palm

Springs resort area and portions of both Anza-Borrego State Park and Joshua Tree National Park are in Riverside County, while San Bernardino County contains the northern gateways to Joshua Tree National Park.

San Bernardino County extends up into the San Bernardino Mountains, the tallest in Southern California, with Mt. San Gorgonio weighing in at 11,499 feet. Big Bear Lake is the main attraction in that area, and several rides are included to explore that scenic region (BB1, 2 and 3). North of the mountains is high desert land occupied by the Mojave National Preserve, and cities such as Victorville and Barstow, a primary stopover spot along I-15 on the way to Las Vegas. We did not identify any qualifying rides from that area. The rides included from the IE are along the Santa Ana River from Riverside to San Bernardino (R1), a tour of Riverside's revived citrus district (R2), and the new Pacific Electric rail trail (PET) centered in Rancho Cucamonga. The leafy college town of Claremont is just across the border in Los Angeles County but is also included (CL1 and 2) since it is connected to the PET. Temecula is a popular place to ride via tours on wine country roads. Our style rides connect Old Town to a portion of wine country (T1, 2). Lake Perris near Moreno Valley has a fabulous 9 mile paved scenic trail around it (LP1). Diamond Valley Lake near Hemet is also beautiful but its 22 mile strenuous Lakeside Trail loop is not covered in this book (see dvlake.com for info).

Climate Data for Riverside (Source: Weather.com)													
Month	Jan	Feb	Mar	Apr	May	Jun	Jul	Aug	Sep	Oct	Nov	Dec	Totals
Average High °F	68.1	68.7	71.8	73.8	78.9	85.7	92.3	93.1	90.8	81.0	75.3	66.6	78.8
Average Low °F	46.5	46.1	48.3	51.2	55.5	60.1	66.0	65.2	63.5	57.8	51.7	45.6	54.8
Precipitation, inches	2.33	2.50	1.69	0.68	0.20	0.09	0.04	0.09	0.16	0.46	0.81	1.37	10.42

Climate Data for Ontario (Source: Weather.com)													
Month	Jan	Feb	Mar	Apr	May	Jun	Jul	Aug	Sep	Oct	Nov	Dec	Totals
Average High °F	68	69	71	76	79	84	90	92	89	80	74	68	78.3
Average Low °F	43	45	47	49	54	58	62	62	60	55	47	42	52
Precipitation, inches	3.11	4.26	2.63	1.20	0.23	0.09	0.00	0.03	0.15	1.05	1.62	2.45	16.82

Riverside

In the late 1800s and early 1900s when citrus was king in Southern California, Riverside was the center of it all. Fertile soil and mild climate create an ideal combination for navel oranges, which made the area extremely prosperous. While the heyday is long since gone, some of the heritage has been preserved around the city. The Victoria Avenue thoroughfare southwest of downtown is being restored to its citrus era heyday, with rows of orange trees once again alongside it while an adjacent 7-mile Class I trail keeps you away from vehicles (ride R2). The California Citrus State Historic Park near that boulevard preserves the citrus culture as well.

The original Mile Square of downtown is still apparent with 25 historic buildings that give the district its character. The most prominent is the Mission Inn, which is regarded as the largest example of Mission Revival Style architecture in the U.S. The Inn's Christmas festivities and decorations are a regional tradition, and their Sunday brunch is one of the finest in the land. The adjacent 3-block pedestrian promenade

INLAND EMPIRE OF RIVERSIDE AND SAN BERNARDINO COUNTIES

evokes a European vibe. Riverside (population 320,00) is the seat of Riverside County, both named for the Santa Ana River that flows through it. The Santa Ana River Trail (SART, ride R1) is its main cycling feature, spanning the width of the city from Norco to the west, all the way into San Bernardino to the northeast.

Mount Rubidoux is Riverside's prominent geographic feature. At 1,337-feet elevation, this cactus-covered granite hill towers over the SART (elevation 780 ft) to its northwest and downtown Riverside (850 ft) to its southeast. On a clear day a ride up the mountain on its paved path with a gradual grade yields panoramic vistas. Ride R1 - Option 3 is a great 10 mile loop combining this climb, a downtown historic Riverside tour, a scenic stretch of SART, and a visit to Fairmount Park. This gem on the eastern edge of downtown was designed in the early 1900s by the same firm responsible for New York's Central Park. It contains the meandering Lake Evans, a rose garden, lawn bowling, and lots of bikable trails running through it (also R1's Option 2 on its own).

Local bike club: riversidebicycleclub.com
City Bike Program: riversideca.gov/publicworks/traffic/bicycleprogram/
Event: Citrus Classic Ride and bike festival (October)
City code, bike riding on sidewalks: Prohibited unless signed otherwise.

Riverside and the Santa Ana River Trail R1

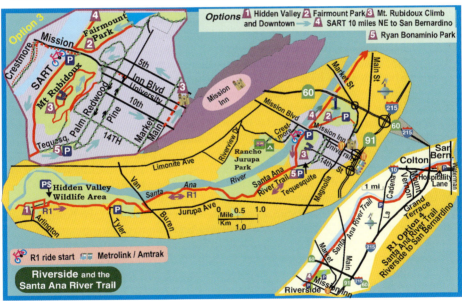

The suggested ride through this area takes you 9 miles along the most scenic section of the Santa Ana River Trail to its western terminus at the beautiful Hidden Valley Wildlife Area, which is the most scenic part of the ride. Through the Riverside area the wide river basin has a natural bottom filled with palms, pepper trees, sycamore, and many other varieties, as well as exotics such as Brazilian cane grass. Bird watching along the trail can be quite rewarding. On a clear sunny day in winter or spring when tall snow-covered mountains form the backdrop behind palm trees, the viewscape while cycling is spectacular, even in the segments that are not as scenic otherwise. Added options include a cycle around Fairmount Park near your starting point, a jaunt on Class II roadways to the historic downtown core for your Bike 'n Brunch, or a cycle up Mt. Rubidoux. Or, cycle the SART 10 miles northeast along the mostly concrete-lined Santa Ana River to San Bernardino (restaurants), enjoying an unobstructed workout with pretty mountain views.

Tunes: Riverside by America; Down by the Riverside by Peter Paul & Mary; Ride the River by JJ Cale and Eric Clapton; Roadhouse Blues by The Doors
Eats: Lunch on outdoor table amongst eclectic sculptures at Tio's Tacos.

Distance: 16.4 miles up and back + options. Time: Average of 1.5 hours.
Route & Bike: Easy to moderate depending on distance. Paved Class I; some Class II and III in the options. Any bike. Mostly flat with some occasional small hills and grades between the river level and the adjacent bluffs. Option 3: Mt. Rubidoux climb is 400 ft in 2 miles: E-bike edge; also for hills in town close to mountain.
Seasons: All. Mornings in summer. Best on sunny clear spring day with wildflowers blooming and snow covered mountains visible in the distance.
Facilities: Restrooms and water at Ryan Bonaminio Park, Fairmount Park, Anza Narrows Park. Water at Carlson Park. Porta-potties at Hidden Valley Nature Center.
Knocks & Hazards: Riverside experiences some of the worst air quality in the country. On a hot smoggy day in summer or fall you would not want to cycle here, unless perhaps if you got out early. Because of the urban nature of the surroundings it is not advisable to cycle at night on the more deserted trails, and it is always better to cycle with a friend. Plenty of homeless encampments are in the river basin. Signs at trailheads warn not to leave valuables in your car, even at Hidden Valley Nature Center where there have also been break-ins. Clueless peds may be on trail, especially on Mt. Rubidoux. Be courteous to them. Street crossings and bike lanes next to traffic in the optional rides. Rattlesnakes. Wild dog packs. Possible cougars.
Bike Shop: Pedals Bicycle Shop, 3674 Sunnyside Dr, 951.683.5343. Rental: See below.
Camp 'n Ride: Pleasant, popular Rancho Jurupa Regional Park (Riverside County), has camping for tents and RV's with hookups. Bike rentals. 4800 Crestmore Rd, Jurupa Valley, 951.684.7032. Reserve: rivcoparks.org.. To R1 trailhead from the park entrance, turn right and ride 1.2 miles along wide Class II Crestmore Rd or sidewalk to Mission Blvd. The river trail is across the bridge to the right. "Walk" your bike on the sidewalk to cross the bridge. Turn right into Carlson Park if the gate is open to get to our referenced trailhead. Otherwise, just over the bridge, follow the dirt path down to the paved trail and begin there.
Bike 'n Brunch: Find great grub in downtown Riverside. See Options 2 and 3 for the routes from SART. The closest on-road access is via Class II Market St, 0.8 mile west from the southwest corner of Fairmount Park. Lots of cafes are along the pedestrian mall and around downtown. The Mission Inn has several pricy restaurants, some with outdoor patios. Offerings include Sunday Brunch and high tea. missioninn.com (bring a spare shirt). Don't miss the wildly eclectic grounds of Tio's Tacos at 3948 Mission Inn Ave. The northeast end of the SART at Hospitality Lane in San Bernardino offers lots of dining options (see Option 4).
Further Info: Friends of the Santa Ana River Trail: trailsafetypatrol.com. Check for trail closures here. Trail users website: santaanarivertrail.com. Hidden Valley Nature Center: rivcoparks.org. Click on "Nature Centers." Ph: 951.785.7452. Downtown Info: raincrosssquare.com.

Access: Choose from several starting points with free parking unless quoted:

Downtown: From SR 91 (Riverside Freeway) take the Downtown/Mission Inn Blvd. exit, and head northwest. Drive through downtown. In 1.4 miles just before a bridge turn left into the parking lot for the Carlson Dog Park (park closed Monday 6-noon and after dark). Park here and ride to the opening in the gate at the southwest, far end of the lot. Fairmount Park is another staging option near downtown.

Ryan Bonaminio Park: From Mission Inn Blvd take Redwood Dr southwest. It becomes Palm. Turn right on Tequesquite to the park. SART skirts the end of the block.

West end, Hidden Valley Nature Center: From SR 91 take I-15 north to 6th Street east into Norco, with its horse-themed buildings and businesses, horse trails instead of sidewalks, and late summer fair that highlights the city's traditions. In 1.6 miles turn left on California St and in 1 mile right on North St that turns into Arlington Ave. Look for the sign for the nature center in 0.8 mile on the left. A paved road leads to the nature center parking lot ($5/person) in 0.5 mile. A Class I bike trail starts near the entrance gate and runs downhill parallel to the road to the nature center where the trail continues eastward. If the facility is closed, people park in the small lot outside of the gate, or at the end of Tyler and Jurupa Streets. Continue east on Arlington and turn left on Tyler until it ends at Jurupa to find street parking near the trail.

Rail 'n Ride: Metrolink stops at 4066 Vine St in downtown Riverside, just east of the 91 Freeway. You can ride about 1 mile west on MLK/14th Street to meet up with the downtown bike routes and access the river trail.

The Ride (described from the downtown starting point): Begin riding on the trail along the south bank of the Santa Ana River. Mile 0 is the exit out of the west end of Carlson Park. As you head west, it will be a slight downhill grade with some ups and downs as you go back and forth to the level of the river. Prevailing winds will be mostly against you westbound. The portion of the trail near downtown is very scenic because it is between the river basin to the north and Mount Rubidoux to

West end of the SART near Rutland Park.

the south. At the far end of the mountain, the trail hits an abandoned road and directs you to the right onto it (mile 1.0). The new Ryan Bonaminio Park is to the left here, and Tequesquite Avenue that is behind the barricade is part of the Class II/III Downtown Bike Loop (and our Option 3) that leads across to historic downtown and Fairmount Park. Continue along the Class I trail another mile, which now runs behind a fenced-off facility that appears to be a landfill, but then emerges between the river basin and residential neighborhoods. Reach Marsha McLean Anza Narrows Regional Park (3.0), another potential staging point, equipped with odd roofless restrooms.

The trail curves left and goes under a concrete arch railroad bridge at Anza Narrows (3.7), and then farther along the river the trail ducks under a pipeline bridge (4.5). Mile 4.9 brings a large sewage treatment plant on the landward side. During the low-flow periods of summer and fall most of the water in the Santa Ana River is actually from treated sewage effluent and irrigation runoff. The trail turns to the right to dip under Van Buren Boulevard (5.5), and to the left up its other side. It runs parallel to the roadway before turning to the right again (6.0), next to Jurupa Avenue. Where the trail bends right once more, behind a neighborhood, look for Rutland Park, a community park with water but no restrooms, across the street (6.2). The trail runs along a riverside bluff behind a neighborhood, then passes a vacant area called "Agricultural Park," which is undergoing PCB remediation so that homes can be built on it (6.5).

Another potential access point is reached as the trail ascends a hill and arrives at the end of Jurupa Avenue at Tyler Street (7.3) where there is free on-street parking. Saving the best for last, the trail ends at the Hidden Valley Wildlife Area park property. It curves along atop the bluffs next to a bridle path, backed by hilly ranchland to the south, the leafy river basin to the north, and awesome mountain views on clear days. Reach the parking lot for the Nature Center facilities (open Saturdays) at mile 8.2, which overlooks large seasonal wetland ponds that have walking paths around them at the level of the river. There are only porta-potties at the Nature Center and no water, however more permanent facilities are proposed. This is our turnaround point.

Option 1: Hidden Valley *About 3.5 miles total, easy to moderate on paved paths.* The rest of the very scenic Hidden Valley Wildlife Area property is hilly but worth exploring, especially during spring wildflower season. Continue west on the main path to the second trail junction (9.2). The path straight ahead continues up the hill to the Arlington Avenue entrance (in 0.5 mile). Choose the path to the right that leads to equestrian parking (porta-potty here), then dips down toward the river. At the first junction (9.4) go straight, to the end (at time of writing) of the IE's segment of the SART (9.9). Turn around, return to the previous junction and turn left, looping eastward back around and up the hill. Cross the park road to continue on the path and go left, back to the Nature Center (11.7).

Return to the east along the trail to your starting point downtown for a total mileage of 16.4 miles (or 19.9 miles with the extra spin through Hidden Valley). On the ride eastbound enjoy views of Mt. Rubidoux that gets gradually closer as you proceed. On clear days the peaks of the San Gabriel Mountains, and farther along the San Bernardino Mountains, may create a stunning backdrop.

Trail up Mt. Rubidoux approaches the landmark World Peace Bridge.

Option 2: Fairmount Park *About 3.2 miles total, easy.* Once you return to your starting point, try an easy excursion through Fairmount Park. Assuming the west entrance to Carlson Park is mile 0, cycle to the northeast, under Mission Inn Avenue, and at the first trail intersection turn right and ride through the wooded area, reaching pretty Lake Evans at mile 0.8. Continue on the sidewalk bike path and make your way all around the park at your whim. This excursion will add on about 3.2 miles to your ride. It will be much more enjoyable on a weekday morning than on a crowded weekend, and is not recommended after dark. The downtown core can be accessed from Class II Market Street at the east end of the park. Ride southwest 0.9 mile to Mission Inn Ave. The Mission Inn is one block to the left. Otherwise, upon returning to the river trail, either return to your starting point to the left, or, for more of a workout, continue to the northeast (right) (see Option 4).

Option 3: Historic Downtown Riverside and Mt. Rubidoux Climb 4 *E-bike edge*
9.9 miles total loop (less if combined with main ride or Option 2), moderate+, Class I /II /III
From SART at Bonaminio Park (0.0) head up Tequesquite. Go left on one-way Class II Pine (0.5). Go right on 10th St (1.0) that has signals to cross busy Brockton and Market Streets. At Main, go left (1.6) to "walk" through the City Hall complex, and cross 9th St to enter the pedestrian mall with sidewalk cafes and the Mission Inn between Mission Inn Ave and 6th, where it ends. Ride on Main one block to 5th St and turn left (2.0). Cycle through the residential district to Redwood (2.6). *To avoid the Mt. Rubidoux climb, go right, to Fairmount Park.* We cross Redwood and ride up Mt. Rubidoux Dr, past mansions of Mt. Rubidoux Historic District. Cross the stone bridge over Mission Inn Ave. The entrance to Mt. Rubidoux Park is after 9th St (3.0). Begin a gradual scenic climb on a wide asphalt path. At a junction at another park sign (3.5) follow the asphalt path to the right around a hairpin turn. Eventually cross under the World Peace Bridge, and reach the summit (5.0). Return the same way, curtailing downhill speed. After the stone bridge go left on Ladera Lane (7.2). Ascend the hill past the mansions. Merge onto Indian Hill Rd that overlooks Fairmount Park. At Redwood (7.7) turn left and cruise down the hill. Go left on Dexter into Fairmount Park (8.0). Turn left onto the trail that begins across from the lake (8.1) and follow it to SART (8.6). Turn left to complete the loop (9.9).

Option 4: Santa Ana River Trail continuation to San Bernardino 3
10 miles each way, easy to moderate depending on wind (e-bike edge).
This flat, nicely paved bike highway with minimal ped traffic and no speed limit makes a great workout ride. It follows the wide river channel that is mostly natural in appearance with more concrete lining toward the east. The rural open viewscape is backed by great mountain views on clear days, from the San Gabriels, including Mt. Baldy, to the San Bernardino's farther east, including So Cal's tallest, Mt. San Gorgonio. It's best to ride with a friend since it's isolated most of the way, and we noticed an abundance of homeless in the river and even a pack of wild dogs. More shopping carts and graffiti appear toward San Bernardino, but the Hospitality Lane area is modern and clean.

From our downtown starting point along the river trail, continue under Mission Blvd, then under Market St (1.3) and SR 60, then under Main St (2.4); pass trailheads at La Cadena in Colton (5.8), Mt. Vernon St (7.9), and in San Bernardino, South E St north of Hospitality Lane (8.6) and South Waterman north of Vanderbilt Way (10.0). Check out the many restaurants in the Hospitality Lane district.

Historic Victoria Avenue and the Citrus District R2 4

Journey back in time to when citrus was king and the smell of orange blossoms permeated the senses in springtime. While those days are sadly gone for the most part, the feeling lives on in the Arlington Heights district of Riverside. Victoria Avenue is a product of that era, a 10-mile boulevard from 1892 that is listed on the National Register of Historic Places, and along 8 of those miles it feels like you have been transported back to the time when orchards dominated the landscape. For the most part, the road is one lane in each direction with a bike lane, and a landscaped median throughout. The Class I Rosanna Scott Memorial Bike Trail runs for about 7 miles along the north side of the road, with one break.

There are so many trees along the boulevard that Joni Mitchell might say that when they paved the citrus paradise, they took all the trees and put them in this tree museum. Over 6,000 trees of 140 different species line the route, including gigantic eucalyptus and ubiquitous palms, as well as exotic flowering trees like magnolia, mulberry,

and tulip, varieties of nut trees and lots of citrus, many of which have been re-planted as part of a renaissance revitalization project conducted by the City of Riverside and the Victoria Avenue Forever organization. They have improved landscaping and maintenance of the median, and rejuvenated the rare ragged robin roses along most of the median that only grow here and have been re-propagated from this stock since the 1800s. Next to the road, especially in its southwest segment, are several working orchards along with rural properties, and some classic citrus-era estates.

A cycle on side streets takes you past some of these orchards and leads to a hidden gem, the California Citrus State Historic Park. Try to plan your ride so you can visit this park when the Visitor Center and museum are open, Friday to Sunday. It has working orchards, a varietal grove with 100 trees, a museum, and replicas of buildings that would have been found in citrus orchards. Presently bikes are welcome to cruise along the paved and decomposed granite paths that lead through the park to scenic viewpoints but be courteous to peds so bikes do not become banned.

On clear days you can take in amazing vistas of the surrounding

The Rosanna Scott bike trail parallels historic Victoria Avenue past some rare remaining SoCal orange orchards.

regional mountains beyond the orchards and palm trees. When we rode through this area in early April, the scent of the orange blossoms was pleasantly overwhelming. You have several choices of where to turn around and which portions of the Avenue to see. The roadway is popular with locals out for a scenic drive and with bicyclists out for a scenic cruise, most of whom keep to the bike lane rather than the bike trail. The area is also accessible by Metrolink via short rides from both ends of the Avenue.

Delightful paths wind through the California Citrus State Historic Park

Tunes: Orange Blossom Special by Seatrain; The Balance by The Moody Blues; Victoria by the Kinks; Ginza Samba by Vince Guaraldi
Eats: Buy some produce at a stand near the southwest end, or take a detour to the shopping center near the Metrolink station at La Sierra and Indiana.

Distance: Take a short spin, or do the total ride, which is about 20 miles. Add 2 miles total if you arrive at the La Sierra Metrolink station and/or wish to ride to a lunch stop near the station. Time: Up to 2.5 hours.
Route & Bike: Easy to moderate depending on distance. Main trail is Class I, with some easy Class II. Route to Citrus Park is Class III. Park trails are paved with options of some packed dirt trails. Hybrid or mountain bike opens up the most opportunities, but any bike is fine. Good brakes needed for side trip to Citrus Park. Mostly flat with a slight gradual grade rising to the northeast. A few small rolling hills. E-bike edge: Hilly route to the Citrus Park, and the park itself is fairly hilly but nothing too steep or difficult. Some may be able to ride a longer distance.
Seasons: All. Best on sunny spring day with the delightful smell of citrus blooming, or clear winter day when snow blankets the surrounding mountains. If coming by train, Friday is best when all of the Citrus Park's facilities are open and Metrolink runs a full schedule. By car, Friday through Sunday are best when the Citrus Park is in full swing. The bike trail is not all that crowded even on weekends, and you can always opt for the bike lane.
Facilities: Restrooms and water found only at the Citrus Park when open.
Knocks & Hazards: Clueless peds may be on trail. Avoid before and after school when kids use the Class I trail to commute. Possible lurkers. Many street crossings. Picking of citrus is not allowed in the state park or on private orchards. Avoid summer heat/smog. A cyclist was killed in the Victoria Ave bike lane near Meyers in 2019.
Rent 'n Ride/Camp 'n Ride: See R1
Bike 'n Brunch: Nothing along trail. Closest is 0.3 mile north on Van Buren: Denny's, McDonalds, Subway, sushi. North on La Sierra about 0.75 mile near Indiana are Carl's Jr, Starbucks, Jack-in-the-Box, pizza, Greek, Mexican, and Stater Bros

market. Another Stater Bros is 1 block north on Mary Street (east of Washington).
Further Info: victoriaavenue.org; victoriaavenueforever.org; californiacitruspark.com; www.parks.ca.gov/?page_id=649

Access: From the 91 Freeway in the Riverside area, take La Sierra Avenue southbound about 1 mile to Victoria Avenue and turn left, then start looking for parking on the cross streets. The first street is actually called Cross Street in 0.4 mile. Parking is not allowed on Victoria Avenue itself. If you choose to park in the State Historic Park (a good option if there are non-riders in your group) there is a $5 parking fee, though no fee to cycle in. The entrance is off of Dufferin just east of Van Buren.

Rail 'n Ride: The La Sierra Metrolink Station is an easy 1 mile ride along Class II La Sierra Avenue south to Victoria Avenue. The Downtown Riverside Metrolink Station is less than 0.5 mile from Victoria Avenue via 14th Street, however this end of Victoria Avenue requires street riding through the downtown district. The station-to-station ride via Victoria Avenue is about 10 miles, not including the 2-mile excursion to the Citrus Historic Park. *Metrolink schedules to these stations are very limited on weekends.*

The Ride: Start anywhere along the route. We prefer the more rural southwest end with a side trip into the California Citrus Park. Assuming Victoria Avenue at La Sierra is mile 0, cycle northeastward. This description is of the Class I bike trail, but you can ride in the nice Class II bike lane as most cyclists do. The cruise is a delightfully peaceful one, but use caution at any driveway or residential street crossing. When you reach Tyler Street (mile 0.9) the bike trail ends temporarily, so you'll need to carefully cross Victoria Avenue to reach the bike lane on the other side if you are heading northeast. On the return you can easily just switch to the bike lane for this stretch.

When you reach Harrison Street (1.6) you have the option of crossing back onto the bike trail. Shortly the residences disappear from the north side of the road and the area is carpeted with citrus groves (1.7). Van Buren Boulevard is the first major signaled crossing (2.1). There are a few dining options 0.3 mile to the north here. Cross at the signal and continue along, past a sports park and then more orange groves. At Jackson Street is your first option to ride to the Citrus Park (2.6). It is narrow and has a steep hill, so we prefer the next street, Irving, that is wider and has barely a grade (2.9). On the return you can try Jackson if you are headed west. The Citrus Park is well worth a visit, or at least a pleasant cycle through this orange grove area. Cycle up Irving past Cleveland Avenue and reach Dufferin Avenue (3.4). Turn right and ride gradually up a small grade past orange groves. The road then pitches down into a valley (3.9) and then back up to reach the entrance to the park on the left (4.1). Bikes enter for free.

Pedal up the entrance road and start a freeform exploration. You can pick up a trail map at the entry kiosk, or at the visitor center, which is at the end of the paved road straight ahead. There are not that many trails, but you can have a great time exploring them all, some of which go through groves, and one to a scenic viewpoint that has all of the mountain views labeled. Most of the trails are concrete walkways, while others are decomposed granite or dirt. You can get in a couple of miles of very enjoyable riding and sightseeing through the park. Unfortunately the adjacent reservoir shown on the map is off-limits. Return to the park entrance at Dufferin (6.0). Turn left for the moment and go to Van Buren Boulevard to pose next to the nifty giant orange that is the directional sign for the park. Turn around and go back on Dufferin past the park entrance. Continue to Irving Street (or Jackson if you'd like a change and the thrill of a hill, but be careful), and return to Victoria Avenue (7.4). Turn right into the bike lane or cross over onto the bike trail. Otherwise, if you'd like to keep your ride to 10 miles, head left on Victoria to the ride start.

Ride pleasantly along, checking out all the different planted trees. Orchards continue along the sides of the avenue, but starting at Adams you can begin to see some industrial areas to the north beyond (8.2). After Washington Street (9.75), residential areas come close to the avenue on both sides, and the closer to the avenue the nicer the houses. The Class I bike trail ends at Arlington Avenue (11.4), but Victoria Avenue continues with its beautiful median, and still as a Class II roadway, although now with two lanes in each direction. Ride through this very nice neighborhood, then cross at signaled Central Avenue (11.9).

When Victoria Avenue curves to the right as the median ends, carefully turn left on Myrtle Avenue (12.1). Myrtle curves around to the right past large homes and becomes a one-way street. It circles around the base of Victoria Hill and returns to Victoria Avenue (12.5). A bridge over an arroyo is to the left. There is not much of interest beyond there unless you need to cycle to the downtown Metrolink station (north on 14th Street off Victoria) or visit the downtown district. Otherwise, turn right on Victoria, continue circling around this toney neighborhood to the point where you turned on Myrtle (12.8) and return down Victoria to the ride start at La Sierra (20.3). From that point there is a shopping center with tempting restaurants about 0.75 mile north on Class II La Sierra.

Temecula and the Southern Wine Country

The pastoral Temecula Valley Southern California wine Country with its 40+ wineries, vineyards, horse ranches, resorts and restaurants lies along the I-15 corridor in Riverside County just north of the San Diego County line. Temecula is steeped in history as a major stop of the Butterfield Stagecoach and rail lines between San Diego and San Bernardino, and Old Town Temecula preserves numerous old west buildings, a major attraction with its restaurants, antique shops, and year round festivals including bluegrass in March. Lake Skinner Regional Park located east of town is a good place for RV camping and the site of the June Balloon and Wine Festival. Pechanga Casino south of town is a popular entertainment venue with an RV park as well.

Temecula Bike Routes   T1 ⭐ and T2 ⭐

Rent 'n Ride: Wine Country e-bike rentals: uyswines.com/ebikes; Tours/Rentals: uncorkedtemecula.com/uncorked-e-bike-tour. Shop: The Bike Shop, 32835 Temecula Pkwy, 951.303.9477

As shown on the map, Old Town is on the west edge of town, while the Wine Country is to the east. In between are mostly neighborhoods and commercial districts of this fast growing Inland Empire city. Although plans include the Class I/II Temecula Loop around the city perimeter and the Wine Country Path connecting Old Town to Wine Country, cyclists currently have to settle for mostly Class II riding to get through

INLAND EMPIRE OF RIVERSIDE AND SAN BERNARDINO COUNTIES

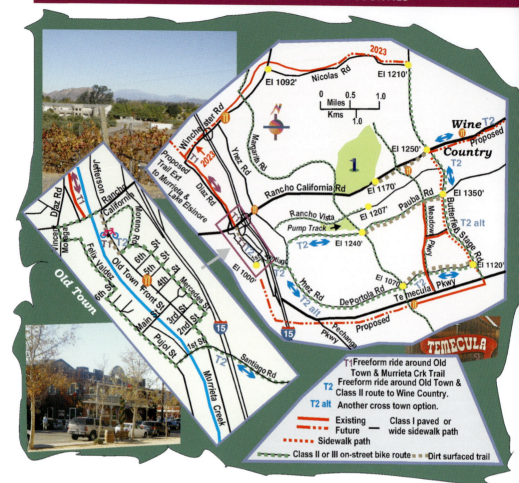

T1 Freeform ride around Old Town & Murrieta Crk Trail
T2 Freeform ride around Old Town & Class II route to Wine Country.
T2 alt Another cross town option.

— Existing
--- Future
••• Sidewalk path
— Class I paved or wide sidewalk path
═══ Class II or III on-street bike route
■ ■ ■ Dirt surfaced trail

this hilly city, plus a few miles of dirt horse/MTB trails, incorporated into our T2 route. An e-bike will have an edge on those hills. Although riding through Wine Country consists of shoulders along busy roadways, numerous wineries are situated along the first two miles of Rancho California Rd once you leave the Class II city roadways, more than enough to keep you occupied for your day's excursion. For winery info see temeculawines.org. It's best to avoid weekends there. Cyclists comfortable riding in traffic can attempt further exploration, and participating in a bike tour may introduce

Murrieta Creek Trail near Old Town Temecula. A small piece of things to come, eventually reaching Lake Elsinore.

you to some interesting back roads. There was some talk of Riverside County building a bike path through Wine Country, but that has not yet materialized.

Along Murrieta Creek 1.5 miles of the planned Murrieta Creek regional trail is completed north of Old Town, allowing a nice jaunt to combine with an exploration of Old Town, considered to be our ride T1. For a map of the city's current routes and future plans see temeculaca.gov/485/Bicycle-Lanes-Trails. Note that city code bans cycling on sidewalks on bridges, and next to commercial districts and schools, although it's rarely enforced, especially on I-15 crossings to avoid dangerous roadways.

Claremont

Claremont, which resembles a New England college town with palm trees, is a true delight, from its leafy downtown village to its adjacent 560-acre college district where cyclists have the right of way. This silver-rated "Bicycle Friendly" city is known first and foremost as the home of the Claremont Colleges, a consortium of five undergraduate liberal arts schools (Claremont McKenna, Harvey Mudd, Pitzer, Pomona, and Scripps Colleges), and two graduate schools (Claremont Graduate U and Keck Graduate Institute of Applied Life Sciences), grouped similarly to the Oxford-Cambridge model.

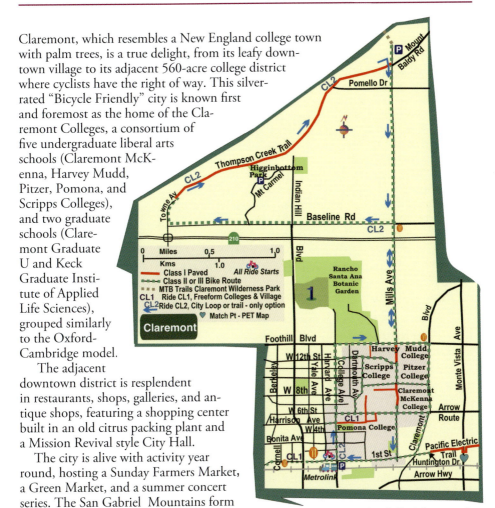

The adjacent downtown district is resplendent in restaurants, shops, galleries, and antique shops, featuring a shopping center built in an old citrus packing plant and a Mission Revival style City Hall.

The city is alive with activity year round, hosting a Sunday Farmers Market, a Green Market, and a summer concert series. The San Gabriel Mountains form a dramatic backdrop to the city that slopes gradually north to the foothills. The paved Thompson Creek Trail is a short but sweet path along the edge of the foothills that leads to Claremont Hills Wilderness Park for MTB's. Class II routes connect that path to the downtown district. The Pacific Electric Trail (ride PET) starts east of downtown and extends 21 miles through Montclair, Upland, Rancho Cucamonga, Fontana and Rialto.

Access: Claremont is located at the eastern edge of Los Angeles County, in the San Gabriel Valley, bordering the Inland Empire of San Bernardino County. From I-10 exit Indian Hill Blvd. Go north to downtown, across the train tracks to 1st St. From the 210 freeway exit on Baseline and follow it west to Indian Hill. Turn left to get to downtown. Set GPS for the Claremont Metrolink station for best parking options.

- **Rail 'n Ride:** Metrolink San Bernardino Line station is at 200 W 1st St near College.
- **Bike Shop:** Jax Bicycle Center, 217 W 1st St (across from Metrolink), 909.621.5827.
- **Camp 'n Ride:** None nearby. See ride LA10.
- **Bike 'n Brunch:** The restaurants are concentrated downtown. Wander around and check out the menus: Some Crust Bakery at 119 Yale; Saca's Med, 248 W 2nd St; several at the historic Claremont Packing House feat. Eureka 's great patio, (1st and Cornel) or Claremont Village Square (2nd & Oberlin) feat. Back Abbey gastropub. On the bike route there are a few casual eateries at Baseline and Mills.
- **Facilities:** Restrooms and water at parks around town including Blaisdell Park, 440 College Ave; Cahuilla Park, Indian Hill Blvd and Scripps Dr; College Park, 100 College Ave (just south of the Metrolink tracks); El Barrio Park, 400 block of Claremont Blvd; Griffith Park, 1800 Woodbend Dr; Higginbotham Park, Mt. Carmel Dr (along Thompson Creek Trail); June Vail Park, Grand Ave and Bluefield Dr; La Puerta Sports Park, 2430 N Indian Hill Blvd; Larkin Park, 660 N Mountain Ave; Lewis Park, 881 Syracuse Dr; Mallows Park, 520 N Indian Hill Blvd; Memorial Park, 840 N Indian Hill Blvd; and Wheeler Park, 626 Vista Dr. Porta-potties at Claremont Hills Wilderness Park trailhead.
- **City code, bike riding on sidewalks:** Defer to state law and be courteous of peds.
- **Further Info:** City of Claremont (activities, maps, City Bicycle Plan): www.ci.claremont.ca.us; Claremont Colleges: claremont.edu.
- **Bike Clubs:** Claremont Cycling Club: www.meetup.com/CCC-CYCLING/ Older crowd: claremontseniorbikegroup.org

Claremont Village and the Colleges CL1

Details: About 6 miles and 1 hour. Easy, paved, any bike. Class I, II, III including sharrows. Land slopes gently to north. **Knocks & Hazards:** Although the town is very bike friendly, you are still comingling with autos. Downtown is full of cars parking.

This is a freeform ride, using the map. The Bike Priority Zone (BPZ) emphasizes safe bike routes, bike parking and improved bike access, in the village, college district, and residential sectors between 1st and Foothill. The college district is a 3-mile square surrounded by College, Foothill, Claremont and 1st, all Class III/sharrows or Class II with some sidewalks available. Inside are paths and streets closed to cars that you can explore, such as southbound Mill Ave that ends at Foothill for cars but not bikes that can continue through Harvey Mudd College to 1st St. From Harrison Ave (5th St) at Harvard, cyclists can ride east through a parking lot, cross College Avenue, and ride east down Stover and Draper Walks through the heart of Pomona College. You can meander through the colleges on various roads and paths unless prohibited by signs.

The adjacent downtown commercial district is roughly bordered by 4th Street to the north (or Bonita Avenue where west of Indian Hill Boulevard), Harvard to the east, 1st Street to the south and Cornell to the west, where the Packing House restaurant and shopping complex is located inside an old citrus packing facility. The perimeter of the downtown "village" totals about a mile, and you can wander through the streets to add to that mileage. Or, you may just want to lock your bike and walk this portion. First Street continues east to join the Pacific Electric Trail, past Claremont Boulevard, in less than a mile from the Metrolink depot. See that ride (PET) for details.

INLAND EMPIRE OF RIVERSIDE AND SAN BERNARDINO COUNTIES

Athletic fields of Pomona and Pitzer Colleges with a San Gabriel Mountains backdrop.

Thompson Creek Trail

Thompson Creek Trail—City Loop or Trail Only CL2

Details: 4.2 or 10 miles, 30 minutes to 1.5 hours. Moderate, paved, Class I (trail), II and III (city loop). Any bike. Area slopes uphill to the northeast. Some e-bike edge.

Knocks & Hazards: Loop ride involves riding in bike lanes next to traffic. Gradual grade on trail. Watch downhill speed. Clueless peds. Potential for rattlesnakes, mountain lions and black bears at urban/wilderness interface in foothills.

Access: Either start from the CL1 trailhead, or, for a shorter ride, drive to the Thompson Creek Trail directly as follows: Take Indian Hill Blvd north, past Baseline Rd, and turn left on Mt. Carmel Dr, then drive a few blocks to Higginbotham Park and park on the street. Ride through the park (restrooms available) to reach the trail. From there the trail is slightly downhill to the left, and more significantly uphill to the right.

The Ride: City Loop:
From Metrolink station ride north on Yale or Campus Ave. Go right (east) on 6th St to Mills Ave (mile 1.0). Head north on Mills on a combination of road and path, past Foothill Blvd. Continue on this Class II route, gradually uphill, over the 210 Freeway to Baseline and turn left (2.5). Cycle down the gradual slope in the bike lane to Towne Ave and turn right (4.2). Reach the obvious drainage channel and paved Thompson Creek Trail, and ride to the right (4.3). The scenic path winds against the foothills, under a leafy canopy, past a well-disguised neighborhood on the right. When riding in the northeasterly direction keep left at forks. The path rises gradually and reaches beautiful Higginbotham Park, with restrooms near the trail. After passing the end of Pomello Dr the viewscape opens up with vistas of the San Gabriel Mountains, and the uphill grade steepens, as high-tension power lines come into view. The path ends at Mills Ave, and the trail's main parking lot (6.4), just north of Mount Baldy Road. To the left up Mills the road ends at another parking lot and trailhead for Claremont Hills Wilderness Park. The doubletrack fire road trails start gently but lead to much steeper terrain. See the city's website for information and a map.

To return to town, simply ride south on Mills, past Baseline (7.6) through the colleges to 1st Street (9.4). If you'd like to get in some more mileage you can turn left (east) and ride 0.8 mile to the trailhead of the Pacific Electric Trail that extends for 21 miles into Rialto. If schedules allow you can even take the Metrolink back to Claremont from stations in Upland, Rancho Cucamonga, or Fontana. Otherwise, turn right (west) to return to your ride start (10.0).

Lake Perris Loop Camp 'n Ride LP1 ⭐

Now that Perris Reservoir's 2-mile long dam has been shored up and is open to bicycling, the loop ride around the lake ticks all the boxes for an awesome easy scenic SoCal bike ride; a paved 9.5-mile loop trail, iconic SoCal scenery including coastal sage habitat with mountain backdrops, and abundant wildlife viewing. Lake Perris State Recreation Area is an 8,800 acre urban oasis amidst the Inland Empire's sprawl between Perris and Moreno Valley. The dam completed in 1973 impounds an 1,800 acre reservoir, southernmost of the California State Water Project. It is heavily used for recreation, such as fishermen vying for largemouth bass and other stocked fish. Summers can be overly crowded here, with the 200 boat slots filling up in advance. Perris Beach's white sands draws crowds for swimming. Picnic areas abound. The park is situated in a broad valley surrounded by low granitic ridges on three sides, with the region's larger ranges beyond. Bring binoculars to view some 100 species of birds from road runners to bald eagles. Wildflowers bloom in winter and spring, and in some wet years they put on quite a show. Visit the Ya'i Heki' Regional Indian Museum to learn of the rich native heritage here, including the park's petroglyphs. A campground for tents and RV's (max 31 ft, W&E, dump station) provides an ideal base to explore, observe, or just exercise.

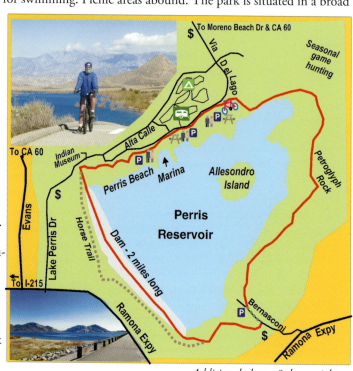

Additional photo p8, lower right.

Details: 9.5 miles per loop, 45-70 minutes. Easy to moderate with gradual hills, one short steep hill. Easy for e-bikes. Mostly Class I paved, some rough pavement on dam.

Knocks & Hazards: Park can get very crowded and noisy with motorboats. Best during off times. Hot smoggy IE summers. Rattlesnakes, coyotes. Clueless peds in busy areas.

Access: From CA 60 head south on Moreno Beach Rd to the north entrance. From I-215 take Ramona Expy east to the south entrance. Pay $10/vehicle, park in a lot and find the trail either north of the lot or within the lot on a wide sidewalk.

The Ride: It's only a 9.5-mile loop, so why not ride it both ways to take in the different viewscapes? Start anywhere, but from lot 10/11 find the trail uphill from the lot and head left. At times it cuts through parking lots on sidewalks then re-emerges as a Class I path. Pass pretty Perris Beach. The trail winds down to reach the dam entrance. An alternate path leads to the unpaved horse trail below the dam. Ride 2 flat miles across the dam, with great mountain vistas over the lake on clear days, then head left at the end, riding behind the dam's mechanics. At a gate go left on the Bernasconi day use access road, then right back onto the trail. There's no more junctions the rest of the way, so enjoy the ride, the interesting rock formations, view of the island, and great birding in the shallower end. For detailed park info see parks.ca.gov/?page_id=651.

The Pacific Electric Trail (PET)— The Inland Empire's Route 66 for Bikes

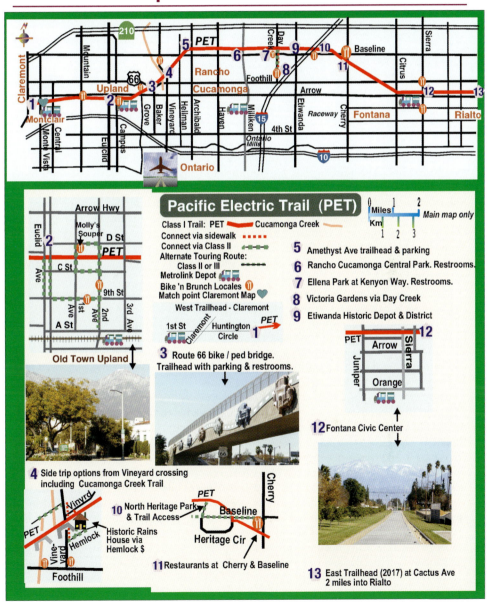

The retro Route 66 bike bridge celebrates the past historic highway and the Red Cars of the Pacific Electric Railroad at the same time

At the foot of the San Gabriel Mountains, the former empire of orange groves—where you could cruise on Route 66 and stop at an orange juice stand or stay at a cheesy motel—has evolved into urban sprawl with shopping malls, chain restaurants, and large commercial and industrial complexes. The mountains remain, of course, and in the winter they can provide a beautiful snow-covered backdrop. If you look carefully you can also spot some leftover relics from the Route 66 era that are usually accompanied by a historical sign along what is now Foothill Boulevard.

One feature of days gone by was the Pacific Electric Railroad that connected San Bernardino with Los Angeles. Its famous Red Cars had wooden benches running lengthwise to transport passengers, while the Southern Pacific rail company used the line to move freight cars loaded with citrus and wine products along the same route. The service discontinued in the 1950s with the advent of the LA freeway system, and the right of way has been transformed into a multi-use rail trail. The Pacific Electric Trail (PET) begins at the east edge of Claremont, running eastward through the San Bernardino County cities of Montclair, Upland, Rancho Cucamonga, Fontana and into Rialto.

One of the original train depots is being restored in Rancho Cucamonga where the trail intersects Etiwanda Avenue. Other points of interest along the way are downtown Claremont and the Claremont Colleges just past the west trailhead (see "Claremont"), historic Old Town Upland, Rancho Cucamonga's Victoria Gardens mega dining/shopping center village (south via a sidewalk or bike lane along Day Creek), Rancho Cucamonga's parks and its spiffy new Route 66 bike/ped bridge, and Fontana's North Heritage Park and Civic Center.

The cities along the route have each done their part to provide this much-needed paved multi-use commuter and recreation trail available to the hordes of residents of the Inland Empire. Its character changes from city to city, with the standout being Rancho Cucamonga that has done a bang-up job with parallel 10-foot wide paths, concrete for bikers and decomposed granite for runners, walkers, and equestrians. Fontana and Rialto also completed impressive concrete paths. Those three cities installed lighting and signals at most street crossings. Upland's path is simple patched asphalt that works fine, but some of their street crossings leave something to be desired. Montclair's short section is basic with several signaled street crossings.

Most of the trail is not very scenic, running between various types of development, sometimes with eucalyptus windrows shielding civilization. However, when the mountains are out on a clear day, there can be some spectacular backdrops to whatever you are looking at. Heading eastward, Mount San Gorgonio will stand as a snowy sentinel in winter, with the much closer San Gabriel Mountains forming a dramatic backdrop to the north. From various places along the trail Palm Springs' Mount San Jacinto is also visible to the southeast and Orange County's distinctive Saddleback Mountain can be seen to the south. The most scenic stretches are those that traverse parkland and vacant land, and others that are elevated over the surrounding countryside that offer sweeping views of the valley.

You can ride on a restored Pacific Electric Red Car at the Orange Empire Museum in Perris (oerm.org), or on replicas in Disney's California Adventure. Hopefully they will return to the San Pedro waterfront after redevelopment is completed there (LA3). Red Cars are also on display in Seal Beach (SE1) and National City (SD7- Opt 2).

Tunes: Route 66 by Nat King Cole; Riding on the Railroad by James Taylor; Take the "A" Train by Duke Ellington.

Eats: Apple pancakes or chef salad at Molly's Souper, Old Town Upland.

Distance: Up to 21 miles each way. Recommended: Old Town Upland to Cherry Avenue, Fontana, 10.3 miles each way; or Old Town Upland to Rancho Cucamonga's Central Park, 6 miles each way. Time: 1 to 3 hours total.

Route & Bike: Easy to moderate depending on distance and winds. Concrete and asphalt. Class I with numerous street crossings, most signaled. Any bike. Because of gaps between concrete segments, wider tires may be more comfortable. Flat with some gradual rail trail style grades. E-bike edge: Headwinds and increased distance.

Seasons: All. Mornings better when hot. Best on sunny clear winter or spring day when mountains are snow-covered.

Facilities: Water fountains along route. Restrooms in some of the Rancho Cucamonga parks including the new Route 66 trailhead, Central Park, and Ellena Park. In Fontana, Seville Park is where PET crosses Cypress Avenue. Find facilities in Fontana Civic Center buildings on weekdays.

Knocks & Hazards: Clueless peds. Although the trail is too new to have an extensive safety record, assume possible lurkers and gang activity in some of the areas so ride with a friend, especially at night, and especially east of Cherry Avenue in Fontana through Rialto. A gazillion street crossings, though most are signaled. Watch for cars running red lights at signaled crossings. Upland has some unmarked street crossings that could be very dangerous if cyclists are not cautious. Be careful of the closed gates at road crossings in Rancho Cucamonga. Summer/fall smog can be nasty here. Windy conditions are common coming out of Cajon Pass to the north, so judge your downwind distance accordingly. Potential for rattlesnakes in some areas.

Rent 'n Ride: Pedego E-Bikes, 310 N. Mountain, Upland, 0.5 mile south of trail, 909.660.5666. Shops: Cyclery USA, 7890 Haven (RC), 1 mi S, 909.466.5444; Incycle, 9110 Foothill (RC), 0.5 mi SE via Vineyard, 483.1991; Mark's Bicycle, 8605 Baseline at Carnelian (RC), 0.75 mi N, 466.1529; Competitive Edge, 9889 Foothill Blvd (RC), 1.5 mi E, 483.2453, and 1869 W Foothill (Upland), 0.9 mi N, 985.2453; Roy's Giant, 106 E 9th St, (Old Town Upland), 982.8849; Hector Bike Shop, 17312 Foothill, Fontana, 0.4 m N, 829.2626.

Camp 'n Ride: Nothing nearby. See listings under Claremont and Riverside.

Bike 'n Brunch: See ride description. Most eats in Claremont, Old Town Upland, at cross streets including Day Creek near trail and a mile detour to Victoria Gardens center, in western Fontana at Baseline and Cherry, and downtown Fontana.

City code, bike riding on sidewalks: (in case you wander off of the PET): Allowed except when signed otherwise (always be courteous of peds per state law) in Claremont, Montclair, Rancho Cucamonga and Rialto. In Upland and Fontana: Prohibited on all sidewalks.

Further Info: Friends of the PET: petrail.org; Upland's Friends of the PET: petrail. weebly.com/upland.html; City sites: Rancho Cucamonga: cityofrc.us; Fontana: fontana.org; Upland: upland.ca.us; Montclair: cityofmontclair.org; Rialto: yourrialto.org; Claremont: ci.claremont.ca.us.

Access: See the map for routes to the trail vicinity. Rancho Cucamonga Trail Access: Central Park, 11200 Baseline Rd; Ellena Park, 7139 Kenyon Way; Red Hill Park, 7484 Vineyard Ave; Route 66 trailhead on Foothill Boulevard and Baker (recommended); Etiwanda Depot at Etiwanda Ave north of Foothill (pending at time of writing); Amethyst Avenue trailhead. In Upland park anywhere in Old Town: Head north on Euclid from I-10 and turn right on 9th Street. In central Fontana park at the Civic Center (north on Sierra Avenue from I-10, just past Arrow Route, on the right). In western Fontana near I-15 park at the commercial center near the trail at Cherry and Baseline, or at the north end of Heritage Circle North (from I-15 take Baseline east 0.4 mile and turn left). In other areas find street parking near the trail as allowed.

Rail 'n Ride: Metrolink stops in downtown Claremont (see that ride) with easy access to the west end of the trail. In Montclair, where the PET crosses Monte Vista at the Richton signal, the Metrolink station is at the southeast corner. In Upland, the station is on A Street at the south end of Old Town between 2nd and 3rd Avenues. The PET can be accessed by riding north a few blocks (0.2 mile) on 2nd through the center of downtown past the historic bandstand, or along less crowded 3rd Avenue, to the trail between C and D Streets. In Rancho Cucamonga the station is off Milliken Avenue 2.3 miles south of the PET, just south of Jersey Boulevard. It requires a cycle along busy Class II Milliken (with a sidewalk option), and a 250-foot elevation gain. In Fontana the station is downtown at the corner of Bennett Avenue and Orange Way. The PET is 0.5 mile to the north, with no great way to get there. You can try going west (left) on Orange Way from the station and then north on Juniper Avenue to meet the trail just north of Spring Street, perhaps "walking" your bike along sidewalks where the road seems dangerous. From that point, the Civic Center is down the PET across Sierra Avenue to the east.

The Ride: Catch the trail anywhere along the route, perhaps exploring different sections each time. The most noteworthy stretch is the 6 miles within Rancho Cucamonga, which is a state of the art trail accomplishment. From the Route 66 trailhead consider riding west to Old Town Upland, and east to Cherry Avenue in Fontana. It is especially scenic starting west of Hellman Avenue (limited street parking available), where there is a 2-mile stretch west to Grove Avenue with no intersections, as well as above Rancho Cucamonga Central Park west of Milliken. The trail is elevated above the valley a bit along these stretches, providing a great valley vista in addition to the more frequent mountain vistas. Extending your ride to Old Town Upland provides a nice excursion for your Bike 'n Brunch. In Fontana the stretch between I-15 and Cherry Avenue is nice because of the wide open spaces and great mountain views, as well as a lot of Bike 'n Brunch opportunities along the trail in this newer section of town. The following describes the entire trail from west to east.

Claremont to Montclair

From the Claremont Depot the PET trailhead is 0.8 mile away, east down 1st Street, across Claremont Boulevard, to the end of Huntington Drive. See the Claremont ride. From the trailhead (mile 0) it heads into the city of Montclair in San Bernardino County where some road crossings are better than others, as many require a detour to a nearby intersection to be able to safely cross at the light, however the first one across Monte Vista Ave (0.25) has been improved. Although it is fairly commercial/light industrial through this stretch there can be exceptional San Gabriel Mountain vistas as the trail rambles to the northeast. The next street crossing is Central Avenue (0.8). Riding about 0.3 mile south along sidewalks on either Monte Vista or Central will bring you to a major commercial center with many restaurants to choose from including Chinese, pizza, Olive Garden, and Applebee's, around the venerable Montclair Place (aka Plaza) mall.

Upland

Continue across Benson Avenue (1.3) and Mountain Avenue (2.0), which is the road that leads all the way up to Mt Baldy. Bombdiggity Dogs Burgers & Brew is down to the right here, and Pedego E-bikes is ahead on the right. PET continues through uninteresting commercial, industrial and residential zones, daylighting at San Antonio Avenue (2.5). Go left to the signal to cross

Old Town Upland is a great destination by bike or Metrolink train

here. Next carefully cross several unsignaled secondary streets before reaching the majestic Euclid Avenue, the main boulevard of Upland, with four lanes separated by a lush treed median. Cross Euclid at a new signaled crossing, eliminating a previous detour. On the east side of Euclid begins historic nicely preserved leafy Old Town Upland. Ride up and down the streets to explore, starting with 1st Street. Popular Molly's Souper is one block north at D Street, serving breakfast and lunch in the historic house or pooch patio (cash/debit only).

Old Town Upland centers around 9th St and 2nd Ave, south of the PET, site of its central bandstand. Check out the Grove Theatre, Roy's Cyclery, antique shops, and lots of restaurants including coffee and tea shops, pizza, a sports bar, deli, Italian, and the yummy Local Baker (est 1895) on 9th. During the Covid-19 pandemic some streets were closed to allow for outdoor dining. The Metrolink station is at A and 3rd. To return to the PET turn left on 2nd or 3rd Avenue (3.4) and then turn right onto the PET, which runs between C and D Streets (3.5). To find Old Town from the other direction look for 2nd Avenue and turn left to reach the center of town.

Continuing eastward on PET, after carefully crossing busy unsignaled Campus Ave (3.9), the trail runs along the median of Washington Boulevard, requiring a couple of unsignaled residential street crossings through 11th Avenue. Reach Arrow Highway at mile 4.4, where there is a crossing signal, and then Grove Avenue (4.7).

Rancho Cucamonga

Across Grove begins one of the newer sections of trail and the start of the superior Rancho Cucamonga trail segment, leading up to the highlight at mile 5.2. Here the trail uses the new Route 66 bike/ped bridge over Foothill Boulevard, across which

Parallel bike and equestrian paths through Rancho Cucamonga with a backdrop of Mt. San Gorgonio

ramps lead from the trail down to restrooms, a water fountain, and a parking area. Check out the cars and Route 66 states sculpted into both sides of the whimsical bridge. You can take a little detour and ride to the circa 1848 Sycamore Inn, once Billy Rubottom's that served Butterfield Stage customers and later Route 66 travelers. The restaurant has been a prime evening steakhouse in recent decades, located at 8318 Foothill just west of the bridge. The circa 1932 Oso Bear statue in front is in recognition of the early pioneers. Another Route 66 classic, Magic Lamp Inn across Foothill, is open for lunch, dinner and Sunday brunch buffet.

The next 1.5 miles of PET is scenic, as it is more elevated, providing great views of the valley and is somewhat farther away from development. Just before reaching the bike/ped bridge over Vineyard Avenue (5.8) a spur trail leads north to Red Hill Country Club Drive (Option 1).

> Option 1: Food Stop or Historic Tour: Take the spur trail down and then up to a low traffic street, Red Hill Country Club Dr. Hungry? Ride to the left a short distance over the channel and turn left on the paved path, then ride down to Foothill Blvd. To the left at Vineyard are several fast food joints, coffee and Incycle bike shop.
>
> To visit the historic Casa de Rancho Cucamonga (aka Rains House, circa 1860), turn right at Red Hill Country Club instead, and cross over Carnelian Street to the far sidewalk. Go to the right, cross Vineyard, go under the PET bridge, and turn left onto Hemlock. On the left is the entrance to the Rains house, the second oldest burned brick structure in Southern California, once part of a large rancho. Tours are available from the Rancho Cucamonga Historical Society: 909.989.4970.

The PET next crosses Hellman Avenue (6.7), busy Baseline Road (6.9), Amethyst Avenue (7.0), Archibald Avenue (7.3), Ramona Avenue (7.6), Hermosa Avenue (7.8), and then Haven Avenue (8.4). Two blocks south on Haven is a Ralph's shopping center with some casual restaurants including a Starbucks. Pass a flood control channel (8.8) and then reach some vacant land and impressive Central Park, where there are great valley views, and on a clear day a panorama of all of the surrounding mountains in the region. Reach Milliken Avenue (9.3) and the vehicle entrance to Central Park, another good staging spot. Back through the mass of newer suburbia, cross Kenyon Way (9.8) and reach Ellena Park on the right, another potential place to park, with easily accessible restrooms.

Cross Rochester Avenue (10.1) then cross a welcome open space/flood control corridor (10.3). At Day Creek Boulevard (10.6) the trail jogs to the right to share a signal across Day Creek with the beautiful Craftsman-style Day Creek Firehouse. Next to it is a new (2017) flagship Stater Bros market, pizza, sushi, bbq, subs, coffee, and more.

Option 2: Victoria Gardens Bike 'n Brunch

To visit Victoria Gardens, a modern mega-mall built like a downtown core with lots of interesting restaurants and stores, detour south down Class II Day Creek. It is a fairly busy street, so you may prefer to ride on the continuous east sidewalk. At the southeast corner of Baseline is a Sprouts shopping center with casual restaurants. Turn left on Main Street after 0.9 mile to get to the center where you will find a Cheesecake Factory, King's Fish House, Yard House, PF Chang's, Chipotle, California Pizza Kitchen, and others including Japanese, Italian, French, and BBQ restaurants.

PET (10.8) carries on between the housing developments, through the nice Victoria Park area and across a bike/ped bridge over, but with no access to, Victoria Park Lane. Across Etiwanda Avenue (11.5) is one of the original depots, which is slated for renovation and trailhead parking. Circa 1914, its curved tower parapet is an example of Mission Revival style. Just south on Etiwanda Avenue are the 1902 Victorian style Etiwanda Congregational Church and the Chaffey Garcia House from 1874. Cycle onward on the PET and cross East Avenue (12.0) then go under the I-15 Freeway to Fontana (12.25).

Fontana and Rialto

Fontana's portion of the trail starts east of I-15 and runs through the city into Rialto. Fontana has done a good job with a wide concrete path with lighting and traffic signals and street signs at the major intersections. This segment begins next to a newer neighborhood to the south of the trail and a vast vacant area to the east and north, allowing for fabulous mountain views on clear days, especially once you pass the high tension power lines. Cross over another flood control channel at North Heritage Park (12.6), where there is some parking.

Wide open spaces of western Fontana just east of I-15

Option 3: Eats

A detour down North Heritage Circle then west on Class II Baseline leads to a Comfort Inn, Denny's, Logan's Roadhouse, Starbucks, and others. From there you have the option to ride east on Class II Baseline to rejoin the PET past the second junction of Heritage Circle.

Ride between more neighborhoods and welcome undeveloped land as the trail bends to the southeast, then reaches a signal to cross Baseline Avenue, across which is Heritage Circle. It next follows a pleasant greenbelt to Cherry Avenue (13.8). Between the PET and Baseline along Cherry is a Vons supermarket shopping center containing a Subway, Mongolian BBQ, Panda Express, Wendy's, and others. Across Baseline are Thai, KFC and more choices. This is one of the recommended turnaround poins.

To continue, cross Cherry to go through an industrial area and the newest section of Fontana's trail. Past Sultana Avenue (15.0) is an open area, followed by a bike/ped bridge over Foothill Boulevard (15.3). Next cross Almeria Avenue (15.6), then travel through more industrial areas, across Tokay Avenue (15.9) and busy signaled Citrus Avenue (16.1), entering more of a residential zone. Cross Oleander Avenue (16.3) and Cypress Avenue (16.6) across which is Seville Park. Cross Juniper Avenue at the signal (16.9) and begin a nicely landscaped stretch through downtown Fontana. Cross Sierra Avenue with a jog at the light (17.1).

Most of the local restaurants, predominantly Mexican food, are south on Sierra, while some fast food outlets are along Foothill, 0.4 mile to the north. The buildings of the Civic Center area east of Sierra are your best bet for finding public restrooms, on weekdays at least. This east-west stretch is especially scenic on clear days because heading east it looks like the PET leads right up to Mt. San Gorgonio. Continue on the PET next to Miller Park and cross its parking entrance at the south end of Emerald Avenue (17.3). Carefully cross Mango Avenue (17.4) and pass Fontana Middle School. Cross Palmetto Avenue (17.6), Tamarind Avenue (17.9) through yet more industrial and residential areas to Alder Avenue (18.1), across which are San Bernardino County court buildings. Next comes Laurel Avenue (18.4) and Locust Avenue (18.6) where there is a Stater Brothers market alongside the trail. After crossing Maple Avenue (18.9) the newest section of trail extends 2 miles into Rialto, ending at Cactus Avenue (20.9).

Big Bear Lake

One of the most popular getaways for Los Angeles area residents is the Big Bear Lake resort area in the San Bernardino Mountains. The reservoir lies 100 miles northeast of LA and contains 22 miles of shoreline lined with both private holdings and public lands. Its elevation of 6,750 feet allows about 5 feet of snow to fall each year on average at the lake and more at the higher elevations. The climate is much cooler than the San Bernardino Valley below it, with average summer high temperatures in the 80°F's and January highs in the 40°F's, with lows in the 20°F's or much lower. People visit the area year round for winter skiing at Snow Summit and Bear Mountain and for hiking, biking, boating, fishing, and horseback riding the rest of the year. The charming alpine Village in Big Bear Lake along Pine Knot is the central focus for tourists.

The city of Big Bear Lake and adjacent Big Bear City are the main communities around the lake, with a combined population of about 22,000. However, on any particular weekend, there may be 100,000 people enjoying the amenities of the area. Wildlife in the region includes some black bears, mountain lions, rattlesnakes, coyotes, bobcats, and the largest population of wintering bald eagles in Southern California. For easy scenic cycling try the fabulous 3.2 mile paved path along the northeast lakeshore and forest (BB1), a downhill mountain bike cruise from a Snow Summit chairlift (BB2), and pleasant on-road bike routes connecting those features with the Village area for fabulous Bike 'n Brunch rides (BB3). Also find advanced mountain biking and road biking, and lots of great hiking in the region. Start at the Visitor Center at Big Bear Blvd & Pine Knot for a bike route map, and hiking and general info. For biking/hiking trails see www.fs.usda.gov/sbnf; trailsfoundation.org.

INLAND EMPIRE OF RIVERSIDE AND SAN BERNARDINO COUNTIES

Tunes: Bears by Lyle Lovett; Bear Gone Fishing by Widespread Panic; Big Bear Lake by Mel Blanc (1949)
Eats: Picnic along Alpine Pedal Path or Lunch at Himalayan in The Village

Rent 'n Ride: Chains Required Bike Shop, 41869 Big Bear Blvd @ Summit, 909.878.3268; Bear Valley Bikes, 40298 Big Bear Blvd @ Talmadge (Lakeview Loop), 866.8000; Also find lots of other places to rent bikes around town, in marina's, resorts, etc.

Camp 'n Ride: North Shore, along Alpine Pedal Path, via SR 38 west of Stanfield Cutoff: Serrano (US Forest Service), in forest, for tents, RV's, some hookups, open Mar - Nov, reserve: recreation.gov; lakeside are Big Bear Shores RV Resort (owner site rentals $$$), 40751 North Shore Dr, Big Bear City, 866.4151; and Lighthouse Trailer Resort, 40545 North Shore Dr, BBC, 866.9464. Pine Tree RV, 1/4 mile east of BB1 trailhead, 42144 N Shore Dr, Fawnskin, 866.2025. South Shore: Pineknot USFS campground, near base of Snow Summit, south end of Summit Rd (tents, smaller RV), Holloway's Marina & RV Park, 398 Edgemoor Rd, Big Bear Lake, on the Lakeview Loop, 1 mile west of The Village), 866.5706. Numerous USFS campgrounds are located in the region, mostly suited for tents and RV's with no hookups. On recreation.gov enter "San Bernardino National Forest" for a summary. From some of the campgrounds, such as Barton

Flats, you can try pleasant rides on surrounding forest trails and roads.
Bike 'n Brunch:
Restaurants are along Big Bear Blvd (BBB) from Vons/Stater centers through The Village: Himalayan (Nepalese), 672 Pine Knot; Mexican (with patios): Azteca, 40199 BBB; El Jacalito, 535 Pine Knot. Italian: Paoli's, 40821 Village Dr; Bakery with demos: Copper Q, 645 Pine Knot. Breakfast: Teddy Bear, 583 Pine Knot; the quirky small place with big lines Grizzly Manor Café, 41268 BBB; Grind & Grill, 42011 BBB. Snow Summit may have a mountaintop BBQ. In Fawnskin North Shore Cafe is popular. Chains along BBB include El Pollo Loco, Sizzler, Carl's Jr, McD's, Denny's and Taco Bell.

Facilities: In most City and USFS parks and The Village. **Club:** BigBearCycling.com
Event: tourdebigbear.com (August) **Info:** citybigbearlake.com

Getting to Big Bear Lake:
- SR 330 to SR 18 is the fastest and easiest route, although it tends to get congested at peak times. SR 330 begins at the 210 Freeway in San Bernardino, at the "Mountain Resorts" exit, then winds uphill into the mountains, intersecting SR 18 in Running Springs. SR 18 continues past Arrowbear and Snow Valley, over 7,200-foot Lake Vista Summit, and across the 15-mile "Arctic Circle" for a total distance of 33 miles. At the Big Bear Lake dam, SR 18 continues to the south shore of the lake, and SR 38 proceeds to the north shore.
- "The Back Way" via SR 38 is longer but more scenic with less traffic than SR 330/18. Take I-10 to Redlands and Exit 80/University Street. Turn north, on University St for 1 mile to E Lugonia Ave/SR 38 and turn right. Climb SR 38, over 8,440-foot Onyx Summit, onto Big Bear Blvd in Big Bear City, about 52 miles from I-10. Trucks go this way and many RV'ers favor it.
- SR 18 through the Lucerne Valley travels over a pass into Baldwin Lake and through the north side of the Big Bear area into Big Bear City. From Victorville take either SR 18 east if you are heading south on I-15, or Bear Valley Road east to SR 18 if you are heading north. Although this route has the least amount of mountain driving, RV'ers should be aware that there is an 11 percent grade and hairpin turns on the pass north of Baldwin Lake.

Alpine Pedal Path BB1

Distance: 5 to 6.4 miles round trip. Time: 45 minutes to 1.5 hours.
Route & Bike: Easy to moderate depending on acclimation to altitude. Class I, wide paved path for any bike. Mostly gentle rolling hills. E-bike edge for hills/altitude.
Knocks & Hazards: Rare rattlesnake, black bear, cougar. Short distance on its own. Clueless peds/dog walkers (especially weekends), though widened trail has helped.
Seasons: Spring to fall; winter when free of snow and ice (X-country ski otherwise). Best on warm sunny summer weekday with strong scent of pines in the air.

Access: On the north shore of the lake, park at Juniper Point or Meadow's Edge Picnic Areas, or Cougar Pass Trailhead (Adventure Pass or National Lands access pass required) or free at Discovery Center or along the Stanfield Cutoff.

The Ride: The only substantial paved Class I path in the region parallels the north shore of Big Bear Lake from the Stanfield Cutoff to just west of the Solar Observatory. From Stanfield Cutoff (mile 0) the path reaches Carol Morrison boat launch facility, then begins a scenic stretch between North Shore Drive and the lake, sometimes close to its shore, with Snow Summit's slopes beyond. Reach the lot for Juniper Point Picnic area (1.0), then ride through a beautiful meadow before entering forest (1.2).

Keep right at an unsigned junction (1.4) to Meadows Edge picnic area. On the return perhaps pedal around its paved paths. Carefully cross Big Bear Lane (1.6) near the entrance to Serrano Campground. A junction up ahead to the right leads through a bike/ped tunnel under Hwy 38 (North Shore Drive) to the Cougar Crest Trailhead parking lot. From there that paved path curves over a hill, east to the Discovery Center. Add 1.4 miles round trip for this pretty excursion. The main trail continues past the Serrano Campground, crossing the Serrano entry road, and runs roughly parallel to the north of North Shore Lane through the forest. Loops of Serrano Campground are to the north and private RV resorts are south of North Shore Lane along the lake in this area. Lighthouse Trailer Resort has a general store for refreshments. The path wanders through the forest as it curves north (2.25), then west, ending at North Shore Lane just south of its intersection with Hwy 38 (2.5). A dirt path across the road leads to the lake, with a view to the Solar Observatory to the left.

Snow Summit to Bear Mountain Downhill MTB   BB2

Enjoy a scenic lift up the mountain and great views of Big Bear Lake and surrounding mountains, followed by a pleasant cruise down the mountain on an unpaved fire road, or roughly parallel singletrack, returning on residential side streets and Forest Service road with lots of options to extend/combine the ride.

Distance: 5-mile loop with lift, with options to extend. Riding time: 1 hour.
Route & Bike: Easy (to moderate depending on acclimation to altitude), dirt fire road and paved city streets, MTB. Skill level advanced novice MTB for downhill ride. Descend from 8,200 feet at the summit to 7,000 feet at the base, then rolling terrain back to ride start. Options for more difficult routes.
Knocks 'n Hazards: Bear, cougar, rattlesnake, thunderstorm, cars on 2N10, $$$ lift.
Season: Spring to fall, exact dates vary. See bigbearmountainresort.com for current season info and map. Fees: Snow Summit adult lift ticket is ~$25/ride or ~$40/day.

Access: From SR 18 west of the Stanfield Cutoff take Summit Boulevard south to the parking lot for Snow Summit. Address: 880 Summit Blvd, Big Bear Lake.

The Ride: Take your bike up the Scenic Sky Chair lift to the top of the Snow Summit ski area. Skyline Taphouse offers summer bbq and great vistas. Follow signs to get to nicely graded Skyline Rd (FS 2N10) heading east. It meanders along small rolling hills through the forest, with occasional vistas of the lake, then drops down more steeply to the Club View trailhead (2.3). *Intermediates will much prefer the new parallel singletrack Skyline Trail, and can continue across the Club View parking lot on Skyline Trail to Fern Trail to Bristlecone Rd.* Club View descends steeply (careful!) to Bear Mountain base station. For the shortest return route turn left on Cedar Ave (3.4). Just after Elm, turn left onto FS 2N99 "Bristlecone" Road (3.8). It passes Pineknot campground and ends at the Snow Summit base station (4.7 total). Or, for a longer return route, pass Cedar and stay on Club View to Moonridge (left, 3.6). The new Big Bear Alpine Zoo is at this corner, home of a grizzly family. Turn left on Evergreen (4.1), and left on Summit (4.8) to the lift area (5.0). With an all day lift pass you can repeat this or other rides. The new Going Green to Towne Trail is a novice+ route from the summit to the lifts. A more intermediate ride takes you from the summit west on 2N10 or Skyline Trail, to the spectacular Grand View vista point, down the hill via 2N08 to Towne Trail, then either to the lifts, or down a steep hill to Knickerbocker and The Village (~8 mi).

Option 1: BB2 and BB1 ★

About 15 miles total: 8.2 miles including ride BB2 and connect through town, plus 6.4 miles on Alpine Pedal Path (BB1).

Big Bear Lake plans to connect the terminus of FS 2N10 to Alpine Pedal Path, including a Class I trail along the Rathbun Creek corridor parallel to Moonridge. Elm St to Big Bear Blvd was completed in 2020. Until the rest is built, generally follow Moonridge to Big Bear Blvd and take your choice of routes to the Stanfield Cutoff and to the Alpine Pedal Path. To get to Big Bear Village, follow the routes shown on the map. These are mostly city-designated bike routes with sharrows. In general the routes closer to the lake are less hilly. Towne Trail is a scenic hilly novice pathway that connects Snow Summit's Slopeside Rental Shop to The Village.

Forest Service Rd 2N10 down from the Sky Chair.
Photo By Conley/MacMillan

Big Bear Easy Bike 'n Brunch BB3 ★

The best of Big Bear Lake: Alpine Pedal Path, The Village, and the City Bike Loops.
Distance 14 miles +/-, Paved, any bike. Easy with options. Town portion is Class II & III bike routes.

Big Bear Lake's bike infrastructure is a work in progress per their 2014 master plan, but it is already a wonderful town to enjoy a scenic pedal with stops at a great variety of restaurants. You can park anywhere in town, but we'll start by parking on Stanfield Cutoff, and cycling the Alpine Pedal Path (BB1). Ride back, past your vehicle (~6.0) along a multi-use path on the west side of the Cutoff. Turn right on Big Bear Blvd on the sidewalk (or bike path planned 2021), then right again on wide Class II Sandalwood before Vons (6.5). Turn right on Fox Farm and cross Garstin, onto Swan (7.2). Turn right onto Marina Point Dr (7.4) to begin the very pleasant, low-traffic Eagle Point Loop, and ride past some of the nicest homes in town, along the lake. Follow the bike route signs around the point to Park Ave (9.1). Turn right. Visit Ski Beach Park at road's end. The "Transition Route" goes left up Knight Ave to Big Bear Blvd at the Taco Bell (9.7). Go right (sidewalk or bike lane) until you reach Big Bear Village's waterfront area, exploring the parks and the Pine Knot Marina (10.2). The Village district extends up Pine Knot Ave several blocks, then west along Village Dr. Use the Class I path between Pine Knot and Knickerbocker in one direction. After exploring this area (~11.2) head back the same way (from Park turn left on Wren this time) (14.0), or try the hillier interior bike route starting east on Village Dr to Pennsylvania (see map) (14.0).

> Options: West of The Village is the 2.8-mile Lakeview Loop (see map inset). Inland of SR18 it passes Aspen Glen picnic area (and hiking trailhead) but it gets hillier and the two unsignaled Hwy 18 crossings can be difficult. The 6.5-mile Moonridge Loop (see map) leads to Bear Mountain and the Alpine Zoo, but involves lots of hills and steady climbs southbound (e-bike edge). The City's "Bicycle Routes" map contains turn by turn detail.

9. The Deserts

When one conjures up a vision of the California desert, it probably includes palm trees, swimming pools, sunshine, and golf greens in a region with the generic name of Palm Springs. Although Palm Springs and environs is all that, there is much more to the California deserts. There are actually two deserts in Southern California, created by the rainshadow effects of the mountain ranges that span the spine of the state.

The Mojave Desert extends from southeast of the Central Valley and the Sierra Nevada Range, through Death Valley and into Nevada and Arizona. With the exception of Death Valley, it is mostly found at elevations of 3,500 to 4,500 feet. Summer temperatures are usually in the high 90°F's (much higher in Death Valley), while winter can see low temperatures under 20°F. Rainfall ranges between 4 and 15 inches per year, to only about 2 inches in Death Valley. The creosote bush is the most common plant in the Mojave, which also contains Mojave yucca and Joshua tree forests.

Palm Springs is in the Colorado Desert, located at the southwest corner of California, an extension of the Sonoran Desert of Mexico and Arizona. The Colorado Desert is found below 2,000 feet elevation. Average annual rainfall is typically 1 to 5 inches, and summer temperatures soar over 100°F. Natural habitat includes creosote bush scrub, mixed scrub (including yucca and cholla cactus), desert saltbush, sandy soil grasslands, and desert dunes.

Our rides are found in Palm Springs and the surrounding Coachella Valley and Anza-Borrego State Park in the Colorado Desert, and the portion of Joshua Tree National Park that lies within the Mojave Desert.

Windmills north of Palm Springs

Palm Springs and the Coachella Valley

The Palm Springs resort region in the Coachella Valley can be a wonderful place to hang out from about November through April, and even October and May depending on your tolerance for a bit of heat. The weather is frequently picture perfect, barren hills can turn green in wetter years, and beyond the lush golf course greenery and stately palms stand towering peaks in the distance that are frequently blanketed with snow at higher elevations. The 10,839-foot Mount San Jacinto to the west, upon which the Palm Springs Aerial Tramway ascends, is the sixth largest escarpment (change in elevation of a mountain from base to summit per distance) in the Lower 48, while other interesting mountains of the San Jacinto Range such as Tahquitz Peak help shield Palm Springs from much of the rain that falls along the coast. Also visible from the valley is Mount San Gorgonio in the San Bernardino Mountains to the northwest, the tallest peak in Southern California at 11,503 feet. To the north are the Little San Bernardino Mountains within nearby Joshua Tree National Park, while the more barren Mecca Hills are to the east. The distinctive colored Chocolate Mountains are toward the southeast, and are within an off-limits military zone. The Santa Rosa Mountains are to the south, which form the backdrop beyond La Quinta and Palm Desert, featuring Toro Peak that rises to 8,716 feet elevation.

The 15-mile wide Coachella Valley spreads out for 45 miles from the northwest at the base of the San Bernardino Mountains southeast to the 376-square mile Salton Sea, which lies below sea level. Formed when the Colorado River was accidentally diverted in 1905, it is now mostly maintained by irrigation runoff and is a very important inland bird habitat, especially due to the loss of 90 percent of California's wetlands. If you see squadrons of white pelicans flying overhead or around artificial ponds in the valley, they are part of the Salton Sea's winter bird population. The valley is flanked by the mighty San Andreas Fault along its northern extremity that appears as a ribbon of green across the otherwise barren landscape. This is indeed a seismically active area, and the next "big one" is expected to happen in this area ... any time now. The mostly flat topography of the Coachella Valley means that easy scenic bike riding is the rule, while the surrounding mountains provide challenges for heartier mountain bikers.

Although the Palm Springs region has become known as a place where the Colorado Desert was dug up and green lawns and golf courses were laid down in its place, there has been a movement to return to more natural desert vegetation that uses less water and is more harmonious with the environment. At the various outlying preserves, native vegetation will be on display, whereas in the developed areas, seeing native vegetation depends on plantings by the various cities or property owners. They typically choose colorful varieties, making a lot of the cycling around the valley a very refreshing experience. It is not unusual to have a vista that incorporates a red flowering bougainvillea, green palm trees, blue skies, and brown and white snow-capped mountains simultaneously.

In addition to the native plants such as creosote bush and mixed scrub, surplus moisture supplied by summer monsoon rainfall fosters the germination of summer annual plants and supports smoketree, ironwood, and palo verde trees. Many herbaceous annual wildflowers pop to life in early spring during wet years. At higher elevations surrounding the deserts are piñon pine, California juniper, manzanita, and Coulter pine.

Common wildlife includes mule deer, desert kangaroo rat, cactus mouse, black-tailed jackrabbit, bobcat, coyote, Gambel's quail, roadrunner, and red-diamond rattlesnake. Rare and sensitive species include Coachella Valley fringe-toed lizard, desert tortoise, prairie falcon, and the Peninsular bighorn sheep. Mountain lions and black bears are also found in the wilderness areas, with bears mostly sticking to the higher elevations.

Climate Data for Palm Desert (NOAA 1981 to 2010 normals)												
Month	Jan	Feb	Mar	Apr	May	Jun	Jul	Aug	Sep	Oct	Nov	Dec	Totals
Average High °F	71.9	75.3	81.3	87.5	95.7	103.1	107.3	106.6	102.0	91.9	79.6	71.0	89.5
Average Low °F	44.6	48.0	54.7	60.9	67.7	74.4	80.3	80.3	74.0	63.7	51.8	44.2	62.1
Precipitation, inches	0.56	0.64	0.43	0.05	0.07	0.01	0.00	0.54	0.04	0.26	0.18	0.62	3.44

The Bike-Friendly Cities of the Desert

Palm Springs (population 48,500) is the most well known, and northwestern-most of the small cities that comprise the Coachella Valley. The rich and famous made Palm Springs their playground in the mid-twentieth century, and unique mid-century modern architecture dominates many neighborhoods. The city had its rises and falls, with the main downtown corridor bustling, then deteriorating, then rebounding with redevelopment in the 1990s thanks largely to the gays and lesbians that have flocked to the city. A massive redevelopment project was recently completed downtown.

Palm Springs offers the lion's share of attractions, including its appealing downtown core, easily accessible via the Star Tour (PS1) ride. Restaurants, theatres, galleries, and plenty of shops make it the most popular place to visit in the valley. Palm Springs Art Museum is a cultural centerpiece, located along ride PS1. Thursday evening's Villagefest transforms downtown into a pedestrian mall, and the Palm Springs Film Festival held in January has become one of the nation's largest, held at various theatres around town. The Palm Springs Air Museum at Palm Springs Airport contains one of the world's largest collections of flying WWII airplanes, and is accessible via sidewalk bikeways from downtown to the Gene Autry Bikeway (PS4).

Southeast of Palm Springs is Cathedral, or "Cat" City, which is mostly a working residential community (population 51,200) but has a few resorts of note and the interesting Mary Pickford Civic Center along Highway 111 with a casino, restaurants, and theatres. The Whitewater Trail (CC1) enables a cross-valley cycle avoiding major roadways. Farther southeast are Rancho Mirage, Palm Desert, Indian Wells, and La Quinta, which are dominated by gated resort communities and world-famous country clubs. The Coachella Valley is one of the premier golfing destinations in the world with about 140 courses. That is great for golfers, however, *cyclists need to be mindful of the occasional wayward golf ball when riding next to golf courses*, even if they are behind walls. Wearing helmets and sturdy protective eyeware couldn't hurt. We find 1 or 2 balls per ride in the golf resort areas, and on rare occasions they are still rolling.

Rancho Mirage (population 17,200) extends from I-10 to the foothills of the Santa Rosa Mountains and contains country clubs such as Mission Hills (site of the Dinah Shore, or ANA Inspiration LPGA golf tournament in April), lots of upscale residential communities, and its share of restaurants and shopping centers, mostly along Highway 111's Restaurant Row. The River is the most interesting center in the valley with its refreshing reflective pools surrounding movie theatres, restaurants, and shops. Sunnylands (the Annenberg Estate), is popular for its visitors center, gardens, and tours.

Palm Desert (population 48,500) contains the ritzy El Paseo shopping district, the College of the Desert with the McCallum Theatre and a popular weekend outdoor marketplace, and miles of boulevards alongside gated country club communities. It also extends from I-10 to Highway 111 and beyond, and is the base of the Palms to Pines Highway (SR 74) that winds up to the quaint resort town of Idyllwild in the San Jacinto Mountains. Palm Desert sponsors "Art in Public Places" around the city, and from the Art Map available at palm-desert.org you can do a scavenger hunt for the installations during your cycling excursions. A satellite of the Palm Springs Art Museum, The Galen, with a sculpture garden, is in the El Paseo district, and art pieces line the median of El Paseo's main boulevard.

Adjacent Palm Desert and Rancho Mirage not only have extensive bike lanes, but bikes are welcome on their lovely sidewalks. When strung together they form an impressive network of Class I-ish bike trails, or sidepaths, that enable long bike rides away from traffic and make it possible to easily and safely visit the area's highlights by bike. Portions of the cities sit on a high point in the valley (around 400 feet) offering 360-degree views of all of the surrounding mountain ranges (RM1 and 2, PD1).

Indian Wells (population 5,000) is located south of Palm Desert and west of La Quinta, and consists mostly of upscale golf course communities and exclusive resorts. The Indian Wells Tennis Garden is home of the BNP Paribas Open in March, one of biggest on the ATP and WTA circuit. A sidewalk path (formerly called a "Bike Path") along Hwy 111 (IW1) through Indian Wells connects Palm Desert to La Quinta (population 37,500), which has constructed wide boulevards and beautiful sidewalks in the newer areas, and offers charming cycling destinations such as Old Town and the densely packed La Quinta Cove district with its rare Class I trail (LQ1, 2, and 3). Besides its suburban-style residential neighborhoods, La Quinta also has high-end developments, such as PGA West and the venerable La Quinta Country Club, plus a long strip of new retail development along Highway 111. The lake in Lake Cahuilla Regional Park is one of the only bodies of water that the public can ride next to in the desert, where most lakes are associated with private golf course developments.

Indio, to the east of La Quinta, was the original city by way of its history as a railroad stop and agricultural center. It contains the valley's largest population (85,600) and hosts some of the region's premier events such as the fun Tamale Festival in December where its downtown core becomes a pedestrian mall with food stands and live music. Downtown is also worth checking out because of its series of murals that depict the history of the Coachella Valley. The National Date Festival in February is Riverside County's annual fair, celebrating the region's legacy as the world's date capital. Hugely popular concerts such as the Coachella Music and Art Festival (indie and mainstream rock bands) and Stagecoach Festival (country performers) are held in April, and various festivals are featured in October at the Empire Polo Club grounds at the south end of town near the La Quinta border. Most of Indio and cities to the east do not have much to offer the easy scenic cyclist, but that will soon change.

The Coachella Valley or CV Link path has begun construction throughout the valley. When completed it will run along the Whitewater River channel in much of Palm Springs and Cathedral City, and a 3-mile section is already completed. Rancho Mirage has banned it, and Palm Desert's section, to be completed in 2021, is mostly along existing roadways. Indian Wells has banned it, but the 14 miles from La Quinta through Indio and Coachella will be continuous along the channel. For precise maps and approximate construction dates see coachellavalleylink.com. The modern path is open to bikes, peds, and Neighborhood Electric Vehicles (NEV's). Some communities are also designating connector routes to access the path. Besides CV Link there is a paucity of Class I bike paths, but many of the valley sidepaths/walks mimic them.

For those who prefer to keep to the bike lanes, next to every great sidepath there is typically also a bike lane, so you can do the same rides on the road, but if the bike lane disappears you can hop back on the sidewalk, where allowed, for your safety.

Novice mountain bikers are mostly left in the lurch in the Coachella Valley. Bikes are either banned from the most popular trails, the trails are too sandy, or the terrain is too hilly to be of interest to us, such as the great hiking trails in the Santa Rosa and San Jacinto Mountains National Monument. Its Visitor Center and trailhead, on Hwy 74, 3.6 miles south of El Paseo, is worth a visit and hike from there. We can recommend biking the short loop trails at La Quinta Cove (LQ1), and possibly Indio Hills at Golf Center & 42nd (map p350), but besides that the closest rides in this genre are in nearby Joshua Tree National Park to the north (JT1), and the flat but mostly sandy rides at Anza-Borrego State Park to the south (AB1 through 4), all described later.

You can, however, cycle to hiking trailheads from a few of our easy scenic rides. Two areas are on the Agua Caliente Indian Reservation that was founded in 1896. It occupies 31,610 acres, 6,700 acres of which are within Palm Springs, and the remainder in neighboring cities and unincorporated areas. The reservation is laid out in a checkerboard pattern, with half the land owned by the Indians and the other half privately owned, leading to significant ownership implications with regards to land leases. Besides housing the popular casinos that attract top name entertainment to the valley, reservation land is also the site of the best easy hiking in the region, and fees are charged for the privilege. The controlled entry helps limit vandalism of the land that holds such importance to the Agua Caliente Band of Cahuilla Indians.

Indian Canyons is at the south end of Palm Springs, down South Palm Canyon Drive, with the trailhead to the beautiful palm oases about 3.5 miles (285 feet elevation gain) down a paved road from the closest point along the South Palm Springs loop ride (PS2). Tahquitz Canyon is at the west end of Mesquite Avenue, just southwest of downtown, and contains a great hike to a beautiful waterfall. The trailhead is up a hill, about 0.8-mile (100 feet elevation gain) from the closest point of ride PS1. The visitor's centers at both sites are good places to learn about the history of the Cahuilla Indians in the region (fees charged).

In Palm Desert, the Living Desert has a great zoo with local flora and fauna, hiking trails, and a popular winter festival. It is about 1.4 miles (and 165 feet elevation gain) south on Portola Avenue from El Paseo, or via a loop ride as shown on the RM1,2 map.

Sidewalks Under the Palms

In many areas bike riding is forbidden and/or undesirable on sidewalks, however this is not the case in the Coachella Valley. In fact, it is more the exception to the rule, and we tend to refer to the nicest sidewalk trails as sidepaths. The cities of Palm Desert, Rancho Mirage, and Indio allow biking on most of their sidewalks. In Palm Springs, Indian Wells, Cathedral City, and La Quinta, sidewalks must

Beautiful sidepaths like this one along ride IW1 are commonplace in the valley.

be designated as bike routes to allow cycling, but they have sidewalk bike routes along many of the main roads. Where bikes are banned outright, such as in the core business district of downtown Palm Springs, signs are usually posted to indicate this. In the other areas citations are rarely issued to well-behaved cyclists, i.e. they are "functionally allowed." However, they will cite cyclists that create a nuisance and are not courteous to pedestrians. So, make your own evaluation whether you want to risk an unlikely citation under the circumstances described versus risking riding with traffic.

Thankfully for the cyclist, much of the valley consists of large, usually gated, subdivisions that have a minimum of access roads across the sidepaths, thus limiting interruptions to the ride. You can take endless rides, easily 5, 10, 25, and up to 40 miles, by just staying on sidepaths, imagining them as Class I trails. You will notice that the character of the sidewalks change as you pass by the various developments, since each is responsible for its own sidewalk. They range from beautiful, wide, lushly landscaped winding sidepaths to more old fashioned straight boring sidewalks. Sometimes there is no sidewalk at all, so it is best to do a reconnaissance of your route beforehand if you want to keep away from traffic. We have done much of that for you, but conditions do change and we did not map out all the sidewalks in the entire valley.

Although most of the main roads have nice ample bike lanes, the speed limits on surface streets can be as high as 55 or 60 mph with up to 3 lanes of traffic each way. The vast majority of cyclists in the valley stick to the streets, but we prefer to be the uncool ones riding safely and calmly on sidepaths, enjoying the magnificent vistas rather than hoping the cars whizzing by won't kill us. However, we do like to ride on low-traffic and low-speed limit roads, especially in un-gated neighborhoods between Palm Springs and La Quinta.

Ride safely! Sidewalks or sidepaths have their own set of hazards, so use as much caution as on a roadway, and wear a helmet in case you fall and head meets concrete. Sprinklers can make paths very slippery, so proceed slowly. Avoid high wind events when palm fronds or entire trees can fall onto the path. Be wary of golf balls next to golf courses. Ride at a safe speed, single file. Some cities elsewhere have a 15 mph limit on sidewalks. If you encounter peds the law requires to signal your arrival and slow way down. Watch for obstacles, especially if you're unfamiliar with the path. Identify the ramp on the opposite curb in advance to avoid a tumble. Just as in road biking the greatest danger exists anytime you cross an intersection or driveway. Always analyze the situation and only proceed when safe; don't take risks. If you're riding against traffic on the sidewalk a driver waiting to turn may not be looking in your direction. Never ride through a red light, and it's best to wait for the walk signal if using the crosswalk. Beware of "right hooks" where a vehicle goes around you and then cuts in front of you, also a cause of accidents for road bikers.

Getting to and Around the Desert

The I-10 Freeway is the main route into the Coachella Valley, and is the freeway that joins most of the desert communities, providing a quick route across town, depending on how far your destination is from the freeway. The main eastbound exit to Palm Springs is Highway 111, which is about 120 miles east of Los Angeles International Airport (LAX). For the east side of our ride area (Indio/La Quinta/Palm Desert), the exit of Washington Street is about 25 miles farther east. It is also about 260 miles west of Sky Harbor Airport in Phoenix. Palm Springs International Airport offers non-stop service to many airports in the U.S. and Canada, more so in peak season. Amtrak has a stop in North Palm Springs but with very sporadic service. The Amtrak bus service from other major stations offers more frequent stops at locations throughout the valley. The Sunbus system operates in the Coachella Valley. Each bus carries up to two bikes. See sunline.org for routes and schedules. Riverside County Transit has a Palm Desert to Riverside route that carries bikes. From Riverside you can board a Metrolink train and then connect to other rail systems as well.

Season: Mid October to mid May, with variations. When hot, ride very early in the morning. During intense heat periods in summer don't risk being caught out in the heat, which typically exceeds 100°F and may reach 120°F on occasion. Best on any sunny, mild day with minimal wind, especially scenic when mountains have snow.

Rent 'n Ride: Bike PalmSpgs, 194 S Indian Cyn, 760.832.8912; Tri-A-Bike, 44841 San Pablo, PD, 340.2840; PalmDes Bike, 73-865 Hwy 111, 340.3861; Pedego E-Bikes, 62950 20th, PSP, 537.7603 & 78-075 Main, LQ, 972.4017; Big Wheel Tours, PSP 548.0500 & PD 779.1837; Village Peddler, 50855 Washington, LQ, 777.RIDE; Shops: Joel's, 42226 Varner, 343.2271; Palm Springs Cyclery, 611 S Palm Canyon, 325.9319; Palm Desert Cyclery, 77750 Country Club, 345.9096; Bikeman, 42280 Beacon Hill, PD, 341.5022; Velo Bum, 71430 Hwy 111, RM, 341.2463.

Camp 'n Ride: *Palm Springs:* Happy Traveler RV Park's sites are separated by tall shrubs. Best location for the Palm Springs rides, 211 W Mesquite, 760.325.8518. *Cathedral City:* Cathedral Palms RV Resort, along Whitewater Trail (CC1) with access to Palm Springs and Rancho Mirage, 35901 Cathedral Canyon Dr, 760.324.8244; Desert Shadows RV Resort, 68901 Ramon Rd, 760.321.7676; Outdoor Resort Palm Springs, 69411 Ramon Rd, 760.328.3834; Palm Springs Oasis RV Resort (55+), 36100 Date Palm Drive, 1.877.570.2267.
Palm Desert: Emerald Desert RV Resort, 76000 Frank Sinatra Drive, 877.624.4140, (near rides RM1 and 2, PD1). Thousand Trails (membership), 77500 Varner Road, 760.345.2236 (closed in summer).
La Quinta: Lake Cahuilla Regional Park, 58075 Jefferson St, 760.564.4712, Reserve: rivcoparks.org. RV sites with partial hookups, tent and equestrian sites. Ride 12 miles to Old Town La Quinta (LQ2). Ride to the Polo Grounds (Coachella Festival, etc), 4.4 miles to Ave 52 and Madison. Both sidewalks and bike lanes are available except for a 1/3-mile low-traffic stretch from park entrance road.
Indio: Indian Wells Carefree RV Resort (near La Quinta's Costco), 47-340 Jefferson St, 760.347.0895; Shadow Hills RV Resort, 40-655 Jefferson St, 760.360.4040; Indian Waters RV Resort, 47-202 Jackson St, 760.342.8100; Riverside County Fairgrounds has RV hookup sites, subject to closure for events and Jan and Feb; fairground entrance is Gate 4, 46290 Arabia, 760.863.8762, datefest.org.

Event: Tour de Palm Springs, late Jan/early Feb, raises money for local charities. Downtown Palm Springs is closed to vehicles and turned into a sea of bicycles for the weekend, choose from ride distances from 5 to 50 miles, tourdepalmsprings.com.

Further info: City websites: cathedralcity.gov; cityofindianwells.org; indio.org; la-quinta.org; cityofpalmdesert.org; palmspringsca.gov; ranchomirageca.gov. Coachella Valley Association of Governments (CVAG): cvag.org.
CV Link Trail (CVAG): coachellavalleylink.com. Also friendsofcvlink.org.
Desert Bicycle Club: cycleclub.com. Facebook: Coachella Valley Bicycle Coalition
Info sites: visitpalmsprings.org; desertsun.com; kmir.com.

Palm Springs and Cathedral City

Palm Springs has designated a series of overlapping bike routes that are mostly on roadways and some sections on designated sidewalk bike paths. See the website visitpalmsprings.com for a map of those routes. We have put together rides that incorporate portions of these bike routes in some cases, and entire bike routes in others. These include our featured ride, a fun journey that is somewhat of a scavenger hunt for vintage stars' former homes and incorporates Palm Springs' most famous neighborhoods (ride PS1). The downtown shopping and entertainment district is easily accessible from that ride. Another shows you around South Palm Springs, a favorite district for many (PS2). Tahquitz Creek Loop (PS3) encircles scenic golf courses and is partially along the CV Link trail network, as is a portion of the Airport-Whitewater loop next to the airport and the wash (PS4). All rides can be connected including the Coachella Valley Bikeway through Cat City to Rancho Mirage (CC1). The pending CV Link trail through Cat City will improve that route.

A group pauses at the former residence of Clark Gable and Carol Lombard to recite appropriate movie lines

1 Via Lola: Sidney Sheldon (375,425, 467), Kirk Douglas (515)
1A Donna Reed (1184 Cam Mirasol)
1B Joseph Barbera (533 Cam Norte)
1C Cam Norte: Alan Ladd (323)
   H Hughes (335) Mary Martin (365)
2 LiberaceGuestHouse(1441Kaweah)
3 Kaufman House (470 Vista Chino)
4 Debbie Reynolds (670 Stevens)
5 Marilyn Monroe (1326 Rose)
   Nat King&Natalie Cole(1258 Rose)
6 Elvis Honeymoon (1350 Ladera)
7 Peter Lawford (1295 Monte Vista)
   Dean Martin (1123 Monte Vista)
7A Charisse / T.Martin (697 CamSur)
8 Hermosa:A Miller (457),Liz Taylor (417), D Shore/Leo Dicapr(432)
9 Kate Hepburn/Spencer Tracy(776)
10 Lily Tomlin "Lily Pad"(443 Merito)
   Lena Horne (465 Merito)
11 Mary Pickford (701 Patencio)
   Burns & Allen/G Hamilton (591)
12 Pioneer Cemetery
13 Jewish Community Center
14 Sammy Davis Jr (444 Chino)
15 Gable/Lombard (222 Chino)
16 Casa Liberace
17 McDonnell Golf Course
18 Chamber of Commerce
19 PS Art Museum; "Marilyn"
20 Historic Tennis Club
   Spencer's restaurant
21 Tahquitz Canyon (Hiking)
22 Deepwell District
   Loretta Young (1075 Manzanita)
   Eva Gabor (1509 Manzanita)
   Liberace (1516 Manzanita)
   William Holden (1323 Driftwood)
   Jerry Lewis (1349 Sagebrush)
   Carmen Miranda (1044 Rolph)
23 Frank Sinatra (1145 Via Colusa)
24 El Alameda: Heddy Lamar (1232); Bob Hope (1188) also 24A
   Dorothy Lamour (1029)
   Bing Crosby (1011)
25 Harold Lloyd (899 Ave Palmas)
26 Cary Grant (987 Ave Palmas)
27 Jack Benny (987 Palos Verdes)
   Dinah Shore/G Montgomery (877)
28 Wellness Park
29 Lucy & Desi (1194 Miraleste)
30 Desert Regional Medical Center
31 Chino Canyon & Little Tuscany
   Zsa Zsa Gabor (595 Chino Cnyn)
   Elvis Presley (845 Chino Cnyn)
   Frederick Loewe (815 Panorama)
   Hearst Home (701 Panorama)

THE DESERTS

Palm Springs Vintage Star Tour—Where YOU Are the Star! PS1

This fun tour combines great scenery, history, pop culture, adventure, and Bike 'n Brunch opportunities. Our route takes you on a treasure hunt past homes once occupied by celebrities that older folks will recognize as household names, and young'uns will know if they pay attention to classic movies or music from the 1920s to the early '80s. It was a golden age when the stars could get away from the pressures of the Hollywood scene and relax in the desert, although they did create their fair share of melodrama out here as well. The stars don't flock here as they used to, and the ones that stayed have mostly passed on. Although some lived in mansions on hillsides in areas not accessible to the general public, most settled in three neighborhoods—Las Palmas, Deepwell, and Movie Colony/Ruth Hardy Park.

Short but sweet bike path along Riverside Drive North

These remain some of the most sought-after neighborhoods today, and combine for a nice tour. We are known to invite our guests to pose in front of the various homes and recite the former occupants' signature lines or songs, and we have supplied some hints to get you started in case you want to do the same. There are many more celebrity homes not mentioned; we picked only the most well known ones so that you are not stopping every minute. For a more complete tour you can buy The Tour of the Stars map from the Palm Springs visitor's center. If you don't really care who owned the various homes, this tour still takes you past some of the most interesting architecture in Palm Springs, including the mid-century modern homes that are a trademark here. Your Bike 'n Brunch options are mostly along Palm Canyon Drive, the main drag of Palm Springs. That avenue is so-so for cycling (a sharrowed lane between Ramon and Alejo, also on Indian Canyon) and bikes are banned from the sidewalks. However, from many segments of PS1 you can ride a block or two to reach the dining district, and walk your bike along the sidewalk there to find your perfect café for an al fresco repast. Some restaurants also have rear entrances from the western side streets.

Tunes: Celluloid Heroes by The Kinks; Diamonds are a Girl's Best Friend by Marilyn Monroe; Some Enchanted Evening by Bing Crosby; Summer Wind by Frank Sinatra; September Song by Liberace; Love is a Many Splendored Thing by The Four Aces. TV Themes: I Love Lucy; Patty Duke Show; I Dream of Jeannie; Green Acres, etc.

Eats: Three-course brunch on Lulu's patio or interesting creations at Cheeky's.

Distance: Up to 11.7 miles + options. Time: Up to 1.5 hours + sightseeing time.
Route & Bike: Easy to moderate. Mostly Class III residential streets with some Class I trail and sidewalk. Paved, any bike. Flat except small to moderate hills in Las Palmas district.

Knocks & Hazards: Mostly on-street riding through residential neighborhoods. May be confusing to navigate in places because of detailed directions. A few hills. Although the stars no longer live in the homes, others do, so do not trespass or disturb.

Facilities: Bring plenty of your own water. Restrooms and water in Ruth Hardy Park. Downtown, public restrooms are next to Il Corso restaurant (111 N Palm Canyon Drive) across from the Rowan Hotel, next to the "Isabelle" sculpture. Also the Hyatt hotel lobby at 285 N Palm Canyon.

Bike 'n Brunch: Tons of options along Palm Canyon Dr, including Cheeky's at 622 N Palm Canyon and Lulu's patio at 200 S Palm Canyon. There's Thai, tapas, gourmet burgers, Mexican, coffee, you name it. See ride description for others.

Access: This is a loop, so start anywhere along it, parking in any of the neighborhoods. We'll start in the Las Palmas neighborhood west of the downtown corridor. If you are driving south from I-10 on Hwy 111, after passing Vista Chino, watch for the light for Tachevah, then take an immediate right onto Via Lola. Park along the street.

The Ride: Pedal west on Via Lola, past Mission. Kick it off with:

#375, 425, 467, 3 home compound of Sidney Sheldon, bestselling author and TV writer. Try acting out a scene from his *I Dream of Jeannie* or *The Patty Duke Show*.

#515 Kirk Douglas (Painting with one ear missing, or a thoughtful gladiator pose?).

Turn around, make the first left on Mission, left on Cam Sur, and right on Mirasol. The corner house after #1144 on the right was Donna Reed's. Act Domestic! On the left corner before Cam Norte (#533) was Joseph Barbera's house. Be Astro? or Fred F? To the right on Cam Norte is the house Alan Ladd od'd in (#323), Howard Hughes' estate (#335), Mary Martin's estate (#365) (fly like Peter pan?), then Dinah Shore/George Montgomery (#317). Make a quick left onto Kaweah. On the corner, on the left, is Liberace's guest house (#1441). Check out the piano mailbox (photo, below).

Turn left on Stevens then right on Via Norte (1.1). At Vista Chino is a decision point. The option below leads you on a hilly adventure (e-bike edge):

> Option 1: Chino Canyon and Little Tuscany (1.4 miles extra): This is a very beautiful but hilly section in the San Jacinto foothills, so depending on how much energy you want to expend on this ride (if no e-bike) you may consider saving it for last. From Vista Chino continue north on Via Norte and turn left on Chino Canyon Road, ascending a gradual hill to Zsa Zsa Gabor, dahling, at #595, "The Arches." Next comes a fairly steep hill climb to an Elvis Presley home at #845 (you know what to do here). It is one of two owned at the time of his death, the other being Graceland, and one of two Elvis homes on this tour. Sadly, the creepy Elvis silhouette (below) was painted over by unappreciative new owners. At the top of the hill continue around the bend to the left to Panorama to return. Frederick Loewe's estate is at #815. Sing the weather forecast if you wish, but the rain does not stay mainly on the plain in these parts. Home #701 was the residence of the son of William Randolph Hearst. Read a newspaper? Continue the loop to Chino Canyon, right on Via Norte and right (west) on Vista Chino.

Ride to the west (toward the mountains) on Vista Chino. Just before the road ascends a small hill, a plaque at #470 indicates that this was The Kaufmann House, a work of art in itself (1.3). Built in 1946 by a Pittsburgh department store magnate and later owned by Barry Manilow in the 1970s, it is one of the most recognizable homes in the desert. Mr. Manilow still lives in an estate in South Palm Springs, so if you sing

The Kaufmann House

"Mandy" (softly please) maybe he'll hear it. Ascend the small hill, round the bend to the left onto Monte Vista, then glide down the hill and turn right on Stevens (1.5). Atop the next small hill, look for Debbie Reynolds' former house at #670. I know you want to sing "Tammy's In Love" for the camera!

Head downhill and left onto Rose Avenue (1.8). Pause halfway down the hill to see:

#1326 Marilyn Monroe is reported to have rented this 1961 bungalow. Perhaps a famous Marilyn pose here?

#1258 Singer Nat King Cole and later daughter Natalie. It's Unforgettable!

Make the first left onto Via Vadera and a quick left onto Abrigo. On the top of the small hill at the end of a cul de sac off to the left is the Elvis and Priscilla Presley honeymoon home (#1350 Ladera Circle), where they lived during 1967–68 (2.1). This is a popular attraction; you may have an audience for your rendition of "Hound Dog" as many pose for photos here in front of architect Robert Alexander's showpiece home. A tour of the home and property was available in the past, but alas new owners are unlikely to continue that business.

The road is now South Via Las Palmas. Bear left down the hill to stay on this street, then right at Via Monte Vista (2.3). On the right are several former celebrity homes:

#1295 Peter Lawford: The Rat Pack actor was married to a Kennedy, and JFK would visit—"Ask not what your country can do for you …" A 50's Alexander home.

#1197 Singer/actor Tony Martin (sing "Begin the Beguine") and dancer/actress Cyd Charisse (perform the Broadway Medley finale from "Singin' in the Rain.") whose marriage lasted sixty years. Their main home was 697 Camino Sur around the corner.

#1123 Dean and Jeannie Martin in a classic Alexander home. Sing "Everybody Loves Somebody."

Make a quick right/left jog on Camino Sur to continue on Monte Vista, then turn left at Mountain View (2.7). Turn left at Patencio, and right on Hermosa. The 6-acre estate on the corner (457 Hermosa) was home to tap dancer Ann Miller in 1961, while the large estate on the southwest corner of Mission (417 Hermosa) was occupied for a time by Elizabeth Taylor; "I am the Nile!" And remember, big girls need big diamonds. At 432 Hermosa is the iconic Wexler home built for Dinah Shore & George M in 1964 and now owned by Leonardo Dicaprio, available for $$$rental. Watch for golfing bears!

Turn right on Mission, and notice #776 that was possibly a getaway house for Spencer Tracy and Kathryn Hepburn. Try reciting some classic lines, though don't ring the bell, the new owners will certainly not want to guess who's coming to dinner. Curve right on Merito (3.1). Lily Tomlin's ex-"Lilly Pad" is #443; "One ringy-dingy." Singing great Lena Horne lived at #465 (can you sing "Stormy Weather"?), while #481 was built by cowboy actor Hoot Gibson and later occupied by Mario Lanza. Try your best opera voice (softly), since he was "The Great Caruso" in 1951.

Turn left on Patencio. At #701 lived Mary Pickford, a Canadian-born actress and queen of the silent movie era, with husband Buddy Rogers. The Mary Pickford Theatre in Cathedral City contains Pickford memorabilia. Act melodramatic (and silent). House #591 was occupied by notables such as George Burns and Gracie Allen, Walter Winchell, and George Hamilton, who signed the right side of the driveway. Have you been getting enough sun to pose next to that? Peek left at #444 Chino, former home of Sammy Davis Jr. and try to break out into "That Old Black Magic." Bear left down Vine toward Alejo (3.5). This is a city bike route and we'll follow Heritage Trail part of the way. Welwood Murray Cemetery on the right is the resting place of early Palm Springs settlers including Dr. Murray who opened Palm Springs' first hotel in 1886, and Desert Inn founder Nellie N. Coffman, "Mother of Palm Springs." Go left on Cahuilla and right on Chino. Find #222 "Casa del Corazon" (pic p326) and glimpse the house once owned by Clark Gable and Carole Lombard. In a tribute to the sudden tragic end of their marriage from the plane crash that left Gable devastated, let's change his Gone With the Wind tag line to "Frankly my dear, I DO give

An enCYCLE ride pauses at the iconic Elvis Honeymoon House.

a damn." Turn right on Belardo (3.8). The large estate on the right corner of Alejo is the newly remodeled Liberace estate where he used to "Cry all the way to the bank." Make a left/right jog on Alejo to continue on Belardo Road (3.9).

> Option 2: At this point you are just a block west of and parallel to the downtown commercial corridor. Alejo daylights on Palm Canyon Drive at the point where the fascinating Rainmaker fountain is located, along with several fun restaurants, including Blue Coyote. Walk your bike on the sidewalk two blocks north to Granvia Valmonte for Cheeky's (breakfast/lunch) or Jake's, or Trio at Merito Place.

The tour continues south on the Heritage Trail Class I bikeway on the left side of Belardo Rd, with private McDonnell Golf Course on the right. At Amando cross to the bike lane (4.2). Straight ahead Belardo leads to the new Palm Springs redevelopment area. Our route curves west on Museum Dr to the Palm Springs Art Museum exhibiting a combination of art and natural history (4.4). On Thursdays after 4:00 admission is free, followed by Palm Springs Villagefest (5:00–9:00 p.m.) along Palm Canyon Drive that closes the road to traffic. Across from the museum is a park with the giant "Forever Marilyn" statue, lawns and amphitheatres. Turn left on Tahquitz Canyon Rd and quick right on Cahuilla Road. Make the first right on Arenas to tour the historic Tennis Club District. Go left at the T, and at Baristo reach Spencer's restaurant, one of Palm Springs' premier al fresco breakfast and lunch options. Ride back to Cahuilla and turn right, then left on Ramon (5.0). At Belardo is Melvyn's, a favorite of Sinatra's back in the day. Head right, up Belardo.

Follow Belardo along a scenic elevated stretch to Sunny Dunes (5.3). PS1's main route turns left down Sunny Dunes. Or consider Option 3:

> Option 3: A bridge straight ahead on Belardo provides a shortcut to the South Palm Springs area (ride PS2) and access to the Tahquitz Canyon Preserve hiking area (fee) at the west end of Mesquite Avenue.

Cross South Palm Canyon at the light (5.5), then enter the CV Link feeder path along the right side of North Riverside Drive. The path brings you alongside the frequently flowing Tahquitz Creek drainage. In a few blocks watch for a nifty bike/ped bridge that spans the creek and connects to the Deepwell area. The CV Link/Riverside path runs for 0.75 mile to Sunrise Way. If you like, take a quick detour to the end of the trail and back, enjoying fabulous views of the mountains heading west. Perhaps connect to Ride PS3 at Sunrise. Return to the bridge and cross it, possibly pausing on it to photograph the view of the creek with the mountains beyond, then check out the cute Presbyterian church across the bridge on the right (5.9).

Our tour continues to the left down South Riverside Drive. Ride parallel to the creek until the first opportunity to turn right onto Hermosa (6.2). Next, turn right at the T on Mesquite, then the first left onto Manzanita (6.4), and come to the first group of the celebrity former homes to check out:

#1075 Loretta Young. How about, "Ladies and Gentlemen, tonight I want to ask you for the most precious thing you own: your vote." (*The Farmer's Daughter*, 1947).

#1509 Eva Gabor "I just adore a penthouse view." Anyone for hotcakes?

#1516 Liberace owned yet another house. If you haven't displayed your bling yet, now's the time. At Deepwell, turn left, then left again at Driftwood (6.8). A landmark on this block is the large contemporary Japanese-style home of William Holden at #1323. Although not that impressive from the street, don't miss this many splendored thing. As you know, "a great many mistakes are made in the name of loneliness."

Turn right on Ocotillo, then left on Rolph (7.2). At 1044, the Brazilian Bombshell, Carmen Miranda, known for wearing a fruit hat in *The Gang's All Here* (1943), spent her last years here with her husband in the early 1950s. If you brought fruit and a camera, you know what to do!

> Option 4: Ride PS1 included only an abbreviated tour of the Deepwell district. Feel free to explore the other streets freeform. Those from France may want to see 1349 Sagebrush, the former Jerry Lewis home, "Well, just don't do something, sit there!" (*The Nutty Professor*, 1963).

The tour reaches Mesquite Avenue. Turn right and ride to Sunrise Way (7.4). Cross Sunrise with the light to the east sidepath.

> Option 5: This is a connecting point with the Tahquitz Creek Loop ride (PS3), which we recommend doing in the counter clockwise direction (to the right/south).

PS1 turns left (north) along Sunrise. Although the sidewalk bike trail runs along the busy thoroughfare, there are great mountain views to temper the traffic annoyance. You will reach Sunny Dunes/Desert Chapel on the right (7.7), which is where the old Tahquitz Creek Loop (PS3) returns to Sunrise. Across Sunrise at Ramon are lots of casual restaurants including Monsoon Indian with a lunch buffet (7.9).

At Alejo Road (8.9) cross Sunrise with the light, then ride in the ample bike lane and make the 5th right at Hermosa to enter the East Movie Colony neighborhood. Make the first left on Via Colusa. On the left at #1145 is Frank Sinatra's first valley residence. Twin Palms was designed by E. Stewart Williams and built in 1947. Frank lived here with his first wife Nancy until their divorce in 1951, and then second wife Ava Gardner until their split a few years later. The 4 bedroom, 7 bath, 4,500 sf home features a pool shaped like a grand piano. His parties were frequented by A-list celebs. It is now available for rentals. Frank's long time valley estate is along rides RM1 and 2.

Return to Hermosa and turn left. In 5 blocks reach El Alameda. At the northeast corner, #1232 is Heddy Lamar's house, a movie star known for films Algiers (1938) and Samson and Delilah (1949), and a noted inventor of "signal hopping" during WWII which became the basis for all modern wireless communications.

Head west (left) onto El Alameda. Former celebrity homes on this block are:

#1188 Bob & Delores Hope's 2nd home (1946). 1014 Buena Vista (1941) was 1st. "A bank is a place that'll lend you money if you can prove that you don't need it."

#1029 Dorothy Lamour "Are you a man who's afraid of danger?" (*My Favorite Brunette,* 1947).

#1011 Bing Crosby. Sure, sing White Christmas (to the ghosts of JFK and Marilyn who likely hooked up here). Hope, Crosby, and Lamour starred in the "Road To …" film series, so if you play patty-cake (before throwing a punch toward the camera) on this block people will realize you are re-enacting the Hope-Crosby con man scenes.

Arrive at beautiful Ruth Hardy Park where facilities and picnic tables are available (9.8). Turn left down Caballeros, then right on Tamarisk alongside the park, where there is also a parallel paved pathway. Cross Via Miraleste, then right onto Avenida Palmas (10.2). Comic silent film star Harold Lloyd, known for his daring gags (no, please don't try one with your bike) built the estate on the left at #899 in the 1920s. "Las Palomas" at #928 on the right is the "Cary Grant Estate," a historic and recently restored Andalusian farmhouse that Grant shared with wives Betsy Drake and later Dyan Cannon. A plaque and model of the farmhouse are on display for tourists. Please don't say "Judy, Judy, Judy," since he never actually said that. He did say "Insanity runs in my family, it practically gallops" (*Arsenic and Old Lace*).

Once you reach Via Eytel, our route turns right down a sidewalk (not the private driveway) next to the medical buildings' parking lot. Or, consider Option 6 here.

Option 6: More Homes and Lunch: Go left on Via Eytel. The home straight ahead at #987 Palos Verdes that has a "B" on the gate was Jack Benny's ..."Well!" Farther down Palos Verdes is #877 at the corner of El Alameda, another residence of western star George Montgomery and wife, singer Dinah Shore. Men can do something westerny in front of it, and women can swing a golf club while singing "Chantez-Chantez," or vice versa. If you continue across Tamarisk and go right on Altamira you'll reach bike-friendly and fun El Mirasol for an al fresco lunch option.

The sidewalk path eastward from Via Eytel leads to Via Miraleste (10.5). Across the street is the interesting Wellness Park. Stay on the sidewalk by turning left, then carefully cross Tachevah. Desert Regional Medical Center is on the northwest corner.

Option 7, Lucy: For Lucy and Desi fans, ride up Miraleste another block to #1194 to catch a glimpse of their possible first desert home on the right, now a multi-million dollar estate. The gate around the corner is a good place to have some 'esplainin' to do to the camera, but dun't block the gate, Lucy! Return to Tachevah. They eventually lived in gated Thunderbird Country Club in Rancho Mirage (along Ride RM2), but when that golf club banned Desi because he was Cuban, they moved to Indian Wells and opened the inclusive Indian Wells Resort Hotel. Their nearby home at 75805 Altamira can be seen on rides IW1 or RM2-Option 2b.

Our route continues on Tachevah, heading west in the bike lane, then sidewalk trail. Cross Indian Canyon (10.8) and Palm Canyon, jog to the left at the light, then right to Via Lola where you started (11.1).

Option 8: After-Ride Bike 'n Brunch: To head downtown to all the great restaurants, you can take side streets to avoid busy Palm Canyon. From Via Lola turn left on Cahuilla, left on Hermosa, right on Prescott, and left on Merito; or continue south on Belardo to Alejo, turning left there or farther along to meet Palm Canyon. Sidewalk riding is prohibited, but there are sharrows on Palm Canyon from Alejo to Ramon, also on Indian Canyon. Palm Canyon is one-way southbound from Alejo to beyond Ramon.

South Palm Springs
PS2

South Palm Springs is one of our favorite places to ride in this area and a preferred part of town to to live in for many. Close to pretty hills with towering mountains beyond, it has a peaceful easy feeling with mid-century modern architecture dominating the wide boulevards. On any given weekend, scores of people are out walking, jogging, or biking. The Canyon Country Club area, a 1960s golf course and housing development, is now called Palm Springs National Golf and Country Club. At the south end of Palm Canyon Boulevard (beyond our loop) is Indian Canyons, the most popular and beautiful place to hike in Palm Springs (fee charged). This ride can be an extension of PS1 or PS3, or done on its own. Using the map you can just explore this area freeform since most of the roadways are good cycling streets. The map shows the main suggested route, and some of the better alternate routes. South Palm Canyon Drive is fairly busy through the residential district, however, many cycle it.

Tunes: Groovin' by The Rascals; Peaceful Easy Feeling by The Eagles; Indian Names by Natalie Merchant; Somewhere Down the Road by Barry Manilow.
Eats: Brunch at South Course Restaurant on Murray Canyon Dr.

Distance: About 6 miles + option. Time: 45 minutes to 1 hour.
Route & Bike: Easy. Mostly Class II and III residential streets. Paved, any bike. Gradually sloping terrain.
Knocks & Hazards: Wide residential streets with traffic, some busier than others. Be extra careful at all intersections.

Facilities: No public facilities. Commercial centers along Hwy 111.

Access: From the Palm Springs Star Tour ride (PS1) you can add this ride from the point where the route crosses the bridge over Tahquitz Creek between North and South Riverside Drives. Instead of turning left on South Riverside to follow PS1, continue straight on El Camino Real. It merges into Indian Trail just before ending at East Palm Canyon Drive. Ride or walk your bike along the East Palm Canyon sidewalk for a block to the left (east), then cross Palm Canyon at the light at Camino Real in front of the Biltmore, passing Koffi on the other side. Make a left onto Twin Palms and ride next to the upgraded mid-century modern homes until the street ends at La Verne. Across the street is Smoke Tree Village Shopping Center with a supermarket and restaurants including the vegetarian Native Foods, Subway, and Viet Fusion. Alternatively, reach this point from the Tahquitz Creek Loop (PS3) by pedaling south from the corner of Sunrise Way and East Palm Canyon. To do this ride on its own, drive to the neighborhood south of East Palm Canyon and Sunrise, and park where allowed.

The Ride: Cycle south on Laverne and very carefully turn left onto Toledo. After passing Sierra Way turn right onto Canyon Estates Drive to enter the Canyon Country Club neighborhood. Turn left on Madrona, curve around to the right on Paseo Del Rey, then head north to Sierra Way. Turn left, then reach Camino Real and turn left, then left again on Yosemite. Turn right on Sequoia, then left on Alhambra, back to Camino Real. Turn left and continue to Murray Canyon. If you're up for brunch, detour to the left to go to the South Course Restaurant at the golf course. Otherwise turn right, and ride west to Sierra Madre Drive. (See Option 1 for an optional moderately strenuous ride from here to the Indian Canyons hiking area.) Turn right, then bend right onto Santiago Way and left onto Calle Palo Fierro. Follow it all the way to Twin Palms and turn right.

If you want a coffee/light meal stop, detour down El Camino Real a block to Hwy 111 to the popular Koffi. Continue east on Twin Palms to return to ride start. Otherwise, take one of many alternate routes using the map. For example, from Calle Palo Fierro turn right on pleasant Sierra Way before reaching Laverne and take it to Toledo, then turn left to ride start. Another option (Option 2 below) allows you to check out the Mesa neighborhood and a new shortcut to downtown and the Old Las Palmas neighborhoods via a route starting from Twin Palms Drive westbound.

Option 1: Bike and Hike Indian Canyons Area
2.4 to 12.7 miles round trip. Easy to strenuous. E-bike edge.

Just past Sierra Madre Dr, Murray Canyon ends at South Palm Canyon Dr (elevation 525 ft, mile 0). The ride to the left is popular with road cyclists and perhaps the most scenic in the area, especially during wildflower season. Most is on-road with little shoulder, low traffic, and low speed limit. Option: In 0.3 mile Bogert Trail leads 2 miles through upscale residential, with the 2nd mile up a steep hill to great vistas and a hiking trailhead. Along Palm Canyon a toll booth at 1.2 miles (elev 590 ft) charges $9 each ($7 seniors, season pass available) to enter the Agua Caliente Band of Cahuilla Indian lands. At mile 1.3 the road to the right leads 0.8 mile up to the trailhead (825 ft) for the Andreas Canyon creekside hike amongst the palms, and Murray Canyon hike. Continue up the main road to the Palm Canyon area. It reaches the main parking area and Visitor's Center/Trading Post at the top of a steep hill (3.5 miles, 810 feet). Palm Canyon contains a 15-mile long oasis with native Washingtonia filifera, considered the world's largest California Fan Palm Oasis. Hike alongside streams, through oases, and up on ridges. The Cahuilla Indians would winter in these lush canyons as well as Tahquitz and Chino Canyons to the north.

Option 2: Mesa Neighborhood and Connection to Downtown and Las Palmas Area

The beautiful Mesa neighborhood lies in the foothills to the west of South Palm Canyon Dr. See the map for this option to bypass 0.5 mile of the main road by riding on Mesa Dr. E-bikers may enjoy the hilly interior Ridge/Crestview/Overlook Rd loop. The Class II Belardo Rd connection to downtown daylights a short distance north on S Palm Canyon, off to the left (west). It ascends an incline to a bridge over Tahquitz Creek and meets up with ride PS1 at Belardo and Sunny Dunes in 0.8 mile.

Palm Springs' Tahquitz Creek Loop PS3

A loop of paved Class I bike trails and sidewalks takes you through the golf course area along Tahquitz Creek in eastern Palm Springs. Doing the route counter-clockwise takes advantage of great vistas as you cycle westward past the pretty golf courses with dramatic mountain backdrops. The ride is described as an extension of PS1, which it overlaps along Sunrise Way between Mesquite Avenue and the Desert Chapel cul de sac. However you can start anywhere, including Tahquitz Creek Golf Resort. The new CV Link ("New PS3" on map) provides an option between Sunrise and El Cielo.

Tune: Mambo 2000 by Warren Hill; A Little Traveling Music by Barry Manilow.
Eats: Thick deli sandwich al fresco at Manhattan Deli.

Distance: About 7.7 miles. Time: 1 hour
Route & Bike: Easy. Paved (about 0.2 mile of rough broken asphalt). Class I including some sidewalk routes, and Class II. Any bike possible, but hybrid preferred for the segment through the rough asphalt. Mostly flat, some gradually sloping terrain.
Knocks & Hazards: Be extra careful at all intersections. Some Class II riding next to traffic. Significant golf ball hazard at several spots.
Facilities: Restrooms/water at Demuth Park and city's Tahquitz Creek Golf Course.

The Ride: From the east sidewalk of Sunrise at Mesquite cycle to the right (south) 0.5 mile to East Palm Canyon, and turn left along the sidewalk trail. Follow it for 2.5 miles, sometimes melding with frontage roads, crossing a wooden bike bridge over a wide drainage, and navigating several road crossings. Along the way, once you reach the signal at Farrell you have the option to cross East Palm Canyon and visit restaurants such as Chipotle or Jersey Mike's Subs to the west or Manhattan Deli to the east. Continue to Golf Club Drive and turn left onto its Class II bike lane. Just past Los Pueblos Condos reach the junction with a Class I trail to the right, eventually reconstructed as CV Link heading southeast (our CC1). PS3 stays in the bike lane here, but if CV Link has been installed on the west side of the road, then take it. In 0.3 mile carefully cross Golf Club to reach Tahquitz Creek Golf Resort's lot. It is a good staging spot, with restrooms and food. A CV Link feeder will someday run east down 34th St here connecting to the main channel route and Dinah Shore at the bridge.

From the parking lot, cycle north on the west sidepath (CV Link in 2021) between Golf Club Drive and the driving range. Caution! Just one more reason to wear a helmet. We actually ride across the street here. Then curve around the end of the driving range to the left. Ride down a fenced, treed corridor between sandy settling ponds and a water treatment plant, with great mountain views in front of you. In 0.5 mile from Golf Club Drive reach Palm Springs Surf Club, which will look awfully enticing on a hot day. The trail bends to the right then reaches a junction. Straight ahead the "Coachella Bikeway" leads to Gene Autry Trail and after Ramon the adjacent Gene Autry Bikeway (see PS4). Our PS3/CV Link route heads to the left.

Approach an interesting golf water feature. You may want to wait if someone is teeing off toward you. The path curves to the left then right, dipping under Gene Autry Trail. Continue riding along the edge of the golf course, enjoying the mountain views ahead. This is another area of significant golf ball hazard. It may also be your best desert/mountain photo opportunity of the ride, especially earlier in the day. In about 0.5 mile from Gene Autry the usually busy Demuth Park (restrooms, pickleball) appears, with a break in the fencing to access it. CV Link continues around its perimeter, bending to the right to reach Mesquite Ave (6.0), then left. The Link crosses El Cielo and as of 2021 or 2022 it heads left (south), which is the new route for PS3. See the map for this route, which skirts the south end of Mesquite Golf Course and then follows Mesquite Ave to Sunrise.

The original PS3 route follows the sidepath to the right, along El Cielo. Turn right (north) on the sidepath and skirt the northern perimeter of the Mesquite Golf Course and Country Club by keeping on the sidewalk paths along Sunny Dunes to the left,

Tahquitz Creek Loop winds past a signature golf hole

then Compadre to the right. Next, a paved path connects to the left between the Mesquite Country Club golf course and condos. Signs warn of golf ball hazard throughout the golf course sections. Follow this path, enjoying more golf course and mountain views, to Farrell Road. To cross the road, follow the sidewalk trail to the left to the signal, and then cross Farrell. Turn right on the opposite sidewalk, and continue to a trail junction on the left that leads between the course and another group of condos. After crossing a narrow bridge over a small creek, reach the cul de sac of Desert Chapel, then ride one block to Sunrise Way, which is along the Star Tour route (PS1). If this is an extension of that ride, turn right here along the Sunrise east sidewalk path. Otherwise, your starting point for this ride is only 0.3 mile to the left down the east sidewalk. You can also connect to the South Palm Springs ride (PS2) by continuing south on Sunrise, crossing East Palm Canyon, and meeting up with the route at Twin Palms around the bend.

Airport - Whitewater CV Link Loop ⭐ PS4 *6-10 miles, easy, any bike*

Two parallel scenic bike paths run between Vista Chino and Ramon Roads; the 2.2-mile Gene Autry Trail next to Palm Springs Airport, and the original 2.3-mile segment of the CV Link regional trail along the Whitewater River. A loop is possible as they are only 0.3 mile apart in the north and 0.7 mile in the south. They can also be combined with any of the other Palm Springs or Cathedral City rides. See the Palm Springs East /PS3 map for those connections. Trail photo is on book's cover.

Ride PS4 starts at the northwest corner of Ramon and Gene Autry, across from the large shopping centers where you can park. Find eats at Panera Bread and others here and south of Ramon. Head north on the bike trail along Gene Autry adjacent to the airport. Views of planes in the air and on the ground, backed by mountains, can be very dramatic. The Palm Springs Air Museum (1.4) contains an impressive World War II aircraft collection and puts on special events. At Tachevah (2.1) cross Gene Autry with the light and head left on the sidepath, rounding the bend to the right at Vista Chino. The next light is the entrance to Escena golf resort, with a popular view patio restaurant 0.6 mile down the road. The CV Link Vista Chino trailhead is ahead (2.6). Ride it south, adjacent to the Cimarron Golf Course, to Ramon (4.9). CV Link will continue under Ramon when the new bridge is built. Check map for future ride options to connect to PS3, CC1 and points southeast. The bridge should also enable safer connections to Rancho Mirage. 'Til then, to complete the loop, either take scary Ramon two blocks west to existing sidewalks (5.7), go back 0.6 mile to an exit path to Chia and cut through a neighborhood, or ride the route in reverse (9.8 miles). To connect to PS3 take the east Gene Autry sidewalk south of Ramon to trail connections at Palm Springs Surf Club, or use Class II Crossley. Via Escuela is a bike-friendly road to reach downtown and PS1. Ramon also has OK sidewalks.

The Coachella Valley Bikeway/Whitewater Trail/ 2 Future CV Link 3 CC1

To avoid roadways while traversing Cathedral City follow this section of the Coachella Valley Bikeway aka Jenkins Trail. It is in rough shape but will be upgraded to CV Link standards. CC1 connects the Tahquitz Creek Loop in Palm Springs (PS3) to the Rancho Mirage–Palm Desert Loops (RM1 and 2) that start at Wolfson Park in Rancho Mirage. Another option from PS3 at Golf Center Dr is 34th St, a future CV Linker, to a dirt path (paved in the future) up to the Dinah Shore Bridge. A signed bike route on its south sidewalk leads 3 miles into Rancho Mirage, then right on Da Vall. Also, Gerald Ford's north sidepath is mostly continuous between Date Palm and Cook St.

Distance: About 3.5 miles each way. Time: 30 minutes

Route & Bike: Easy. Paved Class I for any bike, but hybrid or wider tire preferred for rough pavement and possible sandy spot in wash. Mostly flat, some dips under bridges. E-bike edge for extra distance. CV Link will improve the surface.

Knocks & Hazards: Be extra careful at all intersections, especially the ped/bike warning signal at busy Cathedral Canyon Drive. Golf ball hazard west of Cathedral Canyon Drive. Possible lurkers. Stay out of wash during flow periods.

Facilities: No public facilities. Palm Springs' Tahquitz Creek Golf Course at ride start has restrooms, and Wolfson Park at ride end has water fountain. Rancho Mirage Civic Center at Frank Sinatra west of Hwy 111 is open weekdays and has facilities.

Access: As mentioned in Tahquitz Creek Loop (PS3), the Coachella Valley Bikeway/aka Whitewater Trail continues to the southeast off Golf Club Drive 0.5 mile north of Hwy 111, and 0.3 mile south of the Tahquitz Creek Golf Course parking lot, where you can stage from. It begins just north of Los Pueblos Condos, and there is an unsignaled crosswalk at that point across Golf Club Dr. It will be signed for CV Link.

The Ride: The best part of the trail is the first section as it heads southeast, adjacent to the golf course. Looking back in the other direction the views toward the mountains can be stunning. After it crosses a residential street (Calle Ariba) in 0.25 mile it makes a hairpin turn to the right, while CV Link will continue straight. The old path then runs between a mobile home park and Cathedral Canyon Country Club residences, with some terrible bumps along the way. Another hairpin turn to the left takes the trail between a fenced-off fairway and the backs of car dealerships. More sharp turns to the left and then right puts you behind Cathedral Palms RV Resort, then brings you to busy Cathedral Canyon Dr (mile 1.5). Plans call for CV Link meeting up here again after having crossed the channel twice. The road crossing will likely be improved, but currently it is just a blinking bike/ped warning light, so use caution.

Across Cathedral Canyon the current path and future CV Link replacement run along the top of the Whitewater River levee to Date Palm Dr. The current path dives under Date Palm and continues along the bottom of the channel until it is mired in sand unless it has been cleared, and emerges at Officer Germain Gibson Ave. CV Link will run atop the levee and also exit here, near the Rancho Mirage border. That city has banned it. Ride the short block to Hwy 111, then turn left on the designated bikeway sidepath on the north side of 111. To continue on the most direct route to Palm Desert stay on the 111 north sidepath, crossing to the south side at Peterson or before. To enjoy a nice park and bike trail, bend left at Frank Sinatra and cross the channel in the bike path (subject to closure after flow). Cross at the light to reach hidden gem Wolfson Park at mile 3.5 (See RM1). At the central main entrance push the button on the post to be greeted by Frank Sinatra himself! Signs instruct to walk bikes in the park. The Butler-Abrams trailhead is at the far end of the small park.

Beautiful vistas await as you pedal around the desert (RM1)

Other Options to Wolfson Park/RM1 Once you reach the Date Palm bridge, if the path ahead is not yet available, take sidewalk routes. To the right take Date Palm, then left on the north side of Hwy 111. To the left take the west sidewalk over the bridge, to the north sidewalk along Gerald Ford, to the east sidewalk along Da Vall to Wolfson Park.

Rancho Mirage and Palm Desert

These two upscale resort cities have a great system of sidepaths that imitate Class I paths. As of mid 2021 Palm Desert will have a CV Link corridor that crosses the city from west to east. Rancho Mirage, which has banned CV Link, has a couple of Class I paths. Most of the major high-speed boulevards have bike lanes to keep fast road bikers happy, so those cyclists can parallel the routes described in this section, and hop onto a sidepath if the going gets uncomfortable. Use the map to plot your own routes, or follow our suggested tours: RM1, 2 and 3 and PD 1. Where RM1, 2 and PD1 overlap, they are described in most detail in RM1.

Rancho Mirage and Palm Desert Sidepath Loop   RM1 ⭐

Exclusive gated enclaves and country club communities dominate the area of Rancho Mirage and Palm Desert covered in this ride. Wide bike/golf cart sidepaths and a Class I bike trail makes for a delightful loop with plenty of great scenery and lots of options for a Bike 'n Brunch. The east end of the loop is at a high point in the valley, with great mountain and desert vistas in every direction, and short ride PD1 (Desert Willow Loop) is a subset of RM1 that takes it in, while RM2 expands the ride to cover more area highlights. Extensions of the rides are possible in all directions, from Palm Springs to La Quinta.

THE DESERTS

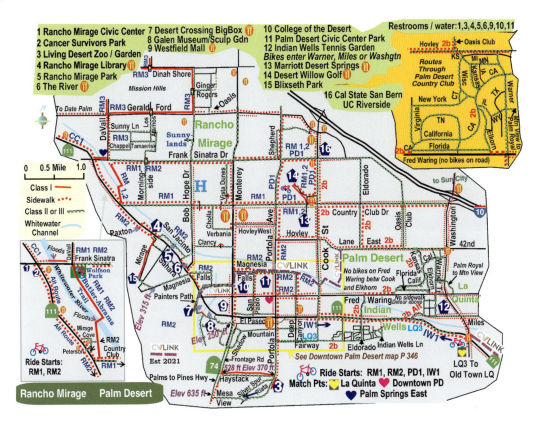

Tunes: Midnight at the Oasis by Maria Muldaur; You Will Be Loved by Maroon 5 & Buena Vista Social Club

Eats: A hearty deli sandwich on Sherman's Deli Patio (Country Club & Monterey) or Grilled Chicken and Pear Salad at Lakeview Terrace (Desert Willow).

Distance: 11.5 miles. **Time:** 1.5 hours

Route & Bike: Easy to moderate difficulty. Paved, any bike. Mostly "Class I" sidepath trail, except for 1.2-mile Class I paved path and 0.5-mile on-street, plus numerous street crossings. Gradual slope up from west to east, from the river channel to the plateau. E-bike edge for crossing the Whitewater Channel and gradual grades.

Facilities: Water in Wolfson Park. Restrooms in commercial establishments, or detours to public parks as described.

Knocks & Hazards: For sidepath riders, road and driveway crossings require extreme caution to ensure safety (see p 324). Those who opt for the Class II/III roadways are subject to the usual dangers of high-speed traffic. All must obey traffic signals. Ride single file. Occasional pedestrians and infrequent golf carts on trail and sidewalks. More walkers tend to be out in the mornings. Possible rattlesnakes. High wind events can cause falling debris from trees onto sidewalks. Slippery sidewalks. Stay out of dips through the Whitewater River drainage during flood events. Butler-Abrams Trail may be closed midway during and after flood for extended periods.

Bike 'n Brunch: At Cook and Country Club are the popular City Wok with outdoor patio, while across the street Marriott Desert Springs has several restaurants and a Starbucks. To the west down Country Club are shopping centers both east and west of Monterey. Choose from the popular Sherman's Deli with outdoor patio, a Bristol

Farms market with a deli and outdoor tables, the Country Club Café that serves breakfast all day plus lunch and dinner, as well as sub shops, Japanese, Chinese, Starbucks, pizza, burgers, Greek, and other restaurants in these complexes. At Cook and Frank Sinatra is an Applebee's. A detour north down the hill on Cook brings you to several other options, including Solano's Bar and Grill, JT's Diner, and farther down the hill Coldstone Creamery, Billy Q's pizza, Firehouse Grill, Bucatini, Pueblo Viejo, Hula's, Carl's Jr, Jack in Box, Starbucks, and Subway. At the west end of the ride, you can detour to Hwy 111 from Frank Sinatra and turn right on the sidewalk path to reach the bounteous Emperor Buffet. To the left is Rancho Mirage's Restaurant Row, including our favorite al fresco breakfast at Palms Café, as well as popular Las Casuelas Nuevas (Sunday brunch).

Access: Start from anywhere along the circuit. We will begin at the Class I Butler-Abrams trail for the benefit of those who only wish to do the 2.4-mile round trip of this usually dry riverside jaunt. From I-10 take Date Palm Drive south about 5 miles to Hwy 111 and turn left, then turn left on Frank Sinatra. Drive through the drainage channel and park next to Wolfson Park after the signal, on the right. If no parking is available, continue another mile to the first light and turn left on Thompson, then park after the No Parking signs end. Then ride across Frank Sinatra and turn right onto the sidepath to the park. Desert Willow Golf Course has a large public lot with no signed restrictions and makes another good staging spot.

The Ride: The paved multi-use Joe Butler–Bruce Abrams Trail begins at Michael S. Wolfson Park off Frank Sinatra Dr just east of Hwy 111 in Rancho Mirage (mile 0). The park is adorned with beautiful colorful desert vegetation and great mountain views. Popular with dog owners, it has benches, picnic tables, a fountain, and the only public water fountains along the route. The Butler-Abrams Trail runs for 1.2 miles, first above the usually dry Whitewater River and then descends steeply into the channel and ends atop the west bank leading to Country Club Drive next to Morningside Golf Course. A picket fence lines the south end of trail, which has a very pastoral feel, and an equestrian trail runs parallel to it. From the trail there are great views to Mt. San Jacinto, Tahquitz Peak, Mt. San Gorgonio and the Santa Rosa mountains. It is a popular trail with strollers and dog-walkers, but takes less than 30 minutes round trip on a bike. The wash portion may be closed and/or covered with sand after a rare period of flow. From the end point at Country Club (1.2) you have options, described later. RM1 goes left (east) on the north sidewalk along Country Club, dips to the wash in a 2-way bike lane, to a sidewalk to meet Morningside (1.7). Either stay on the north sidewalk (there's one narrow spot at a mailbox) or the Class II lane (tho parking is allowed). Go left on Keenan (2.1) and right on Kaye Ballard Ln. At Kersten, her former home is on the left. Go right, then back to the north sidewalk (2.5). Cross Bob Hope (3.0). At the next light (JL Sinn Rd, 3.2) cross to the south sidewalk, which is actually continuous all the way to Washington. A bunch of restaurant options appear at Monterey (4.2) some with outdoor tables. Past Monterey is a Sherman's Deli.

At Portola (5.0) you have rejoined the main ride RM2 as well as met ride PD1. If you are tiring you can shorten the ride by 3 miles by taking Portola's east sidepath to the left (north) to Frank Sinatra. Our main route crosses Portola and to the north sidepath of Country Club. After entrances to various complexes, enjoy riding next to

Wolfson Park, the ride start, is a beautiful oasis with water, benches, and fabulous vistas

The gardens and Visitor's Center of Sunnylands, the Annenberg Estate, is open free to the public

the unique metal fence surrounding Desert Willow Golf Course on a nicely landscaped stretch across from the huge Marriott Desert Springs resort. Pass a sculpted bus stop, a Palm Desert art piece. At the next light (5.7) consider exploring the Marriott's grounds and checking out its flock of flamingos.

RM1, RM2 and PD1 go left at Desert Willow instead. Stay on the sidepath as it bends to the left. The pretty sidepath ascends two short hills, past restrooms, and around some timeshare facilities, then returns next to Desert Willow. Cross over Willow Ridge and continue on the absolutely beautiful sidepath as it takes you over very gentle hills next to the golf course, with San Jacinto Mountain vistas beyond. This may just be the most beautiful half-mile stretch of bikepath in the valley. It is a high point in the desert, so the mountain views are dramatic. The path ends next to a roundabout (6.3). Our ride continues around the perimeter of the roundabout, ridden clockwise on the sidewalk. Notice the large parking area, which is another potential staging point for rides in the area.

Beautiful Desert Willow Golf Course was once a private club that was taken over by the city of Palm Desert. The Lakeview Terrace restaurant at the stunning clubhouse ("clubhouse attire" required) offers a fabulous setting for breakfast, lunch, or afternoon appetizers indoors or out, overlooking a lake and mountains beyond. The ride continues onto the north sidewalk (opposite traffic) past the roundabout. It is another great sidepath to ride on, with a little downhill slant this time, and golf course views with the more barren Little San Bernardino Mountains beyond in this direction. Slow down as the hill takes you down to an intersection, which is Market Place (6.9).

Carefully bend to the left on the sidewalk along Market Place, behind the Ralph's shopping center at Country Club and Cook. If you need refreshments or a restroom, turn up the access road to the Ralph's supermarket or you can check out one of the restaurants in the center. IW Coffee & Chai Bar with its outdoor tables is a popular stop for cyclists (lock bike here). Also worth checking out is the life-size Komodo dragons sculpture on the waterfall at the corner of Cook and Country Club.

In either case, follow Market Place to Cook Street (7.2) and head north on the sidepath, then follow this beautifully landscaped winding pathway, crossing a couple of low-traffic community entrances, to Frank Sinatra. An Applebee's restaurant and a Marriott's Courtyard Motel and Residence Inn are on that corner. To continue on our tour, turn left staying on the south sidewalk of Frank Sinatra (8.0). Hungry? There are also lots of restaurants down the hill along Cook Street. Back on Frank Sinatra, a very scenic ride awaits. The sidewalk is once again adjacent to the Desert Willow Golf Course, with occasional views available of the course and mountains beyond. Because of all the vacant land on the north side of Frank Sinatra at time of writing, the views of desert and mountains from this elevated plateau as you ride westbound are unobstructed. At Portola (8.8) the sidewalk continues on the north side, so carefully cross both Portola and Frank Sinatra with the light to get there. It ends at Monterey where there is a convenience market (9.9). Our sidewalk route continues on the south side after Monterey. Carefully cross Monterey, then Frank Sinatra to its south sidewalk. You can also use the next left turn lane. A pretty stretch of sidewalk path next leads down a small hill to Bob Hope Dr (10.9). Be extremely careful if the sidewalk is wet!

Option 1: Sunnylands *1.2 mile total, easy*
The 200-acre Annenberg Estate called Sunnylands has been open to the public since March 2012. There is no charge to visit the impressionist gardens with 1.2 miles of walking paths and a visitor's center with introductory movie and delightful al fresco café. It is open Thursdays through Sundays, closed in summer and for special events. The house tour on the main part of the estate costs $48 with advance purchase required. To get there from our route, head north (right) in the bike lane up the hill along Bob Hope for 0.5 mile, and very carefully cross over to the entrance on the left. Return to Frank Sinatra and cross at the light, then go to the right along the south sidewalk. Info: sunnylands.org

As you continue west on the south sidepath of Frank Sinatra past Bob Hope, look toward the north where pink walls border the Sunnylands property and its private golf course. Cross Morningside Dr (12.0), or explore Option 4 from this point to the right on Thompson. In another 0.25 mile, just past the entrance to the Morningside Country Club, Old Blue Eyes' former estate is across the street at 70588 Frank Sinatra, next to Tamarisk Country Club (12.25). A dedication plaque at the gate states that Frank lived there from 1954 to 1995. It is mostly hidden behind a stone wall, but imagine an 8,000-square foot mansion, a 4,500-square foot guesthouse, and a railroad car reflecting his love of trains. Proceed down the sidepath along Frank Sinatra, which is smooth sailing except for a blip near the end (12.8) where a pseudo sidewalk takes you onto the street past several driveways against traffic. Use extra caution, perhaps even walking your bike the short distance, and/or waiting for any traffic to go by. Return to your starting point at Wolfson Park (12.9).

Additional Options from the Country Club end of the Joe Butler–Bruce Abrams Trail:

Option 2: Trail Only
Just turn around and return the same way for a 2.4-mile trail ride.

Option 3: 111 Loop
Do a loop using Hwy 111. Turn right on the Country Club sidewalk and ride down to Hwy 111, curving right along its sidewalk. Along the way pass various restaurants. At The Atrium center is a Farmers Market Friday mornings and Palms II Cafe. Cross Hwy 111 at Frank Sinatra to visit the beautiful and inspirational Cancer Survivor's Park adjacent to the south of Rancho Mirage City Hall (restrooms available on weekdays). Cross back over Hwy 111. Either ride the sidewalk

path northwest toward Cathedral City, with options to continue on to the CC1 or CV Link to Palm Springs, or you can complete the 3.5-mile loop by riding on the west sidewalk along Frank Sinatra to the bike trail across the wash (subject to closure after river flow), then up the small hill to Wolfson Park.

Option 4: Rancho Mirage Loops on sidewalks, bike lanes and residential streets 🌟
Turn left (east) on Country Club's sidewalk and 2-way bike lane, then left on Class II Morningside. At Frank Sinatra, either turn left onto the sidewalk and return to your ride start (3.6 miles), or cross to explore a beautiful historic Rancho Mirage neighborhood. Follow Thompson, which curves right (La Paz) then left (Los Reyes). Make the first left on Tamarisk. The 2nd right is Andrews Circle, where the famous sisters lived in the houses at the cul du sac. An iconic mid-century modern home is at 70551 Tamarisk Ln. At Palm View Rd starting at the northwest corner are two clusters of sixteen Tamarisk Ranchos homes, each surrounding a pool, where the Marx Brothers would hang out. To the left at the end of the Palm View is the inclusive Tamarisk Golf Course, created by the Marx Bros, George Burns, Sintatra and others. Explore more of this area per the maps, then exit on Da Vall and go left on the sidewalk back to Wolfson Park (5-8 miles)

Option 5: Expand to Ride RM2 to central Palm Desert 🌟 See ride description below.

The River Grand Sidewalk Loop   RM2 🌟

This loop incorporates half of ride RM1, but skips most of the less interesting Country Club Drive return segment, and substitutes it with a longer option that includes The River complex, an El Paseo district option, and the central area of Palm Desert. It has a lot of pesky commercial driveway and road crossings but the destinations make it worthwhile, and you get to experience Palm Desert's new CV Link path. See ride RM1 for detail on the last segment that this ride has in common with.

Tunes: Come to The River by The Jayhawks; The Four Seasons (Spring) by Vivaldi
Eats: Brunch al fresco at Acqua California Bistro

Distance: 19 miles. Opt 2a adds 2 miles; Opt 2b adds 3.2 miles. Time: 2-2.5 hours
Route & Bike: Easy to moderate. Paved, any bike. Class I sidewalk trail with many road crossings. CV Link Class IV cyclcetracks. Class III routes through El Paseo area. Gradual slope up to the north toward Frank Sinatra high point from all directions.
Knocks & Hazards: Many street and commercial facility entry crossings. Use caution!
Facilities: Restrooms at Rancho Mirage Park, College of the Desert, Palm Desert Civic Center Park, and commercial establishments. Short detours to restrooms at: Rancho Mirage City Hall (weekdays), Palma Village Park (De Anza & San Carlos N of 111), and Magnesia Falls Park at Rutlidge, across from CV Link east of Portola.
Bike 'n Brunch: There are endless options on this route along Hwy 111 including The River and through El Paseo as described in The Ride.

Access: See RM1. Or, start somewhere along the route, such as the El Paseo area, Palm Desert Civic Center Park, The River, Rancho Mirage Park, etc.

The Ride: Start from Wolfson Park as in RM1, and take the Butler-Abrams trail. In 0.2 mile from the top of the west bank look for a couple of signs, a break in the fence, and a wide dirt path (0.8). Take it into a neighborhood, passing an interesting literary wall, then a goat farm, on Desert Cove Ave. Turn left at Peterson, then cross 111 at the light to the far sidewalk (1.3). Go left. You can also take the B-A trail to Country

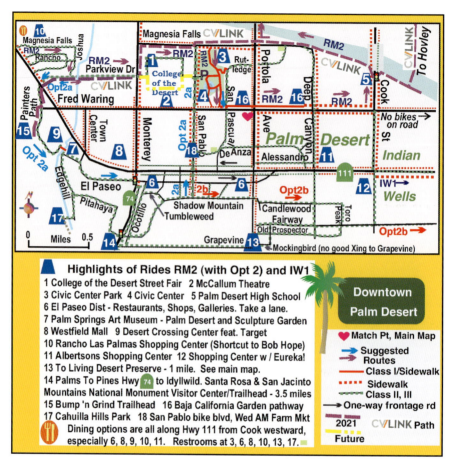

Club, go right and cross 111, but we prefer the Peterson crossing. Both go left along its west/south sidewalk, in a park-like setting including a wooden bike/ped bridge. Cross 111 at Rancho Mirage Library/Observatory (2.6). Go right on the sidewalk.

> Option 1 Instead of crossing 111 at the library, take a more uninterrupted residential route. When the sidewalk forks ahead go right on a Class I trail over a ped bridge. It bends to the right before Mirage. You can ride the gradual grade 0.3 mile up to Blixseth Park, or exit at the first yellow grate onto Mirage, and then left on Sahara, a good biking street that ends on Magnesia Falls. Go left, cross 111, and rejoin main route (top p 347).

Turn left on San Jacinto (2.7), a low-traffic street. Reach Rancho Mirage Park (3.0) (restrooms). San Jacinto ends at Rancho Las Palmas Dr across which are parking lots for The River, an impressive dining and entertainment complex (3.4).

Make your way back to the east sidewalk along 111 from there via the parking lots or the Rancho Las Palmas north sidewalk. The 111 sidewalk runs alongside The River's lovely man-made "river" or reflective ponds, a great photo op. Try the inviting Acqua California lakeside patio, Cheesecake Factory, Babe's BBQ, Yard House, Five Guys, or P.F. Chang's. Take in a flick at the 12-plex, shop in one of the stores or galleries, perhaps listen to some live music at the outdoor amphitheater, or skate on a floating winter rink. Be extra careful of cars coming and going from 111, including those turning left from 111, at the one unsignaled entrance along this stretch.

Arrive at Bob Hope Drive (3.8). Taking Bob Hope to the left allows you to complete a shorter loop of about 8 miles if you ride the east sidewalk to Frank Sinatra. Horsey Clancy Lane between Bob Hope and Monterey is worth checking out.

Reach Magnesia Falls (rejoining Option 1 here). Go left down the hill, right on Joshua, then cross to CV Link along the south side of Parkview (4.6). Here is a decision point. Our main ride heads left on the CV Link Class IV cycletrack. To extend the ride to the El Paseo district and south Palm Desert, take CV Link to the right via Option 2a.

Option 2a: El Paseo District

Follow CV Link west, across 111 next to what is now Painters path (5.0). On the left are an Olive Garden and Red Lobster. At Fred Waring CV Link crosses

Riding past The River center is a highlight of the ride, but you may not get past the inviting patio of Acqua California Bistro.

to the west side of the road, and ends at the trailhead for the popular Bump 'n Grind and Mike Schuler Trails. These very steep trails provide great views of the valley from the hilltops, but we don't recommend biking them. The big box center to the left contains lots of restaurants and an ALDI supermarket. When Painters Path is interrupted by a wash, curve to the left and cycle next to Target until you see a bike/ped bridge (5.8) that goes over the wash to the right, leading to a sidewalk for the continuation of Painter's Path. Edgehill straight ahead leads up to Cahuilla Hills Park and hilly south Palm Desert. Our route goes left in the bike lane. Pass "The Galen" art museum and sculpture garden, worth a stop (free). Painters Path ends at El Paseo (6.1). Turn right and follow the road or sidewalk past several restaurants to Hwy 74 (Palms to Pines Hwy) (6.6). Cross the highway at the signal. From here you can either explore the El Paseo district straight ahead, or for a hilly loop go right on the Hwy 74 east frontage road/paths and follow the route on the map, crossing to Portola via Haystack on path or bike lane. The Living Desert is to the right there (restrooms).

The El Paseo District is the Beverly Hills of the desert, with high end shops, galleries, a variety of restaurants, and sculptures in the boulevard's median and gardens. Cyclists tend to stop at The Coffee Bean west of San Pablo. Popular breakfast/lunch spots are Wilma & Frieda in The Gardens and Café Des Beaux-Artes, both with patios. In addition to El Paseo there are countless restaurants along parallel Hwy 111.

You can cycle, as many do, among the slow-moving vehicles down four-lane El Paseo, ("take a lane" to avoid the car doors opening). Early in the morning when not much is open is optimal. We don't recommend cycling the sidewalk here. To bypass this busy stretch by bike, once you've crossed Hwy 74, take the sidewalk to the right and make a quick left into a parking lot behind the St Johns Store. Exit the lot on Ocotillo and turn right, then a quick left on Tumbleweed. Follow it to Shadow Mountain and turn left (6.9) (Taking this road to the right opens up lots of opportunities to explore South Palm Desert as shown on the map). This area is a good staging option. Cross-streets to the left allow access to prime sections of El Paseo. Option 2a turns left on San Pablo (7.1), while Option 2b, described below, continues straight. Take San Pablo past El Paseo and 111 to the new "Main Street of Palm Desert" with bike friendly design, and site of a Wednesday morning Farmers Market. Pass Tri-A-Bike and the delicious Italian Deli and Bakery. Cross Fred Waring (7.9) and enter the sidepath along San Pablo, then go right on a path into Palm Desert Municipal Park. Explore the park, as described in the main ride. End up at the east end of the park, past the Holocaust Memorial and exit at Fred Waring (8.7) where we rejoin the main ride RM2, at its mile (6.9) found on the next page. Opt 2a added 2 miles over main ride.

Option 2b Loop Back Through Indian Wells Continue on Shadow Mountain. After crossing Portola (7.6) bear left around the bend onto Candlewood. Near the end of the road turn right on Toro Peak, and reach Fairway (8.6). Another day continue on Toro Pk for more exploring. For now, turn left on Class II Fairway. At Cl II Eldorado turn left (9.9). (Option: Check out Lucy & Ricky's house at 75805 Altamira to the left.) Follow Eldorado across 111 (10.4). To the right is the Eisenhower Walk of Honor. Take Eldorado to Fred Waring (11.0). Cross to the far sidepath and go right, up a gradual hill to California Dr in Palm Desert County Club (11.4). Carefully cross to the street from the sidewalk. See map inset for its street layout for various route options through this ungated community. Take California past the main clubhouse to Kansas (13.0). Unless you need food or facilities via the large center straight ahead on California to Ave of the States, turn left on Kansas. Follow it to just before Hovley, and carefully cross to the west sidewalk, then bend around to the left a short distance to a crossing signal at Oasis Club (13.3). From here, those who yearn for more street riding in nice bike lanes should head down Oasis Club to Country Club and take Country Club west to Cook. Our route crosses to the nicely landscaped sidepath along the north side of Hovley, goes left (west) then bends right at Eldorado (14.3). Go left on either sidepath of Country Club (15.3), to Cook St's east sidepath, northbound (16.3). Cross Cook at Frank Sinatra to its south sidepath (17.3). Head west. This joins main ride RM2 at mile 14.1. Opt 2b added 3.2 miles.

Continue east (left) on CV Link along Parkview. CV Link crosses Monterey (5.1) in front of College of the Desert (COD), and turns left (north) along Monterey. On the right the gigantic COD Street Fair operates weekends (7 a.m. – 2 p.m; June-Sept til noon). Vendors sell new products, artworks, and produce. You can catch a meal at a food cart and find restrooms. CV Link rounds the bend and runs along the south side of Magnesia Falls, then crosses to the north side of the road at the San Pablo roundabout. (5.9). San Pablo was reconstructed in 2020-2021 as a bike friendly linker from CV Link to El Paseo. Our route continues straight on the south side of Magnesia Falls' sidepath, and right on the first path into Palm Desert Civic Center Park.

Cycle through the beautiful park, past the impressive aquatic center, waterfalls and lagoons with ducks and turtles, rose garden, and art installations including the Peace Memorial, Dreamer, and Desert Dessert. The huge park has beach volleyball, tennis, restrooms and water fountains. End up on the park path that is farthest to the east and visit the Holocaust Memorial, then reach Fred Waring Drive (6.9). Option 2a re-joins the main route here. Turn left on the sidewalk, and cross San Pascual. The next block begins Baja California Park, which contains an extensive display of native plants found in the Baja ecosystem, in a park that runs parallel to the roadway. Its wide sidewalk pathway winds across several blocks, with features including a giant metal agave plant, an elaborate sculpted tropical rest area on the corner of Primrose, some organ pipe cacti, and then a stone sign explaining it all at its eastern endpoint at Florine (7.6), just before Deep Canyon. Our route continues on the sidewalk along Fred Waring to Cook St, then turns to the left on Cook's west sidewalk (8.2).

A welcome sculpted rest area along the Baja California Garden path

Ride to the light at Aztec, the entrance to Palm Desert High School. CV Link crosses here. To the right CV Link runs along the channel, then crosses it and leads to Hovley Ln East, a path worth checking out (pending, 2021). Use the map for routes from there. RM2 heads west on CV Link along the channel levee. The vista in this direction toward Mt. San Jacinto can be quite impressive. The trail turns into a Class IV cycletrack along Magnesia Falls halfway to Portola Ave. Turn right onto the Portola sidewalk or bike lane (9.5) and follow it up the hill past Hovley (10.3) (use extra caution crossing here), and up a nicely landscaped sidepath to Country Club (11.0).

Cross Country Club and take its sidepath to the right. At this point you have met up with rides RM1 and PD1. See ride RM1 (starting at its mile 5.0 page 342) for detail on the remaining segments. Reach Desert Willow (11.8), stay on the sidepath to the left, climb a small hill, then ride along a beautiful path that leads to a roundabout at the clubhouse (12.4). Then return via the opposite sidewalk. Slow down before reaching the bottom of the hill and follow the sidepath around to the left along Market Place (13.0). The Ralph's shopping center is to the right here.

Head northbound along Cook Street on its west sidepath, to Frank Sinatra (14.1). Turn left on its south sidepath and continue as described in ride RM1, crossing to the north sidepath at Portola (14.9), then back to the south sidepath at Monterey (16.0) (cross Monterey first, then Frank Sinatra for better visibility). Remain on the south sidepath all the way back across Bob Hope (17.0) (Sunnylands is to the right here), and Morningside (18.0), to your starting point at Wolfson Park (19.0).

Desert Willow Loop   PD1 ⭐3

Details: 6 miles, 45 minutes, easy, paved for any bike

One of the best bang for the buck scenic sidepath rides in the valley is the square route that goes around and into Desert Willow Golf Course in Palm Desert. This is a great option for a quick and beautiful ride for those staying in the area, including Marriott Desert Springs or Desert Falls. Most of this loop is also included in the Rancho Mirage Palm Desert loops (RM1 and 2). See ride RM1 (mile 5.4) for detail. Stage from the Desert Willow Golf Course lot. Ride on the north sidepath, carefully around the bend at Market Place, then north on Cook. Head west (left) on the pretty sidepath trail along Frank Sinatra. At the corner of Portola, the sidepath curves to the left, uninterrupted. Check out the great view over the golf course with ponds and plenty of birds. The sidepath heading south along Portola snakes gradually downhill next to a new development, with impressive views of the mountains to the south and west. Use caution at timeshare entrance roads. Near the corner of Country Club are several entrances to an office park. At Country Club you have re-joined rides RM1 (at its mile 4.7) and RM2 (at its mile 11.0). Return to your Desert Willow ride start by traveling east (left) on the Country Club sidepath and bending left on the sidepath at the Desert Willow signal.

Beautiful pathway to the Desert Willow Clubhouse

Mission Hills Loops of North Rancho Mirage RM3

Details: 6-14 miles, 30-90 minutes, easy to moderate, e-bike edge. Maps pages 336, 341

Some of Rancho Mirage's best designated bike sidepaths with great vistas and lush landscaping surround the large gated Mission Hills property. Start from the north sidepath of Gerald Ford at Los Alamos (to connect from RM1,2). Head east, to Bob Hope and bend left (1.0) (restaurants, grocery). Ride to Dinah shore (2.0) and bend left again. For a 6-mile ride continue to Da Vall's west sidepath, back on Gerald Ford. To extend, from D Shore take the west sidepath of Los Alamos (3.0) north to Ramon. Bend left (4.0). At Rattler (4.5) see map for a 2 mile loop (restrooms at Century Park). Reach Da Vall (5.0). At its northwest corner is Desert Memorial Park (Sinatras, Sonny Bono, open weekdays). Bend left. At Dinah Shore cross to Da Vall's west sidepath (6.0). Return to Gerald Ford (7.0), left to ride start (8.0). Option: Explore the neighborhood described in RM1 Opt 4 via Los Alamos or Da Vall's east sidewalk to Sunny Lane. See our website for more detail.

La Quinta Indian Wells and Indio

Some of our favorite easy scenic riding in the Coachella Valley is in La Quinta, located on the opposite end of the valley and a good 45-minute drive from

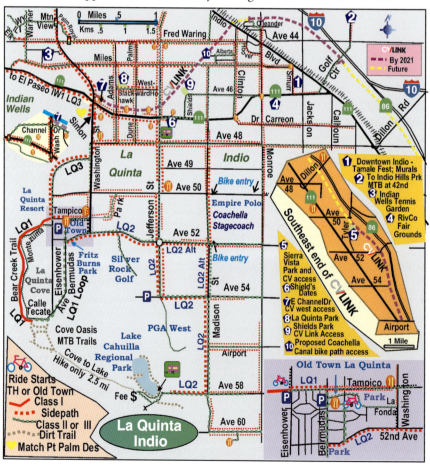

Palm Springs. The city offers desirable scenic sidewalk bike rides to explore, plus a scenic Class I path located next to the La Quinta Cove district and Old Town La Quinta, a great place to go out for a meal. Most of the main roads are equipped with bike lanes for those that prefer, and when the lanes end cyclists are typically diverted onto the sidewalk trails. Indian Wells has a scenic 3.6-mile sidewalk path adjacent to Hwy 111 that also connects to rides and points of interest in Palm Desert and La Quinta. CV Link will provide La Quinta, Indio and points east with a great cycling feature when completed.

Indian Wells Hwy 111 Connector and Neighborhoods IW1

Details: 3.6 miles one way, 20 mins, paved sidepath or road shoulder, easy. Map P 341.
The Ride: This connector between Palm Desert and La Quinta along busy Hwy 111 has a wide shoulder used by most cyclists. Use caution since parking is allowed. A scenic sidepath through pretty greenbelts along the south side of 111 enables safer passage, and cycling is "functionally allowed." The east end is near Washington St west of La Quinta's Vons center (restaurants). Long stretches between road crossings and San Jacinto Mountain views, slightly uphill westbound, makes for a pleasant ride. At Club Dr a similar path starts along the north side of 111. Use caution when wet since it can be slippery. Ride RM2 Opt 2b, a route to El Paseo, crosses at Eldorado. Access Indian Wells' interesting neighborhoods from Eldorado south of 111. Lucy & Ricky's house is at 75805 Altamira, off Eldorado. To get to the main RM1 ride take the east sidepath or lane north along Cook to Aztec and Palm Desert's CV Link. For the La Quinta-Indio CV Link cross 111 at the Channel Dr light (west of Washington) and take it across Washington to a path access. Indian Wells banned CV Link from its borders. See Ride LQ3 for the route to Old Town La Quinta. Indian Wells Tennis Garden is accessible on sidewalks from 111 on the south side of Miles and the west side of Washington, and always open to cycle around. Our patio dining choice is Eureka! at 111 and Cook St.

CV Link East Valley *14 miles long when completed. Flat with undergrossings. Any bike.*

Construction of the CV Link spanning the east valley cities of La Quinta, Indio, and Coachella is just beginning at time of this writing in early 2021. Some sections will be completed sooner than others, depending on factors such as rights-of-way, as indicated on the La Quinta map. The path will follow the Whitewater River channel, passing most roadways with undercrossings. It will also cross the channel a couple of times. Since it winds around in an arch, vistas of the surrounding mountains will change, and riding it back and forth will double the viewing opportunities. It will be a wide path, accommodating peds, bikes, golf carts and neighborhood electric vehicles (NEV's). One of the first segments to be built is through La Quinta, from Washington St and Channel Dr East, running atop the levee behind the Hwy 111 commercial district, then turning northeast under Miles and Fred Waring in Indio, ending at Indio Blvd until a right-of-way is procured to cross under the road and adjacent railroad tracks.

This 3.75-mile segment makes a great addition to nearby rides. Combine it via ride IW1 with Palm Desert/Rancho Mirage rides or with La Quinta ride LQ3. Using the map you can make it into a loop using rideable sidewalks, but riding CV Link back and forth will be much more enjoyable than a sidewalk ride. La Quinta has some nice new sidepaths, especially Miles west of CV Link, but Indio has mostly older sidewalks. Community feeder paths and Class II routes are also planned to meet the link.

Until CV Link crosses under Indio Blvd and the tracks, cyclists will have to detour using sidewalks over the Monroe bridge to access the next 2021 segment at Monroe or the adjacent industrial park, as shown on the map. From there it runs east along the levee 2.5 miles to Golf Ctr Pkwy. The following section that passes Dillon Rd and Ave 50 awaits right-of-way negotiation. It will end at Sierra Vista Park along Tyler St, where cyclists can pick up the final 2021-start segment and ride about 3.3 miles south past Ave 52 to an access on Airport Blvd. Another 11 miles of trail to the Salton Sea may be approved at a later date. *See coachellavalleylink.com for maps and updates. Also see this book's site.*

Future CV Link vista: Adams to the west.

La Quinta Cove and Old Town LQ1

This enjoyable excursion combines a pedal up the paved Bear Creek Trail with an optional easy mountain bike cruise in the Cove Oasis, topped off by brunch in Old Town La Quinta, and great options to extend the ride on sidewalks or bike lanes along wide beautiful boulevards in the newer portions of town.

Tune: Recuerdame (with Marc Anthony) and Me Muero by La Quinta Estacion; A Horse With No Name by America

Eats: Napa Valley Pizza on the Stuft Pizza patio, Old Town

Distance: 5.8 miles (paved portion only) with optional extensions. Time: 45 minutes to 1 hour.

Route & Bike: Moderate difficulty. Paved, any bike. Optional MTB. Mostly Class I, some easy Class II and III. Bear Creek Trail ascends 350 feet in 2 miles (e-bike edge).

Facilities: Restrooms and water at Fritz Burns Park and on Main Street, Old Town. Water fountains along Bear Creek Trail. Bring plenty of water, even more on hot days.

A Napa Valley pizza on the Stuft Pizza patio in Old Town is the perfect reward for a scenic La Quinta cycle

Knocks & Hazards: Peds/dog walkers on Bear Creek Trail. Comingle with autos in Old Town. Street crossings. Bike lanes next to traffic. Rattlesnakes, scorpions, coyotes. Also possible mountain lions at wilderness interface in the Cove area. The city does not officially allow cycling on non-designated sidewalks, but they seem to tolerate courteous cyclists.

Camp 'n Ride: Lake Cahuilla Regional Park has camping for RV's (hookups) and tents.

Access: Take Washington Street 4.7 miles south from I-10, past Highway 111 to Eisenhower and turn right. Go 1.8 miles to the light at Calle Tampico, where trailhead parking is on the right. You can also park in Old Town La Quinta, which is to the left down Calle Tampico several blocks, then right on Avenida Bermudas, and left on any of the side streets. Also plenty of street parking in La Quinta Cove district.

The Ride: Start cycling on the Class I paved path through the palm trees for 0.25 mile to Avenida Caranza. The official Bear Creek Trailhead is on the right side of the road. The 2.5-mile paved path for bikes and pedestrians runs between the base of the Santa Rosa Mountains and the interesting and quirky La Quinta Cove neighborhood, known for its densely packed colorful Santa Fe-style homes. The trail begins adjacent to an upscale neighborhood, requires a short blip onto a residential street (obey stop signs), then quickly reaches the banks of the usually dry channeled Bear Creek. Many cyclists prefer to ride up adjacent Montezuma Avenue.

The trail climbs gradually and gains about 350 feet elevation along its length, eventually moving away from the houses of the adjacent Cove neighborhood. You will mostly feel the elevation gain on hot days. The seemingly barren but starkly beautiful Santa Rosa Mountains form a dramatic backdrop to the colorful landscaped desert vegetation found along the trail. Along the way are a couple of ramadas with water fountains, including doggie bowls. The trail ends at Calle Tecata and the entrance to the Cove Oasis. Mountain bikers can explore Option 1.

Bear Creek Trail next to the Cove neighborhood leads to the foothills of the Santa Rosa Mountains

Option 1: Mountain Biking in the Cove Oasis ⭐2 *3 miles, novice MTB*
The 114-acre Cove Oasis is a natural open space area with gently sloping terrain and wide packed dirt and rock trails suitable for novice mountain bikers. The west trailhead on Calle Tecate, which is next to the Bear Creek Trail entrance, leads south to ramadas and a palm oasis in about 0.4 mile, and then onward to the top of a dike, where you can ride to the left (east) another 0.4 mile and to a trail junction. Cycling sharply to the left will take you to another trail junction in about 0.4 mile. Taking that trail to the left will bring you back to the west trailhead in about 0.7 mile.

Otherwise, you can just ride to the east trailhead, and continue along your La Quinta Cove loop ride. You can get in several miles of riding here by exploring all of the trails, some more official than others. Advanced mountain bikers can attempt some more challenging terrain on the other side of the dike, where allowed. There is a water fountain at the west trailhead, but no restrooms up here. The area is very scenic, with views of the nearby Santa Rosa Mountains, and sweeping views down over La Quinta and across the Coachella Valley to the Little San Bernardino Mountains of Joshua Tree National Park. The impressive flood control retention basin and dam is intended to protect the Cove neighborhood from inundation. Although bikes (and dogs) are not allowed, you can hike on the Cove to Lake trail over a small ridge all the way to Lake Cahuilla Regional Park in about 2.5 miles. Some years bighorn sheep make frequent winter appearances along that trail.

Either ride back the way you came down the Bear Creek Trail, or make it into a loop ride using bike lanes on surface streets. We recommend returning on the trail on uncrowded days to enjoy the easy cruise with great views toward the valley, and cycling down the street when the trail is being heavily used. Either way, you will be delighted that it is downhill. If you choose the loop option, follow the bike lane of Calle Tecate heading east, which turns into Avenida Bermudas heading north. At the bottom of the hill is Fritz Burns Park at the corner of Ave 52 with facilities and picnic tables (5.0). Cross Ave 52 and follow the narrow bike lane for a few blocks to Old Town La Quinta, on the right. We like to lock our bikes in the racks at the corner of La Fonda and grab a patio table at Stuft Pizza. Try walking all around Old Town, including the next block (Main Street) with plenty of restaurants, and a Sunday morning farmers' market. Old Town Coffee Company is a popular place with locals and cyclists for casual breakfast on their sidewalk patio. To return to the start, turn left onto the Tampico sidewalk and cross Eisenhower to the trailhead. Another option is to park and start/end the ride in Old Town.

Extend the ride: Combine ride LQ1 with LQ2. A ride that encompasses Bear Creek Trail, Old Town, and round trip to Lake Cahuilla is 24 miles, and takes about 2 to 2.5 hours.

The La Quinta Boulevards and Lake Cahuilla Regional Park LQ2

One of our favorite roads to ride along is the 1.5-mile stretch of Avenue 52 between Avenida Bermudas and Jefferson Street. It is easily combined with LQ1 and can be extended all the way to Lake Cahuilla Regional Park where camping is available.

Distance: Up to 24 miles round trip. Turn around at any point to control length.
Time: Up to 3 hours.
Route & Bike: Easy to moderate. Class II bike lanes or sidewalks for any bike. Area near Lake Cahuilla is Class III plus optional flat MTB options. Very gradual downhill to east; as golfers say "Your ball always rolls towards Indio." E-bike edge for distance.
Camp 'n Ride: Ride this route in reverse from Lake Cahuilla Regional Park to get to Old Town and La Quinta Cove. See page 325 for campground details.
Bike 'n Brunch: See Ride LQ1.

Access: Stage from the Old Town La Quinta area, at the corner of Avenida La Fonda and Avenida Bermudas. From Hwy 111, drive south on Washington to Tampico. Turn right, then left on Bermudas, and find parking in Old Town.

The Ride: From Old Town, head south on Desert Club Drive, which borders Old Town to the east. It has no bike lane, but is lightly traveled. You can also opt to take Class II Bermudas to the south. From either road make your way to the sidepath or bike lane along Ave 52 heading east. Pass a lovely pond and waterfalls at the entrance/traffic signal for the renowned Silver Rock Golf Course. You can ride your bike up the access road to get a look at it. This is a possible turnaround point if you are adding this ride to LQ1.

Otherwise, continue to the east along Ave 52 to the traffic circle at Jefferson, another potential turnaround point. To ride farther, once reaching the traffic circle (mile 2.2), turn right on Jefferson, and ride down that sidepath or bike lane on a very gradual downhill trajectory to Ave 54, across which is the PGA West community (3.2). You can ride around the un-gated portions of that development, although there is no other exit. The main route turns left (east) onto lovely Ave 54 and follows the south sidepath or bike lane to Madison Street (4.2). Turn right and follow the west sidepath or bike lane, past the light at Airport Road (5.2), all the way to Ave 58 (6.2).

From here, turn around, or you can ride to scenic Lake Cahuilla Regional Park in a few more miles: Turn right onto Ave 58. After both the sidewalk and bike lane end, the road bends to the left (7.2) and ascends a small hill onto a levee. You will see an RV campground on the right, which is part of the Regional Park. Descend the hill off of the levee. To the left are trailheads for some relatively easy, but sandy, MTB trails. Veer to the right onto the Lake Cahuilla access road (7.5) where the entrance to the gated Quarry development is straight ahead. Pedal up the hill past the entrance kiosk (8.1). The fee is $6 per biker if you intend to "use the park" or free to "turn around."

Lake Cahuilla Regional Park contains picnic areas, water, restrooms with pay showers, and a concrete-rimmed irrigation reservoir that is open for shore fishing but not for swimming or use of private boats. During April to September boat rentals and a large swimming pool are available to the public Fridays, Saturdays and Sundays.

To the right down the road are the main day use picnic area and the RV/tent campground.

Lake Cahuilla Regional Park is popular with sea & shorebirds and winter snowbirds at the RV campground

To the left the paved road turns to dirt and leads to the equestrian campground (hookups as well) and restrooms.

You can bike along the lake and onto its berms, however the far half-mile is fenced off at the irrigation canal so you would need to walk your bike along the terraced shore of the lake through there to do a loop.

For a pleasant ride, cycle down the small hill from the entrance kiosk toward the lake and turn right. Follow the paved park road past the campground and around the bend. It leads to a wide gravel area (road bikers turn around here or proceed on foot) between the lake and the adjacent Jack Nicklaus golf course at PGA West. As the shoreline curves, great views open up back over the lake toward the Santa Rosa Mountains. Sea and shore birds frequent this lake including great blue herons, white pelicans, cormorants, and night herons. When you reach the fenced-off area (9.6), we recommend turning around, perhaps enjoying a rest break and moment of solitude (provided the adjacent county sheriffs' shooting range is not active).

Ride back along the gravel access road or the rough concrete apron along the lake where not occupied by fishermen, all the way around past the campground. Follow the lakeshore and reach the beach area. Ride on the firm-packed area at the top of the beach, past the main day-use area, and to a dirt road that leads to the equestrian campground. You can also ride toward the lake past the hydraulic control structure (10.0) and most of the way across the lake on a berm that is popular with fishermen (10.7).

Sea and shore birds perch on the trees along the berm. Return back down the dirt road that becomes paved as it nears the park exit (12.6). Return via the same route. The desert and mountain scenery is most spectacular when riding westbound (20.7).

> Option 1: Cycle Lake Cahuilla Park ⭐2 *About 4.5 miles total, easy.* For an easy and scenic bike ride, pay the $6 per person fee to drive into the park and take your time cycling around the scenic lake, perhaps combining it with a picnic. Ride next to the lake as described in LQ2. Those with skinny tires may be limited to a couple of miles on the park roads. Perhaps try fishing here. Or, take a hike (no bikes) along the scenic 2.5-mile Cove to Lake, aka Morrow Trail, maybe spotting bighorn sheep. It starts to the west of the entry kiosk, parallels the private Quarry Golf Course, and leads to The Cove (LQ1).

Old Town La Quinta through Indian Wells to El Paseo LQ3 ⭐3

Details: 18 miles round trip; 2 hours, moderate due to distance (e-bike edge); Sidepath and Class III.

From Old Town La Quinta, the best route north is along Eisenhower Drive that is accessed a few blocks to the west along Calle Tampico. Its west sidewalk bends to the right to meet Washington Street (2.0). Cross Washington to the east sidewalk and ride to the left. At Ave 48 when bike lanes end all bikes are directed to the sidepath. For a nice diversion Caleo Way runs parallel to the east between Ave 48 and Ave 47. It passes the lakes of the Lake La Quinta development. South of Ave 47 are a couple of restaurants including Louise's Pantry for breakfast.

La Quinta's new Old Town is a great place for your Bike 'n Brunch

To the north at Simon are El Pollo Loco, In-N-Out, Trader Joe's, and ALDI. Cross Washington at Simon/Point Happy (3.3), then ride along Washington's west sidewalk to Hwy 111. At the corner is a large Vons shopping center with several restaurants. Heading west on the sidepath along the south side of Hwy 111, enter Indian Wells' nice sidepath at a bike/ped bridge (3.75). See Indian Wells ride IW1 for a description from this point. The Indian Wells sidepath leads to Cook Street (7.0), and then about 2 more miles will get you through El Paseo (9.0). Ride RM2 Opt 2b crosses at Eldorado, and you can go left for a back roads route to El Paseo. To connect to the La Quinta CV Link section, don't cross Washington at Simon. Cross Hwy 111 and reach an access to the path to the right at the next light, East Channel Dr. Expect this CV Link segment by late 2021.

Beyond the Coachella Valley

Much of the vast desert region of southeastern California has been preserved in Federal and State parkland. The most popular of these areas are Joshua Tree National Park and Anza-Borrego Desert State Park. Rides in those parks are presented.

Joshua Tree National Park

Joshua Tree National Park (JTNP) preserves 800,000 acres of land including both the Colorado Desert and Mojave Desert ecosystems. The Colorado Desert portion, below 3,000 feet elevation, is predominantly covered in creosote bush and beautifully adorned in ocotillo, jumping cholla cactus, and palo verde. Amazing spring wildflower blooms occur during March or April in wet years. The main attraction of the park, however, is the area encompassing the Mojave Desert ecosystem, above 3,000 feet elevation, which is dominated by the Joshua tree. This wide-armed yucca plant (as opposed to an actual tree) spreads out in beautiful desert forests, surrounded by spectacular monzogranite boulder piles and mountains, creating a landscape so spectacular that it could only be found in a national park.

The monzogranite was created below the surface by plutonic intrusions of magma some 100 million years ago, then formed joints that were infiltrated by water, which eventually eroded them into various shapes. Flash floods contributed to the formation of the boulder piles in today's park. A third ecosystem exists above 4,000 feet elevation in the western portion of the park that preserves piñon pine/juniper woodland in the Little San Bernardino Mountains.

Birds to watch for include the birds of prey red-tailed hawk, American kestrel, Cooper's hawk, golden eagle, and prairie falcon. Roadrunner and Gambel's quail may dart across your path. Look for the cactus wren in the Joshua trees as well as sage sparrow, bushtit, ladder-backed woodpecker, black-throated sparrow, oak titmouse, black-tailed and blue-gray gnatcatchers, phainopepla, mockingbird, verdin, rock wren, mourning dove, and Le Conte's thrasher. Check the NPS website under "Things to Do/Birding" for a more complete list of the seasonal and transient birds that frequent the park, especially during the spring and fall migrations along the Pacific Flyway.

Wet winters can produce dazzling displays of spring wildflowers in Joshua Tree National Park.

Desert animals are mostly nocturnal to avoid the heat of day, but you may see ground squirrels, various lizards, and perhaps a desert tortoise. If you are lucky you may glimpse some of the 250 bighorn sheep that roam the park, mostly up in the hills. Some of the nocturnal animals may be seen closer to dusk and dawn, including kangaroo rat, black tail jackrabbit, and coyote. There are 25 varieties of snakes in the park, including 6 species of rattlesnakes. Although snakes are mostly nocturnal they sometimes seek the warmth of the trail or road during the day as well. If you'd prefer not to see snakes, plan your visit for mid-winter.

JTNP is known more for its fantastic rock climbing and hiking than its biking, and bicycles are restricted to paved and unpaved JTNP roads that are open to vehicles. Many enjoy cycling the main paved roads that are hilly with soft shoulders and blind curves. However, the dirt roads see only a tiny proportion of JTNP traffic and are a much better bet for our style of cycling.

Climate Data for Joshua Tree (NOAA 1981 to 2010 normals)													
Month	Jan	Feb	Mar	Apr	May	Jun	Jul	Aug	Sep	Oct	Nov	Dec	Totals
Average High °F	62.2	61.5	69.8	76.4	86.0	93.9	101.1	100.4	95.8	81.2	69.1	58.2	79.6
Average Low °F	37.9	37.5	41.0	46.0	53.4	60.0	70.8	70.1	65.8	53.4	43.0	35.8	51.2
Precipitation, inches	0.62	0.48	0.39	0.13	0.17	0.01	0.33	0.50	0.33	0.33	0.61	0.79	4.69

Queen Valley—A Fabulous MTB 'n Hike JT1

While some of Joshua Tree's dirt roads will take you on epic climbs over mountains, the roads in Queen Valley in the central portion of the park are fairly flat, situated on a gently sloping valley in a little-used area. Queen Valley Road extends from the Barker Dam trailhead area with its beautiful conglomeration of monzogranite boulders to the east out into a wide-open valley filled with Joshua trees and granitic mountains in the distance. This is a place of solitude, reminiscent of the Old West. The ride is

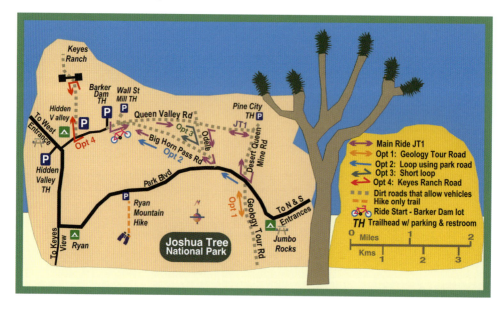

generally slightly uphill out and downhill back, just as we like it. A couple of loop options are available among the approximate 8.5 miles of dirt roads open to motorized vehicles and bikes. We also recommend cycling the nearby 1-mile road toward Keys Ranch. End your ride with a short but fabulous hike from the trailhead and perhaps drive to several others.

Tunes: The Joshua Tree album by U2

Eats: Messy Jessie for breakfast at Crossroads Café in Joshua Tree, on Hwy 62 west of Park Blvd, or bring a picnic to the park.

Distance: 11.4 miles total with options to shorten or lengthen. Time: 1.5 to 2 hours.

Route & Bike: Easy to moderate. Mostly packed sand with some gravel and some washboard areas depending on park road maintenance schedule. MTB. Skill: Novice, not technical. Very gently sloping valley. E-bike edge for 4,200 ft park elevation.

Seasons: Fall through spring. On hot summer days in early mornings only. Best on sunny, warm, El Nino-year spring weekday when wildflowers are peaking and the distant mountains are cloaked in snow but the dirt roads are dry.

Facilities: Chemical toilets at most trailheads and parking lots, including Barker Dam trailhead and Pine City backcountry trailhead mid-route. No water inside main portion of park, only at campgrounds, ranger stations, and Visitor Centers at the park's perimeter.

Knocks & Hazards: Roads are sand with some soft spots, and attention is required to stay on the most compacted sections. Dirt roads are shared with vehicles en route to hiking trails, speed limit 25 mph. Ride on weekdays to limit traffic. On our 1.5-hour weekday rides, only 6 vehicles passed the first day, even fewer on the second day. All were courteous. Paved park road option involves 0.7 mile of downhill grade (about 5 minutes) with no shoulders, speed limit 45 mph. Wildlife: Rattlesnakes, scorpions, coyotes, possible mountain lion. No pets are allowed on the trails. Elevation is around 4,200 feet, which may take some getting used to. Be aware of low-lying washes during rain events.

Rent 'n Ride: Joshua Tree Bicycle Shop, 6416 Hallee Rd, Joshua Tree, 760.366.3377.

Camp 'n Ride: Hidden Valley Campground is 1.5 miles on paved access road to our trailhead. It is a beautiful primitive campground among granite boulders, usually full with rock climbers. RV's under 25 feet only. No reservations. Check the NPS website for the other campgrounds, including Black Rock in the west section of the park, a good choice for RV's (no hookups) and great hiking. Reserve: recreation.gov. For RV hookups, Yucca Valley RV Park (760.365.5596) in town is about 24 miles from this ride's Barker Dam trailhead.

Bike 'n Brunch: No food service in park. Cute cafés outside the Joshua Tree entrance on Hwy 62 near Park Boulevard, such as Crossroads Café.

Emergency: Call San Bernardino Dispatch, 909.383.5651 (call collect). Cell phone coverage is spotty in the park. Emergency phones: Intersection Rock parking area bathroom next to Hidden Valley Campground and at the ranger station at Indian Cove. An emergency room is located at Hi-Desert Medical Center, 6601 White Feather Rd, Joshua Tree, 760.366.3711.

Fees: 7-day passes are $25 per non-commercial carload or $12 per bicyclist. Annual passes are available and federal lands passes are honored. No day-use fee is required for the separate Black Rock area.

Further Info: The park's website is nps.gov/jotr

Access: Joshua Tree National Park is located between I-10 and SR 62 to the north of Palm Springs and the Coachella Valley. To get to the main Mojave Desert section of JTNP from Los Angeles, take I-10 about 100 miles east, past SR 111/ Palm Springs, to Twentynine Palms Highway (62) north. Or, from Palm Springs, take Indian Canyon north to I-10 west, then exit on SR 62 north. Follow it a total of 28 miles, up over 3,000 feet in elevation, past busy Yucca Valley, home of the major stores in the region, as well as access to the Black Rock section of JTNP (Joshua Lane at 21 miles). Continue on to the next town of Joshua Tree, following the signs to the Joshua Tree Visitor's Center at Park Boulevard. Turn right, and stop there for helpful information and advice about current conditions. The quaint cafés at Park Boulevard and Hwy 62 are your last chances for food and water (make sure to bring some) before entering the park.

Follow Park Boulevard 5 miles to the park entrance kiosk, and then drive up into JTNP, reaching an elevation of about 4,200 feet. Just after the Hidden Valley trail access road, turn left onto the road to Barker Dam. Pass the Hidden Valley Campground, and note the dirt road to Keyes Ranch (for later), then reach the obvious Barker Dam trailhead parking lot at the end of the paved road in 1.5 miles. Just before reaching the parking lot, the dirt road that intersects and heads to the east is Queen Valley Road.

The Ride: Begin cycling east down Queen Valley Road (QVR) with a very gradual, easy, uphill climb. You will be instantly thrilled with the experience of cycling among the Joshua trees and granite boulders. The first junction on the left is a short road that leads to the Wall Street Mill trailhead (with a chemical toilet), which you may want to come back to for a hike later. At 0.9 mile is a fork in the road. Take the narrower road straight ahead to stay on QVR rather than the wider road to the right, which is Big Horn Pass Road. Although the granite boulders disappear as the valley opens up, you still have plenty of Joshua trees and granitic mountains in the distance to gaze at, such as Queen Mountain to the north. At 2.3 miles, look for an obvious cross road (not trail), labeled Odelle Road on the park map. This is an option for a shorter 5.6 mile loop if you turn right and meet up with the ride as described in Option 3. Otherwise, continue on QVR across the valley until you arrive at a junction with signage to "Jumbo Rocks" going off hard to the right.

Continue straight ahead just past the junction to the Pine City backcountry trailhead (with toilet) at mile 3.9. This is another hiking option. Turn around, and at the immediate junction veer to the left toward "Jumbo Rocks." Cycle scenic Desert Queen Mine Road to reach the paved Park Boulevard at mile 5.2. We recommend turning

Cycling through Queen Valley among the Joshua trees and granite boulders

around and returning the way you came to see the beautiful landscape from the other direction. However you also have two other options from this point in the ride:

Option 1: 4WD Geology Tour Road ⭐ or ⭐ with lift up. *Up to 17 miles, strenuous, MTB*
For some extra mileage cross the paved park road and cycle down the dirt Geology Tour Road as far as you want. Pick up a trail guide at the turnoff that describes the features, and cycle 5.5 miles down a sandy, bumpy washboard-surfaced road that drops 1,000 feet in elevation. At Squaw Tank is a 6-mile one-way circuit through Pleasant Valley, resulting in a total ride of about 17 miles. Despite the very interesting landscape and geology along this ride, we do not like it because of the rough road conditions, dust from vehicles, and the elevation gain on the return ride. However, if you can arrange for a friend to pick you up at Pleasant Valley to avoid the return uphill climb, it would make for a much easier 11-mile downhill scenic ride. E-bikes make sure to leave enough charge for the uphill.

Option 2: JT1 as a Loop Ride ⭐ *Easy MTB*
To turn the ride into a loop, and shave off 2.4 miles from the main ride, turn right onto the paved Park Boulevard. The speed limit is 45 mph and there is no shoulder so cars have to swerve to avoid you. Ride single file! It is downhill, so it should only take 5 minutes to reach the next junction in 0.7 mile. Turn right on Big Horn Pass Road, which is mostly flat easy riding besides one small rise, on packed sand and gravel. The south end of the Odelle Road cutoff is reached in 0.5 mile (mile 6.4), and you have now met up with the main ride.

If you chose not to do Options 1 or 2, turn around at the park road and pedal north the way you came up Desert Queen Mine Road, then make a hard left at the junction to QVR prior to the Pine City Trailhead (6.5). As you head west you will be treated to views of Mt. San Jacinto and/or Mt. San Gorgonio most days, which if the lighting is right (mostly during the morning to mid-day), can look spectacular, especially if they are snow-covered. To add some variety and a bit of distance, turn left at the road junction with Odelle Road at mile 8.1, follow it to its end at Big Horn Pass Road (8.7), and turn right. At this point, Option 2 continues as well.

As you pedal closer to the granite boulder area, the viewscapes become that much more spectacular. Reach the original junction with QVR (10.6) and return down a nice gentle grade to the parking lot at mile 11.4 (or mile 9.0 via Option 2), plus any mileage added via Option 1.

Option 3: A Shorter Loop Ride on QVR ⭐ *5.6-miles total, easy MTB*
Begin by riding east on QVR as in the main ride, skipping the spur road to Wall Street Mill trailhead, then keeping left at the next fork at mile 0.9. Turn right down Odelle Road (the first dirt road crossing) at mile 2.3 and follow it for 0.6 mile until it meets up with Big Horn Pass Road (2.9). Turn right and follow it back past the original trail junction with Queen Valley Road (4.8) and to the start at mile 5.6.

Option 4: Keys Ranch Ride ⭐ *5 miles extra, easy MTB*
Add this very scenic side trip to any of the other ride options. Once back to the beginning of QVR, ride (or transport your bikes via your vehicle) for 1.5 miles on the scenic paved park access road to the Keys Ranch access road. The paved road here is just a trailhead access road and not a through road, so it is pleasant to ride on. Turn right on the obvious wide gravel road toward Keys Ranch that leads at first to a gravel parking lot with a toilet. This is a very scenic area with lots of granite boulders to gaze at, and on weekends rock climbers will be on each one. Follow the dirt road on a slightly downhill trajectory, past the first, usually open, gate for about 1 mile through this beautiful stretch

of Joshua tree forest and granite boulders until you reach the signed gate for the Keys Ranch tours. A toilet is available here. Do not proceed through the gate or risk a $75 fine. Rangers lead walking tours of the ranch once occupied by successful homesteaders Bill and Frances Keys. Get tickets ($10) the same day at the Oasis Visitor Center. Return the same way. The road is packed sand, but may not be as compacted as QVR.

Forests of Joshua trees around every bend

Bike 'n Hike: Some of the most spectacular scenery is accessed by foot path only, and you can reach several trailheads on your bike, then lock up and stroll. From our trailhead access parking lot, try the 1.1-mile Barker Dam loop. This very scenic hike through the trees and boulders leads to a small pond that was once used by the cattle of early ranchers and is now a popular spot for foraging birds. If you are lucky enough to be here when the pond is full of water after a particularly wet period, and perhaps wildflowers are blooming, you will be in for a treat. Some native petroglyphs are also found on this trail, although most were ruined by a film crew that "enhanced" them years back.

Another fabulous bang for the buck hike is the 1-mile Hidden Valley Trail loop. From our ride starting point, its trailhead is to the west, beyond Hidden Valley Campground, then a short jog to the right/left on the main park road. Cattle rustlers used to hide among the amazing collection of monzogranite boulders, and you will have your camera out around each twist and turn of the trail photographing the vistas. Actually, all of the short nature trails in the park are worthwhile, which you can access by packing up your bikes and driving to their trailheads.

Keys View is a must-see on a clear day. At 5,185 feet there is a great view across to the Coachella Valley desert and surrounding mountains. Check out the trace of the mighty San Andreas Fault in the valley below as depicted by the signboard. This is also one of the best places in Southern California to come for celestial events like eclipses, meteor showers, and comets. Once we saw a lunar eclipse and the Hale Bop comet simultaneously here.

For more of a workout, take the popular 1.5-mile trail to the summit of 5,462-foot Ryan Mountain. The 1,100-foot elevation gain over the valley provides awesome views. In other sections of the park, we recommend the 3-mile Mastodon Peak loop in the lower Cottonwood section, a great area to visit during spring wildflower season. Park at the end of the access road past the Cottonwood Campground and follow the signs. We typically take the "unmaintained trail" spur that leads to the summit for a picnic, with views out to the Salton Sea and across the park. The trails out of Black Rock Campground are also worthwhile, with great views west to the mountain ranges.

Anza-Borrego Desert State Park and Borrego Springs

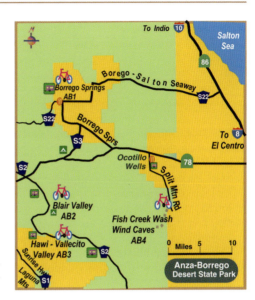

Anza-Borrego Desert State Park is the largest state park in California, containing 500,000 acres of California desert from low-lying badlands and washes to mile-high eroded peaks lined with palm canyons. The Santa Rosa Mountains separate the region from the Coachella Valley to the north, and the Laguna Mountains of the Peninsular Range rise steeply to the west, where Sunrise Highway and Julian perch over 4,000 feet above the desert floor in a contrasting oak and pine forest, as described in ride LM1 in the San Diego chapter. To the east is the vast Salton Sea, an eternal remnant of a leaking aqueduct from the early twentieth century. The park lies mostly in San Diego County, and extends north into Riverside County and east into Imperial County.

Anza-Borrego is named for the Spanish explorer Juan Batista de Anza, and the Spanish word "borrego" for bighorn sheep. These endangered and protected animals can be seen around the park if you are lucky, usually in the morning. Some of the better places to see them are along road S-2 (between mileposts 12.5 and 13.5) and along the trails, including the park's popular Borrego Palm Canyon hiking trail that starts from the Borrego Palm Canyon Campground.

Borrego Springs is surrounded by the State Park and is its main gateway town. Sleepy in summer, it bustles in winter with visitors who stay at the B&B's or RV resorts and frequent its restaurants, spas, and golf courses. The town explodes with activity if there is a good wildflower season, which can occur from late February through March in wetter years. Blooms are also possible in the early fall if the summer monsoons materialize. Wildflower displays can range from small patches of colorful flowers to entire fields of pink sand verbena, while cacti bloom at various times depending on conditions and elevation.

Anza-Borrego is not an easy scenic cycling destination, but more of a place where cyclists enjoy the hilly winding highways through mountain passes and canyons alongside cars and RV's traveling at a high rate of speed. Alternatively, mountain bikers can ride over varied terrain for many miles on sandy dirt roads without ever hitting pavement. For easy bikers, we still recommend visiting this unique park with bikes in tow, as we have identified some fun riding opportunities. Any bike will work on the easy road ride around Borrego Springs and the main facilities of Anza-Borrego State Park (ride AB1). Bikes are not allowed on hiking trails within the park, but can be ridden on paved park roads and the 500 miles of dirt roads also open to all motorized vehicles. However, in the more recently added Hawi-Vallecito area (ride AB3), vehicles are prohibited on the dirt roads.

Rides AB2, AB3, and AB4 require driving to more remote areas of the park on scenic paved roadways. These rides are along sandy back roads and after a rainstorm they can become muddy and unrideable. Even when dry, large sections can be too sandy to ride comfortably without the proper equipment. You should have tires at least 2.4-inches wide inflated to no more than 25 PSI, and make sure to bring patch kits or spare tubes because of thorns from desert vegetation. You can still ride portions of these routes without the ideal tire configurations, but you will most likely get bogged down in sand before too long and it will become a Bike 'n Hike. The ideal bike for sandy conditions is a wide-tired e-bike, like what surfers use at the beach.

Beware of rattlesnakes, mountain lions, extreme summer heat, and flash floods, especially during summer monsoon season. Bring plenty of water.

Rent 'n Ride: Bike Borrego, 583 Palm Canyon Dr, 760.767.4255

Camp 'n Ride: Borrego Palm Canyon Campground in the State Park has sites for tents and RV's with hookups. Camping is also allowed in Blair Valley as signed. For other State Park campgrounds around the park (no RV hookups) see the park website, or look up other private parks in the region. Outside of the State Park, camping is allowed on BLM land. Borrego Springs has RV parks, hotels, B&B's, and restaurants.

Further Info: CA State Parks site: www.parks.ca.gov/?page_id=638; Anza-Borrego Foundation: theabf.org. Wildflower Reports: Hotline: 760.767.4684; Anza-Borrego Desert Natural History Association: abdnha.org/pages/03flora/reports/current.htm; Desert USA: desertusa.com/wildflo/ca_abdsp.html.

Access: To get to Borrego Springs and the main part of Anza-Borrego State Park: From Palm Springs/Coachella Valley: Take I-10 east to Indio and then the SR 86-S Freeway south toward El Centro, to Salton City. Follow Borrego-Salton Seaway (S-22) westbound (the first couple of miles are very bumpy, no fun for RV's) about 30 minutes into Christmas Circle in central Borrego Springs.

In wet years visitors flock here in spring to see the colorful display

Anza-Borrego and Borrego Springs
Bike, Brunch 'n Hike   AB1 ⭐

Details: About 5 miles. Easy, paved surfaces for any bike.

Start at the visitor's center where there is free parking. Take the Class I paved path 0.7 mile down the gradual hill through the interesting desert vegetation to the campground, then ride to the left up the park road on a gradual grade to road's end, and the trailhead for the 3.5-mile Borrego Palm Canyon hike. The hike is still worthwhile even after 70 percent of the native fan palms were destroyed in a 2004 flash flood. Return to the visitor's center, then ride into the town, as shown on the map.

Path between visitor's center and campground allows bikes

Blair Valley MTB 'n Hike   AB2 ⭐

Details: 10.6 miles MTB plus hiking. Moderate to strenuous. Packed dirt to loose sand. Impassible when wet. Vehicles are allowed on the road (4WD recommended).

The Blair Valley turnoff is about 25 miles south of Christmas Circle in Borrego Springs. Take Borrego Springs Rd (S-3) 5.1 miles south to Yaqui Pass Rd. Turn right and go 6.8 miles to SR 78 and turn right (west) toward Julian. Follow it 7 miles to The Great Overland Stage Route (S-2). Turn left and drive about 5.9 miles. After rounding a bend down a small pass look for a sign that reads "Butterfield Stage Route—2 miles" and a sign for "Blair Valley" on the left (GPS 33°02'13.9820",-116° 24'38.7017"). Drive a short distance up the dirt road for trailhead parking (restroom, no water).

The first 1.5 miles of cycling are along a nice flat stretch on compacted dirt roadway with great vistas west across the valley to the Laguna Mountains. Beyond there, be prepared for deeper sand. Reach the Ghost Mountain/Marshal South Homesite trail in 3.1 miles. A rugged hiking-only trail climbs 420 feet in one mile to the remains of the site of a poet's family home from the 1930s. Next, cycle east to the Morteros Trail (3.8) that leads to Native American mortars in the granite. This hiking trail is level and only 0.5-mile round trip. The road then climbs gradually to the northeast ending at the Pictograph Trail's trailhead (5.3) (GPS 33°01'10.1566", -116°21'36.8117"). The 1.5-mile sandy hiking trail climbs about 160 feet. At 0.4-mile watch for the pictographs in the rock, then continue on through the piñon juniper woodland to the saddle and a vista point with a view of the valley.

Riding the sandy roads in Blair Valley

The Hawi-Vallecito Valley Cultural Preserve MTB   AB3

Details: 8–10 miles, Easy to strenuous, MTB. Flat to gradual grade. Sandy roads. No facilities

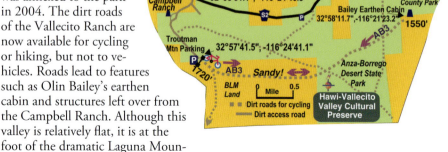

This 3,400-acre parcel was annexed to the park in 2004. The dirt roads of the Vallecito Ranch are now available for cycling or hiking, but not to vehicles. Roads lead to features such as Olin Bailey's earthen cabin and structures left over from the Campbell Ranch. Although this valley is relatively flat, it is at the foot of the dramatic Laguna Mountains. Garnet Peak is due west and 5,905 feet in elevation. It's an optional hike on the Laguna Mountain ride (LM1) in the San Diego chapter.

Trailhead for the sandy route to Bailey Cabin

To access AB3 follow the instructions for ride AB2. After passing the Butterfield Stage sign for Blair Valley continue approximately 7.9 miles farther (13.8 miles altogether from SR 78). At the bottom of a hill look for a turnoff signed "Hawi-Vallecito," "Vallecito Ranch," on the right. Bear right at the first fork on this dirt road, then curve left around the gated Thompson Ranch historic property, and continue for a total of about 1.25 miles to the gate at the day-use parking area. Ride east from the gate, and stay left at the first fork. The right fork just leads up into BLM land. Reach Baily Cabin, a picnic spot, in about 3.1 miles (GPS 32°58'11.6940", -116°21'23.1660"). Explore any road you like in this area, but beware conditions are not the greatest, with deep sand in places, and potential desert thorns causing flat tires.

Fish Creek Wash MTB 'n Hike   AB4

Details: 10.2 miles MTB plus 1.5-mile loop hike. Moderate. Sandy 4WD road.
No facilities

From Christmas Circle in Borrego Springs head south on Borrego Springs Road (S-3) to its end at SR 78 in 11.4 miles. Turn left (east) and drive 6.6 miles to Split Mountain Road near Ocotillo Airport. Turn right on the paved road and drive south. About 5 miles along the road is a 1-mile loop nature trail to the elephant tree grove, a tree common in Mexico that exists only here and in the Santa Rosa Mountains at the northern extent of its range. At around 8 miles Split Mountain Road becomes Fish Creek Wash, 2 miles before the main road ends at a gypsum mine. Fish Creek Wash is our route (GPS 33°02'19.1", -116°05'49.3").

This desolate canyon is bisected by a sandy dirt road that can potentially be ridden by bikes with wide enough tires inflated properly. Cycle up the wash to the southwest about 4 miles to the junction with North Fork Fish Creek Wash and the trailhead for the Wind Caves hiking trail (GPS 32°59'24.0", -116°07'05.2"). The 1.5-mile loop trail climbs about 630 feet and provides a great view of the Carrizo Badlands from the top. Back to your bike, you can continue cycling up the various arms of the canyon. This route is very sandy and 4wd vehicles going by may throw dirt up in your face. Common sense dictates not to be caught in washes if there are severe rainstorms in the region, and it is best to do this trail on weekdays to reduce encounters with motorized vehicles.

ENCORE!

Southern California has a fabulous wealth of bike trails. Here are a few more rides to explore:

Point Mugu State Park Camp 'n MTB—Southwest Ventura County   VE5   *No e-bikes*

Located in the Santa Monica Mountains, Point Mugu State Park extends along 5 miles of ocean shoreline and inland into rugged hills and uplands. Two major river canyons and wide grassy valleys contain sycamores, oaks, and a few native walnuts. The Big Sycamore Canyon Trail is a scenic novice MTB along a fire road through lush riparian woodlands. From the Sycamore Canyon campground to Deer Camp Junction is 6.5 miles round trip, with 200-foot elevation gain, or to Ranch Center Road is 9 miles round trip with an approximate 375-foot gain. In winter, stream crossings may be encountered. Other options are available for more challenging rides. The campground is one of the best places to observe wintering monarch butterflies. Thornhill Broome campground, about 1 mile northwest of the Sycamore Canyon park entrance on Hwy 1, offers primitive oceanfront camping as well as access to fabulous scenic hiking in the La Jolla Valley Natural Preserve across the road. The park is about 15 miles south of Oxnard, or 30 miles west of Los Angeles, along scenic Hwy 1. Day use parking: $12 or $3/hour. See www.parks.ca.gov/?page_id=630 for info.

Orange Line Busway Path LA6   and Chandler Bikeway LA7   in LA's San Fernando Valley

The Orange Line Busway bike path cuts through the Sepulveda Basin (LA5), offering options to extend that ride west and east, however the section between Sepulveda and Woodman can be sacry. The route is depicted on the LA County locator map. It is mostly utilitarian with numerous street crossings and not especially scenic, alongside LA Metro's Orange Line Busway. It extends 12-miles from NoHo (North Hollywood) near Coldwater Canyon and Chandler west to Canoga, just north of Victory in Woodland Hills, then turns north, parallel to the west of Chatsworth Ave, ending at Chatsworth Station (Amtrak, Metrolink). The east end of the path connects with a 2-mile Class II bike lane along Chandler near Metro Red Line's NoHo Station. It leads to the 2.8-mile Chandler Bikeway (LA7), for a combined route of about 21 miles. LA7 runs along and in the center median of Chandler between Vineland and Mariposa, ending a few blocks shy of I-5 (Burbank Blvd west exit). The pleasant path, with public art along it, is popular with local familes out for an excursion.

Malibu Creek State Park Camp 'n MTB—West Los Angeles County   LA8   *No e-bikes*

This beautiful park in the Santa Monica Mountains contains 7,000 acres of rolling tall grass plains, oak savannahs, and dramatic peaks, bisected by Malibu Creek. A campground is near the park entrance, and most park-goers walk the short trail from the day-use lot ($12 fee) that leads south to rock pools along the creek. Crags Road is a 3.8-mile advanced-novice MTB path that is mostly flat, compacted double-track as it follows Malibu Creek, but it also encounters some riding within a rocky streambed, and an elevation gain of about 200 feet plus some hills en route. It can be very busy with cyclists and clueless peds on peak use days. The route is not well signed, but from the main parking lot head toward the Visitors Center and then Century Lake, popular for fishing. The property was once owned by 20th Century Fox studios, and at about 3 miles reach the refurbished location of the M*A*S*H set, complete with an ambulance and a covered picnic area at the location of the mess tent. The trail ends at the park boundary in another 0.8 mile. For further info and maps see malibucreekstatepark.org and www.parks.ca.gov/?page_id=614. From US 101 in Calabasas take Las Virgenes Road south about 4 miles to just past Mulholland, or from US 1 at the Malibu coast take Malibu Canyon Road about 7 miles north.

Santa Clarita Class I Trails—North Los Angeles County   LA9

This suburb along I-5 and SR14 to the north of the San Fernando Valley of Los Angeles is developing an impressive system of Class I bike trails known as "The Cloverleaf" that connect Santa Clarita's communities of Newhall, Saugus, Canyon Country, and Valencia. Although most parallel roadways, some of the trails can be fairly scenic, especially when they run next to the rare non-channelized Santa Clara River. Metrolink also provides good access to points along the trails. Already in place are the 8-mile Santa Clara River Trail, the Chuck Pontus Commuter Rail Trail, the San Francisquito Creek Trail, and the Bouquet Creek Trail. Magic Mountain amusement park is located here. See bikesantaclarita.com for a trail map.

Whittier Greenway Rail Trail—South Los Angeles County   LA11

This award-winning 4.7-mile long rail trail follows a Union Pacific right of way and celebrates Whittier's history as a major citrus and walnut producer with informative displays at several "stations." The trail is punctuated by pleasant landscaping and features interesting kinetic wind sculptures, though it also has twelve on-grade road crossings. Trail extensions are planned. Coyote Creek Trail is 4 miles way (P 103). For detailed information and a map see www.cityofwhittier.org/depts/prcs/parks/greenway_trail.asp.

INDEX

Aera Park, Bakersfield BA1   288, 289
Agua Caliente Band of Cahuilla Indians   323, 335
Alamitos Bay LO1, 2   97, 99, 100
Alisco-Serrano Trail SV5, 6   211, 216
Aliso & Wood Canyons Park SV3, 4   147, 148, 206, 213–215
Aliso Canyon Trail, Chino Hills State Park   204
Aliso Creek Trail SV1   206–211, 213, 214, 216
Aliso Viejo Community Park SV1   209
Alpine Pedal Path BB1   315–318
Alta Laguna Park, Laguna Beach LB1   146–148, 213
Anaheim   128, 163, 164, 169–175, 189, 192, 194, 199, 309
Andre Clark Bird Refuge SB1   62
Angels Gate Park LA3   92
Angels Stadium SAR2   164, 169–172
Anisqoyo Park, Isla Vista SB2   67
Anthony C. Beilenson Park LA5   117
Anza-Borrego State Park AB1, 2, 3, 4   222, 281, 284, 292, 319, 323, 357, 363–365
Anza Narrows Park R1   294, 295
Aquarium of the Pacific, Long Beach LO1   92, 94, 95
Arch Beach Heights, Laguna Beach LB1   147, 148
Arlington Heights District, Riverside R2   297
Arroyo Seco Bike Trail PA1   121–124
Arroyo Seco Canyon PA2   121, 123, 124
Arroyo Simi Rail Trail, Simi Valley   70
Arroyo Trabuco MTB Trail SV8   216–220
ARTIC, Anaheim SAR2   170, 171
Autry Western Heritage Center & Museum LA4   112
Avalon, Catalina Island CAT1   125, 126
Avila Beach AV1   28, 41–43
Azusa SGR3   101, 102, 108, 109

Back Bay Wildlife Refuge NB2   133–135, 138–142, 180, 181
Back Bay, Newport Beach   134, 138–142, 179, 180, 185–187
Baja California Garden Path, Palm Desert RM2   348
Bakersfield   285–290
Bakersfield Sound (Country Music)   285
Balboa Ferry and Fun Zone NB1   134
Balboa Isle & the Newport Beaches NB1   131, 133–139
Ballona Creek Trail LA1   86, 88
Barker Dam Loop Hike, Joshua Tree JT1   362
Basque Restaurants, Bakersfield   285, 287, 289
Bayshore Bikeway SD7   271
Bayside Park, Chula Vista SD7   272
BBQ Tri–Tip, Santa Maria   53
Beach Park, Bakersfield BA1   287, 289
Beach riding   47, 228
Beaches
    Arroyo Burro Beach County Park SB1   63
    Best surfing   19
    Black's Beach (c/o) SDC1   20
    Cabrillo Beach LA3   90, 92
    Clothing Optional (c/o)   20, 41, 69, 162
    Corallina Cove MB2   39
    Coronado Beach SD7   266
    Dockweiller State Beach LA2   84
    Dog Beach, Huntington Beach HB1   130
    Dog Beach, Ocean Beach Park SD3   256
    Doheny State Beach DP1   151, 152
    El Segundo City Beach LA2   87
    Faria Beach, Ventura VE4   73
    Goleta Beach Park SB2   63, 65, 66, 69
    Harbor Beach, Oceanside OC1   226
    Hermosa City Beach LA2   88
    Hobson Beach, Ventura VE4   73
    Huntington City Beach HB1   131
    Huntington State Beach HB1   131
    Jalama Beach County Park   60
    Lasuen, San Clemente SC1   157
    Lost Winds, San Clemente SC1   157
    Manhattan County Beach LA2   87
    Moonstone Beach, Cambria CA1   30
    North Beach, San Clemente SC1   157
    North Carlsbad State Beach SDC1   225
    North Gate, San Clemente SC1   157
    Ocean Beach County Park, Lompoc LOM1   59
    Ocean Beach Park, San Diego OC3   256
    Pismo State Beach PB1, 2   47
    Pirates Cove Beach (c/o) Avila Beach AV1   41
    Poche, San Clemente SC1   157
    Quarry Cove MB2   39
    Redondo County Beach LA2   88
    Riviera, San Clemente SC1   157
    Royal Palms County Beach LA3   92
    Salt Creek Beach SV2   206, 213
    San Buenaventura State Beach VE1   73, 74
    San Clemente State Beach SC1, 2   157–159
    Santa Monica State Beach LA1   85
    Silver Strand State Park SD7   270
    Spooner's Cove MB2   39
    Surfers Point Park, Ventura VE1   74
    T-Street, San Clemente SC1   157
    The Hole, San Clemente SC1   157
    Torrance County Beach LA2   82, 83, 88
    Trails, San Onofre State Park SC3   162
    Trestles, San Clemente SC3   157, 160, 162
    Venice City Beach LA1   85, 86
    Will Rogers State Beach LA1   82, 84
    Windansea Beach, La Jolla SD2   253
Bear Creek Trail, La Quinta LQ1   352, 353
Bear Mountain Ski Area BB2   314, 317
Belmont Pier, Long Beach LO1   94, 95
Belmont Shore, Long Beach LO1, 2   92, 95, 96, 98
Bernardo Bay trails, Lake Hodges LH1   236, 237
Betty Davis Park, Glendale LA4   115
Beverly Hills   81
Bicentennial Korean Friendship Bell LA3   92
Big Bear City   314, 316
Big Bear Discovery Center BB1   316, 317
Big Bear Lake   163, 164, 292, 314–318
Big Bear Lake, City of   314
Big Bear Village   316, 318
Big Laguna Lake, Laguna Mountains LM1   283
Big Sur   27
Big Sycamore Canyon Trail, Point Mugu SP   368
Bike 'n Brunch, explained   16
Bird watching   20, 36, 43, 62, 130, 132, 134, 189, 235, 253, 269, 276, 286, 288, 306, 320, 355, 357
Bixby, Mark Memorial Bike Path 92, 96
Black Bears   16, 108
Bluebird Park, Laguna Beach LB2   149
Bluff Park, Huntington Beach HB1   128

INDEX

Bluff Trail, Montana de Oro SP MB2   39
Bluffs Overlook Trail, Goleta SB2   68
Boat Canyon Park, Laguna Beach LB2   149
Bob Jones Trail, Avila Beach AV1   28, 40–44, 49
Boden Canyon, San Diego County   239
Bolsa Chica Ecological Reserve HB1   20, 129, 130
Bonelli Regional Park (Puddingstone) LA10   118-119
Bonner Canyon, Irvine IR2   183
Borrego Canyon Trail SV5   213
Borrego Palm Canyon Hike AB1   363, 365
Borrego Springs   222, 363–367
Bouquet Creek Trail, Santa Clarita   368
Brea   204
Brea Dam, Fullerton F1, 2   201, 203
Bristlecone Loop MTB Big Bear BB2   318
Broadway Pier, San Diego SD4   268, 272
Brown Trail, Newport Beach NB2   140
Browns Creek Bike Path, Chatsworth   119
Buck Owens Crystal Palace, Bakersfield BA1   285, 286, 289
Bud Turner Trail, Fullerton F1, 2   201, 203
Buena Park   169
Bump 'n Grind Hiking Trail, Palm Desert RM2   347
Burbank   111, 116
Butler-Abrams Trail RM1, 2   339, 340, 342, 344, 345, 350

Cabrillo Aquarium LA3   90
Cabrillo National Monument SD5   241, 262
Cal State Bakersfield BA1   286, 288
Cal State San Marcos SMR1   231–233
Caliente Mountain & Range CP1   50
California Citrus State Historic Park R2   292, 298, 300
California Living Museum (CALM) BA1   290
California Polytechnic State University   40
Calumet Park, La Jolla SD2   253
Cambria and Scarecrow Festival CA1   19, 27–32
Camp 'n Ride, explained   16
Camp Pendleton Marine Base SC3   157, 160–163, 222–225
Campus Point SB2   67
Cancer Survivor's Park, Rancho Mirage RM1   344
Canoga Park   111, 116
Canyon Country Club District PS2   335
Canyon View Park, Aliso Viejo SV4   214, 215
Capistrano Beach Park, Dana Point DP1   153
Carlsbad SDC1   20, 22, 24, 225, 228, 229, 231
Carlson Dog Park, Riverside R1   292, 295
Carpinteria & Carpinteria State Beach   60, 64
Carrizo Plain Natl Monument CP1   20, 28, 49–51, 285
Casa de Rancho Cucamonga PET   312
Caspers Wilderness Park SV11   206, 220
Castaways Park, Newport Beach NB2   140
Castlewood Trail F2   203
Catalina Conservancy   125
Catalina Island 26, 80, 81, 85, 90, 92, 125, 126, 130, 142, 147
Catalina Island Boat Terminals   91, 92, 96, 125, 142, 150
Cathedral City   323, 325, 326, 331, 338, 345, 350
Cathedral City Whitewater River Trail   338
Cave Landing Trail   48
Centennial Regional Park, Santa Ana   167
Central Park, Rancho Cucamonga PET   309, 310, 312
Century Lake, Malibu Creek State Park   368
Cerro de las Posas Mountains, SMR1   233
Chandler Bikeway LA7   111, 368
Channel Islands Harbor   70
Channel Islands Natl Park   52, 60, 66, 70, 72, 74, 75
Chapman University, Orange OR1   190
Chase Palm Park SB1   62
Chatsworth   111, 116
Cherry Park, Lake Forest SV1   210
Chinatown Los Angeles   81
Chino Hills State Park   204–205
Chocolate Mountains   320
Chuck Pontus Commuter Rail Trail, Santa Clarita   368
Chula Vista; Chula Vista Marina SD7   270, 271

CicLAvia   81
Citrus Culture   11, 190, 291–293, 297–299, 303, 368
Citrus Ranch Park, Tustin TU1   188
Civic Center Park, Irvine IR1   180, 187
Claremont & Colleges CL1, 2   81, 292, 303–310
Claremont Hills Wilderness Park   304, 306
Clarington Park, Laguna Hills SV1   209
Class I, II, III paths explained   14
Cleveland National Forest   239, 281
Climate Data:
    Anaheim   128
    Bakersfield   285
    Burbank   82
    Joshua Tree   358
    Long Beach   82
    Newport Beach   127
    Ojai   70
    Ontario   292
    Palm Desert   321
    Riverside   292
    San Diego   222
    Santa Barbara   53
    San Luis Obispo   28
    Ventura   70
Cloisters Community Park MB1   34–36
Coachella Music and Art Festival, Indio   322, 325
Coachella Valley   20, 319–321, 353, 363
Coachella Valley Bikeway CC1   339, 350
Coal Oil Point SB2   67
Coast to Crest Trail, San Diego County   235
College of the Desert, Palm Desert RM2   322, 348
Colorado Desert   222, 281, 319, 357
Colorado River   276, 291, 320
Colorado Street Bridge PA2   124
Cook's Corner SV1   208, 211
Corona   164, 175, 291
Corona Del Mar NB1   127, 131, 135, 137–139, 143, 144
Coronado Ferry Landing SD7   267, 268, 272
Coronado/Silver Strand SD7 18, 180, 241, 248, 256, 258-272
Costa Mesa SAR1   164–169, 190, 192, 193
Cove Oasis MTB Trails, La Quinta LQ1   352, 353
Cove to Lake (Morrow) Hiking Trail LQ2   355
Coyote Creek Bikeway SGR1   102, 103
Coyote Hills F2   200
Crags Road Trail, Malibu Creek State Park   368
Crescent Bay Point Park, Laguna Beach LB2   148
Cross-country skiing, Laguna Mountains LM1   281
Crown Shores Park, San Diego SD1   244
Crystal Cove Historic District NB3   144
Crystal Cove State Park NB3,4 127,131,135,138,142–145
Crystal Pier SD1   244
CV Link Regional Trail 322, 325, 326, 338, 339, 345, 351,356
Cycle-Way of LA PA1   122

Dan Henry Bike Route SO1   58
Dana Point DP1   125, 127, 146, 149–153, 157, 206
Dana Point Harbor DP1   127, 151, 152, 155
David Keitzer Lake Hodges Ribbon Bridge LH1   235–239
De Anza Cove Park, San Diego SD1   245
Death Valley National Park   292, 319
Deepwell District, Palm Springs PS1   332
Del Dios & Community Park LH2   235, 237, 239, 240
Del Dios Gorge Trail LH2   240
Del Mar   229, 231
Demuth Park, Palm Springs PS3   337
Descanso Park, San Juan Capistrano   155, 156
Desert Hot Springs   322
Desert Willow Loop, Palm Desert PD1   340–344, 349
Devereux Slough SB2   66
Diablo Canyon Nuclear Power Plant   38, 44
Dinosaur Caves Park PB3   48
Discovery Lake & Creek, San Marcos SMR1   231–233
Discovery Science Center OR1   192, 194

INDEX

Disneyland and California Adventure   169, 309
Doheny Blues Festival DP1   150
Double Peak Regional Park, San Marcos   233
Downtown Bike Loop, Riverside R1   294, 295, 297
Dreamworks Animation facility LA4   113, 115

Edison MTB Trail, Lake Forest SV1   210
Edward White Park, Fullerton F2   202
El Dorado Park, Long Beach SGR1   81, 101–104
El Monte   101, 105
El Paseo District, Palm Desert RM2   322, 345–356
El Segundo   87
El Toro Park, Lake Forest   SV1 209
Eldwayan Ocean Park PB3   48
Electric Avenue Path, Seal Beach   101
Elephant Seals   8, 27, 30, 32, 39
Ellen Browning Scripps Park SD2   251, 253
Ellena Park, Rancho Cucamonga PET   309–312
Elwood Mesa SB2   68
Embarcadero Harborwalk MB1   34, 35
Embarcadero Marina Park, San Diego SD4   260
Emma Wood State Park VE1, 4   72–74
Empire Polo Club, Indio   322, 325, 350
Encanto Park SGR3   102, 108–111
Encino LA5   111, 116–118
Escena Golf Club, Palm Springs PS4   336, 338
Escondido & Bike Path   234, 235

Fairmount Park, Riverside R1   293–297
Fairview Park, Costa Mesa SAR1   166–168
Fanuel Street Park SD1   244
Father Junipero Serra   21, 40, 71, 153, 279
Father Junipero Serra Trail SD12   279
Fay Avenue Path, La Jolla SD2   252
Featherly Regional Park SAR3   173
Fiesta Island, San Diego SD1   245
Fiscalini Ranch Preserve CA1   29–31
Fish Creek Wash Bike 'n Hike AB4   367
Fisher Park, Santa Ana SAR2   172, 194
Fontana PET   304, 307–310, 313, 314
Fontana Civic Center PET   309, 314
Foster Park VE3   76, 77
Fountain Valley   164, 165, 167–169
Foxen Wine Trail SO1   54
Fritz Burns Park, La Quinta LQ1, 2   352, 354
Fullerton F1, 2   20, 169, 198–203
Fullerton Loop Trail F2   199–203
Fullerton, Historic Downtown   198, 202

Galaxy View Park, Newport Beach NB2   140
Garnet Peak LM1   284, 366
Gaslamp Quarter, San Diego SD4   261, 272
Gene Autry Bikeway, Palm Springs PS4   321, 326–338
Getty Museums Los Angeles   80, 84
Glendale Narrows Riverwalk LA4   113, 115
Glenn Trail Camp, West Fork SGR4   111
Glorietta Bay Park, Coronado SD7   269
Golden Shores Preserve, Long Beach LO1   96
Goleta SB2   52, 53, 57, 60, 63, 65, 66, 68, 69
Great Park of Orange County   178
Griffith Park LA4   81, 111–115
Grijalva Community Park, Orange OR2   193
Guajome Regional Park, Oceanside OC1   224, 227

Hahamonga Watershed Park PA2   124
Harbor Beach, Oceanside OC1   226
Harbor Island, San Diego SD4   257, 259
Harford Pier, AV1   44
Harry Bridges Memorial Park, Long Beach, LO1   96
Hart Memorial Park, Bakersfield BA1   286, 287, 290
Hart Park, Orange OR1   192–195
Harvard Athletic Park TU1   187
Hawi-Vallecito Valley Cultural Preserve AB3   366

Hazards, Southern California   16
Heisler Park, Laguna Beach LB2   127, 146, 148
Heritage Square Museum PA1   122, 123
Hermosa Beach LA2   19, 82, 84, 87, 88
Heroes Park, Lake Forest SV1   210
Hidden Valley Hike 'n Camp, Joshua Tree JT1   359–362
Hidden Valley Nature/Wildlife Area R1   164, 293–296
Higginbottom Park, Claremont CL2   306
Hillcrest District SD6   241, 262–266
Historic Districts
    Fullerton F1, 2   198, 202
    Orange OR1   172, 189–191, 194, 198
    Pasadena PA2   121, 123, 124
    Riverside R1   292, 294–297
    San Diego SD1   248, 249
    San Juan Capistrano SJ1   156
    Temecula T1   301, 302
    Upland PET   311
    Victoria Avenue Citrus District R2   297–301
Hollywood, Los Angeles   11, 80, 111, 112, 328
Honda Center (The Pond), Anaheim SAR2   169–171
Hotel Circle San Diego SD1   245, 248–250, 255
Hotel Del Coronado SD7   266, 268, 269, 271
Hotels   16
Huntington Beach HB1   19, 20, 92, 98–101, 127–132, 135, 137, 163–166, 208
Huntington Beach Central Park/Library HB2   20, 132
Huntington Library & Gardens PA3   81, 121, 125
Hurless Barton Park, Yorba Linda YL1   176

Idyllwild   322
Imperial Beach   266, 270, 271
Imperial County   222, 292, 363
Indian Canyons, Palm Springs PS2   323, 335
Indian Wells/Tennis IW1   321–323, 350, 351, 356
Indio, festivals in   322, 323, 325
Inland Empire   15, 291
Inland Rail Trail, San Marcos-Escondido SMR2   234
Irvine and Irvine Ranch   127, 177, 178
Irvine Ranch Historical Park TU1   188
Irvine Regional Park OR2   141, 186–189, 194–198
Irvine Spectrum IR1   178–181
Isla Vista SB2   65–68
Islay Creek Road Trail MB2   38–40

Jack's Pond Park, San Marcos   232–234
Jeffrey Open Space Trail, Irvine IR3   184
Joshua Tree National Park   292, 319, 323, 353, 357–362
Juanita Cooke Trail F1, 2   200–203
Julian LM1   235, 281, 282, 284, 363, 365

Kenneth Newell Bikeway, Pasadena PA2 123, 124
Kern County/Kern River   285–288
Kern River County Park, Bakersfield BA1   286
Kern River Parkway Trail BA1   286
Keys Ranch/Keys View Joshua Tree Natl Park JT1   362
King Harbor, Redondo Beach LA2   88
Kwaaymii Point LM1   284

La Jolla Bike Path SD2   252
La Jolla SD2   20, 231, 241, 244, 245, 250–253, 277, 278
La Quinta/La Quina Cove LQ1   320–323, 350–353
LA Zoo, Los Angeles LA5   111–114
Lacy Park, San Marino PA3   125
Laguna Beach LB1, 2   24, 127, 137, 142–149, 157, 177, 206, 208, 213, 215
Laguna Coast Wilderness Park   145–147
Laguna Lake Park, Fullerton F1, 2   200–203
Laguna Mountain Recreation Area LM1   222, 281, 363, 366
Laguna Niguel   206
Laguna Niguel Regional Park SV2   211, 214
Laguna Village to Crescent Bay LB2   148
Lake Cahuilla Reg Park LQ2   20, 322, 325, 352–356
Lake Forest SV1   206, 208, 210

INDEX

Lake Hodges Dam LH2 236, 240
Lake Hodges LH1, 2 20, 222, 232, 235–240, 273
Lake Ming, Bakersfield BA1 286, 287
Lake Miramar, San Diego SD9 275, 276
Lake Murray, San Diego SD13 280
Lake Perris State Recreation Area LP1 20, 306, 307
Lake Skinner Regional Park, Temecula 301
Lakeview Park, San Marcos SMR1 232, 233
Las Palmas neighborhood PS1 328–331, 335, 336
League of American Bicyclists 92, 177, 224
Least Tern Preserve, Coronado SD7 269
Leffingwell Landing State Park CA1 30
Legg Lake, Whittier Narrows SGR2 20, 104, 105
Lido Isle, Newport Beach NB1 137
Limestone Canyon SV5, 6 215
Little San Bernardino Mountains 320, 343, 353, 357
Live Oak Canyon 216
Living Desert, Palm Desert RM2 323
Lompoc LOM1 21, 24, 52, 53, 59
Long Beach LO1, 2 16, 19, 22, 52, 80–82, 90–106, 112, 125
Lopez Canyon Trail, San Diego SD8 274
Los Angeles Live Steamers Railroad Museum LA4 113
Los Angeles Maritime Museum LA3 90, 91
Los Angeles River LA4, 5 93, 96, 106, 111–118
Los Angeles River Trail LA4 100, 112–115
Los Angeles/Rio Hondo (LARIO) Trail 93, 96, 106, 115
Los Flores Ranch Park SAM2 54
Los Olivos SO1 52–58
Los Osos 38
Los Padres National Forest 28, 52
Los Penasquitos Canyon Preserve SD8 273–275
Los Rios Historic District SJ1 153–157
Lower Arroyo Park, Pasadena 124

Malibu 70, 81, 82, 84
Malibu Creek State Park, LA County 368
Manhattan Beach LA2 19, 82, 84, 87
Margot Dodd Park PB3 48
Marian Bear Memorial Park, San Diego SD10 277
Marie Ignacio Trail SB2 69
M*A*S*H set 368
Marina Del Rey LA1, 2 82, 84, 86
Marina Green Park, Long Beach LO1 95
Marine Stadium, Long Beach LO2 98
Marine Studies Institute, Dana Point DP1 152
Martin Luther King Promenade SD4 260, 261, 272
Marvin Braude Trail LA1 82
Mastodon Peak Loop Hike, Joshua Tree NP 362
Max Berg Plaza Park, San Clemente SC2 160
Mecca Hills 320
Mesa Neighborhood, South Palm Springs PS2 336
Metro Rail Gold Line 121, 123, 124
Metrolink Bike Car 22, 23
Mexico 222, 241, 270, 319
Mid-century modern architecture 321, 328, 334, 335
Midway aircraft carrier, San Diego SD4 259, 260
Mike Gotch Memorial Bridge SD1 244
Mile Square Park, Fountain Valley FV1, SAR1 165, 167, 169
Miller Park, Fontana PET 314
Mission Bay & Ocean Front Walk SD1 20, 241, 250–256
Mission Bay Park, San Diego SD1 245
Mission Beach SD1 241, 242
Mission Inn, Riverside R1 292, 294
Mission La Purisima Concepcion 21
Mission San Buenaventura VE1 21, 71
Mission San Diego de Alcala 21
Mission San Fernando Rey de Espana 21
Mission San Gabriel Arcangel 21
Mission San Juan Capistrano SJ1 21, 153, 156
Mission San Luis Obispo de Tolosa 21, 28, 40

Mission San Luis Rey de Francia OC1 21, 223–226
Mission San Miguel Arcangel 21, 28
Mission Santa Barbara 21, 60
Mission Santa Ines SO1 21, 57
Mission Trails Regional Park SD12 112, 278–280
Mission Valley Preserve SD1 248
Mission Viejo 206, 213, 217
Mojave Desert 319, 357
Mojave National Preserve 292
Monarch butterflies 45–47, 68, 368
Montana de Oro State Park MB2 28, 32, 37–39
Montclair PET 304, 308–310
Montecito SB1 64
Montecito Heights Recreation Center PA1 122
Monterey pine trees CA1 30
Moon Park, Costa Mesa SAR1 167
More Mesa Open Space, Goleta SB2 69
Morro Bay MB1 19, 20, 28, 32–36, 38–41
Morro Bay Museum of Natural History MB1 35
Morro Bay State Park MB1 34
Morro Estuary Natural Preserve MB1 36
Morro Rock MB1 28, 32, 35, 39
Morro Strand State Beach MB1 34–37
Mountain lion attacks 215, 220, 274
Mountain lions 16, 40, 42, 108, 113, 122, 123, 216, 282
Mountains to the Sea Trail TU1 135, 140, 141, 178, 185–190, 194, 198, 206
Mt. Hollywood, Griffith Park LA4 112, 115
Mt. Rubidoux, Riverside R1 293–297
Mt. San Antonio (Mt Baldy) 80, 297, 311
Mt. San Gorgonio 292, 297, 308, 312, 314, 320, 342, 361
Mt. San Jacinto 308, 320, 342, 343, 349, 361
Movie Colony District, Palm Springs PS1 333
Mule Hill Trail, Lake Hodges LH1 236–238
Murrieta 301
Murrieta Creek Trail, Temecula T1 302

Naples Isle & gondolas, Long Beach LO1&2 92, 94, 97, 98
NASA Jet Propulsion Laboratories (JPL) PA2 124
National City SD7 271, 272
Naval Base Point Loma SD5 261
Newport Back Bay Ride NB2 *See* Back Bay
Newport Beach NB1, 2 19, 125, 127, 128, 130, 131, 133–142, 144, 146, 166, 177–179, 181, 184–187, 208
Newport Center 133, 140
Newport Harbor 134, 138, 140
Newport-Inglewood Fault 136
Nine Sisters volcanoes 28
Nixon, Richard and library YL1 157, 176, 216
No Ho (North Hollywood) LA7 119
Noble Canyon Trail, Laguna Mountains 282
Noguchi Garden, Costa Mesa SAR1 164
Nora Kuttner Recreation Trail, F2 203
Norco 291, 295
North Harbor Dr Bike Path, San Diego SD4 259
North Heritage Park, Fontana PET 308, 313
North Shore Trail, Lake Hodges LH1 236–239
Northern/Kendall-Forst Reserve SD1 244
Norton Simon Museum, Pasadena PA2 81

O'Neill Regional Park SV7–10 206, 208, 216–219
Obern Trail, Goleta SB2 63, 65, 66, 68, 69
Ocean Beach Bike Path SD1, 3 246–249, 255–257
Ocean Beach SD3 241, 242, 245, 247, 254–257, 261
Oceanside and Oceanside Harbor OC1 20, 21, 23–25, 127, 157, 159–161, 163, 222–229, 234
Ojai and the Ojai Valley Trail VE3 72, 74–78
Old Globe Theatre, Balboa Park SD6 262
Old Mission Beach District SD1 244
Old Pasadena 121, 123, 124
Old Rincon Highway 64, 73, 79 *See also* Rincon Bike Trail
Old Town Kern, Bakersfield 287, 288

INDEX

Old Town La Quinta LQ1   322, 351–356
Old Town San Diego SD1   241, 245, 248–250, 261
Old Town Tustin   185
Old Town Upland PET   311
Old Towne Orange OR1   172, 189–191, 194, 198
Olvera Street Los Angeles   81
Ontario   291, 292
Orange, city of. *See* Old Towne Orange
Orange County Great Park IR3   184
Orange County Zoo OR2   191
Orange Line Busway Bike Path LA6   111, 368
Outlets at Orange, The   168, 172
Oxnard   22, 24, 64, 70, 368

Pacific Beach SD1, 2   20, 241–244, 250
Pacific Coast Railroad   42
Pacific Crest Trail   281
Pacific Electric Railroad Red Cars   20, 90, 91, 308, 309
Pacific Electric Trail (PET)   20, 292, 304–308
Pacific Flyway   20, 50, 132, 134, 235, 357
Pacific Palisades LA1   81, 82, 84
Pageant of the Masters, Laguna Beach   146
Painted Rock, Carrizo Plain CP1   50, 51
Palm Desert RM1, 2, PD1   19, 24, 320–325, 339–352
Palm Desert Civic Center Park RM2   345, 348
Palm Springs   12, 14, 19, 22, 291, 308, 319–328, 331, 332, 334–336, 338, 339, 345, 347, 350, 351, 360, 364
Palm Springs Air Museum PS4   321, 338
Palm Springs Art Museum
      PS1   321, 331
      "The Galen" RM2   322, 347
Palm Springs, South PS2   323, 326, 332, 334–336, 338
Palm Springs Vintage Star Tour PS1   19, 321, 323, 326–338
Palms to Pines Highway   322, 347
Panorama Park, Bakersfield BA1   289
Pasadena   21, 81, 120–125
Paso Robles   21, 27, 28, 41
Peters Canyon (Regional) Park TU2   178, 185–190
Peters Canyon Trail TU1   180, 186–188, 190
Peters Canyon Wash TU1   178, 180, 186, 187
Pictograph Trail, Anza-Borrego AB3   366
Piedras Blancas Lighthouse CA2   30, 32
Piedras Pintadas trails, Lake Hodges   236
Pismo Beach PB1, 2, 3   19, 27, 28, 40–49
Playa Del Rey LA2   82, 84, 87, 88
Point Conception   52
Point Fermin Park & Lighthouse LA3   90, 92
Point Loma Peninsula SD5   241, 248, 257, 261, 270, 272
Point Mugu State Park   368
Pomona College CL1   303, 305
Port of Long Beach LO1   92, 95
Port of Los Angeles LA3   89–92, 309
Ports O' Call Village LA3   90
Prado Dam   163, 164, 172, 175
Presidio Park, SD1   249, 250, 261
Purddingstone Reservoir   118-119

Quail Hill Community Park, Irvine IR2   184
Queen Mary LO1   92, 94–96
Queen Valley Rd, Joshua Tree NP JT1   358–362
Queensway Bridge, Long Beach LO1   96

Rainbow Lagoon Park, Long Beach LO1   95
Ralph C. Bren Memorial Park, Irvine IR2   183
Rancho Bernardo   235
Rancho Bernardo Community Park LH1   237
Rancho Cucamonga PET   292, 304, 307–312
Rancho de los Penasquitos SD8   273, 274
Rancho Jurupa Regional Park, Riverside R1   294
Rancho Mirage RM1, 2   19, 321–326, 339–349
Rancho Mirage Civic Center Park RM1   339, 344
Rancho Mirage-Palm Desert Loop RM1, 2   339–349
Rancho Santa Margarita   206, 216

Raptor Ridge, San Pasqual Valley Trail LH1   238
Raptor Road/Serrano Cow Trail SV2   216
Rattlesakes   16
Rattlesnake Trail, Bakersfield BA1   286, 289
Red Hill Park, Rancho Cucamonga PET   310, 312
Redondo Beach   82–84, 88
Rialto PET   307–310, 313, 314
Rincon Bike Path and Seaside Cruise VE4   19, 64, 73, 77, 79
Rio Hondo Trail   93, 102, 105–107
River Oaks Park, Bakersfield BA1   288
River Walk Park & Center Bakersfield BA1   286–288
Riverdale Park, Anaheim SAR2, 3   171, 172
Riverside, City of R1, 2   20, 24, 77, 163, 164, 175, 291–301
Riverside North Path, Palm Springs PS1   332
Rosanna Scott Memorial Bike Trail R2   297, 298
Rose Bowl, Pasadena PA2   81, 121–124
Rose Canyon Bike Path SD11   277
Rose Canyon Open Space SD11   277, 278
Rose Creek Trail, San Diego SD1   245
Roundhouse Marine Studies Lab and Aquarium LA2   87
Route 66   20, 90, 307–312
Ruth Hardy Park, Palm Springs PS1   329, 333
Rutland Park, Riverside R1   296
RV Rentals   22
Ryan Bonaminio Park, Riverside R1   294, 295, 297
Ryan Mountain Hike, Joshua Tree JT1   362
Rynerson Park, SGRT   102

Saddleback Mtn   155, 168, 183, 205, 206, 219, 220, 309
Saddleback Valley   183, 205, 206
Salinas River Walk (Paso Robles)   28
Salt Creek Beach Park, Dana Point SV2   19, 206, 211, 213
Salt Creek Corridor Trail SV2   211–213
Salton Sea   20, 281, 320, 322, 362–364
San Andreas Fault   50, 51, 320, 362
San Antonio Creek   77
San Bernardino, City of   164, 291
San Bernardino Mountains 110, 291, 292, 296, 297, 314, 320
San Bernardino National Forest   164, 316
San Clemente Canyon SD10   277
San Clemente Island   80
San Clemente SC1, 2, 3   18–20, 26, 80, 127, 151, 153, 157–163
San Diego Bay   266
San Diego Bayfront Park SD4   260
San Diego Coast Route SDC1   20, 163, 222, 224, 225, 228, 229
San Diego Convention Center SD4   257, 260, 272
San Diego Creek Trail IR1   135, 140, 177–181, 184, 187
San Diego Harbor Tour SD4   18, 241, 248, 250, 257–262, 266, 268, 272
San Diego Maritime Museum SD4   259
San Diego National Wildlife Refuge SD7   271
San Diego Padres Petco Park SD4   257, 260, 261, 272
San Diego River   245, 246, 248, 249, 254–256, 278–280
San Diego Zoo SD6   222, 241, 262, 266
San Diego Zoo Safari Park LH1   237, 239, 241
San Diego, City of   222, 240, 241, 250, 271
San Dieguito River Park, San Diego County   235
San Elijo State Beach, Cardiff-By-The-Sea SDC1   231
San Fernando Valley   21, 22, 70, 80, 81, 111, 112, 368
San Franciscuito Creek Trail, Santa Clarita   368
San Gabriel Canyon SGR3   102, 109
San Gabriel Mountains   99, 101, 105–111, 113, 163, 166, 168, 170, 179, 181, 192, 291, 296, 297, 304, 306, 308, 310
San Gabriel River Trail   13, 81, 92, 99–111, 127
San Gabriel River West Fork SGR4   111
San Gabriel Valley   80, 81, 101, 110, 304
San Gorgonio Wilderness   314
San Jacinto Mountains 291, 320, 322, 323, 329, 343, 351
San Joaquin Valley and River   285, 286
San Jose Creek, SGRT   102

San Juan Capistrano SJ1   20, 21, 127, 151–157, 161, 206, 220
San Juan Creek and Trail SJ1   152, 154, 155, 157, 220
San Luis Obispo, City of   28, 40, 41, 44, 46, 52, 53, 59
San Luis Obispo Creek   42–44
San Luis Rey River Trail OC1   21, 163, 222, 224–227
San Marco Park, Irvine IR1   180
San Marcos/South San Marcos Tour SMR1   231–234
San Marino PA3   21, 81, 120, 121, 124, 125
San Mateo Creek   162
San Onofre to Oceanside Ride SC3   20, 127, 157–163, 222, 224, 225, 229
San Pasqual Valley Trail, Lake Hodges LH1   236–238
San Pedro/LA Harbor LA3   81, 89–92, 125, 309
San Rafael Mountains   52, 54
San Simeon State Park CA2   30–32
Santa Ana, City of SAR1   164, 166–169, 172, 185, 191–194
Santa Ana Mountains   90, 163, 179, 191, 205, 206, 215, 220
Santa Ana River,   127, 131, 170, 174, 292
Santa Ana River Trail SAR1   127, 131, 135, 137, 164–169
Santa Ana River Trail SAR2   164, 168, 170–172, 174, 194
Santa Ana River Trail SAR3   164, 170, 172–176
Santa Barbara, City of   16, 19–22, 52–54, 57–64, 71–75, 257
Santa Barbara Harbor SB1   63, 75
Santa Barbara Museum of Natural History SB1   63
Santa Barbara Shores Park SB2   68
Santa Barbara Zoo SB1   62
Santa Catalina Island (see Catalina Island)
Santa Clara River Trail, Santa Clarita   368
Santa Clarita Class I trail system   368
Santa Claus Lane SB1   64
Santa Fe Dam Recreation Area SGR3   101, 102, 107–110
Santa Fe Train Depot
    Fullerton F1, 2   198
    San Juan Capistrano SJ1   153
    San Diego SD4   250, 259, 261, 268
Santa Lucia Mountains   40
Santa Maria River Trail & Santa Maria Valley SAM1   53
Santa Monica and Santa Monica Bay LA1   70, 82–85
Santa Monica Bike Trail LA1   82–86
Santa Monica Mountains   84, 87, 111, 112, 368
Santa Rosa and San Jacinto Mountains NM   323
Santa Rosa Mountains   320, 321, 342, 353, 355, 363, 367
Santa Susanna Mountains   111, 118
Santa Ynez, Town of SO1   41, 55–58
Santa Ynez Valley & Mountains SO1   52, 54, 59–61, 76
Santiago Creek Trail OR1, 2   170–172, 186, 189–198
Santiago Creek Wildlife & Watershed Ctr OR1   194
Santiago Oaks Park OR2   186, 189, 191, 194–197
Santiago Retention Basin OR1   193
Sawdust Festival, Laguna Beach   146
Sea World, San Diego, SD1   222, 241, 243–246
Seal Beach SE1   13, 19, 92, 97–104, 127
Seaport Village, San Diego SD4   257–260
See Canyon Road, Avila Beach AV1   43
Segerstrom Center for the Arts, Costa Mesa SAR1   164
Sepulveda Basin LA5   81, 111, 115–118
Sepulveda Japanese Garden LA5   117
Seven Oaks Dam, Santa Ana River   164
Seville Park, Fontana PET   309, 314
Shady Canyon Public Trail IR2   183
Shady Canyon/Turtle Rock IR2   140, 178–184, 187
Shamel County Park, Cambria CA1   30
Sharrows, explained   15
Sheep Hills Park, Aliso Viejo SV1   209
Shelter Island, San Diego SD4   257, 258, 260
Shipley Nature Center HB2   132
Shoreline Marine Village/Park LO1   92, 95
Shoreline Park, Santa Barabara SB1   63
Sidewalk cycling and safety measures   323, 324

Sierra Madre Mountains   52
Sikes Adobe, Lake Hodges LH1   237, 238
Silver Strand Bikeway SD7   20, 241, 248, 262, 266–272
Sinatra, Frank estates PS1 326, 333; RM1&2   344
Six Flags Magic Mountain/Hurricane Harbor   368
Slabtown Rollers CA1   10, 30
SLO Railroad Safety Trail   40
Snow Summit/Bear Mt Downhill BB2   314–318
SOCO District, Fullerton F1, 2   198, 200, 202
Soda Lake, Carrizo Plain NM   50, 51
Solvang SO1   21, 24, 52–59
South Bay Trail LA2   82, 83, 86–88
South Carlsbad State Beach SDC1   231
South Coast Plaza, Costa Mesa SAR1   164, 167
South El Monte SGR2   104, 105
South Pasadena PA2   121–123
South Shores Park, San Diego SD1   245
South Wildlife Refuge, San Diego SD1   246
Southern California Bight   52
Spanish Landing Park, San Diego SD4   259, 260
Stadium Promenade, Orange SAR2   172
Stagecoach Music Festival, Indio   322, 325
Stearns Wharf, Santa Barbara SB1   62
Strawberry Festival, Oxnard   70
Sulfur Creek Park, Laguna Niguel SV2   213
Summerland SB1   64
Sundowners Park, Lake Forest SV1   210
Sunnylands, Rancho Mirage RM1   322, 343, 344, 349
Sunset Beach   101, 129, 130
Sunset Cliffs Natural Park SD3   254–257
Sunset Trail, Laguna Mountains LM1   283
Surf City HB1   128, 129, 137, 264, 166
Swallows, San Juan Capistrano SJ1   153
Sweetwater Bikeway, San Diego SD7   272
Sweetwater Marsh Wildlife Refuge SD7   272
Sweetwater Summit Regional Park SD7   272
Swiss Park, Chula Vista SD7   271

Tahquitz Canyon PS1   323, 329, 331, 332
Tahquitz Creek Loop PS3   326, 332, 334–339
Tahquitz Peak   320, 342
Talbert Marsh Trail HB2   131, 166
Talbert Regional Park, Costa Mesa SAR1   166–168
Tamale Festival, Indio   322
Tecate Peak   270
Telegraph Canyon Trail CH1   127, 204, 205
Temblor Mountains   50
Temecula & Wine Country T1, 2   11, 24, 222, 292, 301–303
Temecula Valley Wine and Balloon Festival   301
Templeton   28
The Market Place - Tustin/Irvine TU1   186, 188
The River, Rancho Mirage RM2   321, 340, 345–347
The Strand, Oceanside OC1   163, 222–228
Thompson Creek Trail & City Loop CL2   304, 306
Tidelands Park, Coronado SD7   268
Tijeras Spur Trail SV8   218
Top O' Laguna Ride LB1   146–148
Top of the World, Laguna Beach LB1   146, 147
Toro Peak   320
Torrey Pines State Reserve SDC1   20, 231
Tour de Palm Springs   325
Tournament of Roses Parade, Pasadena   81, 121
Towne Park Trail MTB, Big Bear BB2   318
Trabuco Canyon   206, 216–220
Trabuco Creek   154–156, 217, 219
Trabuco Creek Bikeway SV9   216–220
Trabuco Mesa Park SV9   219
Travel Town Museum LA4   113, 115
Truxton Lake, Bakersfield BA1   289
Tulare Lake   286
Tule elk   49, 285

INDEX

Turtle Rock Community Park IR2   182, 183
Turtle Rock, Irvine IR2   178, 182, 183
Tustin TU1, 2   127, 141, 178, 185–190, 194, 198
Tustin Marine Corps Air Station TU1   180, 187
Two Harbors, Catalina Island   125
Ty Warner Sea Center SB1   62

UCSB Lagoon SB2   65–68
Union Station, Los Angeles   23, 52, 81
Universal Studios, Los Angeles   80, 111
Univ of California, Irvine IR1, 2, 3   140, 178, 180, 184
Univ of California Santa Barbara SB2   60, 63, 65–68
Upland PET   304, 307–311
Upper Newport Bay NB2   20, 134, 138, 139
Upper Newport Bay Muth Interpretive Ctr NB2   139
Upper Newport Bay Regional Park NB2   134
Upper Trail, Bakersfield BA1   286
USS *Iowa* LA3   90

Vacation Island SD1   243–247
Valencia Park, Tustin TU1   188
Van Nuys   116, 117
Vandenberg Air Force Base   52, 59
Venice Beach and Canals LA1   19, 82–86
Ventura VE1   18, 21, 64, 70–77
Ventura Harbor/Village VE1   71–75
Ventura River and Trail VE2   74–77
Verdugo Mountains   111
Verdugo Wash   114, 115
Victoria Avenue, Riverside R2   292, 297–301
Victoria Gardens Center PET   308, 309, 313
Victorville   292, 316
Villa Park/Villa Park Dam OR1, 2   191–197
Vincent Thomas Bridge   91
Virgil Grissom Park, Fullerton F2   202

Walnut Trail, Irvine TU1   187
Weir Canyon Loop TU1   185, 189
West Bernardo Bike Trail LH1   237
West Coyote Hills Tree Park, Fullerton F2   202
Wet 'n Wild Palm Springs PS3   337, 338
Whitewater Park, Rancho Mirage RM2   345, 346
Whitewater River   322, 339, 341, 342, 346, 349
Whitewater Trail CC1   321, 325, 326, 337–339, 345, 350
Whiting Ranch Park SV5, 6   206, 208, 210, 211, 215
Whittier Greenway Trail   368
Whittier Narrows Dam SGR2   81, 102, 106
Whittier Narrows Nature Area SGR2   105, 106
Whittier Narrows Recreation Area SGR2   101–105
Wilderness Park SGRT   102
Wildfires near the rides
  Cedar Fire Laguna Mountains (2003) LM1   281
  Freeway Complex Fire (2008) CH1   204
  Laguna Beach Fire (1993)   145 (NB4), 147(LB1)
  Santiago Fire (2007) SV5, 6, 215
  Windy Ridge Fire (2007) Orange OR2   191
  Witch Creek Fire (2007) San Diego LH1, 2   235
William Mason Regional Park IR2   140, 178, 180–183
Windrow Park, Irvine IR1   181
Wolfson Park, Rancho Mirage RM1, 2   339–347, 349, 350
Wood Canyon Trail SV4   214, 215
Woodbridge Community Park, Irvine IR1   181
Woodfield Park, Aliso Viejo SV1   209
Woodland Hills   119
WR Hearst Memorial State Beach CA2   30
Wrigley Botanical Garden, Catalina Island   126

Yokuts Park, Bakersfield BA1   289
Yorba Linda SAR3, YL1   164, 170, 172–176
Yorba Linda Recreation Trail YL1   176
Yorba Regional Park SAR3   173, 174

RIDE NUMBERS
Quick Reference with Page Numbers

AB1…365	LO2…96	SD3…254
AB2…365	LOM1…59	SD4…257
AB3…366	LP1…306	SD5…261
AB4…367	LQ1…352	SD6…262
AV1…42	LQ2…354	SD7…266
BA1…286	LQ3…356	SD8…273
BB1…316	MB1…34	SD9…275
BB2…317	MB2…37	SD10…277
BB3…318	NB1…135	SD11…277
CA1…30	NB2…139	SD12…278
CA2…32	NB3…143	SD13…280
CAT1…125	NB4…145	SDC1…229
CC1…339	OC1…224	SE1…100
CH1…204	OR1…191	SGR1…103
CL1…305	OR2…195	SGR2…104
CL2…306	PA1…122	SGR3…107
CP1…50	PA2…123	SGR4…111
CP2…50	PA3…125	SGRT…101
CP3…50	PB1…47	SJ1…154
DP1…151	PB2…47	SMR1…231
F1…201	PB3…48	SMR2…234
F2…202	PD1…349	SO1…55
FV1…168	PET…307	SV1…206
HB1…128	PS1…327	SV2…210
HB2…132	PS2…334	SV3…213
IR1…179	PS3…336	SV4…214
IR2…182	PS4…338	SV5…215
IR3…184	R1…293	SV6…215
IW1…351	R2…297	SV7…217
JT1…358	RM1…340	SV8…217
LA1…82	RM2…345	SV9…218
LA2…82	RM3…339	SV10…219
LA3…89	SAM1…53	SV11…220
LA4…112	SAM2…54	T1…302
LA5…116	SAR1…165	T2…302
LA6 - 9..368	SAR2…170	TU1…185
LA10…118	SAR3…172	TU2…189
LA11…368	SB1…60	VE1…72
LB1…147	SB2…65	VE2…75
LB2…148	SC1…158	VE3…76
LH1…238	SC2…159	VE4…79
LH2…239	SC3…160	VE5…368
LM1…281	SD1…241	YL1…176
LO1…93	SD2…250	

Richard Fox (author, cartographer, photographer) is a lifelong avid cyclist whose biggest thrill is discovering scenic bike trails while exploring the U.S. and Canada in an RV with his partner of 29 years, 3rd generation Southern Californian Steve Fisher (consultant, photographer, primary photo model). After receiving an M.S. in Hydrology from UC Davis, the biking capital of America, Fox worked in environmental and water resources consulting out of Southern California, writing or editing hundreds of scientific reports over 25 years. He delved into the guidebook world with *The Pender Islands Handbook* (©2006, 2009, 2016). The 400-page tome reflects his love for that beautiful southern British Columbia island, and it remains its main source book covering hiking, boating, biking and many other topics. The team continues to explore, and the results are posted on enCYCLEpedia.net, which also contains links to the enCYCLEpedia bike blog and Facebook page, special features, and supplementary articles.

Photos from rides: Above, LQ2, CAT1, DP1, RM1, BB1. Below, CAT1, Webster Demner, my Mews.